CONSUMING RUSSIA

CONSUMING

POPULAR

CULTURE,

SEX, AND

SOCIETY

SINCE

GORBACHEV

RUSSIA

EDITED BY ADELE MARIE BARKER

DURHAM + LONDON 1999

DUKE UNIVERSITY PRESS ■

© 1999 Duke University Press

All rights reserved

Printed in the United States of America

on acid-free paper ∞

Designed by Deborah Wong

Typeset in Times Roman by Keystone Typesetting, Inc.

Library of Congress Cataloging-in-Publication Data

appear on the last printed page of this book.

To the memory of my Father

Jack Porter Barker

(1911–1998)

and

Charles Isenberg

(1944–1997)

CONTENTS

ILLUSTRATIONS

ACKNOWLEDGMENTS

This book, like most, is the product of many hands, conversations, conferences, books, and friendships. It is a pleasure to take this opportunity to extend my hand in thanks.

A fellowship at the Udall Center for the Study of Public Policy at the University of Arizona provided me with the kind of environment I needed — my first office with both porch and fireplace — to read and think my way through cultural life in the new Russia. Special thanks are due to Bob Varady for his help and generosity. A grant from the Office of the Vice-President for Research sustained me in my travels to Moscow; and the provost's Authors' Support Fund made it possible to include all the chapters we wanted to in this book. My thanks also to Dean Charles Tatum of the College of Humanities, who helped me through a difficult time and gave me the slack I needed in order to complete this project.

During the past four years I have had the privilege of being affiliated with the Program in Comparative Cultural and Literary Studies at the University of Arizona. It is my association with this program and with my colleagues from other disciplines that first led me to think seriously about many of the questions that are asked in this volume. In particular, I thank my colleague and friend Eileen Meehan, whose love of the media is matched only by her generosity in sharing her knowledge of it. My graduate students in cultural studies have invariably kept me on track. Smart and sophisticated in their thinking, they keep teaching me new ways to think about old problems.

As anyone doing work in the field of post-Soviet studies knows, it is increasingly difficult to keep up with the changes taking place in the new Russia. Scholarship often becomes a communal effort as we increasingly depend on each other for sources of information. Many of the contributors to this volume went way out of their way to provide me with materials and to help me when I needed to be at home more than I needed to be in Russia. Susan Larsen shared

Seans with me; Bob Edelman shipped conference papers to me; Cathy Nepomnyashchy sent Marinina to me; Eliot Borenstein managed to get hold of a particularly elusive issue of *Novoe literaturnoe obozrenie;* Alexei Yurchak shipped articles from *Litsa;* and Anna Krylova, who was in Moscow on an IREX grant, found herself the recipient of some phenomenally silly questions from me and cheerfully thumbed through the Moscow phone directory in order to get the answers.

Friends and colleagues took time out from their own busy schedules to involve themselves in this book. I am particularly grateful to Thomas Lahusen, Jeffrey Brooks, Sibelan Forrester, and James von Geldern for their thoughtful comments and helpful suggestions.

Sustenance, ideas, and good cheer came from many quarters. Many of my deepest thanks go to the group at Duke University Press with whom I have had the privilege of working on this project and others. The two anonymous readers for the press gave this manuscript a timely and very close read and offered good, cogent suggestions that helped bring this manuscript together. Laura Barneby, senior editorial assistant at the press, sensed that I was organizationally challenged and thus made doubly sure that all the pieces of this project came together in just the right way. Pam Morrison, as always, went over this manuscript as if it were her own. Mindy Conner's impeccable eye and editorial skill extraordinaire brought this volume together. My greatest debt is to my editor, Valerie Millholland, whose every conversation was punctuated with "this is going to be a great book" and who has the rare gift of knowing when to push an author and when to suggest the ocean instead.

This volume came together in several different cities. In Moscow, Ekaterina Stetsenko and Vladimir Alpatov, Maya Koreneva, Nadezhda Azhgikhina, Natal'ia Dmitrieva, Larissa Morozova, Alexei at Betkhoven, and Valerii Varlakov all helped me with everything from logistics to pets and with much in between, often incredulous at the sorts of things that academic scholarship is up to in the United States these days. At the University of Illinois, Peter Maggs helped access a phenomenal number of databases and went out of his way through numerous acts of kindness. In Tucson, Gary Kabakoff's wondrous technical expertise freed me from the infuriating detail of formatting a manuscript just about to go into production. My thanks also to Dawn Winsor-Hibble, Jodi Kelber, Jane Hill, Mia Schnaible, Brett Soulages, Travis Vandell, and Sabrina Lee. Special thanks are due to my friend and colleague Sabrina Ramet at the University of Washington, with whom many of the ideas for this volume were originally hatched and who gave so much of her time and energy in the initial stages of the project.

Sometimes the most generous help comes from those who aren't involved in the project at all. Mary and Xavier Leon, Jill McCartney, Jane Arons, and Ivanna Abril helped in innumerable ways. Georgia Maas, Julia Clancy-Smith, Del and Lafon Phillips, and Marian and Dawn Binder provided deep and sustaining friendship. In Paris Marty Reubin, Jacqueline Wales, Serena, and Samara were there for us as we were settling in. And Susan Aiken, my sister, listened like only a sister can, gave my prose its most generous and critical read, and urged me throughout "not to give away Peaches."

Acknowledgments frequently end with thanks to one's family for putting up with all those things families put up with when books are being written. Rather than sit around and wait for the book to be done, my son Noah decided to join in, becoming an intrepid traveler in the process and a great researcher of Moscow's pet sites.

This book is dedicated to the memory of two dear friends. To that of my father, Jack Porter Barker, a kind and gentle man from Tennessee, whose life was inscribed with an abiding love of nature and of the written word, and an inherent sense of justice and commitment to the work he chose to do. My father did not live to see this volume completed. But he lived long enough to see the changes in the new Russia and to both marvel and ruminate upon them as I have. It is dedicated as well to the memory of my friend and colleague Chuck Isenberg, whose love of teaching and whose gifts as a reader were matched only by his generosity of spirit and modesty about his own accomplishments.

Part I INTRODUCTION

■ **CHAPTER 1**
ADELE MARIE BARKER

REREADING RUSSIA

Sometime in the spring of 1993, I had occasion to spend more than an hour in a cab with a Moscow taxi driver hurling and honking his way through the streets in our mutual quest for an address that had been given to me. After an hour of precipitous stops — as the driver leaned out, hailed passersby, asked for directions, and engaged in protracted discussions over how to find the elusive address — we arrived at our destination, only to have the embarrassed driver confess that he knew all along where the address was and would have gotten us there sooner if only the "bastards" at the top hadn't changed the names of all the streets in Moscow.

This taxi ride suggests the kinds of disorienting surface changes that abound in post-Soviet society. Streets metamorphose, their "old" familiar revolutionary names giving way to even older, less familiar names from the prerevolutionary past. Billboards advertise everything from the laundry delights of

3

Prokter i Gembl to *dzhinsy* Wrangler or Levi-Strauss. A cathedral erected to celebrate Russia's victory over Napoleon, then subsequently blown up in 1931 to make room for Stalin's Palace of Soviets but turned instead into a swimming pool, now rises again out of the cavernous mass that once housed the pool. Oddly inappropriate buildings — office high-rises, a neighborhood Orthodox church, and a McDonalds — eye each other uncomfortably on property once state owned, now privatized. And living spaces — once communal and scarcely able to contain those who dwelt within them — now squeeze out their former inhabitants as the New Russians remodel and renovate this former domestic territory. The geographic and physical landscapes of urban Russia today — ruptured, defamiliarized, jolting to the eye and to other senses as well — speak of other kinds of displacements and permutations at work, this time in the cultural landscape of the new Russia. These dislocations may best be summed up by Anna Krylova in her chapter in this volume on Soviet and post-Soviet anecdotes ("Saying 'Lenin' and Meaning 'Party': Subversion and Laughter in Soviet and Post-Soviet Society"): Krylova recounts an evening in 1994 spent at a performance of Erofeev's play *Moskva-Petushki,* a play she had first seen in 1988. Returning to Russia after six years, she sat in the audience and noticed that something had changed. "The audience was laughing, but it was not laughing the way I remembered it, expected it, and wanted it to laugh. But," she adds, "I [myself] did not know when to laugh."

I begin my introduction to this volume on popular culture, sex, and society since Gorbachev with these two moments from post-Soviet life because they represent the enormous changes that have taken place in Russian society and culture over the past ten years and the kinds of questions we need to ask about these changes. Like the construction sites themselves, which seem to throw together past and present, disparate styles, or no style at all, so too does the new cultural landscape of Russia present itself as an indecipherable and some-times impenetrable maze of everything from high fashion to rave clubs, from sushi parlors to shi-shi dog-grooming studios, at once imitative and original, and all reflective of the new popular culture that is emerging in this newly emerging nation.

The transformative changes that have taken hold of Russian society since the mid-1980s, unprecedented as anything that has occurred in that country since the Bolshevik Revolution, have brought with them a restructuring not only of the political and economic landscape but of cultural life as well. One of the most obvious changes in the life of the nation has been the emergence of a new popular culture: new kinds of TV programming, pulp fiction, cruising strips, and tattoo parlors. Like Russia itself, this new popular culture finds itself torn between its own heritage and that of the West, between its revulsion with the past and its nostalgic desire to re-create the markers of it, between the lure of the lowbrow and the pressures to return to the elitist prerevolutionary past.

The contributors to this volume have attempted to navigate through the maze of popular culture in the new Russia. Although there are numerous areas in which the popular has made its mark, not all could be included in this volume. Much remains to be done, for example, on the relationship between structures of ownership and control of culture in post-Soviet Russia, on fashion, reading habits, and popular culture in the rural areas — to name just a few — that for reasons of space could not be included. The chapters that do appear here raise some of the most salient questions regarding popular culture in contemporary Russia: How, for example, are Russians negotiating cultural stereotypes from their past in the production of this new culture? How have notions of the public and the private realm changed? What is the relationship between the producers and consumers of this culture and between elitist and popular culture in post-Soviet society? And finally, to what extent are Western paradigms applicable to both the production and the study of this culture? Many of the issues raised here may serve as a guide to research in other areas of the popular culture boom in Russia today. For example, Eliot Borenstein's insights on the new religious cults ("Suspending Disbelief") might serve as a framework within which to examine alternative realities and the UFO craze in Russia today; Nancy Condee's analysis of tattooing the postcommunist body ("Body Graphics"), Laurie Essig's chapter ("Publicly Queer"), and my own chapter ("Going to the Dogs") might provide an entrée for those wishing to study configurations of public and private in postcommunist Russia.

This volume is divided into sections dealing with popular culture, sexualities, society, and social artifacts. Just as studies of popular culture examine how culture, gender, economics, and national identity come together in the formation of culture, a similar kind of weaving is at work between the various chapters in this volume. Although Alexei Yurchak's "Gagarin and the Rave Kids" and Theresa Sabonis-Chafee's "Communism as Kitsch" appear in different sections, both are engaged with patterns of consumption in the transition from the Soviet to the post-Soviet state, specifically with what happens when certain signs and symbols lose their ideological value in the new order. Similarly, Julia Friedman and Adam Weiner's "Between a Rock and a Hard Place," which explores the nationalistic strain among some Russian rockers today, and Essig's "Publicly Queer" both look at issues pertinent to the construction of identity. Essig argues that the notion of identity as it is understood in the West is simply not applicable to queer life in Russia today, which she sees as being more accurately defined as a set of subjectivities. Similarly, Friedman and Weiner explore the desire among certain Russian rockers not only to move explicitly away from any identification with the West but to find a way to negotiate the Russian past, which, in the authors' words, is simultaneously rock's "saving grace and deadliest temptation." Similarly, the complex and not easily resolvable issue of the past — where to put it, how to think about it — is fundamental to several chapters, notably Friedman and Weiner's chapter, Larsen's "In Search of an Audience," Boym's "From the Toilet to the Museum," Bushnell's "Paranoid Graffiti at Execution Wall," Judith Kornblatt's "Christianity, Antisemitism, Nationalism," and Eliot Borenstein's "Suspending Disbelief."

This volume is both descriptive and theoretical. It is an attempt both to chart some of the manifestations of a newly emerging popular culture and to understand how this new culture is informed by models from both past and present, from both within and without. In Chapter 2, "The Culture Factory," I look at what happens to Western theories of popular culture transplanted onto Russian soil. Western culture critics continue to debate the precise nature of the relationship between elite culture and popular culture, a question complicated by the fact that popular culture is often produced by an elite class for the benefit of the masses. And thus this phenomenon potentially raises the question of whether the production of that culture becomes a form of social control. I trace the evolving history of the relationship between elite and popular within Soviet society and examine one of the fundamental premises to the study of popular culture in the West — the concept of everyday life — and how that concept is nuanced differently for those who lived under Soviet rule and those in the West who study Soviet society. Specifically, I suggest that the ambiguous nature of the public-private dichotomy in Soviet history is still a felt presence in post-Soviet life, pointing to the often complex interaction between older social and cultural patterns and the popular culture of today. Indeed, any study of TV viewing habits in the new Russia would have to take account of this public and private dyad. Television viewing in early post-Soviet society is exposing domestic spaces — Russian and foreign — to the public sphere. The average post-Soviet viewer is being treated vicariously to people's private lives, an area Soviet citizens protected zealously precisely because the state implicitly condoned intrusion into those lives through its infamous system of *donosy* (denunciations).

The chapters in part 2 are all concerned in some way with what Dick Hebdige defines as "a set of generally available artifacts,"[1] under which he includes films, music, TV programs, pulp fiction, jokes, and so on. Within the Russian context those artifacts would be those pastimes and forms of entertainment generally available to the average Russian today in the urban areas.

Several of the chapters in this section take up the production and consumption of culture since the collapse of the Soviet Union. Although not market based, the Soviet Union was nevertheless a consumer society. What was produced was ideology; what was consumed was some portion thereof, depending on the degree to which the average Soviet identified with the ideology and the degree to which the ideology happened to match the needs of the people at various times. Ideology had its own *reklamy* (advertisements) in the form of billboards heralding larger-than-life figures engaged in the process of moving the country into the "radiant future" (*svetloe budushchee*). But there are differences, and very important ones, between Soviet and post-Soviet society in matters of consumption.[2] Most important is the fact that the Soviet Union was not a monied economy. Although people had money — some a great deal more than others — privilege, not money, was the determinant of power. And that privilege was predicated on whom one knew and, in the case of Russia's writers, on the traditionally semisanctified role of the Russian writer. In "Markets, Mirrors, and Mayhem," Catharine Nepomnyashchy discusses what happens to the writer's, and more specifically the female writer's, authority as the traditional role of the Russian writer is supplanted by the market. These differences between Soviet and post-Soviet society are crucial in understanding the situation that the hapless Russian television viewer faced in the summer of 1994, as narrated by Eliot Borenstein in "Public Offerings: MMM and the Marketing of Melodrama." Borenstein recounts the infamous MMM scandal that mesmerized all of Russia in the summer of 1994. MMM was just one of many pyramid schemes that came into being in Eastern Europe and Russia between 1990 and 1994 (the largest and perhaps most outrageous by all accounts being the infamous Caritas scheme in Romania),[3] set up ostensibly to help the beleaguered citizens of these countries survive the transition from a socialist to a market economy by multiplying depositors' funds within a matter of months. MMM was not just another pyramid scheme. One of its distinctive features was the way characters in soap operas were used to entice the Russian viewer to invest, promising her new furniture, trips, and even romance.[4] Borenstein explores what happened when Russian viewers, formerly such astute readers of party ideology, allowed themselves to become not only the TV viewers but the partners and even the coauthors of a narrative that most failed to read correctly.

Issues of how products and the ideologies they implicitly advertise are marketed in the new Russia are also taken up by Elizabeth Zelensky in "Popular Children's Culture in Post-Perestroika Russia." Zelensky focuses her attention on how Russia's children are negotiating their way through the maze of new consumer products and integrating models from their own past with the Americanized life around them. The effect of the transformative economic and social changes on Russia's children is far from clear. Recent studies have shown that children are among the biggest consumers of TV and billboard ads in Russia. Slogans from the ads have crept into the language of the youth subculture, a fact the older generation finds extremely worrisome and which has increased nationalistic sentiment among them as they respond to the increasing Americanization of Russia and Russian values. My chapter "Going to the Dogs" looks at the new pet culture not only as an example of what has happened to traditional notions of public and private in the new Russia but at what happens when economics transforms popular culture from a potential site of resistance back into the domain of elitist culture.

One of the underlying tensions in Russian popular culture today, no less than in other forms of post-Soviet life, is the still unresolved relationship with the Soviet and prerevolutionary past. Alexei Yurchak's "Gagarin and the Rave Kids" is an anthropologist's view of how Russia's youth, particularly its rock groups and the organizers of its nightlife, have been negotiating the disappearance of what he calls "the cultural logic of late socialism." Yurchak sees cultural production in postcommunist Russia as being framed by a "symbolic creativity" within which many of the traditional Soviet symbols, such as that of the cosmonaut Yury Gagarin, have been lifted out of the context of Soviet ideology and made to seem relevant to a youth culture for whom the figure of Gagarin is ideologically meaningless.

Anna Krylova's chapter, "Saying 'Lenin' and Meaning 'Party'," like Yurchak's, examines how forms of resistance come about and what happens when a cultural artifact such as a joke ceases to circulate as oppositional discourse and enters the "free marketplace of ideas." Both Krylova and Yurchak identify moments in Soviet life during which Soviet citizens operated simultaneously within official and nonofficial cultures, thus suggesting that in Russia, as in the West, the origins of countercultures often lie within authoritative and dominant discourses. Nancy Condee's "Body Graphics: Tattooing the Fall of Communism" similarly looks at what happens when the symbolic import of nonofficial culture falls away. Condee traces the fate of the symbolic designs of skin decoration in light of the disappearance from post-Soviet life of the social and political context within which they were once produced. She argues that tattooing in Russia has changed to reflect people's reappropriation of their bodies from state control. Theresa Sabonis-Chafee looks at how the past has carved out a place for itself in the nostalgia bank of postcommunist culture through the symbols of communist kitsch, most of which are happily consumed by the postcommunist consumer. John Bushnell provides another take on this tension between past and present in "Paranoid Graffiti at Execution Wall," which details how the old Russian custom of creating martyrs for the cause is reflected in the transition to the new order. Similarly, Robert Edelman, in "There Are No Rules on Planet Russia," suggests that post-Soviet sport is still as much a contested terrain as it was under communism, although it is no longer the party vying for control of that terrain with the people, but rather a struggle between various members of the newly emerging elites. In a slightly different take on this relationship between the post-Soviet present and the Soviet past, Svetlana Boym, in "From the Toilet to the Museum," explores the dialectic between past and present in postcommunist Russia by asking what happens when an artist such as Ilya Kabakov begins to tamper with nostalgia and collective forgetting and alters the popular narrative of nostalgia.

Several of the chapters examine intersections between gender and popular culture — from ownership of one's body to power and pornography. In "Markets, Mirrors, and Mayhem," Catharine Theimer Nepomnyashchy examines detective writer Aleksandra Marinina, whose novels are topping the best-seller list in Russia. Marinina's female protagonist, Anastasiia Kamenskaia, overturns many of Russia's most hallowed female stereotypes. Kamenskaia, a police lieutenant colonel who works as an analyst at central police headquarters in Moscow, eschews the domestic, rewriting the narrative that Russian tradition appropriated to women. She earns respect less through maternal qualities (of which she seems utterly devoid) than through her sharp analytical mind, which enables her to solve from behind her desk the bizarre and often dastardly crimes in the new Russia.

Other chapters move more explicitly from issues of gender to those of sexuality. Paul Goldschmidt's "Pornography in Russia" provides a historical over-view of pornography in Russia and then focuses on some recent legal battles over what constitutes pornography. Goldschmidt focuses on the role of the erotic in popular culture today, in Russia and elsewhere. It is the play on the potentially transgressive nature of the erotic that informs much of popular culture, from Madonna to rock music, and it is that transgressivity that is at issue in the pornography debate in post-Soviet Russia. In "Queer Perfor-mance" Tim Scholl takes on the St. Petersburg Muzhskoi balet (Male Ballet), a group that was never intended to be a gay ballet, as an example of this trans-gressivity. The Male Ballet's "self-presentation" exposes the tensions between high and low art, Western and Russian, male and female, gay and straight, and sacred and profane found in Russian society in the early post-Soviet era.

As the chapters in this volume suggest, popular culture is ultimately insepar-able from the process of social change and the re-formations of identity that accompany it. As Russian history reveals all too clearly, the impetus toward social change as well as the forces that have retarded it are often characterized by a powerful religious element. This trend is as true today as it was in pre-revolutionary or communist Russia. Susan Larsen's "In Search of an Au-dience: The New Russian Cinema of Reconciliation" picks up on the theme of the "Russian idea" introduced by Friedman and Weiner and discusses its fate and that of Orthodoxy in general in the new Russian cinema. In "Christianity. Antisemitism. Nationalism," Judith Deutsch Kornblatt argues that despite the factionalism both inside and outside the church, many Russians still believe in an "all-pervasive single Russian idea," although one no longer grounded in adequate spiritual training. Eliot Borenstein's thought-provoking essay on the new religious cult of Maria Devi, "Suspending Disbelief," correctly suggests that the emergence of cults in the unstable days of the new order, whether or not they are ascribed to pernicious foreign influence, is suggestive of a nostalgia for a mystical spiritual haven, a place of retreat from the instabilities of the present, which many believe are leading Russia once again toward an apocalypse.

Why popular culture? Because as Russians search for answers to the uncer-tainties of the present and try to forge a new discourse and a new culture for themselves, they must inevitably confront the fact that they no longer have a dominant discourse, if there ever was one to begin with. No longer is there a party rhetoric, or even a discourse of an elitist intelligentsia, seeking to pre-serve "high" culture, however one chooses to define it. That Russia's popular culture during the Soviet era was often conflated with both elitist and mass cultures may account for the enthusiasm with which popular culture from the West, which makes no claim to being other than what it is, is greeted in Russia today. In examining this evolving cultural palate, each chapter implicitly struggles with the question of whether Russia can resuscitate its cultural life, not in elitist terms but in the new forms of "people's" culture it is experimenting with and experiencing today.

Note on Transliteration

In general, we have adhered to the Library of Congress transliteration system.

Notes

1 Dick Hebdige, *Hiding in the Light: On Images and Things* (London: Routledge, 1988), p. 47.

2 It is important to note that the prevalence of this culture does not automatically guarantee that Russians can participate in it. Most Russians, for example, have TV sets, but most cannot begin to afford the products directed at the New Russians that are advertised on it. Pampers, for example, is a luxury item — seen in ads by everyone but consumed by only a few. Procter and Gamble has made interesting use of this Soviet determinant of status in ads that say, "Prokter i gambel zhaesh'?" (Procter and Gamble, do you know it?). Here the marketers are deliberately alluding to a Soviet marker of status in which one person might say to another, "Do you know Ivan?" (Ivana zhaesh'?). For more on the use of Soviet linguistic and social forms in the new advertising, see, Aleksei Levinson, "Zametki po sotsiologii i antropologii reklamy," *Novoe literaturnoe obozrenie,* no. 22 (1996), pp. 101–28.

3 For an account of the Caritas pyramid scheme in Romania, see Katherine Verdery, *What Was Socialism and What Comes Next?* (Princeton: Princeton University Press, 1996), ch. 7, "Faith, Hope, and Caritas in the Land of the Pyramids, Romania 1990–1994." For most of us in the West, it was the dissident movement in the socialist countries that signaled the fiction of the facade. But on an everyday level for those who lived there, the existence of the second economy in which most dabbled in order to make ends meet and the various layers of Soviet official and unofficial discourse were all marks of a culture in which there were degrees of resistance at virtually every turn.

4 One of the reasons Russians were so successfully duped by the pyramid scheme was the average Russian viewer's identification with the characters on the TV program. The actor Vladimir Permiakov, who played the character of Lenia Golubkov, stated in an interview that Mosfil'm was looking for someone with peasantlike features (*muzhitskaia vneshnost'*) to play the role of Lenia, and he fit the bill. See *Litsa,* no. 3 (March 1998), pp. 33–36.

THE CULTURE FACTORY: THEORIZING THE POPULAR IN THE OLD AND NEW RUSSIA

About eight kilometers north of the center of Moscow lies a neighborhood I have come to know rather well over the past twenty years. I have had occasion to get lost there, to shop there, to visit friends there, and to stay there. Like most neighborhoods in Moscow this one is most easily reached from the metro, whose ornate décor once contrasted sharply with the drabness of the life one encountered on emerging from its depths onto the street. Things have changed now. There is still a certain contrast, but it is no longer contrast between monumentalism and the gray exterior. Instead it might best be summed up as that between the old Soviet style underground and the chaos of styles aboveground, which consequently leaves one with the impression of no style at all. Not long ago the only voice that could be heard over the PA system on the escalator in this metro station was an official one exhorting the public to stay to the right on the escalator. Since the early 1990s, less official voices advertise package tours to Tunisia, Morocco, or the Canary Islands, places that in the past the average Soviet could only dream about. Ironically, such destinations remain equally unattainable now, as the salaries of the average Russian have failed to keep up with the goods proffered on the market.

On this particular day I emerge with the throng onto the street and head toward one of the many hastily constructed stalls selling everything from the magazine *Andrei* (the Russian version of *Playboy*) to other "pet" magazines (animals, this time), to brochures on the history of the Orthodox Church in Russia. I share the space near one particular book and magazine stall with a couple of young guys with spiked hair who are thumbing through rock magazines and *Ptiuch,* the trendy new magazine for Russia's youth, while surreptitiously surveying the offerings in *Andrei,* which the vendor recommends to me as "better" than the American *Playboy*. People of varying ages, shopping on their way home from work, elbow their way through the crush of stalls. Several of those who pass by appear to have been touched little if at all by the changes in the new Russia. Further on — the boundaries between stalls becoming indistinguishable at a certain point — sellers proffer the latest Vladimir Bezymianny thriller or the more introspective detective fiction of Nikolai Leonov, both of which soon give way to the salacious offerings of Sidney Sheldon, Harold Robbins, and the darling of the romance set, Barbara Cartland. Extracting myself from the sea of kiosks, I notice the inevitable line — one of the many holdovers from Soviet times. But this one is not for food or hard-to-get items, but for currency exchange at the local bank.

This bustling new consumer culture — free of the constraints of censorship and party ideology, although not altogether devoid of other kinds of ideology — still bears the economic marks of a past from which it will take decades to make the final break. One feels the persistent hold of that past in the bizarre and often random nature of the offerings in the stalls that have sprung up outside most metro stations in Moscow. In March 1997 the food kiosk I visited to get some salmon for my friend Katya prominently displayed imported baby food and French liqueurs alongside one another on the front shelves.[1] This phenomenon — so sharp a break from the past in terms of what was being offered, so like it in the seemingly random nature of its offerings — spoke volumes about the complexity of the transition from socialist to market economy that had already begun to emerge in the last years of socialism.

I pass through an eighteenth-century arch into a world little changed over the twenty years I have been visiting Moscow. Before me stands a small eighteenth-century Orthodox church whose interior and the life it represents bespeak a world untainted by what lies outside. Not far from this place is a park that once housed a hospital for those injured in World War I. The dead were buried in a cemetery that lies along its now demolished walls. But even here small signs of the new order are omnipresent. On my daily strolls I pass a Chinese teahouse — an architectural jewel with virtually no customers since it has priced itself out of the market in this particular neighborhood. Instead the locals throng to the formerly state-owned *prodovol'stvennyi magazin* (food store) down the street, now privatized and run by an Azerbaijani family; it stocks and sells local and imported products priced more in accordance with most people's pocketbooks.

My walk has taken me through the sights, sounds, and textures of some of the many manifestations of what can be termed popular culture in Russia today: the *makulatura* (pulp fiction) on the bookstands, the bustling consumer culture (for those who can afford it), the sites of resistance to that same culture, the cultivation of travel and leisure time, what is viewed and listened to — in short, life as it is lived by the average post-Soviet *Homo consumptor* in Moscow today. And it is precisely this new consumer culture — much of which has been inspired by the West, and much of which is anything but elitist — that has become the focus of lively debate and study in both Russia and the West. While the New Russians are buying up Cartier watches as fast as they come into the Almaz Jewelry Store or putting down fifty-five thousand dollars in cash at a GM dealership for a Chevy Caprice, many of the older generation are digging in their heels and refusing to go along. What perturbs them is not just the spending habits of the New Russians, but the lack of *kul'tura* that seems to accompany these habits.[2] It is not surprising that some of the most stringent objections to this new "culture" come from the older generation of Russians, many of whom are from the intelligentsia and, regardless of class allegiance, perceive themselves to have been unceremoniously dumped into the miasma of post-Soviet culture. Interestingly, class affiliation under the Soviet regime has become much less a marker of how former Soviet citizens are responding to post-Soviet culture than is the fact that Soviet citizens, irrespective of class, were educated to regard culture in general and literature in particular as more than mere entertainment. Thus, for them, some of the most disturbing moments in post-Soviet life center on their discomfort with this new culture, which ostensibly seems to have little to redeem it, either socially or ideologically. As a colleague of mine from the Gorky Institute of World Literature, lamenting what she sees as the demise of culture in the new Russia, recently put it: "The point is not whether Russians are reading Tolstoy or Sidney Sheldon but whether they will even be able to read Tolstoy or appreciate real art after being exposed to what is available to them today." Most disturbing to the aesthetic sensibilities of some has been the recent establishment of the Association for Mass Literature (Assotsiatsiia massovoi literatury), which now awards prizes for the best works in detective fiction, sci-fi, and thrillers as well as providing data banks on the economics, sociology, and aesthetics of the new fiction.[3] Although in one sense no one will argue that what we are seeing in the new Russia is as decisive a break from the past as anything the country has witnessed since the Bolshevik Revolution, my colleague's argument is, in fact, an old one that reflects a debate among Russian Marxists even before the revolution: could the proletariat best be served by absorbing the culture of the so-called civilized world or by fashioning a separate proletariat culture of its own in forging the revolution?[4] Ironically, as the members of a once-cohesive intelligentsia continue to argue vehemently for the cultural richness of Russia's past in the face-off with post-Soviet culture, the very reforms set in motion through glasnost under Gorbachev were accomplished precisely with the intelligentsia in mind. Hoping to secure their support in the political and economic arenas, Gorbachev introduced the free marketplace of ideas whose cultural products the former intelligentsia now see as the scourge of the tradition they cherished and often sacrificed their lives to preserve.[5]

In the pages that follow, I will look at how some of the questions we are asking about popular culture in the West play themselves out on Russian soil today. The current vogue in the West for studying everything from shopping malls to sporting events has also begun to attract the attention of Russian critics searching for ways to interpret the new popular culture craze in their own country.[6] By understanding this phenomenon, Russian sociologists, economists, culture critics, and consumers alike hope to negotiate a middle-of-the-road position between the massive consumption of the popular and the desire not to be ultimately consumed by it.

The study of popular culture in the West is part of the larger field of cultural studies that has made its way into the academy during the past ten years, helping academics rethink the boundaries of knowledge and traditional notions of disciplinarity.[7] In its scrutiny of long-standing notions in traditional disciplines about what constitutes high versus low culture, dominant versus marginalized, and the appropriate venues of academic study, to name but a few, cultural studies has concerned itself in almost every sense with what Michael Holquist calls "the negotiation of borders."[8] It is precisely the study of popular culture that has brought many of these issues to the foreground. Moreover, traditional approaches to the concept of text saw the writing of literature, and its implied status as high art, as the principal form within which to speak about textuality. Within the sphere of popular culture, *text* has taken on a very different meaning. I have in mind here the work of people such as David Morley, Stuart Hall, Dick Hebdige, John Fiske, Megan Morris, Tony Bennett, and others who posit that symbolic configurations of all sorts — what we wear, what we buy, the kind of music we make and listen to, the sports we play, and even where we walk — constitute forms of textuality in our lives that are every bit as important to "read" as what is inscribed in the written text.

A colleague of mine remarked not long ago that she is glad popular culture is now part of the academic curriculum because it legitimizes what most of us do on the sly anyway when we are not engaged in teaching high art — namely, consuming a certain amount of junk TV, reading trash novels, or even secretly stealing a peek at *People* or the *Enquirer* in the grocery store checkout line. But whether we consume these products or not, they have become compelling objects of interest in their own right as they have helped culture critics piece together the relationship between the production and the consumption of culture — between high and low art, between gender and cultural production, and between marketing and ideology, to name but a few. For many critics, the lure of popular culture is not just that it is great fun but that finally it becomes a way of defining what it means to be a consumer in the cultural production line of late capitalism. Certain critics such as Adorno and Horkheimer and other members of the Frankfurt school take a pessimistic view of the role of the consumer in this dyad, viewing popular culture as just another means by which capitalism secures its tenacious hold on society. In their view, those of us who consume this culture, passively and unthinkingly, become "cultural dupes."[9] Other critics, however, such as John Fiske and members of the cultural populist school, predicate the study of the popular on the assumption that it is not just a degraded form of high culture imposed on us from above for purposes of control and profit. In Fiske's view, we are, in fact, creative consumers of the culture that is produced for us, acting on it rather than letting it act on us.[10] For Fiske, then, the study of popular culture demands that we look not only at who is producing the cultural products but at ourselves as consumers and at the ways we use these products. Thus, acknowledging the economic or ideological power of such culture conglomerates as Disney or Reebok or McDonalds is not the same as acknowledging the influence they have on us.

Two interesting examples from Soviet and post-Soviet popular culture illustrate how Fiske's thesis might work within a Russian context. High Stalinism, as I will discuss later, was a complex merging of elitist and lowbrow cultures designed to create a culture for the masses, who became both its producers and its consumers. The culture that evolved in the 1930s was meant to be consumed in a very specific way, as illustrated by the number of readers' clubs (*chitatel'nye kluby*) that were created under Stalin with the express purpose of ensuring that the literature being produced in the people's name would be read properly.[11] Problems arose when Soviet "consumers" failed to consume the culture as they should. But according to whom? Although it was relatively easy for censors and for the literary establishment as a whole to police a work in an effort to ascertain whether it was written, composed, or painted in the spirit of the times, how was that same establishment to keep tabs on whether readers were reading as they ought to or responding with the appropriate level of fervor to the mass parades celebrating various socialist holidays? People went to the movies, participated in the requisite parades, and read official literature that often stirred them deeply, as Thomas Lahusen's recent study of Vasilii Azhaev's novel *Far from Moscow* (*Daleko iz Moskvy*) shows.[12] The real policing of public response to literature and other areas of Soviet life came not from above but from Soviet citizens themselves, many of whom welcomed the values of the system, internalized them, and proceeded to apply them by engaging in *samokritika,* or "self-criticism." Thus it was that in memoirs and biographies of the time the failure to consume properly made itself felt not in any expressed desire to subvert the system but rather in feelings of unworthiness among writers and readers alike, who frequently felt that they didn't measure up to the goals set forth in the literature they read. A case in point is the Soviet novelist and poet Vera Inber, whose notebooks written in the 1930s lament her feeling that she is an outsider — "a stepdaughter" — to Soviet literature because of her petit bourgeois origins, which have kept her from ever having a "proper" biography. Her writings communicate her sense of failure because her background did not conform to the sort of heroic life the times demanded. Alas, she laments, "I was not lucky with my biography."[13] Similarly, in her diary written between the years 1932 and 1936, Galina Vladimirovna Shtange talks about her community work for the party in Moscow: "I was terrified: would I be able to do as much as I should? Noblesse oblige! Tomorrow I'll get down to work, I'll try to measure up to those expectations that Pogrebinsky talked about."[14]

The phenomenon of billboard advertising that increasingly saturates the urban landscape in Russia's larger cities is another area in which Fiske's theories of the popular can be tested. Interestingly, a billboard advertising Wrangler jeans, for instance, proffers something many Russians were consuming long before perestroika through gifts from Western friends, the black market, or *blat*. Thus the assumptions on which much American advertising is predicated — that consumers will purchase a product as a result of seeing an ad — are not necessarily applicable to the Russian experience given the history of how consumption was determined in the Soviet Union. There are two important issues here. First of all, advertising functioned very differently in the Soviet Union than in the West and was used as a way to reenforce party policy. Because advertising was intrinsically political, it was strictly forbidden to advertise Western products. Nevertheless, Soviet citizens procured Western products aplenty without the benefit of advertising — and continue to do so now perhaps in spite of it — a fact that tends to support Fiske's thesis that consumers "consume" very differently than producers intend.[15] Fiske sees a constant tension in the culture industry between the production of popular culture and the way the consumer receives it, a tension created by the fact that we are refashioners of that culture even as we seem to be its passive recipients.[16]

As we begin to look at the explosion of popular culture in post-Soviet Russia, we will need to shift our gaze more than geographically. The fact that many of the groundbreaking works on contemporary popular culture have been produced by British and American scholars has shaped our theoretical reflections, and also suggests that we need to decontextualize these reflections as we carry them into Russia. Moreover, as we export everything from Disney to Barbie and Reeboks to the new Russia, we are exporting not only products but also the markers of an entire complex ideology. Indeed, the very theory we use — most of it Western in origin — to interpret the new culture in Russia may, if we are not careful, become yet another colonizing strategy on the part of the West over the postcommunist world. One of the questions we might ask is whether we are assuming that we can study the fate of American popular culture and cultural products in Russia in the same way that we study them in the United States. The comments that follow suggest why that question is important.

I. Popular Culture and the Party

When we speak of popular culture within a Western context, what we generally have in mind are the sorts of activities and pastimes that Dick Hebdige refers to when he defines popular culture as "the set of generally available artifacts" such as TV, films, music, jokes, and various subcultures.[17] While Western culture critics often disagree over how this culture is consumed or over the relationship between producers and consumers, there is general agreement as to what lies within the domain of the popular. The question of what exactly popular culture *is* becomes much more problematic when transplanted onto Russian soil. For one thing, as several of the essays in this volume make explicit, popular culture in Russia today is heavily nostalgic, although in a very different way than nostalgia is usually understood in the West. Although much cultural production—from rave parties to anecdotes and art installations—in the new Russia deals with the past, it does so not merely to remember and to mourn but to rewrite the nostalgic text, often by domesticating, familiarizing, and even trivializing outworn symbols of oppression or by returning to what is familiar from a safe enough distance to preclude any real return to what is both mourned and despised. It is precisely because of this nostalgic tendency that much of the rock music scene simply cannot be studied the same way it is studied in the West. This retrospective stance of much of post-Soviet popular culture also suggests the complex intersection of past and present that informs post-Soviet life today. One of the questions we must ask as we begin to study post-Soviet popular culture is to what degree the experience of the past seventy-five years is a felt presence in the culture industry in contemporary Russia. On the one hand, many of the consumers and even producers of this new culture have only the memory of the latter days of socialism, and even fewer have direct experience with the ravages of Stalinism. On the other hand, collective memory, which derives much of its power from a realm outside individual experience, has also been a powerful stimulus in the production of culture in post-Soviet Russia, thus suggesting that the vestiges of lived experience among the older generation still play into the imaginations of the young.

Our understanding of post-Soviet popular culture is further complicated by the fact that the paradigms we use to describe popular culture in the West don't hold up very well when applied to the Soviet experience. I have in mind the distinction between high versus low, or elite versus popular, culture, and where—if at all—the two intersect. The issue is a complex one because the boundaries between the two apparent opposites are often elusive. Moreover, the study of popular culture inevitably leads into issues of class, which, whether we take an elitist stance or not, is consumer based. How culture is produced is often, although not always, determined by the class of people for whom it is intended. Decisions about TV programming in the United States, what airs when, and who the sponsors will be are intricately bound up with the construction of economic and social privilege in U.S. society. Further, the assumption that the upper classes, although they may be heavily involved in both the production and consumption of popular culture, are by and large also the perpetuators and conservators of elitist culture suggests that the boundaries between the two realms may not always be clearly delineated.[18]

The history of Russian popular culture in this century suggests if nothing else that the relationship between elite and popular has been vastly more complicated than Western models might lead us to believe, resulting in the virtual collapse of this distinction, at least in theory, from the 1930s on.[19] To begin with, the identities and positions of the elite were really a function of whether we were looking at Soviet society from within or without. Sovietologists in the West tended to place the elitist culture on the fringes of official Soviet culture, and defined the elite as those who belonged to the dissident community and carved out their own path to create a cultural life that became an alternate source of power. Further, if official literature was associated with a locus of power — political, cultural, and even economic — it was precisely the location of certain kinds of cultural products on the margins of acceptability, or, sometimes, in a place of total unacceptability, that defined their centrality for many Sovietologists and Western intellectuals. Certainly the degree of influence writers such as Alexander Solzhenitsyn, Andrei Sinyavsky, Boris Pasternak, or Anna Akhmatova wielded over our literary imaginations and our social consciousness was directly proportional to the distance those same writers occupied from the center of Soviet power, whether or not they were formally members of the dissident community.[20] But it is also important to remember that the disaffected intelligentsia constituted an extremely powerful intellectual subculture that challenged the official culture through the power of moral persuasion it exercised on Western intellectuals and, through nonofficial channels, on Soviet society itself. As the critic Lev Anninskii has noted, the literature that was part of that periphery and was passed hand to hand through samizdat from the 1960s on created the moral conscience of an entire generation of thinkers and writers long before those works were permitted publication

in the Soviet Union.[21] This power emanating from the margins of Soviet society, while not overtly political, had important political ramifications and
suggested the uneasy relationship — sometimes accommodating, sometimes
clearly hostile — that characterized the dealings between the center of political power and those who occupied a place on its margins during the 1960s
and 1970s.

The tendency in the West to champion those writers who ran afoul of the
Soviet system was linked to a much broader tendency to view the Soviet Union
as a monolithic totalitarian entity in which the relationship between rulers and
ruled was one of domination and subordination — rulership and resistance.[22]
The totalitarian model led many westerners to see a country of indoctrinated
Communists, on the one hand, and dissidents, on the other. That some Sovietologists in the West retained the concept of Soviet society as two monologic
nonintersecting narratives may, in fact, have accounted for the disbelief expressed by many in the West at the reforms perestroika set in motion. The
tendency most recently in Soviet and post-Soviet studies has been to view
Soviet society as made up of "sites of contestation,"[23] in Stuart Hall's words, in
which nonofficial life and daily life were engaged in various struggles with the
dominant party line.

Although our proclivity to view everyday forms of resistance as radical
contestations has undoubtedly been influenced by Western cultural studies
theory, much of which is based on how marginalized groups and discourses find
voice and access to power, this approach has also been useful in studying the
Soviet experience because it has brought us much closer to the reality of Soviet
life as lived by the average Soviet citizen. For Soviet artists, cultural life was
characterized by a series of small victories and ideological compromises waged
on behalf of works of art. Dmitry Shostakovich survived the Stalin era to
compose his Symphony No. 10 and subsequent works because he made concessions after his opera *Lady Macbeth of Mtsensk* was suppressed in January
1937. Likewise, several of the new generation of poets in the 1960s, the most
notable being Evgeny Evtushenko, were criticized yet tolerated by the government for their liberal views because they toed the party line when they had to.
And in the sphere of daily life, the struggle was waged, often on an unconscious
level, by the people themselves as they sought to live within the strictures
imposed by the regime.

Yet, these small victories and signs of so-called resistance, such as the flour-
ishing "second economy" or the existence of unofficial clubs or unofficial art,

were not necessarily tantamount to dissent. Between the party line and dissent lay a vast arena where the infamous Soviet anecdote proliferated, where people purchased and sold on the black market, where Soviet citizens lived in cities where they were not registered (*propisan*),[24] where they procured what they needed through *blat* and did what they did not so much as a measure of dissent but as a survival strategy in a system whose economic and social realities fell far short of the promises it made on paper.[25] It was precisely in this area of the unofficial that most of Soviet life flourished. It was here in the everyday that the grand master narrative of the Soviet Union moved in a Bakhtinian sense from the monologic to the polylogic as Soviet citizens proceeded to reformulate or subvert it — not with the intent of bringing down the system, but simply to buy a decent pair of shoes, a Hungarian umbrella at Balaton, or some nice French cognac, or to find a good book at the black market down by the river on a Saturday.

Clearly for many in the West, Soviet elitist culture was an oxymoron, for what Western observers often perceived as elite lay on the fringes or under the surface of official Soviet life. But the perception of elitist culture from inside the party was an entirely different matter, particularly since party ideologues (ironically like some cultural studies scholars today) spent the better part of the twentieth century attempting to do away with the notion that there even *was* a distinction between popular and elitist culture. The early Bolsheviks attempted to forge a culture for the masses that would abolish this distinction. What the early Soviet leaders inherited was a population whose own culture was taken largely from the sphere of the popular, by which was meant anything from the traditional, prerevolutionary culture of the rural people to the culture of the urban masses or the various subcultures within Russian society with their own songs, traditions, theater, and mores.[26]

The problem in the early 1920s was that an enormous gap separated the revolutionary elite from the peasants and workers in whose name the former had made a revolution. That gap was both political and cultural. While the early Bolshevik leaders denied their own elitist position in Russian society, preferring instead to see the intelligentsia as the guardians of prerevolutionary high culture, the fact remains that the early Bolshevik revolutionaries themselves came from an intellectual elite that shared the intelligentsia's vision of a special class whose job it was to bring enlightenment to the masses below.[27] The early Bolsheviks were also elitist in that they dismissed urban popular culture at the time as being philistine, vulgar, and trivial, despite the fact that the new so-called elite that came into being under Stalin managed to exhibit shockingly bourgeois tastes in their own right, in everything from home furnishings to ersatz art, as they sought to replicate old prerevolutionary culture as the mark of having acquired status in the new order.[28] As the early architects of the state drew up new cultural directives for the masses, they endeavored to forge a proletarian culture that would speak to the peasants and the workers and would eventually supersede both the culture of the prerevolutionary elite and the "vulgar" urban culture of the day.

The history of this early proletarian culture contained the seeds of the distinction between elite and popular as it came to be understood during much of the Soviet era. If many of the early Bolsheviks themselves came from an intellectual elite that they sought to repudiate even while seeking a new form of elitism, they also looked toward a time when there would be essentially no difference between elitist culture and so-called popular culture, a time when, with the withering away of class distinctions, the divisions between the art and culture of the various classes would also disappear. This dream supposedly reached its culmination in the creation of socialist realism as the artistic credo in the 1930s. Ultimately the culture that emerged from the revolution would be a proletarian one.

This vision was all well and good as an example of solid utopian thinking, but in actuality the gulf separating rulers from ruled was very real and remained so, although unstated, throughout the Soviet era. This fact is poignantly brought out by the Soviet writer Mikhail Zoshchenko, whose satirical stories of the 1920s describe the plight of the simple Soviet citizen simultaneously aspiring to emulate the high culture of Russia's prerevolutionary past and that of the new Soviet proletariat, and failing miserably at both. Although early proletarian culture drew on forms from Russian peasant and urban culture, it remained essentially elitist, the brainchild of the upper echelons of the party, who put no small effort into creating the ideology behind the production of the new culture. Thus, by the end of the 1920s, Soviet society was structured in such a way that *kul'tura* as it was understood was the product of an ideology designed by a small group of party elite for everybody else.[29] In order to reinforce their power and strengthen the ideological underpinnings of Soviet society, the party created a culture that, through its use of the popular tradition, both obfuscated and in some sense perpetuated the gulf separating the masses from those who ran the party and created its ideology.

Defining the relationship between elite and so-called popular culture under

Stalin is both simpler and ironically more complex. While there was still a substantial gap between elitist culture and that of the people during the early 1920s, that gap began to close by the late 1920s and the early 1930s with the institution of the First Five-Year Plan. The goals of the plan were to bring the city to the countryside by introducing technology, electricity, and education to Russia's rural peasantry, thereby bridging the gulf that had long separated Russia's urban classes from its rural one. Some party leaders felt that it was enough to introduce modernization to the countryside; others sought to bridge the gap by resettling large numbers of people from the urban areas into rural Russia. If the countryside was slowly becoming urbanized as a result of the efforts of the First Five-Year Plan, so too were the cities becoming ruralized as peasants, responding to the enormous need for labor in the cities and resisting collectivization, resettled in the cities en masse. Thus demographic shifts, some carefully planned to eliminate cultural gaps and some that came about in a way completely unforeseen by the leadership, were as responsible for the general merging of elitist and popular culture under Stalin as were cultural mandates from above. This fact suggests that one of the real differences that must be taken into account as we try to understand how culture was produced from the 1920s on were not just those between the party and the masses but those between city and country as well.[30]

If demographics helped to close the gap between city and country and thus to some degree between elitist culture and that of the people, Stalin's method of dealing with this gap was to close it by force, linking what Hans Gunther calls the culture "from above" with that "from below."[31] To this end Stalin and his cultural ideologues created a prodigious culture machine that produced and directed culture for the masses — everything from lavish parades to Stalinist musicals in the spirit of the Hollywood extravaganzas of Busby Berkeley, to the resurrection of folklore in order to create a kind of pseudofolklore in state-sponsored form. Traditional folk motifs and formulas were hauled into the service of the state in surprisingly new juxtapositions, such as: "It is not a prophetic bird talking / It is Soviet radio."[32] Or this song, composed by the bard Marfa Kriukova, one of many who employed models from Russian folklore to fashion a new folklore based on the heroic exploits of the heroes of the day:

It was not the White Sea beginning to undulate —
It was a hero's heart beginning to beat faster;
His mighty shoulders had stirred,

Joseph-light had begun to think,
He thought a strong thought.
He sat through dark nights
And whole days thinking.
He decided to go into a great battle for the working people,
He got ready quickly,
And hurried off on his journey.[33]

If Lenin, following Marx's precepts, had perceived the distinction between high and low art as ultimately collapsible given time and social shift, Stalin perceived the creation of a mass culture (*massovaia kul'tura*) as the most effective way of controlling and socializing the population. He accomplished this in several ways. Early in the 1920s it was clear that the old prerevolutionary culture of Russia was completely incomprehensible to the new Soviet worker. The comments of one worker after seeing a production of *Swan Lake* speak volumes about the cultural level of the masses: "So, for four acts' time this most boring of all stories drags on, the story nobody needs, about the love of a 'prince' for a 'swan-princess.' " On Shakespeare's *Antony and Cleopatra*: "Why does a worker who works hard all day need to look at this moldy historical trash?" Or this on Ilya Ehrenburg's *Julio Jurenito*: "They ought to beat up authors who make up a new grammar."[34] The problem was what to do about this cultural abyss.

One solution was to make high art accessible to the people, thereby blurring the distinction between the two cultures. One of the most prominent examples of how this process took place was the Sovietizing of Russia's great poet Alexander Pushkin, who became, in honor of the one hundredth anniversary of his death, the posthumous recipient of countless activities organized in his name by the All-Union Pushkin Committee to bring his work to the people. Collective farms and factories, schoolchildren, chocolate factories, libraries, pioneer groups, and more were mobilized to create Pushkin memorabilia, compose songs, or organize literary evenings in memory of the great poet who, with a little help from the party, was now appropriated by the *narod* as their bard.[35] Pushkin would no doubt have been more than slightly surprised to hear a peasant from the May Morning Commune declare in one of the commune's reading groups, "If we were to take apart every line of his [Pushkin's], every principle of his, then we'd get historical materialism from his poetry."[36]

This blurring of the distinction between elite and popular was masterminded under Stalin through the creation of a new, comprehensible workers' culture. In order to understand how this workers' culture was formulated, we need to look at how the concept of culture was reconstituted under Stalin. From the 1930s on, Soviet culture was invested with a very different set of associations than it has in the West or even than it had in Lenin's time. Culture, as Katerina Clark notes in *The Soviet Novel: History as Ritual,* was much more than listening to Bach, reading Shakespeare, or obtaining a university degree. It was that entire spectrum of changes that occur in a person's life as s/he makes the transition from a wooden hut to a more urban and Westernized way of life.[37] It included the acquisition of certain social graces, learning polite forms of expression, learning how to put one's napkin in one's lap, and acquiring a certain *comme il faut.* This *kul'turnost'* to which the new Soviet man and woman were busily aspiring was anything but high class. For example, peasants and workers desiring to be *kul'turnyi* accumulated everything from doilies to pink lampshades to collections of cut glass and figurines, which they saw as the symbols of having entered the world of *kul'tura.* The most spectacular example of the above is Stalinist wedding-cake architecture — an elaborate and overdesigned mélange of styles combining neogothic, baroque, and Stalinist kitsch that dotted the Moscow skyline. This particular understanding of culture and what it meant to acquire it characterized most of the Soviet period well after Stalin's time. For example, when I was a student in the Soviet Union in the 1970s, one of the most commonly heard criticisms of someone was that he or she was *nekul'turnyi* (uncultured).

It was this understanding of culture — more all encompassing yet more banal than culture's usual definition — that determined how literature was read and composed during the 1930s. Like culture in general, literature was meant to become universally accessible, thus paving the way for the formulation of socialist realism in the early 1930s.[38] Drawn up originally as a blueprint for the arts, socialist realism nevertheless managed to infect virtually every branch of Soviet society as it became the order of the day in everything from fiction to journalism to factory production statistics.[39] The official mandate was no longer the elevation of education and aesthetic consciousness but rather the lowering of art to the public level.

Socialist realism was as successful as it was for many reasons: under Stalin the elite was constituted very differently than it had been under Lenin. By the late 1920s the new Soviet elite had incorporated into its ranks a worker-peasant intelligentsia, or *vydvizhentsy,* whose roots were not to be found in the traditional educated classes but who nevertheless formulated cultural and party policy in a vastly different way than the early Bolshevik leadership envisioned it. Further, socialist realism became much more than an artistic credo due to the evolving relationship between the producers and the consumers of this new culture. If we look at how culture was produced during the Soviet era in general and the Stalin era in particular, we need to understand how the party perceived its relationship to the *narod* as the class for whom this ideology was packaged. I use the word *consumers* intentionally to stress the fact that the Soviet Union, long before the advent of the current market economy, was predicated on the relationship between those who produced the goods — in this case the ideology — and those for whom that ideology was intended. And as in any consumer society, there was a symbiotic relationship between those who fashioned the product and those who "bought" it. Much of westerners' thinking about consumption is based on our understanding of it within the context of a market economy. And yet in a sense, every culture, regardless of its economic system, is consumer based insofar as it exists in relation to those who view it, listen to it, read it, act on it, and reflect on it. Further, Soviet society, as Nancy Condee and Vladimir Padunov have pointed out, has long been consumer based in the literal sense of the term in that numerous Soviet citizens blithely dealt in the black market — the necessary response to a command economy that attempted to create new needs rather than meeting the fundamental needs of the average Soviet citizen. Further, Soviets were almost invariably engaged in making a little on the side (*podrabatyvat'*) or pushing papers through a bureaucratic maze for a small fee in an effort to extend the limits of what the socialist economy made possible in their daily lives.[40] Even leaving aside the incipient market economy that has existed on the fringes of Soviet society for years, Soviet society under Stalin became heavily consumer based as a new middle class was created in the building of socialism with promises of perks and privileges in return for service to the party. Thus Soviet citizens, contrary to what official labels suggest, were clearly involved for decades in consuming much more than mere ideology.

In the early Soviet era the concept of the *narod* (masses) as consumers was defined by the ideologues and producers of Soviet mass culture. However, the way the party understood the *narod*-consumer was both ambiguous and subject to change depending on the current party ideology and political platform. The shifting nature of the *narod*'s role as consumer of mass culture was also determined by the fact that the Soviet Union was, as I have already suggested, not a monolithic entity whose leaders issued strict edicts that were blindly followed by the unsuspecting masses. In *Russia/USSR/Russia: The Drive and Drift of a Superstate,* Moshe Lewin argues that the notion of the party as the all-encompassing organization responsible for the direction taken by the state was beginning to change dramatically by the 1930s.[41] Lewin suggests that the state — all-powerful in the early days of Bolshevik rule as both maker and mediator of ideology, policy, and cultural politics — was by the 1930s well on its way to devolving into an enormous bureaucracy that gradually swallowed up the party and the various functions it performed. Even when there were clear cultural directives from the top, there was often a good deal of slippage between those directives and the way they were actually carried out.[42]

If one accepts Lewin's thesis about the gradually devolving role of the party in the fashioning and implementation of ideology, then the question arises as to how cultural policy became adapted and integrated into daily life. The answer is simple when we look at Bolshevik culture in the 1920s. The early Bolsheviks saw the production of culture for the masses as the vehicle through which revolutionary consciousness would be instilled in the people. Many, Lenin included, rejected the notion of popular culture as having too many petit bourgeois antecedents and advocated a culture that would educate and ennoble the masses.[43] Lenin viewed the *narod* as a potential elite, but one seriously deficient in the cultural level demanded by a proletarian state and even by bourgeois society.[44] He believed that this cultural level had to be raised (*podniato*) through education in order for the masses to be able to understand the new proletarian art produced for them and to appreciate the art of the past that the *narod* was both repudiating and inheriting.[45] Unlike Zinoviev and Stalin, who unilaterally rejected Russia's cultural past because it had no obvious relation to the present, Lenin, along with Trotsky and Bukharin, set about rehabilitating that past partly for its own sake and partly because he needed the chief advocates of that culture, the intelligentsia, to be ideologically in sync with the party.[46]

Stalin, as we have seen, seemed to have a very different take on the *narod* as consumers of the culture that had been designed for them. Whether he deliberately misread Lenin's call to raise (*podniat'*) the cultural level of the *narod,* changing it instead to *poniat'* (understood) is something we do not know.[47] What we do know is that under Stalin the onus was no longer on artists, educators, and ideologues to *raise* the collective cultural level of the masses, but on the artists themselves to make their work accessible or *understandable* to those same people — a concept that should find resonance with anyone concerned about the cultural "dumbing down" of America today. Whether intentional or not, Stalin's "misreading" of Lenin's directive had devastating consequences for the party's understanding of its mission vis-à-vis the masses.

Although there is no doubt that the masses consumed this public culture — both because they were enjoined to do so and because the culture frequently fit their needs — just how this process was actually accomplished is still open to debate.[48] A compelling argument, and one that supports what Lewin has to say about the transformation of the party in the 1930s, is made by Evgeny Dobrenko in *The Making of the State Reader*. Dobrenko shows that one reason the canon of socialist realism worked as well as it did was that it was not, in fact, ideologically constructed from above but in a very real sense was the product of the masses from below, answering their need for accessibility and a particular kind of realism in art. In Dobrenko's words, socialist realism became "the encounter and cultural compromise of two currents — that of the masses and that of authority" in the production of culture.[49] Thus the masses became not only the consumers of Soviet culture but also its producers, as most mainstream party-line writers from the late 1920s on were workers. Further, the worker as reader also became the critic par excellence, whose critique of a work often replaced the text itself in terms of ideological importance.[50] Thus, in an extension of Lewin's thesis, Dobrenko sees the making of culture as much less a product of party mandate and much more a function of the *narod* as the prime movers of their own culture.

How tightly the producers and consumers of this culture were intertwined is still an open question. Dobrenko implies that the intersection of the roles of producers and consumers was so tight that the product would automatically be "bought." Boris Groys argues similarly that although the aesthetic was completely alien to the tastes of the people, marketing conditions ruled out the possibility that the ideology would not be bought.[51] I think it is also possible to argue that although ideology guaranteed that the culture would be consumed to some extent, it was not entirely clear that it would always be consumed exactly as its planners hoped it would be.

A final factor needs to be considered as we look at the gradual conflation of high and low cultures in the 1930s: the creation of the Soviet Union's middle class. While no Soviet history admits as much, under Stalin a de facto middle class came into being consisting of those whom Stalin co-opted into service for the state with promises of rewards, perks, and privileges. Along with the emergence of a middle class in postwar Stalinist Russia came a literature that reflected the tastes and desires of this new class. Much of this middlebrow fiction came into prominence in the works of Natalia Baranskaia, Maia Ganina, and Viktoriia Tokareva in the 1960s and 1970s. Although they often eschewed any identification with the new class, these and other writers were implicitly writing with it in mind.[52] The appearance of the middle class is particularly important because its very presence forces us to look outside the traditional categories of elitist and mass cultures that have defined critical approaches to the study of Soviet culture. If under Stalin elitist and popular cultures became conflated, a third simultaneously came into being which, because it ran counter to the ideological thrust of the party, went unacknowledged and thus has been little studied in terms of its relationship to the other cultural products of the Stalin and post-Stalin eras.

What effect, if any, this long-standing and complex relationship between the producers and consumers of culture and between so-called elitist and nonelitist cultures in the Soviet Union will have on cultural production in the new Russia is far from clear. A few tentative ideas emerge, however. For one thing, however we choose to define elitist culture, popular culture, or the relationship between the two during the Soviet era, culture — dissident, popular, and elitist — was informed by its relationship to the center. With the collapse of the Soviet Union, there is no longer a dominant culture to which all other cultures — whether dissident, official, or nonofficial — stand in some relation. As Friedman and Weiner make clear in their chapter on rock music, many rock groups in the former Soviet Union happily defined themselves as underground, or at the very least as on the margins of acceptability, and it was out of these margins that their self-identity was born. If cultural life for them became more difficult when their art "suffered" the transition from the margins to the center, popular culture today finds itself in that peculiar liminal place outside the confines of what both we in the West and Russians themselves once defined as either elitist or popular — no longer official, yet no longer sequestered under the umbrella of the nonofficial either. In short, there is no longer a dominant culture at Russia's center that defines the space one inhabits as either a producer or a consumer of that culture. Similarly, it is far from obvious how changing Soviet notions of the relations between the producers and consumers of culture will affect relations between production and consumption in the new Russia. What is obvious is that the new Russian consumer is still powerfully engaged with many of the cultural artifacts, paradigms, and stereotypes of the past, partially as a way of disengaging from that past, partially as an expression of the longing for what Anna Krylova terms "the lost position of the Soviet subject."[53]

The question of how culture is consumed in Russia today may in the long run be affected by the experience of the past eighty years during which Soviets were both the producers, the passive recipients, and the creative consumers of their culture. Although many of the most avid consumers in Russia today have no recollection of the Leninist or even the Stalinist state, collective memory is deeply rooted, reaching back to a time when the state not only created an official culture for the masses but attempted to create the identity of those who would consume it as well. And because the relationship between the state and the people was not static or monolithic, most Soviets learned to negotiate their way within mass culture, utilizing it when necessary to form bonds between self and state, using it for their own amusement sometimes, and rejecting it or ignoring it at others.[54]

II. La Vie privée and *Byt*

The study of everyday life — what historian Henri Lefebvre calls "la vie quotidienne" — is often subsumed within the study of popular culture. Once considered outside the parameters of the historian's craft, the study of the everyday and of those once erased from the historical process now occupies center stage for those who study microhistory, partially because it is here that we find potential sites of resistance to the grand historical narratives that were traditionally the focus of the historians' craft.[55]

What exactly do we mean when we talk about "la vie quotidienne," and specifically what form does it take within the context of Soviet and post-Soviet experience? If, as Lefebvre suggests, the everyday is made up of the repetitive gestures of work and consumption that mask the changes that take place in our lives, the particular quality of that ritualized behavior undergoes permutations from culture to culture.[56] The French critic Michel de Certeau sees ordinary life as something like a guerilla war that people implicitly wage against prescribed official ideologies.[57] Thus, for de Certeau, the ordinary will always swim against the prevailing tide of inscribed official ideology or state or cultural myths. Likewise, Bakhtin, who approached the problem from the vantage point of a Russian *intelligent* who suffered under Stalinism, was looking for ways in which common, ordinary life might conceivably function as a site of resistance against the prevailing ideology.[58]

As we begin to investigate everyday life in Soviet and post-Soviet society, we must remember that for the greater part of this century, everyday life (that is to say, unofficial life) in the Soviet Union has been invested with a specific set of associations that lie outside our experience in the West. While Western scholars were not urged to explore this facet of Soviet life, it was shockingly easy for American professors and students to gain access into nonofficial Soviet life. Sitting until the early hours of the morning in the kitchens of the intelligentsia was one of the ways Western students and academics were able to find out what was really going on in lives lived outside the prescriptive norms propagated by the media or by official discourse. We needed that nonofficial version, the version that took us beyond "life as it is becoming" to "life as it is" to construct for ourselves that more complete picture of Soviet life.[59] And just as important, the intelligentsia needed us because we were the conduit to the West that was otherwise inaccessible to them.

Much, though not all, of this nonofficial life was contained under the heading of what the Russians call *byt,* a term the late writer Yury Trifonov calls "perhaps the most enigmatic, multidimensional, incomprehensible word in the Russian language." It explains "how husbands and wives get on together, and parents and children, and close and distant relations — that too. . . . And the interrelationships of friends and people at work, love, quarrels, jealousy, envy — all this, too, is byt. This is what life consists of! . . . We are all enmeshed in byt in our own network of everyday concerns."[60] For students of Soviet society, there was often a truth in the study of *byt* that simply was not available through the study of official culture. *Byt* became the means of access to that elusive other half that told us what was going on behind the facade of the official story. For example, Nadezhda Mandelshtam's *Vospominaniia* is, in Donald Fanger's words, "a treasure house of *byt* in the thirties" because of its wealth of information about surveillance and search and arrest techniques under Stalin.[61] In a similar vein, Aleksei German's film *Moi drug Ivan Lapshin (My Friend Ivan Lapshin,* completed in 1982, but not released until 1985) — the tale of a police inspector in a provincial town in the mid-1930s out to capture a band of criminals who sell the bodies of their victims to compensate for the meat shortage — contains descriptions of *byt* that complicated the reception of German's film in the Soviet Union. Not only does German present the catastrophic state of human relationships during Stalin's time, but he also subverts the official version of what life was supposed to be like through his descriptions of the deplorable living and moral conditions to which Soviet life had descended.[62]

Critics in the West connect the study of quotidian existence to the study of private life. In the Russian and Soviet experience, however, this identification does not always hold. *Byt,* while omnipresent in every Russian's personal life (including Stalin's!), was not contained by it. In other words, private life was and is often made up of *byt,* but *byt,* in and of itself, was not always private. The most telling example of this discontinuity is the nefarious and ubiquitous phenomenon of the *kommunalka* (communal apartment). Full to overflowing with *byt,* the *kommunalka* was anything but private, as the shared living and psychological spaces often culminating in the infamous *donosy* (denunciations) by one's neighbors during the Stalinist era testify.[63] I make this distinction between the everyday and the private precisely because private life (what is usually referred to in Russian as *chastnaia* or *lichnaia zhizn'*) has traditionally carried a complicated set of associations for Russians, particularly in this century. From the time Lenin declared the private life dead shortly after the revolution, people's attempts to garner some sort of personal privacy have been fraught with emotional ambiguity and even political risk. As Svetlana Boym notes in her book *Common Places,* there has even been a sense of publicly sanctioned guilt associated with personal life in Soviet Russia.[64] Further, the party under Stalin exerted every effort to make the public and the private virtually indistinguishable. Under Stalin, for example, motherhood became a public act, and countless faces of mother-heroines beamed out from the covers of magazines such as *Ogonek, Krest'ianka,* and *Sovetskaia zhenshchina,* exhorting Soviet women to produce more Soviet citizens (read "sons") for the motherland. Similarly, the infamous partition that was supposed to afford a modicum of privacy in the *kommunalka* only served to reinforce the notion that privacy was altogether impossible in such a setting.[65] Ironically, even if privatization has brought some the opportunity for privacy, it has also brought a nostalgia not only for the past but for the present, as many fear leaving the familiarity of their communal situations.[66]

The effect in the new Russia of the blurring of the lines between public and private for much of this century is not yet clear. If, as has been often argued, fiction enjoys the special privilege in Russia of providing the key to social and political issues (witness here Solzhenitsyn's famous remark that in Russia the writer is a kind of "second government"), then the prose of the contemporary writer Liudmila Petrushevskaia provides one possible take on the consequences of this blurring. In story after story Petrushevskaia's characters relate their most intimate lives to perfect strangers — to passengers in cabs, anonymous colleagues at work, strangers in stairwells — people who have no vested interest in what the teller has to say. Petrushevskaia's stories suggest the psychological, emotional, and linguistic evisceration that has taken place in a world in which public and private are still hopelessly conflated.[67]

Other possible results of the ambiguous nature of the public-private dichotomy that informed so much of Soviet society are visible in Russian popular culture today. For example, the recent spate of pornography that has glutted the market since the collapse of censorship in 1991 has not been confined to magazines and newspapers that are explicitly pornographic. Porn has also appeared in mainstream newspapers and magazines. In 1991 an economics journal, *Ekonomika,* displayed a bare-breasted woman on one of its covers for reasons that may or may not have had anything to do with Russia's economic assets, while *Ogonek* has on more than one occasion used bare breasts and fleshy buttocks as lead-ins to stories that had nothing to do with the flesh proffered in the photos.[68] An analogous situation in the United States would be the appearance of pornography on the cover of *Time* or *US News and World Report.* This phenomenon is an interesting reflection of post-Soviet commercial culture in several ways. Catriona Kelly argues that this confusing juxtaposition of advertising in seemingly inappropriate venues is partly because niche marketing is not yet well developed in post-Soviet society.[69] Further, while one can argue endlessly over whether these photos are pornographic or merely highly erotic, and over the economic motive behind their appearance in magazines that are suddenly forced to compete in a cutthroat market economy, the photos are equally interesting in the way they illustrate traditional notions of public and private. In essence, what we are seeing is a kind of revenge of the private on the public. After years of the "public" invasion of "private" space and discourse (even sex becoming a public act in the Soviet communal apartment), private discourse and experience, or at least that which was blatantly barred from the public realm, seem to be reversing that process by insinuating themselves into the public arena, transgressively invading spaces where they "ought not to be."[70] In this sense, the new pornography in Russia can be seen not simply as a reaction to the demise of censorship, but as a response to the constantly shifting boundaries — no less in the new Russia than in the old — between what counts as "public" and "private," particularly in the sphere of ownership of one's body, formerly part of the communality of Soviet life.[71]

III. Marx and the Post-Soviet Popular

Like much of Russian history itself, the popular culture craze in Russia today is laced with ironies, not the least of which is that it is Marx to whom popular culture theorists owe much of their debt in framing the questions about the production and consumption of culture, even as his statues are hauled off to the same storage vaults that house Lenin, Stalin, and other fallen idols of the revolution. It is Marx's understanding of history and culture as being indissolubly linked and of culture as a site of ideology that has informed studies of popular culture in the United States and Great Britain. It was also one of Marx's assumptions that culture is a site wherein various struggles are waged between classes, between competing ideologies and generations, and between meanings that an elite group or dominant social group seeks to impose on a subordinate group. Thus culture, and popular culture in particular, becomes less a retreat from ideology than a place that reflects the ideological underpinnings of any given society; it is where the battle is fought between those who produce the ideology and those who are supposed to consume it.

In another interesting ironic reversal Marx saw commodity fetishism as a function of capitalist economies, perhaps little realizing the extent to which commodities could become fetishized in economic systems philosophically opposed to capitalism. Long before the advent of the market economy, Soviet citizens were consuming much more than ideology as they sought out fancy crabmeat, booked cruises up and down the Volga, waited years for cars, and collected rare and prized items of travel paraphernalia ranging from travel posters to beer cans or cookie tins reminiscent of places most people had never been. That these consumer products were proffered in ways that did not always conform to the demands of the marketplace should not detract from the essential fact that the Soviet consumer since Stalin's time has been an active partaker in consumer life, the more so because so many of these longed-for items have been simultaneously available yet unobtainable.

Along with the proliferating ironies of Marx's importation back into Russia come a host of questions that lie outside the scope of this chapter but beg for study, in particular, issues dealing with the culture industry and how that evolving industry works in the new Russia. When we speak of the current popular culture industry in the West, we generally have in mind those conglomerates from Disney to Reebok that produce the products that enter the realm of popular culture. When we speak about the culture industry in America we tend to forget that the culture industry, in a somewhat different form, has been around in Russia and the Soviet Union much longer than our appropriation of the term to describe it. Indeed, for a good portion of this century, the Stalinist culture machine regularly ground out culture for the masses on a scale unrivaled by anyone in this century but Disney. Similarly, the reception of Western pop culture within Russia can potentially tell us a great deal about ideology and consumption in the former Soviet Union. Although the influx of Western culture into the new Russia is impressive in both quantity and scope, it is certainly not the first invasion of Western popular culture into Russia. In the early period of NEP under Lenin, Russian women swooned over Douglas Fairbanks, and Russians in general followed the adventures of Tarzan and savored the detective exploits of Nick Carter, Nat Pinkerton, and Sherlock Holmes. In the early and mid- 1930s American jazz was all the rage, and Russians happily danced to American dances from the foxtrot to the Boston waltz — until the purges hit. Whether officially accessible or not, Western popular culture has always been in the air. What this culture has meant for the average Russian and how that meaning has changed throughout this century is crucial as we attempt to make sense of cultural life and its almost imponderable permutations in Russia since Gorbachev.

As we ponder the possible influence of Western culture on Russians themselves and on the Russian market, I will close with a story. Last year my friends in Moscow were watching *Santa Barbara* and *Dynasty* reruns, incredulous that an American viewer didn't always follow the episodes sequentially! Other serials were running too. An informal survey taken in the apartment building where I was staying revealed that *Love and Secrets of Sunset Beach* (USA), *Prime Suspect* (Britain), *Stolen Love* (Mexico), and *Babylon 5* (USA) were being watched with as much regularity as was *Santa Barbara* in our flat. I chastised my friends for watching this trash, and a heated argument ensued over the depths to which Russia's once great intelligentsia had descended!

And indeed, perhaps at no time in the past eighty years has the gulf separating highbrow and lowbrow been this immense, a fact due partially to the enormous infusion of the lowbrow into Russia, but also due to the collapse of a system and a way of life that were designed to conflate the two cultures. But if the gulf between the two cultures is very real, there is also a crossing over on the part of the intellectual elite as they sample a culture at once threatening to their heritage yet all the more tempting because it remained out of reach for so long. In a recent article in *Novoe literaturnoe obozrenie,* Alexei Levinson remarks that one cannot really dispute the interest on the part of Russians of all classes in TV soaps from the West that advertise a life that is still blissful escapism from difficult times.[72] But in a somewhat different vein and with a profoundly different message, Russians are now the recipients of a new ideology and set of values, many of them produced in Tinsel Town or Mexico City, which may in the long run be no less insidious than the state-sponsored programming once predictably aired on state-controlled channels. According to a recent article by Michiko Kakutani in the *New York Times,* the days when we exported the best of American culture are gone. Now we seem to be taking out the trash, treating the rest of the world as a "vast toxic waste dump" into which we are pouring the absolute worst that our culture has to offer.[73]

Classical Marxists, replicating the same arguments we voiced at the lot of the Soviet citizen under communism, would have it that capitalist consumers become inexorably molded into passive, standardized culture dupes whose identity has already been fixed by those who produce our culture for us. And as Borenstein's chapter on the MMM scandal reveals, there is indeed reason for pessimism; the neophyte post-Soviet consumer is having some difficulty distinguishing the plots of TV soaps from real life, having been schooled in a system that expected art to be a model for real life. But the past eighty years may also provide some reason for optimism. If the ideological rigors of the Soviet period established the parameters within which the average Soviet citizen was exhorted to function, so did they, albeit unwittingly, provide opportunities for the decoding of that ideology and for tremendous individual creativity. As the new Russian consumers move into an economic order that, like the system from which they have emerged, creates both ideologies and identities but whose final configuration is still far from clear, they may already be involved in the process of making the creative adjustments necessary to extract themselves from the forces of yet another ideology. In the meantime, my friends and I resolved our dispute by switching channels to *The Thornbirds.*

Notes

My thanks to Eliot Borenstein, Helena Goscilo, Jodi Kelber, Anna Krylova, Tamara Petrovna Krylova, Susan Larsen, Peter Maggs, Ekaterina Stetsenko, and Alexei Yurchak for procuring materials for this chapter. Special thanks to Dean Charles Tatum for giving me the time I needed this year to write; and to Susan Aiken, Jehanne Gheith, and Thomas Lahusen, for their smart and sensitive readings.

1 This random assemblage of mostly Western goods first made its appearance under
   Andropov when products formerly available to the elite and to the foreign community through special stores began to filter down into the first economy on a limited
   and random basis, resulting in such spectacular combinations as Christian Dior
   perfume and bananas being sold at the same kiosk.

2 On July 31, 1993, Celestine Bohlen reported in the *New York Times* that diamond
   earrings at the Almaz store were going for $250,000, women's suits were selling for
   $2,000 at the Escada shop on the second floor of the old GUM, and Rolls-Royces cost
   from $140,000 to $260,000. See "Russia's New Rich on a Giant Buying Spree,"
   New York Times, p. 1. Five years later, Cartier watches sell for $8,000 to $10,000 and
   new Chevy Caprices go for $50,000. My thanks to Anna Krylova for obtaining some
   of this information for me.

3 O. Vronskaia, "Na podstupakh k Zolotomu pistoletu," *Literaturnaia gazeta,* no. 9
   (1998): 9. According to a recent survey, the number of people reading detective
   fiction and thrillers increased from 26 to 32 percent between 1994 and 1997; readers
   of romance novels increased from 23 to 27 percent, and readers of science fiction
   from 11 to 15 percent during the same period.

4 See Jeffrey Brooks, *When Russia Learned to Read: Literacy and Popular Literature
   1861–1917* (Princeton: Princeton University Press, 1985), pp. 328ff.

5 The plight of the Russian intelligentsia has been the subject of numerous articles in
   the press. For a sampling of approaches to the problem, see in particular Vadim
   Belotserkovskii, "Rossiia ostaetsia bez intelligentsii," *Literaturnaia gazeta,* no. 44
   (October 30, 1996), p. 1, in which the author discusses why Andrei Sakharov has
   been all but forgotten. For a discussion of how the intelligentsia has accommodated
   itself to the new consumer economy, see Kira Kovalkina and Alexei Levinson, "The
   Intelligentsia in Post-Soviet Times," *Moscow News,* March 11, 1994. The critic Lev
   Anninskii makes an interesting distinction between the terms *elitist* and *intelligentsia* in his article "Vytesnenie intelligentsii," in *Novaia volna: Russkaia kul'tura i
   subkul'tury na rubezhe 80-9-x godov,* comp. N. I. Azhgikhina (Moskva: Moskovskii
   rabochii, 1994), pp. 19–24. What Anninskii sees in the new Russia is the crowding
   out of the intelligentsia by the elite. Andrei Sinyavsky's *The Russian Intelligentsia,*
   trans. Lynn Visson (New York: Columbia University Press, 1997), looks at the
   intelligentsia's relationship to the people, to bread, and to democracy. For an over-
   view of the plight of the intelligentsia after communism, see Masha Gessen, *Dead
   Again: The Russian Intelligentsia after Communism* (London: Verso, 1997).

   As Nancy Condee and Vladimir Padunov note in "The ABC of Russian Consumer Culture: Readings, Ratings, and Real Estate," in *Soviet Hieroglyphics: Visual
   Culture in Late Twentieth Century Russia,* ed. Nancy Condee (Bloomington: Indiana
   University Press, 1995), there have been both economic and geographic displacements of high culture in Moscow out literally onto the periphery of the city and onto
   the periphery of the bookstalls, where at best one might find a "stray token of one
   historical, philosophical, or theological book" (p. 141).

6 A recent issue of *Novoe literaturnoe obozrenie* (no. 22, 1996) is devoted to alterna-

tive literature and popular culture and contains a number of interesting articles on topics as diverse as TV advertising, billboards, recent detective fiction, and pornography.

7 In particular, see *Russian Cultural Studies: An Introduction,* ed. Catriona Kelly and David Shepherd (Oxford: Oxford University Press, 1998).

8 Quoted in Marc Wortman, "The Coming of Cultural Studies," *Yale Alumni Magazine* 56, no. 6 (1993): 26–31.

9 See Theodor Adorno, *The Culture Industry* (London: Routledge, 1991).

10 See John Fiske, *Understanding Popular Culture* (London: Routledge, 1989), ch. 1.

11 Evgeny Dobrenko makes the point that by the 1930s Soviet aesthetics had arrived at a point at which literary criticism simultaneously became the "conduit of popular opinion" and "educator." The goal on the part of party ideologues was to achieve "total control of the reader in the library." See Dobrenko, *The Making of the State Reader: Social and Aesthetic Contexts of the Reception of Soviet Literature,* trans. Jesse M. Savage (Stanford: Stanford University Press, 1997), pp. 20, 34.

12 Thomas Lahusen, *How Life Writes the Book: Real Socialism and Socialist Realism in Stalin's Russia* (Ithaca: Cornell University Press, 1997).

13 See Anna Krylova's chapter "In Their Own Words? Soviet Women Writers and the Search for Self," in *A History of Women's Writing in Russia,* ed. Adele Barker and Jehanne Gheith (Cambridge University Press, forthcoming).

14 Excerpts from Shtange's diary are translated in *Intimacy and Terror: Soviet Diaries of the 1930s,* ed. Veronique Garros, Natalia Korenevskaia, and Thomas Lahusen, trans. Carol A. Flath (New York: New Press, 1995), p. 172.

15 At present the advertising industry functions very differently in Russia than it does in the West. Nancy Condee and Vladimir Padunov make the point that in the new Russia most billboards and magazine ads contain verbal messages in languages from English to Japanese that are for the most part unknown to the average consumer. This suggests that what is most important to the advertisers is not verbal understanding on the part of the consumer of what is being advertised but consumer recognition of products and brand names. See Condee and Padunov, "Pair-a-dice Lost: The Socialist Gamble, Market Determinism, and Compulsory Postmodernism," in *Postcommunism: Rethinking the Second World,* special issue of *New Formations,* no. 22 (spring 1994), p. 78. See also "Vashe blagorodie, gospozha reklama . . . ," *Ogonek* 27–28 (1994): 25; and Julie Hessler, "A Postwar Perestroika? Toward a History of Private Enterprise in the USSR," *Slavic Review* (fall 1998): 516–42.

16 John Fiske, *Understanding Popular Culture,* pp. 32–37. A similar point is made by John Storey in *Cultural Studies and the Study of Popular Culture* (Athens: University of Georgia Press, 1996), pp. 5–6.

17 Dick Hebdige, *Hiding in the Light: On Images and Things* (London: Routledge, 1988), p. 44.

18 A classic example of this conflation of boundaries between elitist and popular culture is David Lean's film version of Pasternak's novel *Doctor Zhivago,* which completely ignores the philosophical implications of the novel. A more recent example

of this conflation of the two spheres is the film version of Shakespeare's *Romeo and Juliet* directed by Baz Luhrmann, retold within a contemporary setting. The question these renditions raises is to which cultural sphere do these films belong — elite or popular?

19 This ambivalence between elite and popular culture is still felt in many post-Soviet magazines, which often contain an unusual mix of high culture and low culture within their covers. *Ona,* for example, the Russian version of *Elle,* seems to be covering all possible bases as to potential audience by including highbrow and lowbrow elements. See Greta N. Slobin, "Ona: The New Elle-Literacy and the Post-Soviet Woman," in *Writing New Identities: Gender, Nation, and Immigration in Contemporary Europe,* ed. Gisela Brinker-Gabler and Sidonie Smith (Minneapolis: University of Minnesota Press, 1997), pp. 337–57.

20 See Adele Barker, "Reading the Texts — Rereading Ourselves," in *Women and Russian Culture: Projections and Self-Perceptions,* ed. R. J. Marsh (Oxford: Berghahn Books, 1998), pp. 42–58.

21 Lev Anninskii made this point in a talk given at a Social Sciences Research Council summer seminar on "Soviet Literature and Film of the Eighties," at Yale University, 1985. The Russian critic Dmitry Urnov has long argued that the West failed to access accurately the state of Soviet letters in this century because of westerners' tendency to overvalue works that were marginalized in their own country. He makes a similar point in an article on the new alternative prose, which is enjoying great popularity but which he finds unreadable. See "Plokhaia proza," *Literaturnaia gazeta,* no. 6 (1989), p. 4.

22 An example of this tendency to dichotomize rulers and ruled can be seen in George Breslauer's "The Nature of Soviet Politics and the Gorbachev Leadership," in *The Gorbachev Era,* ed. Alexander Dallin and Condoleezza Rice (Stanford: Stanford Alumni Assoc., 1986), p. 11. Mikhail Epstein also supports the paradigm of a strong ideology on top versus critical citizens who resisted that ideology on the bottom in *After the Future: The Paradoxes of Postmodernism and Contemporary Russian Culture* (Amherst: University of Massachusetts Press, 1995). Some recent works, however, provide a more textured analysis of the intricate relationship between ideology and daily life in the Soviet Union and Eastern Europe. See Katherine Verdery, *What Was Socialism and What Comes Next?* (Princeton: Princeton University Press, 1996); and Alexei Yurchak, "The Cynical Reason of Late Socialism: Language, Ideology and Culture of the Last Soviet Generation" (Ph.D. diss., Duke University, 1997).

23 Stuart Hall, "Notes on Deconstructing 'The Popular,' " in *People's History and Socialist Theory* (London: Routledge and Kegan Paul, 1981), p. 227.

24 *Propiski* (residence permits) were one of the ways the Soviet government kept track of its citizens. Basically one needed a *propiska* to live in a particular city. One could not get the *propiska* unless one had a job there; but one could not get a job unless one had a *propiska.* Further, the amount of room one was allowed to inhabit in square meters depended on the number of persons living in the apartment. In order to get

around these laws, Soviet citizens traded apartments unofficially, resulting in large numbers of people living in apartments for which they had no *propiska*. In general, the situation regarding *propiski* has changed very little since Soviet times. In Moscow, for example, one still must be registered in the city in order to be hired by an official agency. Situations in which people own apartments in Moscow but do not have the legal right to live there, and therefore to work there, are very common. It is possible to buy a *propiska,* but the price of one (usually somewhere between $50,000 and $70,000) is more expensive than the cheapest apartment, which usually runs from $25,000 to $30,000. Thus the right to live in Moscow costs at least $100,000. People who have managed to amass $30,000 but no more usually buy apartments in other cities. For a literary treatment of the phenomenon of the exchange in Soviet times, see Yury Trifonov's novella *Obmen* (*The Exchange*).

25 See Verdery, *What Was Socialism,* ch. 1, in which she tracks the interactions between the official and the nonofficial economies of Romania. Many of Verdery's insights are equally applicable to the Soviet experience.

26 Regine Robin discusses the difficulty of defining popular culture in "Stalinism and Popular Culture," in *The Culture of the Stalin Period,* ed. Hans Gunther (London: Macmillan, 1990), pp. 15–40. Zara Abdullaeva's "Popular Culture," in *Russian Culture at the Crossroads,* ed. Dmitri N. Shalin (Boulder: Westview Press, 1996), pp. 209–38, sees the root of Soviet popular culture precisely in folk culture.

27 Sheila Fitzpatrick discusses this implicit link between the early Bolsheviks and the intelligentsia in *The Cultural Front: Power and Culture in Revolutionary Russia* (Ithaca: Cornell University Press, 1992), pp. 3–5.

28 Ibid., p. 5. Richard Stites makes this point in *Russian Popular Culture: Entertainment and Society since 1900* (Cambridge: Cambridge University Press, 1992), p. 65.

29 In this sense, the Soviet construction of culture under Stalin, so antibourgeois in its aims, ironically reinforces Harold Bloom's definition of the Western canon as reflecting the taste of the ruling elite within which the muse becomes an elitist one. Harold Bloom, *The Western Canon: The Books and School of the Ages* (New York: Harcourt Brace, 1994), p. 34. Bloom similarly maintains that "literary criticism, as an art, always was and always will be an elitist phenomenon" (p. 17).

30 My thanks to Thomas Lahusen for reminding me of this important distinction.

31 See Hans Gunther, introduction to *The Culture of the Stalin Period,* xvi–xxi.

32 Quoted from Frank J. Miller, *Folklore for Stalin: Russian Folklore and Pseudofolklore of the Stalin Era* (Armonk, N.Y.: M. E. Sharpe, 1990), p. 69.

33 Ibid., p. 159.

34 Quoted in Dobrenko, *The Making of the State Reader,* pp. 118–19.

35 For a discussion of the furor over Pushkin in the 1930s, see Marcus C. Levitt, *Russian Literary Politics and the Pushkin Celebration of 1880* (Ithaca: Cornell University Press, 1989), pp. 162ff.

36 Ibid., p. 104.

37 Katerina Clark, *The Soviet Novel: History as Ritual* (Chicago: University of Chicago Press, 1981), p. 197.

38 See Robin, "Stalinism and Popular Culture," p. 31.

39 See Fitzpatrick, *The Cultural Front,* p. 217.

40 See Condee and Padunov, "The ABC of Russian Consumer Culture," p. 136.

41 See Moshe Lewin, *Russia/USSR/Russia: The Drive and Drift of a Superstate* (New York: New Press, 1995), particularly chs. 5, 8, and 10. Lewin, in fact, sees Soviet socialism as a case of "mislabeling" in which the terms we were encouraged to apply to it by the system itself were "not adequate to the reality" of the state but only to that which was created by an enormous propaganda machine (p. 159).

42 For more on this point, see Katerina Clark, "From a Directed Culture to an Autonomous Cultural Model?" in *Stanford Slavic Studies,* vol. 7: *Russian Culture in Transition,* ed. Gregory Freidin, pp. 25–52.

43 See Richard Stites on the differing approaches taken by the early Bolsheviks and Stalin to the issue of popular culture, in *Russian Popular Culture,* chs. 2 and 3.

44 Lenin parted ways with some of the early Bolshevik ideologues who felt that it was their job to first create a real proletarian culture for the masses. He said, "For a start, we should be satisfied with real bourgeois culture; for a start we should be glad to dispense with the cruder types of pre-bourgeois culture, i.e., bureaucratic culture or serf culture, etc." (V. I. Lenin, *Collected Works,* vol. 33 [Moscow: Progress, 1966], p. 487).

45 In the early days of the Bolshevik Revolution there was still a great deal of debate — which came to a precipitous halt under Stalin — as to the role high culture and popular culture should play in the people's education. For example, the Proletcult organization, founded in 1917, championed the new revolutionary culture but found that the *narod* wanted to perpetuate both the oral traditions and the high culture of the past. Moreover, during the NEP period, 1921–28, much of popular culture from the prerevolutionary era, outlawed in the early days of the revolution, reappeared with the restoration of private business. See Stites, *Russian Popular Culture,* pp. 40–41.

46 See Boris Kagarlitsky, *The Thinking Reed: Intellectuals and the Soviet State, 1917 to the Present,* trans. Brian Pearce (London: Verso, 1988), pp. 57–58.

47 My thanks to Tatiana Tolstaia for first bringing this distinction to my attention.

48 In their introduction to *Mass Culture in Soviet Russia: Tales, Poems, Songs, Movies, Plays, and Folklore, 1917–1953* (Bloomington: Indiana University Press, 1995), James von Geldern and Richard Stites make the point that the Stalinist myths, replete in songs, films, and, literature of the 1930s, were consumed by the *narod* with conviction, particularly as the country headed into war and citizens felt the need to bond together collectively through their shared suffering (p. xxi). See also the special issue of the *Journal of Popular Culture,* "Birches, Bolsheviks, and Balalaikas: Popular Culture in Russian History," ed. James von Geldern and Hubertus Jahn, 31, no. 4 (spring 1998).

49 Dobrenko, *The Making of the State Reader,* p. 139.

50 See ibid., p. 105.

51 In *The Total Art of Stalinism: Avant-Garde, Aesthetic Dictatorship and Beyond,*

trans. Charles Rougle (Princeton: Princeton University Press, 1992), Boris Groys makes the point that socialist realism was the product of an elite who had "assimilated the experience of the avant-garde," which had nothing in common with the actual tastes of the *narod*. Further, he argues, socialist realism bridged the gap between elitism and kitsch by making "visual kitsch" the vehicle of elitist ideas (pp. 9–11).

52 Beth Holmgren discusses the appearance of middlebrow literature among postwar women writers in "Writing the Female Body Politic (1945–1985)," in *A History of Women's Writing in Russia,* ed. Adele Barker and Jehanne Gheith (Cambridge University Press, forthcoming).

53 See Svetlana Boym, *Common Places: Mythologies of Everyday Life in Russia* (Cambridge: Harvard University Press, 1994).

54 See von Geldern and Stites, *Mass Culture in Soviet Russia,* pp. xi–xvii. However, that same mass culture no longer worked as effectively on the population after the war because many of the values that culture celebrated, such as traditional family roles and socialist values, were not borne out by the experiences of most Soviets during the war, particularly soldiers who got to see a world outside Stalin's Russia.

55 See Fiske, *Understanding Popular Culture,* p. 19.

56 Henri Lefebvre, "The Everyday and Everydayness," trans. Christine Levich, *Yale French Studies* 73 (1987): 7–11.

57 Michel de Certeau, in *The Practice of Everyday Life,* trans. Steven Rendell (Berkeley: University of California Press, 1984), argues that everyday life consists in the art of "making do" through a series of subterfuges and ruses that enable us to undermine official ideologies and the producers of culture.

58 Mikhail Bakhtin, *Rabelais and His World,* trans. Helene Iswolsky (Bloomington: Indiana University Press, 1984).

59 Fitzpatrick, *The Cultural Front,* pp. 219–27.

60 Yury Trifonov, "Net, ne o byte — o zhizni!" in *Kak slovo nashe otzovetsia* (Moscow: Sovetskaia Rossiia, 1985), p. 102.

61 Donald Fanger, "Reflections on Byt" (paper given at American Association for the Advancement of Slavic Studies meeting, Boston, 1996).

62 Numerous Soviet works that ran into trouble with the authorities did so because of their depictions of *byt*. I have in mind I. Grekova's novella *Na ispytaniiakh* (*Novyi mir,* no. 4, 1967), which landed her in disfavor both with her institute and with the Writers' Union because she painted a portrait of daily life in the Soviet army without the usual gloss (*lakirovka*) accorded the military. See also Fitzpatrick, *The Cultural Front,* pp. 219–27, in which she contrasts life as it actually *was* in the 1930s versus life as it was becoming.

63 There is some debate about whether privacy was even possible in a communal apartment. Svetlana Boym makes the point that tenants invented all sorts of curtains and screens to mark privacy, but ultimately these barriers were more a *sign* of privacy than a guarantee of it; see Boym, "Everyday Culture," in *Russian Culture at the Crossroads: Paradoxes of Postcommunist Consciousness,* ed. Dmitri Shalin (Boul-

der: Westview Press, 1996), p. 170. Soviet fiction is replete with scenes of overheard conversations behind *kommunalki* partitions.

64 Ibid., p. 183.

65 Svetlana Boym offers a different view of privacy in her chapter in this volume. Boym thinks that voyeurism became nearly obsolete during Soviet times when people learned to avert their gaze from toilets both in communal dwellings and in public spaces because the toilets had no doors. Thus, with everything accessible to one's gaze, one learned to look away.

66 Boym, "Everyday Culture," p. 178. I have two friends in Moscow who still live in a communal apartment, in a room formerly inhabited by one. More and more consumer products — a computer, a standing refrigerator, etc. — have been moved into the room, gradually taking up the space occupied by one person. Now it is a room inhabited by objects and books. See also Celestine Bohlen's article in the *New York Times,* February 28, 1993, "Moscow Privatization Yields Privacy and Problems," p. 1.

67 See in particular Petrushevskaia's stories "Medea," in which a cab driver tells the story of his daughter's death and his wife's arrest for the murder; "Rasskazchitsa" ("The Talker"), about a young woman who assumes an intimacy with her fellow co-workers and is subsequently deeply humiliated by their actions toward her; and "Vremia noch'" ("The Time Night"), in which the narrator not only delves into her daughter's diary but then divulges the daughter's secrets to us, the unknown readers. All are in Petrushevskaia's *Taina doma* (Moskva: Kvadrat, 1995).

68 My thanks to Helena Goscilo for providing me with these "tit bits."

69 Catriona Kelly, "Creating a Consumer: Advertising and Commercialization," in *Russian Cultural Studies: An Introduction,* ed. Catriona Kelly and David Shepherd (Oxford: Oxford University Press, 1998), p. 227.

70 Lynne Attwood makes a similar, though not identical, point in "Sex and the Cinema," in *Sex and Russian Society,* ed. Igor Kon and James Riordan (Bloomington: Indiana University Press, 1993), pp. 69–70. Attwood argues for the symbolic representation of woman in the contemporary Russian cinema as in the past wherein the violence directed against her becomes symbolic of violence directed toward the state. If woman has traditionally represented the sanctified values of motherhood, nature, suffering, and so forth, what we are seeing now is woman shorn of these traditional representations, her sexuality, once veiled behind nationalist needs to exploit the mother image, taking its revenge on a state that denied her such.

71 If the glut of pornography may suggest something about the reversal of the public and the private in the new Russia, its appearance may also be a kind of revenge of the dissident community on the official culture that ostracized it. After dissident writers such as Vasily Aksyonov and Eduard Limonov arrived in the West, many of the older émigrés from the first wave complained bitterly of the pornographic streak in their writing, particularly in that of Limonov, whose *Eta ia Edichka* (*It's Me, Eddie!*) became a kind of *succès de scandale* in the West. With the collapse of censorship and the demise of the Soviet Union, dissident currents in Soviet literature have found

their way into the market with a vengeance. Not only have dissident works published abroad been returning to Russia since the inception of glasnost in 1986, but dissident currents have been increasingly employed in contemporary works of art by Russian artists themselves.

72 See Levinson, "Zametki po sotsiologii i antropologii reklamy," *Novoe literaturnoe obozrenie,* no. 22 (1996): 101–28.

73 Michiko Kakutani, "Taking Out the Trash," *New York Times Magazine,* June 8, 1997, pp. 30–34. Most disturbing is the fact that the rest of the world seems to be consuming our trash. Witness the fact that Kevin Costner's *Waterworld,* which grossed only $90 million at home, brought in $176 million in foreign sales and was for sale in the video stores in Russia even before the final edits were made in Hollywood. Thus the version Russian viewers were treated to was even worse than the one that was released in the United States.

Part II POPULAR CULTURE

PUBLIC OFFERINGS: MMM AND THE
MARKETING OF MELODRAMA

Throughout the Russian Federation in the summer of 1994, people of all ages and backgrounds, from cynical schoolboys to bitter *babushki,* could be heard constantly invoking a certain three-letter word without any trace of shyness; this same word was seen on the walls of public buildings and subways, was prominently featured in national newspapers, and was repeated like a mantra on state-owned television. To those already inclined to believe that the country was going to hell in a handbasket, the word's ubiquity was a clear sign of the degradation of public taste. That word was "MMM." Sergei Mavrodi's MMM, a network of companies whose complexity and mystery have yet to be completely unraveled, was both producer and product of the most effective and unrelenting media campaign in the former Soviet Union since Mother Russia rallied her sons and daughters against the Nazi invaders.

Such an icon as Mother Russia, however, would be out of place in MMM's advertisements, for that stern, maternal symbol exists outside of time: her depiction may vary somewhat depending on the artist, but the Mother Russia of World War II neither aged nor changed. A static figure rather than an episodic hero, she could not develop or be shown to learn. For the MMM advertisements, however, the passage of time would prove to be essential, as the viewers had to be convinced that investing in MMM always led to satisfying results. The act of investment had to be shown as a process, and so the makers of the MMM ads quickly learned the trick of conflating the product being hyped with the genre of entertainment that held its viewers' attention between commercials: the soap opera, probably the only genre named after its corporate sponsor. The success of MMM, a pyramid scheme that defrauded consumers by the millions, was due in large part to its brilliant exploitation of the possibilities inherent in the soap opera genre, a form of entertainment that has rapidly come to prominence in post-Soviet Russia. MMM's foray into soap opera allowed the company to blur the boundaries between production and marketing, fiction and nonfiction, and public and private, to the point where the ads themselves became the company's greatest product: Mavrodi's medium *was* his message.

MMM's use of soap opera was, according to Bakhyt Kilibaev, the ad campaign's director, a happy accident dictated by the nature of the product being sold.[1] Not only did its success surpass the wildest dreams of its creators, but MMM's artificial world rapidly took on a life of its own: its main character, Lenia Golubkov, became the stuff of jokes and urban folklore, burned in effigy by his enemies and emulated by his friends.[2] Moreover, as events overtook Mavrodi, ultimately leading to his arrest, the soap opera of MMM soon became the soap opera *about* MMM. In one of the many bizarre circumstances that would surround the MMM crisis in 1994, news programs revealing damaging evidence of Mavrodi's fraudulent activity were punctuated by the inevitable commercials urging viewers to change their lives by investing in MMM stock. The MMM soap opera, which was intended from the beginning to inspire mimetic desire, spilled over throughout the media that first had carried it and then discussed it. For Russian television and newspapers, this was a melodrama in which the naive, post-Soviet media found themselves cast in the role of gullible heroine tempted by the rich, smooth-talking deceiver (MMM).[3] For MMM, it was the government that played the villain's role, while Mavrodi (and, by extension, his "partners" — the investors he convinced to put money into his scheme) was a martyr fighting against a jealous, authoritarian state. Both Mavrodi and the mass media tirelessly spun new narratives for popular consumption: the pundits demonstratively wrung their hands over the sorry state of the media and exchanged accusations with rival journalists, while Mavrodi paid to have his frequent declarations from prison published in full-page ads in newspapers throughout Russia. Finally, Mavrodi's "partners" joined in the act with their "Letters to MMM," in which one ordinary citizen after the next recounted the tale of successful investments in terms already familiar from MMM's advertising.[4] Although television is often criticized for rendering the viewer passive, MMM's ad campaign had the opposite effect: not only did it prompt millions of Russian citizens to imitate Lenia Golubkov and his friends, and thus turn off their televisions at least long enough to buy shares, but as the crisis developed, MMM's diehard supporters progressed beyond viewers and actors, ultimately becoming the coauthors of MMM's grand narrative, reinscribing their own lives within its parameters and publishing the results in newspaper advertisements for all their fellow Russians to read. To a large extent, MMM's simulation of the stock market (which replaced actual investment with a semblance of entrepreneurial activity) ultimately became a self-perpetuating, all-encompassing master narrative in which MMM's "partners," viewers, and authors could live nearly full time.

To dismiss MMM as simply one in the long list of pyramid schemes that have sprouted up throughout the former Warsaw Pact nations would be to treat the company as merely an economic or political phenomenon. Such a conclusion would be possible only by ignoring the source of MMM's success: its advertising campaign.[5] Although the substance of MMM was, of course, economic (money was made and lost at a staggering rate), the television advertisements focused far more on the achievement of happiness in everyday life. What makes the MMM ad campaign so compelling a case study, however, is the manner in which the "everyday life" depicted so rapidly expanded: by the summer of 1994, there was no aspect of life that could not somehow be subsumed within the omnivorous rhetoric of MMM. MMM had even appropriated the trappings of national executive power, becoming a "hologram state" that flirted with the idea of appropriating supreme governmental authority. Economically, MMM was a classic pyramid scheme (that is, an investment plan in which earlier investors are paid dividends from the money contributed by later investors), distinguished from the more common chain letter only by its scope. But MMM as a cultural phenomenon applied the principles of the pyramid scheme to both advertising and public discussion of the scheme itself: the rhetoric of MMM expanded along with its money, finally reaching a point at which the company's critics came to see it as a symbol of everything that was wrong with post-Soviet Russian life, while its advocates looked on it as the only institution offering a viable alternative to these very same problems.

Initial Mystery

To understand the MMM phenomenon, a few words about the nature and history of the company are in order. MMM was founded by Sergei Mavrodi as a cooperative in 1988. A 1979 graduate of the Moscow Institute of Electronic Machine Building, Mavrodi's involvement in "business" dates back to 1981, years before Gorbachev's reforms would render such activity legal. Over the years, Mavrodi slowly climbed the black-market ladder, selling first jeans and records, then eventually computers and other expensive consumer goods.[6] According to the newspaper *Moskovskie novosti,* Mavrodi spent most of the 1980s registered as an elevator attendant, janitor, and night watchman in order to avoid prosecution for "parasitism" (lack of an official job) while developing his black-market career.[7] For the first few years of its existence, MMM kept a low profile in both the markets and the media; in the late 1980s it was the Alisa company, with its ubiquitous barking dog, that dominated the airwaves. As MMM expanded, its troubles with the law also grew, most notably over the question of taxes. In January 1992, MMM's accountants were arrested for non-payment of taxes and for presenting false balance sheets. In April of the following year, Makhaon, an MMM subsidiary, was prosecuted for hiding one billion rubles. MMM-Bank, another affiliate, was closed in the fall of 1993, but its money disappeared before unpaid taxes could be collected. Soon MMM's run-ins with the law took a burlesque turn that strained credibility even more than its ad campaign: in May 1994, a Toyota carrying important documents relating to eighteen divisions of MMM was mysteriously hijacked on its way to the offices of the tax police; the car was later found, but the documents had vanished for good.[8]

Perhaps not surprisingly, the beginning of MMM's troubled relationship with the authorities roughly coincided with the company's rise to prominence in the public consciousness (1992–94). If the government was intrigued by MMM's activity, ordinary Russians were no less so. From the very beginning, MMM was a creature of Moscow's equivalent of Madison Avenue, a set of mysterious initials and enigmatic advertisements that seemed designed to arouse the public's curiosity. In the early 1990s, MMM lavished money on exquisitely produced billboards displayed in metro stations throughout the country's major cities: one would have had to be blind not to recognize MMM's ever-present butterfly symbol, often accompanied by the enigmatic slogan "из тени в свет перелетая" (Flying out of the dark into the light). Perhaps these words were an announcement that MMM would indeed finally "come to light" and reveal its true nature, but its early television advertisements only increased the mystery, even as they emphasized the company's widespread name recognition.[9] One ad in particular comes to mind, the commercial that might best be called "The Annunciation of MMM." This TV spot immediately stood out for its high production values (still a rarity in 1992) and excellent direction; it was a combination of Western quality with Russian faces. In it, the camera shows us people from a wide variety of backgrounds, at work, at play, engaging in casual conversation. One after another, each one sees a light emanating from the heavens and looks up. Finally, we see what they see: the huge letters "MMM," accompanied by a God-like baritone proclaiming: "нас знают все" ("Everyone knows us," or, more literally, "We are known by all"). In effect, the ad worked like an incantation: endless repetitions of the words "everybody knows us" ultimately rendered them true: who didn't recognize MMM? At the same time, the ad played on a variety of mass traditions: the ever-present Soviet мы (we) that was the subject of so many political slogans had now became an object, нас (us), while the masses became the subject, все (everyone). Although both Soviet propaganda and post-Soviet advertising target the "masses," their different approaches to the populace reflect contradictory metaphors of the body politic: for Soviet propaganda, with its roots in the collectivist romanticism of the proletarian culture movement, the masses moved as one body.[10]

When the masses become consumers, however, the once-nationalized public body becomes fragmented, privatized. Although the advertiser operates on a large scale, he must nevertheless develop the illusion of a personal relationship between the product and the consumer. The MMM ad treated consumers as anything but undifferentiated masses or class types: the revelation of MMM was, like the revelation at Sinai, a collective event experienced by each person individually. Moreover, the Sinai comparison leads to an important point: the advertisement is suffused with a distinctly nonsecular glow. In the United States, such an approach fairly reeks of Protestantism: the skeptical housewife comes to accept Clorox bleach as her personal savior. Appropriately, this MMM ad appeals to a closer, Russian Orthodox context: as the individuals who make up the Russian все each, in turn, look up and display their profiles to the camera, their poses effortlessly switch from the casual to the iconic, and each one basks in the reflected halo of corporate transfiguration.

Eventually, the advertisers lifted the veil of mystery from their product, and MMM was revealed to be an investment group. This, however, was no ordinary fund: first of all, it did not involve the direct purchase of stocks. Instead, MMM's "partners" bought pieces of paper that gave them redemption rights to stocks, which in turn might someday earn dividends. Most investors never redeemed their paper for actual stock; instead, the paper itself was the source of unheard-of profits. MMM newspaper ads repeatedly crowed that "our shares are guaranteed to be liquid" — they could be bought and sold at any time. Moreover, whereas the new capitalist stock market was a source of potential anxiety for consumers who were only just being weaned from a planned economy, MMM's shares came with a guarantee: not only would they always go up in price faster than the rate of inflation, but, in the best traditions of Gosplan (the Soviet governmental entity in charge of central economic planning), their future value was announced several days in advance. There was, however, no rational explanation for such profits; certainly, no investments in Russia at the time could yield such returns, nor could the currency markets (despite the inexorable decline of the ruble); even drug trafficking was less lucrative than the 3,000% annual dividends promised by MMM.[11]

Although a number of hypotheses have been proposed to explain MMM, the prevailing model is quite simple: it was a pyramid scheme that operated on an elegant and simple premise; if enough people were convinced to buy the shares at 1,000 rubles (the original price), even more investors could be persuaded to buy them at 1,200. Some of those who bought in at 1,000 took their money and ran, but others kept it in because the price went up as promised, suggesting further profits. When the company increased the price again, its proven track record of profitability lured new buyers, whose higher investment paid off the old buyers. In a pyramid, old investors are paid off thanks to new investments, but pyramids usually collapse when the price for new stocks gets too high to be affordable, driving down the number of buyers and, eventually, the value of the shares. Shareholders panic and ask for their money back, but the company cannot oblige; the stock undergoes a kind of physical sublimation, and "guaranteed liquidity" gives way to hot air. Investors can certainly make money on pyramids, but only if they get in early enough, since the scheme is based on an inflationary spiral. To put it bluntly, pyramid schemes function very much like a notoriously unreliable method of contraception, in which a calamitous outcome can be avoided only given a timely withdrawal.[12]

Playing the Market

Pyramid schemes succeed in attracting investors only if they can show results; thus, it is essential that an aspiring pyramid builder spread the good word of his successes early on. Television advertising is the perfect means to do that: after abandoning its initial mysterious commercials, MMM devoted its massive resources to filling the airwaves with success stories about investors "just like you." But it was MMM's use of the soap opera format that proved to be a stroke of genius, even though, in retrospect, the choice of this genre seems overdetermined. Although no stranger to melodrama, the Soviet Union did not produce soap operas as such, and before the late perestroika era, the viewing public had seen few examples of soap operas from abroad. When state television began to show the Mexican serial drama *Los ricos lloren tambien* (Богатые тоже плачут, *The Rich Also Cry*), the country was so caught up in the trials and tribulations of Marianna, a street waif turned rich man's wife, that the program had to be shown twice a day in order to avoid a precipitous drop in labor productivity. For the uninitiated, it must be noted that Latin American soap operas differ sharply from those in the United States; the melodrama, unrestrained emotion, and reliance on chance that characterize Mexican and Brazilian soaps make *General Hospital* look positively Pinteresque. Perhaps more ominously for MMM and its "partners," Latin American *telenovelas* also differ from American soaps in terms of time: while *The Guiding Light* has been shining since 1948 (having successfully made the transition from radio to TV),[13] Latin American serials are finite — even if coming to the end of the story means skipping ahead ten or twenty years to allow the heroine's long-lost son to grow up and narrowly avoid marrying his sister.[14] The Latin American model is particularly appropriate for a pyramid scheme, because both reach an inevitable, tear-stained conclusion.[15]

Yet, MMM could not borrow from Latin American soap operas whole cloth; no matter how much the Russian audience might empathize with Marianna, or with the heroine of the most popular soap of the summer of 1994, *Prosto Mariia* (*Simplemente Maria,* or *Just Maria*), there was still an undeniable distance between Russian viewers and Mexican actresses, one that no amount of dubbing could overcome. As mentioned above, MMM had good reasons for choosing the soap opera format: the company could encourage the purchase of MMM shares by offering repeated simulacra of MMM investment success stories. MMM's target audience, however, was neither Mexican nor Brazilian, and thus the company took the *telenovela* and Russified it. The creators of MMM's advertising campaign drew on particularly Russian sources, especially folklore and socialist realism. The connection between aggressively capitalist advertising and official Soviet propaganda might seem unlikely, but MMM cleverly borrowed a number of socialist realist tropes (the ordinary worker as hero, the conflation of personal and collective success), even as it twisted them to suit its own purposes. Moreover, MMM was able to take advantage of an audience that had been raised on socialist realist mass culture, whose idea of mimesis included not only the "accurate" representation of "real" life in art, but the expectation that "real" life can (and perhaps should) use art as its model.

Since MMM was trying to soak up the paltry savings of engineers and pensioners, the heroes and heroines of the company's mini-melodramas were carefully designed to be ordinary; "New Russians" need not apply. Thus Russia was introduced to its new national hero, a man who would displace the butterfly as MMM's primary symbol: Lenia Golubkov, construction worker.[16] Lenia Golubkov was a cross between a Horatio Alger success story, a Russian fairy tale, and a socialist realist nightmare. If the much-maligned protagonist of the socialist realist novel developed an unhealthy attachment to his tractor, machine operator Lenia Golubkov, the Soviet hero's capitalist grandson, was only too happy to strike it rich and give his unlamented excavator a divorce. When first we meet Lenia, he is a typical working stiff who jumps at the chance to buy MMM shares and make money from thin air. Initially, his goals are small, hence the oft-quoted refrain from Lenia's first commercial: "Куплю жене сапоги . . ." (I'll buy my wife some boots . . .). The boots are followed by a fur coat, a dacha, and even, eventually, a trip to California to attend the World Cup soccer championship; indeed, Lenia needed a "family growth chart" to keep track of his burgeoning wealth through 1993, all thanks to MMM. As numerous commentators pointed out at the time, Lenia is a postmodern Ivanushka-durachok (Ivan the Fool), a fairy-tale hero who found the secret to success that involved no effort on his part.[17]

Lenia was quickly joined by an equally colorful supporting cast: his plump, fur-clad wife and his tattooed brother Ivan often shared the camera with him. But there were also other heroes, each designed to appeal to different segments of the audience: Nikolai Fomich and his wife, Elizaveta Andreevna, pensioners who can barely make ends meet. What can possibly save them, other than MMM? Igor and Iuliia, the young, party-loving would-be entrepreneurs of the MMM-TV generation, advise their friends to invest in MMM in order to make money to pay off a business debt. And, of course, there was Marina Sergeevna, a lonely, single woman of a certain age. As we see her leaving her apartment, the announcer tells us that "Марина Сергеевна никому не верит" (Marina Sergeevna trusts no one). Even though she has seen MMM's commercials, she is on her way to the Sberbank to give her hard-earned rubles to the state-owned entity that has defrauded its customers so many times. One of her neighbors tells her about her own success with MMM, and finally she is convinced to put part of her money in the bank and invest part in MMM. A nervous week goes by, and Marina Sergeevna cashes in her shares at an MMM trading point in order to receive the promised profit. Her reaction: "Надо же, не обманули!" (How about that! They were telling the truth!) To which the announcer responds, "Правильно, Марина Сергеевна!" (That's right, Marina Sergeevna!) Like the Wizard of Oz, MMM provides something for everyone: a dog for Nikolai Fomich, a pair of boots for Lenia's wife, and even new love for Marina Sergeevna. Just as Vladimir Zhirinovsky would promise to personally console all of Russia's lonely women with his sexual favors, Marina Sergeevna not only gains much-needed cash, she also meet a man, Volodia.

ANNOUNCER   Marina Sergeevna arrived at her friend's birthday party. But she didn't come alone. There were congratulations. And, as is the custom, they drank and had snacks. Then they danced. And then they talked. The men had their own conversations, and so did the women.
WOMAN   You're so lucky, Marinka! How I envy you! How I envy you, how I envy you!
ANNOUNCER   Marina! You do have something worth envying. A/O[18] MMM.

Ведущий: Марина Сергеевна пришла на день рождения к своей подруге. Но не одна. Звучали поздравления. И, как водится, выпивали и закусывали. Потом были танцы. Ну, а потом разговоры. У мужчин—свои. А у женщин—свои.
Женщина: Счастливая ты, Маринка. Я так тебе завидую! Так завидую, так завидую!
Ведущий: Марина! И есть чему позавидовать А/О "МММ."[19]

Marina Sergeevna's friend feels compelled to express her envy three times in a row. While one might be tempted to ascribe this repetition to the laziness of the script writer, this folkloric triple invocation of envy is actually the key to the commercial. One of the appeals to socialist ideology (if not Soviet reality) is that it promises to eliminate envy by eliminating discrepancies in wealth; while the Soviet Union was hardly egalitarian, the conspicuous consumption of the post-Soviet New Russians has provoked the scorn (and envy) of the majority of citizens still hovering around the poverty level. Marina Sergeevna's economic success is portrayed almost exclusively in terms of her personal happiness, which may be "worth envying" but could hardly invite the hostility so often provoked by wealth. Moreover, even as the woman "envies" Marina Sergeevna, she is also able to celebrate with her, to share in her happiness. To some extent, this is an oblique expansion on Mavrodi's euphemism for his investors: "partners." MMM struck a devious compromise between the values of state socialism and "wild" capitalism: the success of individuals spreads happiness to everyone around them.[20]

Heroes of Khaliava

As time passed, the soap opera elements of the MMM advertising campaign developed on two levels simultaneously: the personal (that is, the financial and romantic successes of MMM "partners" such as Lenia Golubkov and Marina Sergeevna) and the corporate (dispelling rumors that MMM was going to crash). We see Igor and Iuliia dancing around their spacious apartment, accompanied by their own personal soundtrack. The announcer asks them, "Everybody's criticizing MMM. Aren't you worried?" Iuliia's response: "Why should we worry? In our country, people always criticize what's good." In response to public concern over MMM's multi-million-dollar assault on the pathetic remains of the Russian work ethic, Lenia decides that his previous "family growth plan" was "incorrect." Instead of frittering away his profits on luxury items, he will buy back his excavator and start his own business; belatedly, Golubkov is presented as a hero of privatization. We can see an early version of his plans in an ad featuring Lenia and his brother arguing while surrounded by empty vodka bottles and leftover *zakuski:*

ANNOUNCER   This is Lenia Golubkov. And this is his brother, Ivan.
IVAN   You're a *khaliavshchik* [freeloader], Len'ka! A moron. Don't you remember what our father and mother taught us? To do honest work. And here you are running around, making a fuss, buying stocks. You're a *khaliavshchik!*
ANNOUNCER   Leonid thought for a while, and said:

LEONID   You're wrong, brother. I'm not a *khaliavshchik,* brother. I make my money honestly, with my excavator. You wanted to build a factory. You can't build it on your own. But if we all chip in, we can build it, and it'll bring us profit, it'll put food on our table. I'm not a *khaliavshchik,* I'm a partner.
ANNOUNCER   That's right, Lenia. We're partners. A/O MMM.[21]

Ведущий: Это Леня Голубков. А это его брат Иван.

Иван: Да халявщик ты, Ленька! Оболтус. Ты забыл, чему нас отец с матерью учили? Честно работать. А ты тут бегаешь, суетишься, акции покупаешь. Халявщик ты!

Ведущий: Подумал Леонид и сказал . . .

Леонид: Ты не прав, брат. Я не халявщик, брат. Я свои деньги честно на экскаваторе зарабатываю. И вкладываю их в акции, которые мне приносят прибыль. Ты захотел построить завод. Один ты его не построишь. А если мы все сложимся, мы построим его, который будет давать нам прибыль, кормить нас. Я не халявщик, я партнер.

Ведущий: Верно, Леня. Мы-партнеры. A/O "ммм."

The heart of this particular commercial is, of course, Lenia's cri de coeur: "I'm not a *khaliavshchik,* I'm a partner." Here the increasing attacks on MMM are transferred to the familiar, comical realm of the drunken kitchen debate (Ivan's speech is slurred, while Lenia is at great pains to form a coherent sentence), and their discussion highlights the aspect of MMM that was considered most unsavory by the television pundits and the man on the street: the moral quandary posed by easy money. While the source of MMM's profits was cause for curiosity, it was not the legality of Mavrodi's pyramid scheme that was of primary concern; nor did the ethical ramifications of making a profit at the expense of other "partners" seem to bother investors, who were well aware that the pyramid would have to crash eventually.[22] Instead, MMM, a company that seemed to produce nothing but its own commercials, brought into focus the public uneasiness over the concept of labor in the post-Soviet, postindustrial world.[23] Pyramid schemes aside, Russians in the early 1990s watched with discomfort as trade and service began to supplant the Soviet industrial economy. Diehard Communists watched in horror as their apocalyptic visions seemed to come true; Russian factory assembly lines ground to a halt while candy stands selling Snickers popped up at an alarming rate.[24] MMM represented a frontal assault on one of the primary myths of official Soviet culture: labor. The situation, in which production dropped while the circulation of consumer goods increased, was no less paradoxical than the everyday economics of Soviet life, in which the workers' labor produced nothing but shortages.[25] Or, as Vladislav Todorov argues, Soviet factories were "not built to produce commodities," but were rather "allegorical figures of industrialization" resulting in "a deficit of goods, but an overproduction of symbolic meanings."[26] Even if the ineffectiveness of Soviet labor was the butt of endless jokes ("We pretend to work and they pretend to pay us"), respect for the idea of labor was inculcated at the same time that the desire to perform actual labor was suppressed. The Soviet economy may well have been simulative from the very beginning, as Todorov claims, but by unceremoniously dispensing with even the illusion of work, MMM aroused the public's latent anxiety that hard work was obsolete. It also led to the "rehabilitation" of a word previously consigned to oral slang: *khaliava*.

Khaliava refers to anything that can be obtained without effort, whether it be money or possessions. Although the word is by no means obscene, it is safe to say that it was never featured prominently in such respected newspapers as *Izvestiia* and *Literaturnaia gazeta* before the MMM scandal. The term itself became a focal point for the public anxiety over the fate of labor, for while it was often used as a term of derision, a number of commentators recognized *khaliava*'s seductive appeal to what they considered the "Russian soul."[27] Elena Ivanitskaia wrote at the height of the MMM crisis that such pyramid schemes recall Dostoevsky's question: "It's not yet clear which is more awful: Russian outrageousness [*bezobrazie*] or the German method of saving up money with honest work." According to Ivanitskaia, the voucher privatization campaign was "doomed" from the beginning because "it's shameful for us, with our Russian bravado, with the breadth of our soul and our beloved outrage to take such laughable trifles seriously."[28] For their part, MMM's supporters admitted no such "Russian" desire for easy money, and instead objected to their characterization as lazy. As Sergei Bardin wrote at the time in *Nezavisimaia gazeta* (one of MMM's staunchest apologists), "We, the greedy, sly, the stupid . . . who are guilty before the government of desiring to get rich *na khaliavu* [for nothing], still have some positive qualities despite all our negative ones."[29]

Lenia and Ivan's "kitchen debate" did more than simply address the issue of *khaliava* head-on: it attempted to disarm MMM's critics by incorporating their complaints into the ad itself and then immediately superseding them with a new entrepreneurial myth. And yet, like the ad about Marina Sergeevna at the birthday party, this particular commercial managed to package the new "by-your-bootstraps" ethic in terms that would be comprehensible and acceptable to an audience raised on socialist values.[30] Lenia's story is now represented in terms not of mere individual success (which can always breed envy and resentment), but of group effort. Hence the repeated invocation of MMM's brilliant euphemism for its investors: partners. Nothing is accomplished individually, and even the paradise of private ownership that Lenia paints in vodka-enhanced hues is actually more of a cooperative. The dream itself is quaintly "pre-post-industrial": Ivan and Lenia want to build a factory. The kind of factory makes no difference whatsoever; simply the fact of a factory (Todorov's "allegorical figure of industrialization") is enough to show that Lenia's values have not been distorted.

MMM as Shadow Cabinet

Of course, the greatest challenge to Golubkov's creators was the pyramid's collapse in the summer of 1994. As the value of MMM's shares continued to rise, the government intensified its scrutiny of the company's operations. On July 18, the State Anti-Monopoly Commission urged television stations to stop broadcasting MMM's commercials, but the plea fell on deaf ears; 2,666 MMM ads had aired on Russian television in March, April, and May 1994, bringing financially strapped stations much-needed cash.[31] Of far greater consequence was an announcement made by the Tax Inspectorate three days later: MMM's subsidiary Invest-Consulting owed 49.9 billion rubles in taxes, payable immediately. Mavrodi responded the next day (July 22) by upping the ante: if forced to pay, he would shut down MMM and let the government deal with his outraged shareholders. By the time MMM shut down all its trading offices on July 26, panic had already erupted. Huge crowds gathered outside the company's main office on Varshavka — from two to three thousand people on July 26 to an estimated thirteen thousand the following day. Independent dealers were already buying up MMM shares at 65,000–75,000 rubles on the twenty-sixth, down from 115,000–125,000 before the crisis began.[32] Typically, the government and MMM moved to calm down the unruly crowd in their own fashions: Mavrodi recorded a soothing message, while the authorities sent in OMON, the "special forces" that are as inevitable in any post-Soviet mass crisis as a chorus is in a

Greek tragedy. On July 29, MMM, laying the responsibility for the panic entirely at the feet of the government, announced that circumstances had forced it to drop the official price of MMM's shares from 115,000 rubles to 950. By evening, the crowd had stopped traffic on Varshavka, and only OMON could restore order.[33] The next day, Mavrodi issued new MMM "tickets," which the Ministry of Finance announced it would not recognize; for its part, MMM designated these tickets "promotional material" — truth in advertising at last, even if only in the fine print.[34] The new tickets also differed from their predecessors in bearing the likeness of Sergei Mavrodi himself, a wise move from the standpoint of publicity, if not aesthetics, for it suggested that MMM's founder had no plans to try to slip out of the country unnoticed. The tickets' official rate was 1,065 rubles, and despite the assault on MMM's reputation, brisk trading began.[35]

One would think that the results of a battle between the central government and one private company would be a foregone conclusion, and yet the government's campaign against MMM was foundering, at least in part because it did not know how to fight an enemy based entirely on image rather than substance. The government's lack of comprehension of the rules of the narrative game was a definite obstacle to its belated attempt to clamp down on MMM's operations, and it allowed Mavrodi to outmaneuver his enemies every step of the way. As a result, officials made themselves look foolish when they engaged in a war not just with the company, but with its fictional creations as well. One of the more memorable moments came when Prime Minister Viktor Chernomyrdin addressed Marina Sergeevna and Lenia Golubkov on national television, warning them that they should be more careful with their money.[36] Mavrodi then turned the tables on Chernomyrdin: "So, the authorities do not like Lenia Golubkov and Marina Sergeevna," he responded in the nation's newspapers. "But do Lenia Golubkov and Marina Sergeevna like the authorities? No one's asked about that. Yet."[37] If the prime minister and Mavrodi were engaged in a war of words, then Chernomyrdin was well on his way to defeat. He had already ceded important rhetorical ground by invoking MMM's characters as if they were real; in his response, Mavrodi also referred to Lenia and Marina Sergeevna by name, but their enemies, "the authorities," remained abstract. As a result, MMM's heroes not only appeared to be classic "little men" victimized by inhuman bureaucratic forces, they also seemed more "real" than the nameless governmental authorities who opposed them. Moreover, Mavrodi's words contained a thinly veiled threat: if the government closed down MMM, then Mavrodi's "partners" would get their revenge at the ballot box.

Indeed, as events unfolded over the next two years, it became more and more clear that MMM and its "partners" were styling themselves as an alternative not only to the current "party of power," but to the Russian state itself.[38] Mavrodi claimed that MMM was the most powerful political force in the entire Russian Federation, large enough to gather the one million signatures needed to call a referendum on the current government and the constitution. Yeltsin's government was particularly vulnerable at that point, having just put the country through an almost interminable four-question referendum process in a failed attempt to resolve the country's constitutional crisis.[39] By August 8, Mavrodi's "partners" were openly talking of nominating him for president. If only a few years ago the greatest threat to Yeltsin's government seemed to be from the Communists, now MMM appeared to be on its way to taking over the mantle of the opposition; when diehard Communists organized a demonstration commemorating the failed coup attempt against Mikhail Gorbachev on August 19, an MMM rally held on the same day had a far greater turnout.[40]

MMM's newspaper advertisements strongly encouraged a presentation of the company and the government as equivalent forces. In one such ad on August 16, MMM's representatives claimed that the company was the "target of the entire propaganda machine of the Russian state," implying that the battle was unfairly weighted in the government's favor. This "injustice," however, was described in terms more appropriate to a rival company than to a government; the ad expressed outrage that "information from the authorities is published by the newspapers immediately, on the day it is announced, and absolutely free. But information coming from MMM has to be paid for."[41] In any case, MMM's "partners" quickly followed the company's lead, repeatedly making comparisons between the government and MMM, and always to the detriment of the former. In an advertisement run in *Komsomol'skaia pravda* on August 14, four families signed a letter saying that "if the government did even one-tenth of what A/o MMM did for us ordinary mortals," they would have started hailing it long ago.[42] Particularly telling were the investors' suggestions. An economist by the name of B. Dukhnevich wrote on August 5, "It's time for MMM to have its own newspaper, its own savings bank, to become more active in solving social problems, such as housing construction. . . . It would be good if MMM would . . . produce calendars, T-shirts, caps." In other words, MMM should assume all the state functions neglected since the Soviet Union's collapse. Moreover, there was a general expectation that MMM should accord special treatment to the social categories that had special status in Soviet times. It was repeatedly suggested after MMM closed its trading points in July 1994 that the company pay retirees and war veterans first.[43] Dukhnevich's wish list continues: "It would be wonderful if MMM . . . were to help veterans find a place in market relations, arranging a special movie showing for us, or a play, or special literature."[44] If the Soviet state was supposed to take care of the elderly under communism, it should be up to MMM to help them in a market economy.

Enough people believed the promises of MMM to vote Mavrodi into public office. On October 31, 1994, Mavrodi was elected to the state Duma, whereupon he squandered most of his public support by announcing that MMM offices would remain closed until the following year and that all present shares in the company were invalid. Clearly, Mavrodi, who had been released from prison only two weeks earlier, had run for office only to gain parliamentary immunity.[45] His wife, Elena, the former "Miss Zaporozhie 1992," twice ran unsuccessfully for a Duma seat, first in 1995, then in 1997 (when her opponents included chess champion Anatoly Karpov and Yeltsin's former bodyguard, Alexander Korzhakov).[46] If 1994 saw MMM emerge as a political force, 1995 was the year that Mavrodi's political ambitions were crushed. In September, the Central Electoral Commission denied registration to his "Party of People's Capital" because of his decision to pay dividends on MMM shares to party members only. A mere two hundred protesters picketed the commission, a far cry from the glory days of 1994.[47] Mavrodi lost his reelection bid in December, whereupon he announced his candidacy for the Russian presidency in January. By then, however, Mavrodi was facing new criminal charges, and the Electoral Commission refused to register him as a candidate. Although Mavrodi did launch another pyramid scheme (MMM-1996), it has failed to attract anywhere near the attention to which he was once accustomed; clearly, Mavrodi's moment has passed.[48]

Unlimited Partners

In order to understand how MMM could have seemed even a vaguely credible alternative to Russian governmental institutions, it is necessary to return to the critical moment when Chernomyrdin stopped attacking fictional characters and turned his attention to Mavrodi himself. The arrest of Mavrodi was a carefully staged media event that was apparently an attempt to dislodge MMM not only from its central financial position, but from its dominant place on the airwaves as well. Again, however, the measures taken by the authorities lacked subtlety: the government responded to MMM's soap opera with a poorly scripted police drama (OMON's raid of Mavrodi's apartment). If anything, the arrest made

Mavrodi a martyr, an image he would exploit from prison with some success. During the same summer that Americans were treated to the spectacle of the Los Angeles Police Department's low-speed chase of O. J. Simpson, Russian TV viewers watched as members of the special forces scaled the side of Mavrodi's building in order to capture the physically unimpressive little man behind the financial wizard's curtain. The result was bad television, in part because the authorities suffered from generic confusion: a producer who decides to send the cops from *NYPD Blue* to arrest the Bundy family from *Married, with Children* can expect to have to look for a new job.

MMM's counterattack was, as usual, inspired, and it represented the expansion of the soap opera well beyond its accustomed bounds. Recall that MMM's ad campaign represented a rapprochement of the viewing public and the soap opera format: where once all soap opera heroes were exotic, now they were almost laughably familiar. As MMM attempted to inspire confidence in its "partners," it went one step further: the company flew in Victoria Ruffo, star of *Just Maria,* an immensely popular soap opera that was still airing in Russia at the time.[49] In the course of one day, MMM's studio filmed a series of advertisements in which "Just Maria" met with each and every hero of the MMM soap opera.[50] The fact that Ruffo speaks no Russian was scarcely an obstacle (her only words, "Si, si!" vaguely sounded to the Russian ear as though she were calling attention to one of the more prominent features of her anatomy); the ever-present announcer always supplied half the lines.

> ANNOUNCER   Igor and Iuliia felt a bit shy around Maria, and so they made small talk: about the weather, young people's fashions, movies, music, their favorite performers. And then finally they got around to asking for an autograph. "A memento for Igor and Iuliia — Just Maria." A/O "MMM."[51]
>
> Ведущий: Игорь и Юлия чувствовали себя с Марией немного скованно, а потому говорили обо всем подряд: о погоде, о молодежной моде, о кино и о музыке, о любимых артистах. И в конце концов попросили-таки автограф. На память Игорю и Юле. Просто Мария. A/O "MMM."

In another spot from the same series, Marina Sergeevna and Just Maria have just swapped photographs of their respective boyfriends, Volodia and Viktor, when Volodia arrives in person:

MARINA SERGEEVNA   Oh, Maria, I love him so much! It's scary. . . .
What do you think, can I trust him?
ANNOUNCER   . . . Marina Sergeevna asked Just Maria. "An interesting
man," thought Just Maria, "but Victor is better." "Yes, Victor is really
handsome," thought Marina Sergeevna.
MARINA SERGEEVNA   And this is Volodia!
ANNOUNCER   And that's how Volodia and Just Maria met. A/O
"MMM."[52]

Марина Сергеевна: Ах, Мария, я его так люблю! Что мне
страшно. . . . Как ты думаешь, ему можно верить?
Ведущий: делилась Марина Сергеевна с Просто Марией. —
Интересный мужчина,—подумала Просто Мария,—но Виктор
лучше. —Бесспорно, Виктор красив,—подумала Марина
Сергеевна.
Марина Сергеевна: А это Володя!
Ведущий: Так познакомились Володя и Просто Мария. A/O
"MMM."

First the foreign heroes of soap operas were replaced with more familiar Russian characters, who could more easily represent the viewer and therefore attempt to convert the viewer into a "partner" by inducing the mimetic desire to invest. If the ads worked then the viewer, essentially, became the hero of the commercial.[53] Now, as a special treat, the Russian heroes get to meet the Mexicans who served as their inspiration; thus the Russian viewers watched as their stand-ins met the foreign movie star. When Just Maria walked into the apartment of Marina Sergeevna, she entered the home of the viewer as well. After successfully domesticating the soap opera, MMM bridged the distance between its own prosaic heroes and their exotic models.[54] The Russian viewer was only one step away from being a soap opera heroine herself.

But the total participation of MMM's "partners" in the company narrative required two unexpected shifts, one in medium, the other in genre: from television to newsprint, and from domestic melodrama to hagiography.[55] When the authorities turned the spotlight on Mavrodi himself with the televised arrest, Mavrodi told his own story, the slick attempt at autohagiography of a latter-day Avvakum. In full-page ads taken in central newspapers of all political persuasions in August 1994, Mavrodi published a series of letters from prison in which he explains his motivations and gives his "partners" a clearer sense of the company's president. Two components of his strategy are immediately clear: Mavrodi is a martyr; Mavrodi is a saint. The "Biography of Sergei Mavrodi, President of MMM" even includes childhood miracles: when he was in eighth grade, little Seryozha studied higher mathematics on his own, and when his teachers were sick, Seryozha was called on to teach class in their place. In a letter entitled "In the Light of Conscience" (При свете совести), Mavrodi refers to his arrest as "treacherous" (вероломный). "To suffer for the Fatherland is easy and pleasant. Only in short-term solitary confinement have I truly understood the correctness of these words." The letter concludes with an appeal to Mavrodi's public: "Don't let up, and don't let them fool you again; together, we'll win. After all, we're partners."[56] Thus Mavrodi's suffering was our suffering, and Mavrodi's triumph our triumph. The subtext of MMM's entire media campaign was the overcoming of adversity through proper financial planning, and, borrowing liberally from the hagiographic tradition, Mavrodi rewrote his own story to fit the message.

It was in these print ads that MMM succeeded in completely subsuming its "partners" within the corporate master narrative. For if Lenia Golubkov, the representation of the Russian investor, could meet Just Maria on television, "real," nontelevised investors would share space with Mavrodi himself in newspapers throughout the land. In August 1994, entire pages of Russian newspapers were dedicated to "Letters to MMM," in which "partner" after "partner" expressed outrage over Mavrodi's treatment and faith in the miraculous powers of his company. Their faith in Mavrodi's miracle was apparently complete, and was remarkably reminiscent of the faith demanded by an earlier, decidedly anticapitalist culture. Pensioner Dmitri K. wrote, "Your stocks have changed reality, like in a fairy-tale [*skazochnyi*] dream."[57] His words, perhaps unconsciously, reflect a song sung by Soviet schoolchildren in the 1930s, "We were born to turn the fairy tale into reality" (Мы рождены, чтобы сказку сделать былью). Another investor provided a more personal account: "At my most critical moment, MMM saved me from poverty. I'm not talking about a fur coat or vacation resorts, but about my daily bread, since after 35 years of working in the defense industry, the government could provide me only 15 (fifteen) thousand rubles a month; I've got more than a year to go until I retire, so leaving or finding a new job isn't realistic. And besides all that, I'm a woman."[58] By this point, it is no longer clear if the genius of MMM's advertising directors is that they portrayed everyday Russian life so well, or that they created a set of narrative conventions so compelling that the audience was induced to unconsciously replicate the formula in its own letters. The Mukavev family from Perm, headed by a single mother, wrote of its own version of Lenia Golubkov's early, more modest successes: thanks to MMM the daughter bought a leather jacket and the family could eat milk, soup, and meat bouillon every day, with even the possibility of buying the occasional banana at the market. Such stories are, of course, touching, which is the most obvious reason for their inclusion in MMM's print advertisements. But they also represent the total identification of the investors and their "soap opera" heroes. Just as the act of purchasing MMM stock was consistently portrayed in the advertising campaign as a transformative moment, the campaign itself worked its enchantment on its object, changing the soap opera hero into the investor, the TV viewer into the "partner," and the "partner" into not only a player in the MMM narrative, but even, eventually, the narrative's coauthor. For a company targeted by numerous government investigations, this strategy makes sense: if the viewers (and voters) become both heroes and authors, their investment in the company's plot will be at least as great as their investment in company stock; they will do their best to make sure their story has a happy ending.

Notes

The author thanks Mark Lipovetsky and Frances Bernstein for their comments on a draft of this chapter.

1 Viktoriia Dubitskaia, "Bakhyt Kilibaev: Ia i Lenia Golubkov — takie, kak vse," *Iskusstvo kino,* no. 1 (1995), p. 19.

2 On September 14, 1994, the European-Asian News Agency reported that a young man in Ekaterinburg was put in a mental hospital after trying to convince his friends and family that he was Lenia Golubkov. One of the doctors interviewed remarked that extreme reactions to advertisements were not unusual and cited the "Uncle Ben's effect," which causes vomiting in children who have seen the ad for the American rice company too many times. See Agenstvo Evropeisko-aziatskie novosti, "Lzhe-Golubkov popal v psikhushku na Urale," *Komsomol'skaia pravda,* September 14, 1994, p. 1. Like so many feature stories published in Russian newspapers in recent years, this one should certainly be taken with a grain of salt. However, this chapter is concerned with the portrayal and perception of MMM rather than "reality"; one need not subscribe to postmodern notions of "hyperreality" and "simulacra" to recognize that the relationship between the world of commercial advertising and objective reality is tenuous at best. Thus I offer the following disclaimer: In this essay, newspaper articles and television broadcasts are cited not as unimpeachable sources but as contributions to the creation of MMM's public image.

3 Azer Murasliev, noting that only the more financially independent *Segodnia* declined to print MMM's newspaper advertisements during the summer of 1994, ironically refers to the papers' tendency to criticize Mavrodi and print his ads in the same paper as the press's "loss of innocence": the press is now independent of the "government-rapist," but has been "seduced" by Mavrodi ("Chetvertaia vlast' teriaet nevinnost'," *Moskovskie novosti,* August 7, 1994, p. 8).

4 Here, too, some skepticism is also appropriate. It is quite possible that at least the initial letters were fabricated by MMM's advertising arm, although such falsified ads could have served to stimulate letter writing from actual investors.

5 Certainly, commentators were well aware at the time that MMM was more than an economic phenomenon. Aleksei Tarkhanov notes, "Now saying 'I invested in MMM' unites people no less than 'I fought on the Belorussian Front.' But to reply, 'And I invested in *Chara*' [another pyramid scheme] would be the height of poor taste" ("Prostota luchshe vorovstva: Obsuzhdenie reklamnoi kampanii 'MMM,' " *Iskusstvo kino,* no. 1 [1995], p. 7).

6 Irina Savvateeva, "Khorosho schitat' i torgovat' Mavrodi nauchilsia na fakul'tete prikladnoi matematiki," *Izvestiia,* August 4, 1994, p. 4.

7 Vladimir Yemelyanenko, "The State Meets Its Match," *Moscow News,* December 2, 1994.

8 Aleksandr Liasko and Sergei Razin, "Kak govoriat v narode, v sem'e — ne bez Mavrodi!" *Komsomol'skaia pravda,* August 3, 1994, p. 3.

9 Maiia Turovskaia writes that this particular ad "remains a mystery to me: I don't know if one should understand it as a symbol of the movement from the shadow economy to the legal economy, or as a metaphor of poverty-shadow and wealth-light . . . , or as the 'conversion' of [communist] party money" (Maiia Turovskaia, "Lenia Golubkov i drugie," *Iskusstvo kino,* no. 1 [1995], p. 22).

10 For a discussion of the "mass man" in Soviet culture, see Vladislav Todorov, *Red Square, Black Square: Organon for Revolutionary Imagination* (Albany: State University of New York Press, 1995), pp. 94–99. Mayakovsky depicts the Soviet people as one giant body in his epic poem, *150,000,000* (1919). Contemporary readers are most familiar with such imagery in its negative, satiric form, in Evgeny Zamyatin's dystopian novel *We* (1920).

11 Reuters, untitled, September 11, 1994; Nikolai Andreev, "V ianvare — sapogi, v avguste — KPZ," *Chas-Pik,* August 10, 1994, p. 2. Moreover, even if MMM could have sustained such high dividends, it could not have given small investors such as Lenia Golubkov enough money to purchase all the luxuries he would obtain during the course of the advertising campaign (G. Demidov, "Lenia Golubkov bez telegrima," *Argumenty i fakty* 31 [August 1994]: 5).

12 The sexual comparison, although crude, is by no means inappropriate; the constant visual connection drawn between capitalist success and sexually available young women in the post-Soviet mass media lent the free market the air of free love. Moreover, the very language of commerce, with its foreign borrowings and odd circumlocutions, seems almost tailor-made for double entendres. Chubais's plan for

privatization of state enterprises introduced a number of ungainly Anglicisms into the Russian language, most notably the word ваучер (voucher). In certain everyday financial contexts, the term takes on a distinctly risqué overtone when combined with the Russian verb "to invest" (вложить), which literally means "to insert." It is difficult to imagine a Russian man asking a Russian woman, "Where can I invest my voucher?" with a straight face.

13 According to Muriel G. Cantor and Suzanne Pingree, *The Guiding Light* is the only old radio soap opera still on the air. The show first aired in 1937, was dropped briefly in 1941 (and reinstated after angry listeners organized a letter-writing campaign), and was broadcast on television and radio simultaneously for four years until the radio version ended in 1956. As one might imagine, the cast of characters has changed drastically over the last sixty years. Muriel G. Cantor and Suzanne Pingree, *The Soap Opera* (Beverly Hills: Sage, 1983), p. 97.

14 The open-endedness of American soap operas has yet to be completely assimilated by Russian television, leading announcers to alert the viewing audience that at 8:00 P.M. they will be able to watch, for instance, episode 271 of *Santa Barbara.*

15 The radically different time frame of the *telenovela* has led some American scholars to conclude that it cannot be called a soap opera. Cantor and Pingree consign the *telenovela,* which "last[s] for eight or nine months," together with miniseries and "nighttime soaps," to a different generic category: "In South America and other parts of the world the *telenovela,* produced locally by country, has been compared to the American soap opera, but actually resembles the shorter series in form" (*The Soap Opera,* p. 25). Or, as Madeleine Edmonson and David Rounds argue, "Soaps are serials, but not every serial is a soap." For them, soap operas are by definition "stories about American life." See Madeleine Edmonson and David Rounds, *The Soaps: Daytime Serials of Radio and TV* (New York: Stein and Day, 1973), p. 17.

While defining a genre based on its sense of time is compelling, especially to Slavists steeped in Bakhtin's notion of the chronotope, such a narrow definition precludes any international perspective on a form of popular entertainment that knows few boundaries. Indeed, it is a particular characteristic of American television that "seriality" (the extension of plots and the repeated appearances of characters for as long as the market will support them) is integral; most other television cultures (including the ex-USSR) assume that a series will come to an end. Moreover, even if the time frame of the North American soap and the Latin American *telenovela* differs, both serve similar functions in their respective cultures: they provide popular daytime entertainment for a largely female audience. In addition, the heroes and heroines of each genre live in a world in which both fate and chance play a crucial role, a largely domestic world that occasionally opens up to include incursions by organized crime. If we compare Rosa Gómez's "Temas articuladores en el género telenovela," in *Telenovela/Telenovelas: Los relatos de una historia de amor,* ed. Marita Soto (Argentina: Atuel, 1996), pp. 37–50, with Cantor and Pingree's chapter "Soap Opera Content" (*The Soap Opera,* pp. 69–94), we find both variation and common ground. It is worth noting that Latin American scholars (who, thanks to the relentless export of American popular culture are likely to be intimately acquainted with both varieties of daytime drama) do not, as a rule, insist on isolating the soap opera from the *telenovela: "Telenovela, teleteatro, culebrón,* soap opera, televised melodrama — all are names by which society recognizes a series of audiovisual narrative texts. The consumption, criticism, classification, . . . and even parody [have at their basis] a series of common characteristics that distinguish them from other fictional texts, such as humor programs or other types of televised comedies and dramas" (Gustavo Aprea and Rolando C. Martínez Mendoza, "Hacia una definición del género telenovela," in Soto, ed., *Telenovela/Telenovelas,* p. 17). Finally, one must also take into account the reception of the Latin American *telenovela* and the North American soap opera in contemporary Russia; although many viewers may have distinguished between the two, they are usually discussed as variants of the same form of popular entertainment.

16 In interviews, Kilibaev made the relationship between his heroes and their intended audience quite clear: "We wanted the television viewers to identify with our characters" (Dubitskaia, "Bakhyt Kilibaev," p. 14). Critics, however, have argued that such an identification is unlikely. Konstantin Ernst argues that "the viewers identified these characters not with themselves, but with the people who live next to them" ("Prostota," p. 5). Turovskaia puts it more plainly: "Lenia Golubkov has one permanent virtue: he always seems more stupid than any viewer" (Turovskaia, "Lenia Golubkov," p. 23).

17 The comparison is made by Turovskaia ("Lenia Golubkov," p. 23), Marina Shakina ("Sergei Mavrodi kak otets rossiiskoi mechty," *Novoe vremia* 31 [August 1994]: 25), and Tarkhanov ("Prostota," p. 8).

18 "A/O" stands for акционерное общество (*aktsionernoe obshchestvo*), joint-stock company.

19 My thanks to Rebecca Stanley for sharing her *Russian TV Sampler* video cassettes and teachers' guides, from which this text is taken (Stanley, *Russian TV Sampler,* program 103, p. 8). For more information, write to Rebecca Stanley, New York Network, P.O. Box 7012, Albany, NY, 12225; (518) 443-5333; stanlerm@nyn.sunycentral.edu.

20 This theme is also present in an ad starring Nikolai Fomich and Elizaveta Andreevna. Since they are retirees, they claim they don't need much out of life. Thanks to MMM, they've started to "help others," including their retired neighbor (Stanley, *Russian TV Sampler,* program 102, p. 9).

21 Stanley, *Russian TV Sampler,* program 103, p. 8.

22 Indeed, Mavrodi's apologists often argued that MMM was under no obligation to explain how it made its money. In her notorious defense of Mavrodi on the pages of *Nezavisimaia gazeta,* Larisa Piyazheva argued that "all this is his business, and he is free to tell it to society, the state and even his shareholders, or not to tell them; after all, any shareholders who do not like his reticence can pick out another Mavrodi, one

who is more talkative" (Larisa Piyazheva, "Position: Free Sergei Mavrodi! On Entrepreneurial Ethics and the State's Zeal," *Nezavisimaia gazeta,* September 27, 1994, pp. 1, 4; trans. in *Current Digest of the Post-Soviet Press* 46, no. 39 [October 26, 1994]: 12).

23 By the summer of 1994, MMM officials had all but admitted that their only product was their advertising. When Kilibaev announced that there would be a new series of MMM ads despite the company's apparent crash, he said that the new spots were "designed to calm people down, to show them that MMM is alive and producing new commercials" (Mikhail Dubik, "Lyonya Seeks New Life as a Small Businessman," *Moscow Times,* July 29, 1994, p. 2).

24 Thanks to aggressive marketing by the Mars Corporation, Snickers was a lightning rod for popular discontent with the flood of foreign imports. In 1993 and 1994, the Mars Corporation accounted for 80 percent and 63 percent, respectively, of all TV ad time devoted to sweets. Vladimir Zhirinovsky even campaigned to ban Snickers from the airwaves in December 1993. See Ellen Mickiewicz, *Changing Channels: Television and the Struggle for Power in Russia* (Oxford: Oxford University Press, 1997), pp. 236–37.

25 For an extended examination of the Soviet attitude toward labor, see Mikhail Epstein's "Labor of Lust: Erotic Metaphors of Soviet Civilization," in *After the Future: The Paradoxes of Postmodernism in Contemporary Russian Culture* (Amherst: University of Massachusetts Press, 1995), pp. 164–87.

26 Todorov, *Red Square, Black Square,* p. 10.

27 Nikolai Andreev laments that "capitalism in the MMM commercials . . . is portrayed as heaven for do-nothings and the feeble-minded," but also admits that "if you take into account our Russian nature . . . , then such an image of existence couldn't be more appropriate" (Nikolai Andreev, "Khorosho li dlia Rossii to, chto prekrasno dlia 'MMM'?" *Chas-Pik,* August 3, 1994, p. 2).

28 Elena Ivanitskaia, "Metafizika aktsii. Piat' podstupov k teme," *Obshchaia gazeta,* August 5–11, 1994, p. 9.

29 Sergei Bardin, "Nas reshili sdelat' plokhimi, chtoby ne reshat' nashi problemy?" *Nezavisimaia gazeta,* August 12, 1994, p. 7.

30 Vladimir Magun considers Lenia's rejection of *khaliava* a "false move, an idiosyncratic concession to the old values that goes against the general, pro-capitalist orientation of this advertising serial" ("Prostota," p. 11). While the ads are definitely a concession to socialist values, it is difficult to see Lenia's desire to build a factory as inimical to a "pro-capitalist orientation"; here Magun himself seems to identify capitalism with *khaliava.* Turovskaia takes a more nuanced view, recognizing that Lenia's new plans "fit quite well in the Soviet propaganda tradition," but also seeing the new Lenia as a result of MMM's realization that "the ideology of 'khaliava' is still not respectable enough" (Turovskaia, "Lenia Golubkov," p. 23).

31 Julia Wishnevsky, "MMM," *RFE/RL Daily Report,* July 19, 1994; "Na TV emotsii perevodiatsia v tsifry," *Izvestiia,* June 17, 1994, p. 9, as quoted in Mickiewicz, *Changing Channels,* p. 237. The television channels would have been hard-pressed

to stop airing MMM's ads, since the commercials had been paid for in advance (Otto Latsis, "Chto eto za istoriia?" *Izvestiia* August 6, 1994, p. 2).

32 Andrei Kniazev and Alina Kazakova, "AO 'MMM': a ved' vse moglo byt' inache . . . ," *Russkii biznes,* August 1–7, 1994, p. 14.

33 Ibid., p. 14.

34 Andrei Koleshnikov, "Aktsii otchaianiia," *Moskovskie novosti* July 21, 1994, p. 1; Otdel ekonomicheskoi politiki, "Kommentarii," *Kommersant,* August 10, 1994, p. 15.

35 Louisa Vinton, "MMM Pyramid Comes Crashing Down," *RFE/RL Daily Report,* August 1, 1994.

36 "We must warn those like Lenia Golubkov and Marina Sergeevna, the opportunities for easy money in the market will soon begin to disappear" (broadcast by Michael Shuster, "Russian Investors Rocked by Pyramid Scam," *National Public Radio Morning Edition,* August 3, 1994, transcript 1403–4).

37 Sergei Mavrodi. "Ob''iasnenie v neliubvi," *Kuranty,* July 27, 1994, p. 11.

38 This new twist in MMM's self-presentation was by no means lost on Russian commentators at the time. Valentin Aleksandrovich wrote on August 12, 1994, that "capital is now making claims on power. A/O MMM wants to be treated as a sovereign entity, uniting the functions of a party and government, with the right to form popular opinion, issue its own newspapers, and have no outside regulation" (Valentin Aleksandrovich, "Chastnyi sluchai ili krizis politki?" *Nezavisimaia gazeta,* August 12, 1994, p. 7).

39 Indeed, the possible referendum is one of those rare instances that seems even more threatening with the benefit of hindsight; the breakdown of Albania's central government after a series of pyramid scheme failures in 1997 was cited by the head of Russia's Federal Securities Commission as one of the reasons for the commission's decision to refer documents relating to MMM to the General Prosecutor's Office on March 20, 1997, effectively renewing the possibility of criminal proceedings against Mavrodi (Natalia Gurshina, "Pyramid Scheme Documents Given to General Prosecutor," *OMRI Daily Digest,* March 30, 1997).

40 Julia Wishnevsky, "August 1991 Anniversary Roundup," *RFE/RL Daily Report,* August 22, 1994.

41 "V istorii s 'MMM' nezavisimaia pressa okazalas' zavisimoi ot vlastei," *Komsomol'skaia pravda,* August 16, 1994, p. 4.

42 "Pis'ma v MMM," *Komsomol'skaia pravda,* August 14, 1994.

43 See, for example, Bardin, "Nas reshili," p. 8. Soon after the crash, Louisa Vinton reported that MMM, in an attempt "to project the image of a kinder, gentler pyramid scheme," offered to redeem the shares of "selected 'needy' investors at the pre-crash price . . . providing shareholders could prove they needed the money for a funeral, wedding, or other emergency expenses." Meanwhile, an ad hoc investors' committee announced that "the handicapped, Afghan war veterans, and Chernobyl victims will also be able to redeem their shares at the old price" (Louisa Vinton, ". . . While MMM Builds Good Guy Image," *RFE/RL Daily Report,* August 2, 1995).

44 "Pis'ma 'MMM,' " *Pravda,* August 9, 1994.

45 Indeed, an attempt to strip Mavrodi of his immunity on April 7, 1995, failed, and a month later criminal proceedings against him were suspended.

46 This race, which Korzhakov ultimately won, is an amusing footnote on MMM's foray into politics. In 1994, MMM made a concerted effort to appear as though it had more than its own corporate interests at heart, but by 1997, Elena Mavrodi's campaign in Tula was indistinguishable from the pyramid scheme itself. Citizens who signed contracts to become "agitators" for Mrs. Mavrodi were eligible to receive 3,000 rubles (about 55 cents at the time), with the possibility of receiving up to 50 million rubles (then $9,000) after the election, depending on "the election results in your polling area." For each agitator they recruited, they received an additional 3,000 rubles (Laura Belin, "Yelena Mavrodi's Election Pyramid Scheme in Tula," *OMRI Daily Digest,* January 6, 1997). Elena Mavrodi's registration was revoked on the eve of the election (Anna Paretskaya, "Korzhakov Wins Duma Seat," *OMRI Daily Digest,* February 10, 1997).

47 Laura Belin, "MMM Shareholders Picket Central Electoral Commission," *OMRI Daily Digest,* October 5, 1995.

48 Alaistair Macdonald, "Russian Pyramid King Back in Business," *Reuter European Business Report,* January 13, 1997.

49 In December 1993, *Just Maria* (*Prosto Mariia*) was one of the ten most popular shows in Russia, along with its American counterpart, *Santa Barbara* (Mickiewicz, *Changing Channels,* p. 234).

50 Ruffo was later quoted as saying that she knew nothing about MMM, and she expressed her concern that her image was being used to "dupe" people (ITAR-TASS, "Ruffo ne znakoma s Marinoi Sergeevnoi," *Rossiiskaia gazeta,* August 17, 1994, p. 3). It was also alleged that Ruffo planned to sue MMM, but nothing appears to have come of it ("Bakhyt Kilibaev — otets Leni Golubkova," *Argumenty i fakty* 33 [1994]: 8).

51 Stanley, *Russian TV Sampler,* program 102, p. 9.

52 Stanley, *Russian TV Sampler,* program 102, p. 9.

53 Cf. Aleksei Tarkhanov: "the director has turned the consumers of his commercial, and not the commercials' heroes, into his characters" ("Prostota," p. 6).

54 Maiia Turovskaia finds Ruffo's role particularly telling: "By inviting Victoria Ruffo into his serial, Bakhyt Kilibaev openly defined his audience — the circle of people to whom A/O MMM addresses itself" (Turovskaia, "Lenia Golubkov," p. 23). But Konstantin Ernst sees Ruffo's inclusion as "completely unorganic": "the heroes of our commercial simply have nothing to talk about with her, except maybe for 'the weather.' And I don't see this as the director's fault. Such contact could not take place on principle, because 'Maria' is different, she's from another world" ("Prostota," p. 6). Ernst's interpretation of the Ruffo series in general (and Just Maria's meeting with Igor and Iuliia in particular) misses the point; the very fact that their conversation is strained is perfectly consistent with the reaction her starstruck audience would have to meeting her face-to-face. In any case, Just Maria is treated here

as a living icon rather than a thinking subject; if the characters grew too close to her, it would detract from her aura of stardom. Finally, the limits placed on the MMM characters' dialogue (either by invoking "shyness" or through the announcer's monopolization of the spoken text) have an obvious practical purpose: the less the Russians speak, the less we are aware of the fact that Maria herself is incapable of saying a single word in their language.

55 This is not to say that MMM did not print newspaper advertisements before the summer of 1994; on the contrary, full-page ads featuring primitively rendered cartoons could be found in all the major newspapers. However, these print advertisements failed to capture the public's imagination the way that Lenia and his friends did. As a result, they are rarely mentioned by Russian commentators and fall beyond the scope of this essay.

56 Sergei Mavrodi, "Pri svete sovesti," *Nezavisimaia gazeta,* August 18, 1994, p. 6.

57 "Pis'ma v MMM," *Nezavisimaia gazeta,* August 11, 1994.

58 "Pis'ma v MMM," *Sovetskaia Rossiia,* August 9, 1994, p. 4.

So, that pesky and boring Soviet epoch has sunk into oblivion — the epoch when you had nowhere to go in the evenings and at night, and the only thing to do was drink vodka pointlessly in the kitchen with your clever friends or dance in the corner of your communal apartment to some wonderful music, having covered your table lamp with a sweater to create the much-desired pseudo-Western disco atmosphere. Today the only problem is to choose for yourself the right place for nightly entertainment. All you need is some money, vigor, and the endurance not to sleep at night but to move in a beautiful and graceful way in rhythm with new pulsating sounds piercing your body like a quiver of arrows. Where to spend the night? In Sexton, Hermitage, Manhattan, Penthouse, LSDance, Jazz Club? Almost everywhere you can drink the night away, and even buy something else . . . like in normal countries. I am still amazed by this new life . . . because I grew up in the world where to a foreigner's question, where is the nearest night club, we answered in a sadly jocular way: "Probably in Helsinki."[1]

GAGARIN AND THE RAVE KIDS: TRANSFORMING POWER, IDENTITY, AND AESTHETICS IN POST-SOVIET NIGHTLIFE

Post-Soviet Nightlife: The New Russians and the New Young

The emergence of the nightlife subculture, from dance clubs to expensive casinos, has been one of the most noteworthy changes in Russian youth culture in the first post-Soviet decade. In many Russian cities, the nightclub and all-night dance party have become prominent cultural forms, organizing around themselves diverse types of cultural production in the spheres of music, fashion, and language, and serving as venues in which the younger generations reinterpret old Soviet cultural symbols and meanings and experiment with new post-Soviet identities and relations of power. Because of the considerable importance of the nightlife scene in the lives of the young, at least in the big Russian cities, my analysis will first focus on the inner aesthetics of this subculture and then use that subculture as a medium for a broader cultural analysis of the so-called transition from state socialism and its implications for the emerging social identities, relations, and ideologies. I have limited my analysis to St. Petersburg (Leningrad) and Moscow, Russia's largest cities, which have traditionally had more exposure to official, nonofficial, and foreign cultural influences, forms of information, and financial possibilities than other places in Russia. Not surprisingly, the nightlife scene here is more predominant, influential, and cutting edge than elsewhere.

Contemporary nightlife can be divided into three main areas: rock and jazz clubs with live music; expensive clubs, restaurants, and casinos; and dance clubs and all-night dance parties. Nightclubs of the first type, with live rock and jazz, have mixed audiences, are often relatively inexpensive, and continue the tradition started in the 1980s by the Russian independent rock movement. Nightclubs of the second type, with restaurants and casinos, cater predominantly to the *novye russkie* (New Russians, the idiomatic name for Russia's nouveaux riches) and are frequented by members of Mafia groups relaxing from their main occupations. Such clubs are more expensive — the cover charge for some events can reach $100 U.S. or more. They are often spoken of with contempt by young frequenters of the other two types of clubs for their expensive kitschy designs,[2] gambling, striptease shows, and occasional open prostitution. According to a real estate dealer who creates "elite apartments" to fit the expensive tastes of the nouveaux riches in St. Petersburg, some of his clients "go to casinos every night or a few days a week. . . . The daily amount they may lose there is [in the summer 1995] 2 million rubles [$500]." One client told him with a laugh: "You know how much so-and-so lost yesterday? Fifteen million [$3,700]. He won't show up in the casino for two weeks now."[3]

This chapter will focus on the third type of nightlife scene, which is organized around dance clubs and all-night dance parties and raves. This type of night subculture is represented today in Moscow and St. Petersburg by dozens of nightclubs and by frequent and well attended night parties that are often organized in venues other than clubs — theaters, cinemas, houses of culture, museums, and outdoors. The public in these events usually dances to "house music" played by *di-dzhei* (DJs) or techno groups.[4] This night dance scene caters mostly to the younger post-Soviet generation and the artistic communities, often referred to by the new youth media as *modniki* (trendy people), *novye molodye* (the new young), and *reivery* (ravers).[5] This subculture currently occupies a dominant position in Moscow and St. Petersburg and is quickly expanding to other parts of the country. It has its own well-defined style, associated with what is often called rave, techno, or house culture and a particular type of music (the same techno and house styles as everywhere else in the world), language (which draws heavily on the English expressions used in this subculture in the West),[6] clothes, drugs, interior designs, lifestyles, and social relations. Unlike the Soviet discotheques of the 1970s and the independent rock of the 1980s, where the feeling of belonging to a young collective was particularly important, all-night dance parties encourage a certain atomization and self-sufficiency: "Don't forget that you are not supposed to dance in a group!" instructs the new hip magazine, *Ptiuch*.[7]

To analyze some elements of cultural production in that subculture I will turn to Paul Willis's concept of "symbolic creativity,"[8] a process of creative consumption (of clothes, music records, magazines, etc.) in the conditions of a late capitalist market. Since the late-socialist and early postsocialist contexts have little to do with late capitalism,[9] I will use Willis's concept somewhat differently. Here, symbolic creativity is a process of a creative appropriation of cultural symbols through market and nonmarket techniques from state-run cultural spheres, from the official post-Soviet market, and from diverse subcultures and black markets that escape official control. With the collapse of the socialist state and the emergence of the peculiar post-Soviet power relations, youth cultures experienced new structural restrictions and forms of control, but also discovered new forms of symbolic creativity never imaginable in the past.

This chapter focuses predominantly on the group of people who, for the past ten years, have been the producers of the nightlife subculture. They include party organizers, club owners, designers, DJs, musicians, sound and light artists and technicians, sponsors, and journalists. Most of them belong to the last Soviet generation; that is, they were born between the mid-1950s and the early 1970s, grew up in the Soviet era, and are usually five to twenty years older than the party goers at their events. They began their creative work as active producers of nonofficial Soviet culture as members of independent rock music and artistic subcultures before the changes brought about by perestroika, and have continued their involvement into the present. The content and cultural significance of their work today are new, however, having been transformed from the previous nonofficial status.

In their article on rock music in this volume, Julia Friedman and Adam Weiner point out the cultural continuity of Russian rock from the 1980s to the 1990s. This is especially true of the lyrics of such musicians as Boris Grebenshchikov (Akvarium) and Yuryi Shevchuk (DDT). But the persistence of familiar Russian themes and aspirations in some rock poetry did not prevent the rock movement from suffering a major crisis in the early 1900s, at the end of perestroika. The shift in Russian youth culture reflected in this crisis is relevant to the discussion of contemporary nightlife. As an independent form of youth culture, the night dance scene is not only reminiscent of the phenomenon of Soviet independent rock of the 1980s, but for a period in the early 1990s it actually replaced rock as the dominant mode of cultural experimentation. This transformation from rock to dance scene occurred in youth cultures in many countries during the 1990s. The Russian composer Yuryi Orlov expresses a common view in saying that "today a DJ with two turn-tables is more significant than any musician or composer"; and "the new generation is not satisfied by a rock-concert. . . . Today you no longer have to jump close to the stage. Today you can be inside yourself and invent yourself in a dance."[10] In the Russian context, however, this cultural transformation was particularly significant and dramatic. It occurred in the context of the spectacular collapse of the late socialist symbolic order in the early 1990s, and the consequent crisis of independent rock, which played a peculiar role in that symbolic order.

The dance night subculture, as a field of symbolic creativity, did not emerge out of a void; it is genealogically connected to the cultural dynamics of late socialism. Not surprisingly, much of it can be traced to events that took place at a particular time and place — in the St. Petersburg of late perestroika, between 1988 and 1991, in a squat apartment at 145 Fontanka. Without analyzing that historic moment and location, and its roots in the culture of late socialism (the period between the mid-1960s and mid-1980s), we will fail to understand many trends in today's night dance subculture and the continuity between the *nonofficial* culture of socialism and the post-Soviet youth culture. This is why I begin with late socialism and pay special attention to the unusually quick and experimental cultural production of the late 1980s before moving on to discuss the night dance scene today.

The Cultural Logic of Late Socialism:
The Official and Nonofficial Spheres

It is common in analyses of Soviet culture to speak of a certain opposition between a dominant state culture and a "counterculture." For example, in his rich ethnographic study of the community of independent rock musicians in Leningrad in the 1970s–80s, Thomas Cushman describes Soviet culture in

terms of a dichotomy between the " 'normal' culture of Soviet industrial society" and a "counterculture" that opposed it. The latter he defines as "a stock
of knowledge which, quite literally, runs counter to the dominant stock of
knowledge in a society."[11] Although this model is useful in many respects, it is
problematic in at least one: it may suggest that the logic of independent cultural
production in the socialist state, which involved practices and meanings incongruent with those proclaimed officially, was in *countering* the latter.

I argue, however, that the logic of nonofficial discourses and practices in late
socialism was based most of all on attempts to have a meaningful life in spite of
the state's oppression. Hence, the nonofficial (or "countercultural") practices
involved not so much countering, resisting, or opposing state power as simply
avoiding it and carving out symbolically meaningful spaces and identities away
from it. This avoidance included passive conformity to state power, pretense of
supporting it, obliviousness to its ideological messages, and simultaneous involvement in completely incongruent practices and meanings behind its back.
It was this avoidance and pretense-based logic of the relations of power that
led most independent rock musicians to maintain that they were not interested
in politics.[12]

In late socialism, state power depended less and less on Soviet citizens'
belief in the communist ideology, and more and more on their simulation of that
belief. That logic of the relations of power, which concerned both the em-
powered and the powerless, is well summarized in a jocular maxim of the
1970s about production relations in state-run industry: "They pretend that they
pay us and we pretend that we work" (*Oni delaiut vid, chto platiat, a my
delaem vid, chto rabotaem*). As a result, Soviet culture of late socialism included two coexisting, and often incongruent, spheres of everyday life: the
official and the nonofficial spheres. Practices in the official sphere were observed and controlled by the state and involved real and simulated support of
the official ideology. Practices in the nonofficial sphere were usually unob-
served by the state and produced cultural forms and meanings often incompat-
ible with official ideology. Virtually every Soviet citizen participated in both
spheres on a daily basis.[13]

Thus, what is often referred to as "counterculture" was, in fact, an element
of the nonofficial sphere and therefore an organic and indivisible part of the
everyday culture of the Soviet state, not "a stock of knowledge" that ran
counter to it. Russian philosopher Lev Timofeev similarly argues that the term
"second economy," in discussions of the unofficial economy in the Soviet

Union, may confuse the picture: there was "nothing second, disjointed, [or] independent" about it; the official and "second" economies were "united and indivisible from each other." [14]

In these conditions it became important to maximize one's involvement in the nonofficial part of the cultural universe, to carve out a nonofficial existence inside what was perceived as unavoidable and immutable official reality. The logic of nonofficial cultural practice — from independent art to the ubiquitous system of connections (such as *blat*) and the black market of cultural and consumer products — should be understood precisely in terms of that cultural dynamic: these practices provided ways of avoiding immutable, and often oppressive, officialdom, of not participating in it as either supporter or dissenter. In short, it became more relevant (especially for members of the last Soviet generation) not to resist the system overtly but simply to ignore it. The absence of any political attitude, either pro-official or anti-official, was a way of avoiding official meanings, of existing within them — and even pretending to support them — without needing to think about them. Many nonofficial cultural phenomena of the late Soviet and first post-Soviet years, including today's youth night culture, were produced precisely by this double-sided cultural logic of the Soviet universe. To understand how, we need to return to the past.

Stiliagi and X-Ray Plates

A nonofficial cultural sphere existed in all periods of Soviet history. During World War II it received a strong injection of Western influence through such wartime experiences as the American lend-lease and the personal experience of other European countries by millions of Soviet soldiers. Most films shown in Soviet cinemas in the first years after the war were Hollywood and German trophy films. [15] In the early 1950s, palaces of culture in Leningrad organized regular dances to Western music, and orchestras in restaurants played American jazz. Duke Ellington's "Caravan" became a popular tune. Soon, a new type of young people appeared in the big cities. These were "the first devotees of exotic music, the first advocates of an alternative style," [16] who became known as *stiliagi* (from *stil'*, "style"), a name designed by a Soviet newspaper to sound derisive. Dances and clothes were at the center of their existence.

The *stiliagi* of Leningrad gathered in the main street, Nevsky Prospect, which they nicknamed "Brod" after New York's Broadway. [17] Many Soviet cities had "Brodvei" of their own — in Moscow it was the right side of Gorky

Street from the Hotel Moskva to Pushkin Square.[18] The symbolic creativity of that generation produced the first elements of a Westernized youth subculture that became very important in the following decades. Everything in the *stiliagi*'s outfit imparted a dissimilarity from the symbols used in the official sphere of everyday life. Narrow pants, big shoes, long checkered jackets, and colorful ties were not simply Western — in fact, they were often homemade — but openly nonofficial.[19] The official Soviet press sensed that immediately: a typical attack on *stiliagi* in the satirical magazine *Krokodil* (March 10, 1949) stressed that "the most important part of their style of clothing is not to resemble normal people."[20] Despite the criticism, American jazz, Westernized clothes, and the writings of Ernest Hemingway remained part of the expanding nonofficial youth culture in the following decade.

Since traveling to the West was impossible, most cultural information came by way of shortwave broadcasts,[21] through Soviet sailors returning from abroad on commercial ships, or from foreign tourists and diplomats. In the early 1960s, Latvian factories started producing Soviet shortwave transistor radios, and younger Soviet listeners discovered Willis Connover's *Jazz Hour* on the Voice of America.[22] The growing demand for American jazz and the absence of that cultural product in the official sphere led to an ingenious invention of the pre–tape recorder era — homemade music records, which became known as music "on ribs" (*na riobrakh*). Artemy Troitsky explains this ingenious nonofficial technology:

> These were actually X-Ray plates — chest cavities, spinal cords, broken bones — rounded at the edges with scissors, with a small hole in the center and grooves that were barely visible on the surface. Such an extravagant choice of raw material for these "flexidiscs" is easily explained: X-Ray plates were the cheapest and most readily available source of necessary plastic. People bought them by the hundreds from hospitals and clinics for kopecks, after which grooves were cut with the help of special machines (made, they say, from old phonographs by skilled conspiratorial hands). The "ribs" were marketed, naturally, under the table.[23]

Tape Recorders and Bards

Nonofficial cultural production expanded dramatically throughout the 1960s. The Soviet Union started producing reel-to-reel tape recorders for the consumer market, and these quickly became the most efficient tool for multiplying Western and nonofficial Soviet music. Production grew steadily every year, from 128,000 recorders in 1960 to more than 4.7 million in 1985. Altogether in that period Soviet people bought approximately 50 million Soviet-made tape-recorders.[24] In addition, thousands of Western and Japanese recorders brought into the country by Soviet sailors and occasional travelers were sold through secondhand shops and the black market. In late socialism the Soviet Union underwent what Petr Vail and Aleksandr Genis call the *magnitofikatsia* (tape-recorderfication) of the whole country.[25]

Tape-recorded music became easily accessible to most young people, even those who did not own a recorder. The songs of *bardy* (bards) — poets singing to an acoustic guitar — became the first nonofficial cultural objects reproduced in millions of copies and dispersed all over the country by means of home tape-recording. Guardians of the official cultural sphere sensed the significance of that innovation: in 1965 Soviet composer Ivan Dzerzhinskii wrote in *Literaturnaia gazeta:* "the bards of the 1960s are armed with magnetic tape. This presents . . . a certain danger since distribution becomes so easy. . . . Many of these songs invoke in us feelings of shame and bitter offense, and greatly harm the upbringing of youth."[26] The technique became known as *magnitizdat,* by analogy with samizdat (self-publishing of unofficial texts). Unlike the latter, however, *magnitizdat* managed to elude state control by virtue of its technological availability and privacy. Nonofficial cultural products quickly multiplied and were distributed throughout the country by networks of friends and acquaintances.

Western and Soviet Rock

The ultimate effect of *magnitizdat* was the expansion of Western rock music as the dominant, though nonofficial, cultural form practiced by Soviet youth in the 1970s. Although records with the music of Western bands were officially unavailable, the recordings of the Beatles, Led Zeppelin, Deep Purple, and Donna Summer circulated widely all over the country. The great diversity and accessibility of these nonofficial cultural products stimulated the development of new forms of nonofficial symbolic creativity in youth culture. In the 1970s, a local rock movement exploded.

At that time most nonofficial culture depended on the ability of its producers to manipulate the official sphere. This ability was a vital element in the cultural logic of late socialism. In the 1970s there were thousands of unprofessional bands in Moscow alone, and they played regularly even at dances organized by Komsomol.[27] In the late 1970s, a member of the Komsomol Committee of a

Leningrad research institute organized rock concerts of such famous under-ground bands as Moscow's Mashina vremeni (Time Machine) and Leningrad's Mify (Myths), Argonafty (Argonauts), and later Akvarium (Aquarium). In fact, these events were approved by the deputy chairman of the Ideology Depart-ment at the party *raikom* (district committee). All of this became possible through intricate strategies of pretense on the part of both producers of nonoffi-cial culture and local Komsomol activists, who frequently knew each other well. For example, these semiofficial rock concerts were often represented as "Komsomol cultural-mass activities" (*komsomol'skie kul'turno-massovye meropriiatiia*) regardless of the ideologically suspect lyrics and sounds of these bands, which the party officials usually did not care to check.[28]

The Aesthetics of *Stiob*

By the 1980s, the nonofficial cultural sphere occupied a significant part of the everyday life of Soviet youth. Simultaneously, the official ideological messages receded further, and behavior simulating support, combined with indifference, became omnipresent. Daily experience founded on the immense incongruity between messages, and cultural forms in the official and nonofficial spheres shaped a peculiar type of late-socialist humor based on the aesthetics of the absurd, known in slang since the mid-1970s as *stiob*. Since any straightforward criticism of the seemingly "unchangeable" regime smacked not only of politi-cal activism but of banality and lack of taste as well, one type of *stiob* masked itself as ideology's eager supporter. This ironic treatment of ideological sym-bols, a uniquely late-socialist cultural phenomenon, differed from sarcasm or derision. It required a certain *overidentification* with the ideological symbols exposed to such treatment, often to the point that it was almost impossible to tell whether the symbols were supported or subverted by subtle ridicule.

A similar aesthetic appeared in the 1970s–80s in the nonofficial culture of many socialist countries, as evidenced, for example, by the ambiguously "fas-cist" happenings staged by the famous Slovenian rock group Laibach, by communist celebrations staged by the Leningrad rock group AVIA, and by the films of the independent Soviet *parallel'noe kino* (parallel cinema).[29] The logic of Laibach's artistic strategy, Slavoj Žižek explains, is that it " *'frustrates' the system (the ruling ideology) precisely insofar as it is not ironic imitation, but over-identification with it* — by bringing to light the obscene superego under-side of the system, over-identification suspends its efficiency."[30] This aesthetic also included a sudden inappropriate mixing of symbols from various official and nonofficial cultural spheres, perfected by many Eastern European and Soviet nonofficial artists in the period of disintegrating socialism. For example, Žižek describes Laibach's art of that time as "an aggressive inconsistent mixture of Stalinism, Nazism, and *Blut und Boden* ideology."[31] Similarly, Sergei Kuryokhin's Pop-Mekhanika in the mid-1980s mixed official Soviet ideological symbols (military orchestras, ballet dancers from the Kirov, and characters from socialist realist plays) with nonofficial symbols of the cultural underground (rock musicians, experimental fashion shows, and well-recognized characters of the *tusovka*).[32] In the last decade of late socialism, much of nonofficial artistic production, from Leningrad rock to Moscow conceptualist art and *sotsart,* incorporated principles of *stiob* aesthetics.

The Holes in the Symbolic Order and Temporary Autonomous Zones

Reinterpretations of Power and a Face-to-Face Encounter

In the late 1980s, perestroika dramatically changed the political and symbolic contexts of nonofficial cultural production. Soviet borders grew porous, and many members of the last Soviet generation began to travel to the West. The steady drizzle of nonofficial cultural imports turned into a sudden downpour. Concurrently, the relentless public attacks on the party, ideology, and state institutions of power reached their zenith. These factors provided unique material and context for nonofficial symbolic creativity and led to the emergence of a new type of youth subculture organized by a group of nonofficial artists, musicians, and their friends in St. Petersburg, who produced the first all-night dance parties of the Soviet era, ultimately spreading them to the rest of St. Petersburg, to Moscow, and then to other cities.

Many members of the nonofficial cultural scene in St. Petersburg were among the first to travel to the West. They were in a privileged position, because for such travel one needed a legal invitation from someone abroad to obtain a Russian exit visa and a foreign entrance visa. Many of these artists and musicians had foreign friends who traveled to the Soviet Union, including foreign art students, journalists, and even festival organizers and exhibition curators. Westerners also became increasingly interested in the newly available glimpse of Soviet nonofficial art. And for their part, many Soviet artists traveling in Western Europe encountered forms of youth culture, such as dance clubs and all-night raves, that could not exist in Soviet times, even in the nonofficial sphere, for various reasons, not the least of which was state control over time

4.1   DJ Alexei Haas in his home with his equipment and records. Photo by Alexei Yurchak.

and space. Alexei Haas (fig. 4.1), the founder of the first Russian dance club, Tonnel' (Tunnel, opened in St. Petersburg in May 1993),[33] described his first encounter of the West to me: "In 1988 in Stockholm I went to the club called Mars located in a former subway station. The place was full of transvestites. Everyone was happy. I watched all night how the DJ played records and decided that we must have this in Petersburg." Artist and critic Timur Novikov, whom the Russian press has dubbed "the ideologue of youth culture," had a similar experience: "When in 1988 I found myself for the first time abroad and visited night clubs, I thought that this was the most interesting of those things that we did not have in Russia."[34] Through their ability to travel and their unique positions as purveyors of nonofficial cultural forms, these artists were able to emerge as the producers of a new subculture, recognizing which Western cultural material to draw on, yet transforming it to fit existing Russian cultural demands and the temporary vacuum of state power.

The Utopian Places of the Late 1980s

Another late perestroika development was the emergence of a new type of quasi-private place in the city. In the centralized universe of a socialist city, the older buildings at the center were always renovated according to a centrally managed plan. The city administration began the renovation process of a building by moving its inhabitants into new apartments, usually in the suburbs. During late perestroika, however, the city administration unexpectedly underwent tremendous turmoil and turnover (during the first free elections in 1989, for example, the Leningrad City Council was voted out). The country entered a transition period marked by considerably diminished power in the official state institutions. Thus, many buildings previously emptied for renovations were "forgotten" by the authorities. During the general disarray of the period, however, the electricity, heat, and water supplies were often not cut off.

One such "forgotten" building was an old apartment block close to the city center on the embankment of the Fontanka River, number 145. In 1988, a group of artists, musicians, and their friends moved into two of its many large apartments.[35] Since the apartments did not belong to anyone, and were in fact supposed to be demolished, the artists felt free to change the physical layout. They broke down the walls dividing rooms to create a large dance hall ten by twenty meters in size, painted the walls, and restored the molding on the ceilings. Basically, they did what the New Russians started doing several years later when they bought communal apartments and turned them into large, pleasant spaces for themselves.

The building was still connected to electricity, heat, and water, but no municipal agency kept track of their consumption. The new inhabitants even managed to connect to a phone line in the courtyard and could make outgoing phone calls. They started listening to different recordings of Western house music and worked on the design of the place, trying to reproduce the atmosphere of a Western night dance club. Soon they started inviting friends and friends of friends, "a group of young people who liked to have fun,"[36] for the first all-night dance parties to house music.

The birth of such utopian places as 145 Fontanka, controlled by neither the state, the market, nor the previously ubiquitous gaze of the Soviet collective (all the other apartments were unoccupied), was possible only between the late 1980s and the early 1990s. During that "window," the old institutional relations of power had been almost completely suspended but new ones had not yet replaced them. The general critical disposition of society during perestroika and the chaos in state institutions left even the police baffled. During several particularly loud parties, remembers Alexei Haas, a couple of policemen attracted by the noise knocked on the apartment door and asked its new inhabitants to turn down the volume. The policemen were almost apologetic. They thought everything was legal and did not request any residence papers. The idea of squatters was still beyond them, as was any association of techno music with drugs.

Such utopian places can be better understood in terms of Hakim Bey's "temporary autonomous zones" (TAZs), which he defines as decentralized experiments that exist outside the legal framework of state-controlled society, connected by informal networks of communications through a loose and shifting membership. These zones exist in the nonofficial sphere, and often center on extraordinary "peak experiences," which Bey compares to "mini-revolutions" that do not directly confront the state.

> The TAZ is like an uprising which does not engage directly with the State, a guerrilla operation which liberates an area (of land, of time, of imagination) and then dissolves itself to re-form elsewhere/elsewhen, before the State can crush it. Because the State is concerned primarily with Simulation rather than substance, the TAZ can occupy these areas clandestinely and carry on its festal purposes for quite a while in relative peace. . . . Its greatest strength lies in its invisibility — the State cannot recognize it because History has no definition of it. As soon as the TAZ is named (represented, mediated), it must vanish, it will vanish, leaving behind it an empty husk, only to spring up again somewhere else, once again invisible because undefinable in terms of the Spectacle. The TAZ is thus a perfect tactic for an era in which the State is omnipresent and all-powerful and yet simultaneously riddled with cracks and vacancies.[37]

Perhaps Bey's definition of the autonomous is too idealistic and even utopian. In fact, temporary autonomous zones are never quite free from the state. However, the unusually high degree of such freedom in certain moments and spaces makes his concept very potent for our analysis. The apartment on Fontanka 145 became the site of such a TAZ, a space considerably suspended outside the institutional state power, an ideal place for new creative experiments.[38]

Experiments at Fontanka

The inhabitants of the Fontanka apartment experimented with music, light, design, clothes, dance styles, drugs, and ways of organizing a large all-night dance party. The parties were primarily held on Saturdays, and for the first year they were closed and exclusive, with a strict policy of *feis kontrol'* (face control) at the door that preserved the unusually private and relaxed atmosphere of the apartment and the necessary conditions for an unrestrained creative process.

The place functioned as a large, private club. The parties, which became known as *hauz-vecherinki,* continued between the spring of 1989 and 1991 and became popular enough that more people wanted to get in than the place could hold. Eventually the organizers started charging three rubles (then two to three dollars) at the door. These first parties were organized practically for free — rent and electricity were free, and equipment, music tapes and later records, and materials for designs were usually brought from the trips to the West or were gifts from foreign visitors. This situation gradually changed, and by the time the first big public raves took place the organizers had entered into complex financial relationships with new businesses and quasi-criminal groups.

The original regular party goers included several dozen artists, rock musicians, and their local and foreign friends, who represented a visible part of the city's nonofficial cultural scene. Many at the parties looked strikingly different from the Soviet public outside, with rings in ears and noses, dyed hair, and unusual and colorful clothes. Gays, who were forced to keep a low profile in the official sphere, were visible and relaxed. Anyone could openly experiment with transvestism — a marker of club culture in the West. The new house music, in which the DJ played a creative role by constantly mixing and sampling, provided great potential for experimentation and learning. At first, the only house music available for the parties was on tapes brought from Europe that were simply played on a tape recorder all night. Soon, however, several party goers (some later became famous DJs) started mixing music from reels played on reel-to-reel recorders.[39] At the time, the only *real* DJ in the USSR — someone who actually mixed from records and not reels — was Janis from Riga, Latvia. The Latvians, who had strong cultural links with West Germany, learned about the rave culture before anyone else in the country. Janis was invited to play at Fontanka, and he brought his own records and a turntable, thus providing the opportunity for his hosts to experiment with record mixing. Within a year, by 1989, 145 Fontanka had its own turntables and a wider variety of house records brought by friends from Sweden. By that time the scene had also expanded to include younger people, in their late teens and early twenties, many of whom today are active promoters and DJs in the night dance subculture.

Planetarium: The Scene Goes Public

Novye Kompozitory (New Composers), the first nonofficial group in Russia to experiment with recording their own electronic dance music,[40] were among 145 Fontanka's inhabitants and were active participants in its music parties. In the early 1990s the group's members, Igor Verichev and Valerii Alakhov, worked in the Leningrad Planetarium as technicians, preparing music recordings and light equipment for children's shows about the universe (i.e., playing an assortment of the Pink Floyd tracks typical at such shows the world over). Between shows, they used the equipment to mix, sample, and record their own material. In the absence of tight state control, New Composers talked the Planetarium director into letting them use the studio and its audio and light equipment for a private after-hours dance party. They borrowed two lasers from technicians in the nearby Music Hall and again invited Janis. This party, which took place in 1991, was the first nonofficial event of the budding night life staged in a nonprivate space. The number of participants was still relatively small — around 150 people — and the event was spoiled by the appearance of a criminal group that demanded money. But the creative experiment nevertheless occurred. The organizers were learning how to organize, finance, and advertise a public party (e.g., for the first time, Western-type flyers were handed out around the city), how to create a clublike space, and how to keep the public entertained.

The first experiment in the Planetarium was soon repeated on a much larger scale with the famous DJ West Bam from West Berlin. That event became the first large-scale, widely advertised house party on Russian soil. Since the publicity was great and the event was still relatively esoteric (and thus more attractive), the promoters continued to discourage any who might mistake this party for a regular discotheque.[41] For this purpose they set a cover charge of sixty rubles (then nine dollars), several times higher than the cover charge in any discotheque in the city. However, a large portion of the six to seven hundred party goers, mostly active participants in the nonofficial scene, entered for free, through connections or by being placed on the guest list. West Bam and his friend DJ Rocky, also from Berlin, played in the Planetarium for two consecutive nights. The event generated continuing waves of interest — thousands of young people all over the city heard about it and started recording house music, exchanging tapes, and preparing for future events. This spelled the end of the St. Petersburg house scene as an esoteric phenomenon and launched it as a massive phenomenon of youth culture.

Inverted *Stiob* and the Crisis of Underground Rock

By the early 1990s, the official ideological symbols that once marked the seemingly immutable Soviet system had been openly criticized or ridiculed by

the discourses of glasnost to such an extent that their continual public shattering had in itself become a mainstream of official cultural reality. This openly
critical, oppositional stance was a new perestroika-time (post-1986) development markedly different from the late socialist cultural dynamic based on
pretense of support for the official ideology and a simultaneous withdrawal
from the official sphere. This new development gradually rendered many nonofficial subcultures developed in the Soviet years irrelevant and obsolete. It was
in large part responsible for the major crisis in the early 1990s in independent rock, which had been prominent in the country throughout the 1980s but
suddenly found itself in a symbolic void left by the disappearance of its cultural logic.

The reliance of most rock groups on the evaporating aesthetics of late socialism — be it *stiob* (AVIA, Zvuki Mu, NOM, Auktsion, Pop Mekhanika, Nol'),
political commentary (Televizor, Brigada S, Alisa, DDT), or some combination
of the two (Akvarium, Kino, Nautilus Pampilius) — deprived them of much
contemporary cultural appeal. The central problem encountered by independent rock musicians at that time was not so much their inability to deal with the
sudden offensive of the capitalist market (as some studies suggest),[42] but this
mutation in cultural logic from which all nonofficial art drew its inspiration and
on which it based its relevance. Suddenly, the official and nonofficial symbols
and meanings became equally irrelevant. As cultural critic Tatiana Cherednichenko notes, one had to "write about rock-music, like about the Young
Pioneer song, in the past tense."[43] The void produced by this crisis of independent rock became a strong catalyst for the quick expansion of new youth culture
movements, including the night dance subculture of parties and raves.

This change did not lead to an overnight shift of the entire nonofficial cultural aesthetics; some of its elements persisted. For example, *stiob* continued to
remain relevant, but in a new way, through a kind of cultural inversion. Now
stiob was directed not at official Soviet mythology, but at the new post-Soviet
public derision, equally official and ubiquitous, of recently sacred symbolic
material.[44]

The subject's *stiob*-based relation to an official dominant discourse, whereby
the subject subverts it by pretending to take it too seriously, has been reproduced in the post-Soviet period. This is especially true for the members of
the last Soviet generation, who came of age in the late-socialist period when the
stiob-based logic of power relations came to prominence. In terms of Bourdieu's theory of practice, this generation's *habitus,* as a set of *transposable*

dispositions (i.e., as a principle capable of generating practices, perceptions, and attitudes in the areas other than those in which they were originally acquired), inclines them to have a particular *stiob*-based set of relations to any kind of dominant discourse to which they become unavoidably exposed, be it the discourse of anticommunist criticism, market reforms, or Western feminism.[45] This late-socialist cultural disposition informed many creative decisions made by nonofficial artists in the early 1990s, including their ideas for the designs of the first grandiose rave parties in Moscow.

Reinventing Symbols and Patching Up Holes

The Gagarins

The 1991 all-night party with DJ West Bam at the Planetarium made a strong impression on its participants. Zhenya Birman and Ivan Salmaksov, two of the leading promoters to emerge from the Fontanka scene, "suggested doing something huge in Moscow, only this time on a *professional* basis."[46] This big all-night party had to be unprecedented in every way. When preparations began, careful attention was paid to making every element of design and physical structure impeccable, significant, and striking. The choice of the Soviet capital as the host city was obvious and served to intensify the effect. Drawing on the symbolic material that survived the collapse of the Soviet system, the promoters chose as a locale for the dance party the Cosmos Pavilion in the famous Soviet Exhibition of People's Economic Achievements, a central shrine of the Soviet mythology of the Bright Future. Full of spacecrafts, including a Sputnik and the spaceship that flew the first man in space, Yury Gagarin, the pavilion is rich with metaphors of Soviet heroes, explorers, and futuristic technology. It was these metaphors that the event sought to explore as an ideal connection to the new, post-Soviet, futuristic night culture with its techno and science fiction aesthetics.

Although the organization of small night parties at 145 Fontanka did not require substantial financial resources, the big Gagarin Party, which took place on December 14, 1991,[47] was a different story. The rent of the venue, equipment, designer materials, electricity, and heating systems (that winter was particularly cold) required a considerable amount of money, and the Gagarin Party became the first major financial arrangement in the rave scene (fig. 4.2). To secure adequate finances Zhenya Birman arranged for sponsorship from several new private companies. With his appealing post-Soviet image — dressed in

4.2   Flyer for the first Gagarin Party, Moscow, 1991.
Krin was the company sponsor. Photo by Alexei Yurchak.

a suit and tie, he looked and talked like a cross between an articulate intellectual and a new businessman with money — he managed to impress many directors of private businesses and secured their financial support for his unusual projects. Some businesses used their sponsorship as a way to advertise; for others it was a way to launder money they had accumulated in quick, semilegal dealings during the late 1980s. The food company Krin, which sponsored the first 1991 Gagarin Party (apparently its representatives gave Zhenya a bag with ten thousand rubles in cash — a sum close to ten thousand dollars in 1991 prices — for the event), in return got the company's name printed on two thousand flyers distributed around Moscow.

The creative design for the event at the Cosmos Pavilion was equally impressive and unprecedented. It consisted of spaceships, rocket parts, unfolded solar batteries hanging from the ceiling, and a huge portrait of Gagarin specially made for the occasion. Actual cosmonauts in air force uniforms were paid to sit at the bar and chat with party goers.

Alexei Haas described the choice of the name, Gagarin Party: "When perestroika started and all the heroes of the previous years had been shattered to dust, the only remaining, real, tangible hero was Gagarin, the first man in space, and a good guy whom both the elderly and the young trusted. And when someone said 'Gagarin,' the chain [of associations] suddenly connected. New Composers, Sputnik, Gagarin, the Last Hero, Perestroika, Cosmos."[48] A regular participant in night parties explained the understanding prevalent in the scene at the time: "Despite the seeming ridiculousness [komizm] of Gagarin . . . I still consider him to be a people's hero, toward whom the irony is of a pleasant, good-natured kind."

The juxtaposition of Soviet symbols with rave symbols, which may seem ironic and absurd, in fact freed the symbolic meanings attached to Gagarin and the space program from their Soviet pathos and reinvented them, making them accessible for the new cultural production. The symbols were taken away from the context of both the Soviet ideological myth and its incessant public derision of late perestroika period, and were made to seem relevant to the emerging post-Soviet youth culture. The Gagarin Party was a cultural event that offered and celebrated the meaningful and positive cultural continuity of the post-Soviet world.

The crowd at the party consisted of several hundred members of the scene from St. Petersburg, who arrived by an overnight train, and more than two thousand members of the artistic community of Moscow. Among the elements of new symbolic creativity introduced to the capital was *peterburgskii psikhodelizm* (Petersburg psychodelia) — drugs ranging from acid and PCP to the Petersburg specialty, hallucinogenic mushrooms, collected in the fall in the forests around the city.[49]

Tickets to the Gagarin Party cost around ten dollars, but journalist Artemy Troitsky announced the party during his evening TV program, adding that young people dressed with unusual imagination would be admitted free. The promise attracted crowds of creatively dressed Moscow youths. The party was repeated in the spring of 1992 under the name Gagarin Party II, this time organized by Alexei Haas, another founding resident of 145 Fontanka. Both parties are known in the official history of the Russian night dance scene — endorsed today by new youth culture magazines — as Gagariny (the Gagarins).

After the Gagarins, large events were organized in St. Petersburg and Moscow with increasing regularity. Gor'kii Dom (Bitter House) was held in 1992 in St. Petersburg's Gorky House of Culture. Like the Gagarins, that project focused on symbols that had survived perestroika and the collapse of the state. This focus provided grounding and continuity for new, post-Soviet symbolic creativity. The mixing of symbols is evident again even in the name of the event. Here *gor'kii* (bitter) is used to mean both the Soviet writer Maxim Gorky, founder of socialist realism, and "bitter" drugs. *Dom* (house) also refers to both: the Soviet "House of Culture" and "house music." The party began at midnight with the performance of a choir of World War II veterans, who sang war songs familiar to the audience of young ravers from childhood. That performance was received by the audience with utter respect and without any cynicism. Like the space symbols, the traditional patriotic symbols, when put in the context of a rave party, at first seem paradoxical. According to the logic of the inverted *stiob,* however, this procedure freed these traditional symbols from both the ideological Soviet pathos previously attached to them and the public shattering to which they were being subjected by some groups of moralistic intelligentsia (as, for example, in the film *The Russia That We Lost*).

Once again, symbols were reinterpreted and made relevant for the post-Soviet, future-oriented youth culture. This active reinterpretation of recently state-owned and ideologically charged symbols occurred at many rave parties. As with house music — which is continuously remixed, sampled, and quoted in new contexts — here, former official symbols were also *remixed* and presented in new contexts and in a fresh, nonlinear format. They were *sampled* by editing pieces of a heretofore united symbolic tapestry out of their traditional place in the Soviet culture of symbols and out of their new place in anti-Soviet criticism. Thus, the new "symbolic samples," containing quotes from past and recent Soviet meanings, were placed into a dynamic new cultural context.[50]

This dynamic symbolic creativity at the time of the political power vacuum played a significant role in producing new cultural forms and meanings for the coming social order. Groups of artists and designers quickly gathered around the movement, and much creative work went into the preparation of every event. Each night dance party was treated as an important cultural event for which everyone waited impatiently and in which great artistic resources were invested. The phenomenon grew so big that in 1991–92 most art exhibitions ceased in St. Petersburg, having been replaced by the night parties as the most serious, carefully prepared, and massive artistic projects.[51]

The process continues today, although less dynamically. Among the most recent examples is a big night dance party that at the time of my research (in the summer of 1996) was being planned under the name "No to NATO's Expansion to the East" (Net rasshireniiu NATO na vostok), a recent ideological slogan of the Russian government designed to protest the planned admission of several East European countries of the former socialist bloc into NATO. The political rhetoric of the Russian government on this theme has become reminiscent of the hegemonic rhetoric of the Soviet period, and the cultural producers of the youth scene have reacted to this discursive shift with a familiar attitude of *stiob*. The promoter of this party explained its theme to me: "We all keep hearing this new slogan in the media, 'No to NATO's expansion to the East.' So, after a while we decided — why not have a party with this name? This doesn't mean, of course, that we do not care about NATO's expansion. But we actually aren't really interested in saying openly whether we oppose it, support it, or don't give a damn about it." The party as a cultural event would be designed to create a cultural trivialization of pompous state rhetoric and at the same time to reinvent symbols of the state army as nonmilitaristic, familiar, almost family oriented. The transformation would be accomplished according to the principle of *stiob*, by juxtaposing the ideological state rhetoric and its military symbolism (with which the event is overidentified in its overt theme) with everyday mundane symbols connected to the army (field kitchens, porridge, army songs sung to guitars) and by putting both in the context of an all-night rave. The promoter even managed to secure moral, financial, and technical support for the event from the St. Petersburg military garrison: "The military leaders were glad to hear of our interest, complaining that no one respects them anymore."[52]

As these examples illustrate, the post-Soviet symbolic creativity at work in all-night dance culture mobilizes diverse symbolic material, including ideologically charged Soviet and post-Soviet symbols, and reinterprets it by applying diverse cultural procedures, including the aesthetics of *stiob*, that were developed and perfected in the nonofficial cultural sphere of late socialism.

The Rise of Post-Soviet Cultural Logic: The Mafia and Subcultures

The nightlife subculture reinterprets not only cultural symbols but also such central concepts of modern urban life as time and space. All the parties happen late at night — in the past, the time exclusively controlled by the Soviet state, when no public events could take place. Increasingly they have taken place in traditionally state-controlled spaces. For example, the first night dance club in Russia, Tonnel', was launched by Alexei Haas (in 1992 in St. Petersburg) in a former fallout shelter belonging to a nearby factory.[53] This is the post-Soviet reality: bankrupt industrial enterprises, research institutes, museums, and palaces of culture, formerly subsidized by the state, today often stay afloat by renting out their premises to private ventures. Today one can rent almost any place for an all-night party. Among the most expensive locations is the beautiful nineteenth-century Shuvalovskii Palace, now a state-run museum. In the summer of 1996, it cost seven thousand dollars a night to have a party there. But not every appropriate place has emerged as a popular spot for all-night parties. The same promoter explained to me: "Many good places are never used—one example is the cinema Avrora, which would be popular because it's right in the center of Petersburg. However, its director is an old-fashioned *Soviet* (my emphasis) woman who is afraid—for her such all-night dances are anathema. Her cinema is funded to this day by the state budget and she gets her salary every month. Such old-regime people behave like local czars." Most directors are more flexible, however, and often enter into various semilegal arrangements with promoters. This process also reinterprets the former state control over time and space, drawing on the realities of the new official and shadow markets. The arrangement is always semilegal and very lucrative for the director. The promoter continued: "The director and I write a fake contract where the event is presented as if it were jointly organized by us, which means that I pay no rent, but only pay for water and electricity—let's say ninety thousand rubles [twenty dollars in summer 1996] for the night. The actual cost, which is paid but never mentioned on paper, might be around two thousand dollars. This goes straight into the director's pocket. Without such an arrangement no one would let us organize parties anywhere."

The unwritten contract is guaranteed by the Mafia groups, or *kryshi* (roofs), that oversee the arrangements. A system of organized crime based on racketeering emerged in the first years of the post-Soviet era. Today, virtually every business venture, from a small kiosk selling cigarettes and candy to a night club or a large bank has a nonofficial business arrangement with a *krysha*. Once unruly and indiscriminately violent, this system has now developed into a complex organizational structure. No one speaks of being "racketed" any more—instead, businessmen talk about having their own personal *krysha,* which collects a monthly payment from the business. In exchange, the *krysha* not only protects the business from other criminal groups, it also serves as a guarantor that unwritten business agreements between partners will be kept and as an arbitrator in case of conflicts between business parties (conflicts are monitored by the *kryshi* of both businesses following a strict and elaborate unwritten code). Representatives of the *krysha* determine the amount of payment that a business owes them by assessing how much the business can siphon off without failing. In the case of my interviewees from small businesses in St. Petersburg in the summer of 1996, this amount was close to 15 percent of the company's profit. Today, no business operates without a *krysha*. The system of *kryshi* thus constitutes an immense and complex system of nonofficial power relations that permeate most businesses in today's Russia. For example, the same organizer of night parties in St. Petersburg does his work through both official and *krysha* structures: "I come to the meeting with my *krysha* and they [the administration of a house of culture, theater, museum, or wherever he organizes his next dance party] come with theirs. We meet and discuss who will be responsible for what, and what should happen. In the case of any problems their *krysha* will simply beat the money out of you, and if you are in the wrong your *krysha* won't help. . . . Everyone knows that tricking someone is simply not in the cards. These are not government structures and everything is based on your word. If they heard your word, this is enough."

Businessmen often explain that everyone prefers today's system and feels more relaxed in doing business. This is a typical explanation that I heard in the summer 1996: "The *kryshi* behave in a much more civilized way than the indiscriminate Mafia groups of the early 1990s, who could simply demand a random sum from a business, while the police could provide no protection. Today everyone is protected, and you can do business." Nancy Ries argues that one of the features of today's Russian Mafia is that "to a large degree it has become constructed and experienced as a normal, necessary and even comforting presence in day-to-day life." Most social groups tend to perceive it as a socially ordering force.[54] Katherine Verdery further argues that this image of the Mafia, persistent throughout most of postcommunist Eastern Europe, perhaps "gives voice to an anxiety about statelessness, alongside other forms of insecurity."[55] And Mafia *kryshi* do in fact deliver much-needed order, especially in form of relative security and reliability of business procedures and contracts.[56]

We may further add that the cultural logic by which the Mafia emerges as today's ordering and state-supplementing force seems parallel but opposite to the logic according to which official Soviet symbols are reinterpreted, for example, during night raves. While the role of the Mafia here is to fill the void in the state's institutional and power structures (or at least to be perceived by people as fulfilling this role), the role of newly reinterpreted ideological symbols is to fill the void in the state's symbolic structure by providing meaningful and comforting symbolic material for the new postsocialist symbolic order. Both processes may be interpreted as a weaving of the state fabric out of different materials and from different directions to fill the symbolic and institutional void produced by the collapse of the Soviet system. Indeed, these processes often augment each other. For example, the system of criminalized arrangements seems to mix quite naturally with official power on every level in what may seem to be bizarre combinations. The indifferent attitude to authority in late socialism, the power void in the late 1980s to early 1990s, and the ensuing "privatization of power"[57] — all have contributed to a double process in which official power becomes criminalized, and criminal power officialized. Thus, even the anticrime special police force often enters into nonofficial and quasi-criminal types of relations that follow the *krysha* code. At the same time, Mafia *kryshi* regularly secure the arrangements between perfectly respectable and official businesses. My interviewee, the promoter, in fact boasted that he has

> a very serious *krysha* — the MVD [Ministry of Internal Affairs]! This is a double arrangement: as a state anticrime organization they provide official security to people and businesses; at the same time, they can also be your *krysha* and, like all other Mafia groups, they can intimidate or kill people, extort money, the whole thing. . . . So, I have an official contract with the MVD — I pay them fifty thousand rubles a month [ten dollars in the summer of 1996] as a state security organization. But, of course, you understand yourself that this is a ridiculous sum. So, I also have an oral agreement with them, like I would with any *krysha,* and when I organize a party I pay them five hundred dollars unofficially to provide me with protection. This is called "a gentlemen's agreement" [*dzhentel'menskii dogovor*]. . . . I am lucky to have this arrangement because the same guys will protect me from the official law [lawyers are employed by the same ministry and are bribed from the same money] and from the criminal law: as my *krysha* they go to meetings with other *kryshi* and have their ways of resolving conflicts.[58]

New Subculture, New Ideology, New Symbolic Order

With this consolidation of the new power structure and cultural logic, the temporary autonomous zone in which the creative, nonofficial experimentation took place came to a close. The night dance subculture is no longer characterized by uncontrolled symbolic creativity within the space of a temporary power void. Now much of this subculture is controlled by the state, the market, the Mafia, and their various combinations. And it also has new consumers — the truly new, *post-Soviet* generation of the *novye molodye*. These people are at least a decade younger than the organizers and producers of the subculture, who were members of the last Soviet generation who came of age during late socialism.

The night dance subculture now has its own dominant ideology, symbols, and heroes, which are represented and disseminated by such new youth media as the magazines *Ptiuch* and *OM,* house music FM stations and TV programs, and a whole array of music and clothing shops. *Ptiuch,* for example, instructs its young readers in the correct desires, tastes, behaviors, and occupations of the post-Soviet *novye molodye: "svetskaia zhizn'* [trendy life] is art, . . . style, and manner of behavior. Trendy people cannot work"; and "The main place of relaxation for all the young and progressive, is, undoubtedly, the rave party."[59] In its regular rubrics, such as "Odna devushka, odin stil'" (One Girl, One Style), *Ptiuch* quotes the young *modniki* (trendy kids) to describe a new post-Soviet form of symbolic creativity based on creative consumption in the new youth subculture:

> I love to dress up. This is a pleasure which you can enjoy every day if you wish. . . . Picking out clothes is a long, but interesting and creative process. . . . My favorite music is club music to which you can dance . . . artistic and informative music. . . . I go to the parties all the time because this is my way of life. I like being among trendy and beautiful young people, and I like the atmosphere of carelessness and fun.
>
> I am omnivorous in styles. I say yes to everything. What you did not like yesterday you may like today. And vice versa. . . . Parties are a celebration of music and light. . . . I want people to learn how to have fun.[60]

An eighteen-year-old regular party goer in St. Petersburg explained some practical aspects of these "rituals of consumption" to me in the summer of 1996: "*Reivery* [rave kids] help each other to get clothes. My boyfriend's best friend sells lots of designer clothes. I don't know where he gets them but he always does. It's kind of unspoken. He sells Diesel, Levis, Versace, Armani. . . . Among people who regularly go to clubs many don't work anywhere. They live off buying and selling fake designer clothes. They have contacts and they buy clothes and then resell them among their friends." The new discourse, with its symbols and meanings that can be used to mark membership in the trendy post-Soviet generation, now occupies a dominant position. This transformation signifies a near complete closure of the temporary autonomous zones and an institutionalization of the nightlife and other subcultures that originally emerged in them. At the same time, this process is accompanied by the emergence of a whole array of competing discourses and counterdiscourses. For example, many of the first organizers of the nightlife scene complain today about its trivialization and co-optation: "There is less interesting stuff going on than when it was at the peak of sharp sensations. . . . My favorite parties are in the past. They were at Fontanka, the Planetarium, and everything in that period."[61] One also hears the voices of the older intelligentsia complaining about the loss of cultural values and aspirations among the new young. In reaction to such attacks from the intelligentsia, *Ptiuch,* for example, responds: "Some people, including very clever and sophisticated people, do not seem to understand that they cannot push the following generations into a classroom and instruct them in the wisdom of life that they have learned. . . . We have only one chance to live our own life as we want to. . . . And the only thing that we really need . . . is to be left alone by them."[62] One also regularly hears the discourses of nationalists, patriots, Communists, and other proponents of the strong Russian or Soviet state, for whom Westernized youth subcultures symbolize the loss of the country's political, scientific, artistic, and military importance in the world.

This new heteroglossia of ideological discourses has produced a familiar counterreaction of *stiob.* It comes especially from the cultural producers of the last Soviet generation, that is, from the people for whom *stiob* and a particular cynical attitude have been central paradigms in their relations with power and dominant ideology since the 1970s. The new post-Soviet *stiob* is reminiscent of the *stiob* of late perestroika, which reacted against both the ubiquitous symbols of Soviet ideology and their equally ubiquitous public derision. The difference in today's context of ideological heteroglossia is that *stiob* may often position itself vis-à-vis a whole group of different ideological discourses simultaneously, in one text, as in the following example:

> It seems that clubs and discotheques in Moscow are a place for relaxation
> and entertainment.[63] What nonsense! Do Muscovites actually believe
> that discotheques are for dancing and fun! What a loss of any connection
> with tradition! . . . In Piter [Petersburg] discotheques and magazines are

only an excuse to get together and speak about something more dignified. This comes from the tradition: over a glass of wine in Saigon[64] talking about Dante, Tiutchev, Ogarev. . . . Our trendy kids do not pay enough attention to the beauty of their thoughts, to the dignity of their spiritual impulses. Yet today these things are trendy. It is trendy to be a patriot, an intellectual, a scientist, a military person, a politician; it is trendy to discover the new laws of the universe; it is trendy to investigate the life of nature; paleontology, mineralogy, ontology, and epistemology are becoming trendy. Freedom to Cuba![65]

While it is quite obvious that recognizable symbols of various ideologies are scattered throughout the text, the ultimate inversion happens in the last phrase, fashioned as a well-known ideological appeal of Soviet times.

Conclusion: Nightlife as a Post-Soviet Subculture

The cultural logic of late socialism, with its symbiotic relationship between the official and nonofficial spheres and its aesthetics of a type of "cynical" pretense and *stiob* (especially in the case of the last Soviet generation,[66] was integral in creating the experimental nightlife subculture in a unique time and space, between 1988 and 1992. This period was characterized by a considerable power void and by a crisis in the symbolic order of socialism that culminated in the abrupt and unexpected collapse of the system. At that time, large Russian cities witnessed the emergence of particular "utopian" public spaces — temporary autonomous zones — free of the previously ubiquitous control of the state and the collective. In these spaces new forms of information freely circulated and new cultural forms and social relations quickly developed. Such autonomous zones mushroomed in various locales and spheres of activity in the late 1980s and early 1990s and became particularly fertile laboratories of a quick cultural and social transformation of the late-socialist system. The social phenomena that developed in these zones varied from the first quasi-private businesses, evolving within Komsomol committees and state-owned institutions, to the consolidation of organized criminal groups, often in close connection with new businesses and state security organs, to the development of innumerable youth subcultures.[67] The experimental artistic scene of 145 Fontanka, where the post-Soviet night dance subculture emerged and acquired its stylistic and structural identity, was a product of one such temporary autonomous zone.

After the early 1990s the scene experienced major changes. Although the night parties became more common, the symbolic order in the country was increasingly acquiring new official and nonofficial organizational principles, and the power void was being quickly replaced by new relations of power and types of control. It became less easy for producers of the night dance subculture to take advantage of the official and nonofficial powers' ignorance of them. The state, the police, the media, the market, the Mafia, and their various combinations reentered the temporary autonomous zones. For example, such places as 145 Fontanka and 10 Pushkinskaia could not emerge today, although some of them still exist and may still continue to function for quite a while on a limited scale.[68] No longer can one suddenly occupy large official spaces and escape the control of the state, the market, and the Mafia *kryshi*. The changing official laws and the entry of the Mafia into security and business arrangements, and even into sponsoring the night dance parties, played a critical role in the construction of a cohesive subculture. The organizers of night parties had to explore new structural opportunities and limitations, and to become more businesslike and inventive in negotiating and dealing with these official and nonofficial powers.[69] Purely by virtue of its longevity, popularity, and ability to permeate the realm of pop culture, the original closed rave scene was prepared to undergo a transformation.

All these internal and external factors contributed to the closure of the temporary autonomous zone and the transformation of the relatively small and experimental cultural phenomenon of night dances into a large, institutionalized subculture with its own trendy symbols, people, and lifestyles. As is often the case, the transformation occurred through an ever-growing demand for access to the hallowed halls of the subculture's origins, to the primary places of cultural dissemination, through the demand for trendy music, clothes, images, and ideas. And this process in turn has created new economic opportunities for companies that import Western designer clothes and music records, and local pirate companies that produce and sell their illegal copies.

In the mid-1990s, dozens of new clubs mushroomed in Moscow and St. Petersburg. Many can be still linked to the original Fontanka scene. Night dance clubs are also quickly emerging in other big cities throughout the former Soviet Union. Recently *Ptiuch* reported the opening of night dance clubs with house music and DJs in many large and middle-size post-Soviet cities.[70] Nightclubs and dance parties continue to be venues for active cultural production in which the post-Soviet generation draws on diverse symbolic material from

4.3 A poster advertising a rave party ("House Music Energy") in St. Petersburg's Spartak Cinema on August 10, 1996. Two FM radio stations — Evropa Plius and Radio Maksimum — were the party's sponsors. Photo by Alexei Yurchak.

different historical periods and spaces and under different forms of structural control to shape new identities, hierarchies of power, tastes, aspirations, and understandings of time, space, work, leisure, and money within the cultural fields of fashion, music, language, sex, drugs, and business (fig. 4.3).

Notes

I am grateful for assistance during my research to Victor Mazin, Alexei Haas, Marina Albee, Rem Khaibrahmanov, Igor Vygodin, DJ Peter Acid, Oleg and Pasha of Fish Fabrique, and numerous party goers in St. Petersburg; and to David Fisher, Thomas Campbell, and Sarah Phillips for invaluable comments on the draft of this paper.

1 Writer Yegor Radov about Moscow nightlife scene, in *Ptiuch,* no. 2 (1995), p. 13. All Russian quotes in this essay appear in the author's translation.

2 While the New Russians and Mafia members sometimes leave expensive clubs and casinos to visit hip dance clubs for the young, movement in the opposite direction is highly limited.

3 Author's interview. Many of the names of my informants are not mentioned to protect their identity.

4 Most DJs play records of Western house bands and occasional Russian dance music of such bands as Novye kompozitory (New Composers).

5 These media include Moscow-based magazines *Ptiuch* (circulation eighty thousand) and *OM,* both published since 1995; Moscow-based FM stations Radiostantsiia (106.8 Mhz) and Serebriannyi dozhd' (100 Mhz), Petersburg FM station Port and several TV programs on Muz-TV and other channels. See more internet links at http://www.aha.ru/~bradis/raverus.htm (Russian Rave homepage), http://www.ptuch.ru/main.shtml (*Ptiuch* announcements of upcoming dance parties in Moscow), and http://www.bradis.ru (information about clubs, DJs, concerts, etc.).

6 For examples, *feis-kontrol'* (the door policy of "face-control"), *chil-aut* ("chill-out" room in the club), and *di-dzhei* (DJ).

7 "Pis'mo redaktora," in *Ptiuch,* no. 3 (1995).

8 Paul Willis, *Common Culture: Symbolic Work at Play in the Everyday Cultures of the Young* (Boulder: Westview Press, 1990).

9 By *late socialism* I mean the period between the mid-1960s and mid-1980s. See A. Yurchak, "The Cynical Reason of Late Socialism: Power, Pretense and the *Anekdot,*" *Public Culture* 9, no. 2 (1997): 161–62.

10 *Ptiuch,* no. 2 (1995), pp. 15–16.

11 Thomas Cushman, *Notes from Underground: Rock Music Counterculture in Russia* (Albany: State University of New York Press, 1995), p. 8; also see Elena Zdravo-myslova, "Kafe Saigon kak obshchestvennoe mesto," in *Civil Society in the European North,* Centre for Independent Social Research, Materials of the International Seminar (St. Petersburg, 1996), pp. 39–40.

12 See, for example, Cushman, *Notes from Underground,* p. 93.

13 See Yurchak, "The Cynical Reason."

14 Lev Timofeev, "Novaia teoriia sotsializma," *Moscow News,* December 8–15, 1996, p. 16.

15 Maiia Turovskaia, "The Tastes of Soviet Moviegoers during the 1930s," in *Late Soviet Culture: From Perestroika to Novostroika,* ed. Thomas Lahusen and Gene Kuperman (Durham: Duke University Press, 1993), pp. 104–5.

16 Artemy Troitsky, *Back in the USSR: The True Story of Rock in Russia* (London: Omnibus Press, 1987), p. 2.

17 Vasily Aksyonov, *In Search of Melancholy Baby* (New York: Random House, 1987), p. 18.

18 A. Fain and V. Lur'e, *Vsio v kaif!* (St. Petersburg: Lena Productions, 1991), p. 172; Troitsky, *Back in the USSR,* p. 3.

19 Aksyonov, *In Search,* p. 13.

20 Quoted in Richard Stites and J. von Geldern, eds., *Mass Culture in Soviet Russia: Tales, Poems, Songs, Movies, Plays, and Folklore, 1917–1953* (Bloomington: Indiana University Press, 1995), pp. 450–51.

21 After the Twentieth Party Congress (1956) the Soviet Union stopped jamming the Russian-language broadcasts of the Voice of America and the BBC. Jamming resumed in 1968 during the events in Czechoslovakia. See M. Friedberg, "Russian

Culture in the 1980s," *Significant Issues* 7, no. 6 (Washington, D.C.: Center for Strategic and International Studies, Georgetown University, 1985), p. 18.

22 Aksyonov, *In Search,* p. 18.

23 Troitsky, *Back in the USSR,* pp. 7–8.

24 *Narodnoe khoziaistvo SSSR v 1970g. Statisticheskii ezhegodnik* (Moscow: Statistika, 1970), p. 251; and *Narodnoe khoziaistvo SSSR v 1985g, Statisticheskii ezhegodnik* (Moscow: Statistika, 1985), p. 169.

25 Petr Vail and Aleksandr Genis, *60-e, Mir sovetskogo cheloveka* (Ann Arbor: Ardis, 1988), p. 114.

26 Quoted in ibid., p. 114.

27 S. Frederick Starr, *Red and Hot: the Fate of Jazz in the USSR, 1917–1980* (Oxford: Oxford University Press, 1983), p. 291.

28 Author's interview, summer 1995. See also A. Yurchak, "The Cynical Reason of Late Socialism: Language, Culture, and Ideology of the Last Soviet Generation" (Ph.D. diss., Duke University, 1997).

29 An example of *stiob* in the nonofficial cinema of the early 1980s is the Aleinikov brothers' three-part film *Traktoristy* (*Tractor Drivers*): the first part is a parody of an educational film about the tractor's mechanics, the second part portrays the tractor's passion for the land, and the third part describes a female driver's love for her tractor. This is a *stiob* of the official Soviet cinematographic myth about collective farms, in which tractors played a central role. The film neither openly denounces that myth nor openly laughs at it, which made it, for enlightened young audiences, all the more hilarious and subversive. See Viktor Matizen, "Stiob kak fenomen kul'tury," *Iskusstvo kino,* no. 3 (1993), pp. 59–62.

30 Slavoj Žižek, "Why Are Laibach and NSK Not Fascists?" *MARS* 3–4 (1993): 3–4.

31 Laibach's project was not based on subverting the ruling ideology through ironic distancing, since the type of "totalitarian ideology" that existed in late socialism already presupposed the ironic distance of its subjects. To function successfully, it required them only to behave as if they took it at face value, regardless of their cynical lack of any belief or interest. This is why Laibach's anti-ideology project was instead an *overidentification* with that ideology. See Slavoj Žižek, *The Metastases of Enjoyment* (London: Verso, 1994), p. 72; and Žižek, "Why are Laibach and NSK Not Fascists?" AVIA also overidentified with the system's ideological procedures, but did it differently. While Laibach looked too fascist to be fascist, AVIA looked too optimistic, to the point of slight insanity, to be true "young builders of communism." In AVIA's performances, up to twenty actors in workers' overalls shouted slogans and built human pyramids. The group drew on the official Soviet art of the 1920s and 1970s, calling their style "Soviet march-rock." As in the case of Laibach, not everyone in the audience, especially the older generation, was sure what to make of AVIA's act. After one AVIA concert in Kiev in 1987, an elderly couple came backstage to thank the group ("It is so rare today to see young people with such devotion to the spirit of communist construction!"). Later that evening another elderly couple told the group how much they enjoyed laughing at the absurdity of the Soviet system. That couple had survived the Stalinist camps.

32 A slang expression which in this context refers to the cultural underground of the late Soviet period.

33 See *Ptiuch,* no. 3 (1997), p. 18.

34 Timur Novikov, "Kak ia pridumal reiv," *OM,* March 1996, p. 67. For a recent discussion of the role played by Novikov and other artists of the 10 Pushkinskaia scene in the artistic underground of St. Petersburg, see Bruce Sterling, "Art and Corruption," *Wired,* January 1998, pp. 125–40.

35 Among the first regular inhabitants were future DJ Alexei Haas and his brother; artists Timur Novikov, Sergei Bugaev (Afrika), and Georgii Gurianov; musicians of the first Russian techno group, Novye kompozitory, Valerii Alakhov and Igor Verichev; and future rave promoter Ivan Salmaksov.

36 "Iz istorii otechestvennogo reiva. Interv'iu s Alekseem Haasom," *Ptiuch,* no. 2 (1994).

37 Hakim Bey, "The Temporary Autonomous Zone," in *Automedia* (http://www.unicorn.com//lib/zone.html, 1991), pp. 2–3.

38 Another famous example of such a TAZ was a huge building at 10 Pushkinskaia Street, also "forgotten" by the state, which from the late 1980s became home to dozens of spontaneous studios and apartments of independent artists. This place played an incomparable role in the post-Soviet development of independent art in St. Petersburg. For example, see "Fond Svobodnaia Kul'tura. Pushkinskaia, 10" (St. Petersburg: Gumanitarnyi fond Svobodnaia Kul'tura, 1998); "Liudi i skvoty: peterburgskie ugly," *Ptiuch,* no. 11 (1996), pp. 22–27; and Sterling, "Art and Corruption."

39 Haas, "Iz istorii: Interv'iu s Alekseem Haasom."

40 See "Novye kompozitory: skuchno slushat' pesni kak oni est'," *Ptiuch,* no. 4 (1994).

41 For example, the most popular discotheque in the city at the time, Kur'er (Courier), played mainstream Western pop and rock and often simply played video recordings of MTV (recorded from Finnish TV), and closed early (around 11:00 P.M.).

42 See, for example, Cushman, *Notes from Underground.*

43 Tatiana Cherednichenko, *Tipologiia sovetskoi massovoi kul'tury* (Moscow: RIK "Kul'tura," 1994), p. 222.

44 An example of this public derision occurred in 1990–91 with the emergence of a whole stream of publications and rumors obsessed with exposing something cryptic and perverse about the figure of Lenin, formerly the most sacred of Soviet symbols. The 1991 documentary film of director Stanislav Govorukhin, *Rossiia kotoruiu my poteriali* [*The Russia That We Lost*], shown on national TV, presented documents allegedly confirming rumors that Lenin was a German spy during the revolution. The film describes in detail Lenin's non-Russian ethnic composition as a mixture of Chuvash, Kalmyk, German "with some Swedish blood," and Jewish. The *stiob* reaction to the new inverted dominant ideology was swift: in 1991, in his regular TV program *Tikhii dom,* St. Petersburg journalist Sergei Sholokhov, himself an active member of the nonofficial scene, introduced musician Sergei Kuryokhin as a famous political figure, film actor, and scientist who recently had conducted an extensive study of the role of hallucinogenic mushrooms in social revolutions. Kuryokhin,

quoting from philosophical treatises and pointing at diagrams, explained in a perfectly scientific manner that the leader of the world revolution, Lenin, a greater lover of mushrooms, consumed so many of them that eventually he turned into a kind of mushroom himself. This phenomenon, continued Kuryokhin, sheds light on the main mystery of the Great October Socialist Revolution, and is today of great scientific interest. That year a wave of interest in mysticism, parapsychology, and "inexplicable phenomena" swept the country, and Sholokhov later reported that several older viewers called the studio in dismay to ask if the story was true (*Tikhii dom,* St. Petersburg channel, spring 1991; and author's interview with Sergei Kuryokhin, St. Petersburg, summer 1995).

45 Pierre Bourdieu, *Outline of a Theory of Practice* (Cambridge: Cambridge University Press, 1993), p. 72. On such relationship to Western feminist discourse among Russian and East European feminists, see, for example, Larissa Lissyutkina, "Soviet Women at the Crossroads of Perestroika," p. 277; and Hana Havelkova, "A Few Prefeminist Thoughts," pp. 65 and 68, both in *Gender Politics and Post Communism,* ed. Nanette Funk and Magda Mueller (London: Routledge, 1993).

46 Haas, "Iz istorii"; emphasis mine.

47 The DJs invited to play at this event included Janis, Jaokim Garo from France, and the Leningrad groups New Composers and Not Found. See *Ptiuch,* no. 3 (1997), p. 18.

48 "Last Hero" refers to the popular late-1980s song "Poslednii geroi" ("The Last Hero"), by Victor Tsoi (Kino). Haas, "Iz istorii"; emphasis mine.

49 For a discussion of the use of drugs in post-Soviet youth culture, see "Liudi i skvoty"; and Sterling, "Art and Corruption."

50 Another example of this symbolic creativity was the reinterpretation of traditional symbols of high culture, which in Soviet times became charged with ideological significance: Zhenya Birman and Ivan Salmaksov invited a class of ballerinas from Vaganova Ballet School to perform classical *pas* on the balconies during the rave (author's interviews with Mazin and Haas in 1996).

51 This phenomenon was observed by critics Victor Mazin and Olesia Turkina (author's interview, 1996).

52 The promoter described his plans thus: "We will build three big stages in the Winter Stadium. People will walk between armored cars. Camouflage nets will be hanging everywhere. Cafés will be located in field hospital tents, and soldiers will cook porridge in field kitchens. There will also be a shooting gallery for the public. A military orchestra will play, and military singers will sing about love and the difficulties of the military service. This will go on until 6:00 P.M. Entry will be free. After six everything changes — you pay at the door, and there are famous rock groups, a laser show, etc. And at midnight a gigantic rave starts with the best DJs, and the price goes up again" (author's interview with the promoter, 1996).

53 The shelter is still being leased out by the factory on the condition that in the case of war, the club will miraculously turn back into a fallout shelter within twenty-four hours (author's interview with Haas).

54 Nancy Ries, " 'Honest Bandits' and 'Warped People': Russian Narratives about Money, Corruption and Moral Decay," in *Ethnography in Unstable Places,* ed. Carol Greenhouse, Elizabeth Mertz, and Kay Warren (Ithaca: Cornell University Press, in press).

55 Verdery, *What Was Socialism and What Comes Next?* (Princeton: Princeton University Press, 1996), p. 216.

56 See also Jim Leitzel, Clifford Gaddy, and Michael Alexeev, "Mafiosi and Matrioshki. Organized Crime and Russian Reform," *Brookings Review,* winter 1995, p. 28; and Svetlana Glinkina, "K voprosu o kriminalizatsii rossiiskoi ekonomiki," *Politekonom. Russo-German Economic Journal* 1 (1997): 49.

57 I borrowed this term from Katherine Verdery, *What Was Socialism,* p. 216.

58 See also Sterling, "Art and Corruption," p. 121; and Leitzel et al., "Mafiosi and Matrioshki," p. 28.

59 "Pis'mo redaktora," *Ptiuch,* no. 2 and no. 3 (1994).

60 *Ptiuch,* no. 7 (1996), and no. 6 (1995–96).

61 "Interview," *Ptiuch,* no. 5 (1996).

62 Igor Shulinskii, "Zametki redaktora," *Ptiuch,* no. 7 (spring 1996).

63 A reference to the kind of coverage of the night scene that is offered by the magazines *Ptiuch* and *OM.*

64 Slang name of a famous café on Nevsky Prospect which in the 1960s–80s was a trendy hangout for the nonofficial cultural scene.

65 Sergei Kuryokhin, "S novym godom zveria!" *OM,* March 1996, p. 69.

66 See Yurchak, "The Cynical Reason."

67 The number of organized criminal groups more than quadrupled between 1990 and 1993; Leitzel et al., "Mafiosi and Matrioshki," p. 26. See, for example, Hilary Pilkington, ed., *Gender, Generation, and Identity in Contemporary Russia* (London: Routledge, 1996).

68 See "Liudi i skvoty"; and Sterling, "Art and Corruption."

69 The magazine *Ptiuch,* drawing on numerous unlucky experiences of promoters of mass parties, gives the following recommendation to new promoters: "Do not forget that you should absolutely try to avoid getting involved with state structures" ("News," *Ptiuch,* no. 3 [1995], p. 2).

70 On night dance subculture in Novosibirsk, Yaroslavl, Vladimir, Riazan, Omsk, Cheliabinsk, Rostov, Taganrog, Samara, Kemerovo, Minsk, Kiev, and Kharkov, see "News," *Ptiuch,* nos. 3, 5, 6, and 12 (1997), and no. 2 (1998).

■ **CHAPTER 5**
JULIA P. FRIEDMAN AND ADAM WEINER

BETWEEN A ROCK AND A HARD PLACE: HOLY RUS' AND ITS ALTERNATIVES IN RUSSIAN ROCK MUSIC

In *Hole in Our Soul: The Loss of Beauty and Meaning in American Popular Music,* Martha Bayles argues that the "perverse" modernist cult of novelty, with its persistent impulse to break with past values, has had harmful effects on Western rock.[1] Russian rock has been involved in a different dynamic, for while it initially found its inspiration in Western bands, it has been gradually shifting Eastward, homeward, in terms of lyrics and music.[2] Instead of rejecting native, traditional influences, Russian rock artists have sought to transcend aesthetic models they perceive as foreign and inorganic — a situation that recalls T. S. Eliot's admonition that original art is created only from a thorough knowledge of one's origins and traditions. By the mid-1980s many of the most original Russian rock musicians were clearly leaving the shadow of Western rock 'n' roll in search of more "native" traditions in a quest for authenticity that has led to a body of song texts of great artistic and cultural interest. For some of the best songwriters, authentic Russian rock has had much to do with Russianness and, sometimes, Russophilism.[3] Others have used their music to challenge the Russophile tendency in their compatriots. The result is a kind of rock polemic about the meaning of Russian culture. More than merely parroting the motives and devices of Russian folk music, Russianness in rock involves a complex negotiation of traditional and innovative interpretations of Russia's eternal "accursed questions" (*prokliatye voprosy*) concerning national identity and destiny. Tradition, as Eliot said, "cannot be inherited, and if you want it, you must obtain it by great labour."[4]

The image and idea of the homeland acted fatefully on rock, and to a great extent was the music's *rok,* or "fate" — a pun that begs to be made in discussions of Russian rock. Russianness is at once rock's saving grace and its deadliest temptation: the first because it is a force that can deepen rock into meaningful expression of the songwriter's worldview, and the second because this force can grade imperceptibly into either trivialized, *matreshka*-style folksiness or, worse yet, ugly nationalism, both of which are capable of delimiting whatever beauty the music constitutes. Il'ia Smirnov made this point well when he wrote that "any avowal of an idea — especially if we are talking about the 'Russian Idea' — renders it linear and flat. True Russianness [*narodnost'*] threatens to turn into a tasteless imitation [*lubok*]; the word 'Russian' threatens to become not the name of an ethnic group, but a call to action. When spiritual suffering gives birth to gloomy intolerance, good will perhaps suffers its first defeat in a clash on the 'Kalinov Bridge.' "[5]

In this chapter we argue that such leading Russian rockers as Aleksandr Bashlachev, Iurii Shevchuk (DDT), Konstantin Kinchev (Alisa), Iurii Naumov, Iana Diagileva (Ianka), and Boris Grebenshchikov (Akvarium) have all created evocative visions of their homeland in their quest for an original rock aesthetic. By limiting our purview to these groups and artists, we do not intend to suggest that other rock musicians have not contributed to this debate (for they have), nor that there are no groups that have chosen not to enter into it at all (for there are).[6] Neither do we present our conclusions as a comprehensive overview of Russian rock or as a review of Russian rock in the 1990s. Rather, we discuss those artists whose music most vividly depicts their native land, whether as an ideal to achieve or a trap to avoid. It was during the second half of the 1980s, concurrently with the arrival in the capital cities of Bashlachev, that this theme arose and asserted itself in Russian rock, and we follow its subsequent development into the mid-1990s.

Critics and musicians generally recognize Bashlachev (d. 1988) as the first rocker to compose authentic poetry for his songs, and by no mere coincidence it was also Bashlachev whose songs posed the question of Russia's origin and destiny for the first time in Russian rock. It is fitting, then, to begin the current discussion with the poet who led rock out of the dead-end of self-indulgent romantic posing, anti-Soviet satires, and so-called *stiob* into which it had wandered by the mid-1980s.[7] A distinctive feature of Russian rock music — recognized by its practitioners, followers, and critics alike, and first applied to great effect by Bashlachev — is its privileging of the word, as contrasted with Western rock's relatively musical orientation.[8] Yet, the "Russification" of rock is not merely the discovery of a more verbally rich poetic; it is also the engagement of an endemic and venerable polemic about Russia's destiny. The genius of Russian poetry, which is present in the best rock music, is a deeply national, and thus enigmatic, phenomenon. Here we pause on the brink of the perceived gulfs that lie between so-called high art and popular art, and also between national art and universal art.[9] Dostoevsky probably oversimplified the matter when he wrote that all of Russia's great artistic talents "inevitably ended up by turning to the national sentiment, becoming one with the people, Slavophile. Thus, the frivolous Pushkin suddenly, before all of the kireevskiis and khomiakovs, creates the Chronicler of the Chudovyi Monastery."[10] The "Chronicler of the Chudovyi Monastery" is the monk Pimen (from Pushkin's great historical drama, *Boris Godunov*), who was for Dostoevsky an icon of Russian spiritual wisdom, gained through deep insight into the national character. It is perhaps such insight, rather than Slavophile sentiments per se, that is often a wellspring of Russian artistic genius, so that while Bashlachev was hardly a Slavophile in the manner of Kireevskii and Khomiakov (to say nothing of Pimen), he followed Dostoevsky's axiom by turning his art to the mysteries of the national character.

The rock poetry of Bashlachev is a ringing affirmation of Russia and her people, despite all the misery, degradation, and darkness it recognizes there. Bashlachev's arrival in the capitals, after the celebrated liberal Soviet rock critic Artemy Troitsky had "discovered" him in his native Cherepovets, signaled a sea change in rock poetry. In the course of the few years separating Bashlachev's emergence on the rock scene in 1984 and his suicide, he composed sixty or so remarkable lyrics. As his texts testify, Bashlachev sang of Russia's hidden moral life, which the Western-style bureaucratism imported into Russia by Peter I and passed down to Soviet times had not — so affirm Bashlachev's poems — managed to trample down. "The Time of Little Bells" ("Vremia kolokol′chikov")[11] is a paean to the Russian moral past, which the song views against a complex web of native Russian emblems brought into meaningful play with each other: kasha, birches, bells, laments, feasts, cupolas, troikas, and vodka. Although this is a poem that rewards rereading, we are not allowed to forget that it is also a song: its central conceit is to hear echoes of the great bells of the Russian spiritual past in the guitars and loudspeakers of Russian rock, while its verses resonate with external and internal rhyme, alliteration, assonance, and other rich sound orchestration.

The song presents a double vision of time that plays the recent Soviet past against a distant, mythic past, discovering behind the obvious contrasts an essential unity between the two times. The poet traces the path from a great past to a dwarfish present, beginning with the first stanza:

> Долго шли зноем и морозами,
> Все снесли и остались вольными,
> Жрали снег с кашею березовой
> И росли вровень с колокольнями

> We journeyed long in heat and frost.
> Endured it all and remained free.
> Devoured snow with birchy porridge.
> And grew to the height of belfries.

During the first phase of their journey through history, Russians were made free by their ability to suffer hardship (*berezovaia kasha,* "birchy porridge," is a euphemism for a whipping). By feeding on privation and pain, they became spiritual giants among men. This led to a time of ideal communion (or *sobornost′*) among people and between the people and God, whose voice was heard in the tolling of the bells. The Russians of the remote past were indeed united by the bell, in worship, sorrow, celebration, and danger: the bell protected them against enemies and fires, resonated with their emotions and uplifted them.[12]

> Если плач—не жалели соли мы,
> Если пир—сахарного пряника,
> Звонари черными мозолями
> Рвали нерв медного динамика.

When lamenting — we spared no salt.
When feasting — sugar-coated spicecakes.
The bell-tollers, with their black blisters,
Tore at the nerve of the copper loudspeaker.

Bashlachev's point is that, whether in grieving or rejoicing, Russians know no measure. The bell-tollers of old, ringing the enormous bells of medieval Russia until their hands were reduced to black calluses, become an icon of this ancient strenuous emotional and spiritual life. By calling the bell a "loudspeaker," the poet foreshadows the profane present from within the pious past in a surprising metaphor; rockers, it will later emerge, are the modern-day analogue for the bell ringers of yore, tearing painfully at their guitar strings, seeking to reestablish the lost communion of the past, the spiritual harmony that makes giants of men.

Но с каждым днем времена меняются.
Купола растеряли золото.
Звонари по миру слоняются.
Колокола сбиты и расколоты.

But with every day the times change.
Over time the cupolas lost their gilding.
The bell-tollers stumble about the land.
The bells are knocked down and cracked.

The fateful crack in the bells is also the schism of time: it divides present from past and spiritual life from profane. This split evokes the many schisms, heresies, and wrenching Westward reforms imposed on Russia from the reign of Peter the Great until modern times. In this quatrain, Bashlachev vaults into the recent past and present, a time of disharmony ("We don't sing any more. We've forgotten how to sing"), of stasis and stagnation ("Not a single wheel is greased. / The whip is gone. The saddles have been stolen over time"), of dissipation ("We sleep and drink. Whole days and liters"), of profanity ("We've been chewing for ages: a blue streak with prayers"), of darkness ("We've been living for ages — in pitch black darkness"). But most important, the present is a bell-less age, a time of dislocation and solitude, of a vain search for the lost secret of harmonious living:

Что же теперь ходим круг да около
На своём поле, как подпольшики?

Если нам не отлили колокол,
Значит, здесь время колокольчиков.

Why do we beat around the bush
In our field — like underground men?
If no bell has been cast for us,
It means here — is the time of little bells.

Without a great bell, without the unifying idea of the native communal spiritual life, Russians have become uprooted and lost; they drift about the field of time with only their "little bells" to guide them. But in Russian the "little bells" are also the "bluebells" growing in the thawing field after a long winter: they evoke a postcivilization, postindustrial return to the more natural, pagan life that preceded the entire cycle of Russian history just detailed. Through the pun *"podpol'shchiki"* Bashlachev evokes both underground solipsists of the nineteenth century, personified by Dostoevsky's Underground Man, and members of unofficial organizations in the twentieth century — that is, Soviet dissenters, including, of course, the unofficial, underground culture that produced Russian rock and from which Bashlachev emerged. With the decay of the shared cultural values of the past, Russians have been forced into the more Western modes of isolation, individualism, and egoism, which have led to the misery the poem depicts.

The destruction of the great bell of past harmony tolls the coming of the age of small bells, assuredly a more fragmented and crueler epoch, but by no means a hopeless one.

Ты звени, сердце, под рубашкою
Второпях—врассыпную вороны.
Эй! Выводи коренных с пристяжкою
И рванем на четыре стороны.

You ring out, heart, under my shirt
Hurriedly — the crows fly off pell-mell.
Hey! Lead out the shaft horses,
And we'll tear off in all four directions.

The Russian who can still make out the tolling of his own heart has found a secret, internal echo of the great past. And even without knowing where to search for that lost harmony, if one races in all directions with famous Russian abandon, it is just possible that one will prevail. Here Bashlachev rigs up, bell and all, the troika of the final paragraph of *Dead Souls,* Gogol's emblem of Russia's potential for leading the world into either perdition or salvation. The troika has been reduced to a state of dreadful disrepair,

А на дожде—все дороги радугой!
Быть беде. Нынче до смеха ли?
Но если есть колокольчик под дугой,
Так значит, всё. Заряжай, поехали!

But in the rain — all roads lead off in a rainbow!
There's hell to pay. Is this a laughing matter?
But if there's a bell under the shaft-bow,
Then let's go, charge it up, we're off!

The passage suggests that so long as Russians hear the soul, the spiritual bell, in their bodies — and so long as artists (be it Gogol or Bashlachev) can make it resonate — there is hope for Russia.

We're so long waiting. All wandered about dirty.
Because of this we began to look alike,
But under the rain we turned out to be different.
The majority is honest, good.

The Soviet brand of communion attempted forcibly to reestablish the lost harmony of the great Russian past, but it failed because its method was to reduce all to the lowest common denominator of humanity: instead of rerooting Russians in the soil of their spiritual past, in a free brotherhood of mutual faith and love, Soviet life simply trampled them into the mud. The song ends on the note of the singer's faith in his people's miraculous capacity for moral regeneration.

И пусть разбит батюшка Царь-колокол—
Мы пришли с черными гитарами.
. . .
Рок-н-ролл—славное язычество.
Я люблю время колокольчиков.

And though Father King Bell[13] may be crushed —
We have come with our black guitars
. . .

Rock 'n' roll — splendid paganism.
I love the time of little bells.

Here the circle closes. Bashlachev envisages the spirit of contemporary culture, ideally rendered by the art of rock poetry, as a return to Russia's primordial pre-Christian state, described in the first lines of the poem. After the smallness of Bolshevism, Russians have once again begun to discover goodness in their suffering and to grow spiritually as a result. They have rediscovered a sense of direction, have renewed their search for metaphysical grace. In the beginning, the artistic medium best suited to convey this spiritual quest was the bell, a direct means of communication with God in a newly Christened Rus; later, in the age of schisms, this musical expression of harmony was lost and the harmony itself destroyed; then literature, like Gogol's lyrical prose, became the oblique medium through which Russians best conveyed their sorrowful yearning for the cracked bell of past unity; but even literature was enslaved to foreign (Marxist) ideals under socialist realism. Rock poetry is the medium for a new age: combining music and poetry, direct and indirect intimations of harmony, the new bell — the "copper loudspeaker" — overpowers the lies of the recent past with its loud affirmation of an ancient, eternal truth. Bashlachev holds up the past as a sacred time against which he measures the profane present, although he also finds a redemptive value in the suffering of those who have strayed from past ideal into present misery.

As we turn our attention from Bashlachev to his followers and fellow travelers, starting with Iurii Shevchuk, we pause to draw some important connections and distinctions. Russian rock, in becoming a truly national phenomenon, found champions not only in the capitals of St. Petersburg (Grebenshchikov) and Moscow (Kinchev), but throughout the provinces — in Cheropovets (Bashlachev) as in Ufa (Shevchuk) and Novosibirsk (Diagileva and Naumov). The desire to find the native sources of rock brought both Bashlachev and Shevchuk back to Vladimir Vysotskii (d. 1980), one of Russia's great bards and "the first rocker in Russia," if we are to believe Russian punk-rocker "Svin'ia" (Andrei Panov, who, while not always the most reliable source of information, is here, perhaps, not far from the truth).[14] If Bashlachev sustained the humanism, hope, poetic depth, and roughness of expression that distinguished Vysotskii's songs, then Shevchuk found in Vysotskii a model for all the pain, hoarseness, and *nadryv* (a form of expression so emotionally charged as to approach self-laceration) that came to characterize DDT's music. Bashlachev, too, sang with *nadryv,* but never, as in Shevchuk's song "Revolution" ("Revoliutsiia," from *Ottepel'* [*The Thaw*], 1987), as a way of calling his audience to social awareness or activism: "In this world what we want is absent, / But we believe we are capable of changing it: yes!" Bashlachev's understanding of the homeland is more farsighted and metaphysical, Shevchuk's more topical and concrete, but both are remarkable for a Russianness of form and content.

Shevchuk's demeanor is so intrinsically Russian that one of the principal critics of Russian rock called DDT a "Russian folk group."[15] The strength and charm of Shevchuk's songs stem from a profound national feeling that is not quite so raw and uncultivated as it might seem. "In order to write songs," Shevchuk once said, "it's not enough to watch your VCR. You have to read [the famous nineteenth-century Russian historian] Kliuchevskii."[16] Shevchuk's song "The Church" ("Tserkov'"), from *The Thaw,* which is evidently the work of one who has read and internalized Russian history, is a convincing expression of Russian national sentiment. In a saturated, smoky voice, at a sustained scream, Shevchuk produces a long series of extremely evocative negative metaphors which fuse into a vision of Soviet Russia as a great void haunted by the ghost of a spiritually eviscerated past. Perversely enough, the Russian sentiment starts to ring false just as soon as Shevchuk attempts to work it into a conscious expression of his genuine concern for the homeland. "The Big Woman" ("Bol'shaia zhenshchina," *The Thaw*) begins as Russia, represented by "a big woman on the beach, one-sixth the world in size, drowsily uses fences to scratch between her legs," and from there quickly deteriorates into a litany of clichés for Mother Russia — exploited, violated, but, of course, still beloved.[17] Shevchuk's "Homeland" ("Rodina"), from *The Actress Spring* (*Aktrisa vesna,* 1993), is another interesting reflection on Russia.

Еду я на родину,
Пусть кричат—уродина,
А она нам нравится,
Хоть и не красавица,
К сволочи доверчива.

I'm going to my homeland. Let them scream, "Freak,"
But we like her;
Though she's no beauty,
Is too trusting of scoundrels.[18]

More than an underhanded compliment to one's motherland, these verses constitute a confession of love by someone who is fully aware of his beloved's flaws. *The Cossack Infantryman* (*Plastun,* 1991), a politically minded album that came out on the threshold of the new era, returns to DDT's mid-1980s style of colorful lyrics delivered with all the volume of Shevchuk's capacious lungs. Political controversies clearly did not vanish with the Soviet Union, and songs such as "Presentiments of Civil War" ("Predchustvie grazhdanskoi voiny") amount to shouts of execration against the political violence of the Soviet Union and former Soviet people, an admonishment that "nationality votes for blood." We must emphasize that an artist's mere engagement with the age-old debate about the meaning of Russia by no means implies anything about his nationalist sentiment or political tendentiousness: Bashlachev was no jingoist, nor is Shevchuk unpatriotic. Shevchuk continued to pursue the Russian theme in his penultimate album *This Is All* (*Eto vse,* 1995). The suggestively titled "Russian Tango" ("Rossiiskoe tango") gives vent to indignation at the desecration of the Russian soul in a tired rehashing of Bashlachev's metaphors. However, the lyrics fall short of Bashlachev's coherency and poetic vision, and the singer almost admits to becoming lost in his own confusing conceits and mixed metaphors, singing, "I got lost in all these formations."

The Actress Spring is a complex, paradoxical album that is a kind of watershed in DDT's evolution. Musically, it represents a breakthrough with captivating melodies and complex arrangements. Yet, the verses are at times sloppy and awkward, despite the thematic emphasis on poetry throughout: "The Last Autumn" ("Posledniaia osen'") is about Pushkin and the death of poetry; "Rain" ("Dozhd'") describes the poetic inspiration that sweeps over the poet from his open window during a spring shower, "blowing away the bad verses I had written." Some of these bad verses seem to have made it intact into the album, which in places becomes a kind of melodious doggerel, threatening to decay into full-fledged, Western-sounding *estrada* (a word with no precise English equivalent, one of the perversions of Russian rock, something like a cross between lounge and pop music) — a fate from which introverted treatments of literary inspiration and cultural tradition probably cannot save it. The title song, "The Actress Spring," continues the seasonal metaphor of the earlier *Thaw.* The obvious interpretation of this song is that the Soviet winter has finally ended (as it failed to do during the so-called thaws of the 1950s and 1960s). The poet feels his country to be on the verge of the first spring since 1917; all the country — and in fact the entire cosmos, including the sun, sitting like the general secretary in its balcony seat — watches with joy as the Actress Spring performs her spectacle. But Shevchuk ends on a jarring note that threatens the coherency of the song, as, crossing herself, Russia applauds the beginning of the "seventy-fifth theatrical season." Here a sense of continuity unexpectedly undermines the theme of transition and change that had been so pronounced in all the lines leading up to the finale. It now seems that Spring had in fact given this uplifting performance every year from 1917 to 1991 and has continued to do so after the demise of the Soviet Union. Just as the transition from winter to spring seems new each year, so the transitions from tsarist to Soviet and then back to capitalist regimes only appear to bring renewal to Russia while in fact fitting into a universal, eternal rite of spring. Hinting at the timeless continuity of Russian life, Shevchuk comes closest to Bashlachev's clairvoyance, with the important difference that "The Actress Spring" appeared after the end of the Soviet period, whereas Bashlachev's vision dates to a time when few could discern Russia behind the Soviet Union.

Konstantin Kinchev's creativity does not spring, like Shevchuk's, from thoughts about Russia's destiny, and when he finally arrived, in the early 1990s, at a more Russian form of rock, it was under the undeniable and direct influence of Bashlachev. Still, Kinchev had an important role to play in the Russification of rock. Starting with *Energy* (*Energiia,* 1985), his first album as the composer and lead singer of Alisa, he began to focus on the perennial problems of authentic Russian rock, foremost the East-West dialectic and the development of a language both poetical and musical. "The Melomaniac" ("Meloman") satirizes the Western influence that was still pervasive in Russian rock in the mid-1980s. The song's persona actually *lists* reams of Western musical groups, presenting them as his formative influences in a high-velocity jabber that he defines at the end of the song as "r-r-r-ep" (that is, rap).[19] This tirade describes a progression of obsessions from the classics (the Beatles, Rolling Stones, Eric Clapton, Janis Joplin, etc.) to *khard-rok* (hard rock: Black Sabbath, Alice Cooper, Led Zeppelin, etc.) to psychedelic (King Crimson, Robert Fripp, Frank Zappa, Bryan Ino, etc.) to punk and New Wave (Nina Hagan, the Clash, the Sex Pistols, the Police, etc.). Finally, our "melomaniac" confesses to having taken the stage himself:

Now I myself sing and compose, by the way

. . .

In a short time I wrote so much
That much of what I wrote I've already forgotten.

The song seems to suggest that Russian rockers whose credentials and talents are limited to worshipping Western rock can produce nothing memorable or long lasting. The first song of the same album, "We're Together!" ("My vmeste!"), is remarkable for describing the rites of passage for a Russian rocker discovering his own "language" — that is, switching over to Russian from English, the native tongue of rock 'n' roll: "I've begun to sing in my native tongue. / I'm sure it didn't happen all of a sudden." [20]

Kinchev explained in an interview in February 1989 that his most important guide in making these discoveries was Bashlachev, who "taught me, foremost, to treat the word other than I had treated it before. It had seemed to me, a word is just a word, and the hell with it. You can chop it up, stuff it into a verse. For him a word was a piece of life." [21] Bashlachev's death impressed on Kinchev the need to be worthy of the Russian tradition of reverence for the word, particularly in the rock arena. Alisa's 1991 album *The End* (*Shabash*) is, according to Kinchev, "the death of Sasha Bashlachev and his funeral hymn. The whole album is about that." [22] It is, not surprisingly, here that "Twilight" ("Sumerki"), one of Kinchev's most poetic songs, first appears on an album. "Twilight" derives much of its strength from a chain of rock songs with which it forges intertextual links. [23] It resounds with echoes from Russian poetry and music, both folkloric and literary, including Vysotskii, Grebenshchikov, Naumov, and certainly Bashlachev. Kinchev puzzles together in this song a picture made up of the icons and words — "pieces of life" — characteristic of Bashlachev's poetry, but somehow the resulting worldview is like a photographic negative of Bashlachev's. Kinchev's line "With our eyes in the clouds, but our feet in the swamp" resonates with Bashlachev's "Sowing the sky, we trampled the field," but with two important caveats: first, Bashlachev's verse comes from what is probably his most pessimistic song, "Evil" ("Likho"); second, even in this rather morose context, Bashlachev's people destroy the Russian land while attempting to reap a celestial harvest, whereas Kinchev's merely wander into a swamp daydreaming. [24] Kinchev's Russia is plunged into despondent gloom; crows circle; the body throws shadows in all four directions; all around are murky swamps and dead forests; and the singer's thoughts are twilight. As we shall see presently, if Kinchev owes many of his images to Bashlachev, his darkly cynical rendering of them links him more to Naumov. Kinchev's metaphor likening Russia to a swamp and the song's final couplet, "But take a look at the icons, their faces are dark, / And there's no way back" (Да только глядь на образа, а лики-то черные, / И обратной дороги нет), are signature effects of Naumov's art.

Naumov is still less accepting than Kinchev of Bashlachev's sympathetic depiction of Russia. Not Russia but America, the home of rock music, is *his* native land. Naumov, whose song "Styrofoam City" ("Porolonovyi gorod," 1984) tells of how the "city of sounds and music" gave him shelter in his hour of need, has always insisted on the primacy of music over words in his art.[25] This does not detract, however, from the profundity and richness of his own rock lyrics, which paint a ghastly picture of Russia as a land of rapacious violence and eternal horror. Naumov's lyrical heroes, having peered at the Russian soil and recoiled at the elemental violence and demonic cynicism they found there, turn a hopeful eye to the West as a refuge of sanity, hope, and civilization. His powerful "Chastushki" (1986) is characteristic of this tendency: the poem appropriates the humorous, lively, often bawdy poetic folk genre of the *chastushka* in order to present a dismal vision of Russian history and spiritual life. Naumov's Russia is "a swamp tied down with nuts" and bolts; her "sky is somehow evil" (Да только небо какое-то недоброе).[26] The past is presented as a relentless millennial "gang rape" by Russians of their motherland, while "the present smells of garlic" mixed with something sinister, a premonition of things to come: "Wait, bide your time — morning is wiser than night, / Night is stronger than morning, / The worst is still to come" (Погоди, повремени—утро вечера мудренее, / Вечер утра помахровее, / то-то будет вперед). The singer sarcastically undercuts the folk wisdom *"utro vechera mudrenee"* suggesting that insensate brutality is the only lesson Russia's history has to teach. Here even Russia's "Truth, in truth, has eyes blacker than black" — particularly, one suspects, nationalistic, Slavophile truths, at which Naumov hints using words like *pomakhrovee,* which denotes "redoubled" but connotes "more antisemitic." This is one of the means Naumov employs to argue with Bashlachev, Grebenshchikov, and others about the nature of Russianness and Russian destiny. In song after song — "Piataia aveniu," "Moskovskii bugi," "Kosmos," "Emigrantskii bliuz" (to say nothing of his recent songs in English) — Naumov paints the picture of his flight to the West, his exodus from Russia and abandonment of her concerns. "Moscow Boogie" ("Moskovskii bugi," 1989), which dates to and treats of

Naumov's emigration to New York, contains the following two characteristic stanzas:

Великий город—хамелеон,
Который уже миллион на счетах твоих банков,
В твоих ледяных катакомбах
Безумный бильярд, жестокий закон—
От двух бортов в пропасть—ты, я или он . . .
Лубянка . . . ворота в Европу надолго лишатся покоя.

Пока твои крысы бегут с корабля,
Я рысью, без бля, как положено блудному сыну,
До крови пропитанный чувством вины
Пройду по чащобам родной стороны
Трущобам последней гражданской войны
И уйду, только ты не меня в спину.

Oh, great city — chameleon,
How many millions are in your bank accounts,
In your icy catacombs?
Oh, crazy billiards, cruel principle:
Off two banks and into the abyss — you, he, or I . . .
Lubianka . . . the gateway to Europe will bustle for a long time.

While your rats run from the ship,
At a trot, like a good prodigal son, slowly but surely,
Soaked to the blood with a sense of shame,
I'll pass through the swamps of my native land,
Through the slums of the last civil war,
And leave — just don't push me.

The song's two central metaphors for expatriation — rats running from a sinking ship and the Prodigal Son — infuse the poetic persona with a "sense of guilt" at his flight from his homeland. The Westernizer rejects the notion of Russian messianism, but is racked with guilt in doing so. Naumov wryly substitutes the "Petersburg Myth," the literary reflection of the Petersburg period of Russian history, with a new Moscow Myth for the subsequent period of Soviet brutality.

Pushkin's image of Petersburg as Russia's "window onto Europe" yields to Naumov's Lubianka as a "gateway to Europe," an image that implies that Westward flight may be the spiritual counterpart to death in the chambers of Lubianka, yet it is the only answer to one who refuses to build a new cultural edifice on the moral mire of the recent Stalinist past.[27] The persona of Kosmos affirms, "I have no roots in this earth. / Am free to choose captivity, / Free to fly up and leave my captivity." Flight for Naumov is a deeply ambivalent liberation from the Russian land that is at once a miserable "swamp" of violent repression and a rich "soil" of artistic possibilities. Flight is immigration to the physically free but spiritually empty West; it is a guilt-ridden betrayal of the Russian artist's traditional martyrdom and, paradoxically, a new, suicidal kind of martyrdom. But flight is inevitable. Even in Naumov's earlier texts the sense of the minstrel's ephemeral sojourn in his native land is undeniable. Consider, for instance, the ending of his ingenious "Fairytale about Karl" ("Skazka o Karle"), which dates to early 1985:

А я был странники в израненной странной стране
Где продажное "да" и на нет сводят "нет"
Где на тысячу спящих один, что распят,
и пятьсот, что плетутся вдоль стен.

I was a traveler in a wounded, strange land,
Where "yes" is for sale and "no" is not taken for an answer,
Where for a thousand asleep there is one crucified,
and five hundred trudging along the walls.

By intimating that he is but a wayfarer and observer in his own land, Naumov's persona distances himself from all three of the modes of life he presents as possible in Russia: the artist-martyr, the sleeping (i.e., contented) masses, and the many who are malcontent and oppressed with the Russian-Soviet life through which they "trudge," and thirst for life on the other side of "the walls," but will never have the courage either to accept the martyr's cross or to cross over to the other side, the West. The latter is Naumov's option: it entails its own form of daring and is certainly preferable to staying with Russia if that means either selling one's "yes" or falling "asleep." In "Night Flight" ("Nochnoi polet," 1988), a moving tribute to Bashlachev, who had just committed suicide, Naumov compares suicide, emigration, and "overcoming" as methods of escaping from untruth: "To be a suicide / Is probably easier than to overcome, /

But understand—it's even easier to betray." With dreamy lyricism, this poem alone among Naumov's verses envisages what it would be like to flee from the nightmare of Russia's past and present, but into a more ideal Russian future rather than to the West or the grave:

> The earth's slush takes prisoners day after day.
> If I had wings,
> I'd leave my home for a while.
> I'd lift the curse. I'd raise this Earth from her knees.

Characteristically, even in this most Bashlachevian and Russian-looking of Naumov's works, lifting the curse from his homeland, and thus raising up Russia herself, is a magical vision predicated on leaving "home," if only "for a while." Naumov rejects the notion that Russians may find in Russia the secret to the salvation of their culture and nation.

In the songs of Iana Diagileva (d. 1991), as in Naumov's, all is flight and escape, but her flight was less from Russia than from life itself, and her method of escape was not Naumov's (imagination, immigration) but Bashlachev's (death). The flight envisaged by Diagileva's personas in song after song is to a place called "the homeland" (from the song "Angedonia"). But this is neither the homeland of a remote Russian past (Bashlachev's Great Time, Grebenshchikov's Invisible City of Kitezh) nor immigration's home away from home (Naumov's Fifth Avenue). As Diagileva suggests in "Back Home!" ("Domoi!"), from the album *Angedonia* (1989), the homeland is the world beyond the grave, and the hand of death "will extend its finger and point to the doors leading from here / Back home!"[28] Life on earth—especially in Russia—is, in Diagileva, a misshapen journey-turned-imprisonment that leaves us yearning for the home we left in order to enter the false, evil dream of earthly existence and whither we return after "liberation" from this nightmare: "Plus times minus equals liberation / Back home!" This world is "the absurd harmony of an empty sphere," "snow-filled rooms and smoke," "stony systems in swollen heads"—and the singer would flee "from all of this sparkling, ringing and blazing bullshit / Back home!" (От всей сверкающей, звенящей и пылающей хуйни / Домой!). Diagileva's music is the ideal accompaniment to her haunting poetry: like Bashlachev, she played guitar "with the fists," and her eerie, expressive voice sang of this world with horror, anger, or sorrow, seeming to soar up above and away from the tragic scene it described.[29]

This is never as true as in the title song of her first album, *Angedonia*. The rich neologism of the title speaks to the essence of Diagileva's poetics: Angedonia suggests the "anguish" (from the Latin *anga:* to choke, cause distress) of existence. It is even more so the *agonia* of death: "But do you dare switch the places of oblivion and pain / Do you dare to get lost before dawn and fall asleep" (А слабо переставить местами забвенье и боль / Слабо до утра заблудиться в лесу и заснуть).[30] One may summon oblivion to escape the pain of life, but the singer's challenge is to take on a painful death in order to escape the oblivion of living. "Angedonia" evokes the angiology behind the "blood analysis" that the song's "citizens" undergo: "And at eight A.M. blood from the finger analysis for citizens / Accumulated dirt a level permitting of work" (А в восемь утра кровь из пальца анализ для граждан / Осевшая грязь допустимый процент для работ). But when the singer finally defines Angedonia halfway through the song, the diagnosis is much more grave than "accumulated dirt" in the blood; this is a diagnosis that does not permit "work" or indeed life to continue: "Angedonia — a diagnosis of absent joy" (Ангедония—диагноз отсутствия радости). Angedonia is thus the Angel of Death who will escort the anguishing soul to its Homeland. This angel flits into other songs as well, for instance as the "black satellite" of "For Being Smart" ("Ot bol'shogo uma"): "Parallel to the path a black satellite flies / He will comfort and save — he will bring us peace" (Параллельно пути черный спутник летит / Он утешит, спасет—он нам покой принесет).[31] Angedonia, finally, is the "Homeland" of the song's first line — not Russia, and not Rus, but the grave, full of last year's pine needles, rotting and bitter to the taste.

Короткая спичка—судьба возвращаться на родину
По первому снегу, по рыжей крови на тропе
Жрать хвою прошлогоднюю горькую горькую горькую
На сбиты затылками лед насыпать золотые пески.

A short match — destiny: returning to the Homeland
Along the virgin snow, along the red-brown blood on the trail
Wolfing down last year's pine needles bitter bitter bitter
Spreading golden sands over pate-crushed ice.

As is the case with the other musicians discussed here, Diagileva's art finds its impulse — if a negative one — in Russia. For Diagileva, too, Russia was a diabolical place that she never once accorded the status and dignity of "homeland." Her Russia is a KGB interrogation chamber, from a wall of which "Iron

Felix [Dzerzhinsky] smiles down upon us from a portrait."[32] The pain of Bashlachev and Grebenshchikov's songs are *for* the homeland, which they hope may yet be salvaged for good. Diagileva's pain is *from* Russia. Like Naumov, she was crushed by Russia's gloom, by its bloody history and its cruelty toward the individual. Unable to bear the burden of Russian culture, she answered with an art of escape. But where Naumov looked to the West for deliverance, Diagileva looked into the acrid earth itself, into the empty heavens ("Sacred empty places — into the sky from a bridge," "Angedonia"), into the water that became her own grave in 1991. Diagileva's Russian Homeland is primordial and elemental (perhaps feminine) rather than symbolic and mythic, but it is Russian nonetheless. Horror of and flight from Russia are also, paradoxically enough, inscribed by a native cultural tradition that includes great creators of culture from Westernizing thinkers to suicidal poets, Petr Chaadaev, Vissarion Belinskii, Aleksandr Hertzen, Sergei Esenin, Vladimir Maiakovskii, and Marina Tsvetaeva, to name but a few.

After the deaths of Bashlachev (1988) and Diagileva (1991) and the emigration of Naumov (1990), Grebenshchikov (by that time a twenty-year veteran of Russian rock) became the vanguard of this quest for origins. Grebenshchikov — whose lyrics of the 1980s paint the picture of an eclectic land with features of Tolkien's Middle Earth, Arthurian and Druidic legend, Buddhist imagery, and Silver Age symbols — began, with the disintegration of the Soviet Union, to develop Bashlachev's vision of a spiritually charged Rus. Grebenshchikov's songs of the 1990s express a new vision of a people that yearns to be transformed into "Holy Rus" but, due to a tragic spiritual flaw, constantly allows itself to be seduced into becoming something more like "Unholy Rus." Grebenshchikov is warier than Bashlachev (though not so wary as Naumov) about embracing Russianness. Some of his poetic personas chide Russian backwardness with a sophisticated, Western-style levity; others revere Russia with all of her elemental heresies and mystical revelations; still others cast about between these two extremes. "Nikita Riazanskii," a song from the *Russian Album,* describes Russian spiritual history as the fragmentation of an ancient unity of Faith into "nine thousand churches" — terms that recall Bashlachev's artistic vision.[33] The mythical title character "leaves the elders" of the Orthodox Church after first "leav[ing] the city" and civilization behind in order to "laugh and pray" (a combination of activities considered blasphemous by Orthodoxy) with Saint Sophia (a figure suggesting the idiosyncrasies — if not heterodoxies and heresies — of the Eastern faith). Interestingly, this movement away from Western, Christian forms of culture toward a more Russian world-view controls the very composition of the song. In an interview in 1991, Grebenshchikov stated that his first draft of "Nikita Riazanskii" "almost entirely consisted of Old Church Slavonic" from the Russian saints' lives he had been reading, but that in the final version "only one line remained."[34] Like his lyrical hero Riazanskii, Grebenshchikov is tempted to seek Russia's destiny in heretical or pre-Christian religious faith. The poem evokes the ancient legend of the Invisible City of Kitezh, whose denizens pray to God for their city to sink to the bottom of the lake rather than be taken by the besieging Golden Horde. God answers their prayer and the city vanishes under the waves, but the bells, it is said, can be heard once a year emanating from the bottom of the lake. Grebenshchikov, following the Old Believer tradition, makes of Kitezh a symbol of a pure native faith, submerged and preserved in the innermost core of Russia's heart. One must delve into religious schism (Old Belief) and heresy (laughing and praying) in order to resurrect this spiritual Kitezh: "Here, Lord, we are sinking to the bottom, / Teach us to breathe underwater" (Смотри, Господи,—вот мы уходим на дно, / Научи нас дышать под водой).

Like "Nikita Riazanskii," "Wolves and Ravens" ("Volki i vorony"), also from the *Russian Album* (*Russkii al'bom*, 1991), conjures up a vision of a long-submerged Slavonic spiritual past now beckoning to Russians once more. "Here they come with icons — unfamiliar icons, / And icon-lamps light up their path from under the dark water" (Вот идут с образами незнакомыми, / Да светят им лампады из-под темной воды).[35] Perhaps the icons — representing the Orthodox faith — have grown "unfamiliar" to Russians from disuse after seven decades of Soviet "icons" (Lenin, Stalin, etc.). But a still more likely interpretation is that Orthodox Christianity, with all of its trappings, was always "unfamiliar" to Russia. Like Peter's and Lenin's reforms, Christianity was initially something foreign implanted in the Russian soil, where it took dubious root. This observation is not new: the nineteenth-century populists juxtaposed an adopted Christianity with the people's endemic communal spirit. Grebenshchikov suggests that the zealous, slavish adoption of Christianity in Russia is likely, in the present as in the past, only to deaden the Russian spirit, whose native needs it neglects. It was perhaps just such religious deadness, the song suggests, that paved the way for the Soviets, who made the Russian land into a veritable graveyard in the twentieth century: "Loads of crosses were gilded and driven in helter-skelter" (Назолотили крестов, навтыкали, где ни попадя).[36] "Wolves and Ravens" depicts post-Soviet Russia as standing at a crossroads in a state of spiritual crisis: Russians are lost in a "dark and mossy" "high forest" that conceals "either divine grace, or a trap set for us" (first stanza); the "temple" of their religious life is "high, but there's darkness under the dome" (second stanza); they are seeking a path toward spiritual light, but high Russian snowdrifts block the way "in all four directions" (second stanza). Time and again this song depicts the clash between an implanted, synthetic Christianity (temples, icons, crosses) and indigenous Russian nature (snows, dark water, high woods, wolves and ravens, Russia's star), concluding in the end, "But still, only the wolves and ravens ever warmed us / And blessed our journey to the pure star" (А всё равно нас грели только волки да вороны, / И благословили нас до чистой звезды). The bloodthirsty fauna of the song's title and refrain, who animate Russian folklore and imagination, are a perfect emblem of the brutish native element, of the *dvoeverie* (the commingling of pagan and Christian beliefs that is thought to define Russian religious consciousness) that Grebenshchikov identifies as the bane and blessing of Russian spiritual life.[37]

Grebenshchikov's personages stumble from pre-Christian Slavonic paganism to Orthodox heresy, from evil to good, yielding to the enlightened temptations of the West and to the dark destiny of Russia. The refrain of his "Languishing" ("Maetsia," *Navigator,* 1995) describes how the song's hero

> Мается, мается
> То грешит то кается,
> Но всё не признается,
> Что всё дело в нём.

> Languishes, languishes,
> Now sins, now repents,
> But will never admit,
> That the truth lies in him.[38]

"He" is intentionally ambiguous: since the text is sung, capitalization cannot clarify whether "he" is God/Christ (Bog/Khristos), the Russian people (*Russkii narod*), or perhaps the singer's own spirit (*dukh*). More likely, Grebenshchikov intended all three meanings. The mournful melody awakens in this song an ancient native form of art, mixing rock music with the traditional Russian folk lament to great effect. The song depicts Russians as a people cursed forever to seek a truth that will always evade them.

Вроде бы и строишь—а всё разлетается;
Вроде говоришь да всё не про то.
Ежели не выпьешь—то не получается.
А выпьешь—воешь волком, не за что,
     Ни про что.

You seem to be building, but it all flies apart.
You seem to be talking, but always about the wrong thing.
If you don't drink, nothing works out,
But if you drink — you howl like a wolf,
     for no reason at all.

The last verse breaks off into what seems to be stylized folk poetry, not sung like the rest of the song, but rather intoned. In this clearly marked coda, the masculine gender yields to the feminine as the singer appeals directly to the motherland:

In a white little purse are some copper coins,
In the golden baptismal font darkness and prison.
Heaven is on a chain, but its links are torn open;
When you go to fix it — you'll understand yourself [*sama*].

Grebenshchikov's motherland is a complex tapestry woven from images of birth (baptism) and death (the copper coins Russians place on the eyelids of their dead), belief and despair. The christening of Rus has brought physical and spiritual poverty, darkness and enslavement to her people. If only the misery of this world were perceived as a guarantee of salvation in the next, the song might offer some compensation — or at least consolation — for the anguish of Russian life. But the chain binding Orthodox Rus to the bliss of heaven is cleft.

The same strong native sense of *nadryv* pervades an earlier song from the album *Kostroma Mon Amour* (1994). The extremely laconic but plangent "8200," which we cite here in full, is the album's most serious song, and is suggestively located between two works belonging to the mock genre of *stiob*.

Восемь тысяч двести верст пустоты,
А всё равно нам с тобой негде ночевать.
Был бы я весел, если бы не ты,
Если бы не ты, моя родина-мать.

Был бы я весел, да что теперь в том.
Просто здесь красный, где у всех голубой.

Серебром по ветру, по сердцу серпом,
И Сирином моя душа взлетит над тобой.

Eight thousand two hundred versts of emptiness,
And still there's nowhere for us to spend the night.
I'd be happy if not for you,
If not for you, my native mother land.

I'd be happy, but what's the difference now.
It's simply that what is sky blue elsewhere is red here.
Like silver to the wind, like a sickle to the heart,
And like a Sirin my soul will fly up above you.

Like "Maetsia," "8200" conveys the sense of Russia's physical enormity and enormous lost potential. By stating that anguish at the emptiness and poverty of Russia has deprived him of the joy of living, the singer raises his love for his motherland and his pain at her immemorial misery above and apart from the mocking tonalities of the surrounding songs on the album. The second line of the second stanza suggests that Russia has reached her sunset years (the sky is red in Russia, whereas it is still sky blue in other — more Western — lands), and so the dream that Russia has a messianic role to play in history (Gogol's *troika*) is fading away. The decline of both the Soviet Union and the more durable Russia affects the singer like a sickle slash to the heart, and his soul yearns to be freed from his earthly body like silver thrown to the winds. We should note that the singer envisages his soul at death not in Christian terms but as the pre-Christian Sirin (a divine creature of pagan Slavonic legend and old Russian literature, a bird with the head and breasts of a woman). In his sympathy for his dying land, the singer thirsts for death, and somehow the bloody fate of Russia and the Russians is linked to an ancient pagan principle in them that neither a millennium of Christianity nor a century of communism could extirpate.

Although the West is regarded with suspicion in his songs, especially of late, Grebenshchikov never affirms without ambivalence, irony, or reservations that salvation lies in the Russian soil. A review of the general trend of his music from 1991 until the present will demonstrate this principle. In the *Russian Album,* anguish at Russia's condition is tempered with hope that the mad, heretical Russian way may lead to good in the end. *Kostroma Mon Amour* and *Navigator* grow increasingly despondent and at times subtly shift in form from rock to lament (perhaps Russia's counterpart to the blues). In *The Snow Lion* (*Snezhnyi lev,* 1996), the mood darkens yet again. The song "Old-Russian

Sorrow" ("Drevnerusskaia toska") begins with Gogol's oft-quoted question about Russia's direction and destiny, but now the question is not posed in earnest, as it was in Bashlachev and Grebenshchikov's earlier songs:

> Where are you racing, troika?
> Where does your path lie?
> The coachman's drunk again on vodka
> Or just lay down to take a nap.
> . . .
> As foretold by the saints, all is hanging by a thread
> I view this situation with Old-Russian sorrow.[39]

We sense in such mock-tragic music the singer's attempt to don the thick skin of cynicism as a way of disguising his outraged reverence for the shamed motherland. The song goes on to bemoan Russia's commercialization and de-spiritualization, describing a country where "on the field of ancient battle there are neither bones nor spears" because "everything has gone to tourists and visitors for souvenirs." Even the heroes of Russian epic verse (*byliny*) and myth have shamelessly accommodated themselves to the new capitalist order: Dobrynia Nikitich is working in Milan; Alesha Popovich has hocked the iconostasis; and Princess Iaroslavna (from Russia's epic poem *The Igor Tale*) has no time to lament her husband's captivity because of her long work hours. The depiction of the wholesale exploitation of Russianness in this song is lurid:

> А над удолбанной Москвой в небо лезут леса,
> Турки строят муляжи святой Руси за полчаса.
> А у хранителей святыни пляшет палец на курке.
> Знак червонца проступает вместо лика на доске.

> And above stoned Moscow scaffolding climbs into the sky.
> Turks make plaster models of Holy Rus in half an hour.
> And trigger-happy guards watch over the holy of holies.
> The dollar sign emerges on the icon instead of a holy face.

The singer presents blasphemy upon blasphemy with as much sardonic sang-froid as he can muster, "his ancient Russian sorrow" all but drowned out by the frivolous tune, appropriately Western-style rock-'n'-roll rhythm, and ironic tone. The last line halfheartedly admits, "I'm afraid I'm fed up with ancient Russian sorrow," and thus suggests that even selling rock albums on the Russian theme can become just one more way of earning a buck at the expense of Russia's sacred ideals. The sarcasm and *stiob* of Grebenshchikov's last few albums, then, are very probably an attempt to back away from a powerful, original strain of music whose currency the artist does not want to use up, for his sorrow, in the end, is all too serious.

The shape of the lives and careers of Russia's best rock artists confirms the paradigm we have sketched out: Bashlachev and Diagileva lived and died in Russia; Naumov's path took him ever Westward from his childhood in Siberia to the Russian capitals to New York, whither he emigrated in 1991 (he has been writing in English since); finally, Grebenshchikov grew up and rose to fame in the boundary zone of Petersburg, which he began to leave in the late 1980s for extended sojourns now in Paris, the United States, and Canada, now in the heart of Russia, in the Volga and the Black Earth region (today he divides his time between Tibet and Russia). But their various rock poetics converge in the essential matters of word and origin. Bashlachev's "Petersburg Wedding" ("Peterburgskaia svad'ba") searches for the foundations of Peter I's ambivalent creation, the city that emblematizes Russia's identity crisis. It finds in Petersburg two cornerstones: one set by history when Peter decided to "cut a window onto Europe" by building a city with a Western look and imposing a Western administration on Russia from this new capital; the other set by poetry when Pushkin created a national myth of Petersburg, and of Petersburg Russia, in his great poem *The Bronze Horseman*. The question for Bashlachev is which version of Petersburg, and thus Russia, will persevere, the tsar's Western-looking administration or the poet's purely Russian versification of it—for "the two-headed eagles . . . Cannot share the crown between them" (Двуглавые орлы с побитыми крылами / Не могут меж собой корону поделить).[40] Bashlachev answers his own question in the same song: "Beyond the windows—a salute. Tsar-Pushkin is in a new frame" (За окнами—салют. Царь-Пушкин в новой раме). At first glance "Tsar-Pushkin" evokes the famous cannon, Tsar-Pushka, a descendant of which is firing holiday salvos in commemoration of the Bolshevik Revolution in Bashlachev's song,[41] but "Tsar-Pushkin" is, in a deeper sense, a profession of faith: for Bashlachev, it is not some political dictator, but rather Pushkin who is tsar. Russian rock as a whole has declared Pushkin—that is, poetry—to be king, and not politics or history. The rock poets discussed here continue Pushkin's direct, forceful posing of the most fundamental questions concerning Russianness and foreignness. It was Pushkin who first coupled religion and politics in giving the eternal question about Russia's destiny striking artistic form. It is then appropriate that rock, in coming into its own as a national aesthetic, should return to thoughts about Russia, and that precisely these meditations should foster a rock music rich in poetry.

Notes

I express my deep gratitude to Professor Abbott Gleason, without whose inspiring seminar on Russian nationalism this paper would not have been written — JF.

1 Martha Bayles, *Hole in Our Soul: The Loss of Beauty and Meaning in American Popular Music* (Chicago: University of Chicago Press, 1994).

2 Western rock's influence on its Russian counterpart in the 1960s, 1970s, and early 1980s gradually yielded to Russians' discovery and appropriation of ever more native forms and themes, a process of self-realization that continues to unfold. See Didurov's comments on the "derivative" nature of early Russian rock in "Rocking in Russian, or Power Chords from the Underground," *Kyoto Journal* 29 (1995): 107; as well as the discussion of Western influences on Russian rock in Sabrina Petra Ramet, Sergei Zamascikov, and Robert Bird, "The Soviet Rock Scene," in *Rocking the State: Rock Music and Politics in Eastern Europe* (Boulder: Westview Press, 1994), pp. 181, 183, and *passim*.

3 Cf. Il'ia Smirnov's observation that Russian "rock musicians view themselves as the heirs not only of an international rock tradition, but also of their native culture, of the spiritual potential which created that culture over the ages" (*Vremia kolokol'chikov: Zhizn' i smert' russkogo roka* [Moscow: Into, 1994], p. 101).

4 T. S. Eliot, "Tradition and the Individual Talent," in *Selected Essays, 1917–1932* (New York: Harcourt Brace, 1932), p. 4.

5 Smirnov, *Vremia kolokol'chikov*, pp. 256–57. The Kalinov Bridge is the place where the Russian epic hero encounters and vanquishes the forces of evil in folklore.

6 Since the tendency we are describing began in the mid-1980s, we do not discuss earlier groups such as Skomorokhi, Mashina vremeni, Voskresenie, and Zoopark. But even within our time period one can find major rock bands whose principal interest was not the Russian theme as we describe it, including Kino, Televizor, Nautilus Pompilius, Bravo, Brigada S, Zvuki mu, Auktsyon, Strannye igry, Chai F, and Dva samoleta.

7 See Alexei Yurchak's fine discussion of *stiob* in his contribution to this volume. He defines *stiob* as an "ironic treatment of the ideological symbol" that "differed from sarcasm or derision" and "required a certain overidentification with the treated ideological symbol, often to the point that it was almost impossible to tell whether the symbols were supported or subverted by subtle ridicule" (p. 84).

8 On the special importance of words in Russian rock, see Artemy Troitsky, *Back in the USSR: The True Story of Rock in Russia* (Boston: Faber and Faber, 1988), p. 40;

Didurov, "Rocking in Russian," p. 108; Thomas Cushman, *Notes from Underground: Rock Music Counterculture in Russia* (Albany: State University of New York Press, 1995), pp. 103–7; and Smirnov, *Vremia kolokol'chikov,* p. 54.

9 See Cushman's discussion of why Russian rockers consider their music a form of "high" art: "For rock to be authentic, it had to speak 'beyond politics' to the human condition, to the human spirit and soul, and to the great questions of existence" (Notes, p. 103). "To refer to rock music in the Russian context as a form of popular culture is to insult the Petersburg countercultural musician who sees his activity as fundamentally and essentially noncommercial" (*Notes,* p. 129).

10 From Dostoevsky's letter to N. N. Strakhov, May 5, 1871, in F. M. Dostoevsky, *Sobranie sochinenii v tritsati tomakh* (Moscow: Akademiia nauk, 1972), vol. 29, pt. 1, p. 207. See also Dostoevsky's so-called Pushkin Speech (vol. 26, p. 144). Ivan V. Kireevskii (1806–1856) and Aleksei S. Khomiakov (1804–1860) were the principal founders of the nineteenth-century Slavophile movement, which idealized Old Russian traditions, primarily the faith of Russian Orthodoxy and the societal structure of the peasant collective, or *mir.*

11 Bashlachev puns on the word *kolokol'chik* in the title and text of this song: *kolokol'chik* can signify both a small bell (handbell) and a flower, the bluebell. We should note that Bashlachev always played his music with a bracelet of bells around his wrist. "Vremia kolokol'chikov" is cited from Aleksandr Bashlachev, *Pososhok,* ed. Aleksandr Zhitinskii (Leningrad: Lira, 1990), p. 15.

12 Cf. James H. Billington's discussion of bells in Russian culture in *The Icon and the Axe: An Interpretive History of Russian Culture* (New York: Vintage Books, 1970), pp. 39–42.

13 "Father King Bell," or Tsar'-kolokol, is a gigantic bell that originally hung in the Ivanovskoi Belfry of the Moscow Kremlin but fell and cracked during the fire of 1737. Since 1836 it has rested on a granite pedestal next to the Belfry of Ivan the Great.

14 Cited in Smirnov, *Vremia kolokol'chikov,* p. 60.

15 Ibid., p. 20.

16 Cited in ibid., p. 101.

17 All citations of Shevchuk's lyrics refer to Kirill Mazin's DDT homepage on the World Wide Web, 1996, 1997.

18 Shevchuk's play of "*urodina/rodina*" (freak/homeland) is an allusion to the lyrics of Fedor Chistiakov, the leader of the now defunct group Nol', which was usually more remarkable for its use of traditional Russian instruments (Chistiakov plays the Russian accordion, or *baian*) and melodies than for lyrics about Russia. Chistiakov's album *A Song about Unreciprocated Love for the Homeland* (*Pesnia o bezotvetnoi liubvi k rodine,* 1991) contains a song entitled "Lenin Street" ("Ulitsa Lenina"), with the original version of the rhyme parodied by Shevchuk in "Homeland": "As I hate, so I love my homeland. / And there is nothing to marvel at here, comrades. / She's really such a blind, mute freak; / Well, but still there's nothing else for me to love" (Как ненавижу, так и люблю свою родину. / И удивляться здесь,

право, товарищи, ничему. / Такая она уж слепая, глухая уродина, / Ну, а
любить-то мне больше и нечего).

19 "Meloman" is cited from Nina Baranovskaia, *Konstantin Kinchev. Zhizn' i tvorchestvo. Stikhi. Dokumenty. Publikatsii* (St. Petersburg: Novyi Gelikon, 1993),
pp. 87–88.

20 "My vmeste!" is cited from ibid., p. 86.

21 Zhitinskii, ed., *Pososhok,* p. 142.

22 Petr Kamenchenko, "Beseda s Kinchevym," in Baranovskaia, *Konstantin Kinchev,*
p. 219.

23 Cf. Baranovskaia, *Konstantin Kinchev,* p. 42.

24 "Sumerki" is cited from ibid., pp. 115–16.

25 See, for example, his interview with the rock journal *Urlait* (1989, no. 23), in which
Naumov says, "I was raised on Western rock, and when people say that Vysotskii
was the first rocker in Russia, that may be so, but it provokes resistance in me,
because my roots are not there; I 'arose' from sound, and not from the word" (cited
in Aleksandr Zhitinskii, *Puteshestvie rok-diletanta: Muzykal'nyi roman* [Leningrad:
Lenizdat, 1990], p. 265).

26 All citations of Naumov's lyrics refer to manuscripts of the songs provided to us by
Iurii Naumov.

27 Pushkin's phrase, from his narrative poem *The Bronze Horseman* (*Mednyi vsadnik,*
1830), is "V Evropu prorubit' okno" (To cut a window onto Europe). Lubianka is a
word that strikes terror into the hearts of Russians: it was the central Soviet prison in
Moscow, through which political prisoners passed on their way to Siberian exile; it
was also the setting of countless tortures and executions.

28 "Domoi" is cited from Marina Timashevoi, ed., *Russkoe pole eksperimentov* (Moscow: Diuna, 1994), p. 203.

29 The expression *"igrat' kulakami"* (to play with one's fists) is from Bashlachev's
ingenious song "Sluchai v Sibiri"; it evokes the coarse, wild, energetic style of
acoustic guitar playing that Bashlachev employed to such great effect.

30 "Angedoniia" is cited from Timashevoi, ed., *Russkoe pole,* p. 211.

31 "Ot bol'shogo uma" is cited from ibid., p. 206.

32 "А с портрета будет улыбаться нам железный феликс" ("Po tramvainym
rel'sam," 1988).

33 "Nikita Riazanskii" is cited from Boris Grebenshchikov, *Pesni,* ed. B. Nikolaev
(Tver: LEAN, 1996), pp. 207–8.

34 In Ol'ga Sagareva, *Akvarium 1972–1992: Sbornik materialov* (Moscow: Alfavit,
1992), p. 314. The "one line" is evidently the final line of the first stanza: "Оставль
старца и учаше кто млад" (Leaving the elder, the young one began to teach).

35 "Volki i vorony" is cited from Grebenshchikov, *Pesni,* pp. 211–12.

36 Grebenshchikov develops this idea of spiritual death as atonement for evil in the
song "The Graveyard" ("Kladbishche") from *The Navigator,* which ends: "We also
feed with our blood / The glutted boorish bastards; // For so many years — yet they

still want more. / Can we really be so sinful? / Oh, if only the sun would rise soon / Over the graveyard of my homeland" (Grebenshchikov, *Pesni*, p. 289).

37 The wolf figures frequently in the Russian folktale (*skazka*), the raven more in the Russian folk song. In the "Tale of Ivan-Tsarevich, the Firebird and the Gray Wolf" ("Skazka ob Ivane-tsareviche, zhar-ptitse i o serom volke"), the wolf helps the hero time and again, finally resurrecting him from death with the help of the raven. See *Divo divnoe: Russkie narodnye skazki,* ed. A. D. Shavkuta (Moscow: Sovremennik, 1988), pp. 205–13.

38 "Maetsia" is cited from Grebenshchikov, *Pesni,* pp. 291–92.

39 "Drevnerusskaia toska" is cited from Grebenshchikov, *Pesni,* pp. 298–92.

40 "Peterburgskaia svad'ba" is cited from Bashlachev, *Pososhok,* pp. 26–27.

41 The Tsar-Cannon, or Tsar'-Pushka, is an enormous cannon, cast in 1586 and kept in the Moscow Kremlin.

On the golden porch
We once did see
Mickey Mouse and the ducklings three
Tom and Jerry — Scrooge McDuck,
My Little Pony leads the flock.[1]

POPULAR CHILDREN'S CULTURE IN POST-PERESTROIKA RUSSIA: SONGS OF INNOCENCE AND EXPERIENCE REVISITED

Writing about popular children's culture in contemporary Russia is both exciting and troubling. The counting rhyme above is characteristic of the ambiguities that cropped up at every stage of my brief investigation. My first reaction to its image of various characters from American comic books and Saturday morning television shows cavorting on the golden porch of Russian fairy tale and epic tradition was qualified delight. I was charmed by the fact that an ancient poetic form (*schitalka*) had been creatively modified to express a new cultural reality — that of the Westernization of popular culture. The rhyme's use of the Old Church Slavonic form of the adjective "golden," *na zlatom,* rather than the Russian *na zolotom,* however, troubled me; the basic distinction between "high" and "low" style reflected in the two adjectives, which is crucial to the semiotic system of the Russian language and is second nature to any native Russian speaker, seemed to have been purposely ignored by the young author in order to maintain the scanning scheme of the original. What else is being lost, I wondered, in the rush to use Western images to express the new reality of Russian life?

Children, to an uncanny degree, mirror and even exaggerate the contradictions or unresolved dilemmas of the surrounding adult world. Like certain sensitive organisms in the ecosphere, they are the first to express the effects of an imbalance within the social system; they are also the first to react favorably to positive change. Thus, children would seem to be natural subjects for someone studying the impact of post-perestroika political, economic, and social changes on the popular culture of Russia today. It is adults, however, who are the final arbiters of the boundaries of childhood as a social construct — the definition of a "bona fide" childhood invariably stems from adult experiences, from their memories of the past and hopes for the future. Reflecting these complementary but separate problems, this chapter is divided into two parts; in the first part I present the Russian adults' conception of "childhood" and its impact on popular culture; in the second I describe popular Russian children's culture — as presented by the children themselves.

I

"Childhood" as an institution in the West, perhaps as a consequence of the modern world's Weberian disenchantment,[2] remains one of the last enclaves of utopianism. It is a veritable sacred sphere, universally acknowledged by all reputable adults — the religiously and the secularly inclined alike — consciously constructed and guarded from the profane world at large.[3] Russia's Westernized elite actively participated in this Western understanding of childhood both before and after 1917. The contemporary Russian intelligentsia — my cohort — in its definition of "proper" childhood models itself on Russia's prerevolutionary past; dancing lessons, music lessons, foreign languages are all part of the childhood agenda, to the degree that the parents' financial resources allow.

"I want to create a fairy-tale environment for my child," is a cri du coeur often heard by Western observers interviewing Russian parents.[4] The related theme of "childhood as happiness" also informs adult definitions of this stage of life.[5] It seems that in the difficult internal and external circumstances accompanying the first forty years of Soviet rule in Russia, adult citizens strove to find a partial compensation for the innumerable anxieties that darkened their public

and private lives in an idealized and even consciously idyllic view of childhood — thus intensifying the Western privileging of childhood. This understanding of childhood included the following norms: an extremely emotional
parent-child relationship; a prolonging of childhood well into adolescence
through the adults' encouragement of dependency in the child, both physical
and psychological; the conscious separation of the child from objective reality
through the withholding of information by adults; and the encouragement of a
fantasy life.[6] After the death of Stalin, Soviet popular culture transformed this
adult desire for a fairy-tale childhood into a recognizable cultural topos. "It is
only at the close of the 1950s, when the spiritual life of the country entered
a new channel, that children affirm their right to the fairy tale [*pravo na
skazku*]," writes Kornei Chukovskii, venerable author of such children's classics as "Moidodyr" and "Mukha-Tsokotukha." But, of course, it was not the
children who affirmed this right to fantasy, to a childhood unfettered by the
mundane requirements of the real world, but adults like Chukovskii himself.[7]
The recent collapse of the authoritarian welfare state that made the fantasy of
fairy-tale childhood both necessary and, to a certain degree, feasible in the
USSR — through state-subsidized networks of children's resorts, clubs, and
after-school activities — has transformed the parameters of the child-adult relationship in Russia today. Using the medium of popular culture, I will examine
the dimensions and consequences of this change.

While researching this chapter in Moscow, St. Petersburg, and Kostroma I
observed the living processes of cultural formation. The connection between
socioeconomic change and cultural transformation literally jumped from the
pages of my research data. The fact that the sources for this data are, in most
cases, children, however, engendered a disquieting sense of empathy and even
apprehension. I could not help but gauge the emotional and psychological price
that is being paid by these most vulnerable members of Russian society for the
privilege of participating in the reconfiguration of post-perestroika culture. A
redefinition of identity is taking place in Russia among all social groups, including children; this redefinition requires a new lexicon of symbols, and popular culture is one of the means through which this lexicon is being formulated.
Russian sociologist B. V. Dubin claims that

> due to the recent changes in the structure of the old pantheon of collective
> symbols, . . . from year to year, from month to month the contours of a
> collective, common and supragroup area of symbolic solidarity grow

ever narrower. . . . [G]ender and age, along with the newly acquired notion of status, are fast becoming the sole remaining indicators of identity
in Russia. . . . [A] second process taking place currently is the narrowing
of universally recognized authorities. . . . [U]nder these conditions, the
only common sphere with any claims toward unifying the orientation
markers of the various social formations is the system of mass media. . . .
[M]ass culture is a system of symbolic adaptation to the changes taking
place — the adaptation to change through routinization.[8]

Toys, television, and comics are the lingua franca of children in the developed world, and the fact that such stock characters of the American child's
subculture as Tom and Jerry, My Little Pony, and Hughie, Dewey, and Louie
have made it into a counting game improvised by a twelve-year-old in Kostroma — an ancient city on the Volga whose very name connotes "provincial
backwater" in Russia itself — is an indicator of the momentous change in Russia's access to this world's commercial culture. It illustrates the degree to which
the Russian child has become conversant in its lexicon. The point of origin for
these images — the United States — reveals another important aspect of popular
children's culture in Russia today: its Americanization. This, in turn, links the
problem of popular children's culture to a much more broadly studied phenomenon: the semiotic role of "Westernization" within the Russian cultural narrative.[9] If "mass culture shows us society talking about itself in the only way it
could,"[10] then what these children have to tell us about Russia today through
their favorite songs, movies, and television programs, through the choices they
make in creating fashions in clothes, toys, and words, sheds a vivid light on the
processes of social and cultural reconfiguration that are taking place within
their country. To cite Kornei Chukovskii again, "Each child's utterance vividly
reflects the historical moment."[11]

From the very beginning of this project I was confronted with a serious
epistemological problem. My initial impulse was to define contemporary Russian popular children's culture simply in terms of how much it resembled or
differed from American children's culture. Yet, the more I worked with actual
Russian material, and the more Russian children I met and interviewed, the
more I began to feel that such an approach would be at best a distortion and
crude simplification, and at worst a case of covert "ugly Americanism." I
lacked an understanding of the Russians' concept of childhood, without which
it would be impossible to appreciate Russian popular children's culture and

changes therein on its own merits. I needed to reorient myself to a Russian perspective.

To start this reorientation process I interviewed a number of adult child-development professionals and pedagogues in Moscow. I decided to use the first, experimental season of *Ulitsa Sezam* as the common ground for these interviews. *Ulitsa Sezam,* the Russian-language version of *Sesame Street,* was getting ready for its television debut at the time I was in Moscow, in August 1996, and a major effort had been organized by the Children's Television Work-shop — the originators of *Sesame Street* — to acquaint Russian pedagogues with the show and its concepts.[12] *Sesame Street* is currently being aired in ninety countries, and in most cases the American version is simply translated into the local language.[13] Russia, however, chose to create a whole new program, fol-lowing guidelines set up by the Children's Television Workshop but based on a Russian cultural idiom, to answer the needs of children in contemporary Russia as defined by child-development professionals.[14] Everyone I interviewed had participated in the educational seminar organized by the Russian Research Division of the *Ulitsa Sezam* project in June 1996, and thus all were attuned to the problem of children's culture and its transferability, and concerned with the fundamental question of what in Russian children's culture was unique and irreplaceable, and what could and should be changed.[15]

When I asked Rina Sterkina, director of the Preschool Education Division of the Russian Federation's Ministry of Education, to define popular children's culture for me she answered with the following statement:

> This is a most unusual classification. I suppose you mean everything which affects a child's consciousness? There is high culture, based on classics from world and Russian art, literature and music; there's folklore;[16] and there's mass culture, music, television, which also affect the child's psyche. A separate sphere is the children's own subculture, which they create by themselves, among themselves, using elements from all of the above. I would call this subculture "elemental/sponta-neous" [*stikhiinaia kul'tura*]. Within the last five years I have noticed a dramatic shift in children's attitude toward many of the fundamental in-stitutions that structure their young lives. Children no longer eagerly an-ticipate their first day of school, for education is no longer a universally recognized value marker. Parents are no longer universally recognized authorities. The sharp differentiation in levels of material wealth is re-

flected in games such as "playing rich" [*igrat' sia v bogatykh*]. A whole status hierarchy has developed in connection with prestigious toys. This affects the child's relationships with his peers in a way which we, in this country, have not experienced before. A prurient interest in the relationship between men and women fostered by and based on the Latin American and American soap operas which have become a staple of adult television viewing is also influencing the form taken by children's games. Five- to six-year-old girls are particularly prone to games based on the adventures of popular soap opera heroines.

Many of these themes were echoed by Elena Krasnikova, a consultant for the Ministry of Education, who is helping to develop a program of ethical and philosophical education for elementary school and high school programs. Krasnikova, whose doctoral dissertation at Moscow State University was entitled "Hedonism and Western Culture," noted the difficulties involved in the conscious attempt by the Ministry of Education to change the focus of schoolchildren from the collective "we" to the individual "I." The connection between the recognition of pleasure as a positive goal and the development of the individual "I" is a question that particularly interests her: "The word *pleasure* [*naslazhdenie*] still had semirisqué connotations four years ago. It was not something which one openly strove for, and certainly not an acceptable standard by which to measure children's activities in school."

We discussed the Snickers candy bar commercial that was being shown incessantly over Moscow television in August 1996. The protagonist was an adolescent boy, and the culminating point was the slogan "Snickers — Heavenly Pleasure" (*Raiskoe naslazhdenie*). Moscow's advertising executives had clearly overtaken the Ministry of Education in acknowledging the pleasure-child connection. Krasnikova commented on the fact that commercial structures were much more sensitive to changes in popular culture than official institutions — and that children and adolescents were often viewed as bellwethers in this process: "Parents and adults in general have lost a great deal of authority in the eyes of the young. Often children see the adults in their lives completely swamped by the mind-boggling speed with which life in Russia is changing daily. Teachers in many cases cannot compete as sources of information with computers or foreign television. Both have been discredited by history. Thus, children are often the trailblazers in the family as far as adjustment to change is concerned."

Both Sterkina and Krasnikova agreed that the major blind spot in the Russian pedagogue's approach to child development is in helping the child deal with his or her emotions and with negative aspects of social behavior. This thought was taken up by Anna G. Genina, the director of the Russian Department of Research and Content of *Ulitsa Sezam:* "Traditionally, the Russian child had no right to any feeling besides those of happiness. All other feelings were deemed unacceptable, and either suppressed or treated patronizingly. This is where *Ulitsa Sezam* can be of great benefit to future generations. The key to practicing the much higher level of self-discipline required for living in a nonauthoritarian and democratic society is familiarity with and control over one's own personal feelings and the ability to deal constructively with others — voluntarily, not under duress."

Galina Trostnianskaia, the deputy editor for the professional child-development magazine *Doshkol'noe vospitanie* (*Preschool Education*), begged to differ:

> *Sesame Street* was developed for American children in the inner cities and ghettoes. It was developed for Third World children. Our problems are different, which is why I did not agree with what I saw during the educational seminar organized by Children's Television Workshop last June. However, the emphasis on educating children about their feelings could be helpful. We in Russia have always stressed how children should behave, without bothering about inner motivation. There is another problem — that of access to information. It has always been deemed the prerogative and even the duty of Russian parents to limit their children's access to information — in this way letting children remain children for as long as possible. This is not in harmony with your Western attitude concerning the need for freedom and choice for children. It's hard to know where to draw the line.

I protested that many American adults feel a similar sense of anxiety concerning the advisability of limiting children's access to certain information. I specifically mentioned the argument brought forth in a book by Neil Postman, *The Disappearance of Childhood,* which postulates that restricted access to adult information is one of the characteristics of the social construct of childhood as it was understood in Western culture from the Renaissance to the late twentieth century, and that its virtual disappearance in contemporary America is a harbinger of the disappearance of the related concept of childhood.[17]

When I asked these women if any of them planned to incorporate features of the "elemental/spontaneous" children's subculture into their own educational activities, all of them said that they had never thought to do so. Thus, while the need for multivocality is clearly felt in reformist pedagogic circles in contemporary Russia, the psychological and methodological flexibility that would actually bring the children's own culture into the classroom is still to be developed.

Genina allowed me to view video clips of sample *Ulitsa Sezam* audiences. Children ages three to seven were filmed watching *Ulitsa Sezam* in Moscow, Tver, Vyshnii Volochok, and Staritsa, among other towns. The goal was to measure the young viewers' attention span as they watched different segments of the program. As I looked at the children on the screen I was struck by the vivid gender differentiation in clothes, hair, and mannerisms between the boys and the girls, a differentiation that has all but disappeared among American nursery and primary school–aged children. Not one girl out of the approximately eighty I observed was wearing trousers or jeans. Most had long hair; the ones who had short hair invariably wore big bows, as if to stress their femininity — the further from Moscow the location of the group filmed, the larger the bows, until in Vyshnyi Volochok and Staritsa they had reached cabbagelike proportions. The children rarely got up from their chairs, despite the fact that no adults were in the room. The most obvious way they showed their boredom was through fidgeting, whispering to each other, and staring at the floor or the ceiling rather than the screen. What I saw was the traditional image of the Russian child: well disciplined, obedient, lacking in initiative, firmly attached from earliest childhood to static sexual and social roles. Yet, all of the experts I interviewed had stressed how much Russian children had changed within the last decade. Where was I to find the parameters of this change? I would have to go to the children, I decided. I would go to parks, toy stores, and kiosks to see what children were buying, what they were reading, how they were playing. I would watch children's programs on television; and finally, I would ask the children themselves to decipher their popular culture for me.

II

I must warn the reader that this study is a conceptual effort based on subjective impressions alone. I would also like to include a caveat concerning my information pool: the children I interviewed are not representative of the Russian population at large. They were predominantly children of the educated urban former middle class of Russia — the "intelligentsia" — children whose parents, teachers, or scout leaders I knew personally. Besides talking with children of acquaintances and friends in Moscow, St. Petersburg, and Kostroma, I also had a questionnaire distributed to the members of the Ksenia Peterburgskaia Russian Scout Troop in St. Petersburg, and to the children attending an ethnographic summer camp, Camp No. 41, sponsored by the Ipatiev Monastery Historical Museum in Kostroma.[18] The questionnaire asked the following questions:

1   Name
2   Date of birth
3   Telephone and address
4   Tell us about yourself. Your family.
5   What do you want to be when you grow up?
6   Who are your heroes/heroines? Whom would you most like to resemble?
7   What is your favorite fairy story? Give a short summary. How did you first hear it? (Did your parents or teacher read it to you? Did you read it yourself?)
8   What is your favorite book? How many times have you read it? Who introduced you to it? Why do you like it?
9   What is your favorite song? Write the first stanza. Where did you first hear it? Why do you like it?
10   How often do you watch television? How many hours per day? Do your parents set time limits on your TV viewing or forbid you to watch certain programs?
11   Which programs do you like the best? Name your three favorite programs, and tell why you like them. Summarize their content.
12   What is your favorite film? Why do you like it? Briefly summarize its plot.
13   How often do you go to the movies or watch videos?
14   What is your favorite toy? Who gave it to you?
15   What new toy would you like?
16   Do you play different games with your friends? Which games do you play? Describe them.
17   How often do you play with your friends? Where?
18   Who taught you these games?
19   Do you have any games that you play alone?

20   Do you or your friends make up new games?

21   How do you make them up? Do you follow the plots of books or films, or do you simply use your imagination?

22   Do you use counting rhymes in your games? What are your favorite counting rhymes? Write them down.

23   When you play, do you follow the rules of the game?

24   Do you tell your friends stories? Briefly tell us the plot of your favorite story that you heard from a friend.

25   Did you ever make up a story yourself? Tell it to us.

26   What kind of clothes do you like best? Do you like fashionable clothing? How do your friends in school dress? What clothing would you like to have that you don't have?

27   What is your favorite color?

28   Do you have a girl/boyfriend? What do you like about them?

29   What is your favorite food?

30   What do you fear the most?

31   Describe your happiest and your saddest day.

32   What is your most cherished wish?

The information I gained as the result of formally interviewing twenty-seven children, and informally talking with about a dozen more, was extremely interesting. I structured the questions to fit my perception of what it means to be a child; I believe that children spend their childhood in creating and learning to manipulate a system of signs whose mastery gains them the skills necessary to cope with both the outer objective world and their inner subjective universe. Children's popular culture arises at the intersection of three separate but related needs: society's need to integrate the child into its structures, the individual child's need to understand and manipulate the social and material world around him or her, and, in a market economy, commercial concerns that spur the creation of an imaginary universe that attempts both to structure and to answer the questions raised by societal and individual needs. Popular culture is the medium through which most children learn, or in the words of a child, my son Paul Zelensky: "It's what kids think is fun. It's what's not boring. It's what makes them happy." I wanted to understand how Russian children managed to continue their "child's" task of unraveling the mysteries of the universe and their inner selves in the unstable economic and social conditions of present-day Russia.

Under the category of inner life, I was most astonished by the answers I got to question 6. A majority of the children said that they had no heroes or heroines and that they most wanted to be like themselves (sixteen out of the twenty-seven answering the questionnaire). This seems to confirm the impression of the child-development professionals that adults have lost some authority in the eyes of the young. The exceptions prove the rule, since the only admired adult personages were either long deceased, foreign, fictional, or all of the above. Ilya Muromets (a hero from medieval Russian epic poetry), Aleksandr Suvorov (a military commander from the early Napoleonic era), Anna Pavlova (this last chosen by a girl who was studying in the St. Petersburg School of Ballet), Jane Eyre, Tristan (from the French medieval epic *Tristan and Isolde*), child characters portrayed in several Soviet-era adventure films and books, Stirlitz (the master-spy protagonist in a Soviet-era TV spy series), Bruce Willis, Jean-Claude Van Damme, and Marilyn Monroe (this last by a ten-year-old girl from Kostroma) were some of the heroic models mentioned. Only one twelve-year-old girl from Kostroma said that she would most like to be like her mother.

I was also intrigued by the answers to two other questions concerning the children's subjective or inner world, questions 30 and 32. There was remarkable agreement in answers to question 30. All of the boys queried, ranging in age from nine to fifteen, in all three cities I visited answered that they were not afraid of anything. In contrast to this, one girl (age 10) wrote that she did not know what she was afraid of, and the rest had a variety of concrete answers. War and uncertainty about the future (*neizvestnost' budushchego*) were the most frequent answers, followed by the loss of loved ones and loneliness. One girl (14) feared going to Hell, another (13) feared God, while another (11) feared that Russia might perish. I found the degree to which the appearance of stoicism as a marker of masculinity had been internalized by male Russian children quite astonishing. Question 30 revealed that most of the children queried were benevolent in their wishes for themselves and their surrounding world. To attend Moscow State University, to always have a happy family life, to help homeless animals, and a wish that everyone would always tell the truth were all on the wish list. An open desire for wealth and pleasure seemed not to be culturally acceptable, since not one of them answered, "to become a millionaire," "to go to Disney World," or "to go to Paris." One girl (a very pretty fourteen-year-old from Kostroma) did write that she hoped "to marry an American or German and live abroad"; and a boy (14), also from Kostroma, said that his most cherished dream was to own a Volvo, so perhaps the antihedonistic bias has begun to disappear.

While in Moscow, I visited friends at their summer house and informally questioned their nine-year-old grandson and two of his friends from neighboring summer houses, girls twelve and sixteen years old. When queried about their favorite cartoon show, comics, and television programs, the children revealed a balance between old and new popular cultures, but with a palpable undercurrent of anti-Western and anticommercial sentiment. The first thing nine-year-old Serezha told me when I asked him about his favorite cartoon was, "Winnie the Pooh, but not yours — ours." It turned out that he had seen both the Russian cartoon version of the English classic and the Walt Disney version, and he wanted to make sure I knew that he liked the Russian one better. Masha and Anya also told me that while they usually liked Walt Disney feature film cartoons (most Russian children I met had seen *The Little Mermaid, Beauty and the Beast,* and *Pocahontas*) they thought the Russian Winnie was better, and that in general Russian cartoons were "kinder" (*dobree*) than American cartoons, excluding Disney's work. While Serezha was enchanted by Woody Woodpecker, whom he pronounced "impudent, but funny" (*nakhalnyi no smeshnoi*), and Sylvester and Tweety Pie, the girls found these cartoon characters irritating and needlessly violent. All three agreed that the cartoons they most disliked came from China and were badly drawn, boring, and ugly. The theme of China as the source for low-grade or shoddy toys, cartoons, and CDS came up time and again in my conversations with Russian children. I do not know if this is inspired by nationalist sentiments or by the actual quality of the Chinese goods. The Chinese Barbie dolls that I saw being marketed in Kostroma did not look any worse than any of the numerous American Barbie knockoffs.

Serezha said that he liked all sorts of comic books, with both Russian and foreign characters; Donald Duck and Goofy and his gang were his favorites. He greatly enjoyed *Three Cossacks* both as a cartoon serial and as the subject of numerous adventure comics. This television show is produced in Russian by the Kiev Children's Cartoon Studio, in Ukraine. According to Tamara Nikolaeva, producer of the popular science program *In the World of Animals* (*V mire zhivotnykh*) and former producer of *Good-night, Kids* (*Spokoinoi nochi, malyshy*), the Kiev studio is one of the last cartoon studios still producing consistently high-quality children's cartoons. When I looked in Russian kiosks or newsstands I did not see any of the highly violent comic books (e.g., Wolverine,

6.1   Masha Pochukaeva
and Serezha Kolomets.
Photo by Nikita
Zelensky.

The Punishers, or Batman) that in the United States are aimed at a young male adolescent audience. There were, however, historical novels in comic-book form — usually medieval Russian knights fighting Tartars. I saw many adaptations of classical literature as comics, which reminded me of the "Cartoon Classics" series popular among bookish children in the United States in the late 1950s and early 1960s. My most surprising discovery was a religious comic book, which I bought in the portico of a church in Kostroma. Entitled *S nami Bog* (*God Is with Us*), it carried the story of Saint Vladimir's baptism of the Rus'. My own observations and the fact that parents never complained to me about their children reading comic books led me to conclude that the comic book has not yet attained its full potential as a subversive genre in Russia.

I first met Masha and Serezha in 1994 (fig. 6.1), and I traced their development as television viewers over the next two years. At the time of my first visit, they knew numerous television commercials by heart and would belt them out at the top of their lungs at the slightest provocation, much to the chagrin of their grandparents and parents. Commercials were still a great novelty and as such attracted their admiration and attention. By August 1996, however, both Masha and Serezha expressed irritation with and dislike of commercials; in fact, one of their favorite television programs was *Avtopark,* a satiric weekly look at commercials. Soap operas also had fallen by the wayside in their television viewing. Although their grandmothers continued to be faithful fans of *Santa Barbara* and *The Rich Also Weep* (*Bogatye takzhe plachut*), Masha and Serezha pronounced these programs "stupid" and for "old ladies." Their choice in television viewing was consistent with that of most of the children I interviewed: quiz shows for children, such as *Zvezdnyi chas* (*Hour of the Stars*) and *Kto, gde, i kogda* (*Who, Where and When?*); contest shows such as *Gorodok*

(*Small Town*), *Ugadai melodiu* (*Guess That Tune*), and *Pole chudes* (*Field of Dreams*); and comical home video contests such as *Sam sebe rezhiser* (*Be Your Own Director*). Anya — the sixteen-year-old — also admitted to watching *Elen i rebiata* (*Hélène and the Kids*), a French *Beverly Hills 90210* clone, for which she was loudly condemned by Serezha ("How can you watch such sentimental tripe?" [*teliachie nezhnosti*]). My conclusion concerning children's television viewing in Russia is that unlike most youthful American TV viewers, Russian children have not yet learned to be passive recipients of images. They prefer programs from which they gain a sense of vicarious participation — contests, guessing games, amateur hours. There also seems to be a link between large doses of television viewing and a greater affinity toward Western culture, including material culture.

During my stay in Kostroma I concentrated on the subject of children's fashions in clothes, hair, and words because of my close acquaintance with two young denizens of that city — Maria and Katia. Maria, age 14, gave me the lowdown on fashions in high school, while Katia, age 10, covered the elementary school angle. Maria went to public school; Katia was enrolled in a private academy. Neither school required a uniform. "They are always threatening us with uniforms," shuddered Maria. Both schools had unwritten dress codes, whose interpretation usually depended on the teacher. "A girl who wore jeans in my class got sent home, but other teachers allow it," Maria noted. "We are not allowed to wear leggings or tight pants. Trousers with a classic cut, dark skirts, white blouses, blazers. No dresses in school, except to the dances. Nothing flashy or provocative. In third grade I was sent home for wearing earrings, but then my mother wrote the teacher a note."

Katia agreed that this was also the dress code in her school, with the exception of blue jean jumpers, which were allowed and very popular. "Basically, jeans are in — jean jackets, jean skirts, jumpers — all of this is very in."

"True," Maria interrupted. "My friends love everything in denim. We just can't wear denim clothes to school. Denim and army boots and minidresses are all very chic now. Long hair is in again. A couple of years ago everyone was cutting it off — but now a more Russian or 'folksy' look is popular."

I asked about punk fashions, multiple ear piercings, body piercing, and odd hair colors, and was told that only a very few boys and one girl in Maria's high school were into punk. Katia's cousin Daniil, a boy of fifteen, wore an earring, but this was considered quite unusual in Kostroma. He was also the only punk in his private school. He wore ripped blue jeans held together with safety pins, and small bells jingled from his jacket. He did not wear these outfits to school, however; they were worn only on social occasions. What was fashionable, and acceptable, for adolescent boys, according to Maria and Katia, were sneakers with platform soles, green or red double-breasted blazers, and pleated trousers. " 'New Russians' [the nouveaux riches] also wear white socks with black shoes, but we think that's a little too much," finished Maria.

"And we think that's just plain stupid," chimed in Katia. "The whole 'New Russian' thing is stupid, and that's why I won't wear that fur coat." Katia's mother then explained that Katia had been given a real fur coat, which she refused to wear because she did not want to be taken for a "New Russian" child in school.

Katia told me the latest fashion in elementary school were minidresses with tights or, in the summer, nylon pantyhose. "Long hair is in again — French braids — especially in a style called 'Little Dragon' and 'Ear of Corn.' " Adidas were out, both girls agreed, while Nikes and Reeboks were in. This was due, according to Maria's mother, to the law of supply and demand. Adidas had been on the market in Kostroma for several years already, therefore they were not that rare. Nikes and Reeboks were still a relatively new phenomenon, and were coveted as such.

Both girls were eager to tell me the latest slang. First, Katia showed me the special language of signs that everyone in her class knew. Her mother and aunt confirmed that they also had a sign language, similar but not identical to what Katia was showing me, when they attended elementary school some twenty-odd years ago in Kostroma. I found this most intriguing, especially since what Katia was doing did not look like American Standard Sign Language, with which I am familiar. "Sharp" (*chetko*) was the universal term of approval used by Katia, although Maria said this expression was already outdated among the older kids. "Classy" (*klasnyi*) and "steep" (*kruto*) were the words they used most often to express what Katia meant by "sharp." I was astonished to hear Maria use the transposed negative that American teenagers gleefully picked up from the movie *Wayne's World* in the early 1990s: Not! "This guy was smart . . . not," she said, as an example of a current slang expression. When I asked her if she had ever heard of *Wayne's World,* she told me she had not.

Maria also said that it was fashionable to pronounce certain letters nasally and with a burr (*kartavit′*). This revelation astonished me, for such speech mannerisms had been, at least for the last seventy-odd years, associated with the prerevolutionary nobility. I myself had recently watched a cartoon on Moscow television, an animated version of a folktale, in which both of the upper-class villains spoke with a burr. When I asked Maria if she associated this manner of speech with the old aristocracy, she answered that she did not have this association, but that she found everything concerning old Russia interesting, and that she would not trade Pushkin for anyone in the world.

Both girls said they liked Michael Jackson, Mariah Carey, Whitney Houston, the Beatles, and Nirvana, as well as various Russian groups. Petlyura, a sort of Russian "bubblegum" music group that specialized in sentimental ballads about thwarted teen-age love, was their favorite. When I asked Maria if she knew who the real Petlyura was (a Ukrainian anti-Soviet partisan and rabid antisemite), she said no, from which one may assume that the whole anti-establishment subtext carried by the name of the group is probably lost on most of its fans. Another group that was quite popular among the more avant-garde members of her class was a metallica band called Gaza Strip.

Katia, along with every other little girl in Kostroma and Russia, loves Barbie. She herself has almost three Barbies — almost, because the one from China, whose hair turned green, barely counts — and another one, "Kristinka," is a Russian version of the American doll, and so does not really count either. She also has a "Ken" and various accessories. Her friend Olesia, both of whose parents are physicians, has seven authentic (i.e., American-made) Barbies, a cause for solemn awe on the part of Katia. When I asked Katia what it was about this doll that she liked so much, she answered without hesitation: "Because she's so different. Because she doesn't look like any Russian doll. Because she has so many neat things — accessories, furniture, houses, cars, which you can get to go with her."

"So you like her because she's foreign?" I asked.

"Yes!"

Katia's mother told me that Barbie appeared on the horizon of the children's consciousness in 1991. This was the time of the original advertising campaign; first it was Barbie alone, then Ken, then the accessories — an ever-growing network of consumer needs was being created around the toy. As the Barbie phenomenon snowballed the doll became a necessity for a normal social life among Russian girls ages 6 to 13. Girls played only games involving Barbies; all their other toys were forgotten. The culminating point was reached in 1993, when a country-wide contest, "The Doll of My Dreams," was organized by Barbie advertisers. Children, both boys and girls, designed costumes for themselves and their Barbies, and the winner, along with his or her family, received a free trip to Orlando, Florida, to Disney World.

Barbie's alien appearance and her endless train of accessories underscore and confirm her function as a marker of Western abundance and glamour. By owning a Barbie, Russian girls can appropriate a tiny piece of the West's magic, play with it, make it their own. The fact that the Barbies were unique when they appeared, that they did not displace a Russian doll of the same type, makes it possible for their young owners to cherish them without the feelings of guilt or ambivalence that currently mar the choice of foreign goods over domestic products for some children.

I became aware of the fundamental link between Barbie and Western glamour when, on several occasions, I tried to explain to girls with Barbies that actually the name "Barbie" is short for Barbara, and therefore they should call their dolls "Variusha" (a diminutive of Varvara, Russian for Barbara). Not a single girl was convinced — they all preferred the more exotic "Barbie."

Stuffed animals are also popular among Russian children of all ages, both male and female. Giant stuffed animals were the toys most often listed as desiderata on the questionnaire (see question 15). Teen-age boys and girls exchanged stuffed animals as gifts; it was considered very cool to carry around a stuffed teddy bear or kitten given by the object of one's affection. When I asked several youngsters why they liked stuffed animals, their answers were rather vague. "Because they're cute and cuddly. Because they are cozy [*uiut-nenkie*]. Because it's so original." I did not find these answers particularly enlightening. Perhaps it is simply the uncertainty of their young lives — the fear of the future that came out so clearly in their answers to question 30 — that has turned the children of Russia back toward that original symbol of comfort and security, the teddy bear (*mishka*).

While almost all of the children I interviewed watched television, very few had access to VCRs or the means to go to the cinema on a regular basis. Their choices for favorite film are nevertheless quite interesting. For children of both sexes younger than thirteen in all three cities, the musical adventure comedy *The Diamond Arm* (*Brilliantovaia ruka*) was the overall favorite, and the songs from this movie were among those most often mentioned by this age group. A close runner-up was *Prisoner of the Caucasus* (*Kavkazskaia plennitsa*). The most striking fact about these choices is that both movies were produced in the mid to late 1960s. To draw an analogy, imagine American children living in New York, Washington, D.C., and Cleveland in the summer of 1996 consistently picking *The Pink Panther* and *It's A Mad, Mad, Mad, Mad World* as their favorite movies.

I try to explain this anomaly in the following fashion: although both *The*

Diamond Arm and *The Prisoner* carry the requisite element of danger and violence necessary for children to experience dramatic catharsis (since their plots revolve around smuggling, robbery, and kidnapping), their exotic settings (the Tropics and the Caucasus Mountains) neutralize their potential danger, while their ultimately Soviet lifestyle–affirming message reconfirms the children's view of a Soviet Union–centered cosmos. The dramatic action of both films is based on a confrontation between native and alien or foreign characters, with the former emerging victorious over the latter. Both movies are escapist fantasies that present the "fairy-tale" childhood scenario of their adult directors and screen writers and thus confirm the old paradigm of child-adult relations. As relics of a simpler time, these films provide comfort and security in a period of heart-stopping social and economic changes. Their popularity will probably fade within a few years, as the future comes to be perceived as less threatening and the past loses some of its golden glow.

Children thirteen and older were more adventurous in their choices; *Die Hard, Mortal Combat, Twelve Monkeys, The Labyrinth, The Godfather,* and *Gone with the Wind* were all popular foreign films. As for Russian-produced films, the vintage romantic spy thriller *Seventeen Moments of Spring (Semnadtsat' mgnovenii vesny)* and a recently produced film (1993), *Everything Will Be All Right (Vse budet khorosho)* — concerning the difficulties of contemporary life — were the two mentioned most often. *Vii,* a horror film based on a Gothic tale by Gogol, was picked as a favorite film by a fourteen-year-old boy from Kostroma, with the qualification, "Because it is *our* first horror film."

These children were apparently free of the axiom "newest-latest-best," which so influences the movie and video choices of children in the West. The age of *The Diamond Arm,* which was filmed more than thirty years ago, did not affect its reception by the children. I surmise that the foreign film choices were dictated more by availability and gender differentiation than by the actual criteria of personal preference; all of the violent Western thrillers (e.g., *Mortal Combat*) were picked by young adolescent boys in what I took to be an affirmation of their masculinity. Most of the boys who chose them came from St. Petersburg and Moscow, making me suspect that these films were not available in Kostroma. None of the girls and no boys younger than thirteen picked any of these films, which brings me to the subject of violence. The Russian children I met had a much lower tolerance for on-screen violence than their American peers. A universal desire for "kind" films, cartoons, and stories was expressed by the younger boys and most of the girls I interviewed. "It's a 'kind' film [*dobryi*]," was the qualifier most often used when describing *Diamond Arm.* Gender seemed to play a less decisive role in the children's choices of domestic movies; both girls and boys picked the Stirlitz thrillers as among their favorites.

At present, the relationship between Russia and the West, as perceived by the population at large, is quite ambiguous. Russian children's popular culture naturally reflects this circumstance. If three years ago, when I began visiting Russia on a regular basis, any American toy or item of clothing automatically assured its proud possessor a high status in his or her circle of friends, currently the situation is more complex. Not choosing a Western film, toy, or item of clothing has become a valid cultural statement among children, and is treated as such by their peers. What makes this development even more intriguing is that the conscious rejection of "Western" items of popular culture is not based on purely economic indicators. Children of well-to-do parents are as often "Slavophiles" in their preferences as children from poorer families are "Westernizers," and vice versa. Katia, the little girl whose family is wealthy enough to send her to private school and to provide her with a fur coat (which she refused to wear because it made her look like a "New Russian's" child), also did not want me to buy her a Snickers ice cream bar: "I like our Russian ice cream better," she said, and all of the other little girls who were walking with us in the Kostroma city park quickly chimed in their agreement. Serezha's foregrounding of his preference for the Russian version of Winnie the Pooh over that of the Disney studios was another indication of this same phenomenon. Perhaps it was because the questions concerning their foreign/native preferences came from me — a visitor — that these children felt it would be detrimental to the image of their homeland to show a preference for foreign products. If so, this seems to show a heightened sensitivity, on the part of nine -and ten-year-olds, to the question of their country's status on the world stage.

On a more positive note, I was struck by the fact that Russian popular culture, unlike that of the West, has yet to undergo the process of fragmentation into ever-smaller age groups that is so clearly driven by the needs of the advertising industry in its quest for ever-greater marketing efficiency. In Russia, grandchildren and grandparents, sixteen-year-olds and twelve-year-olds, boys and girls together, all participate, to a greater or lesser degree, in the same popular culture. When I heard Masha (age 12) say, without a trace of self-consciousness, "Grandmother and I prefer to listen to Radio Nostalgie" (a "golden oldies"– type radio station in Moscow), to which Serezha (9) retorted, "Grandfather and I won't listen to such tripe," I had to wonder at how much our own children have lost. The almost impenetrable segregation by gender and age that American mass culture encourages among children and between generations has not yet reached Russia.

Conclusion

Contemporary Russia is going through a wrenching period of transition. Popular children's culture reflects the different ways adults and children are coping with this situation. Children's popular culture remains a mirror image of the society that gave it birth. Thus, it reflects both fear of the future and the ambiguities of the country's relationship with the West. These negative features, however, are balanced by the appearance of a more realistic, less utopian and ideological vision of life. The desire to grapple with reality rather than indulge in escapism is apparent in the children's rejection of heroic models in favor of being themselves, and in their refusal to be stampeded into blind acceptance of either foreign or Russian imaginary monopolies within the sphere of popular culture.

The adults I interviewed, in their attempts to come to grips with the true psychological needs of children, and not their idealized adult version of such needs, are also striving to gain a more genuine understanding of childhood. They are gradually abandoning the unquestioning anticommercial biases inculcated during seventy-odd years of socialism, and in the process are coming to accept Russian childhood's "contamination" by market forces.[19] As commercialization shatters the traditional Russian visions of childhood, it simultaneously helps destabilize the binary opposition between profane adult sphere and sacred children's sphere that was one of the building blocks of Russia's authoritarian paradigm for society at large; surely the Russian elite's traditional valorization of the rural masses (i.e., *narod*) is rooted in the same cultural semiotic.[20]

A new approach to childhood is gradually evolving. It is becoming acceptable to treat childhood as a crucial stage in human development rather than a fairy-tale vision of paradise lost. This change lifts a heavy burden both from the parents, whose self-imposed duty it had been to provide paradise, and from the children, who had to constantly prove themselves its worthy beneficiaries. This new realism, coupled with the traditionally deep and supportive human relations that have always enriched life in Russia and the Soviet Union, seems to augur well for Russia's children. I feel privileged to have heard their songs of innocence and experience as I witnessed these processes.

Notes

1   Na zlatom kryltse sideli
    Mickey Mouse, Tom and Jerry.
    Scrooge MacDuck i tri utiatka
    A vodit' ikh budet Pon'ka.
    This variation on a traditional Russian counting game rhyme, related to me by twelve-year-old Anya Malova in Kostroma in 1996, is an indication of the inroads made by Western children's popular culture into Russia. This rhyme may be compared with its traditional version, published in 1988, in S. K. Iakub's *Vspomnim zabytie igry* (Moscow: Detskaia literatura, 1988), p. 13:
    Na zolotom / On golden porch
    Kryl'tse sideli / There did sit
    Tsar', tsarevich / A tsar, a tsar's son
    Korol', korelevich / A king, a king's son
    Sapozhnik, portnoi / A shoemaker and a tailor
    Kto ty budesh takoi / Which one will you be?
    All the materials used in writing this article came from cited published sources or were recorded directly by me during a research trip to Russia in August 1996. All the data I collected are in my possession. I thank the International Research and Exchange Board and the National Endowment for the Humanities (Title VIII) for awarding me a Short-Term Travel Grant in 1996 for the purpose of researching this chapter. I alone am responsible for all views expressed. I also thank Richard Stites for his kind interest in this project.

2 For the concept of a "disenchanted" (i.e., completely secularized) world, see Max Weber's "Science as a Vocation," in *From Max Weber: Essays in Sociology,* trans. and ed. H. H. Gerth and C. Wright Mills (New York: Oxford University Press, 1958), pp. 129–58.

3 The argument, first proposed by Philippe Aries in his book *Centuries of Childhood,* trans. Robert Baldick (New York: Vintage Books, 1962), and later developed by Lawrence Stone in *The Family, Sex and Marriage in England, 1500–1800* (New York: Random House, 1977), that the modern period invented the definition of childhood as a privileged stage of cultural rather than merely biological development, which in turn created a sentimental attitude toward children in Western society at large, has recently been challenged by revisionary reinterpretation, most notably that posited by Barbara A. Hanawalt, *Growing Up in Medieval London* (New York: Oxford University Press, 1993). Russia's experience, however, seems to support Aries's view that this peculiar valorization of childhood as a cultural institution is one of the unique characteristics of the West; access to "childhood" in the Western sense has been one of the Russian elite's cultural markers since the eighteenth century, privileging and setting off its possessors from the rest of the population. See Andrew B. Wachtel, *The Battle for Childhood: Creation of a Russian Myth* (Stanford: Stanford University Press, 1990). Chapter 4, "M. Gorky: Anti-Childhood"

(pp. 131–52) demonstrates the class bias associated with the experience of a "privileged," or Western, childhood.

4 Clementine G. K. Creuziger, *Childhood in Russia. Representation and Reality* (Lan-
ham, Md.: University Press of America, 1996), p. xii.

5 Ibid., p. 83.

6 Urie Bronfenbrenner, *Two Worlds of Childhood: U.S. and U.S.S.R.* (New York:
Russell Sage Foundation, 1970), p. 14; Landon Pearson, *Children of Glasnost.
Growing Up Soviet* (Seattle: University of Washington Press, 1990), p. 110: "In most
respects the pupils of Soviet schools, particularly those in their early to mid-teens,
appear much younger than their North American counterparts."

7 Kornei Chukovskii, *Ot dvukh do piati* (Moscow: Izdatel'stvo "Prosveshchenie,"
1966), p. 208.

8 V. D. Dubin, "Kul'turnaia dinamika i massovaia kul'tura segodnia," in *Kuda idet
Rossiia,* ed. T. I. Zaslavskaia and L. A. Akutinian (Moscow: Interpraks, 1994),
p. 224.

9 The diglossia that is a constant in the Russian cultural narrative, in combination with
the notion of boundary as a primary mechanism for semiotic individuation, makes it
possible for the Russians to accept a mass culture whose primary characteristic is its
markings of "foreignness," whether in the literal or the metaphoric sense. From the
seventeenth century onward this diglossia dovetailed with Russians' perception of
the West as the source of a technologically superior civilization, creating a privileged, if ambiguous, position for the notion of Western within the Russian cultural
narrative. "It is not a matter of an actually foreign origin, but rather the foregrounding of the boundary, the barrier which separates the new image presented by mass
culture, from everyday life" (Dubin, *Kuda* p. 228). Also see Yuri M. Lotman, "The
Notion of Boundary," in *The Universe of the Mind,* trans. Ann Shukman (Bloomington: Indiana University Press, 1990), pp. 131–42; and B. A. Uspenskii and
I. Lotman, "K semioticheskoi tipologii russkoi kultury XVIII veka," in *Khudo-
zhestvennaia kul'tura XVIII veka,* ed. I. E. Danilova (Moscow: Institut istorii
iskusstva, 1977), pp. 259–82.

10 James von Geldern, introduction to *Mass Culture in Soviet Russia: Tales, Poems,
Movies, Plays and Folklore,* ed. James von Geldern and Richard Stites (Bloomington: Indiana University Press, 1995), p. xxvii.

11 Chukovskii, *Ot dvukh,* p. 176.

12 *Ulitsa Sezam* was finally aired on October 22, 1996. See Lee Hockstader's article
"Moscow's Moppets Meet the Muppets," *Washington Post,* October 23, 1996, p. 1. I
thank Dr. Charlotte F. Cole of the Children's Television Workshop for her valuable
help in putting me in contact with the Russian research and content team for *Ulitsa
Sezam.*

13 National Public Radio, *Morning Edition,* January 31, 1996; segment 15: "Bert and
Ernie Take Moscow in Russian *Sesame Street.*"

14 "One of the fundamental ideas of the curriculum plan is to help children understand
and value a democratic society, and to feel at home in a new, open world" (*Ulitsa*

Sezam curriculum). The Soros Foundation helped finance the initial research activity for a Russian version of *Sesame Street* as part of its Civic Society Project.

15 I would advise anyone interested in Russian children's culture to read the "Curriculum of the First Experimental Season of *Ulitsa Sezam,*" published by the Russian Department of Research and Content of the Children's Television Workshop; as well as the "Methodological Recommendations for Pedagogues in Preschool Educational Establishments," written by Anna Genina, director of the Russian Department of Research and Development of the *Ulitsa Sezam* Project, and Rina Sterkina. The familiarity of most Americans with *Sesame Street* makes this an invaluable resource, since it clearly delineates which features of the American children's program carry over into the Russian environment, and which are, culturally speaking, meaningless.

16 The treatment of folklore as an important component of early childhood education is one of the most striking differences between the American and Russian visions of childhood. The addition of the "folkloric" Aunt Dasha to the stock of characters on *Ulitsa Sezam* was one of the Russian changes from the original American script. "The child learns language from the people [*narod*], his only teacher is the people," writes Chukovskii in explaining the importance of folk songs, proverbs, and village games in the development of a child's speech (Chukovskii, *Ot dvukh,* p. 88). I watched numerous cartoons on Russian television that were based on folktales. Children's crossword magazines, which I saw many children solving in trains, frequently use proverbs as sources for words — which shows a remarkable facility with folklore on the part of the ten- to twelve-year-olds who seem to be the target audience for such magazines.

17 Neil Postman, *The Disappearance of Childhood* (New York: Vintage Books, 1994).

18 My thanks to Valentina Aleksandrova and Tatiana Voituk for their invaluable help in distributing my questionnaire.

19 Ellen Sutter, *Sold Separately: Parents and Children in Consumer Culture* (New Brunswick: Rutgers University Press, 1993), p. 3. While it is a commonplace to disparage the value of the consumer culture in children's development, I agree with Sutter that the fact that adult culture in developed countries is anchored in the imagery of consumerism makes it axiomatic that children would play out this adult consumption phenomenon. "All members of modern developed societies depend heavily on commodity consumption, not just for survival, but for participation — inclusion — in social networks. . . . Consumer culture provides children with a shared repository of images, characters, plots and themes; it provides the basis for small talk and play, and does it on a national, even global, scale" (p. 9). "Children are creative in their appropriation of consumer goods and media, . . . children create their own meanings from the stories and symbols of consumer culture" (p. 10).

20 See Cathy A. Frierson, *Peasant Icons. Representations of Rural People in Late Nineteenth Century Russia* (New York: Oxford University Press, 1993).

■ **CHAPTER 7**
CATHARINE THEIMER NEPOMNYASHCHY

MARKETS, MIRRORS, AND MAYHEM:
ALEKSANDRA MARININA AND THE RISE
OF THE NEW RUSSIAN *DETEKTIV*

In the 1985 edition of his book on the history of crime fiction, *Bloody Murder,* the British detective novelist Julian Symons maintains that "crime literature is almost certainly more widely read than any other class of fiction in the United States, the United Kingdom and many other countries not under communist rule. In 1940 Haycraft said that in the United States crime stories represented a quarter of all new fiction, and that most of the copies were sold to rental or public libraries. The proportion is probably not much changed today."[1] Today, just over a decade later, Symons's exclusion of countries "under communist rule" sounds a particularly piquant note. In the wake of the collapse of censorship, and soon after that the collapse of the Soviet Union itself — and with it of those cultural institutions that had for decades given shape to the literary process in Russia — the *detektiv* has arguably become at least as avidly sought after by readers in post-Soviet Russia as it is in the West.[2] As one reviewer observed of the contemporary Russian publishing scene: "Any self-respecting publishing house puts out a detective series."[3] As dramatic as the realignment of forces in Russian culture has been, a brief survey of the history of detective fiction in Russia and the USSR suggests that, like other cultural processes that have come to fruition in the glasnost and post-Soviet periods, the current surge in detective fiction was long in the brewing.

Russia, of course, lacks a tradition of detective fiction to rival that of Britain or the United States, whose writers have historically dominated the genre. Yet quite apart from the vexed issue of whether *Crime and Punishment* and *The Brothers Karamazov* are too "serious" to be subsumed by the category, by the 1870s, now forgotten writers such as Nikolai Dmitrievich Akhsharumov and A. S. Panov were publishing what were then termed *ugolovnye romany* (crime novels). And, as O. Krasnolistov tells us, "at the end of the nineteenth and beginning of the twentieth centuries dozens of detective novellas and novels were published in newspapers, journals, and separate editions. A. A. Shkliarevskii, N. P. Timofeev, N. E. Geintse, A. A. Sokolov, and A. M. Pazukhin may be named among the best-known authors of the detective genre."[4] Nevertheless, detective fiction was generally identified as an "import" from the West, and it experienced its most remarkable periods of popularity in early twentieth-century Russia at transitional moments of social instability when more or less relaxed censorship allowed market considerations to come to the fore. The first spurt came in the wake of the revolutionary upheavals and abolition of censorship in 1905. This "detective boom,"[5] which fed on serialized Russian adaptations of the adventures of such favorites as Sherlock Holmes, Nat Pinkerton, and Nick Carter, was short-lived, peaking in 1908 and dropping off precipitously thereafter.[6] In Russia, as in other countries, the rise of mass fiction aroused emotions little short of horror among the intellectual elite. In a particularly vituperative 1908 article entitled "Nat Pinkerton," Kornei Chukovskii left little doubt as to the issues at stake. Viewing Nat Pinkerton as an emblem of the times, a bastardized offspring of Sherlock Holmes whose fist and greed for financial gain had replaced his predecessor's intellect and devotion to the art of puzzle solving "for art's sake," Chukovskii bemoaned this product of the "savage" taste of the urban petty bourgeoisie (*meshchanstvo*) as a challenge to the intelligentsia's hegemony over culture. With what in the light of hindsight seems almost prophetic acuity, moreover, he linked this looming shift in cultural power relations to a change in the function of the author, to the usurpation of Sherlock Holmes from Arthur Conan Doyle, his "individual creator," by the "nameless authors of the *Adventures of Nat Pinkerton*."[7]

The second spurt in Russian interest in detective fiction came during the relatively freewheeling early years of the NEP, fueled by an unstable and inevitably temporary meeting of literary theory, highbrow parody, a more or less competitive market, and a politically motivated desire simultaneously to encourage literacy and to indoctrinate. The Serapion brother Lev Lunts called on Russian writers to learn plotting from such Western masters as Conan Doyle, while the Formalists studied the plot construction of popular fiction.[8] In 1923, Nikolai Bukharin purportedly called for the creation of "red Pinkertons" as a counterbalance to the literature of entertainment being issued by private publishing houses and to Western *pinkertonovshchina,* which was presumably designed to distract workers from the revolutionary movement.[9] The most touted of these "ideological" detective fictions, apparently inspired directly by Bukharin's challenge, was Marietta Shaginian's *Mess-Mend: A Yankee in Petrograd (Mess-Mend: Yanki v Petrograde,* 1923), published under the pseudonym Jim Dollar.[10] Although the serially published novel was a commercial success, critics judged this attempt (and others like it) to combine entertainment and ideology a failure, and this judgment and the formidable cultural biases from which it sprang in effect guaranteed that detective fiction would remain on the periphery of Soviet literature.

Detective fiction all but ceased to exist in the Soviet Union under Stalin's rule. Beginning already in the 1920s, even such "classics" as the works of Conan Doyle were removed from libraries along with other objectionable "boulevard" literature, and with the shutting down of private publishing houses, detective fiction was no longer published.[11] The reasons for its disappearance were deeply rooted in the driving forces of the culture of socialist realism. The suppression of crime literature and other popular fiction, first of all, stands as a testimony to the curious marriage of politics and highbrow culture that blossomed under Stalin and persisted under his successors. As I noted above in relation to Chukovskii's comments on the prerevolutionary burgeoning of crime fiction, the mass appeal of popular fiction posed a very real threat to the intelligentsia's control over culture. And, as has become eminently clear in the light of the virtual collapse of the educated elite's preeminent status in post-Soviet Russia, despite the unquestionable sufferings endured by members of that group at the hands of the Soviet regime, the intelligentsia survived as a coherent group throughout the Soviet period in no small measure as a result of the regime's artificial inflation of the role of high culture. From the point of view of the political powers that be, literature considered escapist distracted readers from more serious ideological concerns, and the detective novel in particular seemed to incarnate harmful values. As any number of commentators on detective fiction have pointed out, the formula of the genre intrinsically upholds the prevailing social order by exposing and extirpating deviance. In traditional Western detective fiction, crime is directed against private property or rooted in the private realm of passion. In the former case, the unmasking and punishment of the criminal becomes an affirmation of the capitalist structure, while in the latter, crime appears as a universal aspect of human nature. Both sources of crime would have been equally inimical to Soviet socialist utopian ideology, which identified the origins of crime as social and therefore "curable," and moreover, traced them to the injustices of the very capitalist system upheld by Sherlock Holmes and his confreres. Detective fiction did manage, however, to survive in the safe haven of children's literature; for example, in Anatoly Rybakov's *The Dagger* (*Kortik,* 1948). Rybakov's novella — which, in the spirit of the "red Pinkerton," combines an adventure-packed mystery plot with the story of the origins of the Komsomol — was read with apparent pleasure by generations of Soviet adolescents at least up until the glasnost period.[12]

With the coming of the cultural "thaw" after Stalin's death, the detective novel for adults returned to the Soviet Union as well. Among the most popular Soviet writers of the genre were Arkady Adamov and Yulian Semenov, both of whom began publishing in the late 1950s; Lev Ovalov, whose *Adventures of Major Pronin* (*Prikliucheniia Maiora Pronina*) came out in 1957;[13] the brothers Arkady and Grigory Vainer, who had achieved substantial popularity by the late 1960s; and Nikolai Leonov, who published his first *detektiv* in 1970. Like their Western counterparts, these writers created series detectives, including Ovalov's Major Pronin, Adamov's Vitaly Losev, the Vainers' Pal Palych Znamensky, and Leonov's Lev Gurov. The most spectacularly successful of these creations (in the Soviet period, at least) was Semenov's double agent Maksim Isaev, who in the course of the political thrillers chronicling his adventures infiltrated the Nazi high command as Max Otto von Stirlitz.[14] Isaev-Stirlitz, as played by the actor Viacheslav Tikhonov, was further popularized in the television serial *Seventeen Moments of Spring* (*Semnadtsat' mgnovenii vesny*), based on the 1968 Semenov novel of the same name. Works by the Vainer brothers were also adapted for the screen, including the TV movie *The Meeting Place Cannot Be Changed* (*Mesto vstrechi izmenit' nelzia*), based on their 1975 novel *Era of Mercy* (*Era miloserdiia*), which offered a glimpse at the seamier side of life in the USSR during the postwar years.

Detective fiction by foreign authors also reappeared in the Soviet Union in the decades after Stalin's death. A 1971 *Literaturnaia gazeta* article expressed concern that virtually all foreign literature published in Soviet journals consisted of detective fiction, pointing out that fifteen works by Agatha Christie alone had appeared in Soviet journals between 1966 and 1970.[15] One commentator remarked that the predominance of detective fiction in translated literature testified to a "great demand for the detective genre" among Soviet readers, especially when viewed in the light of the fact that "home-produced detective fiction" (*otechestvennye detektivy*) was being issued even in the 1960s in large print-run editions. He concluded that since the time when such "red Pinkertons" as Shaginian's *Mess-Mend* had been sold in editions mounting to "tens and hundreds of thousands of copies," the demand for such works not only had not decreased, but seemed to have increased.[16] V. Kardin, writing during the first glimmerings of glasnost in 1986, provided some rather sobering statistics: only 5–6 percent of readers, including schoolchildren whose reading demands are largely dictated by the academic program, regularly turned to the classics, "the leader of literature."[17] The article suggests that detective fiction, on the other hand, enjoyed a level of popularity in the USSR comparable to that in the West. Thus Kardin goes on to say that "only 10–15 percent of booksellers' orders" for such reading matter were being met, despite the fact that "detective fiction is issued in enormous print runs, published in the mass series Military Adventures [Voennye prikliucheniia], Feat [Podvig], and others."[18] In sum, whatever illusions Western scholars may have entertained about the reading habits of Soviet Russians — illusions most likely fed by a lack of credible statistics for patterns of reading and wishful thinking on the part of the intelligentsia who monopolized the national literary press — well before glasnost Russians were reading a great deal of detective fiction, and were clamoring for more.

The easing and eventual curtailment of censorship along with the increasing orientation of the Soviet publishing industry toward market considerations during the glasnost period created conditions favorable to satisfying the demand for popular reading matter. However, Soviet writers — and their detectives — who had made their reputations earlier found that the changing situation constituted more a crisis than a windfall. Although some Soviet detective novelists, notably Semenov, jumped on the glasnost bandwagon,[19] most writers in the genre found themselves in a situation faintly analogous to but unquestionably far worse than that of such Western cold war best-selling authors as John

Le Carré. Having had to justify its existence to a cultural establishment wary of entertaining literature as well as to conform to rigid oversight by the Ministry of Internal Affairs (MVD),[20] Soviet detective fiction had been ideologically tendentious and populated by squeaky-clean "positive heroes" who represented the now discredited political system and the police force now exposed as riddled with corruption.[21] Of the writers of "canonical" Soviet *detektivy,* only Nikolai Leonov, having successfully recast his inspector Lev Gurov as a "superman" struggling against the forces of the Mafia, remained among the top bestsellers in Russia in 1996.[22] It is thus hardly surprising that by the summer of 1991, hurriedly translated editions of the works of Western writers — foremost among them Agatha Christie and the British author of sensational crime fiction James Hadley Chase[23] — had not only begun to edge out the returning "serious" literature of émigré and previously proscribed Soviet writers from the tables of street vendors in Moscow, but had far outpaced their Soviet counterparts in popularity as well. After the initial dominance of translated literature, however, works by such Russian émigré writers as Eduard Topol' and Fridrikh Neznansky began to make inroads in the market.[24] The most interesting development, however, was the appearance, beginning in the early 1990s, of a new generation of "home-grown" Russian writers, who by mid-decade were more and more frequently topping the best-seller lists (themselves a product of the commercialization of the book market).[25]

Nancy Condee and Vladimir Padunov have aptly termed this radical change in the landscape of Russian literature, driven by a dramatic surge in interest in and availability of all types of formulaic fiction, "the wholesale social displacement of the cult of high culture."[26] This marginalization of the former cultural elite and the collapse, or near collapse,[27] of the government-sponsored institutions that supported its ostensible cultural predominance, along with the sensational proliferation of new publishers and publications, have landed — or stranded — Russian readers in an unfamiliar land governed by different rules and unaccustomed road signs. Readers who took what they could get under the old system now have to get used to making choices, especially given burgeoning book prices and wages eroded by inflation. On the other hand, with big money being made in the popular publishing industry, publishers vie with one another to find new advertising come-ons to lure readers — still unused to high-pressure sales tactics — into parting with their money.

For example, the generic designation *detektiv* (perhaps best translated by Symons's equally ecumenical "crime fiction"), as defined by the assortment of books jumbled together in such series as Lokid's Contemporary Russian Detective Fiction (Sovremennyi rossiiskii detektiv) or Eksmo's Black Cat (Chernaia koshka) series, covers a wide range of formula fiction from *boeviki* (thrillers), even *superboeviki,* and political thrillers to *ostrosiuzhetnye romany,* murder mysteries, and even what at least one critic has categorized as the "woman's roman noir" (*chernyi zhenskii roman*).[28] There is, of course, considerable "leakage" not only between these subdivisions of the *detektiv,* but between the *detektiv* and such other popular genres as fantasy, science fiction, and the romance novel. Nonetheless, the gamut remains broad enough that all works grouped together under a given heading will hardly appeal to all readers. One reviewer deplored in particularly vivid terms the plight of the contemporary Russian fan of popular fiction:

> Take a look at any bookstand — you'll be dazzled by the distorted physiognomies and black muzzles of pistols aimed right at the forehead of the potential reader. And all the same bright, loud, cellophane. . . . Red-blue-black with gold. By the way, very often the picture on the cover has no relationship whatsoever to the text located under that very cover. And the selection of names in series looks just as absurd as their format. Buying books in one and the same series, you may run into quite a powerful *detektiv,* or you may get "something" in a poke. And, truly, it's a shame when Viktor Dotsenko and Aleksandra Marinina stand right next to each other in a stand with identical cellophane covers. If some neophyte happens to buy Dotsenko, he'll shrug his shoulders on the fifth page and won't buy any more books in that series. And too bad. That series is not filled with Dotsenko alone. The opposite can happen: Marinina's intelligent *detektivy* will hardly be to the taste of potential readers of Dotsenko.[29]

Viktor Dotsenko and Aleksandra Marinina do in fact represent the opposite poles of the spectrum covered by the *detektiv* in Russia today. While reviewers and her publisher's advertising copy have dubbed Marinina the "Russian Agatha Christie," the hero at the center of Dotsenko's serial novels — a returning Afghan veteran named Savely Govorkov ("he's Rex, a.k.a. the rabid" [*on zhe Reks, on zhe beshenyi*]) who singlehandedly battles the forces of the Russian Mafia — has been persistently labeled the "Russian Rambo."[30] Aside from suggesting the effectiveness of invoking Western models to help orient the Russian reader in the confusing new book landscape, these slick clichés, even if only loosely accurate, do convey some idea of the distance between Dotsenko's *superboeviki* and Marinina's murder mysteries.[31] Even more interesting, by April 1997, according to *Knizhnoe obozrenie* (*Book Review*), Marinina and Dotsenko were locked in a "best-seller race" for the status of top-selling writer in Russia. Moreover, while Dotsenko had held that position virtually un-challenged for some three years, Marinina seemed to be taking the lead.[32]

Aleksandra Marinina is the pseudonym of Marina Alekseeva, a police lieu-tenant colonel who holds a doctorate in jurisprudence and worked until re-cently in crime analysis and prognostication at the Moscow Juridical Institute. Marinina began writing fiction in 1991, when she coauthored a *detektiv* on the narcotics Mafia which was published in the journal *Police* (*Militsiia*) in 1992. The first two works she wrote on her own, introducing the policewoman who has become her signal character, were also published in *Police*. Only at the end of 1995 did Lokid and Eksmo, major publishers of detective fiction, approach her, and her first two books appeared in the spring of 1995. To date she has published eighteen novels and novellas, which in Russia have sold copies running into the double-digit millions.[33] Like many other detective novelists, then, Marinina produces books with remarkable speed, writing them on the computer at work, at home, and on vacation, thinking through the twists of her convoluted plots as "she makes her way to work on public transport with two transfers in rush hour (an hour and a half each way). At the same time during this time she observes her readers devouring her books."[34] Claiming that the enormous print runs of her books affect her little, since she is paid flat-rate honoraria, Marinina maintained in early interviews that her newfound literary fame had changed her life hardly at all: "Marinina-Alekseeva as before arrives at work around nine, and leaves at seven, rides the subway, wears civilian clothes, which in style and color in no way stick out from the general picture of police surroundings, and the only thing she has allowed herself in her words, from what she has earned as a writer is to buy a new fur coat."[35] The purported normality, even austerity, of Marinina's life, despite her meteoric rise to fame as a writer, led reviewers to compare her with the main character of her books. In this context, one commentator observed: "Although in fact I do not exclude the possibility that the author of best-sellers, whose publishers, if they are not complete fools, must seriously play her up, aiming, potentially, at movie rights as well, could shape her image literally on the fly."[36]

Marinina, then, like other best-selling authors in Russia today, has herself become a salable commodity. Thus, a journalist who attended a recent "presentation" of the new ten-volume edition of Marinina's works noted that while a great deal was made of Marinina during the evening, including the revelation of "incredibly touching details" of her biography, almost nothing was said about the books that were being "presented":

> Finally, . . . at the buffet reception that same literary agent and assistant director of the MVD juridical institute Nathan Zablotskis openly announced that the presentation was part of a big Eksmo advertising campaign, completely devoted not to the books, but to the author. Its component parts include visits by Marinina on television programs of the most diverse character, from Oleinikov's *My Cinema* to cosmetics shows, and the publication of biographical sketches in various publications. The main task is to obtain a recognition reaction [*reaktsii uznavaniia*] from the reading masses. By a remarkable coincidence, Marinina's presentation to journalists took place in the "Tolstoy" hall, and the buffet afterward — in the "Pushkin" hall. Probably, the Eksmo people have the idea that the fashionable detective lady [*modnaia detektivnaia dama*] should take her place in those ranks, not in the sense of the classic quality of her prose, but by [the principle of] automatic association: fruit–apple, detective fiction–Marinina.[37]

This commodification of the author arguably represents the other side of the coin of the anonymity of authorship deplored by Chukovskii early in the twentieth century. (Tellingly, it has recently been rumored that Marinina has become a "collective.")

In the game of images, moreover, all the better if the author's image resembles that of her series detective, which in the given case happens to be so. Marinina's "heroine" is Anastasiia Kamenskaia, like her creator a police lieutenant colonel who works as an analyst (*analytik*). Kamenskaia, however, works not in an institute, but at 38 Petrovka, the central police headquarters in Moscow. Kamenskaia's character is based on the premise that she remain in her Petrovka office, drinking cup after cup of coffee and chain smoking, while her male colleagues do all the legwork of gathering evidence and interviewing suspects. She then solves what are generally devilishly complex crimes by subjecting the material the men gather to cold, machinelike logic combined with an extraordinary imagination, which allows her to (re)construct multiple narratives based on the evidence and ultimately arrive at the "correct" story. While the premise that Kamenskaia works solely out of her office is in fact honored more in the breach, her crime busting is always a function of intellect rather than force, and she fires a gun only at target practice to focus her thoughts. In fact, her physical vulnerability is underscored by the fact that she suffers from chronic back problems and periodic attacks of low blood sugar. Dogged in her pursuit of criminals, Kamenskaia is pathologically lazy away from her job. We are repeatedly told that she can barely drag herself out of bed in the morning, and it takes quantities of her beloved coffee and linguistic exercises in the shower to get her going. (Kamenskaia knows five languages fluently and spends her vacations translating Western detective novels into Russian.) She is particularly "lazy" — and generally incompetent — when it comes to anything that might be termed "women's work," especially cooking. Not only does every male in her life seem to know his way around a kitchen better than she does, but virtually all of them — from her husband, her wheelchair-bound ex-lover, and her stepfather to her colleagues and even the criminals she is tracking — end up cooking for her. Kamenskaia's most distinctive feature, however, is her thoroughly nondescript appearance, underscored by her own conviction that she is physically (and, at least implicitly, sexually) unattractive, a judgment confirmed by the lack of interest she generally inspires in men on first meeting. On the other hand, her face is a "blank slate," a "gift" that allows her, with the aid of makeup, mimicry, and stylish clothing (she generally wears jeans, sweatshirts, and sneakers), to transform herself, quite literally beyond recognition, into a strikingly seductive alter ego. Kamenskaia, however, uses her talent for "disguise" (that is, she uses makeup) only in police work, refusing to dress herself up for those close to her, whether it be her mother or the men in her life. In her demand that people take her as she is, whether it is a question of physical appearance or the way she chooses to prioritize her life, Kamenskaia is consistently classified as different from "normal" Russian women.

While Marinina clearly drew on her own autobiography for her conception of her heroine, she equally clearly took more than a hint or two from the detective fiction she claims to have loved all her life. In one interview she maintained that she aims to combine detective mystery with the romance novel in the manner of Sidney Sheldon, and she named Georges Simenon and the Vainer brothers as her favorite writers in her own genre.[38] Her texts, however, make passing references to other Western models that have left their imprint on her characters and plot structures. Kamenskaia certainly owes her image as a sedentary intellect safely ratiocinating within an interior space locked off from the outside world of crime and criminals in part to Sherlock Holmes's "smarter brother," Mycroft, and in part to Rex Stout's Nero Wolfe, who also passed on to her his proverbial laziness, if not his bulk or refined palate. Marinina's use of an ongoing cast of characters, and particularly her focus on a police team (the "Department for Particularly Dangerous Crimes") whose members — with Kamenskaia as their intellectual center — share the investigative labor, are reminiscent of the 87th Precinct police procedurals of Ed McBain, whose works Kamenskaia translates when on vacation from her police duties. As far as female models are concerned, the persistent invocations of Agatha Christie by critics would seem to have little more than "brand name" value, identifying Marinina as a woman writer of puzzle murder mysteries. More pertinent, perhaps, is a passing reference to the far less well-known American mystery writer Charlotte Armstrong. Particularly interesting in this context is Armstrong's technique of more or less explicitly casting her detective fictions as reworked fairy tales.[39] In what is probably the first work in the Kamenskaia series, *Coincidence* (*Stechenie obstoiatel'stv*), Kamenskaia's ability to transform herself from a mousy, sexually unappealing physical nonentity into a femme fatale is implicitly compared to the fairy-tale-like transformation of Hans Christian Andersen's ugly duckling into a swan and to Cinderella's (Zolushka's) transformation into a desirable mate for a prince.[40] This fairy-tale element in the portrayal of Kamenskaia (which sometimes seems almost to resemble a female variant on Clark Kent as alter ego for Superman, at least as far as sexual power is concerned) runs throughout the series and certainly accounts for some of the appeal of Marinina's fiction to female readers.

Although it would be problematical to identify Marinina as a "feminist" writer in any recognizably Western sense of that word, viewing her works in the light of some Western scholarship on feminist detective fiction may help to explain her popularity with contemporary Russian readers. Sandra Tomc, for example, suggestively contrasts the hard-boiled feminist detective fictions Sue Grafton and Sara Paretsky began writing in the 1980s with what she terms "the feminist mystery after feminism" of the early 1990s, taking as her examples of the latter the British television series *Prime Suspect,* the Patricia D. Cornwell novel *Postmortem,* and the American big-box-office film *The Silence of the Lambs.*[41] She begins by pointing out that it is a fundamental principle of feminist detective fiction to locate the origin of crime in patriarchal social structures. "Moments of metaphoric confusion or mistaken identity" render the female murder victim and the female detective "dangerously interchangeable":

"Within the terms of this feminist polemic, *all* women are subordinated objects, a fact that is driven home precisely through the confusion of the detective — the traditional repository of knowledge and authority in the mystery narrative — with the female murder victim, the one whose knowledge has been annihilated. Frequently, the confusion is literalized as the detective herself becomes a target of the killer; she becomes the victim whose murder she is trying to redress."[42] Grafton's and Paretsky's detectives, Kinsey Milhone and V. I. Warshawski, rebel against these repressive institutions, Tomc argues, by becoming private eyes — loners and outsiders. As in the fictional worlds of male predecessors such as Raymond Chandler and Dashiel Hammett, crime in feminist detective novels is endemic to the social fabric, not an aberration, a temporary disturbance of the order restored by the intellectual victory of Holmes and his successors in classic British detective fiction. "The hard-boiled detective contents himself or herself with defeating a small portion of the chaotic element, usually, in the genre's tradition of individualism, one on one." In the case of the female "dick," "her defeat of the criminal each time is what allows her to entertain options, like living and working alone, since it illustrates to her, and to us, the possibility of her altering the conditions of her victimization."

In contrast, in the "feminist mysteries after feminism" of the 1990s the female detective functions not as an outsider, Tomc says, but rather as a member of a large law enforcement agency. Her vulnerability is underscored by the nature of the crimes themselves, serial acts of sex and violence by men against women, depicted in gruesome detail. While, for example, Clarice Starling's pursuit of investigative threads on her own in *The Silence of the Lambs* leads in the end to the criminal, this dangerous "autonomy" almost puts her in the place of the victim and motivates her return to the protective embrace of "her 'normal' FBI family with its more 'normal' father figure." The moral, Tomc argues, is that "the threatening, even gothic, nature of the criminal acts, together with an emphasis on the female detective's helplessness in the face of them, ensures that packing up and lighting out is never a real option. Full of stalkers, serial killers, and cannibals, the world the detective inhabits is, we are told, too dangerous for a woman working on her own." The price the female detective must pay for protection in the 1990s, Tomc concludes, is the sacrifice of her personal life, which is marred by threatening and abusive relations with men, to her professional life, and of her self-definition as a woman to her self-definition as a professional law enforcement officer, "one of the guys." This inconsistent compromise with the male establishment, Tomc concludes, leaves the female detective trapped in cramped spaces, suffering from claustrophobia.

I have rehashed Tomc's argument at some length because I believe that an examination of the ways in which Marinina's works follow — or, perhaps more to the point, depart from — the paradigms Tomc describes can lead us to one source of their appeal in the form of the anxieties they simultaneously express and neutralize. Kamenskaia certainly shares with her Western opposite numbers the vulnerable status of the female detective as potential victim. In *Coincidence,* not only is the murder victim clearly an alter ego for Kamenskaia, but in the second half of the book, Kamenskaia, in what is apparently her first field assignment, is set up as bait to catch the professional hitman-killer and almost becomes his next victim. In Marinina's second book, *Playing on Another's Field,* one of the murder victims is clearly a surrogate for Kamenskaia. In *Death for the Sake of Death* she again becomes the target of professional hitmen. In *Death and a Little Love,* the novel in which Kamenskaia marries her longtime boyfriend, the bride who takes her place in line at ZAGS when Kamenskaia refuses to go through the full marriage ritual is murdered. Brutal crimes against women abound, in at least two cases lingering as haunting evidence of Kamenskaia's failures. Thus, at the end of *Another's Mask,* after Kamenskaia has brilliantly unraveled a devilishly clever and convoluted series of murders, a rape remains unsolved, a synecdoche for the rampant and random abuse of women afoot in the society. Even more disturbingly, at the end of *Death and a Little Love,* a female rape victim is brutalized and held hostage as a pawn in the duel of wits between Kamenskaia and the male murderer, who resolves to kill the woman by slowly draining the blood from her body. Kamenskaia ingeniously succeeds in keeping the criminal engaged in a telephone conversation with her, thereby distracting him so the male SWAT team can take him by surprise. Despite Kamenskaia's valiant efforts, neither the criminal nor his victim is saved. Tellingly, however, Kamenskaia clearly identifies with the male murderer rather than with his female victim — and is more upset by his death as well.

As the latter episode should make clear, Marinina's works fit snugly into neither of Tomc's paradigms for the feminist detective novel, although they do display a closer affinity to the 1990s texts Tomc examines. Kamenskaia is, after all, not a private detective but a representative of the police. She is, moreover, surrounded by a protective male collective. And although Tomc argues that the woman detective must struggle to gain acceptance from her initially misogynistic male colleagues, Kamenskaia, by the time we meet her, is viewed not with hostility or even mere tolerance but with respect by the men in her department, most notably its head, Viktor Alekseevich Gordeev (affectionately nicknamed

"Kolobok" by his subordinates), Kamenskaia's mentor–father figure who recognized her talent, brought her into his team from the suburban police force, and guides her career with wise paternal advice. Yura Korotkov, Kamenskaia's closest co-worker, who confides the vagaries of his love life to her, and Misha Dotsenko, the youngest member of the team, who stands so in awe of Kamenskaia's superior intellect that he can bring himself neither to address her by the host of diminutives — Nastia, Asia, Nastenka — employed by her other male colleagues nor to use the familiar form of address with her. Tellingly, any hostility Kamenskaia may experience from co-workers outside her department is ascribed not to her gender but to the nature of her unfamiliar position as an *analytik* who remains holed up in her office doing mental labor rather than going into the field. It is only when Kamenskaia leaves the protective confines of her office that she finds herself at risk. More significantly, when Kamenskaia does find herself a potential victim, it is almost always when she is "disguised" as a sexually alluring female. The implicit moral is that it is specifically sexual autonomy that turns woman into victim.

In any case, whenever Kamenskaia is in danger there is always at least one male conveniently around to save the day; and when she does find herself in a one-on-one confrontation with a villain, her protective male collective is never far away. For example, her male colleagues are there to monitor her nightlong vigil with the hitman who plans to take her life in *Coincidence* as well as her verbal duel with the murderer in *Death and a Little Love,* which takes place over the telephone from the safety of her office. If, as Tomc argues, Western female detectives of the 1990s suffer from claustrophobia, constricted by their entrapment within male institutional structures, Kamenskaia suffers from agoraphobia — she cannot stand being in crowds. The fact of the matter is that Kamenskaia is in her element when she is in her office safely surrounded by solicitous men.

Marinina's portrayal of Kamenskaia's private life departs even more markedly from Tomc's feminist detective paradigms. Although her relationships with her sister-in-law, Dasha, and Korotkov's girlfriend, Lusia, are cordial, Kamenskaia has no close female friends, and her relationship with her mother, Nadezhda Rostislavna, a renowned linguistics scholar, is doubly distant, first of all because the latter has spent most of her time in Sweden, and, second, because when she visits and finally returns to Russia, she persistently tries to reform her daughter's inattention to her appearance and dislike of social functions and "proper" eating habits.[43] In contrast, as far as the men in her life are concerned, Kamenskaia is singularly blessed. In place of the wicked step-mother of fairy tales, she has a good stepfather, who has also worked for the police his whole life and who more than makes up for her absent father, serving at home, as Gordeev does at work, as Kamenskaia's mentor. Aleksei Chistakov, a brilliant mathematician, Kamenskaia's boyfriend in the earlier works and later her husband, has been devoted to Kamenskaia since the two met while students. He weathered with fortitude the one passionate affair Kamenskaia has had in her life, and although he himself gets carried away from time to time (at least before the marriage) by bursts of lust, he becomes bored with his sexual partners after two or three days and realizes yet again that Kamenskaia, despite her persistent refusals to marry him over a period of some fifteen years, is the only woman for him. Then there is Kamenskaia's half-brother, Aleksandr, her father's son by his second wife. A successful businessman and physically a male carbon copy of his half-sister, Aleksandr is as devoted to Kamenskaia as her stepfather and boyfriend/husband are. These men, especially Chistakov, form the same type of protective buffer around Kamenskaia outside her office as her male colleagues do on the job. Her physical vulnerability away from work is particularly underscored by her chronic back problems, bouts of which set in whenever she carries anything heavy (generally groceries) and leave her immobilized on the floor of her apartment, sometimes for days, dependent on Chistakov to minister to her needs. Moreover, although Kamenskaia initially lives alone, insisting that she and Chistakov keep their separate apartments even after their marriage (a plan that falls by the wayside in later books), the risk this attempt at geographical autonomy places her in is highlighted when the door of her apartment is rigged to explode when she enters.

Kamenskaia refuses to put on makeup or fashionable clothing to please the men in her life, insisting that they accept her as she is, which they are all more than willing to do. In fact, Chistakov, her stepfather, and her half-brother seem at times to know her better than she knows herself, and with predictable reg-ularity manage to anticipate her every need.[44] Thus, Kamenskaia finally capitu-lates and agrees to marry Chistakov not because she is suddenly overwhelmed by passionate love for him, but because he realizes that she would prefer that he spend their vacation money on a computer she needs for her work. Moreover, he is so certain that she will choose the computer over the trip that he goes out and buys the computer before he hears her answer. When he presents her with this fait accompli, she realizes that no one will ever love her and accept her as he does, including, as the none too subtle symbolism of the computer suggests, understanding that her work will always come first. For all their compatibility (Chistakov is as much of a workaholic as Kamenskaia) and mutual comprehension, their marriage is at best sexually pallid and implicitly infertile.

That female sexuality amounts to little more than an impetus to depersonalization is made clear in *The Stylist,* when Kamenskaia is reunited in the course of a criminal investigation with her old flame, the one passionate love of her life, exactly a year after her marriage. Despite the facts that she initially feels the old attraction and that her former lover, who has been crippled and confined to a wheelchair, claims now to love her, she finds she is no longer interested in him because he does not understand who she truly is, that is, does not comprehend her devotion to her work. By the same token, she discounts the attraction a private detective, with whom she has a one-night stand in *Coincidence,* claims to feel for her, writing it off to her disguise. Kamenskaia shies away from sexual allure, it would seem, because it renders her interchangeable rather than unique. Only her professional persona offers her protection and a distinct identity.

It is hardly surprising that the roots of crime in Marinina's works can be traced to the same anxieties that drive Kamenskaia's professional and private lives, and in this Marinina differs most sharply from her feminist contemporaries in the West — as well as from her male Russian contemporaries, whose heroes expend their energy battling the Mafia and corrupt politicians. As we have seen, Tomc argues that the interchangeability of the female detective with the female murder victim serves as an indication of the vulnerability of women to crime that has its origin in patriarchal institutions. By contrast, in Marinina's tangled plots, in which the true villain is often not the murderer and motives are frequently multiple and confused, it is more difficult to categorize criminals and victims by gender — although, as we shall see below, gender is far from irrelevant. Murders virtually never happen in the singular in Marinina's works, although even what appear to be serial killings by maniacs are never quite what they seem. Arguably, then, the function of the multiple murder plot in Marinina's fiction is somewhat different from that of sexually motivated serial crimes by men against women, which, as Tomc points out, expose the female detective's vulnerability. In Marinina's fictions certainly one motivation for abandoning the classic detective novel's focus on a single murder is to demonstrate Kamenskaia's particular gift for synthesizing plots, for tracing the logical links between apparently disparate acts.[45] On a deeper level, however, the multiple murder seems to be the inevitable consequence and most appropriate demonstration of the origins of crime in Marinina's works. Thus, virtually without exception, murder in Kamenskaia's world is inextricably linked with the villain's acceptance of the dehumanizing premise that people, regardless of gender, are interchangeable — on the basis of their physical appearance. Thus, in *Playing on Another's Field* the victims are all "stars" of "snuff films" chosen solely on the basis of their physical resemblance to the female relatives who have inspired murderous rage in the "clients" who order the films; in *Another's Mask* all three of the murders involve the substitution of one identical twin for another; in *Death and a Little Love* the victims are selected because they are brides, identically dressed in white; and in *The Stylist* the fourteen victims of sodomy and murder are all adolescent boys of Semitic appearance who bear a striking physical resemblance to one another.

Marinina can hardly be considered a political writer, especially when viewed in the context of the lurid political thrillers being penned by her male compatriots. Nonetheless, in some of her books the source of the impulse to dehumanize others from which murder emanates is implicitly traced to lapses in the Soviet past that are tied to the post-Soviet present by the thread of financial gain, charting a disturbing continuity between the systemic abuses, earlier political and later economic, of the two periods. The political critique is most pointed in *Death for the Sake of Death,* which, uncharacteristically for Marinina, borders on dystopian science fiction. On her new computer, Kamenskaia discovers a curious pattern of high incidence of crime in one region of Moscow balanced symmetrically by a correspondingly low incidence of crime in another region. The two areas form a perfect figure eight with a research institute at the center. Kamenskaia's suspicions that the beneficent ray the institute claims to be testing has a reverse effect, transforming ordinary citizens into violent criminals, turns out to be true. The post-Soviet military industrial complex, desperate for vicious soldiers to fight in Chechnya and rebuild the crumbled empire, and the Mafia, which has invested money in the project, vie both in their indifference to the innocent victims of the experiment and in safeguarding the secret of the negative effects of the ray from Kamenskaia's prying. In case we miss the allegory of the ray as a figure of the Soviet utopian experiment gone wrong, creating a link between the political powers of the past and the economic powers of the present, the researcher in charge of the project is a virulent misanthropist whose hatred of all others was bred by his childhood in a cramped Soviet barracks. The money he will get from selling the ray to the highest bidder will allow him to flee to seclusion from the people his Soviet past has taught him to despise. Equally suggestive of allegory is the schizophrenia of the murderer in *Death and a Little Love,* whose incipient mental illness causes him, despite his brilliant intellect, to be rejected from the police force, which, as Kamenskaia says, is mired in dirt and compromise. Unable to leave behind the world of childhood where good and evil were clear and distinct, his twisted sense of justice leads him into particularly sadistic crime. In *Playing on Another's Field* the link between past injustice and present crime is explicit. The ringleader behind the snuff film enterprise is in fact a seemingly innocuous old lady, a crippled Jewish piano teacher. In a twist at the end of the book, we learn that under Stalin she was denied a brilliant career as a concert pianist because of her deformity, and that she suffered for her Jewishness during the campaign against cosmopolitanism and the Doctor's Plot. Embittered and in need of money, since she will only instruct talented students and takes no payment, she has turned to particularly horrible crime. Musing on the woman's equally talented accomplice, a gifted composer and filmmaker, Kamenskaia pointedly, if rhetorically, asks: What is wrong with a society that cannot make use of such talent? The message is clear: the political ills of the past continue to be visited on the present in the form of violent, economically motivated crime. Economics, like politics, devalues human beings, rendering them expendable and replaceable. In other words, while the old Soviet system turned people into political chattel, the new market chaos transforms individuals — and, in Marinina, perhaps especially women and writers — into commodities, valued according to their salability.

Yet if Kamenskaia's forays into the crimes of the past to solve the crimes of the present carry a political charge, it is one that, as a rule, is heavily personalized, psychologized — and gendered. The hand holding the gun, the preferred murder weapon in Marinina's works, is virtually always male.[46] In a number of cases, moreover, a male murderer tries to frame a woman for his evildoing. In *Another's Mask* a romance novelist, who kills his twin brother in order to assume his identity and thereby elude and delude both his publishers and his overbearing mother, tricks a mentally unstable, infatuated female fan into committing the murder. The murderer in *Death and a Little Love,* who claims his motive in killing brides was to commit a perfect crime and therefore prove the police wrong in their rejection of him, constructs a devious scenario leading the police to an older woman, and stages her supposed suicide by shooting her in the mouth when her eyes are closed waiting for him to kiss her. Thus, women stand at greater risk not only as victims, but also as potential fall guys for male violence.[47]

Given the dangers posed by traditional female roles, it is hardly surprising that Kamenskaia retreats to the safety of androgyny.[48] It is, after all, precisely Kamenskaia's refusal to look or act like other women (along with her superior intellect, of course) that constitutes her uniqueness, her nonexchangeability. Kamenskaia's ambiguity in terms of gender classification manifests itself particularly markedly in relationship to her wedding in *Death and a Little Love*. She insists on wearing black to her wedding, the color putatively gendered male by contrast with bridal white in the twisted logic of the murderer, and refuses to go through the full ZAGS ritual; both departures from "normal" female behavior by implication save her life when the woman who takes her place in line is killed apparently in her stead. Shortly before the wedding, moreover, Kamenskaia has a conversation with her half-brother, Aleksandr, significantly stage-managed in such a way that the two siblings, who "strikingly resemble one another,"[49] talk not face-to-face but to their reflections in a mirror. While Sandra Gilbert and Susan Gubar may take issue with Bruno Bettelheim about who speaks from the mirror in "Snow White," the symbolism here is clear. Aleksandr Kamensky becomes Anastasiia's male alter ego; he pointedly asks her if she is sorry she is getting married, if she really would not prefer to be following up a lead in a police investigation rather than going to ZAGS — a question Kamenskaia declines to answer so as not to have to lie. Shortly thereafter, Korotkov, convinced that Kamenskaia was the intended victim of the ZAGS murderer, presses on her, despite her protests, his service revolver. Hiding from her new husband the danger that may hang over her, she confides in Aleksandr:

> "[R]emember that there is a pistol lying in my purse. I would hardly be able to use it."
>
> "Why?"
>
> "I don't know," she shrugged her shoulders. "I'd get flustered, frightened, what does it matter what . . . I'm not used to it."
>
> "You want me to use it?"
>
> "God forbid! Under no circumstances. Just remember that I have it. And if something should happen, watch out that my purse isn't torn away from me or that I don't throw it someplace myself. Who knows what I might do out of fear. By the way, once again, if something happens — remember that it is very effective to hit someone on the head with a purse with a pistol in it. It's certain I wouldn't be able to do that, but you'll take care of it."[50]

Curiously, this gun, which warrants so much comment at the beginning, in flagrant violation of Chekhov's famous dictum that a gun once brought onstage must be fired in the course of the play, is never mentioned again and plays no further role in the plot, which in fact ends with another gun *not* going off. This pointed emasculation of the archetypal phallic symbol of the hard-boiled private "dick's" manhood, squirreled away in a lady's purse, and nonetheless only to be wielded by a man, raises doubts that the female detective suffers from narrative as well as investigative impotence.

If, as Gilbert and Gubar provocatively suggest, a pen is a metaphorical penis, do we have a confusion, whether deliberate or inadvertent, of metaphors here? If guns belong in the hands of men, what of writing implements? Put in other terms, if, as Tomc suggests, the female detective's vulnerability threatens to undermine her authority, what are we to say of the female detective novelist's *author*ity, especially under conditions, such as those inherent in Russia today, in which the traditional role of the Russian writer is being undermined by the commercialization of literature?[51] Not only do members of the creative intelligentsia — sometimes, as we have seen, portrayed as cripples — play central roles in most of Marinina's fictions, but, more important, issues of authorship figure prominently in a significant number of her works. In *Coincidence* the motive for murder originates in plagiarism, in a man's public claim to authorship of a manuscript in fact written by the female murder victim, who is "bumped off" so that her threatened revelation that the now highly placed political figure — who, as it turns out, is also a power in an international drug syndicate — did not write his own dissertation will not lead to closer scrutiny of his other past dealings. Interestingly enough, the female author's motivation in revealing the deception is not pride of authorship. Rather she wrote what should have been her own doctoral dissertation for attribution to someone else in return for the promise of a payment that would have solved her perennial problems with separate living space and thereby put her romantic life in order. Her anger is aroused, then, not by the original misattribution of the manuscript, but by the fact that the "orderer" (*zakazchik*) "stiffed" her, destroying her dreams for a successful love life. Yet Marinina's repetition of the identical term, *zakazchik,* for the party who orders both the dissertation and the murder of its authoress suggests a curious — and distinctly non-Barthesian — metaphorical as well as literal "death of the author." The author, in a sense, consigns herself to death when she agrees simultaneously to sacrifice her career to her love life and to sell her rights to authorship. No longer the product of a "unique" talent, writing becomes a commodity valued merely for the status it imparts to its owner, who, in the given case, can barely rehash its contents intelligibly.

The nature of authorship as defined by the post-Soviet publishing industry is central to the narrative of both *Another's Mask* and *The Stylist,* and in both the impetus to murder is driven by publishers' attempts to bilk authors of their fair share of the enormous profits their best-selling books are generating. In *Another's Mask* the issue of the interconnection of gender and authorship again comes into play. A persistent "red herring" in the case is the suggestion that the putative murder victim, a wildly popular Russian romance novelist, could not have written the books credited to him because it is unlikely that a man could have such a sensitive understanding of female psychology. His wife does indeed claim to be the true author of the books in her negotiations with publishers after her husband's apparent death, insisting that her husband was merely a front, his image as an attractive male being a major selling point for the books. Yet Marinina fans our essentialist biases only to explode them at the end. The books were indeed written by the man, who was not murdered at all, but has merely usurped "another's mask." In *The Stylist* Kamenskaia's ex-lover works as a translator not of Western, but Eastern detective novels. Yet, as it turns out, he is a translator only in the loosest sense. In rendering them into Russian, he completely reworks the texts of a phenomenally productive Japanese graphomaniac with a knack for plotting but no literary talent. Together, and unbeknownst to either, the writer and his "translator" have become the fantastically successful best-selling Japanese "author" Otori Mitio. As it turns out, it was his publishers who arranged to have "the stylist" beaten and left a virtually helpless cripple to keep him from emigrating from Russia. He is too valuable a commodity to be allowed to get away. As this play with the fine line between author and translator underscores, authorship in the new Russia is a risky and potentially violent business, not because of what the author has to say, but because of what he or she might have to sell.

The world of Marinina's fictions, on the face of it, would hardly seem to offer comfort to the reader of pulp. Behind the facade of a friendly neighbor and loving husband may lurk a vicious serial killer, and the course of true love is more likely to end in disillusionment or murder than in happy endings. Far from allowing her readers to escape to exotic climes, Marinina roots her plots and characters firmly in the beleaguered everyday life of Russia today, where politicians are corrupt or ineffectual and police live from paycheck to paycheck, watching their meager wages dwindle with inflation. Yet, if we accept the answer to highbrow critics who dismiss popular fiction as pablum for the uneducated and intellectually lazy masses — that, on the contrary, it fulfills a need — then the rapidly growing sales of Marinina's books suggest that they offer a wide spectrum of readers, which seems to cross boundaries of gender and class, something they not only want but need.[52] The key to her works' popularity may lie at least partly in their overt confrontation with the anxieties and threats posed by the instability of life in Russia today, which are thereby rendered manageable and therefore less frightening. As Umberto Eco has pointed out, it is the very "iterative" nature of formulaic fiction, its predictability, that allows it to offer respite from unsettling *realia,* an argument that goes far toward explaining why such fictions enjoy particular popularity at moments of social instability.[53] After all, it is reassuring that there are honest cops willing to work long hours and forgo the big bucks offered for private security work just for the sake of bringing criminals to justice. Moreover, even if Kamenskaia does not always solve cases fast enough to save the innocent, she inevitably arrives at the correct solution in the end, and the problems she solves are — as in all true detective fictions — riddles of identity, revealing the true person behind the public mask, a particularly consoling message at a time when radically changing values have unsettled long-held assumptions about definitions of the self. For those with a taste for romance, Marinina holds out the hope that, no matter how plain you may be, there is a possibility of finding your true soul mate; and for those fond of intellectual challenge, devious and complicated plots abound. As one male reviewer, apparently of intelligentsia persuasion, observed, his attention was first drawn to Marinina's books when

> one day in the subway I caught sight of two young people who were reading with enthusiasm a new book issued in the "pocket book" series and, to all appearances, written by a woman. What amazed me was that in external appearance these young people did not resemble at all not only readers of women's novels, but any readers at all. No, I don't mean to say that it seemed to me that they didn't know how to read, I would have found it easier to imagine them rather with a plasterer's handbook or the magazine *Radio,* but under no circumstances with "pulp fiction" [*chtivom*].[54]

His interest piqued, he read all of these "women's" novels for himself, concluding, "Now everyone reads Marinina."[55]

Notes

I am grateful to my husband, Viacheslav Nepomnyashchy, for his invaluable help in "surfing the net" to find materials used in this chapter.

1 Julian Symons, *Bloody Murder: From the Detective Story to the Crime Novel: A History*, rev. ed. (New York: Viking Press, 1985), pp. 16–17.

2 A 1995 survey of Russian readers confirmed the assumption of many commentators that crime and adventure fiction was far and away the most popular book category in Russia: 31.82 percent of male respondents and 26.23 percent of women surveyed identified *detektivy, prikliucheniia* (detective and adventure fiction) as their preferred reading. While science fiction came in second in the overall ranking (19.23 percent of men and 12.57 percent of women), only the great demand for *liubovnye romany* (romance novels) among women (22.04 percent as opposed to 9.8 percent of men) came close to challenging the primacy of the *detektiv* ("Kto vy, pokupateli knig?" *Knizhnoe obozrenie,* no. 33 [August 20, 1996], p. 3).

3 T. Kravchenko, "Missis Kholms: Knizhnaia seriia Aleksandry Marininoi," *Russkaia mysl'* (October 23, 1996) (*http://www.relis.ru/*MEDIA*/news/lg/texts/43/0405.html*).

4 O. Krasnolistov, "Ot sostavitelia," in *Staryi russkii detektiv: roman, rasskazy,* issue 1 (Zhitomir, 1992), p. 3. The series Staryi russkii detektiv (Old Russian Detective Fiction) — of which I have been able to find volumes 1–3, all published in Zhitomir in 1992 — consists of re-publications of early Russian examples of the genre, including brief but informative prefaces that make it clear that the series is aimed at capitalizing on the new popularity of detective fiction. By the same token, facsimile reproductions of early Russian serials of the adventures of Nat Pinkerton, Nick Carter, and Sherlock Holmes began to appear in such series as Iz russkoi bul'varnoi klassiki (From the Russian Boulevard Classic) in the early 1990s. On the re-publication of Nikolai Eduardovich Geintse, see Sergei Kamyshan, " 'Bul'var' vchera i segodnia," (special for) *Novaia Sibir'* (*http://www.sicnit.ru/siberia/55/liter_04.htm*).

5 A. F. Britikov, "Detektivnaia povest' v kontekste prikliuchencheskikh zhanrov," in *Russkaia sovetskaia povest' 20–30kh gg.,* ed. V. A. Kovalev (Leningrad: Nauka, 1976), p. 422.

6 Jeffrey Brooks, whose *When Russia Learned to Read: Literacy and Popular Literature, 1861–1917* (Princeton: Princeton University Press, 1985) is the necessary starting point for any study of the Russian popular reading public, describes the "boom" thus:

> The Pinkerton craze, or the *Pinkertonovshchina,* as it was sometimes known, began inauspiciously with the publication of a few stories about Pinkerton and Holmes in 15- and 20-kopeck editions of 5,000 to 10,000 copies in 1907. In 1908 prices fell to 5 and occasionally to 2 and 3 kopecks. The stories sold well, and the size of the editions rose rapidly to 50,000 and 60,000 copies.

During 1908 nearly 10 million copies of detective stories were published at 15 kopecks or less. The detective serials declined swiftly after 1908. The number of copies fell by half in 1909 and by considerably more in 1910. In 1911, 1912, and 1913 only a few hundred thousand copies of the serials appeared, and in 1914 there were none at all. (p. 142)

Kornei Chukovskii, in a 1908 diatribe against the Pinkerton craze deplored the fact that

> in Petersburg . . . in May of this year alone, according to official information, 622,300 copies of detective (*syshchitskoi*) literature were sold.
> That means that in a year something on the order of seven and a half million of these little books must have appeared in Petersburg!
> And here I remembered that while F. M. Dostoevsky was alive, *Crime and Punishment* came out in two thousand copies, and this pitiful two thousand were on sale from 1876 to 1880 and still were not sold out. ("Nat Pinkerton," in Chukovskii's *Sobranie sochinenii v shesti tomakh,* vol. 6 [Moscow: Khudozhestvennaia literatura, 1969], p. 131)

7 Chukovskii, "Nat Pinkerton," pp. 136, 138. Britikov refers to these anonymous writers as "invisible authors" (*avtory-nevidimiki*) "Detektivnaia povest'," p. 423).

8 Lev Lunts, "Na zapad! Rech' na sobranii Serapionovykh brat'ev 2-go dekabria 1922 g.," in his *Zaveshchanie tsaria,* Arbeiten und Texte zur Slavistik, vol. 30, ed. Wolfgang Kasack (Munich: Verlag Otto Sagner, 1983), pp. 115–26. See, for example, Viktor Shklovskii, "Novella tain"; and Boris Eikhenbaum, "V Poiskakh zhanra."

9 A 1934 Soviet encyclopedia entry likens *Pinkertonovshchina* to pornography in "its function of distraction from revolution," and elaborates: "Having arisen in America in the period of the growth of the political power of the capitalist state, the economic flowering of the bourgeoisie, '*Pinkertonovshchina*' was directed against the growing revolutionary workers' movement; it was a weapon in the struggle of the bourgeoisie for influence over the wavering petit bourgeois strata [of society]" (P. Kaletskii, "Pinkertonovshchina," *Literaturnaia entsiklopediia,* vol. 8 [Moscow: Sovetskaia entsiklopediia, 1934], pp. 645, 647–48).

10 On the "Red Pinkerton" in general and *Mess-Mend* in particular, see Britikov, "Detektivnaia povest'"; Robert Russell, "Red Pinkertonism: An Aspect of Soviet Literature of the 1920s," *SEER* 60, no. 3 (1982): 390–412; Kaletskii, "Pinkertonovshchina," pp. 645–49); Carol Avins, *Border Crossings: The West and Russian Identity in Soviet Literature 1917–1934* (Berkeley: University of California Press, 1983), pp. 48–60; Katerina Clark, *Petersburg: Crucible of Cultural Revolution* (Cambridge: Harvard University Press, 1995), pp. 173–82; and Samuel D. Cioran, "Translator's Introduction," in Marietta Shaginian, *Mess-Mend: Yankees in Petrograd,* trans. Samuel D. Cioran (Ann Arbor: Ardis, 1991), pp. 7–21.

11 My thanks to Evgeny Dobrenko, who discussed the subject of detective fiction in the

Soviet Union with me at some length, generously sharing with me his knowledge and insights in this area.

12 In the general realm of crime fiction under Stalin, we might also note the autobiographical cycle, *Notes of an Investigator* (*Zapiski sledovatelia*), by Lev Romanovich Sheinin, who worked in the USSR Prosecutor's Office and participated in the Nuremburg trials, and such postwar, cold war spy novels as Nikolai Nikolaevich Shpanov's *Incendiaries* (*Podzhigateli*, 1949). Shpanov turned to writing detective fiction in the 1950s, creating the series hero Colonel Nil Kruchinin.

13 Pseudonym of Lev Sergeevich Shapovalov.

14 Semenov, whose real name was Lyandres, first achieved wide popularity in the USSR with his novel *Petrovka 38* (1963), which takes its title from the address of central Moscow police headquarters. Of Semenov, Richard Stites writes: "Semenov is immensely popular (some 35 million copies of his sixty or so books in print, many of them filmed) and immensely wealthy" (Richard Stites, *Russian Popular Culture: Entertainment and Society since 1900* [Cambridge: Cambridge University Press, 1992], p. 152). On Semenov, see also Walter Laqueur, "Julian Semyonov and the Soviet Political Novel," *Society* 23, no. 5 (1986): 72–80; A. Vulis, *V mire prikliuchenii: Poetika zhanra* (Moscow: Sovetskii pisatel', 1986), pp. 354–63; V. Kardin, "Sekret uspekha," *Voprosy literatury*, no. 4 (1986), pp. 102–50.

15 G. Andzhaparidze, "Bogachi-filantropy i belye 'mersedesy'. Chto i kak my perevodim," *Literaturnaia gazeta*, January 20, 1971, p. 13.

16 Britikov, "Detektivnaia povest'," p. 434.

17 Kardin, "Sekret uspekha," p. 103.

18 Ibid., p. 108.

19 Richard Stites points out that in the glasnost period, "Semenov began publishing his own books, a journal, and a newspaper and branching out into various enterprises. . . . Detective and science fiction writers, including the Strugatskys and the Vainers, joined forces in the *Detective Story and Political Novel* [*Detektiv i politika*], edited and published by Semenov, containing crime stories, spy thrillers, documents from the Stalin terror, and pro-Gorbachev commentary, thus closing the ranks of practitioners of urban popular fiction along liberal lines" (*Russian Popular Culture*, p. 181). As late as 1994, after Semenov's death, re-publications of the writers' works were still in fifth place on the best-seller list for the year ("Chempiony izdavaemosti 1994 goda," *Knizhnoe obozrenie*, no. 2 [January 10, 1995], p. 3).

20 On the latter point, see Larisa Isarova, "Beskonechnye kilometry detektivov: Koechto o deval'vatsii populiarnogo zhanra," *Literaturnaia gazeta*, April 12, 1989, p. 3.

21 On the difficulties posed to Soviet detective novelists by the changed political and social conditions in Soviet and post-Soviet Russia, see Roman Arbitman, "Dolgoe proshchanie s serzhantom militsii: Sovremennyi rossiiskii detektiv: izdatel' protiv chitatelia," *Znamia*, no. 7 (1995), pp. 201–7; Geilii Riabov's introduction to the anthology *Imenem zakona: Sovremennyi sovetskii detektiv* (Moscow: Sovetskii pisatel' 1989), pp. 3–6; Viktor Toporov, "Pretenzii k poterpevshim" [review of the

Vainers' *Ob''ezzhaite na dorogakh sbitykh koshek i sobak* and *Poterpevshie pretenzii ne imeiut*], *Literaturnoe obozrenie,* no. 2 (1987), pp. 65–69; and Tat'iana Kravchenko, "Losev. Syshchik i dolgozhitel': Sovetskii sledovatel' i postsovetskoe vremia," *Literaturnaia gazeta,* July 12, 1995, p. 4. For a more optimistic view, see the article by Iuliia Latynina (who herself writes detective novels under a male pseudonym) published along with Kravchenko's: "Plokhoi khoroshii detektiv: On podchiniaetsia zakonam rynka, no ne zakonam tusovki," *Literaturnaia gazeta,* July 12, 1995, p. 4.

22 One reviewer argued that Leonov benefited from the liberation from overly narrow subject matter afforded by the new political situation. See Grigorii Revzim, "Sherlok Kholms i Sancho Pansa: Klassicheskii detektiv: igra po pravilam" [review of Nikolai Leonov, *Polnoe sobranie sochinenii v 12 tomakh*], *Ex Libris NG,* no. 2 (February 20, 1997, *http://www.relis.ru/MEDIA/news/exlib/02/1002-75.html*).

23 In a survey asking readers to name their favorite authors taken in May 1992 and repeated in July 1994, Chase and Christie figured among the top twelve writers. (In order of preferences expressed in 1992, the writers named were Pushkin, Sholokhov, Dumas, Pikul', Lev Tolstoy, Chase, Bulgakov, Esenin, Christie, Chekhov, and Solzhenitsyn.) The survey, moreover, registered a predictable variation in preference corresponding to the age of the respondents. For example, there were twice as many Chase admirers among readers younger than twenty-four, and they generally had the smallest home libraries. By 1994, Chase (named as their favorite author by 6.0 percent of the respondents) had outpaced Pushkin (named by 5.1 percent). See Tinatin Zurabishvili, "Liubimye pisateli rossiian," *Knizhnoe obozrenie,* no. 7 (February 14, 1995), p. 3. Viewed in the light of George Orwell's contention that Chase owed his original popularity in Britain in 1940 to the fascism and sadism of his works, this preference for Chase among younger Russians is disturbing. See George Orwell, "Raffles and Miss Blandish," in *The Collected Essays, Journalism, and Letters of George Orwell,* vol. 3: *As I Please, 1943–1945,* ed. Sonia Orwell and Ian Angus (New York: Harcourt, Brace & World, 1968), pp. 212–24.

24 For a comparison between Topol''s most recent political thriller and the American sensation *Primary Colors,* see Alessandra Stanley, "What's Like 'Primary Colors' and Read All Over?" *New York Times,* May 14, 1997, p. A4.

Roman Arbitman, arguing that Russian writers living in their home country were unable to free themselves from the hold of the Soviet tradition of detective fiction, placed his hopes for the future of the genre in Russia on émigré writers. In this context, aside from Topol' and Neznansky, he named Lev Gursky, who made his debut with four novels published in 1995–96. See Arbitman, "Dolgoe proshchanie." The nomination of Gursky's political thriller *Change of Places* (*Peremena mest*), about a plot to replace the Russian president with an impostor, for the Small Booker (Malyi Buker) Prize in 1995 caused something of a scandal because it challenged the still hard line between "high" and "low" culture in Russia. According to one reviewer, "many people" believe Arbitman to be the author of both Gursky's novels and "the image of Gursky, a Russian émigré living in America" (Anna Lapina,

"Fokus udalsia: 'U nas tut chastnyi detektiv, a ne politicheskii triller,' ili Bestseller dlia uzkogo kruga," *Novaia Sibir',* April 21, 1997 (*http://www.sicnit.ru/siberia/47/ artes_06.htm*).

25 Arbitman argues that this phenomenon was spurred by the fact that publishers had exhausted the supply of Western fiction not covered by copyright and were unwilling to pay high royalties for more recent works by Western writers ("Dolgoe pro-shchanie," p. 202). Lev Gursky suggests, on the other hand, that the Russian reader had just grown heartily sick of "foreign names and unfamiliar cities, 'magnums' and 'thompsons,' Texas rangers and corrections to someone else's constitution" (Lev Gurskii, "Nol' tselykh piat' desiatykh" [review of Vitalii Babenko, "Nol'"], *Lit-eraturnaia gazeta,* June 11, 1997 [*http://www.relis.ru/MEDIA/news/Lg/texts/0097/ 23/1102.html]*). I should add that the prospect of sharing, if only in some small measure, in the soaring profits in the publishing industry must also have provided a motivation, especially to intellectuals hard hit by economic change, for Russians to try their hand at detective fiction. Reportedly a number of *intelligenty* write *detektivy* under pseudonyms, and, in some cases, works attributed to one pseudonymous author are written by a number of different people.

26 Nancy Condee and Vladimir Padunov, "The ABC of Russian Consumer Culture: Readings, Ratings, and Real Estate," in *Soviet Hieroglyphics: Visual Culture in Late Twentieth-Century Russia,* ed. Nancy Condee (Bloomington: Indiana University Press, 1995), p. 141.

27 The venerable institution of the "thick" journal, for example, is being kept alive largely by support from the Soros Foundation.

28 Sergei Mitrofanov, "Samaia strashnaia skazochnitsa Rossii," *Ex Libris NG,* no. 3 (March 6, 1997, *http://www.relis.ru/MEDIA/news/exlib/03/1003-74.html*).

29 Kravchenko, "Missis Kholms."

30 See, for example, Mitrofanov, "Samaia strashnaia"; and the advertisement announc-ing Marinina's collected works at the end of an edition of one of her more recent novels: "We present to your attention the complete collected works of the Russian Agatha Christie — A. Marinina" (Aleksandra Marinina, *Svetlyi lik smerti* [Moscow: Eksmo, 1997]).

Dotsenko commented on his hero in a 1996 interview. In answer to the inter-viewer's question ("They call your hero the 'Russian Rambo.' What is your attitude toward this?") Dotsenko responded:

> At first I consciously supported that image. Several articles about my books came out under that title. At that time it was a calculated action. After all, my hero still wasn't well known, therefore it was necessary to let the reader know what kind of hero he was. If you explain at length that he is a former "afganets," that he battles with the Mafia, with traitors — workers for the se-curity forces and law officers, etc., it comes out long and monotonous, but when you say the "Russian Rambo," it immediately becomes clear to every-one, moreover in all countries. In Singapore, when they found out that I was a

writer and director, they asked what I wrote about, and that's what I said: about the "Russian Rambo." ([G. Nezhurin and O. Pogorelova], "Viktor Dotsenko: 'Esli by seichas Khristos vernulsia k nam na zemliu . . . vriad li on stal by podstavliat' vragu vtoruiu shcheku." *Knizhnoe obozrenie,* no. 30 [July 30, 1996], p. 10)

A 1998 interview with Marinina revolved completely around comparisons between the Russian writer and the grande dame of British detective fiction. Notably, however, the questions and Marinina's answers to them addressed only biographical, as opposed to textual, similarities and differences between the two writers. Vlada Vasiukhina, "Dva litsa Aleksandry Marininoi," *Ogonek,* no. 37 [September 14, 1998] (http://www.gornet.ru/ogonyok/win/199837/37-32-39.html).

31   Unfortunately, there are to date no Russian reader surveys studying preference by individual author. However, Dotsenko has identified his most "grateful readers" as veterans of the Afghan war ([L. Goriunova and G. Borisov], " 'Samyi blagodarnyi moi chitatel' — 'afganets' . . .'," *Knizhnoe obozrenie,* no. 15 [1997], p. 3); and Alla Shteinman, director of a publishing house specializing in women's detective literature (which she claims men refer to as "*tetki-press*" or "hag press"), suggested in an interview that, hardly surprisingly, the primary audience for *boeviki* consists of men ([G. Nezhurin], "Alla Shteinman: 'Umenie vzglianut' na situatsiiu s iumorom i samoironiei tol'ko pribavliaet nam shansov vyigrat'," *Knizhnoe obozrenie,* no. 35 [September 3, 1996], p. 6). Arguably, however, the works both of Dotsenko and Marinina, albeit in very different ways, reflect anxiety over changing gender roles in post-Soviet Russian society.

32   Thus the newspaper *New Siberia* (*Novaia Sibir'*) ran the following unattributed report: "In the middle of April the newspaper *Knizhnoe obozrenie* drew some peculiar interim conclusions — counted which authors figured in the bestseller lists of that newspaper (hardcover fiction) during the whole period of existence of the lists (from the first issue of 1995). Viktor Dotsenko, with his 'beshenymi,' came out the victor, followed by D. Koretsky, V. Golovachev, N. Leonov, F. Nezhansky, A. Marinina. Marinina took a stable position on the lists in August of last year with the novel *Don't Get in the Executioner's Way* (*Ne meshaite palachu*), and at present has certainly risen to the first or second position and is successfully competing with the former leader Dotsenko. As the *KO* journalist put it, a true 'Bestseller Race' has begun between these two authors" (*Novaia Sibir'* [http://www.sicnit.ru/siberia/49/artss_08.htm]). A year later Marinina had begun to sign contracts with Western publishers for translations of her books, and the *New York Times* dubbed her "Russia's most successful current crime writer" (Alessandra Stanley, "Russia Solves Its Crime Problem," *New York Times,* March 15, 1998, p. 4).

33   By early 1998, the *New York Times* put the figure at ten million copies (Stanley, "Russia Solves Its Crime Problems," p. 4). Most of the biographical information given here is taken from an interview with Marinina, accompanied by commentary, published in *Ogonek* ([Igor' Semitsvetov], "Aleksandra Marinina: 'Prestupnikov ia

opisyvaiu osobenno liubovno,' " *Ogonek,* no. 19 [May 12, 1997, http://www.gornet. ru/o...i/199719-19-48-50.html]). The proliferation of editions and perhaps even intentional obfuscation on the part of publishers make it almost impossible to figure out the order in which Marinina's books were written. Moreover, Marinina revealed in a recent interview that she coauthored her first book *Six-winged Seraphim* (*Shestikrylyi Serafim*) with a colleague named Aleksandr and that the two decided to use a common pseudonym composed out of their first names: Aleksandra Marinina (Vasiukhina, "Dva litsa Aleksandry Marininoi"). The eighteen works Marinina has published to date are: *Chernyi spisok, Chuzhaia maska, Ia umer vchera* (her most recent work as of this writing), *Igra na chuzhom pole, Illiuziia grekha, Imia poterpevshego: nikto, Muzhskie igry, Ne meshaite palachu, Posmertnyi obraz, Prizrak muzyki, Rekviem, Shesterki umiraiut pervymi, Smert' i nemnogo liubvi, Smert' radi smerti, Stechenie obstoiatel'stv, Stilist, Svetlyi lik smerti, Ubiitsa ponevole, Ukradennyi son,* and *Za vse nado platit'*.

34   "Aleksandra Marinina: 'Prestupnikov.' " In *Svetlyi lik smerti* (*The Radiant Face of Death*), Tat'iana Obraztsova—an episodic character who works as a senior investigator for the St. Petersburg branch of the MVD and who also writes best-selling detective novels under the pseudonym Tat'iana Tomilina and, like Marinina herself, is called the "Russian Agatha Christie"—sees a woman, who will later turn out to be a murder victim, reading one of her books on the metro. This sight leads her to muse on her readership: "As a whole the category of her readers was roughly: all women and men over forty" (Aleksandra Marinina, *Svetlyi lik smerti* [Moscow: Eksmo, 1997], pp. 36–37).

35   Mitrofanov, "Samaia strashnaia." In early 1998, Alekseeva's popularity as a novelist finally prompted her to resign from her job (Stanley, "Russia Solves," p. 4).

36   Ibid.

37   Aleksandr Gavrilov, "Radost' uznavaniia: Izdateli vygodnee torgovat' liud'mi, chem knigami," *Ex Libris NG,* May 19, 1997 (*http://www.relis.ru/MEDIA/news/exlib/04/ 1004-14.html*).

38   "Aleksandra Marinina: 'Prestupnikov.' "

39   Ed McBain's Matthew Hope novels are also tales of detection cast as reworked fairy tales, as a sampling of their titles suggest: *Goldilocks* (1978), *Rumpelstiltskin* (1984), *Snow White and Rose Red* (1985), *Cinderella* (1986). It may not be too much to suggest that detective narratives, with their promise of happy endings, are in a sense fairy tales for adults.

40   The text makes explicit reference to "Zolushka," and Kamenskaia's "pseudonym" is Larisa Lebedeva (swan).

41   Tomc's argument is not without problems even within the context of the Western works she chooses to treat as exemplary. For instance, she passes over in silence the fact that Grafton and Paretsky continue to write in the 1990s. This lapse and others, however, do not affect the applicability of her arguments here.

42   Sandra Tomc, "Questing Women: The Feminist Mystery after Feminism," in *Feminism in Women's Detective Fiction,* ed. Glenwood Irons (Toronto: University of

Toronto Press, 1995), p. 46. For a complementary argument, see Glenwood Irons, "New Women Detectives: G is for Gender-Bending," in *Gender, Language, and Myth: Essays on Popular Narrative,* ed. Irons (Toronto: University of Toronto Press, 1992), pp. 127–41.

43   Kamenskaia's mother returns to Russia and to her husband, apparently for good, in *The Stylist.*

44   In this context, Janice A. Radway's speculation on one of the reasons women may turn to romance novels may apply to Marinina's female readers as well: "[A woman] may well turn to romance reading in an effort to construct a fantasy-world where she is attended, as the heroine is, by a man who reassures her of her special status and unique identity" (Janice A. Radway, "Women Read the Romance: The Interaction of Text and Context," *Feminist Studies* 9, no. 1 [1983]: 62).

45   I am indebted to Richard Borden for this observation.

46   Along with other equally "phallic" weapons, including knives and syringes.

47   In the 1997 novel, *Muzhskie igry (Male games),* which I was able to read only after the text of this essay was completed, Marinina genders crime explicitly male in a way that comes quite close to Tomc's paradigm for the 1990s. As the story opens, Gordeev has been promoted and has been replaced by a new male head of the department. The typically complex plot begins as an investigation of what is apparently a series of serial murders. Kamenskaia's suspicions fall on a female ex–basketball player named Anna Lazareva. As the investigation progresses, however, she begins to question Lazareva's guilt and even whether the murders were actually committed by a single person. The plot thickens as Kamenskaia finds herself embroiled in a parallel murder investigation that seems to lead directly to her own beloved stepfather, and her antipathy to her new boss grows so overwhelming (primarily because he will not allow her to stay in her office and do mental labor rather than going out into the field) that she considers leaving her job and even her profession. In the end, she discovers that all the murders are linked to a complex scheme, located in a special institute funded by the government, to take power in Russia. Her new boss, rather than her stepfather, turns out to be implicated, and, as she learns at the end, Gordeev, who has only pretended to leave the department, and General Zatochnyi, another recurring father-mentor figure, have used her without her knowledge to uncover the threads of the conspiracy. Although Kamenskaia's faith in her stepfather is vindicated, she finds that she — no less than Lazareva, who dies in the course of the novel — has been a pawn in "male games." It is worth noting that at the point of her lowest ebb in the novel, Kamenskaia "remakes herself" in the front of the mirror. This episode appears particularly compelling when we bear in mind that as we learn in an earlier book it was Kamenskaia's stepfather who was originally the "voice in the mirror" from whom Kamenskaia learned both that she was plain and that her plainness represented a gift for disguise, and therefore detection.

48   It is only fair to point out that there are positive female characters who are able to combine motherhood with careers and even the ability to cook — Dasha, Lusia, and Gordeev's wife — but they are episodic.

49 *Smert' i nemnogo liubvi,* p. 23.

50 Ibid., p. 40.

51 While space constraints make it impossible to discuss further here the fascinating relationship between sleuthing and storytelling, not only in Marinina but in the works of other female writers who have created female detectives, it is worth noting that Kamenskaia's talent for detection is repeatedly attributed as much to imagination — to the ability to conceive diverse plots to fit the evidence — as it is to reason. Moreover, we learn that Kamenskaia wrote poetry when she was young, and in *Coincidence,* in a faked biography, she attributes her poems to the female murder victim. In *The Stylist* she demands that her former lover return those poems to her. As discussed in the text, issues of plagiarism and authorship are central to both of those works.

52 See, for example, Radway's arguments concerning the romance novel in "Women Read the Romance" and in her book, *Reading the Romance: Women, Patriarchy, and Popular Literature* (Chapel Hill: University of North Carolina Press, 1984). A recent new report claims that 60 percent of Marinina's readers are female (Stanley, "Russia Solves," p. 4). By early 1998, the *New York Times* put the figure at ten million copies.

53 See, Umberto Eco, "The Myth of Superman," in his *The Role of the Reader: Explorations in the Semiotics of Texts* (Bloomington: Indiana University Press, 1979), pp. 117–22.

54 Mitrofanov, "Samaia strashnaia."

55 Ibid.

What is a national cinema if it doesn't have a national audience?
— Andrew Higson, "The Concept of National Cinema"[1]

IN SEARCH OF AN AUDIENCE: THE NEW
RUSSIAN CINEMA OF RECONCILIATION

Whether viewed as entertainment, a commodity, an art form, a symbol of national prestige, or a means of shaping public opinion, popular cinema in contemporary Russia is on the verge of extinction. The reasons for the current crisis are manifold, but Russian filmmakers and critics increasingly agree that it derives less from the economic difficulties confronting the Russian film industry than from a catastrophic drop in the audience's perception of the social relevance and cultural significance of contemporary cinema. Although fewer Russian films are completed each year, film production continues. Yet the film-going audience, for both Russian and foreign films, has declined precipitously.

Annual feature film production in the former Soviet Union peaked in 1990 at 300 films, then declined in 1991 to 213, in 1992 to 172, in 1993 to 152, in 1994 to 68, and in 1995 to 46.[2] The available sources offer conflicting data for 1996, but indicate that fewer than 30 feature films were completed in the Russian

Federation, with even more drastic declines in the other republics.[3] While the number of films completed in 1996 decreased to roughly one-tenth of the 1990 total, ticket sales in Russian movie theaters in 1996 declined to one-fifteenth of the 1990 total, and the theaters that remain open fill, on average, only 3–8 percent of their seats. The available data indicate that in 1995 Russia ranked lowest among European countries in its sale of movie tickets per capita, averaging less than one ticket per citizen. Another recent survey indicates that in 1996, on average, only one in five residents of Moscow, the center of the nation's film industry, made even a single visit to a movie theater.[4] Moreover, only 10 percent of the films playing in Russian movie theaters were produced in Russia, and of these, only 5 percent were recent productions.[5] The decline in ticket sales per individual film is especially telling: in 1985, 40 of 150 Soviet films made that year sold more than 5 million tickets, but in 1994 no Russian film sold more than 500,000 tickets, and even Hollywood blockbusters sold no more than 2 to 3 million tickets to Russian audiences.[6] As director Sergei Livnev, head of the Gorky Film Studio, remarked in April 1996, "I remember a time when a film that gathered less than 15 million viewers was considered unsuccessful. . . . Now even 100,000 viewers is a rare event."[7]

New Russian films have their best chance of reaching a broad audience on television and videocassette, but here, too, they are far outnumbered by foreign imports, the broadcast rights to which are being "dumped" on the Russian market for fees that are one-tenth to one-third the rate for Russian films.[8] Sergei Solov'ev, first secretary of the Union of Russian Cinematographers, estimated in 1996 that the average cost of producing a Russian film was one million dollars, while the average fee paid to broadcast a Russian film on central Russian television was ten thousand dollars.[9] Moreover, while acknowledging that illegal screenings and broadcasts of both Russian and foreign films have diminished substantially since the early 1990s, I. S. Volkov, director of the Society for the Protection of Authors' Rights, claims that approximately 80 percent of the two thousand television stations on Russian territory continue to broadcast pirated films.[10] Consequently, even the few Russian films screened on Russian television have little chance of recouping their production costs.

The brightest spot on the Russian film industry's bleak horizon is the video market, which has improved dramatically since 1995, when very few Russian films were available for sale, and most of those were pirated copies. Pressure from both foreign and Russian filmmakers' associations led to the passage of new legislation against video piracy in July 1995. Since then, Russian film producers have moved into the legal video market in increasing numbers, often working out informal and ingenious compromises with former pirates. Most-Media, for example, sells limited rights to local video distributors in the form of a single master tape and thousands of empty "licensed" slipcovers with the film's "official" logo and production information. The local distributor then produces the actual videotapes in his own facility. This, claims company director Mikhail Shatin, allows Most-Media to minimize shipping costs and also offers a firmer guarantee that the company will receive payment for each tape sold. Significantly, however, Most-Media conducted its first successful experiment in this form of video distribution with a packet of five Russian films with "relatively weak commercial potential," but intends to concentrate its future efforts on European productions.[11]

Although some recent low-budget films have recouped their production costs with television and video sales, the domestic market has yet to produce the kind of profits that would fund new projects or enable studios to upgrade their outmoded and deteriorating facilities.[12] At the same time, the video market in Russia seems likely to erode ticket sales even further. In the summer of 1997, legal video cassettes were selling in Moscow for between twenty-three and thirty thousand rubles, while tickets to see these same films in the few theaters where they were playing ranged from twenty to thirty thousand rubles. Furthermore, most Russian films appear on videocassette either before or simultaneously with their theatrical release. This is not a case of low-quality films going "straight to video": "arthouse" films such as Kira Muratova's *Three Stories* (*Tri istorii,* 1997) and Vilen Novak's crowd-pleasing vehicle for stars Elena Safonova and Sergei Zhigunov, *The Princess and the Bean* (*Printsessa na bobakh,* 1997), could be purchased on videocassette as soon as they began playing in Moscow theaters. Filmmakers explain their rush to video as a necessary consequence of the drop in ticket sales and the rise in video piracy.[13] Russian filmmakers' only hope for breaking even or making a profit on their films is to sell the foreign distribution and television broadcast rights, but only a few make the leap from the domestic to the foreign market. As Russian funds for film production dwindle, foreign sales have become increasingly important. When asked about his plans and activities in 1997, director Konstantin Lopushanskii told his interviewer to report that "if it weren't for the retrospectives of his films in various foreign countries, and invitations to sit on the jury of major film festivals, he would certainly be dead from hunger."[14]

Responses to the Crisis

In the early 1990s, Russian filmmakers tended to attribute the decline in the production and popularity of their films to causes external to the films themselves: the prevalence of cheap foreign films and television series; the collapse of centralized systems of film distribution; the physical deterioration of film theaters; and the general scarcity of funds, whether for producing films, upgrading studio facilities, mounting advertising campaigns, or renovating film theaters. Typically, Russian filmmakers responded to their economic difficulties by demanding that the government increase its subsidies for local film production while imposing either quotas or special tariffs on the import, exhibition, and broadcast of foreign films.[15] Implicit in these discussions was the assumption that if the circumstances in which Russian films were produced and exhibited improved, then these films would inevitably attract viewers.[16] Increasingly, however, this position has come under attack. Government subsidies are shrinking, and many prominent figures in the film industry have begun to argue that filmmakers must take more financial and moral responsibility for making films that no one wants to watch.

Among the most vocal critics of the current system of government support for filmmaking is the sociologist and cultural critic Daniil Dondurei, editor in chief of Russia's film journal of record, *Iskusstvo kino,* and thus automatically a member of the Russian State Committee on Cinema. Dondurei also heads the "informational-analytic" firm Dubl'-D, the principal source of quantitative information about the contemporary Russian film industry for government, industry, and the news media. Dondurei has repeatedly insisted that the only way out of the current crisis is for filmmakers to start thinking of their work "like any other product or service, from the point of view of its potential consumption."[17] He and other critics deplore Russian filmmakers' tendency to treat "the viewer, theaters, investments, advertisements, and market research as deeply prosaic and third-rate considerations that have to be taken into account only as a result of the inevitable, but despised commercialization of cultural life."[18]

Dondurei's position is shared by many members of the so-called young generation of Russian filmmakers, most of whom began their career in the late 1980s. Among these, the most passionate public exponents of the need to make self-supporting films are Livnev and the director Valerii Todorovskii, both of whom helped to formulate a recent proposal presented by their new Association of Low-Budget Film Studios to the Russian State Committee on Cinema (formerly Roskomkino, now Goskino Rossii). This proposal envisions the production, release, and distribution of a packet of ten low-budget films per year. Each film is allotted a budget of no more than one billion rubles (about $200,000), and projects are approved based on the likelihood that they will recoup their costs.[19] This proposal generated a fair amount of controversy, among older directors in particular, but its first projects have already been released — most notably Aleksei Balabanov's *Brother* (*Brat,* 1994–96), which took prizes for Best Film and Best Actor at the 1997 Open Russian Film Festival in Sochi.

Balabanov's career is indicative of the sea change under way in Russian cinema in the late 1990s. His first two films were loose, hallucinatory adaptations of Samuel Becket and Franz Kafka — *Happy Days* (*Schastlivye dni,* 1991) and *The Castle* (*Zamok,* 1994), respectively — with defiantly uncommercial aspirations to the status of high art. *Brother,* however, is essentially a gangster film about an appealing country bumpkin's assimilation of his older, citified brother's skills as a hired killer for "New Russian" crime bosses. Lingering close-ups of the baby-faced hero (Sergei Bodrov Jr.) as he explores contemporary Russian consumer culture encourage the film's viewers to identify with his folksy innocence, naive xenophobia, and ultimate triumph as an efficient assassin who combines family values with a callous disregard for human life. Balabanov's choice of such aggressively commercial material exemplifies the shift in focus that film critics and directors such as Dondurei, Livnev, and Todorovskii insist Russian filmmakers must make if the Russian film industry is to survive. They are convinced that Russian cinema will perish unless it relinquishes its emphasis on preserving the director's creative freedom and creates, in Livnev's words, "a system oriented toward the audience and one that can live on the money the audience brings to the box office."[20] Or, as an "Appeal to the Plenum of the Filmmakers' Union from the Association of Young Filmmakers" puts it: "National cinema must turn decisively toward the audience. From an industry focused on the beggarly division of [government] subsidies (which are never adequate), cinema must be transformed into a blossoming industry, based on the mechanisms of return and the audience's love. It is the audience's love that must become in future the fundamental and most natural form of support for national cinema."[21]

This new emphasis on the audience is inspired not only by economic concerns, but also by worries that cinema no longer fills a central or "necessary" role in Russian society.[22] Director and producer Sergei Selianov recalls feeling during the filming of his *Angel Day* (*Den' angela,* 1986) as if "we were doing something big not only for ourselves, but also to change the air in the country. . . . There was a particular pathos then, that I would really like to see return. But our field is now, in fact, dying."[23] In the early euphoria of the late 1980s and early 1990s, filmmakers reveled in their newfound freedom from censorship, but many in the younger generation now concur with Sergei Livnev's statement at the 1996 Sochi Film Festival: "Personally, what is important for me now is not to speak out, but to be heard. . . . I am interested in discussing with the widest possible circle of people, the residents of the country, those questions which mutually concern us. This seems to me what is most correct and interesting. That's the point of our work, of its human, aesthetic, and all other value, and not the introduction of innovations in film language."[24]

Statements such as this herald a gradual disengagement from a cult of the film director as almighty auteur and a resurrection of ideas about cinema's social role that derive in large part from the Soviet-era conviction that cinema is both the "most important" and the "most mass" of all the arts.[25] While rejecting the political legacy of the past, contemporary Russian filmmakers long for a return to the prominence that their work once enjoyed in the public life of the nation. "I envy the directors who make [the popular Brazilian television series] *Secret of a Tropical Woman* [*Sekret tropikanki*] and other shows of that sort," director Sergei Ursuliak commented. "They are the masters with, as we say, real resonance among the people."[26]

This longing for "resonance among the people" has led directors and critics to look with increasingly critical eyes at the "hermeticization" of contemporary Russian cinema, which often seems to be made for and seen only by film critics and festival audiences.[27] In the words of Viacheslav Shmyrov, film critic and director of cultural programs at the Moscow Film Center, "Just like a mollusk in its shell, cinema is suffocating from the fact that it is neither in demand nor addressed to anyone. . . . Today, the concept of the audience, however paradoxical it may seem, is no longer only an economic concept, without consideration of which it is impossible to recover the money spent on the production of a film, but also an aesthetic and even an ethical concept, which secures the personal dignity of each person working in the cinema."[28]

This link between the aesthetic and the ethical responsibility of the filmmaker recurs throughout 1995 and 1996 discussions of Russian audiences' indifference to and alienation from contemporary Russian cinema. Critics now tend more frequently to associate Russian viewers' rejection of Russian films with Russian directors' abuse of the freedom they gained with the abolition of government control over film production in the initial period of cinematic perestroika. Film critic Irina Shilova, for example, condemns post-Soviet cinema's preoccupation with apocalyptic and depressing portraits of "slaves, nothings, vagrants, and drug addicts" as a "betrayal of national interests," because cinema is "simply obligated to give hope."[29] Dondurei concurs, arguing that the lifting of artistic, economic, and political controls on filmmakers' work has "left auteurs alone with themselves," but this new liberty has failed to produce the cinematic masterpieces that directors claimed they could make if only given sufficient creative freedom and financial resources. He attributes their failure to the fact that filmmakers, "like the Russian intelligentsia generally . . . apparently do not possess the most important ability today, the ability to create prototypes and models for the future in secure, pressure-free circumstances."[30] Contemporary filmmakers' abdication of what Shilova, Dondurei, and many filmmakers themselves see as cinema's responsibility to its national audience has led, in the words of director Pavel Lungin, to "an absolute absence of collective feeling, of connection to the people, their pain and joy."[31] Ironically, many contemporary laments over the isolation of present-day cinema from its potential audience recall with nostalgia the Soviet-era artistic councils and studio control over both the quality and the content of film production.[32]

Russian Cinema since 1994: Reconciliation or Capitulation?

What kinds of films are being made in this era of disenchanted audiences, disgruntled critics, and disenfranchised film directors? Although no new "big ideas" have emerged in post-Soviet cinema, many Russian films completed between 1994 and 1997 have moved in the direction of what I would tentatively label a "cinema of reconciliation." Thematically, these films emerge from and strive to move beyond the "cinema of repentance" for past sins and the "cinema of little faith" in the present, exemplified, respectively, by Tengiz Abuladze's *Repentance (Pokaianie,* 1984, released in 1986) and Valerii Pichul's *Little Vera (Malen'kaia Vera,* or "little faith," 1988). Elements of the so-called *chernukha* (dark) films of the late 1980s and early 1990s remain, but the bleak view of contemporary Russian life offered by films such as Stanislav Govorukhin's *It's Impossible to Live Like This (Tak zhit' nel'zia,* 1990) and Pavel

Lungin's *Taxi Blues* (*Taksi-Bliuz,* 1992) has been eclipsed by a more lyrical, often comic tone in films such as Aleksandr Rogozhkin's *Particularities of the National Hunt* (*Osobennosti natsional'noi okhoty,* 1995) and Sergei Selianov's *The Time for Sorrow Has Not Yet Come* (*Vremia pechali eshche ne prishlo,* 1995). Even Konstantin Lopushanskii's *Russian Symphony* (*Russkaia simfoniia,* 1994) has been read by at least one critic as a self-parody of that director's earlier visions of apocalypse in *Letters from a Dead Man* and *The Museum Visitor* (*Pis'ma mertvogo cheloveka,* 1986; and *Posetitel' muzeia,* 1989).[33]

Stylistically, these and other recent films attempt to bridge the gap between so-called auteur cinema and popular cinema in a parallel effort not only to chart possible paths toward national and social reconciliation, but also to reunite Russian filmmakers with a population that has lost its taste both for film going in general and for contemporary Russian film production in particular.[34] Attempting to move from the margins to what is widely regarded as the nonexistent "mainstream," films such as Vladimir Khotinenko's *Makarov* (1993) and *Moslem* (*Musul'manin,* 1995), and Vadim Abdrashitov's *Play for a Passenger* (*P'esa dlia passazhira,* 1995), incorporate elements of the supernatural thriller or the gangster movie into socially engaged, character-driven, "serious" dramatic plots.[35] Conversely, Andrei Mikhalkov-Konchalovskii chose to shoot *Chicken Little* (*Kurochka riaba,* 1994), the sequel to his classic of Soviet cinema verité, *The Story of Asia Kliachkina, Who Loved, but Didn't Get Married* (*Istoriia Asi Kliachkinoi, kotoraia liubila, da ne vyshla zamuzh,* 1968, released 1988), as a broadly comic farce. One of the oddest self-proclaimed attempts at bridging commercial and "auteur" cinemas is Dmitrii Astrakhan's critically deplored but popularly acclaimed *Fourth Planet* (*Chetvertaia planeta,* 1994), which is touted as "a mini-Solaris . . . à la Astrakhan, based on motifs from [Ray Bradbury's] *Martian Chronicles.*"[36]

These films also represent a departure from what Svetlana Boym and other critics call the "totalitarian nostalgia" of early postglasnost films for the "big style" and "big themes" of high Stalinism.[37] Other popular films by Astrakhan, Vladimir Men'shov, and Alla Surikova take as their models not the "big movies" of the Stalinist era or the post-Stalin auteurs, but the humbler comedies and melodramas of the 1960s and 1970s. Men'shov's *Topsy-Turvy* (*Shirli-Myrli,* 1995), for example, with its convoluted plot revolving around an elaborate diamond heist, owes major debts to the comedies of Leonid Gaidai, in particular his *Diamond Arm* (*Brilliantovaia ruka,* 1969). Similarly, Astrakhan's *Everything Will Be Fine* (*Vse budet khorosho,* 1995) updates the melodramatic

Cinderella plot of Men'shov's 1979 hit, *Moscow Does Not Believe in Tears* (*Moskva slezam ne verit*).[38] Another 1995 film that enjoyed more popular than critical success, Surikova's *Moscow Holiday* (*Moskovskie kanikuly*), which features an Italian heroine of Russian descent on vacation in Moscow, puts a post-Soviet twist on the plot of William Wilder's 1953 classic, *Roman Holiday*.

In their stance toward Soviet history, Russian films of the mid-1990s also take a more conciliatory position than was the case with most glasnost-era films. The most egregious example is Nikita Mikhalkov's Oscar-winning *Burnt by the Sun* (*Utomlennye solntsem*, 1994), with its sympathetic portrait of a Red Army commander as a tragic hero. In this film, in marked contrast to films such as Abuladze's *Repentance*, support for the activities of the Cheka (a precursor of the KGB) is portrayed as morally legitimate provided it was motivated by a sense of duty rather than fear. This explanation, offered in a moment of postcoital bliss, suffices to shift the commander's wife's sympathies from her first love, a former musician and intellectual who was suborned into the service of the Cheka, back to her cruder, apparently fearless, and more masculine husband.

All of these films aspire to success in all the meanings of the Russian term *narodnoe*, which may be translated as both "national" and "popular." In both plot structure and thematic concerns, these recent films appeal to the nation's people. Attempting to address genuinely "popular" issues in order to gain a truly "popular" audience, many recent films take as their central concern the notion of "Russianness." In this regard, it is significant that the three words that occur most frequently in the titles of Russian films made between 1990 and 1996 are *love* (54 titles), *Russian* (27 titles), and *death* (22 titles). By comparison, the three most frequent title words in Soviet and post-Soviet films between 1917 and 1996 are *love* (221 titles), *day* (69 titles), and *happiness* (61 titles).[39]

National Desire and National Identity in Recent Russian Cinema

The two films in which this new concern with Russianness has been most celebrated are Rogozhkin's *Particularities of the National Hunt* and Khotinenko's *Moslem*, both completed in 1995. I will consider each in some detail in order to clarify the very different ways in which both films attempt to carve out a post-Soviet vision of Russian national identity and a niche in the hearts of post-Soviet audiences.[40] *Particularities* won the Grand Prize at the 1995 Sochi Film Festival, the most important Russian competition, as well as a number of prizes at other festivals.[41] It also appears to have had more commercial success than most other Russian films produced in 1995. According to information provided by the Lenfilm Studio, seventy-five copies of the film were produced and sent out in 1995 to fill distribution contracts that cover 85 percent of Russian territory. The television broadcast rights for *Particularities* were the subject of a bidding war won by the central channel ORT (Public Russian Television), and foreign broadcast rights have been sold to German, Polish, Hungarian, Baltic, Ukrainian, Belorussian, and Kazakh television.[42] According to information collected by the journal *Joker,* the film ranked among the seven most popular videos available in the greater Moscow region from October 1995 through January 1996.[43]

Why was this film such a hit?[44] In the first place, it marks a departure from Rogozhkin's previous "dark" works (*chernukha*) such as *The Guard* (1989), *The Third Planet* (1990), *The Chekist* (1991), and *Life with an Idiot* (1993) in its use of comedy that sometimes verges on slapstick and its repudiation of violence, despite the fact that its plot revolves around the "particularities" of the Russian hunt.[45] Not only do the film's hunters fail to kill a single animal, they also manage not to shoot one another or anyone else.

The film's Russian title has a double meaning that makes its rejection of Rogozhkin's trademark screen violence doubly significant: the Russian word for "hunt," *okhota,* may also be translated as "desire," "wish," or "inclination." This title, I think, transforms the circumstances, or "particularities," of the Russian hunt into a metaphor for Russian national desire. The rejection of violence as a characteristic of what one might therefore term "the Russian pursuit" is underscored throughout the film in scenes that mark the potential for disaster, usually violent, only to deflate it, sometimes literally, as when the hunters fire a rifle into a rubber raft that has inflated by accident in a barn and threatens to crush one of their friends.

The film has almost no plot, only a situation in which a series of gags unfold, most of them arising from the hunters' pursuit of an ideal state of blissful inebriation rather than any actual beast of prey. Crates labeled "ammunition," once even dropped by helicopter, are unpacked, only to reveal a seemingly endless supply of vodka bottles. Most of the hunters are soldiers, and the lodge where they set up camp is in a special military training reserve, but the film presents Russian military power as incapable of causing serious harm. The fantastic harmlessness of the military is particularly marked in the episode in which the hunters bribe a pair of bomber pilots to load a cow into the bay of their fighter plane in order to return her to her "relatives" outside the boundaries of the military reserve. When the base commandant discovers the plan and orders the pilots to return, they decide to jettison their illicit bovine cargo. But when they return and open the bomber's bay, assuring the commandant that there is nothing to see, they discover the cow straddling the edges of the bay, still very much alive. Traumatized, the cow flees, but is later mistaken for an elk and, apparently, shot by the hunters. She recovers, however, just as one hunter pulls out his knife to start carving her into steaks and ribs over the protests of his companions, who insist they should bury the cow, not barbecue her. In each of these scenes, the film teases the viewer with the potential for violence, then turns the moment into a joke.

The film is most "conciliatory" in its visual juxtaposition of scenes from what appears to be an early nineteenth-century Russian hunt with those of the contemporary ersatz hunt. These scenes are presented initially as a young Finnish scholar's dream visions of Russian hunting traditions: the film opens with the nineteenth-century hunt, then cuts to the Finn waking up from a doze in his Russian friend's van. Subsequent scenes of the "real" hunt are framed either by the young Finn's naps or by his perusal of an illustrated volume titled *The Imperial Hunt in Russia.*[46] In contrast to the drunken goofiness of the trigger-happy but harmless contemporary hunters, the scenes from the "traditional" hunt offer colorful panoramas complete with borzoi hounds; elaborately costumed, French-speaking nobles on horseback; and lavish spreads of exotic foods.

In contrast to such films as Karen Shakhnazarov's *Dreams* (*Sny*, 1993), which juxtaposes scenes from 1892 and 1992 in order to accentuate differences between the two eras, Rogozhkin's film argues for a continuity between the prerevolutionary and postcommunist eras despite the often alleged aesthetic and spiritual poverty of the latter. Rogozhkin's rejection of a negative comparison between the leisure pursuits of post-Soviet and tsarist Russia is also indicated in his shortening of the film's working title, *Particularities of the National Hunt in the Autumnal Period* (*Osobennosti natsional'noi okhoty v osennii period*).[47] While the initial version of the title suggested a reading of the film as a portrait of the decline and "fall" of Russian national pursuits, the shorter title implies no negative comparison between the two hunts it depicts onscreen.

In the film's last scene, the contemporary hunters pause for breath as the nineteenth-century hunters ride into the picture, and the young Finn remarks, in Russian for the first time in the film, "It was a good hunt." His comment pertains to both the traditional and the contemporary hunt scenes, but also to the double meaning of the word *okhota*. The key to the desire that drives these hunters and that fueled this film's popularity lies in the short toasts that punctuate the film's protracted drinking scenes: "to beauty," "to friendship," "to brotherhood," "to justice." Comic and resolutely unsentimental as these scenes are, these are the values the film celebrates throughout its episodic structure: the beauty of the landscape, the friendship and playful brotherhood of the hunters, and the "justice" that ensures not only the hunters' safety, but that of their intentional and accidental prey.

The film suggests, however, that the space in which these hunts for beauty, friendship, brotherhood, and justice take place is that of fairy tale and fantasy. Only in the world of fairy tale, after all, could the young Finn suddenly begin to speak Russian, as he does at the end, or the world of his imagination gallop slowly into view. The scene that makes this point most clearly is one in which an Abominable Snowman or Bigfoot runs past the young Finn, who is unable to explain to his Russian-speaking comrades what he has just seen. Other fairy-tale elements include the pineapple that the lodge's caretaker pulls out of his garden, the magical loss and recovery of a policeman's revolver, and the transformation of a bear cub into the hunters' mascot. The bear cub's initial appearance terrifies the hunters, but once they realize he is harmless, they pose with him for a series of comic photographs and read him tracts on the evils of alcohol. The cumulative effect of all these scenes is a cinematic reforging of swords into plowshares: the differences between insiders and outsiders, East and West, past and present are all subtly blurred in a film in which the drunken caretaker of a Russian hunting lodge also tends a Zen garden in which he meditates and from which he plucks the occasional pineapple.[48]

The heart of the film is the interaction between the young Finn, who represents the outside, "civilized" world's preconception of what constitutes Russian national identity, and Kuz'mich, the caretaker, the archetypal Russian peasant (*muzhik*), whose sublime drunkenness the film celebrates as an alternative form of national genius. The young Finn has a static, bookish conception of Russianness that the film presents in its vivid images of the nineteenth-century hunt and in the scenes in which the Finn, like Konstantin Levin in Lev Tolstoy's *Anna Karenina*, tries his hand at mowing hay. He is constantly asking his companions, "When will the hunt begin?" without realizing that the real hunt, or "chase," began when the hunters took their first drink in the boat carrying them from the military base to the isolated hunting reserve. The Finn also

represents "civilization," as his companions note derisively when he stops the
van to pick up a cigarette butt, refuses to drink, and walks around their campsite
picking up litter. His final comment, the first he delivers in Russian in the film,
marks his symbolic acknowledgment that the "hunt" in which he has taken part
was as "good" as the one of which he dreamt.

Kuz'mich, by contrast, is the uncivilized, crafty, "dark" peasant of folklore — a Platon Karataev for post-Soviet times. Viktor Bychkov's inspired performance as Kuz'mich transforms the role from comic stereotype into a sort of
Russian national hero who cultivates his Zen garden, treats animals like human
beings, and conducts long, animated, and often hilarious "conversations" with
the young Finn in Russian. Kuz'mich treats all the creatures in his world as
equals and compatriots. For him, the film suggests, Russianness is the measure
of humanity.

Vladimir Khotinenko's *Moslem* offers a very different and more controversial
view of Russianness in its tale of a young Russian, Kolia Ivanov (Evgenii
Mironov), who converted to Islam during seven years as a prisoner of war in
Afghanistan, then returns to his village home to live with his mother, Sonia
(Nina Usatova), and alcoholic brother, Fed'ka (Aleksandr Baluev).[49] The film's
opening scene — a long shot of a young Orthodox priest striding through a field
and singing a hymn — sets the stage for what the viewer might expect to be a
story of spiritual renewal based in rural life, something like Vasilii Shukshin's
Red Guelder Rose (*Kalina krasnaia,* 1974).[50] As the film unfolds, however, it
presents a vision of contemporary Russian village life that polemicizes with the
idealized portrait of rural "folk" values offered in films like those made by
Shukshin or works of "village prose."[51] While these earlier works of film
and fiction present village life as a repository of traditional, spiritual values,
Khotinenko's film demythologizes the Russian village and Russian Orthodoxy
as a way out of the impasse in which contemporary Russia finds itself. Nor does
the film, as some critics have argued, present the "Moslem" Kolia as the "best
Christian of all."[52]

As many Russian critics quickly observed, *Moslem* is not about a competition between opposing systems of religious belief. "The religious conflicts in
[*Moslem*] are irrelevant," Zara Abdullaeva argues in her review. "They are
simply a pseudonym for the everyday, not the ideological . . . opposition . . . of
diverse culture-multures [*sic*]."[53] Both Dmitrii Bykov and V. Belopol'skaia see
Kolia's ardent practice of Islam as proof of his Russianness. Bykov claims that

the film has nothing to do with the conflict between Islam and Christianity because "this Moslem is himself a Russian . . . [and a] Russian does everything by extremes: if he is a Moslem, then he will be the most methodical and zealous [of Moslems], refusing to back off an inch from his faith."⁵⁴ Similarly, Belopol'skaia argues that Kolia's religious zeal is "simply a means of resistance, of preserving some internal support, with which he was blessed at birth. . . . In the figure of the praying Kolia, the passion, stoic independence, and self-sacrificial yearnings of Boiarina Morozova and Archpriest Avvakum are clearly visible."⁵⁵ For these and other critics, the film is essentially about the intolerance of the "Russian character"; or, in the words of Valerii Turovskii: "In *Moslem* [we see] the struggle between those who are like everyone else and someone who doesn't resemble them."⁵⁶ In short, this film has less to do with particular differences than with Russians' intolerance for difference as such. As several critics, and the filmmakers themselves, have noted, the principal difference at stake in the film is that between characters who believe "sincerely" in some God and those who do not; the precise name by which that God is addressed is unimportant.⁵⁷

Although critic Lev Anninskii reproaches the filmmakers for their frivolous metaphorical use of a conflict that is a "geopolitical reality," Khotinenko and his scriptwriter, Valerii Zalotukha, state unequivocally — and unashamedly — that Kolia's conversion to Islam is only a "provocation," and that "[we] weren't intending at all to make a film about a Moslem, we know almost nothing about Moslems. . . . We made the film about something completely different. The hero himself is not ideological. He simply lives according to rules."⁵⁸ Zalotukha claims that they "didn't want to insult anyone — neither Moslems, nor Russian Orthodox believers." Instead, they envisioned their film as "an investigation of the Russian spirit today, an investigation of the state of the Russian soul."⁵⁹

As "an investigation of the Russian soul," *Moslem* would not appear at first to offer much in the way of "conciliation." Kolia's newfound religious beliefs and his single-minded adherence to them place him at odds with his village and his family, especially his violent ex-convict brother, Fedia. In a key scene, Sonia invites the young Orthodox priest from the film's opening sequence to dinner in hopes of effecting a reconciliation between her two sons. Moved by the priest's homily about the importance of family harmony, Fedia proposes that Kolia kiss a family icon as a sign of their renewed commitment to brotherly love. Kolia's refusal triggers one of the film's most vicious fight scenes, as the much larger Fedia shoves his brother's face into the icon, breaking the glass that protects the holy image. Kolia turns to grab an ax, then marches outside and starts furiously chopping wood, more faithful to his unorthodox religious principles than is his brother to those of his native church.

Fedia is not the only murderous "brother" whose anger threatens Kolia in the film. Kolia is stalked throughout the film by a mysterious stranger whom the final scene reveals to be one of his former "brothers in arms," the lieutenant in charge of political instruction in Kolia's former army unit in Afghanistan. The nameless ex-lieutenant had intended to kill Kolia to avenge the death of a soldier who perished trying to rescue Kolia from the Afghan soldiers who had taken him captive. Convinced that Kolia allowed himself to be captured deliberately, the lieutenant initially considers him a traitor, but after watching Kolia for a month, decides not to kill him. The lieutenant's change of heart is inspired, he claims, by his recent conversion to Russian Orthodoxy and reading of the New Testament. To seal his reconciliation with Kolia, however, the lieutenant wants Kolia to make the sign of the cross "like all normal people," because, he says, that is what has "saved" them both. When Kolia refuses, the lieutenant clutches his head in pain and threatens Kolia with his revolver. As he falls to his knees, still clutching his head and covering his eyes with the gun in his hand, the lieutenant squeezes off a shot. While he seems not to be aiming, or even intending to shoot, the lieutenant kills Kolia in an almost accidental, reflexive gesture of defense against the threat that Kolia's religious convictions pose to the security of his own fragile system of newly acquired beliefs.

The film presents the conflict between Kolia's beliefs and those of the nominally Russian Orthodox villagers, his family, and the ex-lieutenant as a parable about the dangerous futility of attempting to construct a community — whether local, national, or confessional — on the foundation of any single code of rules. When Kolia's former lieutenant explains that he crosses himself with his left hand rather than his right (as is traditional in the Russian Orthodox Church) because he does everything left-handed, "even shooting," it is clear that the lieutenant's beliefs are more lethal than life giving. Similarly, when the lieutenant argues that many of the principles in that "little book," the New Testament, are "outmoded," and gives as an example the pointlessness of "turning the other cheek" in a world in which people use guns rather than hands to "smite" one another, his words indicate the vast distance between the beliefs by which most of the film's characters claim to live and their actions.

This distance between what Homi Bhabha has discussed as the "pedagogy" and "performance" of national identity is particularly marked in Khotinenko's *Moslem*.[60] Of the film's characters, only Kolia lives a life that conforms to his religious beliefs; he refuses to steal, drink vodka, or have sex before marriage; and, most of the time, he also refuses to fight with his brother. He is driven by the desire both to avoid sin and to have "everything be as it should." As he tells Vera, his former girlfriend and now the village floozy, "when [people] learn the real name of God, then everything will be different, everything will be good, everything will be as it should be" (*vse budet pravil'no*). Kolia admits that he doesn't know when this will occur, but "it will definitely happen."

Kolia's confidence in a future that will be better than the present sets him even further apart from his family and fellow villagers, who are characterized less by their lip service to a particular set of beliefs than by their inability to believe in anything. The fatal consequences, as well as the origins, of this lack of belief are most marked in the character of Fedia. An alcoholic like his father, Fedia tries to hang himself from the same hook on which his father hanged himself several years previously, apparently because he, too, sees no reason to live. Kolia cuts him down in the nick of time, then, praying for strength from Allah, yanks the hook from the ceiling and exhorts the assembled villagers not to hang themselves "anymore."

Ironically, Kolia's confidence in a better future and his certainty that "there is no reason to hang yourself" has come to him through his alienation from his "native" environment. The film presents the village as a place of great natural beauty, but one that has been literally "sold down the river" for American dollars by a corrupt bureaucrat to nameless and faceless figures in a military helicopter who are, as the bureaucrat says, "practically not people, but gods." On his way home one evening with a briefcase full of dollars, the bureaucrat stops to take a brief swim. A gigantic pig's head rises up out of the water and hovers over him, terrifying him so that he drops the briefcase in his terror, spilling its contents into the river. The next morning, all of the village's inhabitants — except Kolia — race pell-mell to the river to retrieve the magical dollars that have appeared, as one puts it, like "manna from heaven."

On the one hand, in these scenes the film suggests, none too subtly, that Western materialism has displaced traditional Russian rural, religious values; and it attributes this confusion of the secular with the spiritual to the invasion of the Russian countryside by Western capital and cultural influences. On the other, the vision of the pig's head links the villagers' greed to their Soviet past. The pig's head rises up from the waters of a lake where none of the villagers will swim because its allegedly bottomless depths conceal a church that was immersed when the local Soviet authorities flooded the area to form a lake in the 1930s.[61] The film thus implies that the Soviet destruction of village moral traditions cleared the ground for the villagers' apparently "demonic" possession by Western cultural and social values.[62]

The lieutenant's final speech underscores the film's sense that its characters are possessed by devils far worse than those the country thought it had expelled along with the communist leadership in 1991. In a rambling diatribe the lieutenant compares himself to the man in the New Testament parable whose original devil had moved out, leaving an "empty place," but is then repossessed by the first devil, who returns with seven additional devils "more evil" than himself.[63] While the lieutenant alleges that Kolia is the original devil, who has returned to his "empty" home bringing "seven devils worse than himself," the film suggests that it is instead the vacuum of moral and cultural authority created by the collapse of Soviet power that has thrown both the lieutenant and the villagers into a state the film presents as moral chaos.

Even Kolia's mother, played by Nina Usatova as the archetypal peasant earth mother, throws vodka in his face when he refuses to honor "our laws" by drinking the requisite three shots on his father's grave. She also tells him he must leave the village, because she cannot protect him from Fedia, nor Fedia from himself, as long as Kolia remains. Usatova reports that she found this scene the most difficult to play, because she could not imagine her own mother sending her son away in that manner.[64] The scene does, in fact, run counter to the Russian stereotype of the all-forgiving and loving peasant mother, and thus further emphasizes the destruction of all the former shelters that Russian film and fiction have traditionally offered their viewers from the corruption and degradation of official urban culture. Usatova's performance re-creates the iconic images of peasant mothers made famous in films such as Shukshin's *Red Guelder Rose* and Mikhalkov's *Kinfolk (Rodnia,* 1981) and works of village prose such as Solzhenitsyn's "Matrena's House" ("Matrenin dvor," 1963) and Valentin Rasputin's *Farewell to Matera (Proshchan'e s materoi,* 1976), but the film's script denies her the moral authority and spiritual certainty that these earlier works ascribed to their peasant heroines. Unlike Solzhenitsyn's compulsively honest Matrena, for example, Kolia's mother sees stealing from the collective farm as a matter of family duty. When Kolia refuses to accompany his brother to carry off several bags of feed for their cow, Sonia goes with Fedia herself. Although Sonia loves both her sons, the film insists that she lives in a world in which it is no longer possible for Kolia to find, as he reports that his adoptive Afghan father had told him he would, "paradise at the feet of his mother." The film offers a partial explanation for the peasant mother's power-lessness to give her sons the shelter they seek in her own ignorance of Russian Orthodox religious practice. Sonia turns to the priest to make peace between her two sons more, it seems, from desperation than from any profound religious faith: the film reveals that she does not attend church services and that neither she nor Fedia observes the fasts prescribed by the church calendar, as becomes painfully clear when the priest declines the roast chicken she has prepared in honor of his visit.

In all these scenes the film presents the villagers' claims to Russian "Ortho-doxy" as a superficial explanation for a deep-rooted xenophobia that rules out the possibility of any change in their way of life. At the same time, it is difficult to convict the filmmakers of Russophobia, since the film's visual style runs counter to its plot. The camera work insists, in warmly lit closeups of Nina Usatova and in long tracking shots of fields and forests, on the pastoral beauty of the Russian peasant mother and the Russian countryside.

The key to this film's take on the current state of the "Russian soul" lies in the last line of the New Testament parable that Kolia's former lieutenant cites about the man repossessed by seven devils: "the last state of that man is worse than the first. Even so shall it be also until this wicked generation."[65] Khoti-nenko's *Moslem* presents the post-Soviet Russian soul as eviscerated by the demons of Soviet history and newly possessed by those of a corrupt and unprin-cipled craving for material advantage, unfettered and unguided by any mean-ingful sense of national identity. Its many scenes of thwarted reconciliation and its New Testament references underscore the paradox at the heart of the film: the powerful appeal of universal moral codes in a time of upheaval and the impossibility that any single code of behavior could have universal appeal or "authority" for all.

Although the film begins with an image of a priest striding through luxuriant fields, it ends with a scene of the local cowherd lashing the air furiously with a long whip, as if to chase out all the demons that possess this place and its people. The overall movement of the film, however, suggests that his gestures must be read more as a futile expression of impotent rage than as an act of exorcism. The cowherd has a speech defect that prevents outsiders like the lieutenant from understanding what he is saying; yet it is he who tells the legend of the cursed lake with its drowned church. A reminder of the vanished pastoral idyll of Russian village life, the cowherd remains powerless either to articulate that loss or to remedy it.

Moslem examines contemporary Russian culture from an angle diametrically opposed to that of *Particularities of the National Hunt*. Both films are centrally concerned with Russian national identity in relationship to the past, and both use "outsider" characters as catalysts for the action of their films. But while Rogozhkin's happy-go-lucky hunters absorb the young Finn into their circle and transform him into a hunter like themselves, Khotinenko's self-righteous villagers reject Kolia, unable to tolerate the presence in their midst of a character whose difference consists less in his choice of religion than in his insistence on living a life in which word and deed constitute an organic whole. *Moslem* disrupts both essentialist and chauvinist notions of national and ethnic identity; yet at the same time it indicates the impossibility of organizing new forms of Russian cultural identity outside the parameters of conceptions of Russianness that the film argues no longer exist except as habits of speech and defenses against threatening "others." The film refuses to sustain the illusion that national, familial, or social reconciliation is possible in a country in which both churches and the values they represent have been washed away by history.

Moreover, Rogozhkin positions his vision of collective drunken bliss at the margins of everyday life; his hunters are isolated from the demands of family, job, nation, and moral obligation. Khotinenko hurls his "Moslem" hero into the center of the nation's traditional sense of itself, the Russian rural landscape. Both films, however, convey very powerfully the competing tendencies at the heart of what I am calling the "cinema of reconciliation." *Particularities of the National Hunt* offers a vision of reconciliation with the past that the film repeatedly marks as fantastic and fairy tale–like, while the pathos of *Moslem* derives precisely from its characters' self-destructive quest for a reconciliation with one another that their common history continually resurfaces to prevent.

Notes

Research for this essay was made possible in large part by the generous hospitality of the organizers of the International Film Festival in Sochi, the Moscow International Film Festival, and the St. Petersburg International Film Festival in the summers of 1994–97; and by travel grants from the Committee on Research of the Academic Senate, University of California at San Diego. I am also grateful to Adele Barker, Helena Goscilo, and Vladimir Padunov for their support and thoughtful comments on earlier drafts, and I regret that I was not always able to follow the provocative lines of inquiry they suggested. All responsibility for any errors of fact or interpretation is mine alone.

1 Andrew Higson, "The Concept of National Cinema," *Screen* 30, no. 4 (1989): 46.

2 Statistics for 1990–95 may be found in Miroslava Segida and Sergei Zemlianukhin, *Domashniaia sinemateka. Otechestvennoe kino, 1918–1996* (Moscow: Dubl'-D, 1996), p. 6. The editors claim that these figures include films produced in the non-Russian former Soviet republics that remain members of the Commonwealth of Independent States, as well as those produced in the Russian Federation. As of this writing, the data for 1996 were not yet available, but informed estimates indicated that the total would amount at most to just over thirty films. See Daniil Dondurei, "Rynok vmesto sobesa," *Iskusstvo kino,* no. 10 (1996), p. 28.

3 *Katalog fil'mov stran SNG i Baltiki 1996–97. Informatsionnyi biulleten'* (Moscow: Fond 100-letiia mirovogo kino konfederatsiia soiuzov kinematografistov, 1997). This catalog lists twenty-eight feature-length fiction films completed in Russia in 1996. Another source states that only twenty feature films were released in Russia in 1996 and estimates that not more than twenty-seven films will be released in 1997. See "Spasi i sokhrani," *Kino-glaz,* no. 16 (1997), p. 4.

4 Nataliia Venzher, "Vyzhivat' ili zhit' ''vot v chem vopros," *Iskusstvo kino,* no. 7 (1997), p. 7.

5 Dondurei, "Rynok," pp. 28–30. One recent survey of young Russians indicated that they preferred Soviet-era films to both American films and Russian films made after 1991. See "Pokolenie delaet vybor!" *Kino Park,* no. 0 (March 1997), p. 7.

6 Daniil Dondurei, "Posle imperii: Kinorynok po-russki," *Iskusstvo kino,* no. 11 (1993), p. 7; and Dondurei, "Kinodelo: Na puti k rynku," in *Rossiskoe kino: Paradoksy obnovleniia,* ed. A. G. Dubrovin and M. E. Zak (Moscow: Materik, 1995), p. 132.

7 "V poiskakh molodogo," proceedings of the Meeting of Young Filmmakers, April 23, 1996, *Iskusstvo kino,* no. 7 (1996), p. 26. Unless otherwise indicated, all translations from Russian sources are my own.

8 The impact of television programming on Russian film production is outlined in Dondurei, "Rynok," pp. 28–37.

9 "In''ektsiia real'nosti," proceedings of the Special Session of the Collegium of the Russian State Committee on Film, July 2, 1996, *Iskusstvo kino,* no. 10 (1996), p. 26.

10 I. S. Volkov, "Piratstvo na regional'nom televidenii," *Kinoproizvodstvo,* no. 2 (1996), p. 77.

11 Mikhail Shatin, "Drang nach video, ili Pochemy kompaniia sobiraetsia smenit' orientatsiu," *Kinoproizvodstvo,* no. 2 (1996), p. 13.

12 For a lively discussion of the Russian video market, see Dmitrii Komm, "Shedevry po-prezhnemy ostaiutsia piratskimi," and Sergei Kudriavtsev, "Kholodnaia video-voina," both in *Seans gazeta,* no. 1 (April 1996), p. 8, published as an insert to *Seans,* no. 12 (1996), between pp. 114 and 123.

13 Murad Ibragimbekov, personal communication, August 22, 1997.

14 *Seans gazeta,* no. 3 (May 1997), p. 5, published as an insert to *Seans,* no. 15 (1997), between pp. 128 and 145.

15 See, for example, Aleksandr Golutva, "Den'gi eto vse!" *Iskusstvo kino,* no. 9 (1993), pp. 79–81; the comments of Sergei Solov'ev on the need for a "systematic investment of government money" in "In''ektsiia real'nosti," p. 26; and the 1994 poll of four hundred leading film directors, cinematographers, scriptwriters, actors, and critics, to which 96 percent of those queried replied that "the government is simply obligated to guarantee the development of Russian film; to give money — 92%; to print copies of films at no charge — 80%; to finance advertising — 62%; to institute a special tax on American films — 61%; to introduce a serious tariff on imported films — 65%." Results of the poll are summarized and analyzed in Daniil Dondurei, "Shag vpered, dva shaga nazad: O modernizatsii kinoindustrii v Rossii," *Iskusstvo kino,* no. 7 (1994), p. 18.

16 In 1994, for example, 57 percent of four hundred members of the "filmmaking elite" were convinced that viewers would return to film theaters if they could see recent Russian films there, and 56 percent were convinced that an unregulated market would lead to the complete displacement of Russian films by American imports. See Dondurei, "Shag vpered," pp. 14, 19.

17 Dondurei, "Rynok," p. 33.

18 Dondurei, "Kinodelo," p. 136.

19 "In''ektsiia real'nosti," p. 27. Older directors and film organization bureaucrats are more likely to insist, with Armen Medvedev, chair of the State Committee on Film, that "self-financing [of films] is a utopia," and that the film industry will only survive with government financial support (ibid., p. 22). See also the comments of directors Aleksandr Rogozhkin and Valerii Rubinchik in "Kino kak sredstvo massovoi nekommunikatsii," proceedings of a Round-table at the Kinotavr International Film Festival in Sochi, June 1996, *Iskusstvo kino,* no. 10 (1996), pp. 13–14.

20 "V poiskakh molodogo," p. 28.

21 The "Appeal" was delivered by director Valerii Todorovskii on April 23, 1996. See "V poiskakh molodogo," p. 33.

22 Filmmakers' anxieties about cinema's loss of significance are symptomatic of a much broader cultural phenomenon, what Nancy Condee and Vladimir Padunov describe as the "unprecedented . . . wholesale social displacement of the cult of high culture" in late and post-Soviet Russia. See Nancy Condee and Vladimir Padunov, "The ABC of Russian Consumer Culture: Readings, Ratings, and Real Estate," in *Soviet Hieroglyphics: Visual Culture in Late Twentieth-Century Russia,* ed. Nancy Condee (Bloomington: Indiana University Press, 1995), p. 141.

23 "V poiskakh molodogo," p. 30.

24 For concurrent opinions, see the statements of directors Aleksei Balabanov, Pavel Lungin, and Sergei Ursuliak in "Kino kak sredstvo," pp. 13, 19–20.

25 Even critic Tatiana Moskvina, who persists in asserting an inevitable division between popular and intelligentsia culture and aspirations, acknowledges that contemporary Russian cinema has no "third way" around the alternatives of "national

popularity [*narodnost'*] or death." See Tatiana Moskvina, "O narodnosti v kine-matografe," in *Seans,* no. 12 (1996), p. 156.

26 "Kino kak sredstvo," p. 20.

27 The term is director Pavel Lungin's; see ibid., p. 13.

28 "V poiskakh molodogo," p. 25.

29 Ibid., p. 31.

30 "Katastrofa ili pauza," proceedings of a Round-Table Discussion among Leading Film Critics, *Iskusstvo kino,* no. 8 (1996), pp. 5–6.

31 "Kino kak sredstvo," p. 13.

32 See, for example, Dondurei, "Rynok," p. 37; and Aleksei German, "Mne stalo skuchno," *Iskusstvo kino,* no. 10 (1996), p. 65. For an opposing argument that seeks to debunk the current wave of nostalgia for the allegedly "nationally popular" and "viewer-oriented" cinema of the Soviet past, see Andrei Plakhov, "Inorodnost' i narodnost'," *Seans,* no. 12 (1996), pp. 157–60.

33 Mikhail Trofimenkov, "Pokaianie," *Iskusstvo kino,* no. 2 (1995), pp. 60–63.

34 On the decline in cinema going in Russia since 1990, see Dondurei, "Kinodelo," pp. 126–40. For an excellent discussion of the perceived decline in the aesthetic and technical quality of recent Russian cinema, see "Katastrofa ili pauza," pp. 4–23.

35 On the "nonexistent mainstream" in contemporary Russian cinema and the absence of popular genre films, see the comments of Anatolii Maksimov, producer of film programs for Central Russian Television, in "In''ektsiia real'nosti," p. 25; and those of critic and director Oleg Kovalov in "Kino kak sredstvo," p. 21.

36 This description can be found on the cover of the legally licensed videotapes of this film that were widely available for purchase in Moscow in the summer of 1996.

37 Svetlana Boym, *Common Places: Mythologies of Everyday Life* (Cambridge: Harvard University Press, 1994), p. 247.

38 See Anna Furticheva, "Astrakhan schitaet, chto sochinil skazku na urovne 'Moskva slezam ne verit,' " *Vecherniaia Moskva,* April 9, 1996, p. 7.

39 Overall, *Russian* occurs in a total of thirty-four titles and *death* in a total of forty-six titles between 1917 and 1996. See Zemlianukhin and Segida, *Domashniaia sinema-teka,* p. 8.

40 I have chosen to translate the Russian word *musul'manin* as "Moslem" rather than "Muslim" in part because the filmmakers themselves refer to the film in English as Moslem, with neither a definite nor an indefinite article, and also to preserve the slightly pejorative, old-fashioned, and colonialist overtones of the Russian term. For the filmmakers' comments on their reasons for choosing this name for the film, see Vladimir Khotinenko and Valerii Zalotukha, "Musul'manin kak probnyi kamen' russkoi deistvitel'nosti," interview by Elena Stishova and Lev Karakhan, *Iskusstvo kino,* no. 9 (1995), pp. 14–15.

41 Its other awards include prizes at the 1995 Karlovy-Vary and Vyborg festivals; the 1995 Russian film journalists' award for Best Film at Sochi; and the Golden Ostap. See Zemlianukhin and Segida, *Domashniaia sinemateka,* p. 307.

42 Georgii Mautkin, "Lenfilm on the Market: The Peculiarities of the National Hunt," *Seans Newsletter,* no. 1 (April 1996), p. 4, appended to *Seans,* no. 12 (1996).

43 Cited in Zemlianukhin and Segida, *Domashniaia sinemateka,* p. 307.

44 Representative Russian reviews of the film include Sergei Dobrotvorskii, " 'I ne-medlenno vypil . . .'," *Iskusstvo kino,* no. 12 (1995), pp. 77–79; Lev Karakhan et al., "Osobennosti natsional'noi okhoty: Kritiki o fil'me," *Seans,* no. 12 (1996), p. 25; Irina Liubarskaia, "Utinnye okhoty na plenere," *Seans,* no. 12 (1996), p. 27; and Tatiana Moskvina, "Istochniki zhizni eshche ne issiakli," *Seans,* no. 12 (1996), p. 26.

45 For provocative overviews of Rogozhkin's oeuvre and a comparison of *Particularities* with his earlier works, see Sergei Dobrotvorskii, "I nemedlenno vypil"; and Mikhail Trofimenkov, "Poet klaustrofobii: Aleksandr Rogozhkin," *Seans,* no. 12 (1996), pp. 111–14.

46 This book appears to be the fourth volume in Nikolai Kutepov's *History of the Russian Hunt from the Tenth through the Nineteenth Centuries,* Imperatorskaia okhota na Rusi, konets XVIII i XIX vek (St. Petersburg: Ekspeditsiia zagotovleniia gos. bumag., 1911), which includes illustrations by painters such as V. M. Vasnetsov, N. S. Samoish, I. A. Repin, V. I. Surikov, E. E. Lansere, L. O. Pasternak, A. N. Benua, and other prominent artists from the late nineteenth and early twentieth centuries.

47 The film was listed under this title in the catalog for the 1995 Open Russian Film Festival in Sochi, where it had its world premiere. Otkrytyi rossiiskii kinofestival. Sochi, June 1–13, 1995. *Katalog fil'mov,* p. 14.

48 Natal'ia Sirivlia offers a parallel reading of this film in "Pole chudes," *Seans,* no. 12 (1996), pp. 164–65.

49 Although *Moslem* appears not to have matched the success of Rogozhkin's *Particularities* or Mikhalkov's *Burnt by the Sun,* it received a tremendous amount of attention in the Russian press, was shown on Russian television, and collected a number of prizes at both Russian and international film festivals. It was also the 1995 Russian nominee for the Academy Award for Best Foreign Language Film. Awards won by *Moslem* include the Silver Medal at the 1995 Montreal International Film Festival, selection as one of the three best films of the year by the Association of Russian Film Journalists, and a number of acting prizes. Nina Usatova and Aleksandr Baluev took the top acting prizes at the 1995 Sochi Film Festival, and Usatova and Evgenii Mironov were named Actors of the Year for their roles in *Moslem* by the Association of Film Journalists. For a representative selection of excerpts from the many reviews of the film, see " 'Musul'manin': Pressa fil'ma," *Chital'nyi zal: Kritiko-bibliograficheskii zhurnal o kino,* no. 2 (1995–96), pp. 114–28.

50 As soon as the film appeared, critics commented on its affinities with the work of Shukshin and Nikita Mikhalkov, with whom Khotinenko studied in film school and for whom he worked as assistant director on *Five Evenings* (1978), *Oblomov* (1979), and *Kinfolk* (1982). See Andrei Plakhov, "Predstavlenie o zhizni vsegda bednee zhizni," in *Kommersant-Daily* (Moscow), March 24, 1995, p. 13; V. Belopol'skaia,

" 'Musul'manin': da, aziaty my . . . ," *Ogonek,* no. 23 (June 1995), pp. 68–69; and Liudmila Dziubenko, "Kto tam na puti k vere?" *Moskovskaia pravda,* April 7, 1995, p. 3.

51 On village prose, see Kathleen Parthe, *Russian Village Prose: The Radiant Past* (Princeton: Princeton University Press, 1992). For a brief discussion of Soviet films based on works of village prose, see Anna Lawton, *Kinoglasnost': Soviet Cinema in Our Time* (Cambridge: Cambridge University Press, 1992), pp. 35–36.

52 See, for example, Oleg Goriachev, "Odin khristianin, i tot musul'manin . . . ," *Artfonar',* no. 7 (1995), p. 2; and Anton Charkin, "Patrioticheskaia tragediia. Novyi fil'm Vladimira Khotinenko: ideia edinogo Boga," *Kul'tura* (Moscow), May 20, 1995, p. 7.

53 Zara Abdullaeva, "Zhivye i mertvye," *Iskusstvo kino,* no. 9 (1995), p. 9.

54 Dmitrii Bykov, "Perekhod v Indiiu," *Ekran i stsena,* April 6–13, 1995, p. 4.

55 Belopol'skaia, " 'Musul'manin': da, aziaty''my . . . ," pp. 68–69. Boiarina Morozova and Archpriest Avvakum are well-known religious martyrs who suffered exile, imprisonment, and death for their resistance to the reform of the Russian Orthodox ritual and liturgy in the mid-seventeenth century.

56 Valerii Turovskii, "Khristianin 'Makarov' i 'Musul'manin' Ivanov," *Izvestiia,* April 4, 1995, p. 7.

57 See, for example, Aleksandr Shpagin, "Novyi Vavilon," *Kul'tura,* August 5, 1995, p. 9; and the comments by critic Elena Stishova, Khotinenko, and scriptwriter Valerii Zalotukha in Khotinenko and Zalotukha, "Musul'manin kak probnyi kamen'," p. 15.

58 Lev Anninskii, "Grustno zhit' na etom svete, gospoda . . . ," *Iskusstvo kino,* no. 9 (1995), p. 5; Khotinenko and Zalotukha, "Musul'manin kak probnyi kamen'," p. 15. For more positive takes than Anninskii's on the film's use of Islam as metaphor, see Dmitrii Bykov, "Perekhod v Indiiu," p. 4; and Antonina Kriukova, "Iavlenie, 'Musul'manina' narodu," *Nezavisimaia gazeta* (Moscow), March 31, 1995, p. 7.

59 Khotinenko and Zalotukha, "Musul'manin kak probnyi kamen'," p. 15.

60 Homi Bhabha, "Dissemination: Time, Narrative and the Margins of the Modern Nation," in *The Location of Culture* (London: Routledge, 1994), pp. 139–70.

61 This tale of the flooded church recalls the notorious destruction of the Church of Christ the Savior in Moscow in 1934, on the site of which Stalin intended to erect a giant skyscraping Palace of Soviets. The plan was never realized, and a giant open-air swimming pool was built on the site instead that became notorious in Moscow urban folklore for the illicit sexual activity sheltered by the mist rising from its surface. A smaller version of the original church has just been rebuilt on its old site at the initiative of Moscow mayor Iurii Luzhkov. As Kathleen Parthe notes, images of flooded rural towns and landscapes recur frequently in village prose as a symbol of the disappearance of what she calls the "rural chronotope." The most prominent use of this image occurs in Valentin Rasputin's *Farewell to Matera* (*Proshchan'e s materoi,* 1976). For discussion of this and similar texts, see Parthe, *Russian Village Prose,* pp. 64–65, 71–75. I would argue that the drowned church in *Moslem* fills a

different symbolic function than the flooded landscapes in village prose, which typically serve as a submerged, but nevertheless visible, elegiac reminder of what has been lost. The church in *Moslem* was submerged so long ago, and so deeply, that it can neither be seen nor touched by any but the most persistent divers. Moreover, when the pig's head rises up from the waters of the same lake, it appears to have supplanted the church entirely, suggesting that nothing of the church may remain to resurrect, and that the vacuum created by its absence has been filled irrevocably by demons no longer conquerable by appeals to a vanished way of life and the religious values that sustained it.

62 The encroachment of Western media is apparent throughout the film in the posters for action movies that plaster the walls of Vera's ramshackle cottage and the pop tune "America, the Homewrecker" ("Amerika razluchnitsa"), which the local store-keeper hums on and off throughout the film, at one point ridiculing Sonia for singing an old-fashioned folk lament, because "no one sings like that anymore."

63 The parable to which he refers may be found in Matthew 12:43–45 and Luke 11:24–26.

64 Nina Usatova, "Zametki o russkom," *Iskusstvo kino,* no. 4 (1996), p. 43.

65 Matthew 12:45.

■ **CHAPTER 9**
ROBERT EDELMAN

THERE ARE NO RULES ON PLANET RUSSIA: POST-SOVIET SPECTATOR SPORT

Before the collapse of the USSR, spectator sport was a distinctive form of Soviet popular culture. Inescapably spontaneous, spectator sport was never easy to control; nor did it foster acceptance of communist authority.[1] It was, instead, an arena of "contested terrain" between a powerful but far from omnipotent state and a multifarious but less than civil society.[2] Soviet fans, largely male, watched the sports they wanted to watch, not those the state wanted them to watch. They chose their own heroes, who were not the official heroes of the party, and they consumed the sports spectacles presented by the state in often irreverent ways that transgressed the narrow boundaries of officially approved behavior.[3] The West knew Soviet sport through the warped prism of the Olympics. Internationally, the party sought to "win" the Olympic Games in order to demonstrate the superiority of communism. Domestically, Soviet athletes were to be models of discipline and obedience, fostering acceptance of official values. Victory at this level required the production of athletes across the full range of international sports, major and minor alike. But few Soviet fans paid serious and continuing attention to the gymnasts, figure skaters, weight lifters, and track stars turned out by the "Big Red Machine." Olympic sports were not spectator sports in the USSR for the simple reason that few of them attracted spectators. Only soccer, hockey, and men's basketball regularly drew audiences — primarily men — to stadiums and television sets.[4] The Olympic sport system, a classic product of the command economy, was like the many dams and factories that made the USSR an industrial giant but produced things neither wanted nor needed by the public. By contrast, spectator sport can best be seen as part of the long-suffering, underprioritized consumer sector whose chronic failures played so crucial a role in the erosion of Soviet power.[5]

Instead of generating consent for the regime, as intended, spectator sport afforded male Soviet citizens a place to act irreverently, cheer loudly, and joke among themselves. From 1926 to 1991, soccer riots were part of the Soviet sports scene; athletes often fought with each other on the field. In the various republics, rooting for local teams provided a safe cover for nationalist sentiment, and throughout the USSR open criticism of sports figures was possible in ways unimaginable for most other spheres of activity.[6] The authorities did not foster these behaviors as a safety valve for Soviet life's frustrations. Sports, with their strongly didactic messages, could not be limited to oases of Bakhtinian carnival. Bad behavior by fans, players, and officials was a constant problem, continually bemoaned by a disapproving press and frustrated party.

Unlike many other forms of Soviet popular culture, however, games played by talented, well-rewarded athletes provided a relatively honest spectacle performed at a high level of skill. Print and broadcast descriptions of sports events displayed a core of reality. In the Soviet context, these differences were important. Unlike the Olympic sport system and the monstrous Physical Culture Day parades (both products of the Stalin period), spectator sport gained a measure of autonomy and afforded citizens a space for difficult-to-find pleasure, spontaneity, and fun. Although it would be stretching the argument to claim spectator sport was subversive of communist authority, its effect can, with hindsight, fairly be described as corrosive.[7]

Today, however, spectator sport has lost its exceptional character. It is hard to think of a single sector of public or private life in contemporary Russia that is not "contested terrain." Nor does "transgressive behavior" assume special political or cultural significance when transgressions of all sorts have become common. It turns out that post-Soviet popular culture is less distinctive than Soviet popular culture was. Although a strong latent interest in sport remains, fewer Russians now watch it. Contemporary movies, television, radio, music, and video games, largely but not entirely foreign, are more popular than a great deal of late Soviet fare ever was. Young men, the largest group of spectator sport consumers, have developed other interests. In the country formerly known as the Soviet Union, there are lots of ways to have a good time. Sport has become but one segment of a post-Soviet entertainment industry in which the specifically Russian finds it difficult to resist the impact of an increasingly homogenized global popular culture.[8]

Russian sport spectacles and the athletes who participate in them have become commodities produced and consumed in an intensely competitive world market. The international demand for athletic talent created a "brawn drain" and stripped Russian domestic sports leagues of their stars, causing the level of play to slip and attendance to decline. The drop in playing standards was exacerbated by a completely opposite kind of process — the centrifugal nationalisms that played so crucial a role in the breakup of the USSR. Today, each newly independent state has its own sports leagues, replacing the old All-Union leagues and further lowering the quality of play everywhere.[9] Thus, the contradictory forces of global commodification and localist nationalism have each diminished the attractiveness of domestic sport, which now competes for an audience with more dynamic forms of popular culture.

Despite these problems, powerful forces, both inside and outside the former Soviet Union, are competing for dominance over this segment of the entertainment industry. Privatizers struggle with local and central government officials for control of teams and leagues; commercial entrepreneurs and sports agents seek to profit from Russia's enormous human sporting resources. Lurking behind all this business activity is organized crime, whose precise role is impossible to specify but is, by many accounts, as widespread as it is in any other sphere of business.

Of the two forces, nationalism, curiously enough, had the greater initial impact on post-Soviet spectator sport. Early in 1990, pushed by their struggles for national independence, the Georgians and Lithuanians announced that their clubs would no longer take part in All-Union sports leagues and their athletes would not represent the USSR in international competition. Nearly two years later, when the USSR came apart, each new nation created its own sports leagues, particularly in the most popular sport, soccer. Rigidly following the

European example, each new league, Russia's included, needed roughly twenty teams. Yet, after an initial burst of nationalist enthusiasm, it soon became clear that there were not enough cities large enough or players talented enough to support "big-time" (*bol'shoi*) football. Attendance collapsed nearly everywhere, as fans came to understand that the old multinational Soviet leagues had, in fact, provided a high level of competition.

Nationalism aside, interest in all sports had been waning throughout the years of perestroika. As late as 1987, Soviet league soccer was still attracting a healthy average of twenty-seven thousand fans a game, but by 1991, as the economic crisis worsened, that figure had fallen to twelve thousand. In the economic free fall of terminal perestroika, most Soviet citizens were too busy finding food to show up for games. After the breakup of the USSR, attendance plummeted even further. In the first year of post-Soviet play, an average of less than six thousand fans took in the games of the new Russian league. Elsewhere, the figures were even worse.[10]

The near evaporation of fan interest has today given way to an uneven recovery.[11] As officials have reorganized their leagues and learned the lessons of competition in a capitalist entertainment market, fans have started coming back, some players have returned to work in their homeland, and capital has been drawn to sport. During 1996, soccer crowds finally approached the less than impressive average of the last Soviet season. Basketball established a small, tightly organized, and successful league in 1994, while hockey, despite huge problems, has continued to draw fans outside Moscow, especially in towns where local factories have been successfully privatized.

The Athletic Diaspora

Historically, spectator sport has been entertaining because masses of viewers throughout the world received pleasure from witnessing the extraordinary feats of a talented few. Immediately after the 1917 revolution, this inherent elitism made the watching of sport problematic for early Soviet theorists of physical culture,[12] who were opposed to the professionalization and commodification of athletes engendered by passive spectating. After nearly two decades of debate, however, those qualms were overcome in the course of the Stalinist hierarchicization of culture and society that took place in the mid-1930s.[13] After World War II, spectator sport expanded even further as soccer, in particular, took off as a mass attraction. Previously patronized exclusively by the working class, soccer dramatically expanded its social base, drawing an average of thirty-five thousand spectators per game. Despite the devastations of war and the repressions of Stalin's last years, Soviet fans literally filled stadiums to bursting and consumed these sport spectacles with a joy and spontaneity seen in few other aspects of life.

Soccer's leading players — Lev Iashin, Vsevolod Bobrov, Nikita Simonian, Igor Netto, and Eduard Strel′tsov — were idolized by the public. During the 1970s, such top hockey talents as Valerii Kharlamov and Alexander Iakushev were accorded similar treatment, as were a number of basketball players. While they were relatively privileged, however, these men and women did not live lives of Western-style luxury. Officially amateurs, Soviet sportsmen and women received repeated invitations from Western professional teams, but they were not permitted to play abroad without defecting, an act none chose to take until 1989.

During perestroika, players were able to express their desire to play for and keep big money in the West. At the same time, sport bureaucrats came to realize that players could be a significant source of hard currency. Tentatively, a few veteran soccer players were allowed to go to Austria during 1987. The next year, when the Soviets made the final of the European soccer championship, the demand for their services became overwhelming. Millions of dollars changed hands (little of it going to the athletes) as several top players signed with teams in the powerful Spanish and Italian leagues. Hockey and basketball players soon followed suit.[14]

In the last years of perestroika, the government attempted to control this process, but pressure from players, Western agents, and capitalist teams, eroded away the strictures. Nevertheless, the outflow was limited to a few dozen established figures. After 1992, however, the trickle became a flood. All controls on the talent market evaporated, both in Russia and in the newly independent states. By 1995, more than three hundred soccer, seven hundred hockey, and one hundred basketball players were working in North America, Asia, and Western and Eastern Europe.[15] As in Latin America and Africa, post-Soviet domestic leagues became "farm teams" for capitalist sport.[16] This new and uncomfortable subordinate status made it difficult for Russians to gather their players for international games, collect transfer fees, and get their clubs into lucrative intra-European competitions.[17]

Between 1992 and 1994, athletes from the former Soviet Union were willing to work almost anywhere for almost any wage.[18] Russia and the newly independent states found themselves invaded by hundreds of capitalist talent hunters of widely varying degrees of scrupulousness.[19] Eighteen-year-old soccer players and fifteen-year-old hockey phenoms acquired agents. When Western teams hired Russian scouts, players were discovered not just in Moscow but in the deepest provincial locales. With most former Soviet clubs denuded of institutional support, survival dictated participating in the wholesale transfer of talent, regardless of the consequences for the individuals involved or for the future of sport.[20]

The most visible effect of this talent carousel was felt by the Spartak Moscow soccer team. Founded in 1935 by civilians rather than by the security forces, which had previously dominated big-time sport, Spartak was, and is, the favorite team of the Moscow public and the most popular club throughout Russia. The team dominated the new Russian league during the league's first five years, failing to win the championship only in 1995. It also did well in international competition, and its players were the backbone of the national team. Each year, Spartak's stars attracted the attention of European clubs, and each year the team was forced to reload with young players recruited from throughout the former USSR.[21]

Despite the great exodus, Russian fans maintained a strong interest in former Soviet athletes who left the country. Although few of the soccer players reached stardom in the West, the hockey "legionnaires" in North America did considerably better, exciting great pride in the "Soviet school" of hockey. Yet, these developments have left Russian fans — across a wide range of political opinions — with mixed emotions. To the extent that participation in the global market for sports talent is seen as part of living in a "normal and civilized" world, much of the public, especially its promarket segment, is pleased. Yet, the process of sports globalization confirms Russia's presently subordinate status in the world, making its effect problematic. On the one hand, the athletic diaspora has stimulated among Russians the same kind of nationalist resentments manifested elsewhere in the world against such multinational juggernauts as the U.S.-based International Management Group or the Spanish agency Dorna, both actively involved in buying and selling Russian athletes.[22] On the other hand, the "brawn drain" has had the homogenizing cultural effect of forcing ambivalent post-Soviet sports fans to look outside the old borders for entertainment.

By the middle of 1994, as the larger economy began to experience a measure of stability, Russian spectator sport started a slow and inconsistent recovery.

Muted resistance to the global market was possible, but only by adopting the methods of the outside corporate forces that were driving the hunt for Russian talent. "Business" fortunes were being made, legally and illegally, and a portion of this "new" money gravitated to sport. As the ostentatiously rich "New Russians" went about acquiring the symbols of wealth, sport became one place to put (or hide) their money. Through increased sponsorship — and in a few cases actual ownership by wealthy individuals — Russian clubs in the popular sports acquired the means to retain some of their stars.

It also became possible for Russian teams to attract the best talent from other former Soviet republics. If Russia was weak vis-à-vis the West, it enjoyed advantages over the newly independent states. As it became possible for top stars in the various Russian leagues to make six-figure dollar salaries, the leading Russian clubs took on a curiously neo-Soviet caste. In soccer, Spartak recruited a regular stream of Ukrainians, while Alania, the 1995 champions from the wealthy North Ossetian town of Vladikavkaz, boasted a lineup with several Georgians and a pleiad of Central Asians. Better pay and better play made the Russian league an attractive alternative for young players who had not yet gained the attention of Western scouts. What was good for Russia, however, hurt Ukraine and Georgia, as domestic play there and elsewhere continued to stagnate.

The improved finances also made it possible to attract a number of stars back to Russia. During the second season (1995–96) of Russian basketball's "Super League," several national team players who had been playing with European clubs returned to work in Moscow. Their appearance had a predictably positive impact on team play and attendance.[23] Along the same lines, Spartak succeeded in obtaining the services of three of its former stars for the second half of the 1995 soccer season, enabling the team to make a strong run in the European League of Champions.[24] Second-tier talents also found it more profitable and comfortable to work at home than in the less well endowed European leagues.[25] Hockey players not quite good enough for the NHL found that playing back home had become a viable possibility. Detroit Red Wing forward Viacheslav Kozlov told a U.S. interviewer, "Now they start paying money, good money in Russia. Somebody does not want to go play minor leagues over here [in the United States] because they make enough money over in Russia. When you finish career here, you can go play a couple of more years in Russia."[26] Kozlov's teammate, Viacheslav Fetisov, confirmed that this new trend has had a positive impact on domestic hockey: "Last five years, it was a tough economic situation. People have to worry about family and try to get food. . . . Now it's a situation more stable and people get more interest in hockey and they come to watch hockey games in Russia."[27] As proof of the improved conditions, the aging defenseman Alexei Kasatonov, no longer able to make an NHL roster, came back to play for Central Army in 1996 after several years in the United States, and five former members of the Spartak hockey team, all in their thirties, returned after working in Europe.[28]

Aside from luring back old fan favorites, Russian clubs have become sufficiently well financed to bring in a limited number of foreign players. During the first year (1994–95) of the reorganized basketball league, more than a dozen Americans brought the entertaining U.S. version of the game to Russia. Fans came out to watch the "exotic imports," but few of the visitors performed brilliantly. The players, all African Americans, experienced a high level of racism on and off the court, and it turned out that they were not much better than their Russian competitors.[29] In the league's second year, officials instead invested their money in attracting back former Soviet stars. Attendance continued to grow, and Russian clubs did well in international competition. Along similar lines, a smattering of Brazilians and Nigerians found places in the lineups of several Russian soccer clubs.[30]

None of these deals radically altered the balance of sports trade between Russia and the outside world. The former Soviet Union remained a net exporter of athletic talent. Nevertheless, the new signings indicated that the downward trend of the first post-Soviet years had been reversed. Russia was no longer everybody's victim, but it cannot be said that this shift inspired an orgy of chauvinism. Rather, the new developments blunted communist and nationalist criticism of an excessively Western-oriented sports business world, and when regression in sport began to abate during 1995, opponents of the market turned their criticism to other, nonsport targets.

Meanwhile, in the new, uneven stability, the improved attractiveness of these long-loved pastimes turned them into targets of another kind. A variety of provincial power brokers, not only in business but in government, sought to reinvolve themselves in the sports industry and recapture some of the prestige of association with popular big-time sports. Once again, spectator sport became "contested terrain." Now, however, the contest was not between a didactic central state and a fun-loving, transgressive public; instead, a struggle for control emerged among competing elites.

Reorganizing Leagues and Redesigning Teams

After the collapse of the USSR, each of the three popular spectator sports dealt differently with the task of organizing leagues in the new circumstances. As already noted, soccer formed an entirely Russian league the same size as the old Soviet league.[31] In 1994, the basketball Super League was formed, limited to six well-financed teams located in a geographically compact area to reduce newly expensive travel costs.[32] In hockey, organizers took the deceptively simple step of renaming the old Soviet league, calling it instead the International Hockey League. Since Russians had always dominated hockey, clubs in Ukraine, Belarus, Latvia, and Kazakhstan had to go along with the new arrangement. The league doubled in size to twenty-eight teams, most of which came from provincial cities such as Iaroslavl, Magnitogorsk, and Togliatti, where successfully privatized factories supported strong teams and challenged Moscow's long domination of the sport.[33] This arrangement proved successful in maintaining fan interest, especially on the periphery, despite the mass exodus of talent. Yet, the league and the newly formed national federations soon became involved in jurisdictional disputes, as clubs lost valuable players to international competitions at crucial points in the season. By 1996, this neo-Soviet arrangement had proven unworkable and had been replaced by a purely Russian league.[34]

Of the three approaches, basketball's was, at least for a while, the most successful. Telecasts of league games often drew larger ratings than weekly NBA highlight shows. Russian teams did well in intra-European club competitions, consistently filling their small arenas for international matchups. This progress was accomplished through realism about the limited possibilities for sport in the new Russia, along with an influx of energy and money from new groups and individuals. The driving force behind the new league was a Saratov millionaire named Vladimir Rodionov, who in a typically Russian conflict of interest was simultaneously the owner of his hometown team, Avtodorozhnik (the 1997 champions), and the president of the Super League.

Other business interests, of varying reputations, became sponsors of such longtime Soviet league stalwarts as Central Army Sports Club (Tsentral'nyi sportivnyi klub armii, or TSSKA) and Dynamo Moscow.[35] Yet, this success proved short-lived. The sponsors of TSSKA and Dynamo repeatedly bailed out over the next two seasons. Players were not paid; strikes were threatened; and

Central Army's powerful team was on the verge of extinction until it was taken over by the mighty Oneksimbank late in 1997. On the eve of the 1997–98 season, the principle of a small, financially sound league was abandoned. Eighteen clubs were brought into two geographically distinct divisions, as the basketball federation sought to fill its own coffers from the sizable dues collected from each competing team. With so many weak teams, attendance decreased along with the level of play.

By contrast, there was greater continuity of leadership in hockey and soccer. After an extended power struggle, the hockey league was taken over in 1995 by a longtime Soviet sports bureaucrat named Valentin Sych. Soccer remained under the control of Viacheslav Koloskov, who, from 1986, was president of the old Soviet Football Federation and a vice president of soccer's international governing body, FIFA. Koloskov took over a new group, the Russian Football Union, which replaced the Soviet federation. The union, not formally a state organization, exists in an uneasy relationship with the Professional Football League, a business enterprise that conducts domestic competition.[36] Early in 1997, Sych was murdered in what appeared to be an organized crime dispute over the importing of tobacco, an activity sports federations had been allowed to engage in tax free. However, continuity was maintained with the appointment of Alexander Steblin, a highly experienced sports bureaucrat who was the president of the Dynamo Moscow hockey team. In an unusual development, someone was actually accused of Sych's murder. One of the members of the conspiracy was Robert Cherenkov, the first head of the post-Soviet International Hockey League, who had been forced out of power by Sych.

The soccer league was headed by Nikolai Tolstykh, who was also the president of the Dynamo Moscow Soccer Club. While Rodionov's twin positions did not pose major problems for Russian basketball, the same cannot be said for Tolstykh. In his capacity as Dynamo's leader, Tolstykh threatened referees who made controversial calls against his team. Considering that the league controls the careers of those who judge its games, Tolstykh's actions exposed huge problems in the sport, involving the fixing of games, bribing of referees, and other more subtle forms of corruption.[37]

Problems of this sort are not simply a phenomenon of the more openly dishonest post-Soviet era. The Soviet sport scene was a traditionally notorious arena of dubious practices. Athletes, who had the prized privilege of international travel, often bought dollars on the black market in order to purchase the usual array of *defitsitnye* items. Generally allowed to float past customs, they often disposed of these items with the help of organized crime. This process built relationships, and after their careers many "sportsmen" became bodyguards for Mafia figures. Soviet sports clubs also enjoyed their own legal sources of revenue, primarily ticket sales, and well-endowed teams with wealthy patrons, from both sides of what passed for the law, were able to bend the rules. Like corruption in the rest of society, the range of bribery, money laundering, and influence peddling in the sports industry has expanded since 1992, and only part of this change can be explained by the central government's lack of direct involvement. This continued corruption has slowed privatization of sports enterprises, and the so-called new money has not caused a complete organizational revolution in the way teams are run. Many of the same people have tried to operate by different, as yet unclear, rules, and in the process they have continually contested (not always politely) just what those rules might be.

The leagues have oscillated between organizing themselves as privately held joint-stock companies (*aktsionernye obshchestva zakrytogo tipa*), on the one hand, and so-called social (i.e., nonprofit) organizations, on the other. Some of the more successful clubs have become enterprises whose shareholders are team officials.[38] Conversely, a large number of struggling teams have required assistance from cities or regions. Others, both strong and weak, have become entirely the creatures of provincial government bodies in a process that might be called municipalization.[39] Only two teams in all of Russia — Rotor Volgograd in soccer and Avtodorozhnik Saratov in basketball — are the property of wealthy individuals, and even Rodionov has had to solicit aid from the Saratov mayor's office.[40]

The Spartak Moscow soccer team has been repeatedly reorganized, deriving revenues from the sale of its players and from the generous prize money given to participants in the European Champions' League. Yet, the team refused repeated offers of assistance from the office of Moscow's politically powerful, sports-loving mayor, Iurii Luzhkov.[41] In the fall of 1997, the team's president, Lydia Nechaeva, was murdered in what was rumored to be a dispute over television rights. The 1995 champion, Alania of Vladikavkaz, has, conversely, been lavishly supported by the president of North Ossetia, exciting accusations of corruption and match rigging which themselves raise the specter of anti-Caucasian racism.[42] In yet another sign of the times, one of Moscow's oldest soccer clubs, Torpedo, changed hands in the summer of 1996. For years the team had been supported by the giant ZIL motor works, but the struggling factory could no longer maintain the team and sold it to the private company that controls the vast Luzhniki sports complex.[43]

Some of the most bizarre post-Soviet struggles have surrounded the famed Central Army Sports Club (TSSKA), with its huge campus in northwest Moscow. Immediately after the collapse of the USSR, budget cuts hampered the army's extensive sports operations. In response, the army club became involved in a wide range of business ventures. Several practice facilities were turned into grocery stores. A giant wholesale market took over the indoor soccer stadium, and a Mercedes dealership occupied the lobby of the club's new hockey arena.[44] Army teams in specific sports began to make their own deals, often with mixed results. On the eve of the 1995–96 season, TSSKA's basketball team announced a million-dollar sponsorship agreement with the International Industrial Bank (Mezhprombank). The money was supposed to fund several six-figure contracts the team had signed with its stars, but two months into the season the bank reneged on its deal. A similarly generous sponsor was difficult to locate, and the players were not paid until the very end of the season, working without salaries but quite successfully on the court and at the gate.[45] Similar problems occurred in 1997 when TSSKA, Dynamo, and Spartak Petersburg basketball players threatened strikes after months of not receiving wages. Their performances clearly were affected, and, as noted above, the TSSKA basketball team was on the verge of collapse early in the 1997–98 season.

The most spectacular deal involved the Central Army hockey team's arrangement with the Pittsburgh Penguins of the National Hockey League. TSSKA had been the perennial Soviet champion, but it faced obvious financial difficulties after 1991. In 1993, the Penguins received 50 percent of the army hockey club's marketing rights in return for assuming the extensive costs of promoting and supporting the team. Viktor Tikhonov, TSSKA's dictatorial but highly successful Soviet-era coach, and Valerii Gushin, the team's general manager, retained control of the hockey operation. The team became formally independent of the army but practiced and played in army facilities, which it rented.[46] The Penguins applied contemporary Western promotional techniques to TSSKA's operation, boosting its chronically feeble attendance and enhancing the team's profitability through numerous sponsorship deals. Club jerseys and other paraphernalia were successfully marketed in the West, and at one point the Disney company was prepared to enter into an extensive and multifaceted business relationship.[47]

Unfortunately, the team's best players continually left to play abroad, and its performance on the ice declined. Ongoing difficulties with its Russian partners led Pittsburgh to diminish its involvement after the 1995 season, and Disney also got cold feet about what had been a multi-million-dollar deal. Then, with the Americans all but gone, the army announced in April 1996 that it was unilaterally repossessing the team. Tikhonov and Gushin were removed, and Tikhonov, a colonel, was discharged from the army. New coaches and officials were appointed. Most of the players, several of them subject to military discipline, joined the new team.

Tikhonov organized his own team, hired players, and won recognition from the hockey league. He then took the matter to court, where he and Gushin prevailed. By this time, however, what had once been a profitable relationship with Pittsburgh had withered.[48] Without the Americans' help, attendance in the 1996–97 season returned to the old level. Ironically, Tikhonov, who had long been deemed the most Stalinist figure in Soviet hockey, was now a defender of private property (his own) and an upholder of Russia's extremely tenuous contract law.[49] The army called its "new" team TSSKA, forcing Tikhonov to dub his group the TSSKA Hockey Club (KhK TSSKA). The army's team was required by the league to play the 1996–97 season in the Russian second division, where it earned promotion to the elite league. That success produced the absurd spectacle in the 1997 season of not one but two teams calling themselves TSSKA in the Russian big league.[50]

The army, however, was not chastened by its experience. Early in 1997, the same figures who led the campaign to reclaim TSSKA's hockey club attempted to drive out a group of civilian Russian investors who had gained control of the army's soccer team. Two competing teams with different coaches and players began preparing for the 1997 season, both under the banner of TSSKA. In this case, however, the army succeeded in driving out the "privatizers," and the matter never came to court. Instead, the losing coach and many of his players transferred en masse to the recently privatized Torpedo.[51]

The trend toward privatization in sport, which seemed to be gathering momentum in 1994 and 1995, had slowed by 1997. Today, roughly one-third of Russia's professional sports teams prosper moderately. Another third manage to keep afloat, and the rest slip in and out of bankruptcy. Continuing financial problems, in turn, created demands for a new kind of government involvement, this time at the local level. Provincial political bosses and regional Mafias are becoming the new patrons of sport, enhancing their prestige as providers of contemporary Russia's tattered version of bread and circuses.[52]

Commercialization, Promotion, Sponsorship, and Media

Because Soviet sports clubs had means other than state subsidies to fund their operations, spectator sport in the USSR was never entirely dependent on the government. Ticket sales and foreign tours were two of several revenue streams that ensured the limited financial independence that allowed spectator sport a measure of autonomy, despite the didactic tasks assigned it by the state. Today, the Russian central government is largely out of the sports industry. Even the Olympic system is no longer part of the Ministry of Sport. Instead, it is run by a formally independent Russian Olympic Committee, staffed largely by remnants from the Soviet period and funded primarily by commercial sponsors. Indeed, in a great historical irony, Russia's summer sports federations were able to survive through the Atlanta Olympics by means of a multi-million-dollar deal with the giant shoe and apparel company Reebok, a firm with extensive Russian operations and sales.[53] Scores of athletes, coaches, and bureaucrats, trained in the ways of the old sport system, were able to continue working. One might have predicted that under the new market conditions those sports that never previously enjoyed a mass audience would suffer and perhaps disappear. Instead, the Olympic sports system, a Stalinist anachronism within post-Soviet Russia, was able to survive thanks to one of the giants of global capitalism.

Spectator sport, on the other hand, is unabashedly a creature of an increasingly globalized entertainment market. Alexander Vainshtein, of IMG's Moscow office, made this connection abundantly clear in an interview with the U.S.-based cable sports network, ESPN: "We think that now it's really the right time to start a civilized sports market here in Russia because as it was before . . . it was financed by the government. Now . . . it's really the time for a big commercial structure or some kind of independent company to be involved in. So our experience with Western companies more than successful and unfortunately Russian companies still doesn't want to understand sport everywhere in the world is the most efficient advertiser" (original in English).[54] Many coaches and officials trained in the ways of the Soviet system are unhappy with such explicit statements of capitalist ideology, but the majority of managers, players, and media in the world of big-time sports consider themselves among the winners in the "new" Russia. Like it or not, everyone in the "industry" recognizes that it is now a business.

The Soviet practice of offering cheap tickets has been only episodically altered, and attendance remains less than robust. Money from television is still limited. Therefore, each year Russian clubs must search for sponsors, without which they cannot survive. The most common agreements involve printing a company's name on team jerseys and on signs at games.[55] All the big international sport shoe companies are involved in team sponsorship, and the equipment of virtually every club prominently features well-known company logos. The Italian dairy giant Parmalat, Holsten beer, and Samsung are typical foreign sponsors, while the most heavily involved Russian firms come largely from the energy sector.

For a long time, games in the USSR differed sharply from games in capitalist countries. Specifically, the gaze of Soviet viewers did not land on the extensive advertising long accepted in the West. By the 1980s, however, international matches played on Soviet soil were treated as opportunities for raising hard currency, and today games in Russia look like games played anywhere else. More often than not, signs are not even transliterated into Cyrillic. The old starkness of domestic Soviet league events has been replaced by the standard hoopla of contemporary capitalist sport spectacle production, including dancing girls (and bears), laser shows, and product giveaways.

The cultural practices of spectator sport are not limited to attendance at games, however. Fans watch on television, read newspapers and magazines, and, as they have done for ages, analyze events among themselves in the *dvory* (courtyards) of their apartment houses. Today, these discourses have changed. Even private discussions are different. Before glasnost, there was always a frisson of oppositionism when fans traded rumors that Central Army's center forward was a drunk (an exchange which itself might take place over a bottle of vodka). Today, that same player could well appear in a whiskey ad. Indeed, the practice of sports figures endorsing products has come to Russia. Even the arch-Stalinist Viktor Tikhonov was featured in a commercial for Vick's cough drops.

During the Soviet period, sports media, for all their many distortions, did display a certain core of honesty. The national daily, *Sovetskii sport,* devoted at least one page to straightforward descriptions of games, and television, especially when covering domestic sporting events, was almost entirely apolitical. A fan watching a live telecast of a Soviet league game could be assured that he or she (usually he) was watching an event that was actually taking place. Nor was that fan subjected to commercials, including commentary that could be deemed "commercials" for the party. Finally, it was difficult for Soviet men to turn their wives into football widows for the simple reason that, unlike the United States, there was never an overabundance of televised sports.

By contrast, the post-Soviet media are themselves participants, albeit tentative ones, in the commercialization of spectator sport. Everywhere in the world, television money is the lifeblood of big-time sports. Yet, Russian television, for all its changes, has not led the way in this field. Despite more channels and longer broadcast days, there is less live sport available today than there was in the Soviet period.[56] Under Brezhnev in particular, party leaders were so sports-conscious that regular broadcast schedules were often changed to accommodate big events. By contrast, the present heads of the state and independent channels come largely from the arts, business, or journalism. According to the well-known soccer announcer Viktor Gusev, today's TV executives are less interested in sports than were their predecessors.[57]

Games shown on live television today may be international as opposed to domestic events, and game broadcasts have been replaced by a wide variety of roundup and highlight shows prepackaged by international distributors. Sport shows produced by Russians find it easier to obtain footage of European soccer and NHL hockey than of Russian-league games played outside Moscow. Only the long-running weekly *Football Roundup* (*Futbol'noe obozrenie*) regularly shows highlights from the provinces.[58] Worse yet, when programs made in Russia do prove successful, they may become the subject of internal power struggles. The popular daily program *Seven Days of Sport* was taken off the air when state television (ORT) sought to take control from the show's independent producer.[59]

Although there are restrictions on the number and types of advertisements that can be run, all Russian sports broadcasts have commercials. Most television companies prefer to sell time to independent producers who actually market the commercials. IMG negotiated the first regular *Game of the Week* deal on Russian television, an agreement with the Professional Football League, which receives a guarantee of three million dollars a year. Stimorol gum is the main sponsor, although IMG sells television ads and game signage to a wide variety of foreign firms.

Attempts to work out a similar deal for hockey were not successful, although from 1993 to 1995, Central Army hockey games were shown on national television and the Pittsburgh Penguins sold ads to Western companies, including Gillette, Coca-Cola, and Delta Airlines. This profitable arrangement had ended by the 1996–97 season, after Pittsburgh curtailed its activities in Russia.[60] Instead, ORT decided to show the games of a newly organized European hockey league, ending what had been a successful business relationship.

Post-Soviet sports television has fostered the same kind of globalization and homogenization seen in other forms of popular culture. Since the games of the domestic leagues seem less attractive to viewers in light of the athletic diaspora, Russian events have a harder time getting air time. Ironically, a young phenom from a provincial hockey team may make his Russian TV debut playing for the NHL. Fans, players, coaches, officials, and journalists alike find these trends demoralizing. Russian sporting nationalism, an emotion not exclusive to political nationalists, is wounded by international pop culture developments that underscore Russia's decline as a world power and emphasize its subordinate place in the global sports market.

Unlike television, the print media have been more aggressive in adapting to new conditions. Here, the biggest change has been in the character of the national daily sports paper. From 1924, *Sovetskii sport* provided citizens with news about sports, sandwiched between official political pronouncements and lessons in production gymnastics. With a peak circulation of more than five million, *Sovetskii sport* was the world's most widely read sports publication, and those who worked there were able to pursue professional careers with some degree of honor and self-respect. Yet, because the paper covered the full range of Olympic sports favored by the party, it did not satisfy most fans' hunger for timely and complete news about the truly popular spectator sports. In 1991, after five years of glasnost, a dozen staff writers from *Sovetskii sport,* nearly all of whom covered spectator sport, decided the internal politics of the paper had not kept pace with the changing media atmosphere of late perestroika. They were tired of struggling for space with pieces on what had historically been called "physical culture." The breakaway group planned instead to produce a paper that concentrated on popular sports from an aggressively international perspective. Founded on the eve of the coup, their new daily was called *Sportekspress.*

According to *Sportekspress*'s editor in chief, Vladimir Kuchmi, "Our reasons for quitting were not simply political but also professional. *Sovetskii sport* was a small newspaper, only four pages. . . . There was only one page of sports news for fans; one page for journalists to work in a normal professional man-ner."[61] Following the logic of the market, *Sportekspress* concentrated on the sports that would win the largest readership. It also took a strongly global approach, with full coverage of the major European soccer leagues, as well as the National Basketball Association and National Hockey League. Yet, unlike post-Soviet television, *Sportekspress* also afforded great attention to domestic sports, debating all the complex issues of the new Russia's relationship with the world sporting community. Events in the near abroad, especially Ukrainian soccer, were also covered, as were such loves of the newly wealthy as tennis, professional boxing, and Formula One auto racing.

In the course of five years, *Sportekspress* destroyed the competing *Sovetskii sport,* which now publishes infrequently. By late 1994, *Sportekspress* had come to a crossroad. While the paper's daily run had grown to 400,000, the editors saw possibilities for further growth. In order to acquire the capital for expan-sion, *Sportekspress* eschewed both government assistance and a loan from a Russian bank in order to maintain its independence. Instead, its owners sold 51 percent of their shares to the company that publishes the famous French sports daily, *L'Equipe.* The original editors retained 49 percent. *Sportekspress*'s cir-culation has grown to 900,000, and it has expanded in size to eight pages a day (sixteen on Tuesdays). Ads for phone sex and bookies have been replaced by extensive displays for leading foreign and domestic businesses. The reporters and editors of *Sportekspress* may voice doubts about the impact of global capitalism on Russian sport, but the paper itself is a thoroughly internationalist and capitalist enterprise.

Nationalism and National Teams

Everywhere, the most intense expressions of sporting nationalism surround the performance of national teams. In Eric Hobsbawm's words, "sportsmen repre-senting their nation or state [are] primary expressions of their imagined com-munities."[62] Yet, the historic weaknesses of Russian nationhood and national identity make the relationship between sporting and political nationalism ex-tremely murky.[63] As the dominant group in a multinational empire, Russians before and after 1917 approached the concept of nationalism quite differently from oppressed, subordinate groups. Today, Russians of all sorts, their colonies shorn, are in the process of imagining just what sort of community or commu-nities they may now comprise.[64] Thus, support for *sbornye komandy* (select squads) is not limited to overtly nationalist politicians and their followers. Instead, interest in the fortunes of national teams cuts across political lines, and even the most internationalist of capitalist businesspeople may be passionate partisans of Russia's teams. This politically "liberal" support is especially common in the most popular and professionalized sports, which are thoroughly enmeshed in the market economy. Yet, rather than fanning chauvinism, success in the international arena in spectator, as opposed to Olympic, sports can actually work to the advantage of the so-called reformist forces who now tenuously control the sports industry.

While wins in the short run have been hard to come by in soccer, hockey, and basketball, Russian performances in the popular sports will probably improve in the next generation. Although the Soviet talent pool was enormous, it was spread widely across more than forty winter and summer Olympic sports. This scatter-shot approach actually hampered success in soccer, hockey, and basketball. Many top performers were steered away from these games as young athletes when they demonstrated ability in more obscure but medal-producing sports. In capitalist countries, by contrast, young athletes have historically clustered around a much smaller number of financially rewarding and visible sports. Now free to choose their own games, young Russians have been picking soccer, hockey, and basketball in greater numbers than before. As proof of this shift, there has been no shortage of willing and able participants in the brawn drain. Virtually everywhere, elite Russian athletes are visible participants in global high-performance sports.

Yet, the continued production of individual stars has not been accompanied by success for Russian teams in international competition. Indeed, the last few years have witnessed some spectacular failures. Russia's performances at the 1994 soccer World Cup and the 1996 European Cup were disastrous, culminating in the ultimate calamity: failure to make the final round of the 1998 World Cup. The once dominant hockey team was eliminated in the semifinals of the sport's inaugural World Cup in 1996, and after a surprise Silver Medal at the 1994 World Basketball Championship, the Russians finished only seventh in the next year's European championship, failing to qualify for the Atlanta Olympics. It has proven difficult to mold Russian athletes, regardless of their talents, into cohesive and effective national teams. At the heart of this problem is a massive culture clash between young, increasingly individualistic players and middle-aged or elderly coaches. The athletes are part of an international monoculture of wealthy and privileged elite performers. Yet, to play for Russia, they must work with coaches and officials who have not abandoned Soviet attitudes and habits. Living on their own instead of in dormitories, and pampered by their new clubs, the players are reluctant to return to outmoded training camps with spartan facilities to prepare for international competition under dictatorial coaches.

Before the 1996 hockey World Cup, the players insisted on living at an expensive hotel in the middle of Moscow rather than at the national training center. After a year of struggle with the hockey federation, the players finally got their way.[65] Yet, the resentment did not disappear, leading several stars to refuse to play for Russia in the 1998 Winter Olympics. In 1994 and again in 1996, soccer players rebelled over the size of their bonuses for big competitions.[66] Personality clashes prevented several of the best basketball players from performing for the national team.[67] In the wake of the defeats, some observers accused athletes of a lack of patriotism. Recounting the views of others, Viktor Gusev told ESPN: "Many previous teams were reproached for not having this national feeling, and the best example is our ice hockey team that played in Vienna [1996]. They lost to Canadians, they lost to Americans. . . . These were mostly players coming from NHL, and nobody said bad words about their skills. But the coaches of American and Canadian teams said they were surprised that the Russian team played without heart" (original in English).[68] After Russia's colossal failure at the 1996 European soccer championship, even the highly internationalist *Sportekspress* asked if players who had worked abroad for many years had lost their "Russian souls" and become unwilling "to fight for the honor of their country."[69] Ignoring significant chunks of Soviet sports history, older fans lament the contrast with the previous era. Shortly before his death, famed comic actor Iurii Nikulin told the soccer monthly *Match,* "In no way do our players play like they used to. The makeup of the team is good. They're all 'millionaires,' but there's no team play; no spirit. They're thinking about something other than football."[70]

It is difficult for most Russian coaches, products of the Soviet system, to deal with this alien new world sporting order. In an interview with *Sportekspress,* Boris Maiorov, a hockey star in the 1960s and later a coach, recounted his discomfort when representing the federation in its dealings with NHL players: "Now we seem to be borrowing everything. Words like 'dealer' and 'broker' have appeared in our language. In what kind of circumstances did these new words come into Russian? I now feel a certain sympathy for the person who does not think in English."[71] It will surely be many years before the old attitudes die and a new, entirely post-Soviet generation of coaches and officials who can understand the mentality of the postmodern athlete for whom national borders have little meaning emerges.

Outside the athletic world itself, the broader political implications of the performance of Russia's national teams are skewed and imprecise. In other places and times, success on international playing fields has fanned nationalist pride to the benefit of the political right. In Russia, however, the Yeltsin government has embraced the nation's *sbornye* in order to be in a position to reap gains should there ever be any wins. They understand that in spectator, unlike Olympic sports, international competition is conducted according to capitalist rules. World championships are profitmaking events designed to market a particular sport. With the exception of some coaches and officials, nearly everyone in the Russian sports "industry" understands this reality.

Accordingly, during the 1996 presidential elections, most elite athletes endorsed Yeltsin. Shamil Tarpishchev, then the minister of sport, brandished petitions at rallies, claiming all members of the national teams had indicated their support for the president. In the run-up to the election, television commentators on soccer games, shown on ORT, made sure to include the "pleasant news" that the members of the teams playing that day had indicated their support for Yeltsin.[72] Statements of sympathy for communist candidates had a harder time making it on the air. Basketball commentator Vladimir Gomelsky told an American television interviewer that he knew of members of the national team who were going to vote for the Communist party candidate, Gennady Ziuganov, but Gomelsky claimed to feel pressure from his superiors to exclude the information from his reports.[73]

The interaction between Russian nationalism and the performance of national teams is thus as decidedly ambiguous as Russian nationalism itself. When it has seen fit, the Yeltsin government has been fully capable of playing to nationalist sympathies despite its acceptance of capitalist practices and rejection of xenophobia. Yet, success in contemporary international sport follows the worldwide "golden rule" (the one with the gold makes the rules). The days of Soviet victories achieved on a shoestring by dedicated coaches and athletes ended long before the death of the Soviet Union. If there are to be future triumphs, they will have to come from mastering the procedures of capitalist sports business, not rejecting them. If, in some "bright and shining" future, there are actual victories on the international stage, the glory will most likely go to the partisans of the market.

In the wake of the 1996 Olympics, there can be little doubt that global sport is now thoroughly commercialized. Its practices have changed, even on the playing field. Sponsors, in alliance with television, induce athletes, willy-nilly, to forget team play and become self-promoting individualists in pursuit of endorsements. In the process, the problematic, politically conservative concept of the role model has lost what little meaning it may have had for both capitalist and Soviet audiences. The Soviet Olympic sports machine, a product of the command economy that mass-produced heroes, never really captured the hearts of the citizenry. By contrast, Soviet spectator sport, replete as it may have been with hypocrisies, did seek to differentiate itself from both capitalist and Stalinist sport. In responding to those very hypocrisies, Soviet citizens created an arena of popular culture that was human and genuine, spontaneous and playful.[74] In the vortex of globalized sport, that difference has now been lost. In the country formerly known as the USSR, they buy and sell sneakers just like the rest of us.

Notes

1 Robert Edelman, *Serious Fun: A History of Spectator Sport in the USSR* (Oxford: Oxford University Press, 1993), pp. 7–25.

2 Stuart Hall, "Notes on Deconstructing 'the Popular,'" in *People's History and Socialist Theory,* ed. R. Samuel (London: Routledge, 1981), pp. 227–40. For one of many possible examples of the use of the idea of "contested terrain," see A. Klein, "Sport and Culture as Contested Terrain," *Sociology of Sport Journal* 8 (1991): 79–85. On sport and leisure under Fascism, see Victoria de Grazia, *The Culture of Consent: Mass Organization of Leisure in Fascist Italy* (New York: Cambridge University Press, 1981); and Richard D. Mandell, *The Nazi Olympics* (New York: Macmillan, 1971). See also John Hargreaves, *Sport, Culture and Power* (Cambridge: Polity, 1986), p. 118; Eric Hobsbawm, "Mass-Producing Traditions: Europe, 1870–1914," in *The Invention of Tradition,* ed. Hobsbawm and Terence Ranger (Cambridge: Cambridge University Press, 1983), p. 283; and Pierre Bourdieu, "Sport and Social Class," *Social Science Information* 17, no. 6 (1978): 830.

3 Peter Stallybrass and Allon White, *The Politics and Poetics of Transgression* (Ithaca: Cornell University Press, 1986), p. 18; Michel de Certeau, *The Practice of Everyday Life* (Berkeley: University of California Press, 1984), pp. xii–xiii, xv, xvii.

4 Although all three sports were on the Olympic program, the arcane and ever-changing rules of eligibility made other competitions (the World Cup, NHL, and NBA) the most important championships of these sports.

5 Edelman, *Serious Fun,* p. 250.

6 On both the autonomy of Soviet sports fans and the use of sport as a cover for nationalism, see Simon Kuper, *Football against the Enemy* (London: Phoenix, 1994), pp. 46–47.

7 Richard Stites, *Russian Popular Culture: Entertainment and Society since 1900* (Cambridge: Cambridge University Press, 1992); Svetlana Boym, *Common Places: Mythologies of Everyday Life in Russia* (Cambridge: Harvard University Press, 1994).

8 Interview with Russian television commentator Viktor Gusev, conducted by U.S. television company ESPN, Moscow, June 11, 1996.

9 *Komsomol'skaia pravda* (Moscow), April 25, 1962.

10 *Komsomol'skaia pravda,* June 30, 1992.

11 *Sportekspress* (Moscow), November 11, 1995, and May 17, 1996.

12 James Riordan, "Worker Sport within a Worker State: The Soviet Union," in *The Story of Worker Sport,* ed. Arnd Kruger and Riordan (Champaign, Ill.: Human Kinetics Press, 1996), p. 54.

13 Moshe Lewin, "Society, State and Ideology during the First Five-Year Plan," in *Cultural Revolution in Russia,* ed. Sheila Fitzpatrick (Bloomington: Indiana University Press, 1978), p. 50; Fitzpatrick, "Stalin and the Making of a New Elite," *Slavic Review* 39 (1979): 377–402.

14 *Sportekspress,* December 7, 1995.

15 *Sportekspress,* December 27, 1995.

16 *Sportekspress,* February 8, 1996.

17 *Komsomol'skaia pravda,* March 17, 1992, April 8, 1992, May 30, 1992; *Sportekspress,* March 1, 1996, June 1, 1996.

18 *Sportekspress,* December 7, 1995, January 30, 1996.

19 *New York Times,* July 8, 1995; *Sportekspress,* November 17, 1995, January 23, 1996, March 2, 1996.

20 On the possible consequences for the localities as a result of globalization and on the localities' capacity to resist, see J. Maguire, "Sport, Identity Politics and Globalization: Diminishing Contrasts and Increasing Varieties," *Sociology of Sport Journal* 11 (1994): 398–427.

21 *Sportekspress,* December 8, 1995.

22 Peter Donnelly, "The Local and the Global: Globalization and the Sociology of Sport," *Journal of Sport and Social Issues* 20, no. 3 (1996): 248.

23 *Sportekspress,* November 22, 1995, November 28, 1995.

24 *Sportekspress,* November 19, 1995, January 16, 1996.

25 *Sportekspress,* October 7, 1995, November 18, 1995, December 16, 1995, May 13, 1996, July 5, 1996.

26 Viacheslav Kozlov, interview with ESPN, Detroit, June 3, 1996.

27 Viacheslav Fetisov, interview with ESPN, Detroit, July 11, 1996.

28 *Sportekspress,* September 14, 1996, September 19, 1996.

29 *Sportekspress,* February 7, 1995.

30 *Sportekspress,* July 30, 1996.

31 *Sportekspress,* November 11, 1995, March 19, 1996, April 12, 1996, May 17, 1996, July 19, 1996.

32 *Komsomol'skaia pravda,* January 14, 1992; *Sportekspress,* April 16, 1996.

33 *Sportekspress,* October 31, 1996, November 13, 1995, November 30, 1995, December 16, 1995, January 13, 1996, January 23, 1996, April 4, 1996, July 12, 1996.

34 *Sportekspress,* October 5, 1995, November 2, 1995.

35 *Sportekspress,* November 1, 1995, November 18, 1995, November 9, 1995, November 25, 1995, May 31, 1996, July 24, 1996. Early in the 1996–97 season, however, Dynamo found itself in financial peril as some longtime sponsors withdrew their support.

36 *Komsomol'skaia pravda,* January 3, 1992, February 11, 1992; *Sportekspress,* November 21, 1995.

37 Tolstykh was involved in threatening the referee during and after a March 24, 1996, game between Dynamo and the 1995 champions, Alania. After the referee, Nikolai Chebotarev, called a dubious penalty against Dynamo that allowed Alania to tie the game, Tolstykh invaded the referee's unguarded dressing room and demanded that Chebotarev enter Dynamo's locker room and apologize to the Dynamo players. A few minutes later, Chebotarev was seen running out of the Dynamo locker room with a split lip and blood on his hand. A huge scandal ensued. Meetings were held. Many demanded Tolstykh's ouster. Tolstykh defended himself by claiming he was fighting against "criminal elements" in Russian soccer, referring to widespread rumors that the well-endowed Alania was notorious for fixing games by bribing referees. The scandal briefly lifted the lid on the broader corruption in the game, but after a while the uproar died down. Tolstykh, with Koloskov's backing, remained in power (*Sportekspress,* March 26, 1996, April 17, 1996). On the eve of the season, Tolstykh had responded to a television interviewer's question about "criminal" or "dirty" money by tacitly admitting its role. He claimed that as teams established solid financial bases, the influence of "dirty" money would decrease (interview with Russian State Television [hereafter ORT], March 1, 1996). While rumors abound about the influence of organized crime on spectator sport, no one has publicly admitted or proven anything concrete (for obvious reasons). It should also be noted that Russia is not the only country in which criminal elements play a role in sport. Finally, one should remember that the borderline between the legal and the illegal in the world of Russian business is not clearly drawn.

38 *Sportekspress,* November 26, 1996. According to Tolstykh, 44 percent of Russia's 172 professional soccer teams are *aktsionernye obshchestva,* 33 percent are "social organizations," 12 percent are municipal organs, 6 percent are "noncommercial organizations," and 4 percent are state (federal) supported.

39 *Sportekspress,* September 30, 1995, November 10, 1995, November 11, 1995, November 25, 1995, December 5, 1995, December 16, 1995, December 20, 1995, December 26, 1995, February 2, 1996, May 15, 1996, July 20, 1996, July 26, 1996.

40 *Sportekspress,* March 13, 1996, May 22, 1996.

41 *Sportekspress,* December 18, 1995.

42 Many of the aspersions directed toward Alania carry a racist overtone toward the darker peoples of the Caucasus, who are believed to be dishonest and mercenary. Alania's success is greatly resented by Russians, although almost half the team's players are themselves Russians. The oil-generated wealth of the region gives the team a solid financial base, which is supplemented by funds from the republic's government. Alania has been able to buy top players from all over the former USSR, Georgia in particular. Additionally, the fans of Vladikavkaz regularly fill the team's thirty-eight-thousand-seat stadium, making it the league leader in attendance. See *Sportekspress,* October 18, 1995, November 13, 1995, November 26, 1995, April 2, 1996.

43 *Sportekspress,* December 7, 1995, January 12, 1996, February 29, 1996, July 11, 1996, August 3, 1996, August 13, 1996.

44 Colonel Alexander P. Baranovsky, interview with ESPN, Moscow, June 21, 1996.

45 *Sportekspress,* November 29, 1995, February 1, 1996, February 29, 1996, July 17, 1996.

46 *Sportekspress,* September 11, 1996. In an interview in this edition of *Sportekspress,* Tikhonov did not actually call his arrangement with the army a contract. Some of his understandings with officials from the Ministry of Defense were purely verbal. He also refused to sign the agreement on renting the TSSKA rink because, he claims, he did not have the money back in 1992.

47 The irony of this relationship, based as it was so heavily on the sale of paraphernalia in the West, was that the army hockey team was the only Russian team sufficiently well known in the West to generate sales for its jerseys, etc.; yet, it was well known precisely because it embodied all that was most repugnantly Soviet to the West. While wearing such garments may have generated a frisson of post-Soviet excite-ment among U.S. teenagers, the post-Soviet army proved to be something less than a haven of pro-entrepreneurial attitudes, as Pittsburgh and Disney soon learned.

48 Telephone interview with Steven M. Warshaw, executive vice president for sales and marketing for the Russian Penguins, September 9, 1996.

49 *Sportekspress,* April 19, 1996, August 8, 1996, September 11, 1996.

50 Of the two teams, Tikhonov's club proved far less successful on the ice. It also quickly had financial problems. In September 1997 federal tax officials accused the club of owing some four million dollars in back taxes. In November, players, who had not been paid for several weeks, went out on strike. Tikhonov's team continued to play in the army's rink, which would mysteriously develop lighting and heating problems during his team's games.

51 *Sportekspress,* January 21 and 24, 1997.

52 The president and "owner" of Rotor Volgograd, Vladimir Goriunov, is a member of the state duma. It is unlikely his leadership of one of the nation's strongest soccer teams has hurt his popularity (*Sportekspress,* November 4, 1995).

53 Reebok actually came onboard in 1994. Before that, Soviet Olympic teams had been largely equipped by Adidas, but on the eve of the 1992 Games the relationship

collapsed (*Komsomol'skaia pravda*, January 1, 1992, March 5, 1992). The evidence seems to suggest that the company's support of Russian Olympians has sold Reebok shoes (interview with unnamed Reebok salesperson, ESPN, Moscow, June 20, 1996).

54 Alexander Vainshtein, interview with ESPN, Moscow, June 26, 1996.

55 *Sportekspress,* November 4, 1995, November 13, 1995, November 25, 1995, February 27, 1996, March 6, 1996, April 18, 1996, July 9, 1996; "Seven Days of Sport," ORT, March 1 and 27, May 31, 1996; Colonel Alexander Baranovsky, interview with ESPN, Moscow, June 21, 1996.

56 ORT, March 2, 1996, April 9 and 10, 1996.

57 Viktor Gusev, telephone interview, September 16, 1996.

58 "Futbol'noe obozrenie," ORT, March 24, 1996.

59 Ibid.

60 Steven Warshaw, telephone interview, September 9, 1996.

61 *New York Times,* December 4, 1995.

62 Eric Hobsbawm, *Nations and Nationalism since 1870* (Cambridge: Cambridge University Press, 1990), p. 143; Benedict Anderson, *Imagined Communities: Reflections on the Origins and Spread of Nationalism* (London: Verso, 1973).

63 On the ambiguities of Russian nationalism's relationships with the centrifugal nationalisms that broke up the Soviet Union, see Ronald G. Suny, *The Revenge of the Past: Nationalism, Revolution and the Collapse of the Soviet Union* (Stanford: Stanford University Press, 1993), pp. 1–19. On the peculiar character of prerevolutionary Russian nationalisms, see Hans Roger, *Jewish Policies and Right-Wing Politics in Imperial Russia* (London: Macmillan, 1986), pp. 188–232; and Robert Edelman, *Gentry Politics on the Eve of the Russian Revolution: The Russian Nationalist Party, 1905–1917* (New Brunswick: Rutgers University Press, 1980), p. 104.

64 On nationalism in general, see L. Greenfield, *Nationalism, Five Roads to Modernity* (Cambridge: Harvard University Press, 1992); and Ernst Gellner, *Nations and Nationalism* (Ithaca: Cornell University Press, 1983).

65 *Sportekspress,* April 5, 1996; Viacheslav Kozlov, interview with ESPN, Detroit, June 3, 1996.

66 *Sportekspress,* August 2, 1996, September 20, 1996.

67 *Sportekspress,* January 16, 1996.

68 Viktor Gusev, interview with ESPN, Moscow, July 11, 1996.

69 *Sportekspress,* June 21, 1996.

70 *Match* (Moscow) 1, nos. 11–12 (1996): 58.

71 *Sportekspress,* October 5, 1995.

72 ORT, soccer game Rotor-Alania, May 18, 1996.

73 Vladimir Gomelsky, interview with ESPN, Moscow, June 25, 1996.

74 Edelman, *Serious Fun,* pp. 249–50.

> When we say "Lenin" we mean "Party."
>
> When we say "Party" we mean "Lenin."
>
> For 70 years we've said one thing but meant another.

SAYING "LENIN" AND MEANING "PARTY": SUBVERSION AND LAUGHTER IN SOVIET AND POST-SOVIET SOCIETY

Prologue: Summer 1994, Moscow

Erofeev's play *Moskva-Petushki* was one of many remarkable events of the perestroika era in Moscow. The play examines the past and present of the Soviet state from the perspective of kind, quiet, and heavy-drinking Venychka and his accidental friends. I saw *Moskva-Petushki* for the first time in 1988: the play was drowned in the laughter of an audience grateful for subtle subversive attacks on the October events, the history of Soviet achievements, the present political situation, and the dogma of Soviet-style Marxism-Leninism.

I left the Soviet Union in 1991 and came back to Russia in 1994. That summer I paid twenty thousand rubles for a ticket to the same play. I went to see it not so much to enjoy it as to find out what was in it that appealed to the contemporary viewer. I came to the theater as an observer equipped with what

Raymond Williams calls "distance," from which I could listen to the audience and note its motions and bursts of laughter. I saw myself as part of the audience and separate at the same time. I imagined myself occupying that border position that allows one both to observe the subject and to be a part of it. But I had deceived myself. During the first act, I realized that I held no border position; in fact, I had been ousted from the audience. The feeling from the 1980s of immediate understanding and solidarity with the audience in a collective act of disobedience manifested through laughter was just a memory. I could not achieve unison with the audience's laughter. The audience was laughing, but it was not laughing the way I remembered it, expected it, and wanted it to laugh. The boisterous laughter of the 1980s that forced the actors to slow the performance because the audience had not gotten over the previous joke was sounding only in my mind. That audience had undergone a profound change, a change that manifested itself to me in this new, unfamiliar laughter. I, on the other hand, felt like a stranger — I did not know when to laugh.

Beyond the Social and the Reasonable?

The joke, along with anonymous urban and thieves' songs, is probably the last remnant of oral culture in urban industrial society. It resides in people's minds, traveling through society by means of the spoken word; it lives as long as it is being used, as long as it provokes laughter. The joke needs neither a producer nor a promoter, neither means of transportation nor production space. Everywhere it goes it is followed by laughter, uproarious or subdued, derisive or heartfelt. Laughter is rarely indifferent. It is pleasure, relief, vengeance, challenge. The diversity and richness of jokes and laughter seem to rule out a common denominator hidden at the core, behind the joke's deceptive multiformity. Nevertheless, every attempt to grapple with the enigma of joking or to incorporate jokes into sociocultural analysis produces a definition or contains an assumption of what jokes and their social functions in society *are*.

Sigmund Freud considered jokes simultaneously "the most social of all the mental functions" and antisocial.[1] The labor of telling a joke and laughing at it is inevitably divided between at least two people. One delivers the joke, the other provides laughter — recognition of and witness to a good joke. The joke is also always a reaction to some sociocultural event, process, thing, or person. The joke teller (*shutnik*) assumes that she and the audience share the same interpretive framework and that the content of the joke is intelligible. Although they appear simple and comprehensible, jokes nevertheless pose a mystery: We know what we are laughing at, but we don't know why it is funny. What we don't know, according to Freud, is that joking serves a universal need to liberate oneself from critical, imposed judgment; from "inhibitions of shame and respectability"; from the fetters of social, familial, and marital institutions; and from "proper" speech and "correct" behavior. It is an escape from the results of successful socialization — the ordered organization of life — to a time before the mind was civilized, when the body was not yet fully delineated, responsive, or disciplined.[2]

The escape into the realm of nonsense is accompanied by victorious, pleasurable laughter, a release of energy that functions to keep the mind and body within the limits of civilized thinking and practice. The revolution — the escape — is always stillborn, and the liberation is momentary, followed up by a return to order and meaning, to normalcy. "Jokes," notes Freud, seek "to gain a small yield of pleasure" and not to overturn social constraints.[3] In fact, consideration of any subversive potential of joking is absent from Freud's work. According to the logic of Freud's argument, the return to normalcy is not unfortunate or undesirable, but rather inevitable and intrinsic to social beings who have no choice but to conform to social inhibitions (for this is the only way to be admitted to society), and who, at the same time, ease the pressures of socialization by means of joking.[4] Within the Freudian framework, a joke is a rebel, but one without a cause; it is a safety valve, a pleasure giver, and a folk therapist — in short, it is a true fellow traveler of humankind as old as the first forms of social organization.

Freud's work in general and on the nature of jokes in particular provides many possible points of departure for further inquiries. Mary Douglas, in her fascinating essay "Jokes," conceptualizes joking as a momentary escape from "structure" into "non-structure," a moment of enjoyment "beyond the bounds of reason and society," and as "temporary suspension[s]" of and "little disturbances" in social structures.[5] A number of feminist psychoanalytic critics have questioned what they see as Douglas's pessimistic view of human subversive potentialities. Elizabeth Grosz, for example, hails the theory of subjectivity advanced by psychoanalysis, suggesting that it explains not only "how subjects conform to what is expected of them but [also] why subjects can resist these expectations."[6] Working at the intersection of philosophy, anthropology, and psychoanalysis, Judith Butler proposes that cultural practices of gender parody are capable of subverting and denaturalizing the category of heterosexual normalcy and of revealing the multiplicity and fluidity of gender identities.[7]

It seems, then, that there are dichotomous views on the nature of joking and laughter: humor serves either to reinforce society or to destabilize it. But is it defensible historically to posit a fixed, transhistorical joke-work? In the Soviet and post-Soviet contexts, the role of the joke cannot be reduced to either that of a safety valve or a radical subverter, nor can it be fully understood outside the social milieu within which it operates. The joke performs multiple functions and cannot cross social and cultural boundaries or preserve meanings and uses as readily as can academic categories.

I have chosen to focus exclusively on the political joke because within the universe of Soviet popular humor, the *politicheskii anekdot* (political anecdote) was recognized as a distinct and particularly subversive genre.

A contest was announced for the best political joke.

First prize — fifteen years.

Although present throughout the Soviet years, the political anecdote acquired the status of a symbolic marker in the 1970s and 1980s, the period that is sometimes referred to as the "era of *anekdoty.*" During the Brezhnev years, jokes were told eagerly in people's homes and kitchens, in designated smoking areas at work, in corridors of schools and universities; the laughter that united bosses and employees could often be heard in offices of ministries and party organizations.[8] Political jokes acquired such wide currency despite the fact that before the collapse of the Soviet Union *anekdoty* were never circulated via official media, were never uttered by comedians on the *estrada,* and were never printed on the pages of state-supported satirical publications such as *Krokodil* or *Literaturnaia gazeta*'s well-known "Klub dvenadtsat stul'ev" (Twelve Chairs Club). They circulated via word-of-mouth and constituted a vital portion of Soviet unofficial oral culture.

The immediate post-Soviet period, a transitional moment between the waning Soviet and the emerging post-Soviet cultures, presents a unique opportunity for exploring the complex relationship between jokes and their sociocultural contexts. The early post-Soviet years witnessed a renaissance of Soviet political humor, in which the uses and meanings of *politicheskie anekdoty* changed and included outright statements of victory, mourning for the lost USSR, and public discussions of interpretations of Soviet history. The Soviet jokes that flourished in the immediate post-Soviet context were a popular attempt to reflect on the meaning of the Soviet experience. For the scholar, the phenomenon of the Soviet joke in the post-Soviet context invites a critical reinterpretation of the processes of Soviet identity formation.

Analysis of Soviet and post-Soviet humor holds great potential for scholarly inquiries into what Mikhail Bakhtin calls the "unofficial consciousness" of society.[9] Residing at the very heart of social life, the joke is both the product of a particular society and its articulator. The joke reflects and internalizes the "discourse of authority," and at the same time attacks, reinterprets, and re-imagines it. It offers a unique perspective on society from within, a vantage point unacknowledged in the official realm, and one that has generally escaped scholars of Soviet and post-Soviet society and culture. Of particular interest is the changing gap between the official and unofficial consciousness embodied in the shift from Soviet to post-Soviet jokes, as well as the moments of con-vergence between official and unofficial discourses. Jokes in the Soviet and post-Soviet contexts were not impartial subverters; they were, in fact, very selective in their targets.[10] They delineated the boundaries of subversive jocular possibilities, the line between what can be laughed at and what cannot even be conceived in jest.

Soviet Joking in Post-Soviet Disorder

The immediate post-Soviet period witnessed an explosion of *sovetskie pol-iticheskie anekdoty* (Soviet political anecdotes); they invaded new spheres and acquired a materiality generally denied them during the Soviet period. No longer restricted to small groups of friends and colleagues, they could be heard in concert halls and on theater stages. Post-Soviet radio and television pro-grams gave extensive coverage to Soviet political *anekdoty,* thereby ending their exile from the mass media. The TV show *Popugai (Parrot),* hosted by the famous Soviet clown and actor Iurii Nikulin, for example, devoted many hours to telling *sovetskie politicheskie anekdoty* in the immediate post-Soviet period. Newspapers and journals included Soviet jokes in their articles. Struggling to survive post-Soviet economic hardships, the journal of satire and humor, *Kro-kodil,* began to publish jokes submitted by readers in two new features, "Anek-dot s borodoi" (literally, "Joke with a Beard") and "Anekdot bez borody" ("Joke without a Beard").[11] Contributors of the best jokes received a monetary prize and acknowledgment in the journal. When they entered the realm of commercial entertainment, jokes lost their autonomy and elusive immateriality — the immediate "intimacy" created between *shutnik* and listener(s), in the words of Soviet comedian Roman Kartsev — and were transformed into profitable commodities co-opted by new post-Soviet entrepreneurs. Until recently, jokes were compared, in Kartsev's phrase, with "a bird that could not be caged."[12] Since 1991, however, they have become readily available in booklets and volumes sold on the street, in underground passages, by bus stops, and in metro and train stations. Jokes have invaded very post-Soviet space.

Why did the Soviet political joke become such a hot commodity in the post-Soviet period? What happens to the sociocultural uses and meanings of *anekdoty* when they cease to circulate as oppositional discourse and enter the "free marketplace" of ideas?

The dissolution of the Soviet system deprived Soviet jokes of their oppositional, subversive value. With the authoritative Soviet discourse gone, along with the erasure of distinctively Soviet differences between the official and unofficial realms, the *sovetskii politicheskii anekdot* was left without its nurturing source, its target, and its symbolic space. Nevertheless, it prolonged its existence by appropriating new functions and new meanings. The telling of a Soviet political joke became a particular declaration of freedom, a celebration of social disorganization of a system that *shutniki* had previously perceived and depicted as controlling. In some respects, the experience of the first post-Soviet years nearly approximated the state of freedom (i.e., social disorganization) produced when one controlling system is disintegrating and another is still in the making. The multiple retellings of jokes characteristic of the period allowed the public to relive this sensation of liberation vividly.

Corresponding tensions should not be ignored, however. While laughing heartily over the collapse of the Soviet system, the emergent ex-Soviet society was simultaneously mourning its loss. The abrupt disappearance of the familiar way of life — the destruction of its materiality, the disruption of social roles, positions, and familiar routines with which one had identified — colored the nature of post-Soviet joking with nostalgia. This nostalgic telling of the old Soviet jokes in the new post-Soviet public and private had a healing effect on the mourning post-Soviet subject. It served to help normalize the loss — to master it. The renaissance of Soviet jokes in the 1990s is a powerful example of the multidimensional role of jokes in complex society. In the immediate post-Soviet years, they attended to the complicated emotional life of a society in painful transition.

Yet, longing for the past should not be viewed exclusively as nostalgia for the familiar organization of life. It also suggests nostalgia — despite the prima facie absurdity of the proposition — for the lost position of the Soviet subject. As represented in Soviet jokes, at least, the Soviet subject possessed a clear understanding of the workings of Soviet society and its power relationships. Via the joke, Soviet people took pride in their mastery of the official language and their ability to turn it against itself. They knew how to manipulate and evade the system. Such an "everywhere in control" image only exacerbates the disorientation of post-Soviet society and suggests why post-Soviet humor has some nostalgic qualities.

Playing with the Language

An understanding of the *sovetskii politicheskii anekdot* in the Soviet era presupposed a high level of mastery of the official language on the part of the joke's audience. The mission of Soviet *shutniki* and their *anekdoty* was to expose the gap between the official representational system and the realities of Soviet everyday life. Official slogans, clichés, narrative styles, and stylistic modes were revealed as verbal castles in the air, houses of cards divorced from material reality.

Let us consider the famous Soviet slogan *"Lenin s nami"* (Lenin is with us) in terms of Soviet jokes. Is there anything wrong with it? How is it different from the sentence *"Lenin v mavsolee"* (Lenin is in the mausoleum)? Grammatically these two sentences are virtually identical. As if applying one of Wittgenstein's famous truisms, "the meaning of the word is in its use,"[13] the anonymous critic inserts the slogan into a hypothetical everyday situation:

> Newly married couples are now able to buy a triple bed:
> *Lenin is with us.*

In the context of everyday reality, the slogan turns out to be absurd, to have no meaning, no referent. It appears to be meaningful only if it is left alone and unchallenged on a poster, in the title of an article, or on the lips of a TV commentator. In other words, the coherence and significance of Soviet officialese depends on its not being taken literally. Another example:

> Why such a long line for the eye doctor?
> They said yesterday on the radio: "You can *see* how the well-being of the Soviet people is growing."

The moment the official figure of speech, "you can see" (*na glazakh*), is given back its literal meaning, "to perceive with the eyes," the significance of the whole phrase — "You can see how the well-being of the Soviet people is growing" — is exposed as belonging to the intangible realm of words that people look for but fail to find.

Reinterpreting the Past and the Present: Disorder versus Order

The seemingly innocent joke-play with the official language turned out to be of great significance for the success of the official ideological project. Playful joking helped to discredit officialese as the legitimate language by which Soviet reality was depicted. By revealing the disjuncture between the official system of representation and reality, jokes made the idea of a countersystem of representation conceivable and articulated a need for it. In their attempt to reinterpret the real, jokes created a new language and forged an unofficial public discourse on a wide rage of historical, political, social, and cultural issues — issues presented in official media as *already* having been publicly discussed and ratified. As unofficial discourse, jokes became an autonomous means of public communication, challenging the alienating nature of mass media, a phenomenon characteristic of all modern societies.

In the Soviet case, jokes were not merely momentary safety valves releasing the pressures of the controlling system (this function, of course, cannot be denied), but also constructive functions that served as the venue for communication and discussion. Their opposition was realized both in their subversion of the official language and the system itself, and in their search for alternate meanings. Along with underground songs and samizdat and *tamizdat* (Soviet literature published abroad which then found its way back to the Soviet Union), the joke discourse can be seen as a particular form of social resistance to the tendency of modern society to reduce subjects to passive receptacles of authoritative discourses, and as an attempt to break out of the official interpretive framework by creating a counter framework. Although samizdat, *tamizdat,* and *anekdoty* constituted similar challenges to the Soviet system, I would suggest that jokes played a more important role than underground literature, for the latter was confined to a narrow stratum while jokes circulated much more widely.

Politicheskie anekdoty engaged themselves in reinterpretation of Soviet grand narratives on a gigantic scale. They went beyond attacks on easy and obvious targets such as political leaders to initiate a debate about Soviet history, the organization and operation of the Soviet system, and the place of the Soviet subject in Soviet society. As true revisionist historians, the anecdotes produced their own periodizations and meanings of the Soviet experience. Although they failed to reach consensus on most topics, one theme was undeniably predominant in their interpretation: namely, chaos, lack of control or guidance. The image of the Soviet Union as stagnant or meandering in no particular direction served as an interpretive model for both the entire Soviet era and for particular historical periods.

> Military men were debating: What is the most destructive weapon? One said the atomic bomb; another said the hydrogen bomb.
> No citizens, you are wrong, said the expert on destructive weapons. The most destructive weapon is the cannon on the cruiser *Aurora:* one blank shot, and seventy-two years of ruins.[14]

In this joke, the Soviet period is robbed of its history and is removed from the global historical flow into a timeless realm without change, movement, or development. It is turned into a blank spot and denied both its achievements and its failures. Such ahistoricity is further developed in jokes interpreting the origins of the Soviet state:

> A phone rings at Smol'nyi:[15]
> Hello, is this Smol'nyi?
> Yes, this is Smol'nyi.
> Do you have beer?
> No.
> And who has?
> The guys in the Winter Palace.
> Hurrah! Let's storm the Winter Palace![16]

Here the organized units of revolutionary workers and soldiers from Soviet history textbooks and movies are reduced to an unorganized drunken mob hunting for beer who accidentally decide to take over the Winter Palace. According to the historical revisionism of the *anekdot,* the origins of the Soviet Union were accidental, unplanned, and chaotic. These features are, by extension, held to pervade Soviet society. Within the joke discourse, disorganization became a central theme in the interpretation of Soviet life. As imagined in jokes, the Soviet Union continues to exist not because of its strength or cohesion but only through disorganization, chaos, the unintended random consequences of people's actions. Thus, an American spy dies in Moscow not as the result of the work of the state security apparatus, but because this "normal," "civilized" American man cannot survive even one day under Soviet conditions:

> The CIA sent an agent to find out what military bases were situated around Moscow. He was well trained and given many instructions. The agent got hungry and came out of the forest. He bought a pirogi in a Moscow store and died. The CIA got worried and sent another agent. He got to Moscow safely, got lost in the crowd, and took a tram. There he was trampled.

The work of subversion in jokes of this type deserves close analysis. In their effort to disassemble the official representation of history and society and to escape its imposed ideological structures, the subversive *anekdoty,* indirectly through the help of telling omissions, exhibited a parallel desire for "normal," civilized order. Exposing official language as divorced from reality, uncovering disorganization and chaos beneath official rhetoric, participants in the joke discourse laughed and congratulated themselves on the successful deconstruction of the official symbolic, criticizing it for the lack of order, control, and coherence. The escape into nonstructure was concurrently a demand for structure. Soviet historical development was presented either as ahistorical chaos or as a gradual declension toward leaderlessness.

> A railroad accident: a train went off the track. In Lenin's time, a *subbotnik* would have been organized and the track would have been cleared. In Stalin's time, the engineer, the head of the railroad station, and the switchman would have been shot and the track would have been cleared. In Khrushchev's time, the track would have been taken from behind the train and put in front of it. In Brezhnev's time, they would have started rocking the train and announcing train stations in order to create the illusion of movement. At the height of perestroika, the following order was received: Everyone must look out the windows and scream: "There are no railroad ties! We have run out of tracks! Ahead is the abyss!"

This joke reproduces the standard political periodization of Soviet history and evaluates each historical moment according to the capacity of the respective leader to direct the country. It turns what in previous jokes were lacunae into a narrative about Soviet historical development—from the tangible accomplishments of the 1920s to the illusory existence of the 1970s to the public acknowledgment of complete failure during perestroika. Using the device of effective leadership as a measuring rod, the *anekdot*-historian leaves the joke morally ambiguous. It is insinuated that the forward movement of the 1930s at the expense of human lives was perhaps better than the illusion of movement with no one in control — and no one in immediate danger. However, the unofficial interpreter is not ambiguous in the treatment of perestroika. The image of perestroika as disorderly movement toward the abyss is symptomatic of the joke audience's disillusionment with the ability of the Soviet system to reform itself. Significantly, perestroika is the only period not represented by a leader. It is the last stage of Soviet history, a moment characterized as faceless and leaderless.

The joke discourse failed to identify Gorbachev as the leader of the country but presented him as "one of them," one of many useless *apparatchiki-*Communists. Thus, the following joke, in which Gorbachev appears to be the central figure of derision, exists in several versions. We can readily substitute other members of the Central Committee such as Ligachev and Ryzhkov without changing the meaning of the joke.

> Gorbachev comes to the countryside: How are things going?
> Badly, Mikhail Sergeevich. The cattle are dying, there is no fodder.
> Really? Have you tried to paint the cow sheds green? You see . . . Try it! It helps in other regions very much.
> The collective farmers painted everything green. In a month, Gorbachev phones: How are things going now?
> Badly, Mikhail Sergeevich, all the cows died.
> Really, all? Don't be upset, I have many more interesting ideas!

The effortless replacement of Gorbachev by other communist leaders suggests the dissipation of central power and the absence of an able leader, while the narrative structure of the joke functions as a universal interpretive model for the Soviet apparatus during perestroika. Neither Gorbachev, Ryzhkov, nor Ligachev could possibly comprehend or ameliorate the catastrophic situation of the 1980s. Full of meaningless advice, they were like leader-children playing with the country and the people.

What about Us? Doing and Knowing

Unofficial public discussion did not restrict itself to inquiry into historical and linguistic issues but also engaged in an analysis of the Soviet system and its interaction with citizens. The unofficial discussion further diversified and glorified the *anekdot* as an outstanding linguist-philosopher, a deconstructive historian, and a perceptive social scientist. The joke discourse was the culmination of the analytical and deconstructive capabilities inherent in the unofficial public discourse. Not only did it articulate and label social reality beyond the official order of representation, it also undertook the study of the operation of Soviet society and the production of the Soviet official language itself.

The unreferential official language is presented in the unofficial social analysis as a product of Soviet subjects. It was on the TV screen, on the radio, and in newspapers, as well as in the operations of everyday life. It invaded Soviet factories, plants, and collective farms where people, self-consciously, produced and played with nonexistent facts, passing fake numbers to one another.

> On a collective farm, a pig gave birth to three piglets. A meeting of the party committee was held: "What shall we do? Three — not much better than nothing . . ." They thought and thought and decided to report to the regional committee that the pig gave birth to five piglets.
>
> The regional committee analyzed the data and reported to the Ministry of Agriculture that seven piglets were born.
>
> The ministry thought and reported to the Central Committee: "The plan for the year has been overfulfilled — twelve piglets have been given to the Motherland!"
>
> The people in the Central Committee thought and decided to make Brezhnev happy and reported: "The country has received twenty extra piglets!"
>
> This is very good! said Leonid Il'ich. Three piglets should be given to the workers of Leningrad, three to the hero-city Moscow, five for export, another five to the poor people of Africa, the rest are the strategic reserve. Nobody will get them!

The *anekdot* here functions again in a double role. It is both an entertainer and articulator of social taboos, and a critic exposing to its audience the operation of the Soviet system. The sole rejuvenating force of Soviet society is the Soviet subject himself; the imaginary pigs floating through society are his invention and keep the system going. The *anekdot* presents the Soviet subject as complex and disingenuous. On the one hand, as a producer and user of the official language, the Soviet subject fortifies it, while on the other hand, by refusing to take the system seriously, he subverts it. In producing officialese, he consciously reproduces its falsity. What is especially intriguing about this particular joke is that it makes the distinction between reality and nonreality very ambivalent. Thus far, we have seen a sharp differentiation between social "reality" and the falsity of officialese within the joke narrative. In this joke, the official language and some aspect of social reality do indeed correspond: officialese and practice are both unreal. By producing officialese, the Soviet subject reproduces this unreality.

That the joke discourse mirrors critiques put forth by Soviet and Eastern European dissidents — themselves members of the intelligentsia — suggests that its audience was from the same social stratum.[17] The theme of dual existence and double consciousness pervaded the thinking of contemporary writers such as Slavoj Žižek, Vaclav Havel, Alexander Solzhenitsyn, and Andrei Amalrik, as well as 1920s-era Russian philosopher and literary critic Mikhail Bakhtin.

In theorizing the gap and interaction between official and unofficial ideologies/consciousness, Bakhtin, argues Michael Holquist, was also working through "his own dilemma, the increasing gap between his own religious and metaphysical ideas" and the Soviet official language.[18] The subsequent generation of intelligentsia also perceived "totalitarian" society as divided into two realms. Havel, Amalrik, and Solzhenitsyn unmasked the double life of Soviet subjects and called on them, in Havel's famous phrase, to start "living within the truth" — to display publicly their true identity and dignity.[19] Amalrik identifies the split-personality phenomenon with a particular social group: the "class of specialists" or "creative intelligentsia." "It sometimes appears to me," writes Amalrik, "that the Soviet 'creative intelligentsia' — that is, people accustomed to thinking one thing, saying another and doing a third — is, as a whole, an even more unpleasant phenomenon than the regime that formed it." Within the framework of these dissident writers, the unofficial joke discourse is another expression of "living within a lie" — subversive laughter at the kitchen table and passive obedience in public.[20]

Although dissidents usually counterpoised themselves — active resisters taking risks — to the passively joking Soviet intelligentsia, and even expressed contempt for it, they nevertheless had much in common with it. Coming from the same sociocultural stratum, they shared not only the same conceptualization of "totalitarian" society, but also espoused the same political agenda and cherished the same desire: to liberate themselves from official language and practices. The marked difference between dissident writing and the unofficial joke discourse was that dissidents were publicly exposing the system as a lie while the joke audience only fantasized about it; the dissidents were "living within the truth," while the *shutniki* were merely joking within it.

> Brezhnev is giving a speech before workers: Comrades! Soon we will live even better!
> A voice from the audience: And what about *us* [*a my*]?

This contrasts sharply with the previous joke. While the subject in the former joke passively retreats behind the protective shield of nonexistent proliferating piglets — a practice neither directly challenged nor explicitly criticized within the joke's text — this joke portrays the subject confronting the official discourse and attempting to speak the truth. The subversive *shutnik* imagines a public space in which he announces the double existence of Soviet society, the difference between the official "we" and the unofficial "we." By publicly exposing this gap, the *shutnik* refuses either to acquiesce to official subjectivity or to remain within the limits of the unofficial. The fantasy of public contestation enacted by the outcry "*a my?*" is a plea to abrogate the duality, an entreaty for a new, unified, all-encompassing "we." In other words, it is a demand for a new representational system in which the difference between official and unofficial subjectivity will be erased. Like all forms of historical revisionism, social joking has an implicit agenda. Having unmasked the falseness of the official representation, having learned how to minimize his contact with it, the *shutnik,* in his dreams, leaves the protective shield of official rhetoric and practice and publicly admits his desire to be included in a new whole. Thus, both joke and dissident discourse assume as both possible and desirable a unified subject, one without inner contradictions, "living within the truth."

This dynamic between deconstruction and construction of social order in Soviet jokes invites reconceptualization of notions of subversion as escape to either nonstructure or to the freedom of fragmented, multiple identities. The operation of the Soviet joke discourse challenges the theory of the modern subject as a hopeless cynic, a position most fully developed by Slavoj Žižek. Arguing that Marx's subject, a victim of false consciousness — "Sei wissen das nicht, aber sie tun es" (They don't know it, but they do it) — is outdated, Žižek suggests a view of a modern, cynical subject that is not only quite aware of the "distorted representation," the discrepancies between the real and the represented (the awareness that it demonstrates in jokes), but that takes the distortion for granted: "they know very well that they are doing it but they are still doing it."[21] Žižek's subject is truly postmodern, not because it is aware of the gap between the real and ideological but because it painlessly reconciles itself to this situation of double existence, double consciousness — to the fragmentary nature of its self. It subverts; it deconstructs systems of representation in jokes, laughs at the resulting symbolic ruins, and feels no anxiety over the dissolved false-conscious unity. Žižek's subject has no nostalgia for the modern unitary self. Following Žižek's logic, the cynical subject is beyond change: because discrepancies are perceived not as contradictions but as inescapable givens, the cynical subject is eternally trapped in its fragmentary being. Such a static view of subjectivity cannot contemplate the struggle within the subject between meaninglessness and meaning, a tension ever present but differently manifested in specific sociocultural contexts. In the Soviet case, fragmentation is both desideratum and dread; the *anekdot* always deconstructs a coherent narrative and demands a new one simultaneously. Soviet *shutniki* not only constantly fluctuated between the roles of cynic and idealist, but also attempted to work out systems of representation counter to the Soviet officialese.

Counterorders

The irony of such counterhegemonic undertakings is that they originate within the limits of the authoritative discourse. The West and the pre-Soviet past, designated as the negative Other in the official representation, undergo an interesting inversion. They become the positive, desirable self in the unofficial counternarrative. The subversive, alternative discourse internalized the official Soviet cold war mentality that divided the world into the West and the East, into "capitalists" and "Communists," merely changing the valences. Turned on its head, the official grand narrative survived in jokes, even into the post-Soviet years.

In jokes, images of the West, particularly the United States, provided disenchanted Soviet subjects with a new interpretive framework against which the Soviet system was evaluated and which constructed a social reality without discrepancies between the real and the represented. In these jokes, the desirable capitalist Other is presented as a homogeneous system in which freedom, wealth, and opportunity are not divorced from reality but constitute the very essence of Western everyday existence.[22]

> People's deputies came to Gorbachev and asked: "Mikhail Sergeevich, how do you understand socialism?"

"It is when everyone lives on one's salary and keeps silent."
"What if we give people full freedom and allow them to become rich?"
"Then it will be capitalism — but capitalism is not our way."

According to the joke, the homogeneous capitalist society is inhabited by free, self-sufficient, unitary individuals who, once liberated from the fetters of the state, show their true capacities. The subject of this Other world is depicted as independent from social conditions and social relations, residing in the imagined ideal, conflict-free society. The theme of personal freedom and a coherent and unified social world is echoed in jokes about order and organization, precisely the features that *anekdoty* perceive as lacking in the Soviet system. Contrasts between the convenience, order, and technological prowess of American/Western life and the inconvenience, disorganization, and backwardness of Soviet life organize the narratives of many jokes.

Rabinovich is trying to call Zhmerinka from Moscow.
Operator: I can connect you only after twelve.
Rabinovich: Can you connect me to New York?
Operator: Well, I'll try.
Rabinovich: Hello, New York? Can you connect me to Zhmerinka?
American operator: Yes. No problem. Wait a moment, please.

This longing for organization, discipline, good service, and advanced technology rounds out the unofficial attempt to create a countersystem, an attempt that often borrows from the official discourse. Without questioning the illusive and idealized nature of the countersymbolic, the Soviet subversive subject escapes into its newly constructed dream. It loses its cynical mind and drive to expose in its constructive efforts to find a substitute for the discredited and subverted official system of representation. The West is fancied and presented as forbidden desirable land to which one eternally strives to escape, to immigrate.

What would you do if they opened the border?
I would climb a tree.
Why?
Not to be trampled.

The escape to the West was not the only counternarrative present in unofficial public discourse. Escape into the pre-Soviet, prerevolutionary past constituted the foundation for another countersymbol. Jokes presented another idealized land of abundance and freedom. They interpreted the Soviet period as an interruption of and a deviation from the natural historical path of Russia, as an unnecessary detour to get where the country was going before 1917 and would have been already without the Bolsheviks.

What is communism?
It is when anybody can buy anything. Like in the days of Nicholas II.

In its efforts to articulate alternative systems of meanings, the unofficial public discourse provides a simplified mirror image of the intelligentsia's moods and dissident solutions in the late Soviet period. In his study of the Soviet intelligentsia, Boris Kagarlitsky noted two dominant tendencies within the Soviet intelligentsia and the dissident movement: the liberal-Western, represented by physicist Andrei Sakharov, and the conservative-nationalist, led by writer Alexander Solzhenitsyn. I would suggest that there is a relationship between this divide among the intelligentsia and the bifurcation in the joke discourse. It is a connection that deserves further consideration, a task beyond the scope of this chapter. Nevertheless, it seems likely that the Soviet intelligentsia formed the bulk of the joke audience and, through jokes, revealed its lack of support for the Soviet system. As Kagarlitsky persuasively argues, the loss of faith on the part of the intelligentsia after the 1968 Prague invasion was a key factor in the failure of perestroika of the 1980s. By the late 1980s the system could no longer count on the broad support of the educated classes, but instead was confronted by a range of competing ideologies from the West and from the Russian nationalist movement generated by the intelligentsia itself in the unofficial dissident and public discourses.[23]

Post-Soviet Joking: New Object of Desire?

We have seen that jokes internalize multiple contradictions and inversions, making it impossible to essentialize their function. With the same willingness and artistry, jokes subvert and construct, denaturalize and naturalize, eliminate normalcy and reinscribe it. In their subversions they borrow from the subverted; they subject the authoritative discourse to numerous inversions and reinterpretations. The same jokes acquire different meanings in different sociocultural contexts. Jokes can constitute both unofficial public discourse and collective mourning.

In the post-Soviet years, Soviet jokes underwent another inversion. In a remarkably short period, the unofficial subversive discourse in effect became the new official ideology. What seemed once to be only an unattainable dream promised to become tangible reality. In fact, in the context of the market reforms carried out by the state, jokes like "What if we give people full freedom and allow them to become rich?" began to sound like official propaganda. The joke-as-historical-revisionist and social analyst took part in the collective post-Soviet effort to publicly reinterpret Soviet history and society, and in most cases, to condemn both. In some sense, the collective post-Soviet remembrance of the Soviet past, manifested in thousands and thousands of jokes sent to numerous publishing houses, newspapers, and magazines, is an aggregate attempt to (re)write Soviet history within a public forum.

The transmutation of the unofficial and oppositional into the official and acceptable deprived the *sovetskii politicheskii anekdot* in the post-Soviet context of its role as designator of political and social taboos, and articulator of the subversive unofficial voice. No matter what new functions Soviet political jokes adopted after the disintegration of the Soviet Union — mourning, celebration, or public disclosure — they were displaced by the mid-1990s by new jokes about the new post-Soviet realities. Clearly, any historical interpretation of post-Soviet jokes can only be preliminary and somewhat speculative.

The most interesting recent development in the joke discourse is the constitution of the post-Soviet forbidden, the unofficial; in other words, what is seen as the controlling system in the early and middle 1990s. If the *sovetskii politicheskii anekdot* is used as a standard of reference, the period of the post-Soviet anecdote appears devoid of political content, and the social limits of subversive laughter have withered. Unlike the Soviet joke discourse, which attacked the totality of the Soviet system and its particular manifestations, post-Soviet joking restricts itself to uncoordinated assaults on post-Soviet developments taken out of their broader context. Post-Soviet joking perceives the new reality much as Soviet jokes fantasized the Western and pre-Soviet Other: as lacking in contradictions between the represented and everyday reality. The issue of discrepancies between the two seems to be almost inconceivable at the present time. "Free-market," "free opportunity" rhetoric is neither questioned nor recognized as another official language, and therefore is perceived as reality itself. Jokes seem largely to have shifted their targets from political and social issues to sexual and familial ones. Thus jokes about work are constructed not in relation to the social organization as a whole but in relation to family and married life — and in fact become jokes about familial constraints:

My God! How sick I am of my work! Every day the same thing, the same
thing.
I agree that work is not the most pleasant thing on Earth. But look at it
from a different angle: there must be a place where a man can go every
day to get away from his wife.

Post-Soviet joking approaches the tradition of unofficial political subversion
and criticism in the jokes about New Russians (*novye russkie*), a post-Soviet
sociocultural category widely used in contemporary Russia to refer, usually
unflatteringly, to the group of people who have "made it" under the new
market-economy conditions. Although the *novye russkie* are attacked without
considering the social conditions that made their appearance possible, this
theme registers actual social polarization. Post-Soviet society is represented as
divided between Kolya and Vasya: Kolya is dressed in leather and drives a
Mercedes, while Vasya is dressed unpretentiously and drives a Soviet-made
Zaporozhets.

A Mercedes stands at a red light. Its brakes screeching, a Zaporozhets
rear-ends it at full speed. A *novyi russkii* gets out of the Mercedes, sneers,
and approaches the other car. An unattractive *muzhichek* sits there, looking at the *novyi russkii* like a rabbit at a snake.
"Listen, *muzhik,* don't be afraid," says the *novyi russkii.* "Tell me only
one thing — when I am not here, how do you stop at the light?"

The social hierarchy of the post-Soviet society is offhandedly articulated in
the joke and is not criticized. It is not the target of the joke. It constitutes the
uncontested social reality that provides the joke with its background. The joke
would have been funny no matter who its characters were. Jokes that directly
attack *novye russkie* also present post-Soviet society as taken for granted, as
nonideological. New Russians are ridiculed for being illiterate, ignorant, and
rude. The post-Soviet *shutnik* implicitly counterpoises his/her civilized behavior, moderate spending habits, and erudition in history, geography, literature, theater, and music to the new beneficiaries of the post-Soviet economy.
New Russians are typically portrayed as narrow-minded and boorish.

The wife of a New Russian sees a poster on a kiosk and tells her husband:
"Let's go to hear Mozart."
"Why? Didn't Mozart write here clearly that this concert is not for us but
for the flute?"

New Russians' linguistic shortcomings are also a constant target in post-Soviet humor. Moreover, theirs is the only language of post-Soviet society that is clearly articulated and ridiculed in jokes.

> A New Russian comes back from Paris. His wife asks him: "So, how is Paris?"
>
> "*Blin, klassno, v nature . . . tvoyu mat'! Eta, Fefeleva bashnya . . . tvoyu mat', nu takoi nishtyak! Vashche, blin, klevo, v nature, tvoyu mat'! . . . Man', a Man', ty chego plachesh?*"
>
> "I can't believe how beautiful it is!"[24]

Unable to express their feelings, trapped in the prison of their primitive exclamatory language, and hunted by word-parasites (*blin, v nature, tvoyu mat', vashche*), the language of the New Russian is presented as full-fledged slang.[25] The New Russian is implicitly criticized for his inarticulateness and semiliteracy — an individualistic rather than a social critique.

Jokes about New Russians do not attempt to subvert the new post-Soviet symbolic order grounded on a free-market and "independent individual" system of values. They suggest no alternatives to the current state of affairs, which is characterized by dramatic social polarization and inversion of social status. On the contrary, post-Soviet jokes demonstrate an enormous fascination with the lives of the "rich and ignorant." Detailed descriptions of new lifestyles at home and abroad, luxurious clothes, and exquisite food are turned in the joke text into the desired Other, as in this excerpt from a lengthy *anekdot:*

> The other day I came back from Thailand. What cuisine! I had shark fin soup — amazing thing — I had two bowls. In Paris, they also know how to cook. Filleted frogs' legs have a very savory taste. . . . But this is what I have decided — there is nothing better than Russian food. You know yourself: caviar, sturgeon, *shchi* with sour cabbage, mushrooms with vodka — *kaif!*

The post-Soviet joke discourse seems not to express people's dissatisfaction with the new system, but rather articulates their desire to join it, to become New Russians themselves, albeit "cultured" New Russians. Contemporary *shutniki* acknowledge their marginal position in relation to New Russians; expose the limitations and shortcomings of the new leisure class, noted for their conspicuous consumption; and implicitly offer themselves as much more deserving of the benefits of the new society. Judging by the envy embedded in post-Soviet joking, the post-Soviet subject is a virtually unconditional supporter of the new system, regardless of her actual social position. That official narratives and anecdotes converge in their views of society can be partially explained by the fact that contemporary officialese was so recently at the heart of the counter-discourse. In order to apprehend critically the new reality, *shutniki* must question what in the Soviet era was their forbidden dream. Their questioning is inhibited by the complexity of new Russian society, in which power appears to be decentered and diffused, and in which commercialism, operating to erode boundaries between official and unofficial realms, progressively colonizes all aspects of daily life. Unlike the Soviet era, during which the authoritative discourse was easily recognizable and its dominance and responsibility for social conditions were loudly proclaimed, the post-Soviet system is characterized by an apparent polyphony of political voices and decentralization of power: no group or party claims to be fully in control and responsible for all aspects of people's lives. Thus the articulation of hegemonic discourse and the uncovering of power relationships in society are much more difficult under the new order.

The state of joking in present-day post-Soviet Russia is perceived by many as decadent and vulgar. Tat′yana Pukhova, former editor of the popular satirical Soviet television program *Vokrug smekha,* openly expressed her affinity for Soviet totalitarian joking in her "nostalgic interview" with *Krokodil,* and characterized post-Soviet humor as "a little bit of vulgarity, a drop of humor and an ocean of ambition."[26] From a scholarly perspective, post-Soviet jokes are as revealing about the new order as were Soviet jokes about the old. It is impossible and unwise to predict new forms and themes that post-Soviet jokes will adopt, but the fate of Soviet jokes appears to be clear — they are losing their grip on present reality. Having been transformed from an underground medium to a street-level commodity, they are making the final journey to artifact, and constitute a rich repository of historical material.

Notes

The author thanks the Institute for Global Studies in Culture, Power, and History at Johns Hopkins University for providing funds to undertake research in Moscow in summer 1994; and the Moscow-based publishing house LUNA, which specializes in publishing Soviet and post-Soviet jokes, for assistance in collecting jokes. My joke collection consists of approximately two thousand items, of which five hundred were analyzed for this chapter. Approximately 60 percent of the two thousand jokes were collected in the summer of 1994: (1) through LUNA and (2) by means of interviews and conversations carried out by the author. Forty percent are from private collections initiated in the early 1970s. Most interviewees and owners of joke collections are members of the technical and creative intelligentsia.

1 Sigmund Freud, *Jokes and Their Relation to the Unconscious,* trans. James Strachey (New York: Penguin Books, 1976), p. 238.

2 Ibid., p. 183; also see pp. 174–77.

3 Ibid., p. 238.

4 For further elaboration of this point, see Sigmund Freud, *The Interpretation of Dreams* (New York: Avon Books, 1965), pp. 626–48; Samuel Weber, *The Legend of Freud* (Minneapolis: University of Minnesota Press, 1982).

5 Mary Douglas, "Jokes" in *Rethinking Popular Culture,* ed. Chandra Mukerji and Michael Schudson (Berkeley: University of California Press, 1991), p. 305. Also see Peter Jelavich's analysis of different roles ascribed to satire in modern societies in *Berlin Cabaret* (Cambridge: Harvard University Press, 1993), chs. 2, 6, 7.

6 Elizabeth A. Grosz, *Sexual Subversions: Three French Feminists* (Boston: Allen and Unwin, 1989), pp. 40, 43.

7 Judith Butler, *Gender Trouble: Feminism and the Subversion of Identity* (New York: Routledge, 1990), see pp. 128–49.

8 On the art of joke telling and its interpretation in the 1960s–80s, see Alexei Yurchak, "The Cynical Reason of Late Socialism: Power, Pretense and the Anekdot," *Public Culture* 9 (1997): 174–76.

9 Quoted in Michael Holquist, "The Politics of Representation," in *Allegory and Representation,* ed. Stephen J. Greenblatt (Baltimore: Johns Hopkins University Press, 1981), p. 178.

10 See Douglas, "Jokes," p. 297.

11 "With/without a beard" refers to age and generally does not have gender connotations.

12 Interview with Roman Kartsev, "Anekdot trebuet intimnosti kak seks," *Krokodil,* no. 4 (1995), pp. 6–7.

13 See Ludwig Wittgenstein, *Philosophical Investigations,* trans. G. E. M. Anscombe (New York: Macmillan, 1958), passage 118, 255, 309, 312.

14 The cruiser *Aurora* is an important symbol in the Soviet official narrative of the October Revolution. It was the ship's cannon that gave the signal to the military insurrection in 1917 in Petrograd that led to the victory of the working class over the class of exploiters, to paraphrase the official language.

15 "Smol'nyi" is the Smol'nyi Institute, a St. Petersburg finishing school that was used by the Bolsheviks as the headquarters of the 1917 insurrection.

16 The Winter Palace was the residence of the tsar's family. In the official narrative, the takeover of the Winter Palace by workers and soldiers is the most decisive moment of the October Revolution.

17 For more on the joke audience, see Anna Berchidskaia-Krylova, "The Rise and Fall of Soviet Ideology" (master's thesis, Johns Hopkins University, 1995).

18 Holquist, "The Politics of Representation," p. 180.

19 Vaclav Havel, *Living in Truth* (London: Faber and Faber 1989), p. 55.

20 Andrei Amalrik, *Will the Soviet Union Survive until 1984?* (New York: Harper and Row, 1970), p. x; Havel, *Living in Truth,* p. 45.

21 Slavoj Žižek, *The Sublime Object of Ideology* (London: Verso, 1989), p. 33.

22 On images of the United States in the Soviet press, see Jeffrey Brooks, "The Press and Its Message: Images of America in the 1920s and 1930s," in *Russia in the Era of NEP: Explorations in Soviet Society and Culture,* ed. Sheila Fitzpatrick, Alexander Rabinowitch, and Richard Stites (Bloomington: Indiana University Press, 1991), pp. 231–52.

23 See Boris Kagarlitsky, *The Thinking Reed: Intellectuals and the Soviet State, 1917 to the Present* (London: Verso, 1988).

24 The speech of the New Russians, as presented by the joke discourse, becomes untranslatable since the words the New Russian is using are completely mispronounced and thus deprived of their familiar meaning. What the joke thus presents is a series of words: *blin* (pancake), *klassno* (super), *v nature* (in nature), *tvoiu mat'* (f——k your mother, the second part of the most infamous of Russian curses), *nishtiak* (great), *klevo* (great/super), strung together in such a way that no particular meaning can be attributed to them. This stream of exclamations represents the New Russian's ecstasy over what he saw in Paris, but the emotion is not articulated in the way "educated" people would express these feelings. If the use of modern standard Russian is a sign of one's incorporation into society, then the New Russian is portrayed as still in his presocialized stage. A well-educated person, then, presumably cannot understand the New Russian. The joke suggests that there is such a thing as New Russian language and that it must have some meaning since two people manage to comprehend each other and communicate in it.

25 Examples: *nishtiak* (great), *gonish* (to lie), *Vashche opukh* (to have gone mad).

26 Interview with Tat'iana Pukhova, "Vokrug smekha: Nostal'gicheskoe interv'iu," *Krokodil,* no. 9 (1996), p. 9.

> She's a killing machine, and she'll fight to the end. A terrifying dog. She'll
> guard your house, your car, your family. And she's very good with children.
> — Advertisement for a puppy

GOING TO THE DOGS:
PET LIFE IN THE NEW RUSSIA

One of the unmistakable signs of the times in the new Russia has been the unprecedented boom in the pet industry. Suddenly France, England, and the United States seem to have found a formidable rival in Russia in the amount of attention lavished on pets and pet accoutrements. New shi-shi dog-grooming parlors, kennel clubs, and specialized dog groups have sprung up all over Moscow. Breeders, particularly those of *ovcharki* (sheepdogs or shepherds) and mastiffs, are doing a brisk business, selling puppies for anywhere from $350 to $4,000; state-owned *zoomagaziny,* which formerly sold a paltry variety of unimaginatively produced aquarium and hunting supplies, have been supplanted by *zoosalony* (zoo salons) with names ranging from Liana to Betkhoven, selling everything from imported dog and kitty foods to leashes from Germany and booties and snow jackets from England and France. On Saturdays at Dokat, the largest of the new pet parlors, people gather in front of the

266

video advertising the latest in dog perfume and cosmetics while others eye trendy dog, cat, and rabbit kibble ("Das vollwertige Futter für unsure kleinen Freunde" [Full feed for our little friend] reads the sign under the rabbit food). In a country where homelessness is on the rise, dogs belonging to New Russians can check in at a dog hotel in Moscow and spend their days in "dog college" while their owners are away. Magazines devoted to man's (and woman's) four-footed friends dot the stands: the popular *Kot i Pes* (*Cat and Dog*), which comes out in both magazine and newspaper format; *Four Paws* (*Chetyre lapy*), the Russian version of the Italian magazine *Quattro Zampe,* published in Italy; and the magazine *Drug* — one series for dogs, one for cats, and one for birds. In addition to the Moscow phone directory, one can now purchase a pet directory, a three-hundred-page tome listing the various pet services in Moscow available for pets from dogs to reptiles. Reflective of much of Russian life since 1991, the directory also contains random ads for apartments and dating services, although the relationship of these to the pet world is not always clear.[1] In short, the pet industry has arrived in Russia's large urban areas with a vengeance, having come of age in the West while most urban Russians were forced to confine their love of animals to pictures torn out of magazines and pinned to the walls of their communal apartments. In addition to offering previously unimaginable and unobtainable items for pets, the industry brings potential status for the pet owner and, in a spectacular display of commodity fetishism, incentives to the Russian *cum* consumer to indulge herself in the new consumer life.

The amount of attention accorded Russia's pets — what I term the pet culture — is nothing new, as pet aficionados are quick to point out. The cultural monuments from Russia's prerevolutionary past are replete with images of Russians at work and at play with their favorite four-footed friends. The nineteenth-century painter Valentin Serov immortalized the soon-to-be extinguished nobility through the figure of Madame Yussoupova sitting on her elegant brocaded divan with her equally elegant Pomeranian in the waning days of the Russian empire. One remembers with fondness Turgenev's hunter in *Zapiski okhotnika* (*Sportsman's Sketches*), setting forth through field and stream with his dog, who accompanied him in his ramblings through the Russian countryside around Orel. Even Nikolai Gogol, in a respite from depicting the moral squalor of provincial life, is shown by the nineteenth-century painter I. Volkova in a meditative pose on the porch of his country home surrounded by his two favorite dogs, who, in doglike fashion, are vying for his attention.

The Soviet era was not conducive to the raising of pets. Space and economic restrictions put pet ownership out of reach for many (as, ironically, they do now). Some Russians engaged in it, however, both because they loved animals and because accommodating animals in apartments that were clearly too small for them was one of the ways Soviet citizens domesticated state spaces and also quietly thumbed their noses at the system. But the collapse of state socialism has made its mark no less on pet than on political life. Privatization, larger apartments, and newly acquired wealth for some, coupled with increased access to the West and Western lifestyles, have created a burgeoning pet population and a growing pet industry. It is estimated that there are currently more than a million dogs in Moscow (one for every twelve people) of more than 130 breeds, a huge increase from the Soviet era, when strict controls on dog breeding resulted in no more than 30 official breeds. The current census of the canine population does not necessarily include the bands of dogs, mutts and purebreds alike, that find themselves homeless in a society in which a mixed breed is accorded little or no status, thus suggesting an interesting nostalgia on the part of many Russians for both the Soviet and the prerevolutionary eras. Status and privilege, whether inherited by birth or earned through contacts, have persistently eluded most Russians in this century, and thus it comes as no surprise that Moscow's purebreds are becoming the means by which their owners are attempting to carve out an area of elite status for themselves as the current social and economic climate once again denies many a share of the newly acquired wealth. Meanwhile, the mixed breed is becoming as infinitely disposable as consumer products are in the West.

This chapter explores the pet industry in Moscow today and how that industry reflects some of the directions being taken by popular culture in post-Soviet Russia. I have divided the chapter into vignettes, taking the reader to different sites where the pet culture and industry flourish. Each site suggests a different way that the pet culture and the industry that accompanies it intersect with issues of class and status, with the public and the private, and, as always, with the ubiquitous presence of the West, from which much of this new culture is derived.

Our tour of post-Soviet "pet places" (*mesta domashnykh zhivotnykh*) might well start in front of a Russian TV set, where at least six different animal shows are broadcast weekly, to the delight of young and old alike. Among the most popular airing on ORT and NTV are *Animal World* (*B Mire zhivotnykh*), with Nikolai Drozdov, and *Dog Show* (*Dog shou*), the latter featuring canine participants, all pedigreed, from around the country who vie with one another by performing a variety of tricks before a panel of judges. Prizes range from Chappi dog food to dog shampoo. Such shows highlight not only one's pooch but implicitly the social and economic status that accompanies pet ownership as well. On one particular day on *Dog Show,* a miniature collie was competing against a German shepherd. Interviews with the owners revealed that the miniature collie had been raised as a pet while the German shepherd, belonging to a former border guard, had been trained for a very different purpose. Ownership of a guard dog suggests that one has something to guard and thus imparts to the owner a special status. Indeed, pit bulls, shepherds of different varieties (including German, those from the Caucasus, and Central Asian), rottweilers, and Doberman pinschers are found in abundance in Moscow, where professional dog trainers charge up to fifty dollars a session to teach a dog to bite . . . or worse. In a promotional video circulated by Konstantin Kuznetsov, a trainer of attack dogs, dogs are shown lunging at dummies of criminals in padded suits to the accompaniment of heavy-metal rock in the background.

Anyone who wants to understand more about the social and economic significance of pedigrees in the new Moscow has only to visit a neighborhood park, where the number of people out walking is matched only by the number of dogs by their sides. During a one-week period in March 1997, I counted the following breeds in two different parks adjoining neighborhoods where people of different incomes live: black terriers, Yorkshire terriers, Staffordshires, Dobermans, German shepherds, collies, bulldogs, dalmatians, shar-peis, a borzoi, and a breed I couldn't identify and about whom the owner was reluctant to give information. There was nary a mutt in the group. Purebred dogs are not only status symbols in the new Moscow but ironically seem to be the great levelers between people who otherwise have little in common either economically or socially. Pet ownership confers status through visibility, just as it does throughout most of the world. In Moscow, though, the very visibility of that status differs sharply from the way status and privilege were conferred in Soviet times. Formerly the two were measured not so much by money as by whom one knew — by one's *sviazi* (connections). Moreover, privilege was not advertised because Soviet society, at least on paper, had resolved the problem of social and economic inequality. In the new Russia, however, privilege is increasingly determined not by one's connections but by economic assets, of which pets are one of the visible markers. Pets have also become the markers of the changes to private and public spaces since 1991. Soviet society was characterized by a very clear demarcation between the public and private worlds. That there was little crossover between the two produced at worst a kind of national schizophrenia, at best a private world more zealously guarded and nourished because of its vulnerability to infringement by the state. One of the many reversals in Russian society since the collapse of the Soviet Union has been that between public and private, with the latter now entering into the domain of the former. Dogs, in particular, have begun to function as the markers of how the private has invaded the public sphere. Dog ownership suggests that one's living space can accommodate a pet. Presumably the larger the dog, the greater the number of square meters one has at one's disposal. Thus it is not only the fact of ownership but the size of the dog that has become the barometer of economic privilege.

But there is also a twist. As with any information venue — from tattooing to the Russian media — pet ownership can convey information and disinformation in this new censor-free age. The presence of roving bands of homeless dogs, many of them purebred, and the crisis in animal shelters in Moscow suggest that, whether intentionally or not, some Muscovites are sending out fallacious markers of their social and economic privilege. They buy the dogs they covet but then cannot afford to keep them. People who have experienced some material improvement in their lives since the early 1990s are eager to partake of the new economic elitist culture. Acquiring a pet is the easiest way of showing one's elitist status because dogs are more affordable than Jeep Cherokees and Cartier watches. On the other hand, sustaining and raising that pet on the kind of food the pet industry would like owners to buy is still out of the reach of many. To illustrate, in the spring of 1998, the average wage in Moscow was less than $100 a month. Unskilled workers made approximately $60, Ph.D.'s or the equivalent, $150. Of course, wages varied widely in the private sector, enabling some people to become fabulously wealthy rather quickly. During this period dog grooming cost $50 a session, Staffordshire puppies sold for $350, and a dog-training session for a Doberman averaged around $50. The following items could be purchased at the *zoosalony* in Moscow:

1 box of rabbit food: 15,200 rubles (approximately $2.45)
1 cat bed: 55,000 rubles ($9.00)
1 reptile carrying case (*dom perenoska dlia reptilii*): 45,200 rubles ($7.30)
1 box of Tidy Cat cat litter: 37,800 rubles ($7.00)
1 dog coat: 187,500 rubles ($30.25 — half a month's wages for some workers)

    1 fur-lined dog coat: 250,000 rubles ($40.35 — one week's wage for a
    Ph.D. working at an institute)

Thus, even if one decides against a fur-lined dog coat, feeding Fido with kibble
and meat from the *zoosalony* can average 3,000 rubles a day — approximately
one-fourth of the average daily wage. While this puts pet ownership out of
reach for most, many make the plunge anyway both because, as the editor of
Kot i pes told me, "Russians have always loved their pets," and perhaps equally
because owning a particular kind of pet is a way of vicariously partaking in the
new elitist culture, which is increasingly marked by externalizing the markers
of one's privilege. Ironically, the disinformation (*dezinformatsiia*) that many
Muscovites send out about the true nature of their economic and social status
only reinforces the deep divide between the public representation of self and the
private life that characterized so much of Soviet society for the better part of
this century.

    It is at pet stores such as Betkhoven that one senses another kind of deep
schism, this one dividing the pet culture from the pet industry. Nailed to the wall
near the front door is a small wooden box with a sign reading *"Dlia bezdom-
nykh sobak i poteriannykh"* (For homeless and lost dogs), with a place to put
contributions. Russia as yet has no state-sponsored animal shelters. Fortunately, the age-old tradition of the *kollektiv* is coming to the aid of Moscow's
distressed pets, although it is far from a panacea. Some individuals have taken it
on themselves to bring these strays into their apartments, resulting in a spectacular display of post-Soviet collective living.[2] The shelter advertising its
services at Betkhoven turned out to be someone's dacha outside Moscow,
where fifty-eight dogs picked up off the city streets were being housed when I
inquired. The situation in St. Petersburg is equally grim. A kennel in a St.
Petersburg suburb currently houses more than two hundred dogs and cats in an
enclosure designed for no more than fifty animals. The current crisis in animal
shelters reflects a fledgling market economy that still lacks effective state controls. An example of how the relationship between consumption and control
works within the animal world is provided by the ASPCA, which was founded in
1866 in the United States in order to alleviate pain, fear, and suffering in
animals. The impetus for the establishment of the ASPCA was provided by
progressives in the big cities in the East and Midwest who were concerned
about the sanitation and health problems that accompanied the growing influx
of emigrants into the big cities of the United States, bringing in their wake an

increase in the animal population. Post-Soviet Russia does not yet have such controls, and the use to which the animal population is put is entirely consistent with what happens to conspicuous consumption in a market economy in which effective government and economic controls have not yet been put into place. People purchase and consume until they have either finished consuming or find that they can no longer afford the product. Many Muscovites buy pets as status symbols, exhibit them as such, and then, in an act completely consistent with consumer behavior, discard them when they discover that they can afford neither the food nor the required inoculations.

Much of the current Moscow pet culture is produced outside Russia. The United States, other European countries, and Japan export most of the pet products that Moscow's elite pet owners are buying. Some countries, including the United States, are not only exporting products but producing them on-site, as the recently opened Mars factory outside Moscow testifies. Long known for its chocolate and Mars bars, the Mars company also produces Pedigree dog food. The enormous influx of Western products into Moscow's pet culture and elsewhere is evidence of how Russians are responding to and consuming the West, which has glutted the Russian market with its products.

Since the time of Peter the Great, Russian cultural history has had a long and often tortured relationship with the West. There has long been an undercurrent of belief—which, not surprisingly, many Russians currently support—that Russia could best compete with the outside world not by Westernizing, however, but by looking inward and relying on the sources of its own greatness, most specifically the Orthodox Church and the peasantry. The problem for many Russians, particularly urban Russians in this century, has been their distrust, their devaluation, and even their shame at the peasant culture that for thinkers ranging from the nineteenth-century Slavophile philosopher Alexis Khomiakov to the twentieth-century writer Aleksandr Solzhenitsyn constitutes the fundamental richness of Russia. In Moscow at present, rural Russia and the Slavophile values that Khomiakov and others championed are at loggerheads with urban Russia, the new elitism, and the new ideology of consumerism. And the pet culture is precisely one of the places where this clash takes place.

To look at how old and new Russia are negotiating one another in present-day Moscow, let us visit three pet sites on a Saturday morning in Moscow. The first two are located a block apart not far from the Taganka: a *zoosalon* named

Dokat and the venerable Ptichii rynok (the Bird Market). The third is the Teatr koshek (Moscow Cat Theater).

On Saturday morning, Dokat, the largest of the *zoosalony* in Moscow, although woefully lacking in space by Western standards, is filled to capacity with crowds jostling to eye the latest animal video and pet paraphernalia from around the world. Despite the state taxes, which last year averaged a crippling 70 percent, Dokat has managed to effect a successful transition from a *zoomagazin* that primarily sold hunting equipment to a state-of-the-art store catering to Moscow's proliferating animal kingdom. Unlike Petsmart, the largest pet department store in the United States, there are no long lines at the cashier even though the crowds in the store are so thick that one can barely maneuver through them. Most leave this store empty-handed, not through lack of desire to buy but because they cannot afford the merchandise. At the Bird Market next door, prices are more affordable and one can still barter in a way reminiscent of the old Soviet economy.

Despite its name, the Moscow Bird Market (Ptichii rynok) does a thriving business in dogs and cats, although there are still birds to be had, as there were in the early 1970s when I began visiting it. This venerable institution, an open-air market that conducts its business on weekends, was the center of Moscow's pet culture during the Soviet era. It was here that people came to buy and sell all manner of pets from birds to dogs, rabbits to cats. Villagers came, as they do today, from outlying areas to sell puppies and kittens and sometimes a beloved family pet as a way of supplementing their income and getting through hard times.[3] When I was studying in Moscow in the early 1970s, the Bird Market was on the underground de rigueur tour for American students residing in the city. Like the various farmers' markets — which brought together under one roof the exotica of rural Russia many of us had come in search of but which often eluded us because of restrictions on travel outside the city limits — the Ptichii rynok brought rural Russia within our reach. Here villagers with impossible rural accents using vocabulary that none of us could identify urged us to touch and hold the potential candidate for a family pet. Indeed, in those days pedigree was unimportant; simply locating a pet, irrespective of breed, was the goal. To this day prospective buyers interested in a pedigree deal with breeders or kennel clubs rather than the Bird Market.

The Bird Market retains its decidedly rural cast, although it too shows telltale signs of the changes in the new Russia. Homemade signs exhort passersby not to touch (NE TROGAT') the animals, clear warning that what is being proffered is no longer a potential family pet but a security system that can function as a lethal deterrent. Other concessions to the new order can be found further on down the rows, where entire stalls are now devoted exclusively to selling muzzles.

The very proximity of Dokat and the Bird Market to each other suggests the unresolved dilemma of city versus country — urban versus rural — that informs much popular culture in Russia today and shapes how it is consumed. Russians gravitate to Dokat for the same reason that they buy shi-shi breeds of dogs. Why? Part of the answer lies in the exoticism and sudden availability of products that simply were not part of Soviet consumer life. But another reason, I suggest, why Russians are fascinated by these elitist products and pay enormous sums for them when they can least afford to is their own ambivalent stance on the provincial nature of much of Russian society — and, often, of their own origins. As the introduction to this volume states, the 1930s witnessed the transformation of the entire constituency of Moscow, as peasants moved in from the countryside, fleeing forced collectivization and responding to the need for workers in Stalin's plan to industrialize the nation. As a result, Moscow's population became highly ruralized. Many Muscovites today are profoundly uncomfortable either with their own provincial origins or with what they perceive to be the provincial narrow-mindedness that began to infect urban life in the 1930s.[4] I suggest that it is precisely this discomfort with what many Muscovites perceive as the inadequacy of provincial life, as much as it is any attraction to Western goods, that accounts for their fascination with elitist culture from Versace to doggie shampoo. Regardless of the perspective from which one views it, Moscow's Bird Market seems to function as a site where the urban and the provincial coalesce, but only in an imperfect convergence. It is a site foreigners find compelling because it actualizes their desire for a fetishized rural Russia. Many Muscovites see it differently. They go there because, unlike the store up the street, it is affordable. But it is also a world with which many have an uneasy relationship.

The third site we will visit shows another way that Muscovites are responding to the pet industry: by returning to what I earlier termed the pet culture, or the enjoyment and cultivation of animals in a way not explicitly tied to market concerns. One of the sites in Moscow where this is most in evidence is at 25 Kutuzovsky Prospekt, where the Moscow Cat Theater (Teatr koshek) is housed. Here Yury Kuklachev and his one hundred feline entertainers play to packed houses twice a day on weekends. Kuklachev began his career as a clown with the Moscow Circus, where by accident he discovered that he could train the presumably untrainable felines. He has been performing his cat acts in Moscow for several decades, though he opened his own Cat Theater only recently. His acts feature cats — some decked out in sailor suits — climbing poles, balancing themselves on little platforms, pushing carriages, and generally endearing themselves to audiences of all ages. If the Bird Market is a provincial site over which few wax nostalgic, Teatr koshek provides a site for a different kind of nostalgia, this time for the kind of entertainment with which the Soviet era was replete. It is accessible to everyone, though, as in the Soviet era, tickets are difficult to obtain because the show is wildly popular. The Cat Theater is also reminiscent of the bright, cheerful children's programming that preponderated during Soviet times. As Muscovites are being drawn, albeit vicariously, into the new elitist culture, the presence of such institutions as the Teatr koshek suggests the nostalgic pull of a time when all was not resolved into market forces and when entertainment, whether elitist or not, gave one the illusory impression that all was right with the world.

The pet industry reflects some of the salient issues in post-Soviet cultural life in the new Moscow. How this pet industry is faring in Moscow is in many ways keyed to how class allegiance is formed and how traditional tensions between urban and rural life are being negotiated in the new Russia. Just as in Soviet times, there is still an enormous gap between the elite and the masses, although that elite is constituted very differently now than it was under Soviet rule. What we are seeing is the breaking up of the masses into elitist and nonelitist groups based on economic privilege. Thus, a new elite is being formed, rooted in neither the party elite nor in the intelligentsia but in the subdividing masses themselves, creating a hierarchy of class (and economic) privilege within their own ranks. And this new elitism, the pet industry suggests to us, is a compelling draw for many Russians who have ambivalent feelings about Russia's provincial past and their own relationship to it.

The fate of the pet industry in the new Russia also suggests that the theories advanced by the cultural populists in regard to how culture is consumed may have limited applicability to a society that has recently emerged from a totalitarian past. According to John Fiske and his school, consumers consume in a manner very different than producers intend, thereby, through conscious intent or not, imparting a subversive quality to the act of consumption. The fortunes of the pet industry in Moscow since 1991, however, suggest that the implicit desire on the part of Moscow's consumers is rather to consume in precisely the way they are supposed to, entering vicariously into the elite for whom these goods are intended and yet whose membership continues to elude most Russians, as it did formerly.

Finally, the pet industry and the pet culture in Moscow today suggest the insidious problems inherent in any society where market forces and the conspicuous consumption that accompanies them are allowed to run wild. Purchased one day, "consumed" as symbols of privileged status the next, Fido's and Zhuchka's fortunes in this time of transition may be as tenuous as those of the emerging state in which they live.

Notes

I thank the following people for their help with this chapter: Aleksei at Betkhoven, Noah Barker, Natalia Dmitrieva, Eileen Meehan, Larissa Morozova, Ekaterina Stetsenko, and Valerii Varlakov.

1 *Spravochnik dlia liubitelei zhivotnykh,* 3d ed., comp. Aleksandr Vasil'ev (Moscow: Izd. "Mir Biznesa," 1996).

2 In 1997 the Russian press reported a story of a family living in one of the Khrushchevki apartment buildings who, in addition to their four children, were raising a goat, several cats, a parrot, five dogs, guinea pigs, several geese, and a female bear. See Aleksandr Dobrovol'skii, "Chetyre lapy na kvadratnyi metr," *Argumenty i fakty,* no. 23 (1997), p. 2. Stories such as this abound in the press.

3 In the early 1970s, when I was first studying in the Soviet Union, it was forbidden for foreigners to go more than forty kilometers outside Moscow. Since it was difficult to obtain news about what life was like in the villages, I often visited the Bird Market and the Kazan Railway Station. I learned more about economic hardship and what was *defitsitnyi* (in short supply) in the provinces from observing the number of puppies being sold at the Ptichii rynok and the foodstuffs being loaded onto the trans-Siberian at the Kazan Station than I did reading the paper.

4 In a recent interview the artist Ilya Kabakov discussed this discomfort and reflected on how he strives in his art to find that intersection where the provincial and the capital meet, where the embarrassed "provinciality" meets that elusive "hub," which, when one encounters it, turns out to be no "hub" at all.

> The opposition of the capital city and the countryside is one of the most important themes not only in my works, but also a whole genre of literature and art. What I am concerned with is not so much a "distilled" provinciality, as its encounter with the capital, the intersection where the two meet. I am endlessly drawn to the sections of society that are embarrassed by their "provinciality"

and imagine that there is some sort of hub, a "center" they want to reach. You and I know that when one accomplishes that dream and gets to the capital, one quickly finds that there is no such thing as a "hub" around which the rest of the country revolves, and it is certainly not there. ("Palace" Builder Goes Overseas," *Moscow News,* May 14–20, 1998, p. 9)

Part III SEXUALITIES

PUBLICLY QUEER: REPRESENTATIONS OF
QUEER SUBJECTS AND SUBJECTIVITIES IN
THE ABSENCE OF IDENTITY

In a volume on popular culture, how can we speak of sexual otherness, of queerness, without fixing queerness in the stability of terms such as *identity* or *subculture?*[1] In the United States, queerness is both popularly and theoretically imagined as locatable in a subculture produced by those identified and identifying as queer. Sexual otherness cannot be part of the popular culture; if it were, it would not be queer. But this misses how queerness does manifest itself publicly and popularly, how it seeps into popular culture in a variety of ways.

Queerness is part of any popular culture, but this is especially true in Russia, where sexual otherness, queerness, does not fit into the existing rigid identity structures. Instead, queerness is a discursive regime that does not place its consumers in permanent and stable categories of otherness. The discourse of queerness in Russia, as in the West, has been produced by experts and taken on by those who desire queerly, but the result has not necessarily been "sexual identity."[2] Thus, identifying sexual otherness as "gay and lesbian" or "sexual minorities" forces a series of acts, a verb, to take on the solid properties of a noun. If we look only for "gays and lesbians" in Russia we will blind ourselves to queer performance without identity. The "gay and lesbian" identity is generally imported from the West. "Sexual minorities" is an official categorization. These terms are rarely if ever used in the first person; sexual otherness is not usually found in sexual identity. Persons who participate in same-sex relationships do not necessarily self-identify as "other." In fact, it is not uncommon for one or even both partners in a same-sex pair to consider him/herself "straight" or to refuse to identify in any way on the basis of sexual practices.[3] Other sexual otherness is more closely associated with gender transgression than with sexual practices. For instance, a man who sleeps with other men but does not break the norms of gender performance will often identify as "straight." A typically "feminine" woman who has sexual relationships only with "masculine" women may also identify and be identified as heterosexual. Often the gender-transgressive partner in a lesboerotic pairing identifies as a "transsexual," one who is not necessarily as interested in possessing a male body as s/he is in having a masculine gender.[4] Thus the Russian sexual landscape is full of persons who engage in homoerotic and other nonnormative sexual acts. Some of them identify as "gay" or "lesbian," some identify as "transsexual," but most refuse to self-identify at all, except in very diffuse and difficult-to-translate ways (e.g., people will say they are *nash* [one of us] or *na teme* [on the theme]). Clearly the standard American categorization of persons as either heterosexual or homosexual is not very useful. *Queer* is a dangerous word in American English, fraught with all sorts of unintended meanings. Despite this, I use it here to capture the refusal to fit neatly into binary oppositions and stable categories. I also use *queer* because it can be used in the first person and therefore captures some of the fluidity and momentary self-definition of terms such as "one of us" without cementing itself into the permanence of "gay" or "lesbian" identity.

Even without the safety of identity, queerness represents itself, signifies itself, in ways that are both particular and popular. Queers gather secretly in public places — secret because their queerness is unacknowledged. Sometimes queerness is seen; it becomes part of the public's imagination. A queer play is seen by a large number of people; a queer singer is all the rage. They are "popular" even if being queer is not. Persons who lack a common identity participate in common practices and events (e.g., attend a theater performance).

The common practices and events rely on a common, if heteroglossic, language of queerness. If *identity* and *subculture* are not useful descriptions of this common language, then *subjectivity* is.

Consumers and producers rely on queer subjectivities — a set of signs, symbols, rituals, a "style" — that are readable as queer. Queer subjectivities, unlike queer "subculture" or "identity," are not limited to a well-defined group of persons. Queer subjectivities build an amorphous structure that does not attach itself to individual bodies. Instead, individual bodies participate in creating and consuming queer subjectivities, speaking at times for themselves, at times for others. Queer subjectivities are both culture and subculture, both popular and particular. Queer subjectivities constitute that space of the human collectivity in which sexual otherness is represented by self-speaking subjects and dreamt and even desired by those who do not or cannot speak as queers. This chapter considers how queerness becomes public, not as identity or subculture, but in the flexible and fleeting space of subjectivities. The first section considers local queer subjectivities, the second the leakage of queerness into the popular imagination.

Local Queer Subjectivities

The very ephemeral quality of local queer subjectivities means that not only are they difficult to spot, but once spotted, recorded, and disseminated, they are probably already gone. Yet local queer subjectivities are important because they do not require huge amounts of capital (cultural, economic, or educational). At a local level, queer can go public without paying. What follows are some local moments of queerness that I recorded during 1989, 1994, and the summers of 1991 and 1992.

Dancing to a Different Beat

By 1994, Russia's large cities were awash with discos and clubs, each with its own particular style and clientele. Some of the discos were aimed exclusively at the *nouveau richniki*, those who could afford twenty-five-dollar cover charges and eight-dollar glasses of wine; others were aimed at the "fashionable" youth (e.g., "raves"); and, of course, some discos were for queers. Both Moscow and St. Petersburg had three queer discos in 1994.[5]

Prem'era and Shans (Premiere and Chance) were located in the center of Moscow. Both discos were in theaters and had plenty of room for the three hundred or so revelers who gathered in them each weekend night.[6] The cost of the central discos was relatively high (twenty-five thousand rubles, or about twelve dollars at the time). The language I heard most often inside was Russian, but there was also a fair amount of German and English spoken. The crowd seemed young (under thirty), although there were always a few persons who seemed well into middle age. The majority of the disco patrons were men.[7] The third queer disco, MELZ (an acronym for Moscow Electric Light Factory), was located in a factory complex far from the center of Moscow. Its prices (on entrance fees and drinks) were lower, and the crowd seemed to have more Russians, more women, and greater age diversity.[8] In exchange for the more "democratic" atmosphere at MELZ, however, customers had to live with a far higher risk of violence and exposure. During the first half of 1994, I witnessed or was told about several "gay bashing" incidents near the entrance to the club.[9]

Whatever the costs, whether economic or physical, the payoff seemed worth it to the hundreds, probably thousands, who attended the various queer discos every weekend night. For the hours that they entered that space, despite the dangers of bashing, exposure, and blackmail that lurked right outside the door, queers were free to engage in public significations of their desires. People dressed in ways that were visibly queer (e.g., men wore makeup and women's shoes, women wore no makeup and men's shoes). These were not generally ways people felt comfortable dressing on the streets, and I always noticed disco patrons changing clothes in the morning before braving the Moscow metro. Most of the dancers were same-sex pairs. Many couples found the darkened rooms amenable to kissing and touching. At Chance, the bathrooms, located two floors below, were isolated and easily turned into places for public sex.[10] More important, no one publicly *acting* out queerness was required to *be* a queer as part of the cost of attending a queer disco. Sexual otherness was a verb, a performance, a dance, but not necessarily an identity.

Toilets and Pleshki: *Queer Sex in the Street*

> "Well, and then in Moscow I found out: at Bykovo airport I went into the toilet, it was all written up on the wall, look through such and such a gap, and a guy there signaled to me and gave me a blow-job through a hole in the partition."
> "How did you find out about cruising in the city centre?"
> "Well, that guy told me."
> (Evgenii Kharitonov [1941–1981])

Public toilets are one of the places where men can have completely anonymous, if not completely safe, sexual encounters with other men.[11] Public toilets near cruising areas are "known" as sites of gay male sexual encounters, both by the men who cruise them and by the police who clear them. Unfortunately, men's toilets are not easily accessible to a woman field researcher. Dressed as a man, I twice tried entering a men's toilet near a cruising strip in Moscow. Unfortunately, my "drag" was successful only as long as I did not have to pull down my pants.[12] Once, I was intimidated out of the toilet by a police officer who asked me for "what" (not whom) I was waiting (*"Chego ty zhdesh'?"*). Another time I saw no contact between anyone (perhaps the presence of a nonurinating person made those using the toilet uncomfortable). Fortunately, one source of homoerotic desire in public bathrooms, graffiti, was accessible to me.[13] "I suck" (*sosu*), which does not have the English connotation of being bad at something, but rather refers only to oral sex, was the most popular graffito. Also, men who wanted to be fellated often wrote about their wares (e.g., "Who wants to suck off my big member?"). Some of the transactions were clearly of a commercial nature: "I am looking for an 'active' [a man who penetrates but is not penetrated] man with an apartment. I love to put on makeup and wear women's underwear. I'm 34 years old. Your age doesn't matter. I will give it to you in any position. Write how we can meet . . . I'm ready, Zhana."

Others relied on humor to signify their homosexual desires: "Boys, don't be afraid of sex, a member in the mouth is sweeter than cakes" (this nearly rhymes in the original: "Mal'chiki, ne boites' seksa, chlen vo rtu-poslasche keksa"). As queer desires, much of the graffiti is meant to be all talk and no action. Yet the fact that they exist alerts men — all men who use public toilets — that there is a potential for sexual interaction with other men in such locations. Even if a man knew of no other place in the city to engage in homosexual contacts, he would almost certainly know that it is possible, at least at a textual level, to do so in public rest rooms.

In addition to public rest rooms, large cities have cruising strips where men (and a few women) can go for sexual encounters. In Moscow, the most renowned cruising strip, or *pleshka,*[14] is in front of the Bolshoi Theater. Why the Bolshoi *pleshka* became so popular is unclear, but the fact that it is located in the center of town (easy access) as well as near two separate metro lines (easy escape) may have played a role. The Bolshoi, as the center of both opera and ballet, may have acted as a queer icon, drawing opera queens to its pink exterior with its statues of stallions in all their phallic glory, but few of the men I met at

12.1   Laurie Essig
cruising the *pleshka*.
Photo by Lisa Cowan.

the *pleshka* came for the (high) culture. Instead, during the course of eight outings to the Bolshoi, I mostly met very young men from out of town who were looking for an older and richer man who could put them up for a few days. There were always, of course, older men, often in business suits, sometimes in jogging suits, who were scouting the possibilities.[15]

At the Bolshoi *pleshka* as well as all the others I "cruised" in both Moscow and St. Petersburg (fig. 12.1) there were always other people — families with children, elderly heterosexual couples — who seemed not only uninterested but unaware of the male-male cruising occurring around them.[16] Not only do *pleshki* remain unacknowledged sites of homoerotic desire for many, but the word has also become a pejorative term for anonymous sexual encounters. L, a gay man in his late twenties who is in a committed relationship with another man, told me that for him, "being with men was never about the *pleshka*. I can only be with a man I love. It's more than sex."[17] Dmitrii Lychev, the editor of a gay magazine, argued that in the current age of gay discos and bars, public cruising strips have outlived their usefulness. Those who continue to go there are interested only in sex, and the sex is often commercial, making it an "embarrassment" to the gay community.[18] Despite the opprobrium for the *pleshka* in the eyes of some queers, it continues to thrive, and not just as a metaphor for anonymous homosexual contacts and commercial sex, but as an actual location and located set of activities, none of which require a queer identity or subculture. All the young men I interviewed insisted that desiring another man did not make a person "queer," and almost all of these young men were looking for "straight" men. If a man desires sexual contact with another man, there is a place, in the heart of Russia's cities, where public homosexual sex is both imagined and located, but not necessarily identified.

Journals, Newspapers, and the Publishing of Queer Texts

Sometimes queer is written. Although newspapers and journals are among the major textual expressions of queer subjectivities in Russia, they are more ephemeral than books. And unlike books, journals and newspapers are generally not trying to sell at a national level to a general audience; they usually appear in smaller and more specific editions, something that is possible because they are far easier and cheaper to produce than books. Anyone with access to a copying machine can create these sorts of texts. Many journals and newspapers do not even rely on a typewriter, but use the far more accessible media of paper and pen. Yet the relative ease with which these texts can be produced means that they often remain hidden from view; they may be difficult to find and available only to those "in the know." Journals and newspapers are always in danger of dropping from the public view without the public ever being aware that they were there. In this sense, journals and newspapers are more like discos than books. What follows are descriptions of a few of the newspapers and journals I found mostly in the course of 1994, although a few date from 1990.[19]

In February 1990 *Tema* (again, *na teme* is slang for "queer"), the first newspaper or journal solely about queers, appeared in Moscow. Although some earlier samizdat contained queer material, *Tema* was the first *queer* publication. Its first editions, consisting of eight tabloid pages and cut-and-paste graphics, were difficult to read (especially discreetly). As time went on, *Tema* adopted a magazine format and computer-generated graphics. The first issue explained the formation of the Association of Sexual Minorities, urged queers to "come out,"[20] explained safe sex, and gossiped about foreign queer movie stars (with a sidebar stating that "Soviet stars don't need it advertised"). During its last year

of publication, *Tema* was twice as long (sixteen pages) and more like a magazine than a newspaper. *Tema* had also transformed from a publication for
"sexual minorities" (e.g., gay men, lesbians, bisexuals, transsexuals, sex workers) to an exclusively gay male one. A typical 1992 issue featured Tom of
Finland's homoerotic graphics, articles on Western gay pop stars, and the establishment of a (male-male) cruising strip by one of *Tema*'s editors. All the
personal advertisements were from men as well. One of the few appearances by
a female reader or writer was a letter to the editor from Galina Alekseevna, a
retired schoolteacher from Moscow, who observed that homosexuality, a most
"noxious" and "bourgeois" "infection," must be "burned off (Russian society) with a will of iron."[21] Apparently women were no longer part of *Tema*'s
world, except in the role of "straw men," easily knocked down as homophobic
and communist (i.e., sentinels of the old, long-discredited system). The masculine bent of *Tema* was not unusual. Queer was going public, but it was male
homoeroticism that would take up the most space.

When *Tema* stopped publishing in early 1993, it did not leave a vacuum in its
wake; several other journals of queer subjectivities had already appeared. In
October 1990, just nine months after *Tema*'s first issue, *RISK* began publishing.
A much "slicker" publication than *Tema, RISK* was a magazine published on
higher-quality paper and with well-reproduced graphics. *RISK* contained articles on queer organizational events (e.g., conferences) and culture (e.g., gay
singers and writers), as well as humor, personals, and "centerfold" pictures
(i.e., masturbatory). Like *Tema,* nearly all of the articles and graphics appeared
to be aimed at men. The personals were also almost exclusively male.

The gay male subjectivity expressed in *Tema* and *RISK* was repeated in other
larger-circulation journals and newspapers being sold in Moscow and St. Petersburg. *Ty (You)*, an "illustrated journal for homosexuals and lesbians," did
include political articles on events of interest to men and women, but most of
the articles and all of the images were by and about men. Even the large amount
of AIDS information distributed by *Ty* because of its connection to an AIDS
organization said nothing about safe sexual practices for women.[22]

Significantly, the texts most likely to represent lesbian subjectivities were
those with the smallest circulation. Unlike their larger and more commercial
counterparts, which generally had print runs in the tens of thousands, the
smaller publications generally circulated in the hundreds. One small journal,
Probuzhdenie (Awakening), put out by St. Petersburg activist Olga Krauze, was
specifically for lesbians. Not only was this lesbian journal less circulated than

gay men's journals such as *RISK,* it was also clearly less interested in being widely distributed. The lack of commercialism and fiscal viability, however, also meant that this and other lesbian publications were subject to the vagaries of highly motivated but unpaid individuals. The handful of persons responsible for the publications that spoke to and for women had to juggle large egos and very little money with the demands of publishing in Russia. The result was a few publications that appeared erratically and were extremely difficult to find.

If shouts of queer male subjectivity have barely been heard above the din that is post-Soviet Russia, then queer women's voices are not and have never been louder than a whisper.[23] As the history of queer publications in Russia suggests, queer subjectivities in Russia are gendered, and they are gendered male. The phallic drift of public queerness is interesting for what it says about the gendered distribution of power. Yet even more important than public queerness's gender is its drift into popular culture. Queerness is consumed at a local level in the form of cruising strips, discos, and texts written by and for enthusiasts, but queerness is being consumed throughout Russia as popular music, literature, and theater.

National Queer Subjectivities

Singing Queerly

Boris Moiseev first found fame while performing with Russian pop culture icon Alla Pugacheva. In 1991, after little success in launching his solo career in Russia (in part because of persistent rumors that he had died of AIDS), Moiseev decided to "come out" in the press.[24] Moiseev's homosexual desires were already loudly stated in his work. His performances are permeated with the homoerotic, particularly the homoerotic signified by gender transgression. A video of his song "Egoist" was often shown on the music video program *2 × 2;* that is, to many people who do not identify on the basis of their homosexual desires. The video, which has two versions, plays with gender in decidedly queer ways. One version has Moiseev, unshaven but wearing a lot of lipstick and eye makeup, his hair bleached blonde, singing alongside two female dancers with shaved heads. The dancers bump and grind on one another in lesboerotica that is far from subtle. They wear transparent black shirts with pieces of black tape across their nipples (an apparent reference to pornography and its censorship). Another Moiseev video comes from his show in honor of Freddy

Mercury.[25] The video begins with about twenty men in black tails dancing together to a waltz. Here it is not the dancers' outward appearance, which subverts gender and makes homosexual desire visible, that is striking, but the inappropriate performance of gender (i.e., men twirling men in their arms).

Moiseev's image in the press often plays on gender subversion in order to signify sexual "perversion," specifically homosexuality. A journalist asks what sort of toys he loved in childhood and Moiseev answers, "I played with dolls. And even now I have my favorite dolls at home."[26] Moiseev says his mother described him from birth as a "girl with balls." Later in the same article, Moiseev claims it is his act of wearing a dress that turns his (male) audience on, forces them to stand erect (the double entendre works in English or Russian).[27]

Sergei Penkin is another singer who is both popular and queer. Unlike Moiseev, Penkin does not state his (homo)sexuality publicly.[28] In fact, Penkin publicly denies his homosexuality. In an article that begins with the question "Gay or not gay?" Penkin argues that if he were gay, which he is not, then he would not have been received by high-level officials, which he has been. The author of the article, however, is unconvinced by such arguments and tells us that Penkin's clothes, or more specifically, his "long, red gloves with fake diamonds and fur around his neck . . . speak louder than words." The reader is left to read homosexuality into Penkin's "inappropriate" use of gendered clothing.[29]

Penkin's gender per- and subversion *is* his public image. He appears in his videos wearing women's dresses and wigs, and the front of his *Holiday* CD features Penkin in lace, pearls, silver lamé, a diamond brooch, and eye makeup. In the liner notes to the CD, Penkin admits that "many . . . consider my image . . . shocking, they see in it some sort of . . . scandal. But I try to be just as I am, my main principle is naturalness."[30] Penkin may consider his image "natural" (*natural* is slang for "heterosexual"), but many people, including his interviewer, read queerness in a man wearing lace and pearls.

Queer Books

In 1990, Aleksandr Shatalov founded Glagol Press to publish works by or about queers. Unlike queer magazines and journals, the books were aimed at a far larger audience — those interested in "good" literature regardless of their sexual practices.[31] The first book Shatalov chose was the semi-autobiographical account of Eduard Limonov's émigré years in 1970s Manhattan. Limonov's *It's Me, Eddie* (*Eto ia, Edichka*) chronicles the disintegration of Limonov's national and sexual identity as he moves from heterosexual Russian to bisexual émigré. In addition to *It's Me, Eddie,* Shatalov has published James Baldwin's *Giovanni's Room,* William Burroughs's *Naked Lunch,* and the works of Evgenii Kharitonov, a Russian writer famous before his death in 1981 as a theater director, and since Glagol's publication of his work, as a writer of intensely homoerotic prose. Thus, besides bringing Western homoerotic and homosexual writings to a Russian readership, Shatalov was the first in Russia to publish two queer Russian writers.

Because Glagol Press is the *only* (conscious) source of homoerotic books, it has the onerous task of "representing" queer literature. As with any representation, Glagol's is at best partial. As a *conscious* representation, Glagol is surprisingly particular. All of Glagol's books are "of a time" and generally a place quite separate from their present readership. Baldwin's *Giovanni's Room* was written in 1956 and takes place in Paris; Burroughs's drug-hazed ramblings are also set in the 1950s, in the United States; Limonov's sexcapades are set in New York in the 1970s; and Kharitonov's two-volume works in mid-century Russia.[32]

Shatalov justifies his choices on "artistic" grounds,[33] which are notoriously slippery. Why James Baldwin and not David Leavitt? Why European and American writers and not South American or African? Clearly a lot more is going on here than the publication of the "best" works of art. Glagol's editions speak not just to Shatalov's preferences and prejudices, but to his understanding of what will sell in the Russian market. All of the Glagol books tell similar stories, stories that make sense in Russian.

Baldwin, Burroughs, Kharitonov, and Limonov share neither a common language nor a common culture nor a historical moment. What they *do* share is a recognizable (at least to a Russian reader) concept of queer male sexuality. This sexuality is neither bounded nor fixed. It is not an identity but a practice. The characters are not either gay or straight but both, or neither. They are men who are sexual with both men and with women, not because they identify as bisexual but because their lives are bifurcated. The split between the underworlds and overworlds, the hidden queerness and public normalcy, is most pronounced in *Giovanni's Room.* Baldwin's protagonist, David, is a young American in Paris. In the course of his stay in the city, David moves in with Giovanni, only to abandon him for his female lover, Hella. David leaves Giovanni, and by implication homosexuality, not because he loves Hella more, but because he cannot continue to live "underground." David convinces himself that he can still come out of the queer underground unmarked and unidentified (as queer).[34]

The idiom of a dark and queer underground beneath a brighter aboveground is reversed in Burroughs, where the underground and those who live there — drug abusers, sex workers, homosexuals — are the only objects worthy of interest. Some homosexuals are part of the straight world in Burroughs's book, of course; yet even these "straight homosexuals" are attracted to the underworld. Describing a gay man on the subway, Burroughs's narrator says: "Young, good looking, crew cut, Ivy League, advertising exec type fruit holds the door back for me. I am evidently his idea of a character. You know the type comes on with bartenders and cab drivers . . . a real asshole."[35] For Burroughs, a homosexual, even the most respectable "asshole," is always in danger of being seduced by the underground.

In the disparate works he wrote throughout his lifetime and originally titled *Under House Arrest,* Kharitonov describes homosexual desire in far more detail than did earlier Russian writers. Yet Kharitonov's work is not about sexual "liberation." He describes queer desires as not only inevitable, but inevitably sinful. Kharitonov was a devout Russian Orthodox Christian as well as an insistently queer man,[36] which may explain his obsession with homosexuality as sin. Kharitonov's paradoxical relationship to his sexuality — as both sinful and inevitable, as both hidden and demanding to be recorded in great detail — speaks to the contradictions between his aboveground life as a highly successful theater director and his furtive, underground existence as a gay man in communist Russia.[37]

The above/under separation rings true to a Russian ear, where the metaphor for "coming out of the closet" is "coming out from underground" (*uiti iz podpol'ia*).[38] Yet all Glagol's writers celebrate the underground, especially its darkness. Limonov juxtaposes his passionless heterosexual encounters with his passionate homosexual ones. The homosexual encounters always occur with an air of danger and crossing borders not meant to be crossed. Limonov, the white Russian intellectual, relates his encounters with black and socially marginal American men in a manner that can only be described as radiant.[39]

The strict boundary between queer and normal lives, above and underground, exists to divide not persons but practices. None of the protagonists of the Glagol Press books is a divided person; rather they are all persons who continuously cross over the queer/normal divide. And once on the queer side, these protagonists are not permanently "marked." Instead, they move through these sexual barriers like a pedestrian who must travel from a respectable neighborhood through a red-light district several times in the course of a day, a week, a lifetime. Consider Limonov's Eddie. He does not reveal a "truer" homosexual self. Eddie doesn't feel compelled to announce his newfound sexual practices as part of a previously hidden but more "authentic" identity.[40] In Baldwin, David's female lover discovers his queer practices, but at no point before this happened did he feel compelled to confess his homosexuality to her. Although the queer heroes never reveal themselves, at least willingly, to the hostile straight world in which they also reside, there seems little shame in heterosexuality (and perhaps some pride) in the queer spaces they inhabit. Giovanni and David discuss their female "mistresses" with each other, but the subject seems to arouse neither disgust nor jealousy.[41]

In the same way that "underground" is a powerful description of Russian queers, so is "fluidity of boundaries," the crossing back and forth between straight and queer worlds without ever having to settle permanently in one location or another. The "compulsory heterosexuality" of the Soviet system demanded the label "married" in order to obtain scarce resources such as housing and jobs. Socially it is a lot easier to explain that one is divorced or separated than never married.[42] That nearly everyone had to participate, at least to some extent, in heterosexuality never stopped some from also participating in other sexualities. Since heterosexuality was mandatory, like military service, it did not threaten a person's status as "queer." Many of Russia's leading queer activists are or have been married to someone of the opposite sex. Many young queers, even those active in political organizations, spoke to me of their desire to marry someone of the opposite sex. A twenty-one-year-old member of the Chaikovskii Fund told me he had every intention of marrying a woman in a few years and having children. I asked him whether or not he would tell his hypothetical wife of his homosexual practices. "Absolutely not. I may continue to sleep with men, but I would never tell my wife that. Why should she know about that?"[43] This is the fluidity of boundaries and mandatory nature of heterosexuality that is reflected in Glagol's books. It is not "artistic" merit that Shatalov has defined, but queer subjectivities that mirror the lives of Russian queers.

Staging Queerness

Another major form of popular queer subjectivity, theater, also wraps itself in the cloak of artistic merit. Like queer books, the queer theater is not for queers per se, but for those interested in "art." The "art" happens to represent queerness, but many of its queer producers and consumers seem to feel that is beside the point. Many queers, including movement leaders, when asked which cultural productions are important and why, mentioned queer theater productions. The productions are important, however, not for showing queerness per se but for "showing love." Typically queers argued that theater can "transcend" the banality of a particular sexuality: "[Roman Viktiuk's production of *M. Butterfly*] is far more important than any political organization. This is about love, which is never heterosexual or homosexual"; and "Viktiuk's work does a lot more for us than [queer activists] ever will." Like queer books, queer theater is, despite its protests to the contrary, highly representative of Russian (male) homosexuality. In almost all theatrical stagings of queerness, queer characters are not defined by a coherent and fixed (homo)sexual identity. Instead, the stories consider how men engage one another in love and lust without ever identifying them according to a fixed sexuality.

Since 1989, Jean Genet's *The Maids* (*Les Bonnes*) and David Hwang's *M. Butterfly* have been produced by one of Russia's premier theater personalities, Roman Viktiuk (fig. 12.2).[44] In Genet, the male homoerotica is metamorphosed into the (never overtly) incestuous relationship between the two sisters/maids, Claire and Solange. There is no need to call the men playing the parts of the maids gay, but there is no denying the sexual attraction they feel for each other and Madam/another man. In Viktiuk's production, bare-chested men in skirts and heavy makeup play the women. The effect is not men passing as women, but men *not* passing as women. The Soviet censor originally read queerness into men playing women and tried to ban the show. Audiences also acknowledged the production's queerness.[45] In Viktiuk's *M. Butterfly* the homosexual relationship is literally played out, but one of the lovers is married to a woman, and the gender fluidity of both characters makes it difficult to affix a sexuality to either man. Whether consciously or unconsciously, Viktiuk has chosen to stage plays that speak to intense sexual and emotional attachments between men without ever trying to "identify" those men (especially since they are also women). In fact, Viktiuk explained the homosexuality of one of his productions as "blind faith brings one man to fall in love with another, without ever considering what sex he is."[46]

Viktiuk has not only imported stories that make sense in Russian/Russia; he has also produced an indigenous tale of love and lust between men. When it

12.2   Theater poster advertising the Russian production
of Jean Genet's play *Les Bonnes* (*Sluzhanki*). Photo by
Laurie Essig.

opened in the fall of 1993, the play *Rogatka* (*Slingshot*), written by Nikolai
Koliada, constituted the first time in seventy years that Russian (as opposed to
imported) queer subjectivity was seen onstage. The play itself centers on the
relationship between two men, or more exactly, a man and a boy. The man is
quite clear about what he wants. In the first act he confides that he has never
been with a woman. Later, the man compares his "love" for the boy with a
female neighbor's animalistic "lust," which is no different from that of "rabbits or pigs." The boy, however, is much less certain about his sexual feelings.

He has failed to "perform" with his girlfriend and confesses to being exactly the same as the man in all things. Yet when the boy and the man finally do have sex, the boy wakes up disgusted and angry with himself. He returns in the second act to blackmail the man. Eventually the man kills himself, and only then does the boy admit, in a conversation with his now deceased beloved, that he wishes to be with him.[47]

Rogatka is anything but subtle. The man and the boy sit and eat an imaginary/metaphorical apple, which turns out to be rotten. Dream sequences involve a large swing and an elevator shaft (rather like hot dogs chasing donuts). The overly melodramatic nature of the play did not seem to diminish the audience's enthusiasm for it. On the night I attended, Viktiuk was given a lengthy standing ovation by a crowded house. One of the reasons Viktiuk's belabored show might have been popular with the audience that night (and certainly with many of the queers with whom I spoke, who believed it to be one of the best plays they had ever seen) could very well have been the fact that *Rogatka,* like *M. Butterfly* and *The Maids,* is a story of ill-defined sexualities. The man speaks of dreaming that he is a bird, soaring into the sky, "neither male nor female." The boy, body hairless and long hair falling loosely around his shoulders, also occupies an androgynous space. In the dream sequences, the man and the boy slash and jump their way through walls/borders. Finally, many of the dream sequences, including the finale, include the "lustful" female neighbor. The love may be between two men, but a woman/heterosexuality is omnipresent.

Of course, this is a very particular (i.e., my own) reading of the play. Although I did interview the five persons with whom I attended the show, they all had trouble explaining what exactly they liked about it.[48] One person told me that *Rogatka* was "Russian, and if you're Russian you'll understand." Another said Viktiuk's staging made the show that of a "genius." This person was not, however, able/willing to say what in particular she admired. Yet even if these and other viewers did not vocalize it, what made the play "Russian" and Viktiuk a "genius," at least in terms of presenting homosexuality to the public, was the absolute unwillingness to present homosexuals as a separate species/identity/lifestyle. Sexual love can happen between two men (any two men). No character in the play "is" gay, and the two lovers spend a fair amount of their time speaking about sexual relationships with women. The other obvious message of *Rogatka,* and of Viktiuk's entire oeuvre, is that when sexual love does happen between two men, it often ends in tragedy. The tragedy, however, is not the love between the two men, but rather its denial.

Conclusion: Popularly Queer

Viktiuk's productions, like Glagol's books, allow queers and queer experiences to represent themselves to a much larger public than do the queer-specific magazines and journals, discos, or even bathrooms. The cost of obtaining a large audience is that queer representation seems to be limited to a trope of romantic (never sexual) love and its unimaginative and highly predictable tragic endings. Nevertheless, the rewards of popularly speaking of sexual otherness as "art" are many. First, the pesky imperative for "full" representation disappears. No one assumes that "great art" must also include women (and by shielding themselves in the metaphysical truth of art, popular queer subjectivities are free to ignore the particular and individual truths of queer women). Nor does "great art" include sexual identity, identity politics, or even just sex. No depictions of anonymous sex in a public toilet have pulled themselves up to the level of "art." Queer men who want sex without love are just as invisible as queer women are. Second, a particular political argument about queers is circulated among large numbers of persons without those persons ever recognizing or rejecting it. Queer "artists" are arguing that "love" is the common denominator, the great leveler. "True love," whether between two men or a man and a woman,[49] is universal and should be universally valued. This argument is obviously a useful one to many queers (and nonqueers) because it makes difference meaningless and therefore no longer threatening. The fact that "love" leaves out a whole plethora of queer desires and practices is justified by its status as "art" and therefore above the mundane considerations of representation (while at the same time "art" is representing queerness as "love").

The result is a world of queer subjectivities where men speak more often and louder than women, where queer is represented in some ways and not in others, where other sexual otherness can only be found in a handful of easily erased texts — public bathrooms, cruising strips, texts written by and for enthusiasts. The result is also, however, the proliferation of *some* queer subjectivities among a much wider public. No longer confined to "underground," *some* queers can represent themselves in ways that are readable "aboveground." In this way, queers, who had always been objects (of medical experts, laws, *remontniki,* and a variety of persons or institutions willing to speak for them), have begun to speak for themselves.

Perhaps even more important, queer subjectivity, at least a slice of it, is now part of the "popular imagination." Those who would speak "about them" can

no longer ignore the self-speaking queer subjects who have carved out a surprising amount of space from the public sphere. Queerness has shifted from the
monotonous monologue of objectification to a dialogic exchange between self
and other. The shift from objectification to representation took place not because of a political movement, or because of an attempt to represent queerness
to other queers, but because a small portion of queer subjectivities managed to
enter the gates of popular culture in the belly of the Trojan Horse known as
"true art" and "true love." That these representations of queerness are not the
whole truth is inevitable because not all queer voices would be heard or comprehensible to the public. Instead, queer "reality" (at least as it exists in the
"popular imagination") is represented by those who can speak most loudly and
comprehensibly to a public (both queer and straight) that believes in "love"
and "art," not "identity" and "politics."

Notes

1 According to Michel Foucault and other theorists of sexuality, queerness was transformed in the West from a series of acts to a person through legal and medico-
   psychiatric discourses in the nineteenth century. Thus, according to Foucault, "the
   homosexual species was born." See Michel Foucault, *The History of Sexuality*, vol.
   1 (New York: Vintage Books, 1990). According to Dick Hebdige, "subordinate
   groups" must constantly contest the dominant culture's definition of them. The
   result of the contestation between culture and subculture is a style (e.g., of dress, of
   speech) that can be recognized by both the dominant culture and the subcultures. See
   Dick Hebdige, *Subculture: The Meaning of Style* (London: Routledge, 1979). There
   is certainly a queer style in Russia, but is there a queer subculture? As Hebdige
   himself has pointed out, *subculture* is a term that makes bounded territories out of
   what is in fact a shifting and unbounded landscape. See Hebdige, *Hiding in the
   Light: On Images and Things* (London: Routledge, 1988), p. 212.
2 Sexuality in Russia developed differently than it did in the West. Although the
   meaning of sexual acts was constituted in similar discursive realms, in Russia,
   queerness was never fashioned into the homosexual species. Instead, sexual acts
   between men were seen as a crime and were punishable until 1993 under Article
   121. Lesboerotic acts were and sometimes still are seen as an illness to be "cured,"
   either through electric shock and drug treatments or through a sex-change operation — thereby repositioning desire for a woman onto a (fashioned) male body. In
   both cases, queerness was seen as a set of acts, not an unchangeable core of self-
   identity. For more on the legal and medico-psychiatric discourses on queerness, see
   Laurie Essig, *Queer in Russia: A Story of Sex, Self, and the Other* (Durham: Duke
   University Press, 1999).

3 This is based on surveys of more than one hundred people plus in-depth interviews with more than thirty cultural and/or political figures who are associated with "sexual minorities."

4 For instance, several "transsexuals" I interviewed told me that they were not interested in having a male body (specifically, a penis). One transsexual told me that he obtained the diagnosis so that he could get a job reserved for men and so that he could marry his girlfriend. Another transsexual told me that he had never even seen a man's naked body and that the very idea of having a penis was revolting. This more metaphorical understanding of transsexualism is in line with Soviet/Russian psychiatric and bureaucratic practices that require the diagnosis of transsexual in order to change a person's legal identity. Actual sex-reassignment surgery is not necessary. In the United States, a person must be postoperative before changing his/her legal identity. Interviews with Dmitrii Isaev, August 1994 (Isaev is one of a handful of Russian psychiatrists responsible for making a diagnosis of transsexualism), multiple interviews with ten female-male transsexuals, 1991 and 1994. For more on psychiatric, legal, and medical understandings of transsexualism in the United States, see Elizabeth Cohen, "Biberpeople," *OUT,* May 1995, pp. 87–90.

5 Although I attended two of the St. Petersburg discos several times during 1994, I concentrate on describing the Moscow "scene" because of my far greater familiarity with the discos there. I also met and interviewed far more people in Moscow who go to discos than I did in St. Petersburg. A six-hour stay was not unusual because the high level of crime in Moscow encouraged patrons to get there around midnight and not leave until morning (i.e., when the metro reopened). This was especially true at queer discos, where notices were often posted warning customers about leaving in the middle of the night because of crimes targeted specifically at homosexuals (i.e., gay bashing).

6 These numbers are an average of my best guesstimates because counting dancing and mingling bodies is always an imprecise science. I attended Chance approximately twenty times during 1994 and always tried to count at around 1:00 A.M. (assuming some people had already left and others were to arrive). I would count one quarter of the room I was in and then multiply by four.

7 On average, 80 percent of the disco patrons were men. Given the inaccuracy of my counting as well as the fact that gender, especially in a queer bar, is not always what it appears, I hesitate to make the claim that there were more men than women (but it certainly seemed that way).

8 I attended MELZ only twice in 1994, in part because the second time I witnessed a high level of violence there and often feared for my own well-being. Both times there was a significantly higher percentage of women there (three or four in ten) than in other queer discos. My interviews and surveys support this observation. This may have been due to the lower prices (ten thousand rubles instead of twenty-four thousand) and the fact that Russian women, like women in the United States, tend to earn less money than men do.

9 Generally the stories were the same: someone or a group of people was either

arriving very late or leaving very early and was attacked by a gang of young men (*remontniki,* or "fixers"). The victims were usually robbed and often beaten. Many of them did not go to the police because they were afraid that the police would blackmail them with threats of "outing" them at work or to their families, or that the police were cooperating with the *remontniki,* taking a share of the money in exchange for turning a blind eye to the crimes they were committing regularly and predictably at MELZ.

10 Although I did not patronize the men's bathroom, the women's bathroom was generally used for more purposes than intended. Twice I was propositioned by female prostitutes working the crowd; the going rate was fifty to seventy-five dollars for a visit to the bathroom and whatever could be achieved in one of its stalls.

11 It seems public toilets are only rarely put to such uses by women. With the exception of sex workers, none of the Russian women I interviewed described public toilets as a potential place for anonymous lesbian encounters.

12 Even the most postmodern of theorists must admit to the difficulty of a person without a penis trying to embody herself as male in a public toilet. Perhaps with the right sort of dildo (e.g., one that not only looked "real" but could simulate urination as well) and the right amount of confidence, such a feat could be achieved. I shall leave it to braver and better-equipped researchers than I.

13 Many of the samples that follow are from an unpublished paper, "Istochniki po russkoi gei-istorii" ("Sources for Russian Gay History"), by Viktor Oboin (pseudonym) (1994). According to Oboin, such homoerotic graffiti are visible in "a large number of public toilets" (i.e., not just those near cruising strips), p. 2.

14 *Pleshka* may be the diminutive of the word for bald spot (*plesh'*), indicating the older man/younger boy (commercial) relationships that are often enacted there. It may also be derived from the French *place,* because black marketeers, prostitutes, and "hippies" in Russia also used it. See Vladimir Kozlovsky, *The Argot of the Russian Gay Subculture: Research Materials* (in Russian) (Benson, Vt.: Chalidze Publications, 1986), p. 60.

15 All of the older men whom I approached refused to talk to me with the exception of one man who initially mistook me for a young man and then punched me when he found out that I wasn't.

16 In Moscow, the *pleshki* I "cruised" were the Bolshoi, Kitaigorod, and Gogolevskii Boulevard. In St. Petersburg I met men near the Central Department Store, in front of the Kazan cathedral, and in front of the statue of Catherine the Great.

17 Author's interview with L (and his partner), June 1994.

18 As quoted in Sander Thoenes, "Gay Scene Shifts from Shadows into the Neon," *Moscow Times,* August 31, 1994, pp. 1–2.

19 I asked almost every queer I met to tell me what existed and then tried to obtain copies. Mostly the texts were sold informally, with no consistent or even obvious means of distribution. Sometimes they were available at queer events (e.g., a conference), occasionally they were available at a store or newsstand, but mostly I received them from the editors or writers who produced them.

20 Ironically, the article, entitled "Vyidi iz podpol'ia" ("Come out from the Underground"), was written under a pseudonym.

21 *Tema,* no. 1 (1992).

22 *Ty,* no. 1 (1992).

23 Earning less money and having primary responsibility for children and the home are some of the obvious structural factors that make women's voices less likely to be heard in Russia. See my article (with T. Mamonova), "Perestroika for Women," in *Perestroika from Below,* ed. Judith Sedaitis and Jim Butterfield (Boulder: Westview Press, 1991), 97–112. Not only are most women too tired and too poor to write or act or sing for free, but there are very few women who can act as sponsors for such undertakings.

24 Author's interview with Boris Moiseev, May 9, 1994.

25 Mercury, a singer for the rock group Queen, died of AIDS and is considered by some Moscow and St. Petersburg "sexual minorities" a gay icon.

26 *Chastnaia zhizn',* no. 6 (November 1994), p. 3.

27 *Eshche,* nos. 4–16 (1993), p. 2.

28 As Kevin Moss pointed out to me, Penkin does toy with coming out by telling his audience that all the rumors about him are true, that he is in fact "green" (the play here is on color since light blue is "gay").

29 *Komsomol'skaia pravda,* May 24, 1994, p. 6.

30 Sergei Penkin, *Holiday,* A/O Lad', Moscow.

31 Author's interview with Aleksandr Shatalov, July 1994.

32 James Baldwin, *Giovanni's Room* (New York: Laurel, 1956); William R. Burroughs, *Naked Lunch* (New York: Grover Press, 1959); Eduard Limonov, *Eto Ia, Edichka* (Voronezh: Tsentral'noe chernozemnoe knizhnoe izdatel'stvo, 1993). All future references to these works are from these editions.

33 Interview with Shatalov, July 1994.

34 Baldwin, *Giovanni's Room,* p. 137.

35 Burroughs, *Naked Lunch,* p. 1.

36 Kharitonov was not only religious but fervently nationalist as well. He was also openly anti-Semitic and may have had ties with quasi-fascist leaders who were part of the underground group that later became Pamiat'. The antisemitism is certainly evident in his writing in phrases such as "the Hebrew danger" (*Evreiskaia opasnost'*) and "a generic kike-mason secretive mind" (*obshchii zhidomasonskii tainyi ym*). For more on Kharitonov's antisemitism, see Yaroslav Mogutin, " 'Drugoi' Kharitonov," *Nezavisimaia gazeta,* April 7, 1993, p. 5.

37 Mogutin speaks of this "double life" of Kharitonov, who was a nationally recognized expert on the artistry of mime and the founder of the theater group Poslednii shans (Last Chance), which was still active more than a decade after his death in 1981. Yaroslav Mogutin, "Above Ground at Last," *Moscow Guardian,* February 19, 1993, p. 26.

38 "Underground" is overburdened with significance in Russian because it was the metaphor nineteenth-century Russian writers used for the seamier side of life. To

come out from underground, then, is to move from the dark and dirty vermin-filled spaces underneath the floorboards into the light and clean places of respectability.

39 For example, see the encounter between Eddie and a homeless man in Limonov, *Eto Ia, Edichka,* pp. 329–31.

40 Ibid.

41 Baldwin, *Giovanni's Room,* pp. 215, 104.

42 An article in a gay magazine about gay men married to women begins: "From the point of view of society a normal person must be married. This is how it's supposed to be. This is acceptable. . . . Currently many gays are, in the eyes of the law, in heterosexual unions" (Oleg Zobnin, "Zhenatyi goluboi," *RISK,* nos. 3–4 [1993], p. 20).

43 Author's interview with A, May 1994.

44 It is interesting to note that Roman Viktiuk and Evgenii Kharitonov (discussed above) were "friends — and in many ways — colleagues" (Yaroslav Mogutin, "Val's v invalidnoi koliaske," *Nezavisimaia gazeta,* September 9, 1993, p. 7).

45 Viktiuk was able to circumvent the Soviet censor by beginning the production with Genet's own words that the roles of the maids ought to be played by men. Audience responses included: "Yes, Viktiuk is a pederast, but so what. He's not as rude as Genet" (Author's fieldnotes, March 1994).

46 "Viktiuk igraet tol'ko s molodymi" (Viktiuk plays only with youths) (*Moskovskii komsomolets,* October 27, 1993).

47 Author's fieldnotes, May 1994.

48 One person who hated *Rogatka* was Yaroslav Mogutin, who wrote a highly critical review of Viktiuk's recent work. See Yaroslav Mogutin, "Viktiuk ubivaet napoval," *Nezavisimaia gazeta,* January 5, 1994, p. 7.

49 As I have argued throughout this chapter, love between two women (or sex without love) is not part of *popular* queer subjectivities.

A crowded performance space in 1993. On the stage, eight nearly naked
men dance to the music of Peter Gabriel. After a break, the performers return, but now they dance in drag, as ballerinas. The crowd goes wild, yet the
sense of purpose the dancers bring to the performance creates a profound
sense of disjunction: how should the spectator react?

QUEER PERFORMANCE: "MALE" BALLET

The scene might be imagined in a gay club virtually anywhere in the Western
world: an "erotic dance" followed by a drag show, the two most widely disseminated forms of gay cabaret. Yet this performance occurred in Russia at a
time when male striptease was still a rarity and the drag acts in gay clubs
seemed stuck in the transvestite theater's Mesozoic era, endlessly approximat-
ing the first *La Cage aux Folles*.

   In fact, the performance in question was staged not in a gay nightclub, but in
the cavernous concert hall of Moscow's Rossiia Hotel, a Vegas-style performance space infrequently graced by the likes of Alla Pugacheva or Liza Min-
nelli. Nor were these performers "gay," according to newspaper interviews
given by the group's founder: at least half were family men with wives and
children. The other half were presumed innocent by association.[1] As numerous
articles and interviews would elucidate, these dancers were not the garden

13.1   The *grand pas* from the Male Ballet's production of *Paquita*.
Photo by Natasha Razina.

variety heterosexual cross-dressers that populate newspaper advice columns: this was transvestism in the service of Art.

Founded in 1992 by Valery Mikhailovsky and fellow alumni of Petersburg's most prestigious dance academies and ballet companies,[2] the St. Petersburg Muzhskoi balet (Male Ballet) presented mixed bills of avant-garde choreography and cross-dressed renditions of ballet chestnuts to packed concert halls in St. Petersburg and Moscow (figs. 13.1, 13.2). The headlines that announced the ballet's first season reflect the curiosity, hype, and anxiety that greeted the initial outings of Russia's first drag ballet troupe:[3] "Eight Naked Men and Not a Single Woman," "Only Boys in This Troupe," "Dances Are Men's Work," "Esmeralda Danced by . . . a Gentleman," "Giselle in Size 43 Pointe Shoes," "In Size 42 Pointes," "Maya Plisetskaya: Only Mikhailovsky Dances 'The Swan' Better Than Me," "Mikhailovsky Is Already Here!"[4]

Yet inside the theater, the response was unequivocal, according to dance writer Olga Rozanova: "The huge October Concert Hall is filled to capacity. The audience looks like a swarm of bees, stirred up. Whistles, gales of laughter, applause meld into a rapturous, thunderous roar. And all this fuss for the classics — with one essential difference: the ballerinas here are not women."[5]

Drag performance was not unknown in Russia in the summer of 1993. Local

13.2 *Pas de trois* from the Male Ballet's production of *Paquita.*
Photo by Natasha Razina.

drag queens strutted at Moscow's gay raves, Vladik Mamyshev's Marilyn
Monroe impersonations accorded him a degree of celebrity in Petersburg and
abroad,[6] and theater director Roman Viktiuk's stagings were notable for their
transvestic elements. Yet Mikhailovsky's troupe surpassed all others in scope
and audacity. The company played to large, ebullient audiences in huge concert
halls. And unlike Viktiuk's productions, which often served up drag as an
accompaniment to a "straight" play, the Muzhskoi balet was about little else. In
a 1995 interview, Mikhailovsky assessed the risk: "We were really scared right
up until our first show. Dressing up in women's clothing wasn't just frowned on
in the past, it was banned. Until the curtains parted we had no idea how the
audience would react."[7]

The troupe's slogan, "In Jest and in Earnest" (*I v shutku i v ser'yoz*), pithily
summarizes the duality of the enterprise that presented new modern-dance
works for male dancers as well as choice women's roles from the standard
repertory — although the inherent dualism of the Muzhskoi balet extended well
beyond the programming. What was widely perceived to be a comic drag (or
gay) ballet troupe took pains to present itself as a high-minded organization
intent on "saying" women's choreography and/or reinventing ballet. The name
and high calling of art were invoked at every turn to legitimize the activities of

performers well aware of their marginality on the fringes of the post-Soviet cultural landscape.

The guise of art allowed the Muzhskoi balet to present the two favorite lounge acts of gay cabaret (the burlesque and the drag show) to a broad public. The audience could indulge in guilty pleasures, assured that the venue was proper, the choreography was "classical" (or somehow important, in the case of the contemporary choreography), and the performers were pedigreed artists. Indeed, the somewhat confused, extremely dualistic nature of the group's programming allowed it to carve out a unique place in the vanguard of "queer" performance in Russia. The confusion of genres and genders and the sheer audacity of the Muzhskoi balet's performances reflected the new boldness and volatility of both worlds the group came to represent: the emergent Russian "queer" community and the newly impoverished, newly enterprising domain of Russian dance.

In the Muzhskoi balet's first seasons, the troupe's appearances followed a set order, beginning with Mikhailovsky's own choreography, followed by an intermission and, finally, "effective fragments of the best of classical ballet."[8] The juxtaposition of these diverse dance genres made for a puzzling evening. The first offering of the 1993 season, "In His Own Image" ("Po obrazy i podobiyu"), to music of Peter Gabriel, promised "a choreographic treatment of the meaning of Christ in human consciousness."[9] Devotees of the Muzhskoi balet may not have been surprised when this quasi-religious dance was performed by seven men in dance belts (the lyric stage's answer to a thong), although this costuming option might have seemed less propitious to the typical audience (if such actually exists) for a liturgical ballet. In the 1993 program, a two-page explanation of the dance is superimposed over performance stills. The nearly nude cast, in nets, offers a strange counterpoint to the text:

> He Who has sent comes to find, revive and take away his Envoy. The Envoy asks to give him one more opportunity to arouse kindness and humanness in people, and He Who has sent left him.
>
> The Envoy helps weak and unprotected man to find strength and to believe in himself. But having become strong, a man uses his force against Him Who has helped him to find it.

The expectations raised by this narrative were mostly unfulfilled by the choreography, which closely resembled a favorite Western dance genre of the 1970s: the erotic taffy pull, in which nude or unitarded bodies explore the implications of friction. In a less exalted venue, the performance might have been enjoyed purely as prurience.

The second half of the program—arguably the raison d'être for both audience and performers—consisted mostly of leftover ammunition from the Imperial Ballet's war chest. Titled "Oh! These Masterpieces!" ("Akh, eti shedevry!"), this portion of the program featured the famous bits of nineteenth-century choreography usually reserved for gala nights.[10] If the first half of the Muzhskoi balet program generally met with polite applause, the second enjoyed an audience response bordering on fanaticism: "In the course of the whole [second] ballet, even to the end of the divertissement, the temperature in the hall remained at the boiling point. Perhaps only at children's performances is there such wild, spontaneous joy."[11]

The program's climactic moment belonged to the group's founder and "fat lady," who appeared in an enormous white tutu to dance Michel Fokine's *The Swan,* choreographed for Anna Pavlova and rendered ubiquitous by Maya Plisetskaya, the famous Soviet ballerina of the 1950s, 1960s, and 1970s.[12]

Given that the modern dance movement has flouted propriety since its inception, the Muzhskoi balet's rather risqué first-act presentation of itself has a number of precursors in "legitimate" dance theater, most notably in choreographer Ted Shawn's Men Dancers, a modern dance group founded in the United States in the 1930s.[13] And although "modern" dance remains an underdeveloped art form in Russia (and one with obviously Western roots), it nonetheless offered the Muzhskoi balet more models than classical ballet. Female-to-male cross-dressing was relatively common on the nineteenth-century Western European lyric stage, but extant examples of male-to-female cross-dressing in ballet are generally restricted to occasional bit parts: men cast as hags in a few full-length productions (e.g., Carabosse in *Sleeping Beauty,* Cinderella's wicked stepsisters).[14] Rozanova cites a Russian source, although one not generally known outside the Russian theater world: "These same hilarious drag acts can be seen at the ballet '*kapustniki'* [in-house performances that range from improvisation to outright parody][15] of the Maryinsky, though it's true that these performances are accessible only to a select circle. But to bring backstage antics out for the general public . . . for that one needs courage, and certainly, a fresh view."[16]

If seventy years of Soviet ballet afforded the Muzhskoi balet few models of cross-dressed dance, these could be found readily in the West. Curiously, the Muzhskoi balet's most obvious precedent was precisely the one the group most disdained: Les Ballets Trockadero de Monte Carlo. Founded in New York City in the 1970s, the "Trocks" were one of two all-male drag ballet troupes to emerge in the years of America's dance "boom." Still popular in the United States and abroad, the Ballets Trockadero's broad comic farces suggest an ideal model for the Russian troupe. Nevertheless, Mikhailovsky carefully distanced himself from the U.S. troupe from the start. The Ballets Trockadero were comedians, after all, while the Muzhskoi balet positioned itself as a repository of serious art. "Asked about the decision to found the troupe, Mikhailovsky explained: 'I was watching an evening devoted to a great Russian ballerina on television and shocked by the level of execution. It had nothing to do with [the ballerina being fêted] — neither in manner or style! And that's when I flashed on the idea: even men could do better!' "[17]

In an interview with *Dance Magazine* that was republished in Russia, Mikhailovsky added: "Women doing women's roles nowadays is too, too natural. Men in those roles accent the style, make it noticeable."[18] While Mikhailovsky's interviews are full of ponderings about art, Natch Taylor, the sometime artistic director of the Ballets Trockadero, offered a candid justification for his own troupe's existence: "The best roles have always gone to women. We felt that we should have a crack at them too."[19]

Reviewers of the Muzhskoi balet's performances joined Mikhailovsky's cause, sensing a missionary zeal to save classical ballet from its perceived decline: "Mikhailovsky and his dancers took the case seriously . . . fulfilling the quality of performance of the masterworks of classical choreography."[20] In a review published in *Kommersant Daily,* Pavel Gershenzon identifies the "meaning of the enterprise" as a "search for a lost art," continuing: "The audience didn't even laugh when Valery Mikhailovsky, in Raymonda's variation, played the role not of a mythic ballet princess, but of a Prima Ballerina Assoluta, brilliantly and definitively . . . a touching nostalgia for the artistic scale and place in the scenic hierarchy that is left empty today despite the strivings of ballerina parvenus."[21]

Gershenzon's review then goes to the heart of the matter: "the dancer in drag . . . is capable not only of telling us much about the dancing woman, but of creating her quintessence, a model of ballerina behavior, with her vitality, her art (gay and heroic), from the days when ballerinas encored their codas six times . . . as it was in the old Maryinsky."[22] Rozanova attributes the success of the company to this very quality:

The one goal to which the performers strive is to be sure to dance no worse than Petersburg ballerinas, having grasped and passed on their beauty and charm. . . . Anyway, who, besides a man, could notice what a woman leaves "in the subtext," and thus transform a familiar form . . . ?

The double reembodiment — first to ballerina, then to a concrete form — is a difficult task, and just as enthralling. Mikhailovsky's artists manage this wonderfully, hiding the difficulty, but not their enthusiasm. The mastery achieved by the sweat of their brow becomes a fact of their daring performance, irrepressibly drawing in the audience as participants. How often do you see this in the ballet theater? Probably, the secret of the Muzhskoi balet's attraction rests in this.[23]

The notion that only a man can personify the "true" woman onstage was hardly invented by Mikhailovsky, but it was popularized by a tradition the Muzhskoi balet was anxious to reference: Japanese Kabuki theater. Yoshizawa Ayame, a famous eighteenth-century *onnogata* (a male actor who takes female roles in the Kabuki theater) had articulated a similar prejudice long ago: "If an actress were to appear on the stage she could not express ideal feminine beauty, for she could only rely on the exploitation of her physical characteristics, and therefore not express the synthetic ideal. The ideal woman can be expressed only by an actor."[24]

In his interview with Irina Khmara, Mikhailovsky reminds readers that "there are traditional Japanese and Chinese theaters where all the roles are performed by men." In fact, a text broadcast over the loudspeakers before each of the 1993 performances took pains to reference the Muzhskoi balet's Eastern predecessors and disavow any similarities to the American Ballets Trockaderos.

Mikhailovsky's pronounced anxiety of influence concerning the Ballets Trockadero was only one of the tensions that characterized the Muzhskoi balet enterprise, although it pointed to a number of others. First, the association with the Trockadero suggested the theatrical demimonde of the music hall rather than the lyric stage the performers had previously inhabited (although the venues alone — *estrada* concert halls and hotel theaters — already furnished the damning evidence). In a sidebar to the Gershenzon review, the comparison is made directly: "The only similar company in the world is the American Ballet Trockadero-Monte-Carlo [*sic*], whose work, however, functions in the genre of music hall."[25]

If the specter of the music hall threatened the Muzhskoi balet's artistic reputation, the insinuation of homosexuality hung over the stage like the sword of Damocles. Was the Muzhskoi balet actually a company of, by, and for homosexuals? The question repeats ceaselessly in the company's early press. In *Kuranty:* "[The troupe] could acquire a scandalous reputation . . . if not for its brilliant technique, wonderful taste and nuanced sense of style." [26] In *Shans,* Vadim Mishkin goes further: "Evil tongues immediately christened Valery Mikhailovsky's ballet a show for gays." [27] Mikhailovsky was forced to respond to this charge again and again: "Our work has nothing to do with any kind of sexual anomaly"; [28] "*That* [an appeal to gays] was never our goal"; [29] "art, creation, has nothing to do with any kind of sexual orientation." [30] And finally: "Valery Mikhailovsky prefers not to discuss the issues of 'gayness' in his ballet." [31] Speaking to an American correspondent for *Dance Magazine,* however, Mikhailovsky almost relented: "The goal, says Mikhailovsky, was not to make a gay[32] company, but to make a good dance company — although the sexual question is never far off: 'We can say we aren't; people will say we are.' " [33]

It follows that Mikhailovsky would also choose the high road on the subject of homoeroticism in dance: "Not long ago the American dance group 'Men Dancing' toured here. But I thought it was very tacky. Why, for example, should a performer on the stage suddenly strip naked?" [34] Odd commentary for a choreographer who regularly sent his men onstage in flesh-colored dance belts. The publicity photos and video clips of "In His Own Image" show men in more mascara than clothing, flailing under nets. The effect is not merely lewd (this in a ballet about Christ), it borders on the fetishistic.

In short, the same appeal to art could distance the Muzhskoi balet from both "gayness" and the tawdriness of the music hall. Mikhailovsky and his audiences engaged in a symbiotic conspiracy: the performers pretended to save the ballet; the audience (especially the professional/critical audience) pretended to be grateful. All this as the Muzhskoi balet elevated the two favorite theatrical genres of gay nightlife, now packaged beneath an impervious cover: the guise of art.

The duplicity of the company's slogan, "In Jest and in Earnest," found a reflection in the truly liminal quality of the company's performances. Where the Ballets Trockadero establish a comedic tone from the start, beginning with the parodic names assigned the "ballerinas" (Youbetyabootskaya, for example), the Muzhskoi balet began its performances with a high-minded, scantily

clad ballet about the life of Christ. To further confuse the spectator, the Muzhskoi balet performed much of its drag material "straight," with a minimum
of the clowning that characterizes an evening with the Trocks. A few sight gags
were clearly premeditated: casting the company's shortest dancer as the partner
of the tallest "ballerina" in the *Sylphide* pas de deux; the enormous tutu in
which Mikhailovsky danced *The Swan.* Yet the dancers stuck to the artistic high
ground in most cases, avoiding the hamming and mooning that are the drag
queen's stock in trade. Nonetheless, the veneer of serious intent could not
suppress the inherent comedy: "So what is the troupe's success formula? To
answer directly, without intellectual cunning, the answer would be this: here
they do everything in earnest, and it turns out to be a joke. And if we look
fixedly, then we notice that the humor is unpremeditated, the comedy deliberately excluded."[35]

The unsettling effect of the Muzhskoi balet performances had implications far beyond the stage. The tensions so obviously exposed in the troupe's
self-presentation — "high" art/"low" art, contemporary dance/classical ballet,
Western dance/Russian dance, dances for men/dances for women, nineteenth-
century performance/twentieth-century performance, gay/straight, sacred/
profane, earnest/jest — reflected many of the societal and cultural tensions felt
widely in the initial phase of the post-Soviet era. The questions and issues
raised by the Muzhskoi balet performances spanned the gulf from the personal
to the societal, beginning with those concerning artistic and sexual identity.
Moreover, these very identity crises mirrored those being raised in Russian
society as a whole in the years following the breakup of the Soviet state.

We can easily plot a trajectory of hypothetical questions that establishes
an extratheatrical context for the Muzhskoi balet's performances: If the performers had been respected artists in various Soviet dance troupes and academies, for example, why were they now appearing in an all-male troupe, dancing
nearly nude with other men or dressed as women? How was it that the women
who emerged from these same academies and troupes were now deemed incapable of giving credible performances? Had the Soviet system been harboring
homosexuals in its ballet all along? Were many of the heroic, decorated Soviet
male dancers of the past also homosexual? Had Soviet dance lagged "behind"
Western dance, and was the Muzhskoi's variety of "modern" dance actually
a more significant, if less comprehensible genre? Was classical ballet now
merely a joke? And given that the Soviet Union had so assiduously (and anach-
ronistically?) supported classical ballet, what might this say about the Soviet

arts enterprise? If Soviet ballet (consistently one of the nation's most reliable exports) was now a laughingstock, what about other national points of pride? Such questions could be posited endlessly, but they lead ultimately to ones that challenge and destabilize many of the former Soviet Empire's most cherished values. In short, was the Soviet Union in jest or in earnest?

In *Vested Interests: Cross-Dressing and Cultural Anxiety,* Marjorie Garber locates the transvestite near the epicenter of these societal groundswells. The tensions made manifest by the Muzhskoi balet function as the "category crises" crucial to Garber's discussion of the transvestite in society:[36]

> One of the most consistent and effective functions of the transvestite in culture is to indicate the place of what I call "category crisis," disrupting and calling attention to cultural, social, or aesthetic dissonances. . . .
>
> By "category crisis" I mean a failure of definitional distinction, a borderline that becomes permeable, that permits of border crossings from one (apparently distinct) category to another: black/white, Jew/Christian, noble/bourgeois, master/servant, master/slave. The binarism male/female, one apparent ground of distinction (in contemporary eyes, at least) between "this" and "that," "him" and "me," is itself put in question or under erasure in transvestism, and a transvestite figure, or a transvestite mode, will always function as a sign of overdetermination — a mechanism of displacement from one blurred boundary to another.[37]

Although male ballet dancers *cum* transvestite performers might suggest unlikely signposts of large-scale cultural shifts, they are, to Garber's mind, ideal candidates: "The apparently spontaneous or unexpected or supplementary presence of a transvestite figure in a text (whether fiction or history, verbal or visual, imagistic or 'real') that does not seem, thematically, to be primarily concerned with gender difference or blurred gender indicates a *category crisis elsewhere,* and an irresolvable conflict or epistemological crux that destabilizes comfortable binarity, and displaces the resulting discomfort onto a figure that already inhabits, indeed incarnates, the margin."[38]

Here, the text is a "real" one, and the Muzhskoi balet performers function as incarnations of marginality, carving out a radical new place for themselves as artists as the old social order collapses. If the glory of Soviet ballet lent its male dancers an aura of respectability, then the grim realities of arts subsidization in post-Soviet Russia effectively demoted male dancers to a status they have long held in the West: poorly paid men in tights. And this at a time when Russia's newly free press was opening the closet doors of such dance icons as Rudolf Nureyev and Igor Moiseyev, intimating links between homosexuality and dance that myths of Soviet heroism had long endeavored to mask.

Given the sudden drop in prestige and earning power dancers (especially male dancers lacking "exportable" talent) experienced in post-Soviet Russia, and the scrutiny to which their personal lives were now subjected, it would seem almost natural for the members of the Muzhskoi balet to turn to women's roles. Men have long held second-class status in the ballet world, where ballerinas have enjoyed the spotlight for the past two centuries. The Soviet state had valorized its male dancers as artists and athletes, but as that system was collapsing, members of the Muzhskoi balet effectively staged a revolt of former subordinates, stealing the spotlight from their female partners in the newly liberated world of Russian dance. In effect, the "category crises" the Muzhskoi balet exposed could be described as a conflict between proper and improper artistic presentations, with Mikhailovsky and his dancers playing the role of highly skilled and respected Russian artists now forced to bargain for fame with propriety.

As with any theatrical presentation, the ultimate success of the Muzhskoi balet depended on its appeal to audiences — in effect, on the level of audience participation. On this level, Garber's reading of transvestite performance as an indicator of more generalized cultural anxieties becomes clearer: "Transvestism *on the stage,* and particularly in the kind of entertainment culture that generates the phenomenon known as 'stardom,' is a symptom for the *culture,* rather than the individual performer. In the context of popular culture these transvestic symptoms appear, so to speak, to gratify a social or cultural scenario of desire. The onstage transvestite is the fetishized part-object for the social or culture script of the fan."[39] But what scenario of social or cultural desire did the Muzhskoi balet fill? For all the anxiety regarding the troupe expressed in newspaper accounts, the "anxiety" evident in the theater blended eagerness with unease, enthusiasm with trepidation. The gay presence in the audience was notable, despite the fear still nurtured along with that group's longing for visibility. (Whatever their desire for positive images of themselves, Russian gays were still unused to gathering visibly in public spaces, even as the state prohibition on homosexual activity was being rescinded.) For more mainstream audience members, Mikhailovsky's "spectacles" afforded an opportunity to cast a wary gaze at the society's new margins (performers and audience members alike), exposed only as the fabric of the previous social order was rent. The

Muzhskoi balet was hardly the only drag show in town, but it remained the most accessible. Marilyn Monroe impersonator Vladik Mamyshev offered only impromptu sightings on Nevsky Prospekt, and late-night gay clubs scarcely provided the masses a "safe" space to observe society's margins.

Writing of sumptuary laws (and their transgression) in medieval and Renaissance Europe, Garber notes: "Once again, transvestism was the specter that rose up — both in the theater and in the street — to mark and overdetermine this crisis of social and economic change."[40] In post-Soviet Russia, a similar congruity of cross-dressed pedestrians and performers signaled the nation's most recent socioeconomic transformations. By the same irregularity that allowed Mamyshev to walk Nevsky Prospekt unmolested in a frankly homophobic society, Mikhailovsky's dancers could be the darlings of homosexuals, tourists, balletomanes, and old ladies.[41]

It is worth noting that Mikhailovsky's medium was Russian ballet — the imperial bauble unfailingly evoked to link Soviet Russia with the glamorous prerevolutionary past and provide reliable export revenues. Following a circuitous route to the future through the past, the Muzhskoi balet's adaptation of the nation's most conservative art form had the unwitting effect of creating a space between Culture and comedy, masculinity and femininity, gay and straight, serious and earnest, East and West — and signaling, in turn, the possibility for change in societal attitudes to "open" homosexuality as it marked a watershed in post-Soviet performance. If the founders of the Muzhskoi balet never intended their troupe to become the "gay" ballet many perceived it to be, it remained the queerest performance in Russia in the early 1990s.

Notes

1 The subject of the performers' respective sexual orientations took up large swaths of the column inches devoted to the Muzhskoi balet and will be discussed later. Although it is difficult to imagine a group of heterosexual men — all ballet dancers — deciding to form a cross-dressed ballet troupe, early interviews were adamant. Mikhailovsky first addressed the issue indirectly: "Half the troupe is married and has children" (Larisa Fedorova, "Na puantakh 42-go razmera," *Vechernii Peterburg,* June 23, 1993).

2 The Vaganova school, the ballet of the Maryinsky (formerly Kirov) Theater, Boris Eifman's troupe. In 1993, the troupe consisted of Mikhailovsky, Andrei Rozenblyum, Vladimir Khabalov, Ilya Novoseltsev, Oleg Shikhranov, and Aleksandr Semenchukov.

3 This article examines the initial impact of the Muzhskoi balet and thus focuses on the 1993 season, although the profile of the performers and the programs changed little in successive seasons.

4 *Sankt Peterburgskie vedomosti,* June 25, 1993; *Komsomolets zapoliar'ia* (Murmansk), April 10, 1993, p. 5; *Sovetskii Murman* (Murmansk), April 10, 1993; *Moskovskaia pravda,* April 29, 1993; *Komsomol'skaia pravda* (Moscow), May 6, 1993; *Vechernii Peterburg,* June 23, 1993; *Segognia* (Moscow), no. 34 (1993); *Rybnyi Murman* (Murmansk), April 16, 1993.

5 Quoted in Olga Rozanova, "Balet. Luchshe dlia muzhchiny net," *Peterburgskii teatral'nyi zhurnal,* no. 6 (1994), p. 52.

6 See Michael Neill and Constance Richards, "Hot to Trotsky," *People Weekly* 40, no. 11 (1993): 93–94.

7 Guy Chazan and Marina Vladimirovna, UPI ClariNet, September 18, 1993, on Nexis.

8 In the following years, the general format of the troupe's performances remained relatively unchanged. For the company's New York debut in 1995, "Homo Ecce" (to music of Vangelis et al.) preceded the classical variations, for example. Quoted in program notes accompanying S. L. Samoilov and A. N. Meshkov, *In Earnest and for Fun* (St. Petersburg: EAE, 1993, promotional videocassette, 26 min.).

9 Quoted from the program distributed at the performance.

10 Pas de deux from *Esmeralda* and *La Sylphide;* a variation from *Raymonda;* Anton Dolin's *Pas de Quatre,* a stylized tribute to early nineteenth-century romantic ballet; and "The Lady and the Robber" ("Baryshnia i khuligan"), a more contemporary piece set to Shostakovich's music.

11 Rozanova, "Balet," pp. 53–54.

12 In 1995 Plisetskaia marked her seventieth birthday with a performance of the work on the stage of Moscow's Bolshoi Theater.

13 Mikhailovsky saw Men Dancing, the revival/homage to Shawn that toured the United States, Europe, and Russia in the early 1990s, although he claimed offense at the onstage nudity (quoted in Irina Khmara, "Zhizel' v puantakh 43-go razmera," *Komsomol'skaia pravda,* May 6, 1993).

14 For information on cross-dressing in nineteenth-century European dance, see Lynn Garafola, "The Travesty Dancer in Nineteenth-Century Ballet," in *Crossing the Stage: Controversies on Cross-Dressing,* ed. Lesley Ferris (London: Routledge, 1993), pp. 96–106.

15 The term *kapustniki* is derived from the word *cabbage,* for the cabbage pirogs served at the original Moscow Art Theater. These performances became a part of Russian theatrical life well before the 1917 revolution, and continue to be staged. And while they may take on political implications, they function primarily to satirize the stage. Irina Kliagina of Columbia University provided useful information about this tradition.

16 Rozanova, "Balet," p. 52.

17 Quoted in Larisa Zakharova, "Balet — eto srodni mazokhizmu . . . ," *Stena* (St. Petersburg), June 22, 1993, p. 3.

18 Quoted in Elizabeth Kendall, "Communiqué: St. Petersburg," *Dance Magazine,* June 1993, p. 31.

19 Quoted in Michael F. Moore, *Drag! Male and Female Impersonators on Stage, Screen and Television* (Jefferson, N.C.: McFarland, 1994), p. 152.

20 Quoted in Vadim Zhuravlev, "Pa-de-de," *Nezavisimaia gazeta* (Moscow), April 29, 1993.

21 Quoted in Pavel Gershenzon, "Pateticheskaia nostal'giia po Imperatorskomu baletu," *Kommersant Daily,* July 23, 1993.

22 Ibid.

23 Rozanova, "Balet," p. 54.

24 Quoted in Marjorie Garber, *Vested Interests: Cross-Dressing and Cultural Anxiety* (1992; reprint, New York: HarperCollins, 1993), p. 245.

25 Quoted in Gershenzon, "Nostal'giia." While acknowledging the occasional grotesque of the Muzhskoi balet, Gershenzon focuses on the best-case scenario, the moments when the "real," missing nineteenth-century ballerina is magically reincarnated in Mikhailovsky's body. In the interview with Fedorova (*Vechernii Peterburg,* June 23, 1993), Mikhailovsky acknowledges the problem forthrightly: "The main thing we feared was parody. Like it or not, a man in a woman's costume is already a parody. But we tried to overcome that."

26 Quoted in *Kuranty* (Moscow), April 27, 1993.

27 Quoted in Vadim Mishkin, "Ne topchite, muzhiki, ne skachite, stsenu piatkoyu likhoi ne prolomite!" *Shans* (St. Petersburg), June 1993.

28 Quoted in Zakharova, "Balet," p. 3.

29 Quoted in Khmara, "Zhizel."

30 Quoted in Fedorova, "Na puantakh."

31 Quoted in "Akh, eti zvezdy!" *To da Vse,* no. 26 (June 1993).

32 In the Russian republication of the article, the word *gay* is replaced with *amusing* (*razvlekatel'nyi*). Quoted in Elizabeth Kendall, "Baletnyi Peterburg, otrazhenny v zhurnale '*Dans Magazin,*'" *Nevskoe vremia,* June 16, 1993, trans. from English by Vera Krasovskaia and Vladimir Zenzinov.

33 Quoted in Kendall, "Communiqué," p. 32. If Mikhailovsky's performance drew an inordinate number of gay audience members, the press accounts portray the audiences as a diverse band that included German tourists, elderly women, and serious balletomanes, all wildly enthusiastic. Certainly, the company could not rely solely on a gay audience (in Russia in the early 1990s) to pack large concert halls.

34 Quoted in Khmara, "Zhizel."

35 Rozanova, "Balet," 54.

36 I discuss the cross-dressed portion of the Muzhskoi balet performance here, since the drag show was clearly the focal point for performers and audiences alike, and set the group apart from all others performing in 1993.

37 Garber, *Vested Interests,* pp. 16–17.

38 Ibid., p. 17.

39 Ibid., pp. 366–67. As a prelude to her discussion of Elvis as a female impersonator,

Garber notes: "One of the hallmarks of transvestic display . . . is the detachable part. Wig, false breasts, the codpiece that can conceal male or female parts, or both, or neither" (367). The Muzhskoi balet's "detachable parts" (the oversized tutus and pointe shoes) furnished the subject of much discussion. In the interview with Larisa Zakharova ("Balet," p. 3), Mikhailovsky begins: "What am I wearing now? I just danced Saint-Saens' *Swan,* so I have this enormous swan tutu. Its feathers, feathers, lots of feathers. Lots of decoration [presumably, on the tutu and bodice]. And on my feet I have pointe shoes, which only ballerinas dance in. But these are size 42, which don't exist in nature. They make them for us specially."

40 Garber, *Vested Interests,* p. 17.

41 Straight Russian men are conspicuously absent from any catalog of Muzhskoi balet fans, though in this case, absence accords a degree of consent.

PORNOGRAPHY IN RUSSIA

The collapse of communism carried with it many small revolutions and changes, not the least of which was the large-scale appearance of commercial pornography. Naked bodies adorn even the most mainstream journals and newspapers today, movies (both domestic and imported) regularly feature sex scenes, television portrays explicit sex in regular prime-time hours, and all of these developments do not even skim the surface of the vibrant pornography industry in Russia. Pornographic videos (mostly pirated copies of Western-produced films), magazines, newspapers, live "sex shows," and even porno-graphic homepages on the Internet can be found in Russia today. From a live sex show put on to raise money for rebuilding a church to a Russian erotic-spanking Web site, the Russians have certainly discovered sex, and discovered it with a vengeance.[1] In this chapter I will examine this recent explosion and the state's reaction to it. Russians often argue that their culture (and their solutions

318

to cultural problems) is different from that of the West. We will see whether or not this assertion is true (at least as far as pornography is concerned), but first we must take a brief step backward to examine the historical tradition of pornography in Russian culture and look at the first Russian sex revolution of the 1920s.

Historical Background

Pornography is not particularly new to Russia. The folklorist Alexander Afanas'ev collected a variety of Russian pornographic tales as part of his comprehensive *Russian Folktales* (*Russkie narodnye skazki*). These stories (not published with the rest of Afanas'ev's tales until recently) can be divided into two types: stories of priestly misconduct and erotic material. The latter stories are predominantly about cuckolded husbands, lusty widows, or foolish and sexually naive young people who do not know how to use their "comb" (or some other euphemism for sexual organs) and are tricked into sexual activity. In general, the stories are laced with vulgarity and are more scatological than sexual. In addition to these stories are the *lubok* prints (popular cartoonlike illustrations that had a reputation for being off-color in a suggestive but not obscene fashion), which also date back at least to the seventeenth century.

Famous historical and literary figures have contributed to the pantheon of Russian porn. Alexander S. Pushkin is credited with poems and epigrams of quite a vulgar character (although there has been much exaggeration of his productivity),[2] including the *Gavriliada* and *Tsar Nikita and His Forty Daughters* (*Tsar' Nikita i sorok ego docherei*). Pornography even found its way to the highest levels of authority in the nineteenth century. The court painter to Tsar Alexander II, Mikhail Zichi, was also an accomplished painter of sexual subjects. His series of drawings entitled *Love* (*Liubov'*) features (among other things) a baby masturbating, a semiclad woman making love to a boy, a woman nursing her baby while involved in the act of coitus with a lover, and a prepubescent girl performing fellatio on the artist. Zichi enjoyed official approval of his work and thus was protected from the law. Tsar Alexander II even took drawing classes from Zichi and used the lessons to produce several nude pictures of the empress.[3]

Aside from Afanas'ev's, there are two other erotic anthologies of note from the late nineteenth century: *Among Friends* (*Mezhdu druziami*) and *Eros Russe: Russian Erotica, Not for Ladies* (*Russkii erot ne dlia dam*). *Among Friends* is a two-part collection. The first part consists merely of the unpublished folktales of Afanas'ev; the second part is a collection of works dating back as far as the 1830s. None of the stories is particularly well written, but the collection does include a rare reference to lesbianism ("Two Sisters" ["Dve sestry"]) and a piece on the Emancipation that compares the freeing of the serfs to the breaking of wind ("The Fart" ["Bzdun"]). "The Fart," obviously, was intended as a political critique, not a pornographic work.

Political intent is even more visible in *Eros Russe*. This collection was published in 1879 (around the time of Alexander II's assassination) and mentions real people who were still alive at the time of the printing (thereby slandering them). The book achieved its antiestablishment effect not only in stories that use important officials as characters but also by reprinting a number of poems and stories *written* by famous people. Most of the stories and poems were written in the Junker schools where the tsarist administrators were trained, and the works were embarrassing youthful transgressions for many important people. Among the involuntary contributors is Mikhail Lermontov (whose "Ode to a Commode" ["Oda k nuzhniku"] is included along with two other stories); and one of the people identified as audience participants is Mikhail Loris-Melikov (the minister of internal affairs in 1880–81). The publication of these pieces, and the *timing* of the publication, aimed, as the introduction admits, to reveal the "character" of the country's leaders.[4] Its intent was therefore more political than artistic.

Along with less explicit works such as *The Kreutzer Sonata* and *Sanin*, these works collectively form the foundation for contemporary pornography. Just as *Justine* and *Fanny Hill* are treasured as classics of the genre, the older works (though rarely if ever published until recently) are a means of legitimizing twentieth-century pornography by providing a historical precedent. Even if contemporary works rarely live up to the artistic pretensions of the earlier "classics," they still invoke the titles and authors in order to justify their validity.

Another important influence on current pornography was the first Russian sex revolution of the 1920s. The October Revolution, after the initial disorder of the civil war period, ushered in a series of social experiments in free love. In the cities (and in particular among young people) part of the revolution involved rejecting such "bourgeois" notions as monogamy, marriage, and so on, in favor of amoral sexuality. Tsarist-era pornographic works were published and praised for their promotion of self-determination and "proletarian" values. In addition to the classics, various new pornographic works appeared during this time. Among them were S. I. Malashkhin's novel *Moon from the Right Side* (*Luna s pravoi storony*) and Boris Pilniak's *Mahogany* (*Krasnoe derevo*), both of which deal graphically with the subject of contemporary (i.e., free love) mores. Films also dabbled in the previously socially unacceptable. The 1928 movie *October* (*Oktiabr'*) (the film adaptation of *Ten Days That Shook the World*) originally featured an intertitle, "Fuck your mother!" ("*Tvoiu mat*"), that was left out of later versions but eventually restored in the 1960s.

This sexual revolution, however, was short-lived and restricted to urban areas. At the end of the 1920s it ground to a halt. Having never enjoyed much support among the general public,[5] and with a Stalinist crackdown on immorality taking place, these libertine days were numbered. But they would form the basis on which the second sexual revolution would be built in the 1980s. Social pressure orchestrated by the authorities brought individuals into conformity, while censorship silenced their works. Malashkhin's and Pilniak's works were banned for promoting promiscuity.[6] Plays with sexual themes that appeared in the 1920s, including S. Tretiakov's *I Want a Baby* (*Khochu rebenka*) and *Immaculate Conception* (*Besporzach*), were also shut down. The former was banned before performance and the latter after its first viewing. A reworking of Nikolai Gogol's *The Nose* (*Nos*), updated and changed by making the hero lose another part of his anatomy, was staged quite briefly.[7]

The Second Russian Sexual Revolution

The most recent sexual revolution began around 1987. It began cautiously and slowly. Pictures of topless women (shocking by the standards of the time) began to show up in such newspapers as *Sovetskaia kul'tura,* and a few Russian films flirted with brief nudity. By the end of the decade, however, the revolution was in full bloom. Two events set it off — one political, the other economic.

Mikhail Gorbachev intended his policy of glasnost to be used to publicize the need for political and economic reforms. By relaxing censorship, however, glasnost also introduced new sexually explicit works to Russian culture, the most notorious of which were the films *Little Vera* (*Malen'kaia Vera*) and *Intergirl* (*Interdevochka*), and Viktor Erofeev's novel *Russian Beauty* (*Russkaia krasavitsa*). *Little Vera* gained the most notoriety for its naturalistic and explicit depiction of casual sex, including what was alleged to be the first filmed Soviet sex act and the appearance of its star, Natalia Negoda, in *Playboy* magazine. Up until this time Soviet films had not been sexual. As one Soviet commentator dryly noted, "The Pope even recommended to Catholics that they watch Soviet films because they were highly moral and were not revolutionary."[8]

Under glasnost, many previously banned or expurgated Soviet-era works were published in their complete form for the first time. For example, Anatolii Rybakov's novel *Children of the Arbat (Deti Arbata)*, written in 1969 but published only in 1989, was able to include the word *whore (bliad)* unexpurgated.[9] Glasnost brought back many old tsarist classics as well. The November 1991 issue of *Literaturnoe obozrenie* was devoted completely to the subject of pornographic literature. It also discussed a broad historical range of material from antiquity to the present, with academic studies of the erotic works of Aristophanes, Ivan Barkov, Pushkin, Fedor Dostoevsky, Zinaida Gippius, and others.

The relaxation of censorship certainly had an impact, but the rise of pornography was as much tied to the rise of a free market as to the lifting of censorship. Pornography, like religion and the formerly dissident culture, was in great demand and thus commercially viable. It was that market pressure that encouraged the spread of pornography. When the government called for publishers as well as other industrial managers to achieve a level of financial self-dependence, they were drawn to such ways of making money. The marketing approach was fairly cynical. Pornography's strength as a commodity rested on its forbidden nature. People wanted to feel as if they were getting something *dirty* or they would not buy it — the success of erotica lay in its being seen as "pornographic" (i.e., corrupt and shameful), and as Nancy Condee and Vladimir Padunov have noted, "unless the latter is confused with the former in the Soviet Union, it has no opportunity to be sold."[10]

That commercialism was also visible in films. After *Little Vera* and its success, the sex scene became de rigueur in all new Soviet films. Whether it was necessary to the plot or not, almost every film had sex in it.[11] The sex, moreover, was most often combined with sadism. The 1989 film *Evil Spirit (Zlaia dusha)* has a homosexual gang rape in it.[12] *Burn (Ozhog)* (also from 1989) features an extremely graphic scene in which a group of escaped convicts beat a woman, attempt to rape her, place a hot cigarette lighter between her legs, and then wrap her up in plastic and throw her in a garbage dump.[13]

Most of the pornography in Russia, though, was not domestically produced. Pirated foreign pornographic videos were reported in large numbers as early as 1988.[14] Previously confiscated at the border, pornographic literature poured in from Sweden, Denmark, the Netherlands, Germany, and the United States —

without official approval, but also without interference. Eventually, foreign magazine publishers would produce Russian-language editions, but initially few Russians cared what language the text was in; only the pictures mattered. For those people who *did* want to read the articles, Russian entrepreneurs were ready to fill the gap. Many short-lived samizdat-type publications were created in the late 1980s with titles such as *Seks-katalog* and *Seks klub*. None of these periodicals produced more than a few issues, and none had official permission from Glavlit or the Press Ministry to exist. Like most samizdat before them, these publications lacked solid editorial backing and sound financial support, and were difficult to sustain.

The first major and legal indigenous producers of pornography were *Andrei* and *SPID-Info*. *Andrei* had a short initial life. Professionally produced and published abroad, it was too expensive for most Russian consumers. It eventually went under and the publisher turned to doing live "sex concerts" and pornographic videos in 1993 and 1994 in Moscow.[15] *Andrei* was reborn in 1995, however, and continues to this day to put out high-quality (and expensive) issues.

SPID-Info has a more continuous and low-key history. Founded as a private educational newspaper devoted to spreading the word about venereal disease prevention and sex education, it had achieved a very impressive circulation of nearly five million copies by 1993. In doing so, however, it lost track of its original intention and became less educational and more sensational. The illustrations became more juvenile (in an attempt at humor), and the articles became more gossipy than informative. The result was often quite contradictory in the messages sent. For example, one issue illustrated an article about rape victims with pictures of pornographic models.[16]

The second revolution, like the first, was short-lived. By the early 1990s pictures of naked women were so commonplace that they elicited little attention. There were signs that people had grown bored with sex. For example, when the Moscow cultural center Blitz tried to hold a live-sex "erotic festival," it lost most of its money.[17] As one reporter noted in 1992, ice cream was selling better than pornography.[18] Sex scenes in movies became less sensational. Pornography was less unusual and thus less interesting. The forbidden fruit was available everywhere and thus seemed less forbidden.

Pornography has not disappeared today; sexual representations have simply become more acceptable. Their uses have begun to resemble those of the West. Sex now features prominently in advertisements, particularly for business services. One such advertisement features a woman lying amid a pile of rubles and a computer (the ad is for the computer). She is dressed in a strapless top, tight short skirt, and heels. The pout on her face suggests a prostitute more than a secretary.[19] The message: fast women, copious money, and a new computer go together.

With the exception of a few conservatives and a small number of diehard users, the Russian people have shown little long-term interest in pornography. Sales of pornography dropped off by 1994. Even the venerable *SPID-Info* suffered a decline in circulation.[20] In one sense the situation has normalized. Those people who have a deep interest in pornography pursue it, but the majority have found other ways to occupy their lives.

Yet pornography has found a niche, and a sizable market at that. Western-owned publications dominate the scene. *Playboy*'s Russian-language edition boasts a circulation of 100,000,[21] and *Penthouse* (now defunct) had even more impressive sales figures. Both magazines mixed indigenous material with translations from their international editions. As a rule, they were less explicit than the American editions, and the reason for this softness appears to be cultural. *Penthouse*'s notorious "Forum" column had an odd mix of raunchy American contributions mixed with chaste and relatively innocent Russian imitations. The Russian contributors apparently had not yet learned how to write at the level of their American equivalents.

Public Responses

There has long been a tension between public tolerance of sexuality and official unacceptance. Society itself has been divided between those who held liberal views (or no views at all) and those who did not approve of unrestrained immorality (which was synonymous with anarchy and the rejection of authority). Even after the imposition of atheism with the revolution, official morality persisted and had public supporters. So deeply rooted was that morality that by the 1990s it was possible for one woman to write the following letter to a Russian newspaper:

> I have lived for 52 years, but I know of no sort of sex or perversions. I do not understand the word "heterosexual" or "homosexual." But to-day's youth probably knows. They gather in basements and pursue it, and narcotics and alcoholism too!
>
> One must raise young people in a normal spirit, so that they can create

a good, strong, and orderly family and correctly raise their children, and not think about sex. Not *ever* think about it!

I hold in contempt all this, these prostitutes, drug addicts, alcoholics, homosexuals, and heterosexuals![22]

Such views are extreme, of course, but certainly not uncommon.

Far more Russians seem to tolerate pornography and sexual license today, though, than condemn it. Comprehensive surveys of Russian sexual behavior and attitudes are currently under way, but the following anecdotal statistics illustrate the point: The military, which one would expect to be very conservative in Russia, is not particularly antipornography. A survey published in the military newspaper *Krasnaia zvezda* showed that, although a large number of soldiers perceived a moral decline in society, only 11 percent attributed it to pornography, and only 29 percent felt that pornography should be banned outright. Another survey determined that 22 percent of European Russians read pornography — a figure that placed them second only to Estonia for pornography consumption within the Soviet successor states. Although most Russian adults were concerned about keeping pornography out of the hands of children, they were not so worried about the use of such material by adults. More than three quarters of those surveyed felt that, regardless of any other controls, there should be special sex shops where mature adults could purchase pornographic materials.[23]

State Responses

The state has been slow to develop a response to pornography. Article 242 (formerly Article 228) of the Criminal Code punishes the distribution but not the possession of pornography. Furthermore, the law, created in 1936, was forced on the Soviet Union by its membership in the League of Nations.[24] This law is noted for the vagueness of its legal definitions — a subject that deserves special attention.

Defining Pornography

In enacting a law prohibiting the production or distribution of pornography, the Russian government failed to provide an official definition of what was being prosecuted. Determining how to identify pornography in real court situations thus proved to be quite a challenge for trial judges. Commentary on the Russian Criminal Code in 1960 defined pornographic works as "rudely naturalistic, obscene, cynical [*tsinichno*] portrayals of sexual life that attempt as their goal the unhealthy stimulation of sexual feelings."[25] This legal definition of "pornography" is still the authoritative guide for the Russian criminal justice system.[26]

The first thing that leaps out is the word "naturalistic." The intention, although not explicit here, is that realistic portrayals of sex can be overly done, to the point that they destroy "nature" by making it mechanical. For example, the use of "plumbing shots" (showing the natural functioning of the sex organs) would be considered unnecessarily vulgar (i.e., rude) in a work of "art." Put another way, such shots would destroy the ideal of Love by turning it into a physiological function.

The definition also mentions the word "cynical," which keys into a history of Russian religious philosophy, within which Vladimir Solov'ev, Nikolai Berdiaev, and others delineate between eros (the "true" and spiritually beautiful love) and its poor cousin, pornography. Pornography is seen as blasphemy against Divine Love. It is "cynical," says Solov'ev, because it degrades beauty and destroys the spirituality of love that imparts beauty to life. In many ways, this relates back to the criticism of pornography as "rudely naturalistic."

Finally, there is the statement that pornography creates "the unhealthy stimulation of sexual feelings [or instincts]." The implied point here is that there is such a thing as "healthy stimulation." Although no explanation is provided, it is not too difficult to guess what this phrase means: the "legitimate" relation of sex (with the aim of procreation) between a husband and wife. The concern, then, would be with preventing any "stirring" of sexual desire outside the traditional family structure. Beauty, it is implied, can be preserved only in a lawful relationship — a sex economy controlled by the state.[27] "Healthy stimulation" is the norm. By making the preservation of this norm a law, the state is operating under the assumption that it is obligated to protect the "health" of its citizens. This health, however, is moral, not physical.

Vladimir Borev

Although it is up to the judge to make the final determination, the Russian legal system encourages the use of "expert commissions" (*ekspertiza*) in court proceedings. The assumption is that neither the average judge nor the average person is qualified to determine what is pornographic and what is erotic. The "expert," who has been trained in these matters, is thus invited to give privileged testimony.

The guidelines used by the expert commissions in writing a preliminary study (*sledstvie*) or an expert declaration (*akt ekspertiza*) on pornography were developed by Vladimir Borev. Borev, an art historian by training, became involved in the video business back in 1985 when it was just beginning in the Soviet Union, thereby placing him in an auspicious position during the "video boom" of the late 1980s. His knowledge of Western films combined with his training in art lent him a level of prestige.

Borev's committee developed a very detailed set of instructions for identifying pornographic videos, and these have been modified for use in analyzing texts and still photographs as well. To analyze a film, the committee advised, one first should ask whether the filmmaker *intended* to create pornography. There are several criteria that can be used to identify intent, according to Borev. First of all, does the film identify itself as pornographic (e.g., calling itself "XXX")? Second, is a list of credits absent or do the credits include many pseudonyms? Third, do the sex scenes lack "artistic pretensions"?[28] "Physiological details" (i.e., rude naturalism, no doubt!) and perversions (group sex, bestiality, exhibitionism, etc.) are also signs of pornography, but are not conclusive in themselves. Finally, a work must show naked genitals in order to be pornographic. Otherwise, the work is probably only offensive to tastes and cannot be judged pornographic by legal standards.[29] These standards, although allegedly objective, are really aesthetic and susceptible to subjective interpretation, and thus present a problem of due process.

The really troubling question is not what the committee intended as much as how the standards it produced are actually applied by the experts. Application always involves a number of unstated biases, and attempting to uncover the explicit subjective standards of the committee is difficult work. Understandably, its members are unwilling to confess to such factors in the first place. Natal'ia Krymova (Borev's assistant) spoke of the goal of the committee as seeing whether the object in question had an "artistic" intent or whether its intent was "not so good." As she explained it, they know what "good" cinema is (i.e., what it *should* be) because of their broad knowledge of film and video. When pressed, she evaded the question by citing the good work the commission had done getting innocent people released from prison ("they have written us thank-you notes").[30] In other words, the fact that they are saving "innocent" people should shield their criteria from scrutiny.

Borev himself declared that it is always possible to create boundaries to define pornography and erotica, and he rejected the suggestion that there is a serious degree of subjectivity in his work.[31] But Borev's own written statements are more guarded. The standard introduction to the texts of his *sledstviia* includes an admission that the commission is biased toward permitting the spread of the message "that sexual life is expedient only under conditions of mutual love and marriage." He also believes that even "weak" sexual portrayals are harmful to children because sex then "dominates" the child, disrupting the "harmony" of the various parts of his psyche.[32]

The Case of *Eshche*

Alexei Kostin, publisher of the sex newspaper *Eshche,* was first arrested and charged with violating Article 228 on October 6, 1993, at the height of the October events, but was released after three days. Over the next couple of months, the procurator acquired evidence against Kostin and finally rearrested him on February 4, 1994. In spite of these actions, the magazine itself was not banned. More unusual, the editor was not arrested; according to the Press Law, however, it is the editor who bears the responsibility for the content, not the publisher. The authorities in fact wanted to arrest the editor, Alexander Linderman, but he was living in Riga and refused to come to Moscow. So they arrested Kostin to try to force Linderman to come in.[33] In violation of the law that detainees must be charged within two months of arrest, Kostin's jail stay was prolonged in a further attempt to get Linderman to appear.[34]

It is a bit strange that *Eshche* was prosecuted at all. As sex magazines and newspapers go, *Eshche* is pretty tame. Another publication, *Mr. Eks,* and its subsidiary publications *Miss Eks* and *EksPress,* are much more explicit than *Eshche.* For example, issues of *Mr. Eks* often feature photographs of couples performing explicit bondage and discipline scenes, *EksPress* regularly publishes letters from the readers that describe similar fantasies, and even *Miss Eks* ("an erotic present for the single woman") once depicted a scene with a woman urinating into the mouth of a bound man.[35] In comparison, *Eshche* is soft core.

Various stories have circulated about why *Eshche* was singled out from among all the pornographic publications in Moscow. One of the more obvious reasons would be the Baltic connection, but Vladimir Solodin, who was in charge of the brief operation of censorship during the period of martial law in October 1993, denied this rumor vehemently. The situation, he said, was more complicated than that. *Eshche* is printed (in Latvia) in two editions: one for Latvia, where there is no obscenity code, and another version especially for Russia that is edited to meet the requirements of Article 228 and the "guidelines" of the Ministry of Press and Information. During 1993 Linderman broke this "voluntary" agreement, and (prior to October) the Ministry of Press and Information decided to take action against the newspaper.[36]

As for why *Eshche* was subjected to such strictures in the first place, Solodin said that *Eshche* came to the attention of the authorities because of three factors: it met the basic "criteria of pornography"; it was a permanent journal and thus likely to be around for a while; and it had a special "cleverness and subtleness" that disturbed the censors.[37] *Eshche* is nothing if not unusual in its combination of sophomoric sex humor, satanism, fine art, and other unusual ingredients; but it is unclear how that combination made it more of a threat. The mystery is only partially explained by the judgments that were written about it.

Borev's commission, despite the fact that Borev himself claims no expertise in analyzing printed works, was one of several groups asked to write a judgment on the nature of *Eshche*. The conclusion his commission rendered on December 14, 1993 (and repeated in a second *ekspertiza* from January 18, 1994) was that *Eshche* was, in fact, pornographic. Their second *ekspertiza* concluded that the texts (while sexual in content) did not meet the criteria of pornography. The problem was *Eshche*'s choice of illustrations for these texts. These illustrations fell into two categories of "pornography." The first type, "unintentional," might be forgivable because despite the content, criminal intent could not be proven. As a specific example of such "unintentional pornography," the commission cited a picture of an interview subject (Vova Veselkin — "a sexual terrorist") in the middle of a human sandwich of naked bodies.[38] Most of the pictures in *Eshche*, though, were far worse and belonged to a second category: "The publishers of *Eshche* for the most part have chosen photographs which are pornographic by their very essence, that is, by their structure (when the camera records the minute details of the sexual act or the sexual organs prepared for the sexual act) and their goal (to summon a single specific reaction from the viewer — their interest and sexual stimulation)." The commission provided several examples of this sort of pornography, including a photo spread of two women and a man in a gym copulating, having oral sex, and using various weight-lifting equipment as sexual aids.[39] On the grounds of this *ekspertiza*, Kostin was arrested a second time.

In finding *Eshche* pornographic, Borev's group was operating under an unusual assumption that was not stated in their *ekspertiza*. In Borev's opinion, there was a question of the "consistency" of *Eshche*'s "cultural level."[40] The problem, as Krymova elaborated, is that a newspaper such as *Mr. Eks* is a "simple" pornographic work. Its entire content can be described as being on a low cultural level. *Eshche,* on the other hand, was trying to combine its high-level text with lowbrow pictures. The text was trying to educate people to be comfortable with sex and was serving a "humanitarian" purpose. The pictures, however, were "simple pornography" and would have a detrimental effect. She concluded, "The editor of the newspaper had not found illustrations to match the high level of his text."[41]

By these standards, a magazine that was blatantly pornographic might well not be prosecuted, but one that walked a fine line between pornography and erotica would be. The argument, of course, is as ridiculous as it is contradictory to the guidelines that Borev himself helped to write. *Playboy* would be prosecutable because it could be argued that the text is a trick to get people to open up the centerfold (and thereby corrupt themselves), but a book describing itself openly as a guidebook to child molestation would not be actionable because it does not attempt to hide its intentions.

Civil Suits

As the Criminal Code has failed to address the problem of pornography adequately, new legal routes are now being pursued. One of the more interesting legal strategies has been the use of civil court cases against pornographers. The idea of using civil proceedings to prosecute pornographers that has been suggested elsewhere — in the United States and Canada, the approach is championed by feminist legal theorist Catharine MacKinnon — is an approach that has only recently found usage in Russia.

It is no small matter that the largest damage award for "moral injuries" by a Russian court in 1995 was made to Natal'ia Patsura, a model who appeared nude in the men's magazine *Andrei.* Patsura did not object to her appearance in the magazine — she had, in fact, signed a model release — but she did object to the intimation in the magazine that she used narcotics. The Chertanov district judge agreed and awarded her 35 million rubles ($7,000 US).[42] Apparently, posing in a men's magazine was not deemed in itself to be a moral injury or a fatal character issue, as it might be in the United States.

A far more ambitious attack is the suit filed by the St. Petersburg Center for Gender Studies in June 1996 against the Russian edition of *Playboy,* which earned the center's wrath for its publication of sexually explicit interpretations of portraits of Catherine the Great, Sofia Kovalevskaia, and other famous Russian women. The center charged that "the way they are presented does not stimulate sexual feelings, but treats them as symbols and images of Russian history to be humiliated and degraded on the basis of their gender." The suit asked for a compensation of 100 million rubles for moral damages, payable to the state. Action languished for several months with no word from the Procuracy about whether the case would be heard.[43] Apparently, the authorities preferred to dodge the issue. In early December 1996, the Russian Academy of Sciences took over the complaint to add more weight to the suit and forced the issue.[44] Preliminary hearings were held in May 1997, and formal hearings were scheduled to begin in September of that year. However, in the end, the numerous barriers that were erected by the state eventually led the Gender Center to throw in the towel. In the words of the center's director, Ol'ga Lipovskaia, "unfortunately we were too busy to be more persistent in our campaign." Yet, in Lipovskaia's mind, the Gender Center had won: at least the pictures stopped appearing.[45]

Conclusion: A Russian Pornography?

Is there anything unique about Russian pornography? The literary critic Kornei Chukovskii once remarked, "Russian pornography is not plain pornography such as the French or Germans produce, but pornography with ideas."[46] It is not so clear, though, that Russian pornography *is* unique. Pornography was used historically in Russia, as it was in France and Germany, as a means to criticize the government, and so the authorities got into the habit of treating it as a threat to the state.[47] Even when pornography did not attack the state directly, its attacks on morality were deemed to be transparent attacks against state authority. The authorities feared the spread of sexual license as some sort of political movement. The result was that "moral censorship" in Russia and the Soviet Union became politicized. As one observer put it: "erotic or pornographic books and pictures are not banned because they are morally offensive but because they are subversive."[48] Even folktales were published with the aim of undermining the censorship apparatus, the Orthodox Church, and the rule of the tsars. Later on, NEP-period pornography, while probably not intending to do so, became associated with an ideology of free love that the state found more and more antithetical to its own desire for public control.

But times have changed, and today's pornography is no longer the hallmark of freedom that Russian and some Western libertarians would like to claim it is.

A cursory survey of the works themselves often indicates something quite to the contrary. Violent pornographic images have infiltrated popular Russian culture. A recent advertisement on the popular Moscow-based FM radio station Evropa Plius (Europa Plus), promising listeners that radio commercials have "impact," included the sound effect of a whip crack and a woman groaning to demonstrate the aforementioned influence. The back cover of *Stolitsa* in July 1991 portrayed a woman on her knees in a loose blouse performing fellatio on a pistol.[49] Thus pornography in Russia has taken on the misogynistic messages also found in the West.

On the other hand, we must also entertain the possibility that pornography's semiotic meaning is very different in Russia, and that we will encounter problems with employing feminist paradigms in Russia that may be more cultural than theoretical. With the exception of the recent acts by the Petersburg Center against *Playboy,* pornography in Russia is hardly addressed as a feminist issue. The argument advanced by Andrea Dworkin and Catharine MacKinnon — namely, that pornography exploits women — has not surfaced in Russia. Instead, the debate over pornography seems stuck in a rather archaic 1950s-style dispute between conservatives and libertarians about "free speech" versus "family values."

In a country where condom production was administered during the Soviet period under the Ministry of Chemical and Petroleum Production, Rubber Subdivision,[50] the semiotics of sexuality are likely to take odd turns. Pornography may serve a variety of other purposes ranging from rebellion to symbolism. In the case of the latter, pornographic degradations of women may be, as Lynne Attwood has suggested, a means of striking back at the state (here represented by the woman).[51] Pornography might yet be a means of political rebellion, just as it was in the nineteenth century with *Eros Russe* and *Among Friends.* But whatever the differences of its origins and the motivations behind its current manifestation, pornography in Russia, like that in the West, ultimately cannot be divorced from the economic, political, *and* social context out of which it emerged and to which it contributes.

Notes

1 Andrei Kapustin, "Teatr 'Tete-a-tete': radi khrama snimem posledniuiu rubakhu," *Kommersant,* no. 12 (1992), p. 29.
2 Pushkin has been credited with everything from *Luka Mudishchev* to a "Secret

Journal," which the contemporary émigré pornographer Mikhail Armalinskii claims
to have "discovered"; see A. S. Pushkin [sic], *Tainie zapiski: 1836–1837 godov*
(Minneapolis: MIP, 1986). Another who has been similarly treated is the eighteenth-
century literary figure Ivan Barkov, to whom the most famous of Russian erotic literary products, *Luka Mudishchev,* has been ascribed. This work had been assumed to
be one of the earliest formal examples of Russian pornography, but it is not, as William Hopkins amply proves by noting the nineteenth-century literary anachronisms
in the text; see his "The Development of 'Pornographic' Literature in Eighteenth-
and Early Nineteenth-Century Russia" (Ph.D. diss., Indiana University, 1977).

3 A. Flegon, *Eroticism in Russian Art* (London: Flegon Press, 1976), p. 123. Both
Zichi's and the tsar's pictures are reprinted in Flegon's book. The emperor's pictures
are more tastefully done. Zichi's only recorded encounter with the authorities was a
request from Pavel Viazemskii (head of censorship in 1881–82) for a portrait sitting.
Zichi, being deluged with similar requests, had to refuse; see *Rossiiskii gosudarst-
vennyi arkhiv literatury i iskusstva,* f. 195, op. 1, d. 4216, ll. 1–2.

4 *Eros Russe: Russkii erot ne dlia dam* (Oakland: Scythian Books, 1988), p. 9.

5 Mikhail Stern, *Sex in the USSR* (New York: Times Books, 1979–80), pp. 26–27,
discusses the reaction of the countryside to the urban licentiousness. Richard Stites,
*The Women's Liberation Movement in Russia: Feminism, Nihilism, and Bolshevism,
1860–1930* (1978; Princeton: Princeton University Press, 1990), p. 384, suggests
that the city dwellers were none too pleased with the situation either.

6 Vera Dunham, "Sex: From Free Love to Puritanism," in *Soviet Society: A Book of
Readings,* ed. Alex Inkeles and Kent Geiger (Boston: Houghton Mifflin, 1961),
p. 541. Dunham misidentifies Malashkhin as "Malyshkin" in the article.

7 I am indebted to Stephen P. Hill of the Department of Slavic Languages and Literature, University of Illinois, for these examples, given in correspondence of
February 21, 1992.

8 Rolan Bykov, "Plus Sixty," *Moscow News,* no. 29 (1988), p. 15.

9 Aleksandr Sir, "Erotika i pornografiia," *Knizhnoe obozrenie,* no. 16 (1992), p. 8.
The word *bliad* was banned from at least the time of Catherine the Great, according
to correspondence from Catriona Kelly of January 15, 1997.

10 Nancy Condee and Vladimir Padunov, "Perestroika Suicide: Not by *Bred* Alone,"
Harriman Institute Forum 5, no. 5 (1992): 6. It was not simply pornography that was
available for sale. Sex manuals such as the *Joy of Sex* and the *Kama Sutra* also
appeared in translation at this time.

11 It is worth noting that similar behavior occurs in the West, where the chances that a
young and well-built actress will survive her early years in the film industry without
having to bare her breasts at least once is extraordinarily low.

12 Richard Stites, *Russian Popular Culture: Entertainment and Society since 1900*
(Cambridge: Cambridge University Press, 1992), p. 187.

13 I myself have not seen this film and am relying on an account given of it by
T. Khloppliankina in "Vse razresheno?" *Iskusstvo kino,* July 1989, p. 50. On the
portrayal and treatment of women in Soviet cinema of the 1980s, see Andrew

Horton and Michael Brashinsky, *The Zero Hour: Glasnost and Soviet Cinema in Transition* (Princeton: Princeton University Press, 1992); and Françoise Navailh, "The Image of Women in Contemporary Soviet Cinema," in *The Red Screen: Politics, Society, and Art in Soviet Cinema,* ed. Anna Lawton (New York: Routledge, 1992), pp. 211–30.

14 Pokhmelkin, A. " 'Prestupnaia' videoproduktsiia," *Sotsialisticheskaia zakonnost',* no. 11 (1988), p. 42.

15 Author's interview with Oleg Aliakrinskii, March 25, 1994.

16 See *SPID-Info,* no. 12 (1993), p. 5.

17 *Mir zvezd,* no. 2 (1990), p. 36.

18 Steven Erlanger, "Something There Is in Moscow Still That Doesn't Love a Crumbling Wall," *New York Times,* March 7, 1992, p. A4.

19 *Ogonek,* no. 22 (1991). The irony is that many advertisements were appearing in the press at the time for women "with pleasing exteriors" who wanted to be "secretaries" for businessmen.

20 Moscow Radio Rossii, May 22, 1994, trans. in Foreign Broadcast Information Service, *Daily Report* (Eurasia), May 24, 1994, p. 29.

21 Gordon, Michael R. "Fleshing Out the New Russian Brand of Capitalism," *New York Times,* February 17, 1996, p. 4.

22 "O. B., Child-Care Worker," quoted in V. Shakhidzhanian, *1001 vopros pro eto* (Moscow: Terra, 1993), p. 26.

23 Igor' Kon, "Sex as a Mirror of the Russian Revolution" (lecture presented at the Russian State University for the Humanities, March 9, 1994). No further details (including the dates of these surveys, which are assumed to be recent) were mentioned.

Sex shops *à la russe* are in themselves a strange experience. The store Intim in Moscow is the hangout not of seedy-looking men in trenchcoats but of white-smocked doctors. It is located at a birthing hospital. The prospective customer must first discuss his or her problem with a licensed sexopathologist. The doctor then "prescribes" some sort of regimen for the patient (dildo, inflatable doll, lubricant, etc.), which the patient can have "filled" at the store with the help of a specially trained pharmacist. There are regular articles on the sex shop Intim in *SPID-Info;* for example, see no. 9 (1993), pp. 14–15; no. 11 (1993), p. 19; no. 1 (1994), pp. 19–20; no. 4 (1994), p. 18 — although my information comes from personal observation.

24 On the subject of Article 228 and its creation, see Paul W. Goldschmidt, "Legislation on Pornography in Russia," *Europe-Asia Studies* 47, no. 6 (1995): 909–22. Perhaps the most interesting element of this law is its focus on commercial exchange rather than possession. Soviet law held that possessing pornography for private use was not a crime. A test case in January 1990 upheld this interpretation; see *Biulleten' verkhovnogo suda SSSR,* no. 3 (1990), p. 26.

25 *Kommentarii k ugolovnomu kodeksu RSFSR (1960 g.)* (Leningrad: Izdatel'stvo leningradskogo universiteta, 1962), p. 380. In fairness, we should note that even the United States has never successfully drafted a legal definition of *pornography!*

26 On January 1, 1997, Russia enacted the first major revision of its Criminal Code

since 1961. However, the new code has not attempted to change the state's treatment of pornography. In particular, it has made no attempt to improve the legal definition of what is to be prosecuted. In fact, it has complicated matters because now it punishes only the "illegal distribution of pornographic materials" (see "Ugolovnyi kodeks Rossiiskoi Federatsii," *Rossiiskaia gazeta,* June 20, 1996, p. 6). The implication is clearly that some distribution is now legal, but the law provides little or no help on determining what is legal and what is not, preferring to leave the matter up to a judge or an expert commission.

27 The idea of a state-controlled sex economy dates back at least as far as the Stalinist reforms of the 1930s, when the state desperately tried to increase the population by outlawing abortion and making divorce nearly impossible to accomplish.

28 Prokuratura SSSR, "O praktike primeneniia ugolovnogo zakonodatel'stva ob otvet-stvennosti za rasprostranenie pornograficheskikh predmetov i proizvedenii, propagandiruiushchikh kul't nasiliia i zhestokosti," *Informatsionnoe pis'mo,* no. 12-4d-89 (April 17, 1989), pp. 10–11. This lack of artistic pretensions can be shown "objectively" by observing whether the film lacks "the artistic principles of construction" (i.e., an introduction, development, and conclusion) or whether the scenes merely repeat each other. If this is unclear, one can ask whether the characters have any meaning outside of being representatives of their sex.

29 Ibid., p. 16.

30 Author's interview with Natal'ia Krymova, April 14, 1994.

31 Author's interview with Vladimir Borev, April 14, 1994.

32 I am indebted to Borev and his staff for sharing with me the texts of various *sledstviia* and *akty ekspertizy.* For purposes of preserving privacy, the names of the accused on my copies of these documents was obscured, but otherwise they were left intact.

33 Jean MacKenzie, "Magazine's Publisher Jailed for Pornography," *Moscow Times,* February 9, 1994, p. 2.

34 Jean MacKenzie, "Sex Publisher Gets Longer Jail Term," *Moscow Times,* April 2, 1994, p. 2. As late as December 1, 1994, Kostin was still being held in prison, according to the chairman of the Russian Press Committee, Gryzunov.

35 *Miss Eks,* no. 8 (1993), p. 13.

36 Author's interview with Vladimir Solodin, April 20, 1994.

37 Ibid.

38 See *Eshche,* no. 7 (1993), p. 7.

39 Ibid., pp. 8–9. Once again, I am grateful to Borev and his staff for making the original text of this opinion available to me.

40 Interview with Vladimir Borev, April 14, 1994.

41 Interview with Natal'ia Krymova, April 14, 1994.

42 Irina Belinskaia, "Ne mnogo li chesti," *Ogonek,* no. 3 (1995), p. 77.

43 Quoted from e-mail correspondence (July 1996), reprinted in *WEW* 44 (September 1996), pp. 8–9; updated by correspondence with Julia Zhukova of the center, October 1996.

44 Heidi Schreck, "Nude Drawings of Catherine II Provoke Lawsuit," *Saint Petersburg Times,* December 9–15, 1996, p. 3.

45 Correspondence with Ol'ga Lipovskaia, July 22, 1998 (courtesy of Helena Goscilo).

46 Cited in Laura Engelstein, *The Keys to Happiness: Sex and the Search for Modernity in Fin-de-Siecle Russia* (Ithaca: Cornell University Press, 1992), p. 386.

47 For more about the history of pornography in Western Europe, see Lynn Hunt's introduction to *The Invention of Pornography: Obscenity and the Origins of Modernity, 1500–1800,* ed. Lynn Hunt (New York: Zone Books, 1993).

48 Stern, *Sex in the USSR,* p. 181.

49 *Stolitsa,* no. 23 (1991).

50 Anna Husarska, "Kondomski," *New Republic,* July 27, 1992, p. 28.

51 Lynne Attwood, "Sex and the Cinema," in *Sex and Russian Society,* ed. Igor' Kon and James Riordan (Bloomington: Indiana University Press, 1993), p. 67.

Part IV SOCIETY AND SOCIAL ARTIFACTS

[The First Russian Tattoo Convention] will convey a propagandistic-educational character. A seminar on the practice of tattooing will be held. — Announcement for the First Russian Tattoo Convention, *Intermedia,* April 24, 1995

BODY GRAPHICS:
TATTOOING THE FALL OF COMMUNISM

This announcement — whose style evokes the Red Enlightenment of the mid-1920s — seems to imply that tattoos were little known in Russia until 1995. Yet the Russian tattoo tradition is both richer and — for reasons of politics, crime, and power — far more complex than its Western counterpart. The convention's promised "propagandistic-educational character" exudes mainstream respectability for a practice that, until the 1990s in Russia, was almost exclusively associated with the criminal underground. These two elements — cultural amnesia and a search for new respectability — strongly shape the discourse and social practices of contemporary Russia. Their articulation here is an instance in a larger story about reclaiming a familiar past while forgetting its unprofitable associations.

Throughout the Western world, including Russia, tattoos have been fraught with cultural contradictions. The tattoo is both eternal and fleeting; it lasts a

339

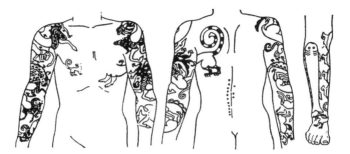

15.1   Scythian tattoos worn by a chieftain; taken from burial
mound 2, Pazirik Valley (Altai). From Tamara Talbot Rice,
The Scythians (New York: Praeger, 1957), p. 115.

lifetime but cannot be preserved. It manifests an internal state of being on the
external surface of the skin. It can be bought but not sold, yet can be infinitely
reproduced. It can transgress social norms while asserting stern, alternative
moral parameters. It is an art form that increasingly confuses traditional institutions of culture such as museums, art schools, galleries, and arts foundations. It
ironically recasts the purchase of an original visual artwork whose ownership
will never be in dispute and whose venue can be uniquely controlled. It raises
the specter of social marginality while providing a conversational opportunity
that facilitates social intercourse. Finally, the tattoo is a commodity fetish that
does not deny its value as fetish; indeed, that fetishistic quality is the direct
connection back to a time before commodities, when culture and fetish were
less ashamed of their family resemblance.

   The most ancient tattoo markings in what would later become the Russian
empire were found on Scythian corpses at the Pazirik Valley burial mounds, on
the southern slopes of the Chulishman range of the Altai Mountains.[1] There in
1924, archaeologist S. I. Rudenko found forty mounds covered with boulders,
which formed a protective ice layer preserving the frozen remains. Mounds 2
and 5 contained two bodies of what are presumably fifth-century A.D. Scythian
chieftains, elaborately decorated with traditional Scythian-style animal tattoos
on their arms, chests, backs, and legs (fig. 15.1).

   This minor footnote in the history of Scythian art matters because, from
about 1987 onward, as the cultural systems of totalitarianism began to collapse, young Russian tattoo artists returned to these ancient Scythian images,
making a fanciful leap back to a community with no knowledge of the West and

no memory of the Romanovs, the Soviets, or any of the bloody history of twentieth-century Russia.

Social prohibition *against* tattooing is a more recent phenomenon, at least in European cultures, where it derives its moral significance from biblical authority (Leviticus 19:28: "Ye shall not make any cuttings in your flesh . . . nor print any marks upon you"). In Russia, from at least the seventeenth century onward, prisoners were branded on the face, usually on the forehead just above and between the eyes, with the Russian letters *KAT* for *katorzhnik* (prisoner) (fig. 15.2) — in a sense, "biblical outcast."

Yet, despite the biblical prohibition, the list of historical figures of European culture who at one point in their lives chose tattoos as a form of "ritual transgression" is as long as it is varied; it includes both Nicholas II (a fire-breathing dragon on his left shoulder, acquired from a renowned Japanese tattoo artist) and Stalin (a death's-head tattoo). Generally, however, tattoos in Russia, as in the West, have fallen within the purview of sailors, rank-and-file soldiers, and criminals. The first Russian known to have voluntarily tattooed himself was the early nineteenth-century traveler Fedor Tolstoi (known as "the American," presumably for his adventurous spirit), who was tattooed by a Polynesian artist in exchange for two axes.[2] By the late nineteenth century, Russian prisoners exiled to Sakhalin Island were decorating themselves with "Sakhalin pictures," establishing a tradition of tattooing as the art most intimately linked with the prison. Although Soviet sailors and soldiers routinely tattooed themselves, nowhere was the sign system as elaborately developed as it was in the penal system. Even in other spheres of Soviet life where tattooing was common — among jockeys, drivers, stablehands, and other official and unofficial horse-track employees — tattooing suggested a prior prison stint (and the tenuous employment record that followed prison). In short, tattooing and the gulag were inseparable concepts, whether or not the individual collector had actually spent time in prison.

The tattoo machine, based on Thomas Edison's electric pen and patented in 1891 by Samuel O'Reilly,[3] remained a rare curiosity in Russia. Instead, a common method of applying the tattoo outside the prison community involved a rubber sheet or wooden board pierced with nails that was used as a template and embedded in the recipient's skin, marking the tattoo all at once. In adult prisons and so-called children's colonies,[4] tattooing was more difficult because inmates were not officially allowed to tattoo, and punishment could involve time in an isolation cell. Although some homemade tattoo "machines" existed

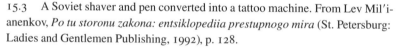

15.2   Seventeenth-century Russian prisoner with forehead brand. From Iurii Dubiagin, *Sleduiushchaia zhertva–ty: Azbuka bezopasnosti* (Moscow: Pechatnoe delo,
1995), p. 224.

15.3   A Soviet shaver and pen converted into a tattoo machine. From Lev Mil'i-
anenkov, *Po tu storonu zakona: entsiklopediia prestupnogo mira* (St. Petersburg:
Ladies and Gentlemen Publishing, 1992), p. 128.

during the Soviet period, such as the spring-powered, wind-up shaver (fig.
15.3) or the rare foreign electric toothbrush (no such item was produced by
Soviet industry), most simple tattoos were done with ordinary sewing needles
encased on all sides with wooden matches and bound with thread. Easy to hide
and to justify as a tool necessary for routine mending, sewing needles provided
a means of expression that could not automatically be confiscated by the prison
authorities. In the absence of needles, any metal wire, such as unwound spiral
notebook wire, could be sharpened and put to use. As ink was not ordinarily
available in prison, soot, dirt, cigarette ash, a burnt match head, or burnt shoe
sole could be mixed with liquid to form a coloring solution. The preferred
choice of liquid was the prisoner's own urine because of its "immunological"
properties.[5]

Throughout the Soviet period, information about the tattoo subculture was
entirely anecdotal, but since the fall of communism in 1991 several small
compilations of prison tattoos have appeared, all sections of larger compendia
of prison culture, including argot, proverbs, card games, coded toponyms, hand

signals, cryptography, ciphers, encoded speech, a prison Morse code, epistolary etiquette, and other sign systems.[6] These rare volumes, intended for police investigators, prison staff, journalists, the curious general reader, and (in one case at least) for the criminal community itself,[7] offer illustrations and cryptic "translations" of the tattoos' meanings, but no analysis of the sign system. The brief remarks here, which draw on oral interviews with former and current inmates, tattoo artists, and collectors, as well as the volumes mentioned above, are a preliminary discussion of that system as a basis for remarks about its post-Soviet transformation.

Soviet prison tattoos had a multitude of functions, many of them replicating Western tattooing purposes: visual autobiography, personal and political philosophy, talismans, declarations of love, and, of course, ornamentation. Indeed, several of the most common Western tattoo genres, such as "men's ruin" (fig. 15.4) and devotional tattoos (fig. 15.5), are familiar within the Soviet prison as well. Specific Soviet prison tattoos also served outside prison as signals of mutual recognition to obtain food, shelter, information, access, and so on. In their own way, these tattoos are no different from recognition systems used by such diverse groups as hobos and Masons. The two simplest recognition tattoos were a series of crosses, placed on the back of the hand below the knuckles, each cross indicating either a prison sentence or a year spent in prison; and a single large dot, placed on the back of the hand between the forefinger and thumb, indicating a previous prison escape. More elaborate signs were the "four towers and a prisoner" (*chetyre vyshki i ZK*) tattoo, traditionally placed on the back of the hand near the wrist below the little finger, and the sign "Greetings, thieves!" (*Privet voram!*), traditionally worn as a ring tattoo (fig. 15.6).

What differentiated Soviet prison tattoos from Western tattoos and other recognition systems was the highly specific and nuanced code of meaning. Tattoos not only communicated the prisoner's status, crime, and family life, they linked those facts together into a syntagma or story that was possible to read across the criminal's body. Both the signs themselves and their placement carried meaning: the upper body (head, neck, shoulders, chest) was reserved for tattoos denoting prestige, while the feet and legs tended to be tattooed with jokes, wordplays, or humorous images.

Of the prestigious tattoos, two in particular held positions of greatest honor, to be worn only by a capo or king of thieves (*pakhan*). The first was a Russian Orthodox church, whose cupolas indicated the number of completed sentences.

15.4   Men's ruin tattoos (Soviet examples). From Iurii Dubiagin, *Sleduiushchaia zhertva–ty:* p. 374; and D. S. Baldaev et al., *Slovar' tiuremno-lagerno-blatnogo zhargona (rechevoi i graficheskii portret sovetskoi tiur'my* (Moscow: Kraia Moskvy, 1992), p. 502.

For reasons that should require no elaboration, the churches were not replicas of actual buildings, but rather imaginary religious monuments drawn from the artist's fantasy (fig. 15.7). A second prestigious tattoo was the Virgin Mother and Child (fig. 15.8). Although this tattoo would seem to the uninitiated to bespeak a belief in Russian Orthodoxy (as would the church tattoo), it in fact had a number of closely related meanings, none of them religious: (1) the bearer was a "multigenerational criminal" (i.e., his father had served time), (2) the bearer began a criminal life very young (as a "babe in arms"), or (3) the bearer considered prison to be home. Although the saying *Tiur'ma — rodnoi dom* (Prison is my original home) was a frequently tattooed slogan, the Virgin and Child was worn only by the most highly placed criminal in the unofficial prison system. As with most prison tattoos associated with criminal power, to wear it without authority was to invite death.

Members of the lesser elite, known as "authorities" (*avtoritety*), signaled their status and loyalty to the king of thieves by tattooed epaulets on the shoulders or by faceted, six- to eight-pointed stars placed below the collarbones (fig. 15.9). Again, these were tattoos earned over the years by multiple prison sentences, service to (including murder for) the *pakhan*, and violence in defense of one's status. Unlike the *pakhan*, who no longer needed to commit physical violence, the authority was a lieutenant in the army of crime, carrying out the orders (but not the errands, which were carried out by a lesser-ranking *shesterka,* who had his own tattoo sign) of the *pakhan.* Taken together, these status tattoos constituted a kind of insignia, a felonious uniform of the body that established and maintained criminal order, parallel and yet opposed to the official prison hierarchy.

Further down the criminal hierarchy, three common subsets of tattoos were available to virtually any prisoner. The first of these communicated family status (or rather its absence): the letters *DD* meant "orphanage" (*detdom*); a circle with a single dot in the center meant "complete [in Russian, 'circular'] orphan" (*kruglyi sirota*); an asterisk in a circle meant "fatherless" (fig. 15.10).

A second subset of tattoos indicated criminal specialty: an apartment key for breaking and entering (fig. 15.11); a heart in a square for rape; a skull, which often (though not always) meant "convicted murderer." A winged arrow or a ship in full sail meant "roving thief." A Nestor-like monk writing at a table meant that the bearer had a skilled "pen" (knife or razor) (fig. 15.12). A portrait of Vladimir Lenin, far from being an advocacy of socialism, meant "thief" (*vor*); Lenin was officially known as "Leader of the October Revolution" (*Vozhd' Oktiabr'skoi Revoliutsii*), thus the initials *V-O-R*. While these permutations would appear to resemble a kind of Cockney slang, a metalanguage removed from the original meaning and deeply indebted to context, their function has less to do with wordplay than with more familiar Russo-Soviet traditions of secrecy, paranoia, Aesopian language, and the use of sacral symbols to express profane intent.

15.5 (*top*)   Devotional tattoos (Soviet examples). From Iurii Dubiagin, *Sleduiushchaia zhertva–ty,* p. 422.
15.6 (*bottom*)   "Four towers and a prisoner" (A) and "Greetings, thieves!" (B). From Iurii Dubiagin, *Sleduiushchaia zhertva–ty,* p. 441; and D. S. Baldaev et al., *Slovar' tiuremno-lagerno-blatnogo zhargona,* p. 471.

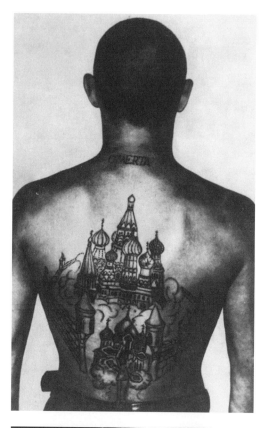

15.7 (*left*)   Russian Orthodox church, a tattoo worn only by high-ranking criminals. From Lev Mil'ianenkov, *Po tu storonu zakona,* p. 193.

15.8 (*below right*)   Virgin Mother and Child tattoo, worn only by a "multigenerational" criminal. From Lev Mil'ianenkov, *Po tu storonu zakona,* p. 256.

15.9 (*below left*)   Epaulets and faceted stars, worn by criminal "lieutenants." From Iurii Dubiagin, *Sleduiushchaia zhertva–ty,* p. 352.

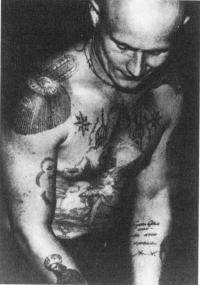

15.10 (*left*)   "Fatherless." From D. S. Baldaev et al., *Slovar' tiuremno-lagerno-blatnogo zhargona*, p. 469.
15.11 (*center*)   "Breaking and entering." From D. S. Baldaev et al., *Slovar' tiuremno-lagerno-blatnogo zhargona*, p. 467.
15.12 (*right*)   "Razor expert." From Lev Mil'ianenkov, *Po tu storonu zakona*, p. 20.

A third subset of tattoos signaled sexual preference. Setting aside the subject of punitive tattoos — that is, the forced branding by a fellow prisoner — sexual preference was declared with a bunny (a man who loves women), a butterfly (not a prostitute, just likes to fool around), a boar (butch) (fig. 15.13), or a violin bow (fem). A pair of eyes tattooed on a man's stomach or groin meant "active gay." This was, however, a rare prison tattoo, insofar as "gay" was largely indistinguishable from "rapable" (involuntarily available for forced anal or oral sex because of physical frailty or some transgression such as nonpayment of a debt), while those who committed the same-sex rape were "merely" deprived heterosexuals.

Rapable men were often forcibly tattooed on the buttocks (with two eyes, a beehive, a poker, or other suggestive images) or on the face (with fake beauty marks by the lips or beneath one eye) (figs. 15.13, 15.14, 15.15). These face brands, reminiscent of the prerevolutionary penal practice of branding convicts, were intended as a warning to other prisoners, who would not associate with these "gay" men in any way, refusing even to touch any object that had been handled by them.

Women's tattoos were more frequently devotional or ornamental; common images were flowers, birds, hearts, angels, and wreaths. Unlike male prison tattoos, which were often prominently displayed on "public skin" (head, neck, hands), women's tattoos were more frequently hidden from view and not associated with the performance of criminal power. They were often autobiographical, recalling a first experience of heterosexual or lesbian sex, marriage, birth,

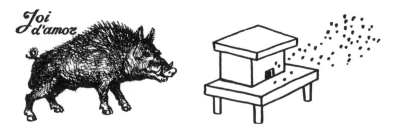

15.13   Active lesbian (*left*) and punitive gay (*right*) tattoos. From Iurii Dubiagin, *Sleduiushchaia zhertva—ty,* p. 410.

or narcotics; or a death, often of a mother or a child. Lesbian relations were often signaled with musical instruments, such as a guitar or violin played by a naked woman. Unlike male homosexual tattoos, women's tattoos seemed to lack a punitive dimension; a pair of eyes on the buttocks, for example, which served among males as a passive gay and therefore punitive tattoo, signaled active lesbian sexuality.

Political tattoos, of which the most common were the Romanov double-headed eagle and the Nazi swastika, constituted another productive category. To the outsider, these symbols would seem to stand, respectively, for distinct political philosophies — Russian autocracy and German fascism — yet, in the language of tattoos, with its perpetual and unfinalizable displacement, they shared nearly identical meanings. Both commonly meant "anticommunist" — that is, opposed to the Communist Party (CPSU) authorities who ran the camp system. Less often (though simultaneously), both meant "beat the Jews," insofar as "communist" and "Jew" were nearly synonymous terms of abuse.

By the curious logic of prison life, the swastika could also mean "Russian patriot" (an assertion of national pride against communist oppression) or "anarchist" (one morally opposed to prison order). In the same spirit, the Latin letters *SS,* traditional sign of the Nazi Schutzstaffel, signaled the Russian abbreviation for "I've preserved my conscience" (*Sokhranil Sovest'*). Nazi regalia thus became, in the language of prison tattoos, a declaration of *Russian* (as opposed to Soviet) moral conscience.

The major difference of meaning between the double-headed eagle and the swastika had nothing to do with Russian versus German (or monarchy versus fascism). Rather, it had to do with the ancient (1917) memory of the eagle versus the recent (1945) memory of the swastika. In this respect, fascist sym-

15.14 "King's crown" punitive tattoo for rapable men. From Iurii Dubiagin, *Sleduiushchaia zhertva–ty,* p. 389.

15.15 "Blow job" punitive tattoo. From Édvard Maksimovskii, *Imperiia strakha* (Moscow: Maket, 1991).

bolism was much closer to home: it was more familiar, more explicitly anti-communist and antisemitic, and (of course) easier to draw than the double-headed eagle.

The Russian prison tattoo system seems enormously complex in part because the symbols simultaneously expressed diverse categories of value, yet none of those categories easily correspond to familiar, Western categories of value. Indeed, the Soviet prison was doubly removed from Western systems of value, first by the Berlin Wall, then by the prison wall. The demand for a particular image or template can be seen, in the most concrete terms, as a measure of a tattoo's value, if by "value" we understand popularity. Yet, other notions of value — such as the declarations of power within the prison caste system (Virgin and Child, epaulets), of professional expertise and specialization (the apartment key for burglary, the heart for rape), of social resistance (the swastika, the Romanov eagle) — functioned not according to demand, but rather according to specific identity relations. Thus, while prison tattoos were unarguably popular culture, the ways in which they were popular were as nuanced and varied as the tattoos themselves.

One can glean from these examples the complexity of the sign system, which committed itself only to a set of potential meanings while affiliating itself with none. The only constant in the potential set of meanings was the performative aspect: the declarative slogan inscribed on the prisoner's body, which was itself a prison environment festooned with declarative slogans.

The tattoo slogans themselves displayed diverse stylistic registers: they could be redolent of Bolshevik enthusiasm ("Crush the régime" [*Davi re-zhim*]), of biblical sanctimony ("Honor thieves' law" [*Chti zakon vorov*]), or of melodrama intertitles ("Became a thief from poverty and injustice" [*Stal vorom ot nishchety i bespraviia*]). Occasionally, in keeping with the Russian association of criminality and card playing, a gambling motif emerged ("Be true to your 'suit' in prison" [*Derzhi mast' v zone*]).[8] This dialogue, so to speak, between the prisoner's sloganed body and the prison administration's sloganed space was intensified by the reality that the body could not be confiscated. It could be mutilated, coerced, controlled, and neglected; but as long as the prisoner lived, his body was a potential interlocutor with the prison administration.

The extent to which the "totalitarian dialogue" served a useful function is exemplified in a 1989 article in the newspaper *Sovetskaia kul'tura* about an unidentified corpse whose life was read by the police in considerable (and, it turned out, accurate) detail *solely* on the basis of his prison tattoos:

> The deceased first landed in prison custody before the age of maturity, apparently for hooliganism. He spent about two years in the children's colony. He had a propensity for violating prison regulations. He was sentenced for theft. He endured abuse from fellow cellmates. He served out his time completely. He apparently was in a strict regime colony. A woman who loved him waited for his release. He dreamt of freedom and was inclined to attempt escape. He was a member of a thieves' gang.[9]

Five things differentiate the Russian tattoos of the 1990s from Soviet tattoos of the 1930s–1980s: (1) the addition of color pigments, (2) a modernized means of production, (3) a socially ambitious consumer, (4), a new reluctance to show tattoos on public skin, and (5) a collapse of the tattooing codes (i.e., who can wear what).

Not all of these differences are worth discussing at length. To summarize the first four points briefly, the importation of Western pigments to produce color tattoos greatly boosted the tattoo's desirability (and profit) while underscoring its difference from gulag tattoos. The introduction of Western tattoo technology (i.e., standardized machines with up to fifteen needles) and the pressure to conform to emerging U.S. hygiene standards transformed a marginal cottage industry into a lucrative business with artistic ambitions and strong Western ties. If Soviet tattoos on public skin had largely been a display of criminal power, then the increasing trend toward tattoos only on private skin (i.e., skin normally covered by a business suit) reflects a consumer committed first to social mobility, which requires "passing" in the untattooed world.

The collapse of the prison tattooing codes in the middle of the perestroika period (1987–88) coincided paradoxically with a renaissance of interest in the tattoo on the part of the next generation of Russian tattoo artists and clients. In addition to being another example of perestroika's general tendency toward Westernization, aestheticization of everyday life, and a gentrification of marginal social practices, this emergence of the tattoo as a design distinct from gulag culture can be traced to four specific changes in Soviet society during the same period.

The first of these changes was perestroika's rediscovery of the body as an object of private ownership, with all the privileges, rights, and abuses that ownership entails, as information about homosexuality, prostitution, drug abuse,[10] and other forms of "illicit ownership" of the body began to be released not only by writers, film directors, and journalists, but also by the Ministry of Health, the police, and other sources. In the context of this radical privatization of the body away from state control, the tattoo collector's gravitation toward individualized, ornamental tattoos was an expression of private aesthetic (or philosophical or religious or sexual) desire rather than the fixed coherence typical of totalitarianism, even in its most deviant prison articulation. In other words, there was an undeniable relationship between the totalitarian "fixing of signs" in official culture and the inflexibility of the sign system of unofficial culture. Far from being a utopian space,[11] where fixity was suspended, unofficial Soviet culture generated its own fixed codes as a strategy of resistance and dialogue. Laudable as the new postcommunist freedoms were, they spelled the death of certain sign systems that existed in articulate and coherent dialogue with the totalitarian state.

A second relevant change during 1987–88 was the outpouring of gulag-related cultural texts. This phenomenon was in some respects, of course, a reiteration of late "thaw" thematics. Both political prisoners and common criminals released during the earliest post-Stalinist "Voroshilov amnesties" had infused the discourse and social practices of the Soviet urban intelligentsia with prison slang, hand gestures, etiquette, social codes, and so-called criminal music (*blatnaia muzyka*), a euphemism for the endearing strains of thieves' speech. A shift in the thaw intelligentsia's identity to include this element of "criminal chic" coincided with the first stirrings of the Soviet dissident movement, for whom a fundamental postulate had been the metonymic relationship between the "little gulag" and the "big gulag" (the Soviet Union itself). For the urban intelligentsia, who had been long trained under Stalin to use euphemisms for incarceration — such as "there" (*tam*) instead of specific prison-site geography (e.g., Abakan, to choose an area familiar from Aleksandr Galich's thaw-era songs) — this flood of released prisoners from the early 1950s on literally opened new geographic, as well as conceptual vistas.[12]

Yet, paradoxically, the very attention during the thaw to prison tattoos as a cultural phenomenon coincided with their loss of coherence as a language system. If, for example, in the 1930s and 1940s, the number of church cupolas on a *pakhan*'s back was a strict accounting of prison terms, by the 1950s it was more an indication of criminal power, without necessarily any "truth in advertising." By the 1990s, which again saw an upsurge of interest in prison culture, the "alphabet" of prison tattoos had ceased to cohere as a language, however much individual "letters" may have survived.

Of the many new perestroika films dealing with the criminal and gulag thematics, Sergei Bodrov's *Freedom Is Paradise* (*SER* [*Svoboda Eto Rai*], 1989) derives its title from a familiar prison tattoo abbreviation. It tells the story of a young boy psychologically driven to run away from the children's colony in search of his own prisoner-father. The boy's tattoo, a visual sign of his prison provenance — genetically *and* geographically — is a verbal sign (Freedom Is Paradise) of his desire to *escape* prison life. It was this very contradiction — the sign of both imprisonment and liberation — that, in the larger framework of the country-as-gulag, enacted the changes of the later perestroika period (1988–91), when much of cultural production turned increasingly to anti-authoritarian (and, by extension, anti-Leninist) rather than parallel-authoritarian (largely neo-Leninist) models.[13]

Perestroika, unlike the thaw, entailed a mass amnesty of texts more than a mass amnesty of prisoners. Alongside the debates generated by the familiar literary and cinematic "perestroika classics" raged intense, public historiographic debates and pro-Stalinist polemics. All of these debates lent credibility to the gulag as a site worthy of study, a place where, in Alice-in-Wonderland fashion, the social practices and norms of both Soviet and prerevolutionary Russian culture were continued, distorted, inverted, and reencoded according to laws not readily apparent to the casual observer.[14] In this context, the tattoo's rehabilitation followed the same trajectory as the other rehabilitations of the perestroika period.

Again unlike the thaw, perestroika was marked by the reappearance of the image of the businessman, whose first, naive instantiation was the NEP-man and the early twentieth-century merchant, but whose later, modern incarnation was a fusion of criminal and nouveau riche businessman, whose expertise — corrupt, illicit, exotic — seemed to spring simultaneously from prison and from the West. Indeed, in a culture where capital was already synonymous with crime, U.S. financial symbols for the cent and dollar had long figured in prison tattoo codes denoting the first and second prison sentences,[15] and the Russian businessman, who could have been (and in some cases was) executed under Soviet law for private enterprise, came to embody a covert, alternative consciousness, a wisdom simultaneously archaic and ultramodern that could lead the way out of communism. The Western-style ornamental tattoo thus successfully conjured up and canceled out both of these provenances, being neither unambiguously from the West nor of the gulag.

A third relevant change in 1987–88 was the new opportunities that opened up for artists,[16] in particular for young artists working officially or unofficially in graphics, fashion, and design. As the professional artistic unions reformed, reconstituted, and then collapsed, state control over artistic space, materials, unofficial income, certification, and means of production gave way to an increasingly entrepreneurial environment that allowed nontraditional artists to use their skills for commercial gain. Tattoo art, a kind of artistic slumming, was a creative deviance that spoofed the Soviet Art Academy's elite norms even as it conjured up a safely distanced memory of the gulag. At the risk of pushing the point too far, these Soviet artists were descendants of the Wanderers (Peredvizhniki), but whereas the Wanderers found new images for their canvas, their descendants found a new canvas for their images.

The fourth development around 1987 was the explosion of so-called informals (*neformaly*): informal clubs, associations, and organizations. Although these had existed unofficially for some time — in the form of innumerable "apartment seminars," unofficial theater groups, and literary groups such as Leningrad's Club-81, named for the year of its founding — by 1987 these informal associations constituted an important part of the genesis story of the new Russia: the first political parties, ecology activists, punks, philanthropic organizers, New Age healers, bikers, legal reformers, spiritualists, businessmen, and tattoo artists. Clustered under such apparently inappropriate but self-consciously inoffensive monikers as "club," these groups sought the company of like-minded members who understood that survival lay in a quiet, gradualist evolution.

These four elements — the rediscovery of the body, the rekindled interest in gulag culture, the new opportunities for artists, and widespread informal associations — converged in 1987–88 to provide an environment within which the new tattoo artists and their clientele (often the same people) sought a living.

They practiced first on those whose boundaries could be transgressed with impunity: if New York and San Francisco artists learned to tattoo on winos and drifters, the Moscow and St. Petersburg artists learned on wives and potatoes, a Russian twist to the ancient, international art.

It must also be borne in mind that Russia, having shaken off the warm embrace of the iron curtain, experienced simultaneously and quite suddenly two scourges that had spread through the United States much more gradually: drugs and AIDS. These two (largely, though not exclusively) needle-driven ills maintained a curious tension with tattooing, for tattooing was self-declaredly *not* drug abuse (nor its "logical extension," AIDS), but instead a ritualistic self-inoculation, immunizing the body from a diseased society awash with dirty, nondisposable needles. Tattoos, historically imbued with mystical qualities, became a protective talisman in an age of needle deaths.

As most tattoo artists and collectors will attest, the first tattoo is usually followed within six months by a second or third. Of the many genres of tattoo stories, the most commonly told "master plot" is the story of the totally tattooed body. Seen in this context, the tattoo is not exactly an addiction, but a kind of constant conjuring up of the potential of the needle to complete its work.[17] That "completed work" is the body-as-thing, the flesh made word, blending visually into an urban environment of advertising slogans, spray-painted graffiti, scarred abandoned buildings, neon signs, Web pages, newspaper headlines, posters, designer wear, shopping bags, and T-shirts. The tattooed body is a camouflaged body, which, far from calling attention to itself, disappears within its ornamented ecosystem. The tattooed body articulates anxiety about the looming obsolescence of humans in an age of intelligent machines, replaceable organs, and computer-generated graphics. The last uncommodified territory, the tattooed body is a potential billboard, subverting its own custody even as it subverts the purposes of capital, whose logos it treats ironically on flesh.

The First Russian Tattoo Convention, organized by New York painter and tattoo artist Kirill Daneliia, was held on April 28–29, 1995, at the Hermitage, a Moscow nightclub, and attended by more than thirty artists from the United States, Canada, Europe, and New Zealand (fig. 15.16).[18] Attendees included many of the best-known Western tattoo artists: San Francisco artist Lyle Tuttle, inventor of new tattoo technologies and founder of the world's most prominent tattoo museum; Shotsie Gorman and Jack Rudy, respectively the East and West Coast godfathers of the American tattoo profession; David Yurkew, who orga-

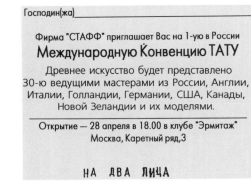

15.16   Advertisement and invitation for the First Russian Tattoo Convention.

nized the first tattoo convention, held at the Sheraton Astrodome Hotel (Houston) in January 1976; Hanky Panky, the most famous of the Dutch tattoo artists, who also runs a tattoo museum in Amsterdam; and Frank Weber (Hells Angels of Berlin). Among the best-known Russian tattoo artists present were Elena Stolarenko and Sergei Pavlov, as well as those artists properly referred to in tattoo subculture only by their monikers: Skull, Credit, the Mouse, Litva (Andrei Litvinov), and Mavrik (Mavrikii Slepnev).

The convention, supported by the Russian investment consulting firm STAFF, GALA Records, and the "rocker brotherhood" *cum* private bodyguards Night Wolves, included music by such major artists and groups as Konstantin Kinchev (Alisa), Garik Sukachev (Brigada S), Aleksandr Shkliar (Va-Bank''), and Kaspar Khauzer, and drew in a broad spectrum of Moscow's beau monde, from young film director Andrei I (*Red Constructor* [*Konstruktor krasnogo tsveta*]) to the leader of the Night Wolves, known by the reassuring moniker "The Surgeon."

As the convention amply demonstrated, the Russian tattoo industry has not yet reached a level of economic development or social respectability that allows it the kind of access afforded other new, post-perestroika businesses. What helps the subculture overcome this obstacle is the long Russian tradition of word-of-mouth as the dominant mode of advertising. Tattoo artists, marked the world over by their marginal status, both hoard and generously circulate supplies, machinery, and information within the parameters of the recognized

15.17   Head tattoo in progress at the Tattoo Fan Club in Moscow. Photo by Nancy Condee.
15.18   Three Whales (Tri Kita) artistic tattoo salon (Moscow). Photo by Nancy Condee.

subculture. Thus, the tightness of the tattoo community compensates for the (as yet) trickle of a ground-floor walk-in clientele. A growing trade in cosmetic tattooing of women's lips and eyeliner is a new, lucrative sideline.

One Moscow tattoo establishment, Vladimir Karelov's biker-style Tattoo Fan Club at 9–14 Meshchanskaia, is office space rented out of an apartment building, where such young artists as Litva, who specializes in extra-large tattoos, and Mikhail Iurov work (fig. 15.17). Unlike other tattoo salons, where certain designs are off-limits, the Tattoo Fan Club draws the line only at genital tattoos. Swastikas present no problem; piercing on Tuesdays. The club is currently trying to branch out beyond Moscow to establish affiliates in Yalta and Kishinev.

The only successful Moscow storefront business is Three Whales (Tri Kita) at 3 Adel'manov Street, where such artists as Elk (Mikhail Sychev), Oleg Mashintsev, Aleksei Minashkin, and Kissel (Pavel Kalinin) work (fig. 15.18). The most Western salon in Moscow, Three Whales meets APT (Alliance of Professional Tattooists) standards of hygiene, including disposable needles, gloves, and autoclave. At the other end of the spectrum is the unnamed salon at

27 Warsaw Highway in the basement of an abandoned, rundown house replete with broken-down cars, more a hangout than a working business. Finally, there are individual masters, such as Aleksei Surkov, who studied art in Fedoskino, and Priest (Sergei Prusakov). Some of the older artists are former inmates who tattooed fellow prisoners in the zone. Their work nowadays, they say, never includes the traditional prison tattoos, although much of their work consists in covering over old prison symbols, much as U.S. ex–gang members cover up the crown tattoo (symbol of the Latin Kings) or the Playboy bunny (tattoo of the Vice Lords).

The popular tattoos of postcommunism are familiar to most Western artists: Chinese dragons, scorpions, skulls, lizards, fanged tigers and panthers, gentle lions; yet some are arcane, traditional Russian symbols, such as the white falcon (incarnation of the Rus'ian pagan deity Rod), the Veles wheel (also from ancient pagan Rus'), the Semargl (half-bird, half-wolf or -dog pagan deity who carried away the souls of fallen warriors), and ancient Scythian and Rus'ian ornamental patterns.[19] Although swastikas are still requested, neither Christ nor women are much in demand: the new tattoo clientele, it was explained to me, have no time for Christ, and tattoos of women's figures are still associated with forced homosexuality.[20]

And what about the children's colony? The forms are maintained there, but the significance has been lost. In the Iksha Educational-Labor Colony, tattooing continues to be an idle and covert preoccupation that in most cases preceded incarceration (fig. 15.19). The most common adolescent tattoos there are traditional thieves' crosses, initials shaped into a design, and rings, all done in crude imitation of traditional prison tattoos, but the symbols have, in effect, reverted to pure ornamentation. If, in the past, the lines emanating from a tattoo ring's "stone" indicated the number of sentences or the years in a single sentence (fig. 15.20), then those same lines have now become sparks that, in the sign system of comic books, video games, and television cartoons, "perform" the ring's value. The customized body is no longer a narrative of incarceration, a political manifesto, or a guide to erotic desire. Instead, it has become a canvas of the prisoner's eclectic aesthetic tastes. Although the symbols are inadvertently eloquent—traditional signs of orphanhood, fatherlessness, life in a children's home—these original meanings are unfamiliar to the inmates, who improvise their own explanations based on specific events in their individual lives.

The only exceptions are the slogan abbreviations tattooed on prisoners' fingers—"LKHSV" (Fuck the Scum, Glory to Thieves! [*Liagavym Khui, Slava*

15.19 (*left*)   Iksha
Educational-Labor Colony.
Photo by Nancy Condee.
15.20 (*above*)   Tattoo
ring's "stone," showing a
seven-year prison sentence
(Soviet explanation) or its
economic value (post-
Soviet explanation). From
Lev Mil'ianenkov, *Po tu
storonu zakona*, p. 24.

Voram!]) — maintaining the grand old narrative of administrative animosity. Only when I began providing information did one adolescent inmate, like a Bronxville newlywed recalling her grandmother's language of flowers, remember that his older brother had been tattooed on his pelvic bones to celebrate his participation in a successful crime.

As tattoos are salvaged from the criminal underworld, a double transformation pertains: on the one hand, gentrification, whereby ornamental tattoos gain ascendancy; and, on the other hand, amnesia, whereby the traditional sign is reproduced now as ornament rather than as codified penal autobiography. The "freeing" of tattoo culture from the criminal world has thus permitted it to circulate among other legalized commodities. The profits are skimmed by precisely that same world (such as the Night Wolves) from which the tattoo culture was "liberated" — liberated as cultural code to be reclaimed as cultural commodity.

Notes

I acknowledge and thank the Hewlett Foundation, whose financial support during the summer of 1996 allowed me to complete my research on this topic. I also thank the following people who supported me in the writing of this chapter: Zheka Akimova, Boris Bagariatskii, Marina and Naum Belenky, Norma and William Condee, Ron Cruder, Galina and Kirill Daneliia, Dmitrii Eliashev, Dan Field, Lucy Fischer, Mario Fischetti, Vivienne Foley, Genevra Gerhart, Henrik Gerritsen, Seth Graham, William Judson, Deb Kaplan, Brad Lewis, Colin MacCabe, Birgit Menzel, Merata Mita, Inna Murav'eva, Vladimir Padunov, Sasha Prokhorov, David Roehler, Andrei Shemiakin, Tina, Elayne Tobin, and Dmitrii Urnov. I am grateful for their interest and assistance in my research; they are in no way responsible for the results.

1 Tamara Talbot Rice, *The Scythians* (New York: Praeger, 1957), pp. 30–31, 114–16.

2 Georgii Marokhovskii, "Eta strannaia moda. Ot igly," *Novoe russkoe slovo* (New York), March 14, 1997, p. 60.

3 Amy Krakow, *The Total Tattoo Book* (New York: Warner, 1995), p. 22.

4 The Soviet children's colony has different degrees of penal severity, up to and including the conditions of an adult prison (barbed wire, spotlights, and twenty-four-hour surveillance), and is intended for criminal adolescents between the ages of fourteen and twenty. My research included oral interviews at the Iksha Educational-Labor Colony, a severe-regime children's colony several hours outside Moscow. Of about five hundred inmates, about a fifth were imprisoned for murder.

5 Urine therapy constitutes an entire branch of Russian folk medicine and is used principally as an antiseptic rub. See Nancy Condee, "Getting By (Part Two): Colic, Curing the Common Cold, and *Mumiyo,*" *Institute of Current World Affairs Newsletter,* April 1, 1986, p. 5.

6 D. S. Baldaev, V. K. Belko, and I. M. Isupov, *Slovar' tiuremno-lagerno-blatnogo zhargona (rechevoi i graficheskii portret sovetskoi tiur'my)* (Moscow: Kraia Moskvy, 1992); Iurii Dubiagin, *Sleduiushchaia zhertva — ty: Abzuka bezopasnosti* (Moscow: Pechatnoe delo, 1995); Èdvard Maksimovskii, *Imperiia strakha* [*Empire of Fear*] (Moscow: Maket Limited, 1991); Lev Mil'ianenkov, *Po tu storonu zakona: entsiklopediia prestupnogo mira* (St. Petersburg: Ladies and Gentlemen Publishing, 1992).

7 Maksimovskii's *Empire of Fear* is a compendium of prison culture sympathetic toward the criminal world, a textual witness to the experience of incarceration. It combines extensive biblical citation and prophesy with prison lyrics by poet-songwriter Aleksandr Galich, a guide to Moscow criminal gangs (playfully entitled "Do Gangsters Want War?" ["Khotiat li gangstery voiny?"] parodying the famous thaw propaganda poem by Evgenii Evtushenko), and extensive tattoo illustrations. Its philosophical position may be gleaned from the opening dedication "To the Unknown Reader":

This book is about the fates of millions of people who went through the meat grinder of the Brezhnev [prison] system. The surviving political prisoners are

writing their memoirs. For some reason, memoirs about the *criminal* prison
life of our time are nowhere to be seen. . . .

Read this book and judge no one.

I thank the Central Asian *pakhan* who provided my husband with this volume,
together with his own additional visual and textual materials.

8 The card-playing tattoo was a rich subgenre all by itself, in which each of the cards
(and each card in various combinations with other cards) had its own small range of
meanings. The most infamous of these was the "king's hat" tattoo, festooned with
diamonds and hearts, the standard punitive tattoo for rapable men. The prison experience was, by extension, a card game or a house of cards; each prisoner had an
assigned face value but could "play himself" so as to acquire the most advantageous
position in the game. The *pakhan* could be reproduced either as a card or, more
often, as the cardplayer, since the mark of a true *pakhan* was his consistent card-
playing success. Another such subgenre was the domino tattoo, of which the most
infamous was also punitive: the diagonal three-dot tattoo, indicating that its wearer
unwillingly performed oral sex.

9 Mil'ianenkov, *Po tu storonu zakona*, p. 7.

10 Murray Feshbach, "Glasnost and Health Issues in the USSR," *Meeting Report*,
October 5, 1987, Kennan Institute for Advanced Russian Studies.

11 It is perhaps ironic that the only Soviet prison tattoos that even remotely approached
utopian, universal accessibility (i.e., that were not strictly defined as to who could
wear them, why, and on what part of the body) were women's tattoos. Although
women's tattoos were not without their own fixed coherence, they were not organized around hierarchical notions of a parallel, totalitarian "universe of criminal
power." An example of this utopianism is one of the most common prison tattoos for
young girls, two drifting seagulls, usually described as "They are not judged" (*Ikh
ne sudiat*) (Mil'ianenkov, *Po tu storonu zakona*, p. 25).

12 It is noteworthy that Galich, whose songs about prison experience were so formative
for the consciousness of the thaw-era intelligentsia, was posthumously readmitted to
the USSR Writers' Union and Union of Soviet Cinema Workers in this same period
(1988).

13 A more extensive argument of this position is contained in the series of articles by
Condee and Padunov: "*Perestroika* Suicide: Not by *Bred* Alone," *New Left Review*
189 (1991): 69–91; "*Makulakul'tura:* Reprocessing Culture," *October* 57 (summer
1991): 79–103; "Frontiers of Soviet Culture: Reaching the Limits?" *Harriman
Institute Forum* 1, no. 5 (1988): 1–8; "The Outposts of Official Art: Recharting
Soviet Cultural History," *Framework* 34 (1987): 59–106. The "signal image" for
this late-1980s antiauthoritarian, anti-Leninist impulse was Iuris Utans's drawing of
Lenin's head, squashed in a rat trap, on the back cover of the alternative journal
Spring [*Rodnik*] 10 (1988).

14 My favorite example in this regard is the long-standing criminal belief that if a thief
can steal anything on Annunciation Day (the Orthodox holiday when Gabriel an-

nounces the Incarnation to Mary) and not get caught, he will thieve successfully for the rest of the year.

15 With characteristic Soviet prudishness, the earliest tattoo compilations identified these signs as "Latin letters with lines drawn through them," so as to avoid explicit mention of the dollar sign (Dubiagin, *Sleduiushchaia zhertva,* p. 427).

16 Among the more important events in 1987 in this sphere, for example, were the First Creative Society exhibition (February), the Hermitage Society exhibition (June), the Kuznetskii Most and Kashirskaia exhibitions, and the Chagall centenary (September).

17 Tattoos seem to bear a constant tangential relationship to addiction, held in check in part by the considerable cost of a large tattoo. The "cigarette measure" (*sigaretnyi razmer*) was the standard unit for tattoo size, price, and length of time: in other words, a tattoo the size of a cigarette pack went for 400,000 rubles (about $80 in 1996) and took about two hours. An arm piece or "stocking" (*chulok*) cost between $250 and $300 dollars. The ultimate tattooed "body suit" (in Russian, "hydrosuit" [*gidrokostium*]) was several thousand dollars.

18 Artists interviewed for this chapter recalled hearing of a meeting of tattoo artists referred to as Tattoo Gulag in a Siberian city in 1992, but no other information was available about this event.

19 Rod, consort of the ancient Slavic fate goddesses, or *rozhanitsy,* is an ancient Slavic deity of dubious authenticity, since he may be confused with the Slavic word for "clan" or "family" (*rod*). See Joanna Hubbs, *Mother Russia: The Feminine Myth in Russian Culture* (Bloomington: Indiana University Press, 1993); V. I. Petrukhin, T. A. Agapkina, L. N. Vinogradova, and S. M. Tolstaia, *Slavianskaia mifologiia: Entsiklopedicheskii slovar'* (Moscow: Ellis Lak, 1995). Veles or Volos is the early Russian and Varangian (Viking) god of wealth and cattle (related concepts), who rules the earth, as opposed to Perun, who rules the skies. See Hubbs, p. 19; V. V. Ivanov and V. N. Toporov, *Issledovaniia v oblasti slavianskikh drevnostei* (Moscow: Nauka, 1974), pp. 55, 62, 164; Petrukhin et al., p. 74; N. I. Tolstoi et al., eds., *Slavianskie drevnosti: Etnolingvisticheskii slovar' v piati tomakh,* vol. 1 [A–G] (Moscow: Mezdunarodnye otnosheniia, 1995), p. 214. On Semargl, see Petrukhin et al., p. 357.

20 I found similar associations at Iksha, where I had brought a number of U.S. tattoo transfers. The adolescents' first choices were the violent images (tigers with bared teeth, skulls, monsters, demons, scorpions, dragons); second were traditional Western tattoos (pirates, lizards, anchors, insects); the female images went unclaimed. Asked in private why, one young man, who chose to go without a transfer rather than take a tattoo of a woman's head, explained apologetically that "to wear a woman is to be a woman."

■ CHAPTER 16
THERESA SABONIS-CHAFEE

COMMUNISM AS KITSCH:
SOVIET SYMBOLS IN POST-SOVIET SOCIETY

Banners, busts, pins of Lenin as a baby, placards exhorting "Revolutionary Zeal!," slogans printed on watches — the kitsch of the Soviet Union has long held a particular fascination for foreigners. To the Western eye, the images of peasant girls and heroic laborers, the slogans on building tops, and the omni-presence of hammers, sickles, and giant sheaves of wheat, all fostered by the canons of socialist realism, seemed too absurd to be persuasive, a kind of self-parody; yet they were an integral part of the Soviet landscape. The manufacture and promotion of heroic communist images was a major industry in the Soviet era. Sentimental images of citizenship, state, and progress were mass produced and distributed for the benefit of the people, to encourage them in right think-ing. Now, after the fall of the Soviet empire, what is the impact of the leftover kitsch debris on the Russian people themselves, and what role does communist kitsch play in contemporary times?

The Soviet approach to the use of these mass-produced symbols can be explained in part through the "hypodermic effects model" of mass media, which assumes that the audience absorbs media information immediately, without altering the message. According to this model, which is examined in Ellen Mickiewicz's *Split Signals: Television and Politics in the Soviet Union,* the media has the power to inject, into the essentially inert audience, both its information and its point of view.[1] It remained the primary theory to which Soviet media theorists subscribed until well into the Gorbachev era.

During the Soviet era, the central message being conveyed to the masses was the importance of the collective and the state. Heroic images of state and citizenship, used with the intention of "injecting" that idea into the masses, encouraged membership in the society, a membership that could be fully enjoyed only by those who shared common definitions of the society's goals and needs.

Totalitarian Vocabulary

In order to understand the mechanisms through which kitsch worked in Soviet society, it is first necessary to understand the notion of "final vocabulary," as articulated by Richard Rorty. Rorty asserts that each individual has a "final vocabulary," a set of words for which s/he has no definition because they are the internal text/test against which all experience is defined and evaluated: The vocabulary is "final in the sense that if doubt is cast on the worth of these words, their user has no noncircular argumentative recourse. Those words are as far as he can go with language."[2] Typically included in this vocabulary are such words as *good, right,* and *beautiful,* but also such words as *revolution,* and *progressive.* Unless an individual is willing to view her own final vocabulary with a bit of irony and appreciation for the final vocabularies of others, she will take for granted that her existing final vocabulary is universal: sufficient to order not only her own life, but also to judge the actions and lives of others. Rorty's work attempts to prove the controversial assumption that a recognition of the inherent relativity of final vocabularies is critical for a successful democracy. Although I find this latter assumption problematic, the import he places on final vocabularies can be very useful in understanding the social-engineering project of Russian communism and the profound crisis of vocabulary now evident among citizens of postcommunist states.

To spell out the text of a citizen's final vocabulary was an explicit goal of the Soviet state, pursued by means of repetition, manufactured sentiment, and punishment for deviation. Once we recognize the extent to which final vocabularies influence an individual's thinking, we can begin to grasp the divergence of the concept of "totalitarian" in the West and the East: after the death of Stalin, the salience of totalitarianism as a model for explaining the Soviet state declined in the West. Even as it declined in the West, however, it increased in use among East European dissident scholars. The West was responding to the improbability that a state could succeed in exercising total control over its citizens' lives, while the East Europeans were responding to the incredible extent to which they had witnessed the state's ability to control how its citizens made sense of their own reality — the way the state had managed, in Rorty's terms, to frame the final vocabulary. Václav Havel, in *The Power of the Powerless,* describes that phenomenon as a critical mechanism of posttotalitarianism: "I do not wish to imply by the prefix 'post' that the system is no longer totalitarian: on the contrary, I mean that it is totalitarian in a way fundamentally different from classical dictatorships, different from totalitarianism as we usually understand it. . . . The social phenomenon of self-preservation is subordinated to something higher, to a kind of blind *automatism* which drives the system."[3] In this system, according to Havel, a legacy of "correct understanding" and the ability to answer any question with the "right" answer lead to the "auto-totality of society." The line of conflict shifts from class conflict to internal conflict, "for everyone in his or her way is both a victim and a supporter of the system."[4] As the vocabulary of the system becomes increasingly internalized — as the "correct" answers become more reflexive — the individual becomes more complicit, even if he or she does not fully believe the words of the vocabulary. In the end, the society arrives at what Havel terms autototalitarianism.

What Is Kitsch?

If control of the final vocabulary can rightly be described as the ideological project of communism, then kitsch must be understood as a critical means to that end. But what is kitsch? The word has its origin in German, in which it is defined as "an object of questionable taste." In English, kitsch is defined as "artistic or literary material held to be of low quality, often produced to appeal to popular taste, and marked especially by sentimentalism, sensationalism and slickness."[5] Milan Kundera, in *The Unbearable Lightness of Being,* defines kitsch in the following manner: "In the realm of kitsch, the dictatorship of the heart reigns supreme. The feeling induced by kitsch must be a kind the multitudes can share. Kitsch may not, therefore, depend on an unusual situation; it must derive from the basic images people have engraved in their memories."[6] In other words, kitsch is manufactured sentimentality. Saul Friedlander's simple definition of kitsch incorporates all these elements: "kitsch is at least something where there is a congruence between content and form, a simplistic message, and the means to stimulate in large numbers of people an unreflective response."[7] For the most part, Western scholarship focuses on kitsch's manipulative uses and employs the word with strong negative connotations. Much of the debate about kitsch in the Western world began with an analysis of the political uses of kitsch, particularly Nazi uses of it. Robert Nozick notes that "kitsch was one of the means developed to arouse emotions and where necessary to mobilize people for sacrifice. When we look at the way that the Nazis and the Stalinists used kitsch, we become nervous because we can see how easily kitsch can be put to bad uses."[8]

In her examination of everyday life in Russia, *Common Places,* Svetlana Boym notes that the word *kitsch* is used in Russia, but it does not bear a moral connotation, as it tends to do in English.[9] Despite the word's apparent innocuousness in the Russian language, most cultural critics regard Soviet kitsch as more dangerous and more potent than its Western versions. And, according to Kundera, kitsch becomes a far more dangerous tool in nations where a single political movement is in power.

Kitsch becomes totalitarian kitsch when it is a state policy, an approved way of understanding reality — dangerous not to admire it, more dangerous still to view it with irony. In such a world, "everything that infringes on kitsch must be banished," and "all answers are given in advance and preclude any questions."[10] If we take this understanding of kitsch and combine it with Rorty's explanation of the final vocabulary, it is possible to get a glimpse of the Orwellian project of communist kitsch symbols. In his assessment of the use of "uplifting kitsch" (meaning mass-produced sentimentality that reinforces the symbols of the regime), Saul Friedlander notes:

> Such kitsch has a clear mobilizing function, probably for the following general reasons: first, what it expresses is easily understood and accessible to the great majority of people; secondly, it calls for an unreflective emotional response; thirdly it handles the core values of a political regime or ideological system as a closed, harmonious entity which has to be endowed with "beauty" to be made more effective. . . . Finally, this

peculiar linkage of "truth" and "beauty" leads to a stylization which tends to capture obvious mythical patterns; political myths and religious myths fuse. In modern societies, political religions are the natural world of uplifting kitsch.[11]

Kitsch played an instrumental propaganda role by providing the masses with a mythology — a shared image of the leaders, the goals, the desired self. In Russian, the word *propaganda* bears no negative connotations; it is simply equivalent to the capitalist term *marketing*. If Soviet propaganda can be considered the marketing of communist ideals, then kitsch should be understood as a particularly favored marketing strategy. Slogans, sculptures, and exhortations, all critical elements of what was called "agitprop" (agitation/propaganda), involved appeals to sentiments that were to be shared and not questioned. These appeals were much more effective if the sentiment could be packaged and offered with an associated image with wide appeal. And it is these images of "manufactured sentimentality" that are the essence of what Kundera and Friedlander recognize as totalitarian kitsch.

We must not assume, as did advocates of the "hypodermic effects" model, that there was no skepticism on the part of the audience. Soviet citizens, like citizens everywhere, decoded words and images in different ways. Some employed the dominant code, and some decoded within an alternative frame of reference, even though they recognized the code preferred by those who manufactured the message.[12] An omnipresent word such as *comrade* may be decoded by the individual as either positive or negative, but the agitprop approach of wrapping the word in a continuous flow of recognizable images with a sentimental appeal was created to encourage the individual to internalize the word as positive: to sell the idea.

Motherland, for example, was typically portrayed in posters in both peacetime and war as a mother in need of protection. *Communism* was portrayed as a future goal, a greatly desired destination. Such words, with their associated ideas, found their way into the final vocabularies of many citizens. For those who found the ideas repulsive and chose to employ an oppositional code, the sentimentalized images had a strong negative impact. For all citizens, communist kitsch images remain recognizable artifacts of the marketing of communist ideology.

Totalitarian kitsch, manifestations of manufactured sentiment that offered answers to every question, permeated the landscape and the Soviet psyche. Now, however, after the collapse of the ideology, the final vocabularies are proving to be far more difficult to remove than those monuments and street signs. Although Rorty enthusiastically advocates an "ironic" stance toward one's own final vocabulary, he offers no prescription for a society in which the final vocabulary of the majority of the population has been humiliated by historical circumstance. Whatever that prescription might be, it must necessarily include caution in dealing with emblems closely associated with the destroyed collective vocabulary.

The Uses of Kitsch

The symbols of communism persist in contemporary Russia. Many of these emblems, integral to architectural monuments, inlaid in glorious detail in ceilings of the metro, or welded onto bridges across the Moskva River, remain simply as artifacts of a collapsed empire. Not all such emblems are kitsch; some are real works of art, created to glorify an empire. But many other symbols — most often kitsch elements of communism deeply embedded in the Russian psyche — are deliberately used today in advertising, campaigning, and contemporary art and music. Communist kitsch has found a solid niche in Russian popular culture.

   Use of communist kitsch may be divided into three types: utopian-nostalgic, ironic-nostalgic, and camp. The first two are derived from Boym's typology of nostalgia. In her examination of post-Soviet Russia, Boym identifies nostalgia as almost inescapable but maintains that it is essential to distinguish between two kinds of nostalgia: utopian and ironic: "The former stresses the first root of the word, *nostos* (home) and puts the emphasis on the return to that mythical place on the island of Utopia where the 'greater patria' has to be rebuilt, according to 'its original authentic design.' Ironic nostalgia puts the emphasis on *algia,* longing, and acknowledges the displacement of the mythical place without trying to rebuild it."[13] According to Boym, utopian nostalgia tends to be collective and lies at the core of nationalist and communist ideologies. It is closely associated with desires for belonging and for reinstating a lost, glorious past. This category often includes wartime kitsch and nationalist as well as governmental applications of kitsch in contemporary efforts at nation building. Ironic nostalgia is, by contrast, inconclusive and fragmentary, focusing on the particular. It remembers the past as a place from which one is exiled and has no plans to return. Boym summarizes it as a fond memory of the neighbors rather than a love of the abstract idea of neighborhood.

The distinction between utopian-nostalgic and ironic-nostalgic uses of kitsch is in the latter's focus on idiosyncratic memories of the era they evoke. Uses in this category include much advertising, as well as political advertisements and a number of popular songs. The third category, camp uses of kitsch, is less often in evidence but of particular interest; it includes deliberately mocking uses of kitsch — a self-conscious playing with the images and meanings.

Utopian-Nostalgic Kitsch

Some elements of communist kitsch remain unquestioned and are still part of the popular canon. Strongest among these is war nostalgia kitsch, which the government (especially in an election year) has seen fit to employ for its own purposes. During the 1996 campaign, the posters for the Victory Day parade, displayed all along the parade route from shop windows and streetlight banners, were reprints of a vintage war poster welcoming the Red Army soldiers back home. The various communist parties complained repeatedly during the 1996 campaign that Yeltsin was co-opting the Great Patriotic War, which was rightfully their political inheritance, not his. Yeltsin, however, apparently assumed that the greatness of Russia was a theme that could be separated from the communist era of that greatness. In a sense, he was trying to have it both ways at once: instituting a campaign for reform and *demokratizatsiia* while appealing simultaneously to those who distrusted the reforms and clung tenaciously to the past. The wartime focus on working together in troubled times was a theme he wanted to use in his efforts to create a new vision for Russia, and so he — like the nationalists and the Communists — was attracted to wartime images.

War nostalgia is a part of what pop culture critic Artemy Troitsky terms "superpower nostalgia,"[14] a longing for Russia to be great again that is shared by almost all political parties. The slow revitalization of parades and the celebration of all the old holidays (with ambiguous names, but falling on the same holiday calendar dates as they did under communism) reflect this common desire to celebrate what is and has been great about Russia.

Although the Yeltsin administration is trying to create new kitsch images that inspire patriotism, these images invariably draw on the familiar old Soviet images in a utopian-nostalgic manner. One curious example is a series of televised public service announcements, titled *Russkii proekt* (*The Russian Project*), that provide two-minute vignettes of life in Russia. The first one in the series features two middle-aged women repairing tracks on the Siberian railroad. Stout and ruddy in the socialist realist way, the women are working and talking. One is crying, telling about how hard her life is and how her husband beats her. She collapses in tears. The second, fearing that her friend has suffered a heart attack, becomes hysterical and tries to revive her. When she realizes that her friend is despairing but not dying, she breaks into a folk song and dance about the beauty of life in Siberia. The final frame offers a wish to the viewers: "God grant you health. A message from the Russian government." What is the viewer to make of such an advertisement? Non-Russian viewers found it incomprehensible, but many Russians enjoyed applying the old skill of decoding Aesopian tales, trying to find the message. My Russian colleagues concluded that the message is: "You are made of strong stock. Protect your health and wait for things to get better. The government is trying."

The *Russkii proekt* has continued to provide these odd vignettes in an attempt to create good feelings about Russia and shared memories that are not politically explosive — the traditional political uses of kitsch. Another immensely popular vignette in the series begins with a young man going off to the Great Patriotic War. As his girl watches from the platform, he breathes on the window and draws a heart with their initials. "Don't cry," he shouts from the window, "I love you!" In the next scene, the same couple — many years older — is mourning the death of their son, apparently in the Prague invasion. As the wife cries, her husband pulls out an old puppet of their son's and makes it say, "Don't cry, I love you!" The third scene shows the old man, now a widower and poverty-stricken pensioner, falling asleep on the metro in the present day. He is ill dressed and disheveled; tears well up in his eyes. Just then, on the window of the train car appears the same heart and initials that he drew so many years before. He spots it, and his eyes sparkle with hope. The final frame offers a wish to the viewers. "We love you. A message from the Russian government."

All of the vignettes in the *Russkii proekt* series are highly sentimental tales of strong people in difficult times, and all draw on the kitsch symbols of the past to create images of a Russia and a people that are great in spite of adversity. Not only does the government consider the project worthy of long-term support, the series also remains rather popular with Russian viewers. The latter vignette,

"Don't Cry, I Love You," was especially popular because the lead actor, Zinovii Gerdt, was a beloved actor from the Soviet period. The scenes of him in his youth were actually clipped from old Soviet films. When Gerdt died, not long after the release of this public service announcement, the vignette was played repeatedly as a tribute to him.

The fact that communist kitsch still finds an enthusiastic audience is hardly surprising. But such utopian-nostalgic uses of kitsch are perhaps the most dangerous, and they are certainly the most politicized. Although Yeltsin has used the strategy extensively, enhanced longing for the past can easily give a political advantage to any of the more extreme communist parties or the various nationalist parties. As Boym notes, "Utopian nostalgia . . . reveals both nostalgia for totalitarianism and the totalitarian nature of nostalgia itself — the longing for a total reconstruction of a past that is gone. It is not accidental that in most post-communist countries today nationalism takes the place of communist ideology. . . . The seduction of nationalism is the seduction of homecoming and total acceptance: one doesn't even have to join the party, one simply belongs." [15]

Utopian-nostalgic kitsch taps into the previous mythology and the people's sense of loss. In spite of its limited current use, it is a potentially lethal political tool, for as Saul Friedlander notes in assessing Nazism, "kitsch does help us to account for the achievement of total mobilization. . . . The ideological arguments, such as they were, were reduced to a few slogans, to a few very potent images. Mobilization took place at the level of simple images." [16]

Ironic-Nostalgic Kitsch

Picture a television commercial for the popular detergent Ariel. The format is a familiar one: a mother speaks about her son getting his good clothes dirty, and about the urgent need to clean them perfectly in time for the "big event." Ariel does the job, saving the family from embarrassment. Although one might expect a mother to be talking about her young son in this commercial, the little boy is instead a young navy recruit who has spilled something on his dress whites, which he needs for the annual parade. The ad is not set in the present — when military service is seldom a source of pride and parades are rare — but it is not set in an actual past either. Rather, it takes place in some never-never land where sons are proud to march in the navy parade and mothers have washing machines at home. In its juxtaposition of old and new, the advertisement does not con-

16.1 *Trud* advertisement: "We are millions — Unite with us!"
Photo by Gavin Helf.

jure up the past. Instead, it deftly makes the suggestion that the consumer can have the trimmings of Western society yet retain traditional Russian values.

This is a prime example of the ironic-nostalgic use of kitsch, a popular advertising tool. In this type of advertising, the company plays on the nostalgic sentiment of its intended consumers and associates its own product with that very sentiment, frequently accomplished with a turn of a recognizably communist phrase. A simple example is the advertising slogan of the worker's newspaper, *Trud* (*Labor*): "We are millions — unite with us!" (*Nas milliony — prisoedinites'*) (fig. 16.1), which echoes the words of the communist anthem, the *Internationale*. Another example, more subtle to the foreign ear, is the slogan of the Russian workingman's cigarette, Iava: "Always beloved and always with you" (*Vsegda liubimaia, vsegda s toboi*) (fig. 16.2). The play on words, obvious to the Russian ear, is in "*Vsegda s toboi*" (always with you), a phrase learned and sung from childhood as "*Lenin vsegda s nami*" (Lenin is always with us).

This commercial play with kitsch is ironic both in the sense used by Boym (the nostalgia evoked is idiosyncratic and personal) and in the more common sense that it is ironic to see the widespread use of communist symbols by commercial organizations as marketing ploys. Not surprisingly, this type of punning on Soviet kitsch is found exclusively in the advertising of Russian products. It is also typically used to advertise objects that appeal to a socioeconomic strata likely to contain substantial numbers of people who would still describe themselves as Communists.

16.2   Iava advertisement: "Always beloved, always with you." Photo by Gavin Helf.

A similar game is also played with familiar images — taking a kitsch visual cue and connecting it to a different agenda. For example, one very prominent image of the 1996 presidential campaign was a poster that appeared in nearly every shop window. The poster was a kind of "before and after" picture. The upper photo, in black and white, showed a (presumably late perestroika era) grocery store with rows of empty shelves. The lower picture, in color, showed a woman surrounded by her happy children and carrying armloads of Russian food products. "Think and Choose" (*Dumai i Vybirai*) admonished the slogan that ran between the two photos. What was curious about the poster is that although it was a pro-Yeltsin campaign poster, and although the bounty of capitalism was showcased, the color photo was done in the style typical of socialist realism with classic communist kitsch images of wealth: a modest but happy everywoman in her kerchief enjoying the bounty of the state, her arms loaded with sausages. Even the use of the mother heroine image was a familiar Soviet visual device. Like the soap commercial, it read like an appeal for Russian values and Western goods. At first viewing, the poster appeared to be an advertisement for the bounty of the early 1970s, not of the uncertain late 1980s.

Ironic-nostalgic uses of kitsch have also permeated music. The televised 1996 and 1997 New Years' programs featured many old songs from the war years that have enjoyed popular revivals through the subsequent years. In fact, the same *Russkii proekt* of the public service announcements has released two albums of these songs, called *Old Songs about the Most Important Things* (*Starye pes'ni o glavnom*). In keeping with an ironic-nostalgic approach to kitsch, the songs included in the two albums are the most popular nonpolitical songs of their era, mostly love songs such as "On the Porch" ("Na krylechke"), and "You Wait, Elizabeth" ("Ty zhdesh', Lizaveta").

Many of the popular videos of 1996 were done in a faux 1950s style and drew on a collage of kitschy Soviet and American images of early rock music and the era in which it was discovered. For a time after the collapse of perestroika, songs with political themes were unpopular. Recently, however, some popular songs have played on the ironic-nostalgic kitsch sentiments of the audience, perhaps most notably the song "We Were Born in the USSR" ("Rodilis' my v SSSR"). This song, recorded by a former member of the extremely popular underground Soviet band Time Machine (Mashina vremeni), reflects the nostalgia and ambivalence of the post-Soviet generation. Against a video background of trash fires and scattered ruins, the song laments, "with nothing in front of us, and everything behind us, we were born in the USSR. . . . Once, in theory, heirs to it all, now we have only ashes. . . . We don't want what was, but now we have nothing." It is a poignant mix of old slogans and new doubts. Ironic-nostalgic kitsch in general, in its efforts to remember fondly but not re-create, is perhaps the most socially constructive use of kitsch in the new Russia.

Kitsch Camp

"Camp sensibility" in the West was first examined by Susan Sontag, who describes it as a kind of deliberate bad taste — an acquired appreciation for things commonly recognized as kitsch or bad art, a "love of the exaggerated, the 'off,' of things-being-what-they-are-not. To perceive Camp in objects and persons is to understand 'Being-as-Playing-a-Role.' "[17] Perhaps the most intriguing example of this is the Stolichnaia "Freedom of Vodka" campaign, which was released only in the United States and used constructivist art in a propaganda poster format to encourage the consumption of Russian vodka. Predictably, this ad campaign is unknown in Moscow, where Stolichnaia, competing against many foreign brands now popular in Russia, takes a patriotic Russian approach to advertising (drink the vodka of the capital city), makes use of tsarist symbols, and has reverted to its prerevolutionary logo.

Even in Moscow, however, there is a market in the camp celebration of kitsch—mostly a tourist market, but a large one. In Moscow in 1992, for example, a hard-currency restaurant called Byloe (The Way It Was) experienced meteoric success with its extensive communist camp décor comprising busts, statues, and banners that had only recently been removed from the surrounding streets. The sale of busts of Lenin has reportedly remained high enough that one of the production factories continues in service to the present day. (More popular among Russians than Lenin busts are Lenin candles, which offer the possibility of melting the all-too-familiar head.) Sales of other kitsch items, mostly in the outdoor markets frequented by tourists, include banners, busts, flags, military hats, political pins, and all the visual trappings of the USSR.

Communism as camp also enjoys popularity in the non-Russian former republics, especially in the Baltic states. Both Latvia and Lithuania, for example, have communist kitsch bars in their capital cities. The Vilnius bar named Iron Felix, after Felix Dzerzhinsky, the Baltic-born director of the Cheka (the precursor to the KGB), displays an extensive collection of propaganda posters, provides a comic menu of communist culinary disasters, and offers patrons a choice of newspaper or real toilet paper in the restrooms. The bar is located just off the square formerly named Lenin Square. The Finnish beer Leningrad Cowboy, which pictures Lenin on its can—sometimes in a cowboy hat, and sometimes with an Elvis-style bouffant—was very popular in the Baltic states in the early independence era. The fact that the kitsch symbols were imposed, but for the most part not absorbed, in the Baltic cultures makes kitsch an easier target for mockery in this region than in Russia.

Even in Russia, a camp artifact occasionally appears that appeals across the generations. The immensely popular "Kommunal'naia kvartira" ("Communal Apartment") music video, for example, shows a wild, tangled burlesque of communal apartment living, full of visual representations of all the familiar anecdotes of its residents, while the chorus repeats, "We live in a communal apartment in a communal country." The song plays with the images of collective living and parodies the slogans of international friendship. Its popularity is due not only to its catchy tune but also to the fact that it parodies a universally unpopular institution of communism—the communal apartment, or *kommunalka* (see Boym's "Communal Apartment" chapter in *Common Places* for a full discussion).

For the most part, however, gleeful use of camp is not common among

Russian citizens. Many kitsch symbols of the Soviet Union evoke strong feelings among Russians, so a camp approach to kitsch remains the province of a
few subcultures. One rare example of the use of camp kitsch in advertising is
the television campaign of the popular *National Enquirer*–style journal, *Sovershenno sekretno* (*Absolutely Secret*). In this ad, Stalin is reading the latest
issue, exclaiming at all the secrets he finds exposed: secrets about the government, space aliens, and Afghanistan. In the end, he calls Beria into his office
and fires him for knowing less than the journal. *Sovershenno sekretno* chose
this ad campaign to reinforce its image as a maverick journal. With its unusual
combination of UFO stories and hard-hitting journalism, *Sovershenno sekretno*
attracts fierce loyalty and harsh criticism.

The camp approach to kitsch appeals most to social groups, such as bikers
and youth subcultures, that traditionally appropriate symbols that are offensive
to the mainstream. Bikers often use communist symbols, much as American
bikers of earlier eras used Nazi symbols: with an intent to offend. Such use of
communist symbols is in part nostalgic, recalling the "glory days" of power
and empire, but it is also an appeal to anarchistic sensibilities, in that use of
communist symbols as camp offends all branches of the Communist party. One
example of this sort of "rebellious use" of camp can be seen in the Iama Bar (a
biker bar on the northwest edge of Moscow; the name means "pit"), which
proudly displays a large communist flag on one wall, and, on the wall directly
across from it, an American rebel flag. In the Iama Bar, however, camp is also
used in a playful manner, such as the display behind the bar of the annual
"Victor in Socialist Competition for Encouraging Worker Productivity" award.

The camp approach to kitsch symbols among youth subcultures reflects the
fact that Soviet symbols never made a strong impression on the younger generation. Adolescents can therefore enjoy the discomfort the kitsch symbols evoke
in their elders without themselves being affected. Acts of youth vandalism
against a school, for example, often take the form of students stealing communist paraphernalia from the school basement and placing it in prominent locations where it can once again embarrass the school authorities or the neighbors.
One former Komsomol club (now an exclusive youth dance club) carefully
maintains the giant murals depicting triumphant socialist youth hard at work on
the outside of the building. And there is a 1997 dance song, rumored to be
popular at raves, whose title (and chorus) is, "I Want to Be a Pioneer, Not a
Millionaire, Mamma" ("Khochu byt' pionerom, ne millionerom"). In the uses

described above, camp plays a role similar to the role Sontag describes for it in America: "something of a private code, a badge of identity, even, among small urban cliques."[18]

The Rise in Ambivalence about Communist Kitsch

In the years surrounding the collapse of the USSR, there was a brief willingness to throw off, and mock, the symbols of the past (fig. 16.3). That willingness has faded with time. In 1991, while elementary students continued (of necessity) to use communist texts, they did so with the ironic commentary of their teachers. One young student I questioned about what she studied answered, "We read the old books. Then the teacher tells us why they are not true." She showed me her textbook, full of doodles and cruel graffiti mocking Lenin.

Today the textbooks are new, extremely well written, and try to repudiate the past more gently, adding a wealth of expanded information about the years before and after the revolutions. *Matreshki* (the nested wooden dolls) at the markets for foreigners no longer bear the cartoon likenesses of leaders of the USSR. They are far more likely to have basketball teams, tsars, or Disney characters. Boym's book bears an illustration of a 1950s "We Build Communism" mural, under which an investment enterprise had painted a billboard-sized advertisement reading "We Are Building a New Russia."[19] At present, that advertisement has been painted over in a large expanse of white, returning the mural as much as possible to its original visual dignity. Photos from 1991–

16.3   Advertisement in Bibloglobus, a Moscow bookstore. Hitler, Nicholas II, Lenin, and Brezhnev hold copies of *Chronicle of History*, a new textbook. Photo by Gavin Helf.

16.4   Broken statue of Stalin on display in the statue park in Moscow. Photo by
Martin Klos.

92 showed toppled statues and graffiti-covered pedestals. Today, those statues
have been cleaned and are displayed in a sculpture garden across from Gorky
Park, on the grounds of the House of Artists. The sculpture garden is a strange
place indeed. Dzerzhinsky, with his pedestal partially scrubbed clean of graffiti,
faces a statue of Brezhnev, who is backed by an enormous seal of the USSR.
Stalin, who was broken, years before, from his pedestal, lies in state on two
stone supports (fig. 16.4). A long row of fallen communist leaders faces a well-
maintained walkway. Since many of the statues were removed from a "statue
graveyard" — a pile in Gorky Park that was created in the wake of the coup of
1991 — it is clear that someone in the government is taking care of images that
are still cherished by many. In part, the Communist party's increased power
accounts for the current protection of the statues.

Unlike camp, which seeks to be deliberately offensive, the vast majority of
communist kitsch is used in contemporary Russia in a gentle and rather fond
way. Advertisers play with it a bit, but most concentrate on prerevolutionary

kitsch: images of tsars and kingdoms. These symbols, from a much more comfortable and distant past, can be manipulated with less risk. The communist past has been universally accepted as dangerous territory, and people are currently exhausted from their reexamination of the ruins.

Communist Kitsch and an Unpredictable Past

A popular one-liner during the late perestroika years, when both Gorbachev and his detractors used the new openness in examining history as a political tool, was "Russia is a country with an unpredictable past." It remains true. In Milan Kundera's novel about totalitarianism and private life, *The Book of Laughter and Forgetting,* the cynical narrator comments, "People are always shouting that they want to create a better future. It's not true. The future is an apathetic void of no interest to anyone. The past is full of life, eager to irritate us, provoke and insult us, tempt us to destroy or repaint it. The only reason people want to be masters of the future is to change the past. They are fighting for access to the laboratories where photographs are retouched and biographies and histories rewritten."[20]

Although everyday society has retreated somewhat into the apolitical, searching for some time in which history is more backdrop than adventure, the symbols of communism retain power over the imaginations of the citizenry. Certain generations cannot eradicate the words and symbols from memory or redefine the final vocabulary. Given that fact, kitsch communist symbols retain the power to become battlegrounds in the conflict over the meaning of history.

In November 1996, the Russian government began releasing yet another series of public service announcements on television, this series titled *Tales for a New Russia.* These shorts were released one by one during the *Vremia* nightly newscast on Channel 1, and — although they assumed a fairy-tale format and were illustrated in childish, crayoned animation — were clearly aimed at the adult viewers of Russia's most popular news program. The most interesting one for our purposes begins, "Once upon a time, in a very red country . . ." and tells a tale about a country where red was considered the only beautiful color;[21] everything was painted red, even the people. The cartoon figures, joyously painting each other red, finally notice that the sky is blue and the clouds are white in spite of all their best efforts, and vow to admire other colors, as the monochrome red screen becomes the three colors of the Russian flag.

The fairy tale is fascinating, both in its plea for tolerance and in its encouragement to viewers to leave the past in the past and render no judgment about it. In its effort to manufacture a sentiment for the mass audience (a sentiment rarely encountered among viewers of the tale), it is a particularly ambitious instance of postcommunist kitsch propaganda. In its use of ancient fairy-tale symbolism, it is implicitly calling the viewers back to a time of pre-Soviet mythology.

It is to be expected that there will be new kitsch, for as Kundera insists, "kitsch is the aesthetic ideal of all political parties and movements."[22] It is also, he says, an integral part of the human condition — something that cannot be eradicated, only critically viewed. Contemporary art in Russia is beginning to examine communist kitsch symbols in a serious way. One particularly interesting treatment of the problem of kitsch and history in contemporary art comes in the current variation on the long-running production of *Jesus Christ Superstar,* at the Mossoviet Theater.

In the era of *magnitizdat* (secretly reproduced and distributed videos and tapes), the American film *Jesus Christ Superstar* was among the most popular. Dozens of translations of it exist, and there were many underground performances of it in Russia before the perestroika era. As soon as it was permitted, the Russian translation of *Jesus Christ Superstar* opened at the Mossoviet Theater, and it continues to play several times a month to full houses. The original production was a faithful translation of the Webber and Rice production. Like the American film, the original production was appreciated both as rare access to biblical history (many young Muscovites cite it as their first exposure to the history of Jesus' life), and as a powerful tale about an intellectual in conflict with the state and the power of ideas to overcome authoritarian control. These themes, also echoed in Bulgakov's *Master and Margarita,* were in need of a new treatment in a post-Soviet Russian society. And so the new version, titled *Jesus Christ Superstar with a Cynical Adaptation,* opened, also at the Mossoviet, where it continues to play to large audiences.

The "cynical adaptations" are substantial, and while the score of Webber and Rice's rock opera is faithfully reproduced, the plot has undergone significant change. As in the original, Jesus is crucified as a result of his politically explosive teachings. In the new version, however, Jesus' teaching is presented as a revolution that falls apart before the leader's death because Jesus' "inner circle" cannot agree what the revolution is about. Everyone betrays Jesus. Mary Magdalene assures Pilate that if he will set Jesus free, she will force Jesus to retire from politics. Simon Zealotis argues that the revolution will be much better off with a martyr and subsequent cult of personality, especially since Jesus seems to be losing heart. Simon Zealotis and Judas argue about the dialectics of revolution.

As the final act unfolds, kitsch symbols proliferate, and the characters take on explicit manifestations of communism: The Sanhedrin becomes the Politburo. Pilate begins quoting Stalin. ("The people," he says, "from time to time need an enemy, and we will provide them with one. But when there is no man, there is no problem.") Simon Zealotis takes on Trotsky's style of dress and speech. Pilate turns and sneers to the audience, "When you have eaten your fill of freedom, and it has made you sick, you will come crawling back to me and say 'Hegemon — for Christ's sake, forgive us!' And for Christ's sake, I will forgive you. But will Christ?"[23] The production, which found its original place in Soviet culture as a lyrical rejection of Soviet values, has become a stunning commentary on the ambivalence of life after the revolution. As his revolution begins to fall apart, Jesus mournfully sings, "Blessed are they who thirst for the truth — they shall find it. Truly blessed are they who can survive that truth."

Surviving the Truth

> "My name is Ozymandias, king of kings:
> Look on my works, ye Mighty, and despair!"
> Nothing besides remains. Round the decay
> of that colossal wreck, boundless and bare
> The lone and level sands stretch far away.[24]

In Shelley's famous poem, it is a neutral traveler who encounters the wreckage of Ozymandias' statue and kingdom. In Russia, however, the observers of the remains of empire are its former citizens, a fact that cannot help but engender profound ambivalence over its displaced statues and long-familiar symbols. One sign of an increasing ability to address the history of the Soviet Union, according to Artemy Troitsky, is that Russians are increasingly making the distinction between communist kitsch and the real art of the Soviet Union.[25] Russians, suggests Troitsky, long unable to appreciate the originality of socialist realism, are now beginning to enjoy it. He cites the success in Moscow of a fall 1996 traveling exhibit titled *Moscow-Berlin* as an example of this phenomenon. The exhibit portrays the art and architecture of twentieth-century authoritarianism and its international impact. According to Troitsky, reclaiming the art of the era of communism is an important aspect of coming to terms with national history.

Drawing distinctions between what is art and what is kitsch, what is history and what are the uses of history, are projects that both demand and aid in the process of developing new final vocabularies. The symbols linked to destroyed final vocabularies remain painful for many citizens and will continue to serve as battlegrounds of the politics of the future. Although the democratic project in Russia is by no means assured, a critical examination of the "marketing tools" of communist ideology may provide individual citizens with the vocabulary necessary for life after the end of the Kitsch Empire.

Notes

1 Ellen Mickiewicz, *Split Signals: Television and Politics in the Soviet Union* (New York: Oxford University Press, 1988), p. 181.

2 Robert Rorty, *Contingency, Irony, and Solidarity* (New York: Cambridge University Press, 1989), p. 73.

3 Václav Havel, "The Power of the Powerless," in *Living in Truth*, ed. Jan Vladislav (London: Faber and Faber, 1989), pp. 41, 44.

4 Ibid., p. 53.

5 *Webster's Third New International Dictionary*, unabridged (Springfield, Mass.: Merriam-Webster, 1981).

6 Milan Kundera, *The Unbearable Lightness of Being*, trans. from Czech by Michael Henry Heim (New York: HarperCollins, 1991), pp. 250–51.

7 Saul Friedlander, in the symposium-debate "On Kitsch," published in *Salmagundi*, no. 85–86 (1990), p. 304.

8 Robert Nozick, in ibid., p. 289.

9 Svetlana Boym, *Common Places: Mythologies of Everyday Life in Russia* (Cambridge: Harvard University Press, 1994), p. 16.

10 Kundera, *The Unbearable Lightness of Being*, pp. 252–54.

11 Saul Friedlander, preface to a symposium: "Kitsch and the Apocalyptic Imagination," *Salmagundi*, nos. 85–86 (1990), p. 203.

12 For a discussion of theories of audience perception, see John Storey, *Cultural Studies and the Study of Popular Culture: Theories and Methods* (Athens: University of Georgia Press, 1996).

13 Boym, *Common Places*, p. 284.

14 Artemy Troitsky, lecture at the Moscow Institute for Advanced Studies, October 15, 1996. Troitsky, a popular music and pop culture critic, is host of the late-night talk show *Kafe Oblomov* (*Slacker's Café*) and is editor of the Russian edition of *Playboy* magazine.

15 Boym, *Common Places,* p. 287.

16 Friedlander, in "On Kitsch."

17 Susan Sontag, "Notes on Camp," in *Against Interpretation and Other Essays* (New York: Octagon Books, 1986), pp. 279–80.

18 Ibid., p. 275.

19 See Boym, *Common Places,* p. 273.

20 Milan Kundera, *The Book of Laughter and Forgetting,* trans. from Czech by Michael Henry Heim (New York: Penguin Books, 1981), p. 22.

21 In Russian, there is an etymological similarity between the words *red* (*krasnyi*) and *beautiful* (*krasivyi*).

22 Kundera, *The Unbearable Lightness of Being,* p. 251.

23 A recording of *Isus Kristos Superzvezda,* translated by Y. Kesler and including the cynical adaptation, is available from Dokument recordings and is sold at the Mossoviet Theater.

24 Percy Bysshe Shelley, "Ozymandias" (1818), in *The Norton Introduction to Literature: Poetry,* ed. J. Paul Hunter (New York: W. W. Norton, 1973), p. 305. Thanks to my colleague Luis Clemens for proposing this analogy in our many discussions about Russia.

25 Artemy Troitsky, lecture at the Moscow Institute for Advanced Studies, October 15, 1996, in response to questions about communist kitsch.

FROM THE TOILET TO THE MUSEUM:
MEMORY AND METAMORPHOSIS OF
SOVIET TRASH

Kitsch, in a celebrated aphorism of Milan Kundera, "is a stopover between being and oblivion."[1] At the end of the era, kitschy souvenirs from the past appear as the last survivors of the cultural cataclysm. The backward glance of nostalgia tends to blur the differences between "high" culture and "popular" culture and between ideology and everyday life.

There is nothing particularly new about post-Soviet nostalgia except its scale. No longer the property of nationalist politicians or ironic postmodern intellectuals, nostalgia has become institutionalized in the new monumental propaganda that flourishes in Moscow. Post-Soviet public memorials, such as newly rebuilt Church of Christ the Savior, the new monument to Peter the Great, and the monumental ensemble on Poklonny Hill dedicated to the Fiftieth Anniversary of the Victory in World War II, nostalgically reconstruct all the grand styles of the past two centuries — from the classical "empire style" to the neo-Byzantine (or pseudo-Russian) style to Stalinist baroque — in a display of monumentalism unseen since Stalin's era. They embody the utopian nostalgia for a powerful homeland, the Rome of the next millennium, and for the architectural grandiosity of the Stalin and Brezhnev eras. The monumental nostalgia promoted by the popular Moscow mayor Iurii Luzhkov goes hand in hand with his support for new entrepreneurship and with the selective forgetting of the dark moments of Russian and Soviet history. Appeals to collective responsibility have become much less popular than they were during glasnost, and, more important, much less marketable. Nostalgia is now a profitable part of the new commercial culture in Russia. Nostalgia arts and crafts include items from different cultural spheres — from popular culture, the dreary Soviet everyday, official propaganda, and state television to the unofficial "tape-recorder culture" (*magnitofonnaia kul'tura*). Soviet slogans, busts of Lenin with and without a cap, beloved musicals from Stalin's time, popular singers from Ludmila Zykina to Vladimir Vysotsky, slow-moving TV serials from the 1970s followed by "nature intermissions" with bubbling brooks, birch trees, and Tchaikovsky's music in the background all acquired a new significance in the cultural recycling. Kitschy souvenirs, everyday objects, and rituals form collective frameworks of memory that are inextricably intertwined with individual remembrances. In Maurice Halbwachs's words, those collective frameworks become visible to us in a "crepuscular light" when we bid farewell to the society and community that nurtured them.[2] Theodor Adorno defines kitsch, specifically commercial mass-reproduced culture of the early twentieth century, as a "parody on catharsis."[3] In the twilight of the era, kitsch might appear sublime, offering a nostalgic catharsis that at once delivers from memory and reassures in the possibility of homecoming and belonging. Nostalgic re-creations of the past acquire particular importance at a time of historical cataclysm and sometimes function as "defense mechanisms" that help survivors cope with major historical changes.

Yet the collective frameworks of memory embodied in popular artifacts and everyday culture of the Soviet era do not offer a single narrative of reconstructing the past. They are signposts on the map of collective tours and individual detours, not exact prescriptions. My focus in this chapter is on the transformation of everyday culture into the topography of memory, and the metamorphosis of Soviet trash into a subversive museum display. I will explore the limits of post-Soviet homesickness through two Soviet memory sites — the

toilets and the Palace of the Future — as reconstructed by the artist Ilya Kabakov. The first installation was presented in Kassel, Germany, in 1992, the
second in Paris, at the Centre Georges Pompidou, in 1995. Together they reflect
the profane and sacred sides of the collective Soviet home.

Ilya Kabakov's fate embodies many of the paradoxes of post-Soviet nostalgia and of the relationship between Russia and the West. Kabakov became
known in the 1970s–80s as one of the alternative artists of Brezhnev's era of
"stagnation," many of whom later gained popularity and publicity in the West
as "artists of perestroika." Kabakov left the Soviet Union in 1988 to work in
Germany and then left permanently in 1992 to live in New York. After the
installation of *The Toilets,* the artist did not return to Russia.

Obviously, installations exhibited outside Russia cannot be considered a part
of post-Soviet popular culture, yet these two artworks remain the best museums
of Soviet kitsch in existence. They inhabit and alienate the past and deter-
ritorialize the Soviet everyday, altering the popular nostalgic narrative. They
challenge some post-Soviet conceptions of national identity and bring the issues of Soviet everyday culture and cultural memory into a global context. For
in spite of his abundant references to the *Soviet* everyday, Kabakov's work is
perfectly translatable into an international artistic context, as a kind of Naboko-
vian invariant in art. This brings us to a comparative discussion of the crisis of
memory at the end of the twentieth century, new ways of recycling popular
culture, and the global nostalgia boom.[4]

Nostalgia is a longing for a home that no longer exists, or perhaps never
existed. The affective geography of nostalgia does not coincide with any historical map. The nostalgic desires to obliterate linear history and turn it into
private or collective mythology, to forget the selectivity of memory itself. Confronted with the irreversibility of time, the nostalgic resorts to the mythical
temporality where Past Imperfect turns into Future Perfect. Although a nostalgic element is inevitably present in any memory work, one can distinguish
between different kinds of nostalgia. Provisionally, I will point out two nostalgic tendencies: the metaphoric one, which is reconstructive, utopian, and ob-
livious of history; and the metonymic one, which is fragmentary, ironic, and
self-reflective.[5]

Nostalgia is at the core of the popular culture in general that flirts with
fashion and newness but in fact remains faithful to traditional forms and stories.
What is recycled in popular nostalgia is a certain narrative of homecoming, of
return to origins. Popular culture is driven by longing for familiarity, for some-

thing repeatable that reminds one of the mythical stability of home. No Wizard of Oz can compete with a friendly uncle or a trickster from the neighborhood. At the end of her foreign travels, Dorothy, from *Kanzas,* or Ellie as she was renamed in the popular Soviet adaptation of the book, agrees that there is "no place like home." If in the 1970s and 1980s popular culture in the Soviet Union was permeated by dreams of escape, Russian popular culture of the 1990s features many stories of return. The encounter between Russia and the West often culminates with the return of the prodigal son, be it an international prostitute or an intellectual music teacher from "Window on Paris" ("Okno v Parizh") who at the end returns to the "Venice of the North."[6]

What happens when one no longer recognizes one's home, or even worse, when one tampers with popular nostalgia and collective forgetting? In this context of the nostalgia boom, Ilya Kabakov's recent projects of reconstructive installations acquire a new meaning. Kabakov's work was often discussed together with that of the Moscow conceptual artists of the late 1970s and early 1980s. Their work was seen as a Soviet parallel to pop art, but with one significant difference: instead of advertisement culture these artists used the trivial and drab rituals of Soviet everyday life, too banal and insignificant to be recorded anywhere else, made taboo not because of their potential political explosiveness but because of their sheer ordinariness, their "all too human" scale. The conceptualists "quoted" both Russian avant-garde and socialist realism, as well as amateur crafts, "bad art," and ordinary people's collections of useless objects.[7] Their artistic language was made out of both Soviet symbols and emblems, and trivial found objects, unoriginal quotes, slogans, and domestic trash. The word and image collaborate in their works to create a rebuslike language of Soviet culture. Kabakov's installations created during the Soviet era often enacted the artist's imagined escape from public embarrassment or private misery — one of his alter-ego little men is saved by UFOs from a meeting of the Housing Committee, another manages to escape naked into the white wall of his crowded room in a communal apartment.

In the post-Soviet context, the meaning of Kabakov's work has shifted. It is no longer about the subversive quotations of the unrepresentable Soviet everyday and the artist's fantastic escapes from it; rather it is about memory, everyday life, and the impossibility of recovering lost time. Kabakov creates the most complete labyrinth of Soviet home abroad with evocative mnemonic sites that use artifacts of popular culture and at the same time challenge contemporary nostalgic narratives. The black hole of the Soviet toilet certainly drives home the experience of the past, but it was hardly regarded as something worthy of public commemoration. Likewise the scaffoldings and temporary barracks of the never completed Palace of the Future evoke utopian aspirations of the past but question their "constructive" principles.

If in the Soviet Union his work took the form of albums and fragmentary collections of Soviet found objects, in exile Kabakov embraced the genre of "total installation." Yet this totality is always precocious, and there is always something incomplete in his works, something about to break or leak. The progression from fragment to totality is not a one-way street. Moreover, each total installation in itself embodies the Kabakovian work of memory. Each creates a complete environment that includes Kabakov's earlier works, fragments from his albums, paintings, everyday objects, collectibles of the obsessive communal apartment neighbors, sketches of the untalented artists, and communal trash. Each installation becomes a kind of museum for Kabakov's earlier work, rather like *matreshka* dolls with many layers of memory.

Another paradox concerns Kabakov's identity. According to the fifth line in his Soviet passport, Kabakov is Jewish; he was born in Dniepropetrovsk, the area in Ukraine most heavily populated by Russians, and spent most of his life in Moscow. Since the breakup of the Soviet Union and his exile, he calls himself neither a Russian nor a Ukrainian artist, but a Soviet artist.[8] That, of course, is an ironic self-definition: the end of the Soviet Union put an end to the myth of the Soviet dissident artist. Sovietness in this case refers not to politics but to common culture. In what way is Kabakov a nostalgic Soviet artist? He embraces the idea of collective art; his installations offer an interactive narrative that could not exist without the viewer. Moreover, he turns himself into a kind of ideal communist collective made up of his own embarrassed alter egos, which include untalented artists, amateur collectors, and the "little men" of nineteenth-century Russian literature — Gogolian characters with Kafkaesque shadows.

Kabakov said in a recent interview that the concept of nomadism is very important for him, yet that the central metaphor for his work is home. Defamiliarizing home and inhabiting the uninhabitable are the two main obsessions that drive his work. We will begin our tour of the Kabakovian home with its most private part — the toilet. Kabakov's installation *The Toilets* was presented in 1992 at the Kassel *Dokumenta* show. It is an exact replica of provincial Soviet toilets, the kind one encountered in bus and train stations. Kabakov describes them as "sad structures with walls of white lime turned dirty and

17.1   Ilya Kabakov, *The Toilets,* Kassel 1992. Photo courtesy of the artist.
17.2   Ilya Kabakov, Installation at *Dokumenta-IX,* Kassel 1992. Photo courtesy of the artist.

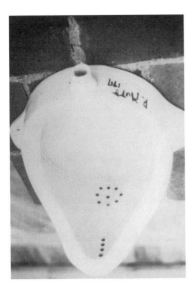

17.3   Ilya Kabakov,
The Toilets, Kassel
1992. Photo courtesy
of the artist.

shabby, covered by obscene graffities [*sic*] that one cannot look at without being overcome with nausea and despair."[9] The original toilets didn't have any stall doors: everyone could see everyone else "answering the call of nature" in what in Russian was called "the eagle position," perched over "the black hole." Toilets were communal, as were ordinary people's residences. Voyeurism became nearly obsolete. Rather one developed the opposite tendency, that of retention of sight; one was less tempted to eavesdrop and more to close one's eyes. Every toilet user accepted the conditions of total visibility. Women's and men's toilets looked alike.

The toilets were placed behind the main building of *Dokumenta,* just where outside toilets would normally be (fig. 17.1). The viewers have to stand in line to enter. Once there, they find themselves inside an ordinary Soviet two-room apartment inhabited by "some respectable and quiet people" (figs. 17.2, 17.3). Here, side by side with the "black hole," everyday life continues uninterrupted. There is a table with a table cloth, a glass cabinet, bookshelves, a sofa with a pillow, a reproduction of an anonymous Dutch painting, and children's toys. There is a sense of a captured presence: the dishes have not yet been cleared, a jacket has been dropped on a chair. Where are the apartment residents? They might have just stepped out for a moment to visit the *Dokumenta* exhibit.

Kabakov's exhibits are never entirely site-specific; rather, they are about displaced homes. And they never include the human figure; the visitor to the exhibit becomes the protagonist in Kabakov's narrative by inhabiting his empty interiors. In an interview, Kabakov revealed that the project has two points of origin: his childhood memories and the circumstances that brought the installation to life.

> The childhood memories date back to the time when I was accepted to the boarding school for art in Moscow and my mother decided to abandon her work [in Dniepropetrovsk] to be near me and to participate in my life at school. . . . She became a laundry cleaner at school. But without an apartment [for one needed special resident permits] the only place she had was the room where she arranged the laundry — table cloths, drapes, pillowcases — which was in the old toilets. . . . Of course, they were not dirty toilets, but typical toilets of the old boy school which were transformed into laundry boards. My mother was chased out by the schoolmistress and unable to rent even a small corner in the city. She once stayed there illegally for a night, in this tiny room practically in the toilets. Then she managed to find a folding bed and she stayed there for a while until a cleaning lady or a teacher informed on her to the director. My mother felt homeless and defenseless vis-à-vis the authorities, while, on the other hand, she was so tidy and meticulous that her honesty and persistence allowed her to survive in the most improbable place. My child psyche was traumatized by the fact that my mother and I never had a corner to ourselves.[10]

The tale of the project's conception is a tongue-in-cheek story of a poor Russian artist summoned to the sanctuary of the Western artistic establishment, the *Dokumenta* show, much to his embarrassment and humiliation:

> With my usual nervousness I had the impression that I had been invited to see the Queen who decides the fate of the arts. For the artist, this is a kind of Olympic Game. . . . The poor soul of a Russian impostor was in agony in front of these legitimate representatives of great contemporary art. . . . Finding myself in this terrifying state, on the verge of suicide, I distanced myself from those great men, approached the window and looked out. . . . "Mama, help" — I begged in silence. It was like during the war. . . . At last, my mother spoke to me from the other world and made me look through the window into the yard — and there I saw the toilettes. Immediately the whole conception of the project was in front of my eyes. I was saved.[11]

The two origins of the toilet project are linked — the mother's embarrassment is reenacted by her artist son, who feels like an impostor, an illegal alien in the home of the Western contemporary art establishment. The toilet becomes the artist's diasporic home, an island of Sovietness with its insuppressible nostalgic smell that persists even in the most sanitized Western museum. Yet the museum space is not completely alien for the artist; it is a space where he can defamiliarize his humiliating experience. Panic and embarrassment are redeemed through humor.

Another origin of Kabakov's toilet is to be found in the Western avant-garde tradition. There is a clear "toiletic intertextuality" between this project and Duchamp's *Fountain* (*La Fontaine*). Duchamp purchased a mass-produced porcelain urinal, placed it on a pedestal, signed it with the pseudonym "R. Mutt," and proposed to exhibit it at the American Society of Independent Artists.[12] The jury rejected the project by saying that while the urinal is a useful object, it is "by no definition, a work of art." In twentieth-century art history, this rejection is seen as the birth of conceptual art, an artistic revolution that took place in 1917 a few months before the Russian Revolution. Subsequently, the original "intimate" urinal splashed by the artist's signature vanished under mysterious circumstances. Only the artistic photograph by Alfred Stieglitz of the lost original survived, which added an aura of uniqueness to a radical avant-garde gesture. A contemporary wrote that the urinal looked "like anything from a Madonna to a Buddha." In 1964 Duchamp himself made an etching of Stieglitz's photograph and signed it with his own name. The permutations of the best-known toilet in art history perform a series of defamiliarizations both of the mass-reproduced everyday object and of the concept of the art itself and challenge the cult of the art. Yet, paradoxically, at the end of the twentieth century we are witnessing an aesthetic reappropriation of Duchamp's ready-mades. Duchamp's artistic cult imbued everything he touched with an artistic aura, securing him a unique place in the modern museum.

In comparison with Kabakov's toilet, Duchamp's urinal really does look like a fountain: it is very clean, "Western," and individualistic. Besides, scatological profanity itself became a kind of avant-garde convention — part of early twentieth-century culture — Bataille, Leiris, etc. Kabakov's installation is not merely about radical defamiliarization and recontextualization but also, more strikingly, about inhabiting the most uninhabitable space, in this case the toilet. Instead of Duchamp's clean, sculpturelike ready-made, we have an intimate environment that invites walking through, storytelling, and touching. The visitors are usually allowed to touch objects in Kabakov's installations. The artist's own artistic touch is visible throughout. Kabakov took great care in arranging the objects and things in the inhabited rooms next to the toilet—metonymical memory triggers of Soviet everyday life.

It is revealing, though, that there is no representation of a human figure in Kabakov's work. One is reminded of Walter Benjamin's description of his memory work in *Berlin Chronicle,* in which the writer speaks of remembering places of his childhood but not the faces of the people. Places appeared emptied, estranged, devoid of their inhabitants, but preserved the aura of their glances, traces of encounters, many archaeological levels of recollections. Kabakov offers a similar kind of topography of memory with the inhabited oases next to the toilet.

Kabakov tried to resist the interpretation of the project as a single symbol or metaphor, but that was beyond his control. The Russian press reviewed the installation very negatively; in spite of the political differences among his reviewers, all seemed to agree that the toilets were an insult to the Russian people and to Russian national pride. Many reviewers evoked a curious Russian proverb: "Do not take your trash out of your hut" (*Ne vynosi sor iz izby*), which means "don't criticize your own people in front of strangers and foreigners." The proverb dates back to an ancient peasant custom in which the trash was swept into a corner and buried inside instead of bringing it outside, the result of a common superstition that evil people could use one's trash to cast magic spells.[13] There is a peculiar superstition against metonymic memory, especially when exhibited in an ambiguous foreign context. Kabakov's evocative domestic trash of the Soviet era was regarded by the Russian reviewers as a profanation of Russia. Kabakov re-created his toilets with such meticulousness—working personally on every crack on the window, every splash of paint, every stain—that the inhabited toilet turned into an evocative memory theater, irreducible to univocal symbolism. But Russian critics expropriated the artist's toilets and reconstructed them as symbols of national shame. National mythology had no place for ironic nostalgia.

It is hard to imagine Duchamp's urinal being interpreted as an insult to French culture. On the other hand, the insults Kabakov received were part of being a "Soviet artist"—a role Kabakov chose for himself not without inner irony and nostalgic sadomasochism.

The largest of Kabakov's total installations was shown at the Centre Pompidou in Paris in the summer of 1995. In a way it was Kabakov's ironic homage to the never realized Palace of the Soviets. The installation, entitled *This Is*

How We Live, presents the Palace of the Future under construction. There is a grand *panneau* representing the city of the future's construction site in the center and barracks around it of different shapes and forms where workers and their families live. In the basement where the foundations of the unfinished Palace of the Future have been laid are several "public rooms" decorated by a single socialist realist painting representing labor, leisure, and the bright communist future, to the accompaniment of cheerful Soviet songs.

As we walk through the exhibit we begin to realize that the construction site has long been abandoned and that the scaffoldings are nothing but ruins and debris. The temporary workers' houses have become permanent; everyday life has taken root on the site of an unfinished utopia. When Benjamin visited Moscow in 1927, one of the few Russian words he learned was *remont* (repairs); the sign was everywhere. In Kabakov's exhibit, "repairs" becomes a key metaphor: the exhibit is a utopia under repair.

The exhibit used the actual basement of the Centre Pompidou, and the imported trash of the Palace of the Future coexisted peacefully with the trash of the Palace of Modern Art. The museum, for Kabakov, is at once a sanctuary and a dump for cultural trash. A visit to the exhibit is all about trespassing the boundaries between aesthetic and everyday life. You are never sure where the total installation begins and ends. You begin the visit to the exhibit by not being able to find it. Instead of a workers' barrack, you think you have mistakenly wandered into the Pompidou's storage area, where someone has collected funky 1950s furniture. It is paradoxical that these nostalgic oases of interrupted Soviet life are the only seemingly unguarded spaces in the museum. Here the museum officials actively encourage you to touch everything. Kabakov promotes tactile conceptualism, he plays hide-and-seek with aesthetic distance itself. You are invited to inhabit the workers' barracks, to relax on the plush sofa, and to touch the personal souvenirs, books, and popular artifacts. You find 1970s Soviet journals, a Russian translation of a Hungarian novel, and post-Soviet commercial magazines with foreign titles such as *Bizness Quarterly, French Family Photographs,* and *Mickey Mouse from Euro-Disney.* Kabakov has internationalized his domestic memorabilia; his souvenirs are no longer exclusively Soviet. The popular culture has become global, yet it still preserves its local colors.

The visitors to the exhibit accepted Kabakov's invitation to touch and to inhabit the mythical barracks of the builders of the Palace of the Future. Indeed, wandering through the exhibit you could always find a couple of exhausted tourists or immigrants reclining here and there. After all, the museum is still a relatively inexpensive urban refuge; it is cheaper than going to a café, and sometimes it is even free.

Kabakov remarks that of all utopian palaces under repair, the Centre Pompidou will probably survive the longest. His total installations reveal a nostalgia for utopia, but they return utopia back to its origins — not in life but in art. While dwelling on his own diasporic souvenirs from Soviet childhood, Kabakov goes to the origins of modern utopia and reveals two contradictory human impulses: to transcend the everyday in some kind of collective fairy tale, and to inhabit the most uninhabitable ruins, to survive and preserve memories. Post-Soviet nostalgia is not the same as nostalgia for the Soviet Union. Sovietness in this case is not merely a political reference, but rather a reference to the common culture of childhood and adolescence, to the common cultural text that is quickly forgotten in the current rewritings of Russian history.

Total installations are Kabakov's homes away from home; they help him dislocate and estrange the topography of his childhood fears and domesticate it again abroad. Lyotard suggests an interesting category: "domestication without domus," which I understand to be a way of inhabiting one's displaced habitats and avoiding the extremes of both the domus of traditional family values and the megapolis of cyberspace.[14] Although the works of some post-Soviet artists reveal the postmodern strategies of multiple narrative, hybridization, and pastiche, they do not engage in euphoric celebrations of nomadism and perpetual identity play. Kabakov's commemorations speak of the pain of estrangement, the embarrassment of memory, and the panic of oblivion. His installations are about the precociousness of the human habitat. In his essay "On Emptiness," written after his departure from Russia, Kabakov remarks in the Russian prophetic mode that at the end of the twentieth century, we all seem to live on tiny islands in the midst of uninhabitable and icy oceans of emptiness. "Of course, one can go visiting, drinking tea or dancing, moving from one tent to another, from the Soviet to the American and vice versa, but we must never forget the emptiness that surrounds us."[15]

Kabakov explores islands of Soviet everyday and ruins of utopia with humor and melancholy, never forgetting the emptiness and gaps surrounding them. Memory can perhaps be best studied through what Carlo Ginzburg called "conjectural science" — the science of hints and traces, of details and synecdoche that operates through associative networks rather than analytic arguments. In this view, everyday souvenirs and popular culture artifacts function as suggestive memory triggers. Kabakov's work is about the selectivity of memory. His fragmented "total installations" become a cautious reminder of gaps, compromises, embarrassments, and black holes in the foundation of any utopian and nostalgic edifice. Ambiguous nostalgic longing is linked to the individual experience of history. Through the combination of empathy and estrangement, ironic nostalgia invites us to reflect on the ethics of remembering.

Ilya Kabakov's museums of Soviet kitsch have been accepted into the Western artistic establishment. In 1997 he was invited to take part in the Whitney Biennial of American Art and in the project of public art in New York City. In my view, Kabakov's appeal in the West is not based on his exoticization of Soviet experience. Rather, the opposite is true. It is not the specific cultural or national home (*nostos*) that his art helps to re-create, but the experience of longing (*algia*), of loss and recovery, to which many international visitors can relate. Kabakov's art goes beyond its immediate cultural specificity and speaks about the complex and politically compromised work of memory and of the cultural recycling of nostalgia that is a part of the global experience of twentieth-century displacements.

Notes

1 Milan Kundera, *The Unbearable Lightness of Being,* trans. Michael Heim (New York: Harper and Row, 1984), p. 278.

2 Maurice Halbwachs, *On Collective Memory,* trans. and ed. Lewis Coser (Chicago: University of Chicago Press, 1992), p. 182.

3 Theodor Adorno, *Aesthetic Theory,* trans. G. Lenhardt (London: Routledge and Kegan Paul, 1984), p. 340.

4 One hope that this will also be a challenge for Western Slavists not to perpetuate the narrow conception of Russian national identity and to examine it in an international context. Kabakov's work is meant not for "émigré audiences," but for Russian and international museum goers alike.

5 For a more detailed discussion of nostalgia, see Jean Starobinsky, "On the Idea of Nostalgia," *Diogenes* 54 (1966): 81–103; David Lowenthal, *The Past Is a Foreign Country* (Cambridge: Cambridge University Press, 1985); and Svetlana Boym, "Nostalgia for the Common Place," in *Common Places: Mythologies of Everyday Life in Russia* (Cambridge: Harvard University Press, 1994).

6 Similarly, many films and popular songs feature émigrés who return. Thus the bruised émigré from the film *Russian Ragtime* summons all his strength, puts on his best clothes, and returns to the USSR of his nightmare. A popular song portrays a lonely Russian woman in Paris who has nobody to spend New Year's Eve with in the

busy West, and in her soul she remains a Muscovite: "*Ona khot' byvshaia, da poddanaia russkaia, ona takaia-zhe moskvichka kak byla*" (She is an ex- but still a Russian citizen, she is a Muscovite, just like she used to be), intones the singer.

7 The artists of the last Soviet unofficial and occasionally underground group, the Moscow conceptualists, became known in the 1970s through a series of apartment art exhibits (called *aptart*), samizdat editions, and events, some of which resulted in direct confrontations with the Soviet police and arrests. (One of their outdoor exhibits was destroyed by bulldozers.) Kabakov, however, never engaged in explicit antigovernment activities.

8 More recently, Kabakov has stopped calling himself a Soviet artist and instead refers to himself simply as an artist.

9 Ilya Kabakov, *Installations 1983–1995* (Paris: Centre Georges Pompidou, 1995), p. 165.

10 Ibid., pp. 162–63; translation mine.

11 Ibid., p. 163. Then Kabakov proceeds to argue with Dante Alighieri that it is not love that inspires art but fear and panic.

12 For an insightful discussion of Duchamp, see Dalia Judovitz, *Unpacking Duchamp: Art in Transit* (Berkeley: University of California Press, 1996), pp. 124–35.

13 Vladimir Dal', *Tolkovyi slovar' zhivogo velikorusskogo iazyka* (St. Petersburg, 1882), vol. 4, p. 275.

14 Jean-François Lyotard, "Domus and Megapolis," in *Inhuman* (Stanford: Stanford University Press, 1992). Andreas Huyssen claims that the current memory boom is not a result of further kitschefication of the past, but "a potentially healthy sign of contestation; a contestation of the informational hyperspace and an expression of the basic human need to live in extended structures of temporality, however they may be organized. In that dystopian vision of high-tech future, amnesia would no longer be part of the dialectics of memory and forgetting. It will be its radical other. It will have sealed itself: 'nothing to remember, nothing to forget' " (Andreas Huyssen, *Twilight Memory* [New York: Routledge, 1995], p. 35).

15 Ilya Kabakov, "On Emptiness," in *Between Spring and Summer: The Late Soviet Art* (Boston: ICA, 1990).

PARANOID GRAFFITI AT EXECUTION WALL: NATIONALIST INTERPRETATIONS OF RUSSIA'S TRAVAIL

The tanks that shelled the Russian White House on October 4, 1993, and the soldiers who fought their way into the building killed several hundred persons, resolved the political stalemate between Boris Yeltsin and his parliamentary opponents in favor of a Bonapartist presidency, and created potent symbols, myths, and martyrology for Russia's antisemitic ultranationalists. The violence broke out at the peak of the political war that Yeltsin and the parliament — seated in the White House — had been waging since early 1992. The war had four main fronts: the proper balance between legislative and executive authority; economic restructuring, which impoverished millions and seemed to threaten the survival of entire industries; the structure of the Russian state; and the fate of the Russian nation, a question as emotionally charged as it was amorphous. These issues intersected in ways that thwarted orderly government. Frustrated by the impasse, on September 21 Yeltsin disbanded parlia-

397

ment; parliament in turn deposed Yeltsin and declared Vice President Aleksandr Rutskoi (by now a bitter enemy of Yeltsin) acting president. Neither side
sought a compromise. When on October 3 armed ultranationalists emerged
from the White House, seized the Moscow mayor's office, and attempted to
shoot their way into the central television studio at Ostankino, the wavering
Russian high command agreed to obey Yeltsin's order to respond in force.[1]

Extreme nationalists were at the center of the political conflict almost by
default. Yeltsin had banned the Communist Party of the Soviet Union in November 1991, and Communist party officials were able to reconstitute themselves as the Communist Party of the Russian Federation only in February
1993. In the meantime, scores of tiny groups on the extreme right and extreme
left had formed a constantly shifting coalition of what came to be known as
"red-browns," who in the absence of a more respectable alternative provided
the vehicle through which Russians could express their antagonism to Yeltsin
and what he seemed to be doing to Russia. Many of these groups came together
as the National Salvation Front (Front Narodnogo spaseniia) in October 1992.
The extreme nationalists and the extreme left (the left combined nationalist
with communist rhetoric) set the tone for the opposition both in parliament and
on the street.

Nationalist rhetoric projected a paranoid view of a mortal threat to Russia.
Red-browns accused Yeltsin and his government of having committed treason
by dissolving the Soviet Union and leaving Russia with a humiliatingly diminished status in the world; selling Russia out to the West; visiting economic
hardship, criminality, and corruption on the Russian people; and destroying
Russian civilization. They blamed Yeltsin for everything that had turned Russia
upside down and disoriented millions of Russians in the past few years. The
reds and browns differed on what Russia should be — how much of the Soviet
past should be restored, for instance — but they had common enemies: the West,
Jews, and "the democrats" who had dismantled the Soviet Union. All red-
browns believed those enemies had by devious means seized power in order to
destroy Russia.[2]

After Yeltsin and the parliament had anathematized and deposed each other,
the red-browns, with the connivance of Acting President Rutskoi and the head
of parliament, Ruslan Khasbulatov hijacked the insurgency and took over the
White House. Self-styled Cossacks fresh from the fighting between Russians
and Moldavians in the newly independent republic of Moldova, the renegade
Russian general Albert Makashov, Aleksandr Terekhov's Union of Officers,

armed volunteers from Aleksandr Barkashov's swastika-sporting Russian National Unity, and assorted other groups became the parliament's self-proclaimed security force. Eager to turn their weapons on the Yeltsin government, these men initiated the fighting, and some of them died when the army responded to the provocation.

No sooner had the insurrection failed than the nationalists began to memorialize their dead. Between October 1993 and March 1995 they covered several hundred yards of a wall near the White House with graffiti celebrating their cause and their martyrs.[3] The wall enclosed a small stadium on the rise behind the White House, and the graffiti — much of it in bold lettering up to three feet high — were the dominant element of a memorial that nationalists created to honor those killed during and, they insisted, after the fighting. Nationalists also displayed pictures of the dead and pasted up dozens of pages of typed and hand-lettered verse. They erected crosses and simulacra of grave plots in the field in front of the stadium gates, and another cross across the street honoring an Orthodox priest said to have died in the White House. They left flowers at these shrines and at the foot of the wall. The graffiti explained their own purpose: "Eternal glory to the heroes!" (*Vechnaia slava geroiam!*); "To those who have fallen for Russia eternal glory" (*Pavshim za rossiiu vechnaia slava!*); "Sleep beloved brethren" (*Spite liubimye brat'ia*).

Remembrance, in the nationalists' view, should promote a thirst for retribution. One graffito used an entire seven-by-fourteen-foot section of wall to link the two:

REVENGE WILL BE OURS!!!
WE WILL REMEMBER EVERY NAME
WE WILL REMEMBER EVERY ONE
THIS IS NOT FOR THE DEAD
BUT FOR THE LIVING!!!

MY OTOMSTIM!!!
VSPOMNIM VSEKH PO IMENAM
VSPOMNIM VSE KAK ODIN
ETO NADO NE MERTVYM
ETO NUZHNO ZHIVYM!!!

Or in the words of "A Russian Mother," the most prolific of the nationalist versifiers:

OH, MY RUSSIAN PEOPLE!
WHERE CAN I FIND EXECRATIONS ENOUGH
TO HURL AT GORBACHEV AND YELTSIN?!
OR TO MAKE OF THEM A BOUQUET
TO FLAY THIS TURNCOAT DUET?!
JUDAS ISCARIOT
HAD NOTHING ON THEM.
THERE HAS NEVER BEEN TREASON MORE FOUL
THAN THAT OF THIS EVIL DUET!
— A RUSSIAN MOTHER

O, RUSSKII MOI NAROD!
GDE MNE PROKLIATII STOL'KO VZIAT',
CHTOB V GORBACHEVA S EL'TSINYM BROSAT'?!
ILI SOSTAVIT' IZ PROKLIATII TEKH BUKET
I OTKHLESTAT' PRODAZHNYI SEI DUET?!
IUDA BYL ISKARIOT,
V PODMETKU NE GODITSIA ETIM TOT.
PREDATEL'STVA GRIAZNEE V MIRE NET.
CHTO DAL NAM ETOT ZLOI DUET!
— RUSSKAIA MAT'

The wall itself was central to nationalist lore. A small graffito still faintly visible on one of the fence posts in August 1996 explained its significance and dated its demolition: "Execution wall torn down in March 1995 by order of Mayor Luzhkov" (*Rasstrel'naia stena snesena v marte 1995 goda po prikazu mera Luzhkova*). According to the myth to which a number of the graffiti were devoted, after the defenders of the White House surrendered, they were stood up against the wall and shot. Some of the graffiti named individual victims and marked the very spots where they had purportedly been executed. A graffito on the footing in 1995 claimed, for instance: "This is where Verevkin, Roman, age 17, was shot" (*Zdes' byl rasstrelian Verevkin Roman 17 let*). Even those who firmly believed in the mass executions probably did not really think they could know, as the graffito claimed, precisely where Roman Verevkin had been shot, because no one had seen any piles of bodies in the aftermath. Some graffiti were devoted to that mystery, and to the widespread nationalist conviction that the government had spirited away hundreds, even thousands, of corpses: "Yeltsin, what did you do with the corpses?" (*El'tsin, kuda del trupy?*) That the dead had numbered in the thousands — "2743 people died 3–4 October 1993" (*3–4 Oktiabria 1993 goda pogiblo 2743 chelovek*) (alongside this, "11,000 people" [*11000 Chelovek*]) — was, and still is, an article of faith among the nationalists. The wall and the ground around it had been consecrated by the blood of heroes and had become the site of genuine devotions by believers.

Nationalists lost the battle, and with it their political war against the Yeltsin government, but they won at least a temporary victory in memorialization. The pathos of martyrdom gave the October losers — who had indeed suffered almost all of the casualties — a self-confident grasp on the moral high ground that the Yeltsin government could not easily loosen. Nor was there even a hint of sentiment to offer a competing memorial to the victors' dead; after October 1993, Muscovites who might have contested the paranoid nationalist point of view felt profound distress and shame. Although the nationalist memorial was an incitement immediately proximate to the very symbol of Yeltsin's authority, city officials moved against it with great circumspection. They painted over the graffiti at least once, with predictable lack of effect. In March 1995, they tore down most of the wall and installed a metal-rail fence in its place. That eliminated the bulk of the surface available for graffiti, but some still appeared on the cement posts and footing, and even on the sides of the metal rails (so that they could be read when viewed from an acute angle). The crosses and memorial grave sites were not touched even then — as though the authorities acknowledged that to do so would amount to profanation — nor was any attempt made to remove the accumulation of nationalist flags and banners that hung from the trees around the shrine.

Memorials do far more than pay tribute to the dead; they also interpret, and this one was no exception: the graffiti offered a mythology through which the nationalists sought to understand their defeat. Some graffiti named heroes and villains. On one side stood the leaders of the insurrection: "Anpilov Hero Makashov Terekhov Barkashov" (*Anpilov Geroi Makashov Terekhov Barkashov*); and "Rutskoi, Konstantinov — Russia's heroes" (*Rutskoi, Konstantinov — geroi rossii*).[4] On the other side, Yeltsin came in for particular abuse: "The bandits Yeltsin and the government are thieves who steal from the Russian and the entire honest people!" (*Bandity El'tsin i pravitel'stvo vory u russkogo i vsego chestnogo naroda!*); "Yeltsin, this is war! Yeltsin is a shit!" (*El'tsin eto voina! El'tsin — svoloch'!*). A picture of a spider was captioned "Yeltsin spider-bane" (*Pauk gore-El'tsin*) (fig. 18.1). A twenty-foot-long composition read "Yeltsin — crematorium filth" (*El'tsin — pasukuda krematorii*),

with an arrow pointing from "crematorium" to a drawing of a naked Yeltsin
with pig hindquarters trotting off, presumably, to the crematorium. Compared
with that rage, "Yeltsin is an alcoholic" (*El'tsin alkogolik*) seemed an objective
statement of fact. Two graffiti singled out then Defense Minister Pavel Grachev
for vilification, "Grachev Pasha — murderer!" (*Grachev Pasha — ubiitsa!*), and
ridicule, "Grachev is a crow in peacock feathers, a crow will never be an eagle"
(*Grachev — vorona v pavlinykh per'iakh vorone sokolom ne byvat'*) (the graffito plays on the fact that in Russian *grach* is a bird, a rook). Other graffiti (like
"A Russian Mother's" broadsides) presented October 1993 as the culmination
of a process of national destruction that had begun with Gorbachev. One (partially obliterated in August 1994) bid "Architect of perestroika — to the gal-
lows!" (*Arkhitektor perestroiki — estafeta!*). Another had a far broader target:
"Democrats are the servants of Satan" (*Demokraty slugy Satany*). And, to give
the spawn of hell a proper name: "Gaidar is a dwarf from a horror tale"
(*Gaidar — karlik iz strashnoi skazki*). Egor Gaidar had not only been the widely
detested architect of Yeltsin's economic policy and acting prime minister in
1992, he had been brought back into the government as first deputy prime
minister in September 1993.

18.1   Graffiti at execution wall. "Yeltsin — Crematorium Filth." Photo by John
Bushnell.

The invocation of Satan and gothic horror tales, and the depiction of Yeltsin as a cloven-hoofed monster on the way to a crematorium, were central to the nationalists' view of politics and history. As the graffiti told the story, the Russian people had been martyred and their land dismembered. Jews were the principal agents of the Devil, but the United States played a supporting role. Yet Russia — or the Soviet Union, conflated with Russia — would eventually rise because the Russian folk were heroic.

Like paranoid antisemites everywhere, Russian ultranationalists identified all of their enemies as Jews, whose machinations were easy to discern. Thus the Russian government was actually a Jewish government: "Death to the governing murderous Jews" (*Smert' pravitel'stvennym krovavym zhidam*). Half of the graffiti denouncing Yeltsin spelled his name with a hard *E* (*e-obratnoe*) rather than the proper soft *E,* because the hard *E* was supposed to indicate that Yeltsin was in fact a Jew with a slightly Russified name, a charge (or so it was taken to be) going back to the Gorbachev years. Newspaper photographs of both Gaidar and Grigorii Iavlinskii (another liberal economist turned politician, but not a member of the government) were defaced with six-pointed stars and the number of the beast, "666." Iavlinskii had had nothing to do with the events of October 1993, but because he was a Democrat and because one of his parents was Jewish, he was necessarily part of the conspiracy of presumptively Jewish reformers that had brought Russia to ruin. Another graffito labeled the OMON, Moscow's tactical police units that had been deployed against the insurgents in the White House, "OMON-kikes": "Omon-kikes, await the reckoning. We will wreak vengeance on the executioners of the Russian people" (*Zhidomon zhdite rasplaty. My otomstim palacham russkogo naroda*). "OMON-kike" (*zhidomon*) was a play on the bête-noire of Russia's antisemites, the "Mason-kike" (*zhidomason*). Russian government television — which the nationalists, convinced that the people would rally to their side if only they knew the truth, tried to seize by force during the insurrection — was of course in Jewish hands: "Ostankino is the synagogue of the accursed murderous Talmudites" (*Ostankino — sinagoga prokliatym krovavym talmudistam*).

These commonplace antisemitic myths were supplemented by a myth specific to the October insurrection: that among the troops who stormed the White House had been an Israeli-trained Jewish strike force, the Betar. The defenders of the White House terrified each other with tales of Betar ferocity, and in the aftermath the right-wing press even specified the location of Betar training camps: Stupino and Odintsovo, outside Moscow.[5] That the Betar had once been a real Zionist youth organization, first in Eastern Europe and then in Palestine, with self-defense units trained in some military skills, illustrates how paranoid antisemites incorporate bits and pieces of reality into their nightmares. The legend of the Betar was as firmly implanted in nationalist folklore as the legend of execution wall, and it found a place on the wall: "Death to the Betar murderers!" (*Smert' Beitaram-ubiitsam!*); "Betar—to the wall" (*Beitar—k rasstrelu*) (the latter graffito also incorporated "Jericho" [*Ierikhon*], connected to "to the wall" by a line); "Betar—the national guard of the bandit Yeltsin" (*Beitar—natsional'naia gvardiia bandita el'tsina*). "Jericho" was, presumably, another Jewish military group of the nationalists' imagining.

Other antisemitic graffiti touched on a range of familiar motifs. "The Jews will answer" (*Otvetiat Iudy*) placed the blame for Russia's misery squarely on Jews. "Beat the kikes" (*Bei zhidov*) evoked Russian tradition; "Tear down the synagogues — the headquarters of kike fascism" (*Snesti sinagogi — shtab zhidofashizma*) the more modern Russian equation of Zionists with Nazis. That identification was also portrayed symbolically, as a swastika inscribed within a Star of David. One graffito borrowed a German theme: "Jews are not a nation, they are a criminal organization" (*Evrei ne natsii eto prestupnaia organizatsiia*).

The United States occupied an instructive second rung in nationalist demonology: "USA—enemy of Russia" (*SShA vrag Rossii*); "Yankee-America out of Russia" (*Ianki-Amerika von iz Rossii*) (fig. 18.2). One graffito accused Viktor Erin, then minister of the interior (and thus commander of the hated OMON), of doing America's bidding: "Erin—lackey of America!" (*Erin kholui Ameriki!*) Another, on the wall of the American embassy compound across from the stadium, seemed to be an outlying part of the memorial collection: "We shall overcome" (this written in English). The contrast between the anti-American and anti-Semitic graffiti indicates whom the nationalists considered their most dangerous enemies. Comparative numbers are less telling than the emotional charge. The nationalists genuinely believed that the United States was an enemy, but their anti-Semitic graffiti revealed both visceral hatred and genuine, if unacknowledged, fear.

It was easier for the nationalists to name their enemy than the country or the people whom Jews were threatening: was it Russia, or was it the Soviet Union? The majority of graffiti identified with Russia, either explicitly or implicitly. Others made a point of hailing the USSR: "Our motherland is the USSR" (*Nasha rodina SSSR*); "Death to the tyrant, the USSR lives" (*Smert' tiranu SSSR zhiv*). Some graffiti consisted only of the Soviet hammer-and-sickle emblem, with or without an accompanying "USSR." The nationalists were not

18.2   Graffiti at execution wall. "Rutskoi, Konstantinov — Russia's Heroes," "NSF [National Salvation Front] Lives," "USA — the Enemy of Russia." Photo by John Bushnell.

necessarily divided between partisans of Russia, on the one hand, and of the Soviet Union, on the other; it was easy enough to conflate the two. Yet, it seems likely that those who singled out the Soviet Union wanted to correct what they thought was an overemphasis on Russia alone.

Whether or not nationalists consciously juxtaposed Russia with the USSR, the graffiti did reveal divergent political attitudes within the red-brown coalition of communist fundamentalists and antisemitic nationalists. Neither the hammer-and-sickle graffiti nor a very large "Communism" (*Kommunizm*) fit comfortably alongside "Orthodoxy will save Russia" (*Pravoslavie spaset Rossiiu*) or "Raise the eight-pointed star of the Virgin on the Kremlin towers" (*Vosmikonechnuiu zvezdu bogoroditsy na bashni Kremlia*). Pro-Soviet graffiti at the very least implied a multiethnic state, but others called for ethnic purity: "Russia for whites" (*Rossia dlia belykh*) was probably directed against interlopers from the Caucasus, and "A Russian government for Russians!" (*Russkim — Russkoe pravitel'stvo!*) may have been directed against Jews, but more likely against all of Russia's many ethnic minorities, who in the nationalist view were constantly showing up in high office.

One anomalous and, on its face, self-contradictory graffito sought to find a place for non-Russians within a nationalist Russia: "Russia for Russians! And for the native peoples of Rus" (*Rossiia dlia Russkikh! I korenykh narodov Rusi*). Rus was the tenth- to thirteenth-century east Slavic polity centered on Kiev to which Russians trace their nation and their state, and which when applied to contemporary Russia conjures up the nation's primordial roots, distinctive culture, and legendary heroes. The explicitly multiethnic "Rus" of this graffito combined an historically evocative assertion of Russians' unique possession of Russia while also legitimating the presence of at least some non-Russians (but certainly not Jews or Georgians). Linking Russia to Rus also permitted a claim (although this graffito did not make one) to Russian reabsorption of their fellow east Slavs, the Ukrainians and Byelorussians.

The Rus graffito was anomalous in its openness to multiethnicity, but the evocation of the heroic legends and myths associated with Rus aligned the graffito with others that employed semifolkloric or pseudofolkloric motifs in their anticipation of Russia's redemption. Just as nationalists drew on the folklore of antisemitism to explain the disaster that had overtaken Russia/ USSR, they drew on folkloric clichés to depict Russia's rebirth. Of course, many vows of revenge employed the most hackneyed clichés: "We will revenge our brothers" (*Otomstim za nashikh brat'ev*); "Blood for blood, death for death" (*Krov' za krov' smert' za smert'*). Sometimes cliché descended into bathos: "Better to fall in battle than live in a yoke" (*Luchshe past' v boiakh chem zhit' v iarme*). One graffito made a nationalist pun: "We beat the fascists, we'll beat the Ebenists" (*Pobedili my fashistov pobedim my Ebenistov*). This is a play on a Russian naming formality: the last name goes first, the first and middle name next (as in the "Verevkin, Roman" graffito above). Ultranationalist newspapers had taken to shortening "Yeltsin, Boris Nikolaevich," to EBN, which suggests the past passive participle of "to fuck," *eben*. The "Ebenists" of the graffito were the government of "the fucked." However, it was the graffiti that took a folkloric view of revenge and redemption that had the greatest resonance. "Rise Russia, shake off your sloth" (*Vstan' Rossia len' vstriakhni*); "Sleep beloved brothers, [soon] our native land will besiege [with an invincible host] the Kremlin walls" (*Spite liubimye brat'ia [skoro] rodnaia strana [nepobedimye rati] dvinet pod steny Kremlia*) (the words in brackets were a later interpolation). One graffito that specified that the object of redemption was the Soviet Union also drew on the image of the awakening people:

I SEE MY MOTHERLAND RISING FROM ITS KNEES,

I SEE MY MOTHERLAND RISING FROM THE ASHES,

I SEE MY SOVIET MOTHERLAND SINGING!

MY MIGHTY PEOPLE IS STRAIGHTENING ITS BACK!!

VIZHU, PODNIMAETSIA S KOLEN MOIA RODINA,

VIZHU, KAK IZ PEPLA VOSSTAET MOIA RODINA,

VIZHU, KAK POET MOIA SOVETSKAIA RODINA!

RAZGIBAET SPINU MOI MOGUCHII NAROD!!

That graffiti such as these were located, on the execution wall, right next to other graffiti presenting the Russian people as the victim of Jewish wiles recalls one of the oldest of nationalist clichés. The innocent people, deceived and victimized by the sophisticated foreigner or Jew, is at the same time unerringly virtuous, collectively heroic, and ultimately triumphant.

As a text, the graffiti at execution wall revealed a great deal about nationalist mythology, but they were more than a text. Any large assemblage of graffiti is an evolving artifact of collective activity. So long as they lasted, the graffiti at the stadium were a work in progress, and the work of many hands. Every contribution invited others: the text recruited its own authors and (remembering the photographs of those killed in the fighting at the White House) illustrators. In 1994, when the weather was fair, right wingers — mostly middle-aged and elderly — gathered at the memorial to socialize, to read the latest graffiti, perhaps to add their own. The graffiti-centered memorial invited participation.

Because execution wall was a site of nationalist sociability, it was a convenient place to post right-wing announcements, some in the form of large graffiti. "April 3 — day of remembrance" (*3 Aprelia — den' pominoveniia*) marked the Orthodox half-year (after October 3) day of remembrance for the dead. "22 June at 6 P.M. at VDNKh" (*22 Iiunia v 18 chasov u VDNKh*) announced a right-wing meeting. "NSF lives!" (*FNS zhiv!*) promised that the National Salvation Front had survived the October defeat. Another group of right-wing militants solicited volunteers: "Registration for the Patriotic Russian Army — 113534, Moscow, P.O. Box 37" (*Zapis' v Patrioticheskuiu Russkuiu Armiiu — 113534, Moskva, A/Ia 37*).

The most elaborate of the extramemorial graffiti amounted to a political program:

THE ELECTION LAW SHOULD INCLUDE

I   THE CANDIDATE MUST SIGN HIS PROGRAM

2   CRIMINAL LIABILITY FOR NONFULFILLMENT

3   ELECTION AT THE WORKPLACE

4   DECISIONS TAKEN ONLY WITH THE KNOWLEDGE AND AGREEMENT
    OF ELECTORS

5   PAYMENT OF SALARY AT THE PLACE OF ELECTION IN ACCORDANCE
    WITH THE EVALUATION OF THOSE WHO ELECTED THE DEPUTY

VVESTI V ZAKON O VYBORAKH

I   PODPISKU KANDIDATA POD DEPUTATSKOI PROGRAMMOI

2   UGOLOVNUIU OTVETSTVENNOST' ZA EE NEVYPOLNENIE

3   VYBORY OT TRUDOVYKH KOLLEKTIVOV

4   PRINIATIE RESHENII S VEDOMA I TOL'KO PO SOGLASOVANIIU S
    IZBIRATELIAMI

5   VYPLATY ZARPLATY PO MESTU IZBRANIA V ZAVISIMOSTI OT OT-
    SENKI IZBRAVSHIKH DEPUTATA

These rules about the mechanics of electoral representation — deputies must stand by their campaign promises or suffer criminal and financial penalties — rested on political assumptions consonant with the execution wall's mythology. The demand that representatives be elected at the workplace recalled a fight over the principles of representation that had broken out when Gorbachev introduced the Congress of People's Deputies. The natural social and therefore electoral unit, orthodox Communists had then argued, is the workforce rather than the quite accidental grouping of people by residence. But that was not enough for the ultranationalists writing at the wall: even deputies rooted in the natural community of the workplace were likely to betray their constituents; only the threat of sanctions would hold them to their word, and only decisions taken in direct consultation with the voters could be trusted. The slightest distance between the people and their designated representatives left an opening for betrayal. In the paranoid nationalist understanding of politics, the people were innately good, but the very men and women they had in their wisdom elected had deceived them and destroyed Russia, and might do so again. Only the closest possible approximation of representative to direct democracy could obviate that danger.

Execution wall was notably free of dissenting opinions. A few crude swastikas that were not elements in graffiti defaming Yeltsin and Jews might have been meant as accusations, but probably were not; some of Russia's most extreme nationalists appropriated the swastika for themselves. There was only a handful of graffiti that had nothing at all to do with politics. One person drew a small hemp leaf with the caption "Only hamp save the world long life the cannabis" (in fractured English in the original). Another graffito, no doubt inscribed at the height of the MMM pyramid scandal, abused MMM's chairman, Sergei Mavrodi: "Mavrodi's a pedophile" (*Mavrodi — pidar*).[6] A fan of the Spartak football club drew a small Spartak emblem. The vast, invitingly white expanse of wall had surely attracted more nonnationalist graffiti than that before the nationalists took it over.

Thus the entire text, the corpus of hundreds of large and small graffiti, was remarkably homogeneous. The fortissimo of virulent antisemitism overwhelmed the very few extraneous notes. The nationalists did not sing in unison, but their graffiti only hinted at the divergent strands within the alliance of racist nationalists and fundamentalist Communists. Antisemitism provided a common idiom and unifying myths: Boris Yeltsin was the leader of a Jewish, even satanic, conspiracy to destroy either Russia writ small or Russia writ large as the Soviet Union; the Russian or Soviet people would rise as one and converge on the Kremlin to reclaim their patrimony; but if the people were innately virtuous, they were also easily deceived.

Antisemitic nationalists produced the graffiti at execution wall in response to the traumatic battle at the White House, and they expressed a distinctive ideology. At the same time, these nationalist graffiti conformed to an established tradition of public graffiti, an evolving genre whose rules governed the structure rather than the content of the public text. The genre had been pioneered in Moscow by gangs of soccer hooligans in the late 1970s, then taken up by a succession of groups. Devotees of heavy metal music, punks, and the hippie counterculture all produced graffiti that identified a particular place with a particular group. Except in the case of the soccer hooligans, the graffiti were not ordinarily defaced by other groups; the texts they collectively produced remained as univocal as the nationalist text at execution wall. A subgenre, memorial graffiti, was inaugurated in 1983, when readers of Mikhail Bulgakov's *The Master and Margarita* covered the walls of an entire five-floor entranceway with graffiti dedicated to Bulgakov and his novel. Although the Bulgakov stairwell became well known, a wall of graffiti memorializing Viktor Tsoi — a rock star who died in a motorcycle accident in the summer of 1990 — was far more public because it was on the Arbat pedestrian mall in the center of

Moscow. The Tsoi wall was followed by the Tal'kov wall, apparently the first public memorial that struck a mildly nationalist note. Igor' Tal'kov, a very popular rock poet with a strongly patriotic (he sang of Rus) and religious message, and a somewhat antidemocratic one as well, was murdered by his Jewish manager during a concert in October 1991 and became a nationalist martyr posthumously.[7] Execution wall was just one more in a series of devotional walls and stairwells.

Subcultural associations were a fundamental component of these collective graffiti texts. The graffiti marked gathering places (*tusovki*, initially counterculture argot that later migrated into mainstream slang) for particular subcultural groups, and the language and referents often rendered the graffiti incomprehensible to outsiders. The texts were interactive — just as at execution wall, author and audience were one — and evolved within a very narrow thematic range. When the graffiti were covered over with fresh paint (as in the Bulgakov stairwell and at execution wall), devotees immediately created a new text. At walls honoring the dead — as at the Tsoi wall, the Tal'kov wall, and execution wall — a handful of mourners stood vigil. The graffiti-marked nationalist *tusovka* at execution wall was, as a form of public and devotional activity, scarcely distinguishable from the Bulgakov, Tsoi, and Tal'kov walls (or from the Grebenshchikov stairwell, or even the Rotunda counterculture site in St. Petersburg).

Execution wall seemed less threatening viewed within the context of counterculture graffiti production than when it was read only as a political statement. Viciously antisemitic graffiti were not widespread in Moscow in 1993–95 or later; they were concentrated at this one site. Concentration magnified their local impact, but even at execution wall both the nationalists and others of more balanced mind treated the graffiti as the private affair of a particular group. This place just happened to be the nationalists' *tusovka*. The graffiti were both a public political memorial and the private property of the nationalists who gathered at the wall. Passersby took little note of either (just as they passed by Tsoi's mourners or hippies congregating outside a coffeehouse *tusovka*), while the nationalists themselves showed no inclination to make their graffiti more public, for instance by inscribing them on city walls at large.

This ultranationalist graffiti lasted for only a year and a half — until March 1995 — but there was an attempt to maintain them even after Mayor Luzhkov had execution wall torn down. In August 1995, two dozen weathered photographs of the original graffiti were on display at the newspaper bulletin board at the edge of the field, and a metal plaque — with an outline of the burning White House, smoke rising, surrounded by the inscription "Memorial Territory" (*Memorial'naia Territoriia*) — had been fixed to the top of the frame. By August 1996 the photographs had disappeared, but the stand was still being used as a bulletin board for right-wing newspaper articles; "A Russian Mother" was still posting her civic verse, and there were still flowers, banners, and symbolic grave plots. Nevertheless, as the graffiti disappeared and then largely faded from memory, the wall ceased to be the nationalists' *tusovka:* by August 1996 they no longer gathered there to gossip and exchange their lore. Without the graffiti, the former site of execution wall was just another memorial, no longer inviting participation or providing an arena for antisemitic sociability.

Nevertheless, in 1997 the red-browns added to the memorial installations: they extended the bulletin board of shame on which they mounted pictures of and articles about their enemies; they set up a separate display devoted to the battle at the White House; they hung a huge banner with photographs of their martyrs; and they constructed new grave plots, a mock barricade, and an execution block with wooden ax surmounted by the sign "Judas." In place of the large graffiti — absent for two years — they hung placards on the fence. The slogans were, in part, reminiscent of the graffiti: "Rus: Don't cower!" (*Rus': Ne trus'!*); "Army: Awake!" (*Armiia: Prosnis'!*); "No to Decree no. 1400! All power to the Soviets!" (*Net Ukazu n 1400! Vsia vlast' Sovetam!*) (Yeltsin disbanded parliament with Decree no. 1400); "Glory to the heroes of the uprising of September–October 1993!" (*Slava geroiam vosstaniia sentiabria–oktiabria 1993 goda!*); "There is the Lord's judgment and there will be the people's Judgment" (*Est' Bozhii sud i budet sud naroda!*); "The criminals will answer" (*Prestupniki k otvetu!*); and others of like sentiment.

Yet these slogans were very different from the original graffiti, if only because they displayed no trace of overt antisemitism. Antisemitic graffiti could still be found, but only through close examination of the photomontage of the nationalists' enemies; antisemitic scribblings in the spirit of 1993–95 defaced many of the photographs. On the walls of the apartment building across the street there was one large painted graffito — "He who has not submitted has not been vanquished" (*Kto ne smirilsia — tot ne pobezhden*) — as well as a few more modest but also more impassioned graffiti: "Yeltsin = Executioner = Crook" (*El'tsin = Palach = Vor*); "They executed we will answer" (*Rasstreliali otvetim*); and (on an old Iavlinskii election poster) "Beat the Kikeocrats" (*Bei zhidokratov*).

These graffiti were proof that the memorial site still attracted antisemites, but also that they had been pushed to the margins. Virulent antisemitism seemed to have been edited out of the placard slogans, as though in a determined effort to make the memorial more respectable. But the cost of respectability was the loss of popular participation. The spontaneous expression of ultranationalist passion was either reduced to penciled slurs on photographs or had retreated across the street, outside the memorial territory. The apartment building itself was no ultranationalist *tusovka:* nationalist graffiti were too few, and they were contested. Right next to the denunciation of Yeltsin was a response, "Communists are pricks" (*Kommunisty mudaki*).

Notes

1 For a concise treatment of the political background and the events leading up to the attack on the White House, see Michael Urban, Vyacheslav Igrunov, and Sergei Mitrokhin, *The Rebirth of Politics in Russia* (Cambridge: Cambridge University Press, 1997), pp. 257–90; for a somewhat more extensive review: Jonathan Steele, *Eternal Russia, Yeltsin, Gorbachev and the Mirage of Democracy* (Cambridge: Harvard University Press, 1994), pp. 267–382. I am skeptical about the view, shared by Urban and Steele, that the Yeltsin government lured the armed parliamentary militants into taking the offensive and thus justified armed repression. While Yeltsin may have wanted an excuse to drive his enemies from the White House, the scenarios of provocation that Urban and Steele sketch seem to me to require too many conspirators, key generals to have been ignorant of the devious plan, and exceptionally coherent reactions to chaotic circumstances on October 3. The journalist Veronika Kutsyllo's *Zapiski iz Belogo Doma. 21 sentiabria–4 oktiabria* (Moscow: Kommersant, 1993) provides the best account of events inside the White House itself.

2 For an interesting, and somewhat different, interpretation of Russian political rhetoric in the early post-Soviet years, see Michael Urban, "The Politics of Identity in Russia's Postcommunist Transition: The Nation against Itself," *Slavic Review* 53, no. 3 (fall 1994): 733–65.

3 Descriptions of the wall and activities around it are based largely on my own observations in August 1994, August 1995, August 1996, and January 1998. There is a brief reference to the wall and the people gathering there in Marina Medvedeva-Khazanova, *Rossiiskie radosti i nevzgody* (St. Petersburg: Astra-Liuks, 1996), p. 24.

4 Viktor Anpilov was the leader of the radical leftist Laboring Russia (Trudovaia Rossiia), which had sparked violent street demonstrations in 1992 and 1993 and contributed combatants to the White House; Il'ia Konstantinov was one of the leaders of an alliance of small ultranationalist parties, Russian Unity (Rossiiskoe edinstvo).

5 See Kutsyllo, *Zapiski iz Belogo Doma,* pp. 136, 150; and the pseudonymous Ivan Ivanov, "Anafema. Zapiski Razvedchika," *Zavtra,* Spetsvypusk no. 2 (August 1994).

6 On Mavrodi and MMM, see Eliot Borenstein, "Public Offerings: MMM and the Marketing of Melodrama," in this volume.

7 On the history of graffiti and graffiti sites through 1988, see John Bushnell, *Moscow
   Graffiti. Language and Subculture* (Boston: Unwin and Hyman, 1990). On the Tsoi
   wall, see John Bushnell, "Organizing a Counter-culture with Graffiti: The Tsoi Wall
   and Its Antecedents," in *Communicating Design. Essays in Visual Communication,*
   ed. Teal Triggs (London: Batsford, 1995), pp. 55–59. The Tal'kov wall is at the rear of
   the columbarium at the Vagan'kov cemetery, right next to Tal'kov's grave; see the
   picture in *Stolitsa,* no. 11 (1995), p. 42. For a sampling of Tal'kov's verse, see
   T. Tal'kova, G. Levkodimov, and N. Shantarenkov, comps., *Pesni, stikhi, proza,
   publitsistika, interv'iu Igoria Tal'kova, otkliki na gibel' russkogo poeta-patriota*
   (Moscow: Molodaia gvardiia, 1993); a small museum devoted to Tal'kov on Cher-
   nigovskii Pereulok presents the singer as a sainted martyr and has a large collection of
   nationalist press commentary on the murder.

   One major change in these graffiti sites is in language. Until the late 1980s, public
   graffiti incorporated English words and symbols with English referents as part of a
   distinctive (and to most Russians, incomprehensible) argot; that is still true of the
   graffiti produced by football hooligans and other youth groups. However, the memorial walls from the beginning were produced mostly in Russian, but since the Tsoi
   wall (1990) English has been largely absent from assemblages of memorial graffiti.

"CHRISTIANITY, ANTISEMITISM, NATIONALISM": RUSSIAN ORTHODOXY IN A REBORN ORTHODOX RUSSIA

The Russian Orthodox Church today finds itself in an enviable position. With the passage of legislation in the fall of 1997 that gives full rights only to religions registered with the government as of 1982, the church has essentially secured for itself the position of state religion.[1] Politicians bow to the perceived voting block of Orthodox citizens, or at least to the vocal opinions of Orthodox officials. Just as in Israel, where otherwise secular prime ministers must be seen wearing yarmulkes to authenticate their status as leaders of the Jewish state, Russian presidents and representatives must attend church services and invite priests to advising sessions in the newly reconstituted "Holy Rus'."[2] Onion domes are de rigeur as official logos, and the largest choir ever assembled sang songs of celebration at the 850th anniversary of Moscow on the steps of the newly rebuilt Cathedral of Christ the Savior.

These public displays by no means prove that all Russians are consciously

414

turning to the Orthodox Church for a sense of identity. Indeed, recent surveys suggest that the number of Russians who regularly attend church is declining, even though those claiming to believe in God is on the rise. In addition, Eliot Borenstein's chapter in this volume on cults and postmodernism in post-Soviet Russia suggests that much of the newfound belief of ex-Soviet citizens has been channeled into apocalyptic cults and/or imported evangelical sects. And the Orthodox Church would not have lobbied so hard for supremacy if it did not fear incursion from other, principally Western, Protestant and New Age denominations.[3] Yet, one cannot help but feel a strong symbolic identification between Russian Orthodoxy and a reborn "Orthodox" Russia, and this in a country that remains factually, if not rhetorically, multiethnic, as was the Soviet republic it succeeds. At least in the capital, Saint George and his slain dragon now adorn banners where the atheist Lenin once smiled.

The church's position today is also unenviable, insofar as it must redefine *itself* at the very same time that Russians are using Orthodoxy to define themselves. The institutional church was severely compromised under Soviet rule, forced to make accommodations with the Kremlin and KGB to ensure its very survival. The "Soviet" clergy has not yet died off, and the official church retains a political as much as spiritual orientation today, as evidenced by its role in the so-called freedom of religion legislation that today guarantees its future. In the near future, at least, the church has much public relations work still to accomplish.

Furthermore, the level of basic knowledge of Christian doctrine and theology, even among regular church goers, is abysmally low. Parishes are scrambling to establish Sunday school and adult education classes on the history of the church, the meaning of the festivals and fasts, and even Old Church Slavonic, so that worshipers can understand the words they pray. Little money is available for such grassroots efforts in a church institution that has not yet undergone its own perestroika and is having difficulty connecting with its constituency.[4] The result is a laity with only the most general, often "folk," appreciation of Christian doctrine. In terms of the concerns of this chapter, the problem is compounded by an unclear understanding of the relationship between Christianity and Russianness, based on widespread notions of Russians as an inherently God-fearing folk and of Moscow as the "third Rome."[5] Russians refer vaguely to a unique Russian spirituality, invoke the "Russian idea" or the "Russian soul," and reprint the works of Russian religious philosophers from the first quarter of the twentieth century in an attempt to construct a post-

Soviet, specifically Russian identity. The church is thus more than the agent for Christ's message on earth, and its representatives must do more than chant liturgy and hear confession. Today the church is in the process of defining what, if anything, is "Russian" about the Russian Orthodox Church, and what is "Orthodox" about Russia.

One way that the institutional church can define itself is in relation to the voices that stand on its extremes. Since the church reemerged in the public arena during glasnost, those voices, for better or for worse, have rallied around the question of the Jews. Jewry functions as the subject of this sometimes frantic debate, serving as archetypical "other" to the Great Russian "self." Chechens and other Caucasians, who are not "true" Russians, also serve this purpose, as can "decadent" Americans or Western Europeans, just as under Soviet rule; and Orthodox religious leaders long before this most recent period of redefinition condemned Islam, Buddhism, and Roman Catholicism as well as Judaism. The difference, however, is crucial. Unlike the Chechens, Jews are seen as a "people" or nation, like the Russians, *at the same time* as they are a religious group, like the Orthodox. In this way, Jews represent a potential model, good or bad, for the integration of Russianness and Orthodoxy. They are, indeed, a rival "chosen people."[6] My purpose in this chapter is to expose the current rhetoric about the Jews on the part of the Orthodox extremes in the figures of one liberal dissident within the church, Zoia Krakhmal'nikova, and of her reactionary enemies, who often speak in the name of, if not always from within, the church. The conclusion will speculate on the extent to which their anti- and philosemitic rhetoric might affect the identity of the Russian Orthodox Church within the new Russia.[7]

Mikhail Agursky, a frequent commentator on Russian-Jewish relations in modern Russia, distinguishes between universalists (or "fundamentalists," for they wish to return to what they see as the original, supranational meaning of Christianity) and conservatives (whom I will call "reactionaries" because of their political as well as religious agenda). The latter insist on the *national* character of the historical church, the former on the universality of Christ's message to all the nations.[8] As we will see, the Jews are important as a rallying cry for both universalists and conservatives because there is more than the traditional charge of antisemitism within the church at stake here. Also at stake is the meaning of Russia as much as of Orthodoxy, the meaning of the nation as much as of the religion — or, rather, a definition of how national identity interacts with religious identity. It is not insignificant that many of the universalist voices come from Jews who have converted to Russian Orthodoxy, Zoia Krakhmal'nikova included. The Jews, after all, are a people *and* a religion. A Jew baptized into Christianity presumably does not become Russian, but remains nationally (or ethnically) Jewish. *Russian* Orthodoxy is also, however, a national identity of sorts. The question posed by universalists is how to take the "national" out of Russian Orthodoxy, how to "supranationalize" and universalize the dominant religion of the state.

Because ultimately the universalist argument is the more philosophically interesting one, I will start instead with the reactionary wing, which in any case appears to have more popular support. Glasnost unleashed freedom of the press that inevitably allowed reactionary as well as democratic speech to find its popular forum. Much of the early discussion surrounded Pamiat', an avowedly chauvinist, antisemitic organization that arose in 1987 and continues to survive in various factions, especially outside the capital, despite its legal abolishment following the attack on the Kremlin in October 1993.[9] *Pamiat'* means memory. Through associations with its name, the founders legitimated the organization's mission by placing it alongside other movements to "remember" Russia's great past and recover her sacred monuments. Observers within and without Russia have long debated the size of the popular base behind Pamiat', and, depending on their political leanings, have either sought or denied evidence that implicated official governmental figures with the ideology of the organization, if not actual membership in it.[10] According to one researcher into right-wing organizations in late Soviet Russia, "the attitude of the party's central organs during this period was ambiguous. Support [for Pamiat'] came from highly placed individuals in the Central Committee, the KGB, and the armed forces; there was more assistance on the regional level."[11] Ironically, Vladimir Zhirinovsky, the chauvinist politician who drew a following as Pamiat' was becoming too fractionalized to wield much political clout, relied on nationalistic rhetoric as he repeatedly attacked the Jews, but was rebuffed by far right organizations as himself a "half-Jew."[12]

Many Pamiat' meetings began with the ringing of church bells.[13] Similarly, many newspapers that profess a strong nationalist ideology also oddly mix symbols of the Orthodox Church with those of the imperialist past. We cannot know exactly who constitutes the audience for these "patriotic quasi-ecclesiastic" publications,[14] but we do know that new titles continue to emerge, supported by the rhetoric of "Great Russian nationalism," "the Russian idea," and some inherent "Russian spirituality" of the people. (We might guess that

19.1   *Nashe Otechestvo* (The Russian Patriotic
Newspaper of the Opposition).

the audience and authors are related to those of the more ephemeral graffiti
described in this volume by John Bushnell in "Paranoid Graffiti at Execution
Wall." As Bushnell points out, the reactionaries often attack the liberal, Westernizing policies of Yeltsin's government by spelling his name with a hard *E,*
supposedly making it sound Jewish.) Antisemitism is discernible throughout,
from specific manifestos calling for the elimination of the Jewish people to the
use of Nazi symbols, ironically transforming a traditional political foe of Russia into an ally in the quest for pure Russian spirituality (fig. 19.1).

In contemporary Russian speech, as in early Russia, spirituality (*dukhovnost'*) need not signify religiosity associated with any specific ritual behavior
(church going, baptism, observing Orthodox fast or feast days), but rather can
suggest a more generalized moral, aesthetic, or psychological depth. The rever-
ent tone with which claims about the "spirit" of the people are uttered evokes
at least a quasi-religious identity, and, for authentication, is often juxtaposed to
popular symbols of the historical Orthodox Church — hence the frequent use of

Old Church Slavonic typeface on mastheads, symbols of the cross and church domes, and articles about religious issues.

Such nationalist rhetoric knows no class boundaries in Russia, and can be found in intellectual as well as popular circles. Western scholars became particularly alarmed in the late 1980s and early 1990s when influential members of the intelligentsia loudly proclaimed their Russian chauvinism, or "radical Slavophilism," and blamed the Jews for Russia's current crises.[15] Popular writers such as Vasilii Belov and Valentin Rasputin, as well as the internationally known painter Il'ia Glazunov, vocally reviled the Jews as corrupters of the pure Russian "soul."

Perhaps the most controversial spokesman to link the three themes of love of Russia, Russian spirituality, and hatred of Jews was Igor' Rostislavovich Shafarevich, an internationally known mathematician and respected member of the dissident community in the 1960s and 1970s.[16] Reacting to Jewish emigration from the Soviet Union in the 1970s, Shafarevich wrote a samizdat pamphlet entitled *Russophobia* that was eventually published in 1989 by the Russian National Union in Munich, and by the conservative journal *Nash sovremennik* in Russia. Even though its composition date is earlier, we can take this publication as emblematic of voices on the reactionary extreme of the debate on the identity of Orthodox Russia, for it continues to evoke argument well into the 1990s. In *Russophobia,* Shafarevich blames Russia's late Soviet woes on the "little nation" (*malyi narod*), a scarcely veiled reference to the Jews (a common antisemitic epithet in Russian is *malanets,* from *malen'kaia* or *malaia natsiia,* "small" or "little nation"), who have somehow created a historically inaccurate and condemnatory picture of Russian identity in an atmosphere of fear and hatred of Russia (hence "Russophobia"). Largely through the writings of Russian Jewish émigrés, the "little nation" has been so persuasive that ethnic Russians have blindly succumbed to this negative picture, and now must be taught the "true" historical facts about the greatness and strength of the Russian people by Shafarevich and other Russophiles like him.

Broad-minded readers have no problem seeing the speciousness of Shafarevich's historical pronouncements. What is more difficult to discern, however, is the underlying presumption of a unique Russian spirit that he, as well as the anonymous authors of the more popular Russophilic and antisemitic publications, tie inextricably to patriotism and hatred of the Jews. Shafarevich himself makes few direct references to the church in *Russophobia,* but he does repeatedly refer to the "spiritual life [*dukhovnaia zhizn'*] of our people," "the spir-

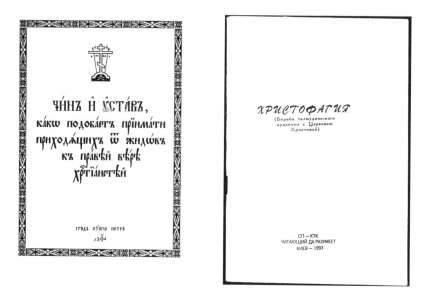

19.2 (*left*)   Cover of antisemitic publication put out by the Union of Orthodox Brotherhoods in St. Petersburg.
19.3 (*right*)   Pamphlet *Christophagia* (*The Devouring of Christ*)

itual cast [*dukhovnyi oblik*] of the people," "Russian spiritual [*dukhovnye*] and historical traditions," and "people of honor, deed, faith [*liudi chesti, dela, very*]."[17] He makes the link to Orthodox spirituality explicit in other writings.

The church did not commission Shafarevich's writings, but neither does it condemn them. Nor does it use its significant political clout to limit the even more explicit use of church symbolism in the popular antisemitic publications. Numerous pamphlets, randomly collected by this author in the years following the fall of the Soviet Union, attack the Jews, including Jewish converts to Russian Orthodoxy, in the name of the church. One, put out by the Union of Orthodox Brotherhoods in St. Petersburg (or, according to the title page, the "City of Saint Peter," with the date of publication printed in Old Church Slavonic characters), reproduces in Old Church Slavonic and corresponding Russian translation ancient rules barring false conversion of Jews, and calls on "Holy Rus'" to preserve the Orthodox faith (fig. 19.2). Oddly, the back cover claims that the publication was necessitated by the "increasingly frequent (and completely ungrounded) accusations of 'antisemitism' and 'intolerance' within Orthodoxy."[18] *Christophagia* [*The Devouring of Christ*]: *Battle between Tal-*

mudic Judaism and the Church of Christ (1993), an unsigned pamphlet, explicitly conflates the "religious question with the national one" and addresses itself to "ethnic Jews" who have accepted Christ (fig. 19.3). The anonymous author concludes that if it is difficult for Russians educated under communism to abandon the ideology they imbibed from childhood and join the church, so much harder (if not impossible) is it for Jews to shake off their "national traits." Those stereotypical traits are defined as curiosity, the unconscious effort to usurp authority over non-Jews, the feeling of collusion with other Jews, a passion for money, hatred of Gentiles, and cleverness, leading to craftiness and impudence.[19]

Again, the central church administration itself did not produce these pamphlets. Nonetheless, the use of church symbolism by the reactionary extreme cannot help but influence the still shaky popular identity of the Russian Orthodox Church proper. Extremist voices can be heard from within as well. As late as 1993, the late Metropolitan Ioann of St. Petersburg published an antisemitic article, using the spurious *Protocols of the Elders of Zion* as proof of the danger the Jews pose to Russia: "Let us look around. What proof does one need in order to understand that against Russia, against the Russian people, a dirty war, well paid, well prepared, unceasing and bitter, is being waged? It is a struggle of life and death. According to the plan of its devilish instigators, our land and people are destined for destruction, and this because of its faithfulness to its historical call and its religious dedication, because through centuries full of rebellion and war, it has defended its religious values."[20]

In his posthumously published book, *Rus' sobornaia* (*United Rus' — sobornaia* is the term used to signify the organic oneness of the nonetheless multivalent church), Metropolitan Ioann frequently uses typical antisemitic catchphrases for the Jews ("Masons," "the alien cosmopolitan bureaucracy") and blames the unrepentant Jews for having murdered God, equated here with the crime of having orchestrated the Bolshevik Revolution.[21]

These words are indeed extreme, and the politically centrist Patriarch Aleksii II, ruling head of the Russian Orthodox Church, ultimately restricted the right of the former metropolitan to speak in the name of the Orthodox Church. In an interview with the paper *Moskovskie novosti* (*Moscow News*), the patriarch of all Rus' stated that "the opinion of one high priest [*ierarkh*] is still not the opinion of the church," recognizing that the result of such antisemitic talk would be "to drive a wedge between the church and society."[22] But Patriarch Aleksii himself apparently does not recognize his own, albeit less extreme, mingling of Russian nationalism with a definition of the church, as exhibited in a speech to a group of American rabbis published as "Your Prophets Are Our Prophets."[23] The patriarch draws on the authority of Russian theologians and religious thinkers who "participated in the defense of Jews against any manifestations of antisemitism," including the religious philosophers Vladimir Solov′ev, Nikolai Berdiaev, and Father Sergei Bulgakov; and he cites examples in which "many priests at local levels actively defended and saved Jews from pogroms and persecutions."[24] Here the Russian patriarch rightfully praises the role of individual Christians in the fight against antisemitism. He goes on, though, to offer the following as proof of the inherent philosemitism of Russians as a nation: "When fighting against Hitler's Germany, the army of our country, at the price of almost twenty million lives, liberated Nazi-occupied countries and thereby prevented the 'final solution of the Jewish question' planned and ruthlessly implemented by the Nazis on these territories. Our army thus saved Jews from total extermination."[25] Factually, he is correct. References to "our army" and "our country," however, read more like the rhetorical nationalism of the patriarch's former communist oppressors than the reasoned argument of a spokesman for a tolerant church centered in a vast, multiethnic nation. "Our country," like all countries, is comprised of philosemites as well as antisemites, not to mention the vast majority with no opinion on the matter whatsoever, and the twenty million Soviets who tragically sacrificed their lives in World War II represented a range of views as well. To claim, no matter how innocently, that Soviet Russians banded together to fight Hitler *in order to* save the Jews is to confuse Christian love with patriotism.

As the Russian Orthodox Church now struggles to define itself, it must respond to the voices on its right, including those of well-known cultural figures who speak of spirituality as they spout chauvinist rhetoric; of a clergy that sometimes confuses Russophilia with faith; and, on the popular level, of ordinary Russians who cannot separate Russianness from their still limited knowledge of the church. And what, asks Zoia Krakhmal′nikova, our primary universalist example, is most shocking about this "spiritual-nationalism"? Even worse, she claims, than the swastikas found on some of the more militant publications is the fact that "they picture the swastika alongside the Orthodox cross, and speak about the church. There are hundreds of such newspapers in St. Petersburg and Moscow alone. But there is not a single Christian newspaper that is prepared to argue with them."[26] The popular press, tolerated on many street corners and even within church walls, creates the impression that love of Russia, and con-comitant adherence to the Russian Orthodox Church, requires antisemitism.[27]

An attractive and soft-spoken grandmother, Zoia Aleksandrovna Krakh-mal'nikova has challenged the assumptions of Russian antisemitism and, like a lone voice in the wilderness, has predicted the demise of a new Russia that allies itself with the reactionary voices described above. Along with her former hus-band, Feliks Svetov, not to mention ideological adversaries such as Shafarevich and Alexander Solzhenitsyn, Krakhmal'nikova participated in the Brezhnev-era dissident community. Born in 1929 to a Jewish mother who was baptized just before her death, Krakhmal'nikova herself became Orthodox in the late 1960s, at a time when a number of Russian Jews converted to Orthodox Chris-tianity, presumably having lost their "faith" in Soviet communism and under-standing their Jewishness in purely ethnic rather than religious terms.[28] Krakh-mal'nikova's Jewish origins are not insignificant here, for they could potentially allow her to see more clearly the national question in Russian Orthodoxy as well. She feels that she can be an Orthodox Christian in Russia without being Russian, and can advocate the establishment of an Orthodox Russia while criticizing the antisemitic aspects of the Russian Orthodox Church today. In the view of antisemites in the church, of course, she and others like her remain "ethnic Jews" who cannot shake off their national traits and must be kept from infecting Russian Orthodoxy through their pseudobaptism. Even if she can dissociate her ethnic and religious identities, her adversaries cannot.[29]

From 1974 to 1982, Krakhmal'nikova produced a series of samizdat pamphlets called *Nadezhda* that she identified as a "*sbornik khristianskogo chteniia*" (collection of Christian teachings).[30] She was arrested in 1982 for this and other church activities, and she served a year in prison and four more in exile in Gornyi Altai before she was granted amnesty under Gorbachev in 1987. Since her release, Krakhmal'nikova has been an outspoken advocate for a "Christian Alternative to the Threat of Russian Fascism," the name of an international association she cofounded in the early 1990s to alert the world to the potential for a new totalitarianism in Russia, based now not on Bolshevik but on "pseudo-Christian" and antisemitic rhetoric.[31]

Krakhmal'nikova's is not the only voice on the left wing of the church, despite her stance as lone prophet.[32] Some of her ideological allies stand, however, further outside the church, including the late Agursky and Sergei Lëzov, a historian of early Christianity, Talmudic Judaism, and contemporary Protestant theology, whose article "Natsional'naia ideia i khristianstvo" ("The

National Idea and Christianity") Krakhmal'nikova has included in one of her collections.[33] Other resonant voices are quieter, involved in private worship rather than public cries for reform. And little popular literature exists to counter the pamphlets and newspapers described above. In 1990 some priests published a short statement in *Vestnik khristianskoi demokratii* (*Messenger of Christian Democracy*) called "An Address to the Jewish People" that condemned the antisemitism of organizations such as Pamiat', and others published an "Announcement by Orthodox Theologians Concerning Antisemitism in Russia," although many felt the words were too few.[34] Perhaps the greatest voice for tolerance within the church was that of the late Father Aleksandr Men', who wrote and spoke often about the Jews. About antisemitic statements that remain embedded in Orthodox liturgy, for example, he stated: "Those texts are a remnant of medieval morals; they have already been removed from Catholicism. When it comes time for the review of Orthodox liturgical texts, I hope that these attacks will also be removed there."[35] The legacy of Father Men' will be revisited in the conclusion to this chapter. In the meantime, the following pages concentrate on the words of Zoia Krakhmal'nikova as the most vocal and colorful response to the "spiritual nationalism" of Shafarevich and his reactionary allies.

Krakhmal'nikova sees great danger for Russia should it continue to define itself as the "big people" (*bol'shoi narod*, in the words of Shafarevich) and find justification for its antisemitism within Orthodoxy or through the appropriation of church symbols. The Soviet Union was a totalitarian state, she says, although that label has more cultural than political significance. The "total monoculture of Bolshevism" that "invaded all spheres of knowledge from psychology to medicine to ecology to philosophy to religion" depleted the riches of Russian culture, a tragedy that only intensified after the fall of communism.

> It is as though there has been an earthquake, or some unimaginable flood, and all that remains in Russia now are pitiful shoots. Everything else has been swept away. Any culture that you chance upon today, even at scholarly conferences, is no more than set dressing. All these scholars and institutes, all these Averintsevs and Likhachevs who seem to you [American Slavists] such luminaries are, from my point of view, no more than academic clerics. They have been deprived of any real culture for so long, deprived of a spiritual culture that could enrich knowledge, that they can now do no more than reinvent the wheel.[36]

Krakhmal'nikova shares with her opponents on the other extreme a rhetoric of biblical proportions. She describes seventy years of Soviet rule as an apocalyptic earthquake, a flood equivalent to God's punishment of the generation of Noah. Life in contemporary Russia is now no more than "pitiful shoots" peeking up from the ravished soil into an "ideological vacuum."[37] These shoots must be properly nourished, but instead are fed a false diet ("set dressing") by "academic clerics" who themselves know only the dead monoculture of communism. The apocalypticism of this vision raises the ante for the future of Russia, evoking as it does the specter of a vulnerable people besieged by the Antichrist.

"We are a powerless people," declares Krakhmal'nikova. "Why are we powerless? Because we are bled of spirituality, of morality. The culture of the lie defeated the spiritual core of our being."[38] At issue here, clearly, is a new definition of Russia following the loss of Soviet ideology that once filled, no matter how poorly, the vacuum of self-identity. Again, the spirituality (*dukhovnost'*) of which Krakhmal'nikova speaks is not purely religious, but moral and aesthetic as well. Yet her continual reference to the Orthodox Church is an indication that more than ethical humanism must now fill the bloodless body of Russia.

How might one imagine an inspiration of spirit, a transfusion of such spiritual blood? Through a new market economy? democratic elections? a more humane socialism? All of these economic, political, or social structures are post-Marxist superstructure, implies Krakhmal'nikova. Instead, hope rests entirely on a retrieval of Christian spirituality, something that can occur, according to Orthodox theology, only through the church. For her, the new Russia is clearly an Orthodox nation. But the church itself is in serious trouble. Too many "reborn" Christians know nothing of the teachings of Christ. Their ignorance, claims Krakhmal'nikova, is evidenced by the active role they take in—or, at best, the blind eye they turn toward—antisemitism in Russia.[39] Father Aleksandr Borisov, a popular universalist-leaning priest and local politician, agrees: "The vast majority of Orthodox Christians are neutral about the question. As for those who take an active position, I'm afraid that anyone who consciously counters antisemitism would be in the minority."[40] Father Borisov places the blame on a problem identified above—inadequate Christian education for the new Orthodox Russians:

Russian society, the Orthodox believers, people who want to come to Christ, are presented with books written in the nineteenth century, put out now in massive copies and only weakly relating to anything happening to us today, one hundred years later. The people who have come relatively recently to the Orthodox Church, therefore, barely have a grip on the very name "Orthodox." For many people, still poorly oriented in Christianity, the church to which they recently came becomes some sort of symbol that provides a bad service: we are orthodox [lit., right belief], and the others are not orthodox, we correctly praise God, and all the rest — incorrectly.[41]

Krakhmal'nikova lays out many of her ideas in two major works: *Rusofobiia. Antisemitizm. Khristianstvo: Zametki ob antirusskoi idee* (*Russophobia. Antisemitism. Christianity: Some Thoughts on an Anti-Russian Idea*), a direct response to Shafarevich's *Russophobia;* and *Russkaia ideia i evrei: rokovoi spor* (*The Russian Idea and the Jews: A Fatal Debate*), a three-part collection of essays published in 1994 that includes reprints of articles on the Jews by earlier Russian Orthodox thinkers, article on the Jews by Krakhmal'nikova and other contemporary intellectuals, and the results of a survey on nationalism in Russia.[42] The collection bears a second subtitle that brings together the three terms crucial to this chapter: "Christianity. Antisemitism. Nationalism." By juxtaposing the three, Krakhmal'nikova apparently means to suggest their incompatibility.[43]

The question of Russian spiritual identity linked to antisemitism is not new in post-Soviet Russia. More than one hundred years ago the Russian religious philosopher Vladimir Solov'ev attempted to discredit Judeophobia among his contemporary Russophiles. This is the same Solov'ev whose works are being bought on the streets of Moscow in the 1990s by antisemites as well as philosemites, and whose words, reproduced in samizdat, brought many dissidents to faith in the 1960s and 1970s.[44] Drawing on the Judeophilia of this earlier religious philosopher to bolster her argument against modern-day Russophiles, Krakhmal'nikova has included Solov'ev's 1884 essay, "Evreistvo i khristianskii vopros" ("Jewry and the Christian Question"), in *Russkaia ideia i evrei.* Solov'ev, as a Russian, identified with the Jews despite the fact that both his background and his philosophical beliefs were steeped in Russian Orthodoxy and a fundamentally trinitarian worldview. As he wrote to a friend with whom he had been quite close, but from whom he had grown apart because of the correspondent's increasingly exclusive Russophilism (what Solov'ev called "neo-Slavophilism" or even "zoological patriotism," and "that zoomorphic idol served by today's nationalists"): "How can Danilevskii's [ultranationalist] theory explain that the purely Russian, Orthodox culture we share does not prevent you from being a Chinaman, and me — a Jew?"[45]

In "Jewry and the Christian Question," Solov'ev accuses Christians of acting "un-Christianly" toward Jews, although the Jews continue to act "Jewishly" toward them: "In relations with us they have never violated their religious law, while we have constantly violated and continue to violate commandments of the Christian religion in relation to them. If the Jewish law is bad, then their stubborn loyalty to that bad law is of course a sad phenomenon. But if it is bad to be loyal to a bad law, then all the worse is it to be unfaithful to a good law, to a testament that is unconditionally perfect. And we have such a testament in the Gospels."[46] For Solov'ev, then, as for Krakhmal'nikova one hundred years later, the greatest marks of un-Christian behavior are exclusive nationalism and concomitant antisemitism. In this sense, both are Christian "fundamentalists," to use Agursky's term. As Krakhmal'nikova states: "There can be no antisemitism in a religion that believes that God was born to a Jewish woman. He was ethnically a Jew, His relatives were Jews, His apostles were Jews. It is absurd, it is ignorance, but a very dangerous ignorance."[47] Even more succinctly: "True Christianity and antisemitism are irreconcilable."[48] Krakhmal'nikova's statement here is theologically (if not always historically) defensible. Her stance becomes more problematic, however, when she inserts the third term of her investigation: nationalism, or, specifically, Russophilia.

In the survey that ends Krakhmal'nikova's collection, nine liberal intellectuals respond to a series of questions about Russophilia in the post-Soviet world. The questions are perhaps more telling than the answers: "How do you account for the fact that the 'national idea' is again becoming one of the central ideas in Russia?" "How do you understand the rise of the national idea in post-totalitarian Russia? Does its development and transformation depend on religion and the church?" and, finally, "In your opinion, will Nazism triumph in its new, Russian variation? What can prevent this threat?"[49] The tone of the questions is at once combative and besieged. The culmination in "Nazism" of the last question seems a foregone conclusion, as though the voice of universalism is shouted out by those of the opposite, reactionary extreme. In fact, the problem exists in the very rhetoric itself, for in framing the question as she has, Krakhmal'nikova is forced to speak from within the voice zone of her opponents. They are the ones invoking Nazism. The reactionaries are also the ones identifying Russia with a "national idea" and connecting Russianness to spirituality. As these questions show, Krakhmal'nikova can merely react to an identity established by others. Agursky pinpoints the problem faced by the universalists in the church by calling the universalist stance "anti-antisemitism."[50]

When Krakhmal'nikova quotes Solov'ev on nationalism, she does try to establish her own voice as more than reactive: "In the nineties of the previous century, V. S. Solov'ev said: 'The ruling idea of our time is the national idea.' A century has passed. In the 1990s of our own age, the national idea is again becoming one of the central ideas in Russia. With what do you connect this phenomenon?"[51] The invocation of Solov'ev lends depth to the question of national identity as related to the Jews, who, that philosopher asserts, have a unique "national-spiritual" identity. For Solov'ev, the "national idea" is not by nature bad. Only when a sense of one's unique national character (one's *natsional'nost'* or *narodnost'* — analogous to one's personal character, or *lichnost'*) reverts to bald nationalism (*natsionalizm* — analogous to an individual's egoism) will a people begin to exhibit "un-Christian" behavior, including antisemitism.[52] In other words, every people has a unique character as well as a unique role to play in the world process, Russians as well as Jews. Each nation must recognize its qualities, but must understand those qualities as they interact with other nations in the universal organism: "*Narodnost' in and of itself* is only an organic part of humanity, able to stand in various relations to the absolute ideal, but in no way equivalent to it."[53] *Natsionalizm,* as opposed to *natsional'nost',* arises when a people rejects the significance of organic interaction of many parts. Thus, the national, or Russian, idea can be a very positive factor only when it operates integrally within the multifaceted "universal organism," and when its multiple internal elements — spiritual and ethnic — are likewise harmoniously integrated. It is indeed possible to be a nation of "religious-national wholeness" (*religiozno-natsional'noe edinstvo*), as opposed to the religious-national separatism (*religiozno-natsional'noe obosoblenie*) of his contemporary Russia, or so claims Solov'ev. Significantly, and ironically for the Shafarevich-Krakhmal'nikova debate, Solov'ev sets up the Jews as the model of "religious-national wholeness."[54] Unlike Solov'ev's contemporary Russians, the Jews are a "chosen people" who can potentially integrate national and spiritual identities.

Despite her own connection to the Jews as a people, however, Krakhmal'nikova does not follow this strain of Solov'ev's thought, which sets up the Jews as independent, *positive* models for so called spiritual nationhood. The Jews for her have significance only as victims of antisemitism — the inevitable result of Russophilia — and thus as symbols of the un-Christian behavior of contemporary Russian nationalists. In her effort to isolate national from religious identity — that is, Russianness from Orthodoxy — she neglects the model for their possible organic integration that Solov'ev had suggested already in the nineteenth century. In addition, by taking a stance that in essence inverts the rhetoric of her adversaries, she also must neglect the Jews as a people. When she became Orthodox, her Jewishness became insignificant; her identity as a Christian became all. Again, she speaks from the voice zone of the other extreme, for "Russian" becomes a merely rhetorical adjective affixed to her Orthodox identity, just as "Orthodox" is often a rhetorical symbol for Russianness on the part of many Russophiles.

It is telling, perhaps, that there is very little dialogue between the universalists within the church and the growing Jewish community in Russia today. Orthodox Russians, whether initially Jewish or not, have made little attempt to *know* Jews and Judaism as it exists now around them.[55] Their sight remains focused on Russia, as is the sight of the reactionaries. Again Krakhmal'nikova falls into the voice of the other extreme: "The national existence of the Russian people, its culture and moral foundations, are built on the Orthodox faith. The treasury of Orthodox spirituality formed the national consciousness."[56] Russians, she asserts, are inherently spiritual, infused with a religious sensibility that is, specifically, Orthodox Christian. Is there room, then, for Volga Germans, Islamic Tatars, and Jews, not to mention New Age Hare Krishnas or even run-of-the-mill Russian atheists in a country called Russia? In this rhetorical sense, as in their apocalyptic vocabulary, the two extremes are not so far apart after all.

So, how, ultimately, will the voices of the extremes affect the identity of the institutional Orthodox Church within the new Russia? How will antisemitic and anti-antisemitic rhetoric shape the relationship between Russianness and Orthodoxy as the new millennium begins? Insofar as the universalists and the conservatives both fall back on an equation of Russianness and spirituality without resolving a more sophisticated relationship of national with religious identity, the church can use both sides to justify its identification with the Russian state. Because the rhetoric of that identification comes largely from the reactionary extreme — the universalists are left with a negation of a negation rather than a positive assertion — the public face of the church will look more and more narrowly Russian and less and less universally Christian. Or so it seems to this observer. An Orthodox Russia, even if it *begins* with Christianity and allows the development of national identity from within, as Krakhmal'ni-kova advocates, still does not allow other national and religious identities to interact within it. Until Orthodoxy becomes the numerically largest, but not the single politically potent, religious identity within an interactive, Solov'evian "organic," multinational Russia, other peoples as well as other religions will be excluded.

There is one curious note to the contrary. In the fall of 1990, Father Alek-sandr Men', an outspoken "universalist" priest within the Orthodox Church, was murdered on his way to mass. Father Men', like Krakhmal'nikova, was born Jewish, and publicly condemned antisemitism throughout his life. Ru-mors began to circulate immediately after the murder that he was killed by extremist elements within the church itself who objected to the "infiltration" of the Jewish people into what they thought should be the *Russian* Orthodox Church. The fact that an inadequate investigation ultimately charged the crime to what many believe to be innocent "hooligans" only increased some people's sense that the church and the state were themselves involved. Orthodox author-ities tried to distance themselves from Men''s memory and his numerous writ-ings, calling them theologically shallow or heretical.

Men' remained a marginal, even denigrated figure within the church for the next six years. As often happens, however, the murdered priest has become something of a martyr to his followers. Many of his spiritual children are baptized Jews like himself, and the others are Christians who share his univer-salist vision. Slowly, their numbers have grown. Finally, Men''s dedicated "heir," Father Aleksandr Borisov, was granted a parish in the center of Mos-cow that is being beautifully renovated as I write. Even more surprising, this author was invited to the opening of an exposition honoring the life of Father Aleksandr Men' at none other than Sergiev Posad, the seat of the established church that once rejected him.

Why this new attention to a voice on an extreme wing of the church? As one participant at a recent conference dedicated to the memory of Father Men' remarked, the Orthodox Church is now faced with a situation analogous to one once faced by the Catholic Church in its relationship to Saint Francis Assisi: it can continue to reject him or choose to absorb him. The former choice would fuel assertions of his martyrdom among his followers. The latter would defuse them. Whether the universalist view his memory represents will now have an effect on the church that is institutionalizing him or, conversely, the church will merely render it harmless remains to be seen.

Notes

1 The law, ironically first introduced by the Communists in parliament, assures full rights only to Islam, Judaism, Buddhism, and the Russian Orthodox Church. Yeltsin originally vetoed the bill, returning it to parliament with revised wording. Despite high hopes in the international community, as well as within Russia on the part of non-Orthodox religious groups, the revisions did not essentially change the law. Although it now tacitly accepts Catholicism and some mainstream Protestant groups, it continues to outlaw all so-called nontraditional denominations. Under the new rules, only those religious organizations that were officially recognized in 1982, under the atheist Soviet state, are allowed to proselytize or do charity work. All others must register with the government annually and cannot establish schools, publish material, or invite clergy from abroad to officiate. In addition, only those religious bodies that can show legal existence for the past fifty years are allowed to include "Russian" in their title. This rule, as explained by Lawrence Uzzell, Moscow representative of the Keston Institute (an independent research center that studies Russian religious life), "explicitly enshrines the church-state relations of Stalin as the norm for today." See David Filipov, "Religious Curbs, Backed by Yeltsin, Passed in Russia," *Boston Globe,* September 20, 1997, p. 1.

2 Gorbachev reinitiated this new form of church-state cooperation in 1988 by inviting the patriarch to a meeting in the Kremlin. The last meeting had taken place in 1943, when Stalin met with church leaders to solicit their support in the war effort in exchange for a short-term easing of communist persecution.

3 The bill was ostensibly introduced to protect Russians from "totalitarian sects" that preach violence, such as the Japanese Aum Shinri Kyo, but extends to other religious groups that have been present, if not officially registered, in Russia for many years, including the peaceable Mennonites, who lived in Russia and Ukraine long before the emigration of many to Canada and the United States. In addition, it recently gave support to the Russian Orthodox Church in its efforts to evict Ukrainian Orthodox monks from land the latter have long possessed.

4 I thank Peter Quimby of the University of Wisconsin for his clear explanation to me of the problems facing the church on two levels: institutional and social.

5 Moscow was first called the "third Rome" in a letter of an Orthodox monk to Grand Prince Vasilii III in the sixteenth century: "Listen and attend, pious tsar, that all Christian empires are gathered in your single one, that two Romes have fallen, and the third one stands, and a fourth one there shall not be" (quoted in Michael Cherniavsky, *Tsar and People: Studies in Russian Myths* [New Haven: Yale University Press, 1961], p. 38). Of the many quasi-religious myths that serve as subject of the

book, Cherniavsky writes: "Some of the Russian epithets which symbolized the myths — 'Little Father Tsar,' 'Holy Russia,' 'Mother Russia,' and, most particularly, the 'Russian Soul' — have become commonplaces outside Russia as well. So much so that even non-Russians began to believe in them" (p. 2).

6 I am currently at work on a book manuscript, "Meeting of the Chosen Peoples: Modern Russian Orthodox Thought and the Jews," that analyzes the works of Vladimir Solov'ev and his philosophical heirs precisely in these terms.

7 The topic of antisemitism in Russia evokes a great deal of outrage even among academics. See the heated and contradictory opinions on the extent of antisemitism in Russia of James L. Gibson, Vicki L. Hesli, Arthur H. Miller, William M. Reisinger, and Robert J. Brym published as research notes in *Slavic Review* 53, no. 3 (1994): 796–855. These notes respond to an article from 1993: Robert J. Brym and Andrei Degtyarev, "Anti-Semitism in Moscow: Results of an October 1992 Survey," *Slavic Review* 52, no. 1 (1993): 1–12. When not citing difficult-to-interpret statistics, observers often resort to anecdote. Thus, Krakhmal'nikova bases her assumption that "there is no antisemitism here among the common people" on the following evidence: "My husband was in a common prison (I was in a rather aristocratic prison, a KGB prison, so I myself had little exposure), and he said that there was no antisemitism there" (Krakhmal'nikova, interview with the author, March 22, 1993).

8 Mikhail Agursky, "Fundamentalist Christian Anti-antisemitism in Modern Russia," *Religion, State and Society* 20, no. 1 (1992): 51–55.

9 In 1991, Mark Deich and Leonid Zhuravlev identified at least eight Pamiat' organizations, and another twelve with views allegedly close to those of Pamiat'. See Mark Deich and Leonid Zhuravlev, eds., *"Pamiat'": Kak ona est'* (Moscow: MP "TSUNAMI," 1991), p. 4. See also Walter Laqueur, *Black Hundred: The Rise of the Extreme Right in Russia* (New York: HarperCollins, 1993), pp. 204–21. After inquiring about antisemitic newspapers and other publications, a recent visitor to the cities within the "Golden Ring" reported numerous invitations to attend Pamiat' meetings. My thanks to Ann Stowell Belyaev for research undertaken in Russia in January 1997.

10 On the back cover of *"Pamiat'": Kak ona est'*, Ales' Adamovich quotes B. Kriuchkov, former head of the KGB, as answering the question: "Why did the agency under your authority relate so loyally to the organization?" with the following: "Pamiat' has done a great deal for the resurrection of historical monuments in Russia." See also William Korey, *Russian Antisemitism, Pamyat, and the Demonology of Zionism* (Chur, Switzerland: Harwood Academic Publishers, 1995).

11 Laqueur, *Black Hundred*, p. 207. See also Eliot Borenstein's chapter in the current volume, "Suspending Disbelief: Cults and Postmodernism in Post-Soviet Russia," in which he points to political rhetoric that blames Russia's problems on the "Jewmasons," a typical bogeyman of Pamiat' and other right-wing organizations.

12 Laqueur, *Black Hundred*, p. 257. This same Zhirinovsky shouted to a crowd protesting the new legislation curtailing religious freedom: "Pack up your bags and go back where you came from" (Filipov, "Religious Curbs," p. 1). Zhirinovsky is an excel-

lent example of a politician who rides the Orthodox platform as a forum for his nationalist views.

13 Laqueur, *Black Hundred,* p. 207.

14 I use this term on the model of "patriotic, quasi-ecclesiastic organizations" (*patrioticheskie okolotserkovnye ob''edineniia*) described in S. Ivanenko, "Novaia religioznaia pressa," *Nauka i religiia,* May 1990, p. 29.

15 For an excellent survey of the "rightist" Russian authors in the final years of the Soviet Union, see Josephine Woll, "Russians and 'Russophobes': Antisemitism on the Russian Literary Scene," *Soviet Jewish Affairs* 19, no. 3 (1989): 3–21. John Garrard looks at antisemitism and extreme Russian nationalism among intellectuals through the lens of a liberal journal in "The Challenge of Glasnost: *Ogonek*'s Handling of Russian Antisemitism," *Nationalities Papers* 19, no. 2 (1991): 228–50. In the same number, Garrard published a translation of a Pamiat' manifesto, followed by the platform of the Nazi party from 1920, and an appendix by the author Tat'iana Tolstaia parodying antisemitic quasi-intellectual pronouncements (pp. 134–43). Tolstaia begins: "Pushkin was a Jew. His real name was Pushkind" (p. 141). See also Laqueur, *Black Hundred,* p. 212.

16 Shafarevich was a member of both the American and the Soviet Academies of Sciences. See the short biography at the end of Alexander Solzhenitsyn's collection of essays by leading dissidents, *Iz-pod glyb* (Paris: YMCA-Press, 1974), to which Shafarevich contributed three articles.

17 Shafarevich, pp. 167, 191, 173, 180: "Sotsializm," "Obosoblenie ili Sblizhenie," and "Est' li u Rossii budushchee?"

18 "Chin i ustav, kako podobaet priimati prikhodiashikh ot zhidov k pravei vere khristiantsei" (Soiuz pravoslavnykh bratstv: Grad sviatago Petra, 1993).

19 *Khristofagiia: Bor'ba talmudicheskogo iudaizma s Tserkov'iu Khristovoi* (Kiev: SP-KTK, Chitaiushchii da razumeet, 1993), pp. 3, 44–47. Although the pamphlet was published in what is now Ukraine, its language is Russian, and it was presumably written for a Russian audience.

20 Metropolitan Ioann of St. Petersburg, "The West Wants Chaos," in *Christianity after Communism: Social, Political, and Cultural Struggle in Russia,* ed. Niels C. Nielsen Jr. (Boulder: Westview Press, 1994), p. 111; translated by Nielsen from *Glaube in der 2. Welt* 21, nos. 7–8 (1993): 43–45.

21 Vysokopreosviashchenneishii Ioann, Mitropolit Sankt-Peterburgskii i Ladozhskii, *Rus' sobornaia: Ocherki khristianskoi gosudarstvennosti* (St. Petersburg: Tsarskoe delo, 1995).

22 Interview with Vladimir Shevelev, *Moskovskie novosti,* no. 16 (April 17–24, 1994); reprinted in *Pravoslavnaia tserkov' i evrei: XIX–XX vv.: Sbornik materialov k teologii mezhkonfessional'nogo dialoga* (Moscow: Rudomino — Bog edin, 1994), pp. 136–37.

23 Nielsen, ed., *Christianity after Communism,* pp. 103–6. The article first appeared in *Moscow News,* February 12, 1992, p. 16; and was reprinted in *Glaube in der 2. Welt* 21, nos. 7–8 (1993): 41–42.

24 Ibid., pp. 104–5.

25 Ibid., p. 105.

26 Krakhmal'nikova, interview, 1993. Many of the publications have telling names. In 1993 Krakhmal'nikova had collected, among others, the following examples: *Soiuz russkogo naroda, Narodnaia volia, Russkii vestnik* ("Well," admitted Krakhmal'nikova, "this one is more 'vegetarian,' not as 'cannibalistic' as others"), *Zemshchina, Sergiev Posad* (which writes of ritual murder and blood libel), *Russkoe voskresenie* (which has openly praised Hitler), and *Patriot.*

27 Krakhmal'nikova's sense of isolation within a society that tolerates such publications is obvious in the following quote from our 1993 interview. She tells the story of a man arrested in the early 1990s for publishing *Mein Kampf:*

> He was arrested, but then acquitted after he claimed that the publication was merely a commercial venture. But the fact is that *he* published *that* book. It wasn't just a commercial venture, since he could have published, let's say, a detective story for a commercial venture; he put out *Mein Kampf* instead. The authorities are silent, Christians are silent. As for me, I was given six years in prison and exile for my Christian activity [see below]. They harassed me, frightened me, mocked me. And all for a book of Christian studies. And the same prosecutors give nothing for *Mein Kampf.* So you can understand what condition society is in.

28 As Svetov asserts, the term *converted* is inappropriate, for it implies "leaving" one religion for another. Instead, he, like Krakhmal'nikova, had never felt himself to be part of the Jewish faith (Feliks Svetov, interview with the author, June 1989). Krakhmal'nikova uses the phrase "brought to faith" to describe her rebirth as a Christian (Krakhmal'nikova, interview, 1993). Unlike Krakhmal'nikova, Svetov claims to have had a strong sense of his Jewish identity, and he wrote of the difficulties of being a Jew in Christian circles, and a Christian in Jewish ones. See Svetov, *Opyt biografii* (Paris: YMCA-Press, 1985); and *Otverzi mi dveri* (Paris: Les Éditeurs réunis, 1978).

29 Compare the words of one baptized Jewish journalist preparing to emigrate: "He went on to say that the real problem was his Jewishness. Although he had been christened, he was terrified of what he was seeing and hearing and reading" (Andrei Sinyavsky, "Russophobia," *Partisan Review* 57, no. 3 [1990]: 340).

30 See the short biography Krakhmal'nikova includes in *Russkaia ideia i evrei: rokovoi spor. Khristianstvo, antisemitizm, natsionalizm,* ed. Z. A. Krakhmal'nikova (Moscow: Nauka, 1994), pp. 242–43.

31 Zoia Krakhmal'nikova, "O mezhdunarodnoi assotsiatsii 'Khristianskaia al'ternativa ugroze russkogo fashizma'" (unpublished typescript, 1993).

32 See, for example, Sinyavsky's cogent reaction to "Russophobia" in Andrei Sinyavsky, "Russophobia," pp. 339–44. More recent critiques of antisemitism in Russia can be found in V. Iliushenko, ed., *Nuzhen li Gitler Rossii?* (Moscow: Nezavisimoe izdatel'stvo PIK, 1996), including a section called "Pravoslavie i totalitarizm."

33 Sergei Lëzov, "Natsional'naia ideia i khristianstvo (Opyt v dvukh chastiakh)," in

Krakhmal'nikova, ed., *Russkaia ideia i evrei,* pp. 99–125. The article was first published in the journal *Oktiabr',* no. 10 (1990), pp. 148–60; and translated in *Religion, State and Society* 20, no. 1 (1992): 29–47.

34 These two documents, along with other essays on the topic of Jews and Orthodoxy from the nineteenth and twentieth centuries, have been collected in *Pravoslavnaia tserkov' i evrei;* see pp. 81 and 82.

35 Protoierei Aleksandr Men', in "Evrei i khristianstvo," an interview with A. Shoi-khet of the journal *Jews in the SSSR* in 1975. The interview is reproduced in *Pravoslavnaia Tserkov' i evrei,* pp. 71–77.

36 Krakhmal'nikova, interview, 1993. She refers here to Sergei Averintsev and Dmitrii Likhachev, respected academics who became spokesmen for spiritual and cultural renewal in Russia during the glasnost years.

37 Such rhetoric is not confined to observers within Russia. Laqueur (*Black Hundred*) also speaks of an "earthquake" (p. viii) and a vacuum (p. ix).

38 Krakhmal'nikova, interview, 1993.

39 Ann Stowell Belyaev reports that the writings of known antisemites are being sold within church walls, and that priests and other church officials hand them out as gifts. She brought back one such "gift": *Bliz est', pri dverekh* [*He Is Near, by the Doors*] (St. Petersburg: OIU-92, 1996), by Sergei Nilus, propagator of the *Protocols of the Elders of the Zion* in the early part of the twentieth century. The present volume is a re-publication of part 2 of his infamous *Velikoe v malom* (*The Great in the Small*), originally titled "Bliz griadushchii antikhrist i tsarstvo diavola na zemle" ("The Coming Antichrist Is Near and the Kingdom of the Devil Is on Earth") and published in 1917 by the Holy Trinity Monastery at Sergiev Posad. For more on Nilus and the resurgence of interest in him, see Michael Hagemeister, "Qui était Sergei Nilus?" *Politica Hermetica* 9 (1995): 141–58.

40 Father Aleksandr Borisov, "Vse liudi — deti edinogo Boga," interview with Mikhail Gorelik for the journal *Shalom,* no. 6 (1990); reprinted in *Pravoslavnaia tserkov' i evrei,* p. 83.

41 Father Aleksandr Borisov, "O natsionalizme v russkoi pravoslavnoi tserkvi," in *Nuzhen li Gitler Rossii?,* pp. 192–93.

42 The pamphlet was circulated in samizdat in January 1990, and officially published in *Neva,* no. 8 (1990), pp. 163–78. It was translated as "Russophobia, Antisemitism and Christianity: Some Remarks on an Anti-Russian Idea," in *Religion, State and Society* 20, no. 1 (1992): 7–28. All further citations are from this translation. The three parts of *Russkaia ideia i evrei* are: "Religioznaia sud'ba Rossii i Izrail'" ("The Religious Fate of Russia and Israel"), with essays by Fedotov, Solov'ev, and S. Bulgakov; "Khristianstvo posle Osventsima i GULAGa" ("Christianity after the Holocaust and the Gulag"), with recent essays by Akhutin, Lezov, Chaikovskii, Protsenko, and Krakhmal'nikova, as well as a translation into Russian of an essay by Emil Fackenheim; and "Natsional'naia ideia v Rossii: Anketa" ("The National Idea in Russia: A Questionnaire").

43 Krakhmal'nikova recently published a book about Mother Maria, a Russian Ortho-

dox nun who died at the Nazi camp Ravensbruch for her work helping the Jews. According to the author, the story of Maria's service "is important, I am sure of this, for many of my fellow Russians." See Zoia Krakhmal'nikova, *Russkaia ideia materi Marii* (Uhldingen, Germany: Stephanus Edition, 1997), p. 2. Although she lives in Moscow, it is significant that Krakhmal'nikova feels she must address her "fellow Russians" from abroad (Germany), and seek international support for her critique of the contemporary Russian church.

44 See the testimony of Father Michael Aksenov-Meerson (born Jewish in Moscow, now rector of Christ the Savior Orthodox Church in New York), "Solov'ev v nashi dni," in S. M. Solov'ev, *Zhizn' i tvorcheskaia evoliutsiia Vladimira Solov'eva* (Brussels: Zhizn' s Bogom, 1977), pp. ix–x. In a series of interviews with Russian Jewish converts to Orthodoxy conducted in Moscow in September 1997, most interviewees mentioned the influence of Solov'ev and Nikolai Berdiaev.

45 V. S. Solov'ev, *Sobranie sochinenii Vladimira Sergeevicha Solov'eva,* 2d ed., 10 vols. (1911–14; reprint ed., with two additional volumes, Brussels: Zhizn' s Bogom, 1966–70), 5:194, 394. Letter to N. N. Strakhov (1890), in *Pis'ma V. S. Solov'eva,* ed. E. L. Radlov, 4 vols. (1908; reprint ed. Brussels: Zhizn' s Bogom, 1970), 1:60. For a detailed study of Solov'ev's writings on the Jews, see Judith Deutsch Kornblatt, "Vladimir Solov'ev on Spiritual Nationhood, Russia and the Jews," *Russian Review* 56, no. 2 (1997): 157–77.

46 Solov'ev, *Sobranie sochinenii,* 4:135; reprinted in Krakhmal'nikova, ed., *Russkaia ideia,* p. 16.

47 Krakhmal'nikova, interview, 1993.

48 Krakhmal'nikova, "Russophobia, Antisemitism, and Christianity," p. 12.

49 Krakhmal'nikova, ed., *Russkaia ideia,* p. 218.

50 Agursky, "Fundamentalist Christian Anti-antisemitism in Modern Russia." It is perhaps telling that Krakhmal'nikova, like the reactive dissidents in the Soviet period, has so often had to look for support abroad.

51 Krakhmal'nikova, ed., *Russkaia ideia,* p. 218.

52 See, for example, Solov'ev, "O narodnosti i narodnykh delakh Rossii," *Sobranie sochinenii,* 5:24–38.

53 Solov'ev, *Sobranie sochinenii,* 5:391. See also 8:316: "Dlia cheloveka v etom vozrozhdennom sostoianii individual'nost',—kak i natsional'nost' i vse drugie osobennosti i otlichiia,—perestaet byt' *granitseiu,* a stanovitsia osnovaniem polozhitel'nogo soedineniia s vospolniaiushchim ego sobiratel'nym vsechelovechestvom ili tserkov'iu (v ee istinnom sushchestve)."

54 Solov'ev, *Sobranie sochinenii,* 6:24.

55 This problem was made clear to me by Mikhail Gorelik, a Moscow journalist who joined the church in the 1960s but has since left, and has now established some ties with the more traditional Jewish community. Although he remains friendly with activists on both sides, he does not integrate the two sides of his own biography. Interview with the author, September 1997.

56 Krakhmal'nikova, "Russophobia, Antisemitism and Christianity," p. 23.

No use blaming the mirror if your mug's on crooked. — Proverb used as the epigraph to Gogol's *Inspector General*

SUSPENDING DISBELIEF: "CULTS" AND POSTMODERNISM IN POST-SOVIET RUSSIA

In the final days of the 1996 Russian election campaign, former dark-horse presidential candidate General Aleksandr Lebed stunned Russian liberals and foreign observers alike by using his first speech on Boris Yeltsin's behalf to launch an attack on an unlikely enemy: "[A]ll these Mormons are mold and filth which have come to destroy the state. The state should outlaw them. They should not exist on our soil."[1] From a purely practical point of view, Lebed's attack might well seem puzzling: one need only open any Russian newspaper at random to be convinced that unchecked organized crime and rampant poverty are far more pressing problems than an influx of earnest, clean-cut young missionaries. Certainly, Lebed was playing to a much smaller and more receptive audience than the international press: this speech to his supporters in the Union of Patriotic and National Organizations of Russia may well have helped deliver a portion of the "patriotic" vote to Yeltsin. But Lebed's attempt to court the Russian chauvinists only opened him up to ridicule at the hands of his Kremlin rival, presidential Chief of Staff Anatoly Chubais: "It is quite possible," quipped Chubais, ". . . that [Lebed] confused Mormons and Masons. Such things happen."[2] Chubais's biting remarks hit the retired general on two fronts simultaneously: first, they made Lebed appear ignorant and barely literate;[3] more important, Chubais was implying that Lebed's rhetoric fit comfortably within the Russian chauvinist anxiety over the "Jewmasons" (*zhidomasony*) who purportedly masterminded the downfall of the Soviet Union and are said to be plotting the imminent collapse of its successor, the Russian Federation. As a result, Chubais's main supporters, the Russian liberal intelligentsia, were unable to set aside the misgivings they already harbored about a general who professed admiration for General Augusto Pinochet of Chile. For his part, Lebed refused to soften his stance, asserting a few days later: "I am categorically against bringing in foreign beliefs which are anti-human."[4]

Lebed's tirade, which was met with predictable outrage by the Church of Latter-Day Saints and the U.S. Senate delegation from Utah, is by no means an isolated incident in contemporary Russia. Ever since the Soviet Union relaxed its restrictions on religious organizations, foreign missionaries and new religious movements have repeatedly come under fire; the Lebed incident is different only in that it was directed at the sixth-largest church in America.[5] Although Lebed's specific target (Mormons) may have been off the mark, the general thrust of his diatribe reflected (and manipulated) the growing anxiety throughout the former USSR regarding new religious movements, popularly known as "cults."[6] Given the unconventional behavior and appearance of some of the more prominent new religious movements' adherents (the Society for Krishna Consciousness immediately comes to mind), it should come as no surprise that such groups are looked on with suspicion. The Supreme Soviet responded to pressure from the Russian Orthodox Church by attempting to ban foreign missionaries on Russian territory in July 1993; in 1997, Yeltsin signed a law severely limiting the activities of all but a select few religious organizations. When politicians like Lebed or religious leaders like Aleksii II rail against foreign missionaries, they express an age-old strain of Russian xenophobia. But the "threat from abroad" is only part of the story: the former Soviet Union has, in a few short years, produced a number of "cults" of its own. Although foreign movements such as the Unification Church hold primacy of place in the Russian nationalist demonology, their homegrown counterparts are also worthy of note. If the Krishnas, Japan's Aum Shinri Kyo, and the followers of Reverend Moon symbolize the danger to Russia's cultural patrimony posed by foreign ideological imports, new Slavic religious movements such as the Mother of God Center (Bogorodichnyi tsentr) and the Great White Brotherhood (Velikoe beloe bratstvo) are, to their opponents, the embodiment of a Russia gone mad, a cultural cancer metastasizing into ever stranger and more virulent growths within the body politic. This metaphor of disease is repeatedly invoked by politicians, religious leaders, and journalists: again and again, new religious movements are denounced as a "plague." In examining the rhetoric surrounding cults in contemporary Russia, I hope to demonstrate that any talk of "disease" is a far from accurate diagnosis. Rather than being a distortion of truly Russian values, new religious movements are, if anything, a distillation of a number of important trends in contemporary Russian culture. The very features that irritate Russian anticultists characterize post-Soviet society in general: both the "cults" in the former USSR and their detractors provide a vivid snapshot of the Russian postmodern condition.

Russian Relativism: From the Silver Age to the New Age

When discussing new religious movements in Russia, it is easy to point the finger at the "ideological void" left by the collapse of communism: today's youth presumably lack a strong set of values by which to make sense of their lives. Such an approach is hardly new, and it has its share of adherents among anticultists in the West as well. Although I do not take issue with this idea (which, given the recent upheavals in the former Eastern bloc, appears self-evident), I propose that we look at the contemporary situation in terms not of lack, but rather of excess: today's God-seeking Russian faces a veritable spiritual smorgasbord whose likes haven't been seen since the Silver Age (1880–1917). The spiritualist legacy of the decades before the revolution was unabashedly eclectic: in the Theosophy of H. P. Blavatsky, Indian mahatmas rubbed elbows with Jesus Christ, and dilettantes throughout Europe peppered their language with exotic Buddhist borrowings. Spiritual seekers in contemporary Russia are equally syncretic, if not to say omnivorous, in their approach: the program of the most noteworthy post-Soviet cult, the Great White Brotherhood, was a New Age goulash of chakras, karma, Kabbalah, and even music theory. On a more anecdotal level, it is not at all uncommon to encounter intelligent, educated Russians who casually refer to the "truths" inherent in astrology and who credit the extrasensory powers of any number of ESPers and swamis, from television's psychic healer Anatoly Kashpirovsky to Brezhnev's favorite clairvoyant, Dzhuna.[7] Many beliefs held by followers of new religious movements seem almost conventional when set against the backdrop of almost daily reports of UFOs and miraculous extrasensory phenomena. The New Age and new religious movements occupy different points on a spectrum of syncretic belief: if the New Age is unrelentingly eclectic, willing to accommodate elements of a nearly infinite set of conflicting belief systems (Christianity, Buddhism, and paganism, for instance), a new religious movement such as the Great White Brotherhood may draw on the same sources but turn the resulting religious mélange into a strict dogma. Nevertheless, it is possible that New Age eclecticism renders the apparent contradictions of cult dogma more palatable, the faculty of skepticism having atrophied for lack of exercise. The post-totalitarian order has proven to be a hotbed of political cynicism, but when it comes to questions of faith, Russians continually astound foreign observers with their capacity for belief.

Although the adherents of "cults" such as Aum Shinri Kyo and the White Brotherhood may appear fanatically committed to a single idea, their dedication is predicated on the ability to reconcile (or at least not question) the widely disparate elements of their faith's doctrine. Here Mikhail Epstein's analysis of Soviet and post-Soviet culture is particularly illuminating: in his "Relativistic Patterns in Totalitarian Thinking," Epstein argues that Soviet Marxism, rather than being "the most rigid and stagnant component of twentieth-century intellectual development," was actually the most relativistic of all possible ideological systems: "it constantly changed and expanded its set of ideas in order to maintain its power."[8] During the Brezhnev era, "ideology was gradually transformed from a system of ideas into an all-encompassing ideological environment that retained all possible alternative philosophical systems as latent components within itself. Existentialism and structuralism, Russophilism and Westernism, technocratic and ecological movements, religious and neo-pagan outlooks — everything was compressed into the forms of Marxism, creating a sort of postmodern pastiche."[9] Conversely, one could argue that the demonizing of all opposing points of view resulted in relativizing everything that was not considered Marxism: fascism and liberal democracy were both simply "anti-Soviet," and thus functionally equivalent. The next step, according to Epstein, occurred under Gorbachev, when totalitarianism gave way to a postcommunist "universalist" ideology: "Universalist ideology tries to eliminate all oppositions and use the entire range of ideas as if they were complementary."[10]

Such relativism could not help but have an impact on questions of faith. Scientific atheism lumped together all religious traditions, from Christianity to Buddhism to paganism. "Soviet atheism," Epstein writes, "produced a type of a believer who is impossible to identify in denominational terms: he is simply a believer, '*veruiushchii.*' " This type of believer does not regularly attend an established church, but neither does he or she rail against organized religion. The faith of the believer is instead what Epstein calls "poor religion" or "minimal religion": a spirituality devoid of rituals and regulations.[11] The believer knows that there is a spiritual dimension to life, but does not think it has been perfectly defined by any particular faith. Such believers, I would argue, believe in nothing in particular and everything at once; their skepticism toward claims to absolute truths is based on a faith in the idea of a "portion of truth" (*dolia pravdy*).

Two surveys conducted in the early 1990s confirm that, far from undergoing a revival of traditional religion, Russia has witnessed the rapid growth of nontraditional belief.[12] Although in the 1990 survey 46 percent of respondents identified themselves as Russian Orthodox, only 19 percent called themselves Orthodox the following year. This sharp decline was not matched by a drop in "believers," however; the main rival to Orthodoxy proved to be neither another established church nor atheism, but rather an amorphous category called "Christians in general": they constituted 22 percent of all respondents in 1990 and 47 percent in 1991.[13] D. E. Furman explains the sharp contrast between the two surveys as largely the result of people identifying themselves with Orthodoxy in 1990 out of a sense that "religion occupies an important place in the bourgeois-democratic societies of the West," along with the expectation that Orthodoxy would play the same role in the new Russia. This "superficial" affiliation quickly wore thin, hence the rise in "Christians in general." Even the term *Christian* must be understood in the loosest possible sense, because a large number of those who chose this identification were "people with the most indefinite, eclectic world view, with a heightened interest in Eastern religious teachings, in spiritualism, in modern parascientific and parareligious mythology built around parapsychology, UFOs, etc."[14] Thus it would seem that Russia has quietly entered the New Age; in spirit if not in climate, the country appears well on its way to becoming the Southern California of Europe.[15]

In terms of sheer variety, then, foreign new religious movements seem to be a manifestation of the same "cultural invasion" that characterizes the Russian marketplace: "cults" are to churches what Snickers bars are to kiosks. Those who fear for Russia's cultural integrity can point to the ingenuity and sheer variety of foreign missionary activity, on a scale made possible by vast financial reserves. Indeed, the manner in which these organizations allocate their resources leaves them open to charges that they are purchasing respectability with foreign currency, as any visitor to the L. Ron Hubbard Reading Room at Moscow State University's Journalism School can attest.[16] The Unification Church, whose leader was received by Mikhail Gorbachev in the Kremlin in 1990, has most recently come under fire from the Russian Commission on Religious Organizations for sponsoring a public school course entitled "The World and I."[17] The Japanese Aum Shinri Kyo, whose activities in its home country have been curtailed while the group is being investigated for allegedly masterminding nerve gas attacks on Tokyo's subway, uses its wealth for a startlingly wide range of activities, from the sinister to the sublime: while Aum's apparent interest in purchasing Russian nuclear weapons has, for good reason, drawn a great deal of attention, the Japanese movement is also said to have contributed eighty thousand dollars in computer equipment to Moscow State University and several hundred thousand dollars worth of medical supplies to Russian hospitals, as well as sponsoring its own Russian symphony orchestra.[18] But the most successful of all foreign groups is also the first one to set roots in Russian soil: the Society of Krishna Consciousness, or the Hare Krishnas. Their presence in the former Soviet Union dates back to 1971, although Krishnas were routinely persecuted until 1988.[19] When the government relaxed its controls on religious activity, it was the Krishnas who developed the first, and most thorough, campaign for Soviet souls. The Krishnas were quite possibly the first group to exploit the commercial potential of the metro in Moscow; in 1991, posters calling on Russians to read *The Bhagavad-Gita as It Is* adorned every metro car; thanks to a model of capitalist efficiency, those who were intrigued by the advertisement had only to step off the train and walk up the stairs to buy the book, which was sold in most major metro stations.[20]

On the surface, the public outrage over "cults" in Russia is a backlash against this very relativism. Orthodox Church leaders are highly defensive against sectarians who poach on "their" territory; and for his part, Lebed framed his rejection of Mormons as a defense of "mono-religious" Russia against Western cultural expansion.[21] Furman distinguishes two tendencies in the new religious consciousness in Russia, both of which are a retreat from Marxist atheism: "The first leads to belief in God and to Orthodoxy. The second, which is 'drowning out' the first, is a movement toward an amorphous, eclectic consciousness that is neither confessional . . . nor even religious or antireligious."[22] Furman argues for a strong correlation between the two opposing religious tendencies and the contemporary political climate; Orthodox respondents to the 1990 and 1991 surveys showed "a very obvious and vivid combination of a purely ideological and symbolic anticommunism with a relative 'softness' toward the actual institutions of Soviet power, strong authoritarianism, and 'anti-Western' tendencies."[23] Even the 1991 attempted coup had, according to Furman, a religious dimension: "The leaders of the attempted coup were supported more by atheists and the Orthodox, while 'Christians in general' and persons with a heightened interest in the *Bhagavad-Gita,* Zen Buddhism, and flying saucers gathered around Yeltsin." Certainly, this is a vast generalization to make on the basis of two surveys, and one could hardly expect Yeltsin's advisers to actively court the "flying saucer" vote. It also underplays the role of supernatural belief on the antidemocratic end of the spectrum.[24] The defenders of Orthodoxy often betray a surprising faith in the very New Age beliefs they so harshly condemn. In *The Black Trail of the White Brotherhood,* the anonymous Russian Orthodox authors assert that the crimes of the Great White Brotherhood should interest all those around the world who are battling "ultra-brain control" (*ul' tramozogovyi kontrol' nad liud'mi*). During their initiation, new members are supposedly subjected to "extrasensory efforts with the help of an upside-down cross," after which a cross with "Kabbalistic signs" places a "code" (*kod*) on the zone of the "third eye," or "agni-chakra."[25] To a large extent, the prophets of new religious movements and the crusaders against them share the same language.

Waiting for the End of the World: The Great White Brotherhood

Although a number of home-grown new religious movements have sprouted throughout the former Soviet Union, one group in particular forced the ex-Soviet public to realize that "cults" were not merely an imported problem: the Great White Brotherhood of Maria Devi Khristos.[26] Most Russians became aware of Maria Devi only in 1993, owing in part to the White Brotherhood's massive campaign of self-promotion. Thanks to the dedication of Maria Devi's followers, who plastered copies of her portrait on practically every window of every metro car in the capitals, millions of people all over the Slavic region of the Commonwealth of Independent States (CIS) quickly became acquainted with the picture of a stern-looking young woman who held the middle and index fingers of her right hand pointed toward heaven as her eyes serenely gazed back at her observers.[27] If the portrait is supposed to supplant its Christian predecessors, as claimed by one young woman who tried to sell me "an icon of the Lord God Jesus-Maria Herself," it is an icon for a less domestic age, displayed in public transportation rather than in a corner at home. Like any divinity worthy of the name, Maria Devi Khristos was omnipresent, at least on paper; indeed, the sheer number of White Brotherhood flyers prompted the Russian newspaper *Komsomol'skaia pravda* to call the special pre-apocalyptic White Brotherhood page of its youth supplement "Cut and Paste Maria Devi!"[28]

Although Maria Devi Khristos was the official head of the Brotherhood (and without a doubt its primary object of worship), the movement was founded by Yuri Andreevich Krivonogov, a scientist who was born in the Voronezh region of the Russian Republic in 1941. At some point not long before the establishment of the brotherhood, Krivonogov abandoned his scientific career in favor of more mystical pursuits. After deciding that he was "Adam and the Sun," he took the name "Iuoann Swami" and founded the Atma Institute of the Soul in 1990. While lecturing on psychic phenomena and "healing" the sick in Donetsk, Ukraine, Krivonogov met Marina Tsvigun, a married thirty-year-old woman whose life before her godhood was as mundane as her later exploits were sensational. In "The Earthly Path of Maria Devi Khristos," Tsvigun describes herself as a journalism graduate of Kiev State University, who, as a reporter, "openly fought the Mafia, lawlessness, and the party *nomenklatura.*"[29] Before meeting Krivonogov, the future Mother of the World had already become convinced of her own divinity after a near-death experience caused by an overdose of anesthetic during an abortion.[30]

Tsvigun and Krivonogov soon developed a following and convinced approximately one thousand people that the world was coming to an end. According to Tsvigun and Krivonogov, the appearance of Maria Devi rounded out a set of trinities that had been left incomplete by Judaism and Christianity: God the Father and God the Son are at last joined by God the Mother, and the Old and New Testaments have been superseded (or fulfilled) by the Final Testament of Maria Devi Khristos.[31] Tsvigun herself is the final incarnation of God, "Jesus-Maria," both Christ and the Mother of Christ.[32] Since June 1, 1991, the "program" of IUSMALOS (an acronym formed from "Iuoann Swami," "Maria Devi Khristos," and "Logos," and used as an alternate name for the brotherhood) had been "activated," and would culminate in the apocalypse 1,260 "biblical" days later.[33] Maria Devi, the "Woman Clothed in the Sun" foretold in Revelation, would fulfill the prophesies of the New Testament and fight the Antichrist Emmanuel, whose power now holds most of the world in its sway.[34] On November 24, 1993, Tsvigun was to crucify herself in Kiev, which was now the "New Jerusalem" of the "promised land" located in the "Slavic region of the CIS."[35] Tsvigun usually referred only to her own sacrifice, but Krivonogov repeatedly claimed that he would die on the cross along with his "wife."[36] Three days after their deaths, Tsvigun and Krivonogov would rise again and lead the faithful to paradise, leaving Maria Devi's enemies behind to perish by fire in a worldwide cataclysm.

Such talk made many in Kiev understandably nervous, especially since Tsvigun's and Krivonogov's (literally) inflammatory rhetoric was compounded by popular misunderstandings of the "program" of IUSMALOS. Reporters and government officials expressed the fear that Maria Devi's followers, who were repeatedly told by Tsvigun and Krivonogov to be prepared for martyrdom, would prepare for the world's end through mass self-immolation, turning the streets of Kiev into a slaughterhouse that would make "Heaven's Gate" and Jonestown look like child's play. Indeed, the government and the media had no idea as to the scope of the problem that faced them. With the benefit of hindsight, it is easy to dismiss the White Brotherhood as an insignificant disturbance of the peace; after all, as headline after headline would eventually declare, the world did not end. But the story being told in November was quite different, as Kiev nervously awaited the anticipated onslaught of 144,000 death-crazed, brainwashed fanatics. By the beginning of November, "Brothers" from all over the former Soviet Union began answering Maria Devi's call to come to the Ukrainian capital, and President Kravchuk authorized "emergency measures."[37] The group's arrival exacerbated tensions between Ukraine and Russia, because most of Maria Devi's followers were Russian citizens, and because a truck from St. Petersburg carrying three tons of White Brotherhood literature had been stopped in Ukraine.[38] Ukrainian government officials made numerous appeals for calm and cooperation in the first week of November, but with little effect. Approximately 250 followers of Maria Devi had been arrested on November 1, and many of them declared a hunger strike.[39] Schoolchildren were given special lessons on how to defend themselves from the Brotherhood, and schools rearranged their class schedules so that children would not have to walk home at night.[40]

The denouement of the whole affair was more comic than tragic, much to the relief of Kiev's citizenry. By mid-November, guards had been posted all around

Saint Sophia Square, the site of Maria Devi's intended crucifixion. On November 11, a group of "Brothers" managed to enter the Saint Sophia cathedral disguised as tourists. Once inside, they threw off their robes, approached the altar, and tried to hold a service.[41] They barricaded themselves within the cathedral, and when OMON (the special forces) attempted to force them out, the "Brothers" attacked them with fire extinguishers (the irony was apparently lost on all concerned). Some members of the special forces suffered minor injuries, and the iconostasis was also damaged, but the brief "last battle" between the forces of the Messiah and the "servants of the Antichrist" was won by OMON.[42] Among those arrested were Krivonogov and the Lord God Herself. On February 9, 1996, Marina Tsvigun received a four-year sentence for seizing public property and endangering the welfare of her followers. Krivonogov, whom Maria Devi had already renounced and divorced, was sentenced to seven years' imprisonment on the same charges and also for creating a public disturbance and resisting arrest. Several dozen of their followers wept as the sentences were read.[43]

Although the activity of the White Brotherhood clearly reached its peak in 1993, not all of Maria Devi's followers abandoned her. The split between Tsvigun and Krivonogov has allowed the "Mother of the World" to claim that her teachings were distorted by "Cain" (the name she now prefers to call the former Iuoann Swami) without renouncing her own divinity. She continued to issue written pronouncements to the faithful from prison, although the size of her flock had shrunk drastically. Of the thirty to forty White Brothers who composed her Petersburg congregation, there are now only eight. Having abandoned both their white robes and their nonstop leafletting, Maria Devi's followers reportedly sing songs based on Tsvigun's poetry and ask for contributions from passersby. The Brotherhood's temporal leadership apparently announced another end of the world (this time scheduled for late 1996), but, like most sequels, the event failed to generate the same excitement as the original.[44] In the summer of 1997, Tsvigun was released from prison to little fanfare.

Sacred Simulacra

Much like the Soviet Union itself, which collapsed under its own weight rather than through any cold war nightmare of nuclear Armageddon, the Great White Brotherhood's downfall was anything but catastrophic: instead of the promised "bang" of the Day of Judgment, Maria Devi's church collapsed with a pathetic juridical whimper. Even Maria Devi's apocalypse was subject to bureaucratic scheduling problems. Although it was originally planned for November 24, 1993, at the end of October Tsvigun and Krivonogov moved it ahead to November 14. Here one recalls Stalin's determination to accomplish the First Five-Year Plan in four years: it is not enough to promise a miracle; the impossible must be achieved in a manner that outpaces the expectations of the believers themselves. Within the context of post-Soviet confusion, the denouement of the Great White Brotherhood had a certain logic: the brief time between the failed coup of August 1991 and Yeltsin's storming of the Russian parliament building in October 1993 was by and large the era of the nonevent. If history had not ended, it had at least paused, thereby only heightening the sensation that something pivotal was about to occur; post-Soviet reality certainly provided fertile ground for fantasies of an apocalypse that would be repeatedly postponed. Like Maria Devi's followers, Russians and their Ukrainian neighbors lived in constant expectation of terrible calamities that doggedly refused to occur: the rumored famines and all-out civil war, the whispers of a plan to sell Lenin's body to the highest bidder at a public auction (a rumor started unintentionally by American humorist Christopher Buckley), and the unsubstantiated allegations that top government officials were trading in a mythical nuclear substance called "red mercury." The claims of both the leaders of the Great White Brotherhood and the movers and shakers of the new political order seemed to grow in scope at the same pace as the ruble's plummet. Indeed, the economic metaphor is perhaps more apt than the "disease" imagery offered by anticultists in the mass media: hyperinflation was, after all, yet another catastrophe that Russia narrowly managed to avoid. Or, more to the point, hyperinflation did occur, but in an entirely different realm from economics: there was a hyperinflation of rhetoric.

When examined closely, the Great White Brotherhood proves to be a fundamentally rhetorical phenomenon — or rather, not a phenomenon at all, but a simulacrum. The scandalous rise and fall of Maria Devi bears all the hallmarks of Jean Baudrillard's "hyperreality," in which reality is supplanted by its representations. As I have argued elsewhere, the Great White Brotherhood was a creature of the mass media; if Maria Devi and her propaganda machine were the movement's mother, its father was not "Swami" Krivonogov but the post-Soviet press.[45] The literature of the Brotherhood repeatedly refers to the 144,000 "saints" who make up Maria Devi's following, and who were to watch her be crucified in Kiev. Most reports took Tsvigun and Krivonogov at their word, neglecting to mention that the figure 144,000 comes directly from Revelation 7:4, and should therefore not necessarily be considered an accurate assessment of the Brotherhood's size. Ironically, in their evaluation of the Brotherhood's unsubstantiated boasting, the reporters for such respected publications as *Izvestiia* and *Komsomol'skaia pravda* (as well as for scandal sheets such as *Shchit i mech'* and *Moskovskii komsomolets*) proved just as gullible as the post-Soviet consumer when faced with the dubious claims of pyramid schemes (MMM) and weight-loss scams (Herbal Life): both journalists and their readers were duped by false advertising. When all was said and done, only about seven or eight hundred followers of Maria Devi were arrested, and there is no evidence to suggest that a significant number of "Brothers" remained at large.[46] If the exaggerations of the group's membership were consistent with the impossible promises of the postcommunist market, they were also positively Gogolian: Maria Devi had saved far more "dead souls" than live ones.

Even if the leaders of the Brotherhood had not been arrested, it is unlikely that events would have unfolded according to the scenario so vividly depicted in the popular press; despite claims by journalists and government officials, it appears that the Great White Brotherhood had no plans to commit mass suicide.[47] Thus the mass media took the already exaggerated claims of the Brotherhood and inflated them further, acting in concert to create the illusion of an enormous threat to civic order. Although one can hardly claim that the leaders of the Brotherhood intended their faith to be a symbol of post-Soviet turpitude, the journalists who covered the movement tended to use the Brotherhood as yet another sign that Russia and Ukraine were suffering from a profound moral crisis. If we set aside all questions of morality (admittedly a difficult task when dealing with questions of faith), we discover, if not a crisis, then a projection of the concerns and anxieties of contemporary Russia. This, too, is probably no credit to Krivonogov and Tsvigun, who need not have been conscious of these issues to exploit them; rather, they resemble the proverbial infinite number of monkeys who, given an equally limitless number of typewriters, randomly hunt and peck their way to the complete works of Shakespeare.

The Russia We Have Lost

The propaganda both for and against the Great White Brotherhood (which, as far as the popular consciousness was concerned, was essentially equivalent to the Brotherhood itself) highlights the problem of the Russian cultural patri-

mony in an age of pluralism and uncertainty. The ubiquitous portrait of Maria
Devi, which deliberately evokes the traditional religious art of Russian Orthodoxy, is both a post-Soviet and a postmodern icon: dressed in a white robe,
headdress, and shawl, with jewelry and a headband, she has a vaguely Eastern
look; but her crucifix, shepherd's staff, and the two raised fingers of her right
hand point to the Christian tradition. Although her face is not at the center of the
portrait, the observer's eye is inevitably drawn to it because the headband and
her right hand enclose it within a partial frame. To the citizens of Russia or
Ukraine, that face bears a distinct and inescapable message: the woman who
has draped herself in this mishmash of Christian and Eastern wardrobe is
unmistakably Slavic.[48]

Maria Devi's Slavic roots were crucial to the Brotherhood's public image,
because the Great White Brotherhood, counter to the usual pattern of sectarian
activity in the former Soviet Union, was a movement that claimed to export
missionaries rather than import them. According to the Brotherhood's pamphlets and its newspaper, *IUSMALOS,* Maria Devi, Iuoann Swami, and their
lieutenants had traveled throughout Eastern and Western Europe, and ITAR-
Tass quoted a Baptist minister's brief account of his encounter with Tsvigun in
Jerusalem.[49] At least to a limited extent, the Great White Brotherhood partook
of a long-standing tradition of Russian messianism, in which "Holy Russia"
will bring salvation to a sinful world. Like the Old Believers and the many
sectarian movements that cropped up in tsarist times, the Brotherhood claimed
to be a more faithful representative of Slavic spirituality than the "corrupt"
Orthodox Church. The leaders of the Brotherhood located themselves within
the tradition of Russian religious dissent both verbally and visually: the ubiquitous icon of Maria Devi shows the Mother of the World making the two-
fingered, Old Believer blessing rather than the three-fingered sign favored by
the Russian Orthodox Church since the reforms that led to the Great Schism of
the seventeenth century.

In their writings, Krivonogov and Tsvigun are unsparing in their criticism of
the official church, casually referring to its priests as the "black cockroaches of
Orthodoxy." Yet the Brotherhood's challenge was based not on a complete
refutation of the Russian church, but rather on the assertion that the church had
strayed from the true path. Such an approach, which facilitated the incorporation of Orthodox symbols and even liturgy within the doctrine of the Brotherhood, made a great deal of sense in the post-Soviet context: as Furman's survey
suggests, the Russian "return to Orthodoxy" was hampered by the church's

close ties with the old regime. When Tsvigun writes that "all the churches today are befouled by the loathsome spirit of Satan," when she asserts that Russian Orthodox priests are "defiling the former sacred place with vomit and orgasms," her admittedly crude phrasing merely recapitulates the accusations that the church made a "deal with the devil" when it made its peace with the communist regime.[50] In the tradition of Avvakum, who referred to the patriarch of the Russian Orthodox Church as the "hound of hell," the Brotherhood managed to attack the church for falling under the sway of the Antichrist while appealing to "true" Orthodox sensibilities; one member of the Brotherhood who claims to be a former priest writes, "I have nothing against Christianity or the church in general; I'm against what is happening in it today!"[51]

In its appropriation of the mantle of "Russianness" from the Orthodox Church, the Great White Brotherhood rather deftly addressed Russia's postimperial malaise. On the surface, the Brotherhood adapted to the new realities much quicker than most inhabitants of the former USSR; at a time when the ungainly "Commonwealth of Independent States" by no means came trippingly off ex-Soviet tongues, Krivonogov's and Tsvigun's diatribes blithely referred to the CIS as though it had existed for decades. The CIS provided the Brotherhood with an easy vehicle for eliding the terminological difficulties posed by the Soviet Union's collapse. Although the movement clearly saw itself in opposition specifically to the Russian church and considered itself the heir to the Russian cultural patrimony, the most significant events relating to the story of the White Brotherhood took place in the now-independent land of Tsvigun's birth: Ukraine. At a time when nationalism threatened to turn Russia and Ukraine into bitter enemies, Maria Devi refused to see any difference between the two. Most of her references to the Commonwealth are directed toward the CIS as it was originally constituted: an umbrella term for the Slavic republics of Russia, Ukraine, and Belarus: "The CIS is becoming the center of Satanism (the Slavic region is the Promised Land)."[52] But Maria Devi's acceptance of the CIS is part and parcel of the "new medievalism" of her message: for her, the fragmentary remains of the Soviet Union are nothing less than the Promised Land of "Ancient Kievan Rus."[53] At the heart of Maria Devi's New Age theology is an appeal to nostalgia for a long-lost, prelapsarian "Russia" that transcends contemporary nationalism. Indeed, the very ubiquity of the Brotherhood's propaganda can be seen as a peculiar bond among the three newly independent states; as one commentator wrote in 1993, "A man from Kiev travels to, say, Moscow, sees [Maria Devi's] photo pasted on the subway

car or on a shop window, and it's as though he never left the Ukrainian capital."[54] Even as Maria Devi's followers look forward to their postapocalyptic
paradise, their rhetoric and tactics also hearken back to a golden age, appealing
to the postimperial nostalgia that quickly took hold in Russia.

The question of Russian identity is crucial to several new religious movements in Russia, and perhaps constitutes the most obvious difference between
home-grown religions and their imported counterparts. The failure of the Russian Orthodox Church, which is seen as having compromised itself in the Soviet period, is always a subtext to the teachings of Russian new religious movements, and many of them make their attacks on official Orthodoxy explicit.
Like the Great White Brotherhood, the Mother of God Center, founded by de-
frocked Orthodox priest Ioann Bereslavsky, styles itself as the "one true faith,"
and considers the official Russian Orthodox Church to be a force for evil. If
Tsvigun and Krivonogov proclaimed IUSMALOS to be the true expression of
Slavic spirituality, Bereslavsky takes these claims even further: the Mother of
God Center is, in fact, the true Russian Orthodox Church, and only the center
can bring back the "truths" of Orthodoxy that were distorted by the Russian
patriarch's "red church."[55] Other new religions, such as the Bazhov Academy
of Secret Knowledge (Bazhovskaia akademiia sokrovennykh znanii), appear
more concerned with reconstructing the lost traditions of "holy" Russian culture than with attacking the Orthodox Church. Founded in the Cheliabinsk
oblast' by Vladimir Sobolev, the Bazhov Academy claims that the Urals are the
"energy center" of all of Russia, and that the navel of the world can be found in
Arkaim, the homeland of a lost people located not far from Magnitogorsk.
Among the key figures in their cosmology is Ermak, the conqueror of Siberia,
whose heroic feat united Europe and Asia. Even contemporary public figures
have their role in the academy's vision of Russia's sacred mission; in Sobolev's
hands, Mikhail Gorbachev becomes the reincarnation of the Grand Prince
Mikhail Romanov, and thus the tsar of all the Russias. Much of the teachings of
the academy are based on interpretations of folktales written by the Sverdlovsk
author Pavel Bazhov (1879–1950), who is said to have encoded sacred truths in
his seemingly innocuous children's stories. Steeped in folklore and national
traditions, the academy sponsors conferences and folklore festivals, and has
close ties with the local government; a Bazhov festival in 1995 is said to have
attracted six thousand participants.[56]

After looking at several different native Russian "cults," one almost gets the
impression that their leaders ransacked the same public library for inspiration,

or that the component parts of the country's national myth were sold off to new religious movements at an ideological privatization auction. In 1992, *Megalopolis Express,* then a new weekly tabloid with a dubious reputation, published a series of articles that purport to expose the existence of a previously unknown community living in secret passageways under Moscow. These so-called Tolstoyites apparently descend from the Tolstoyans who attempted to put the Russian writer's religious ideas into practice, but an editor's note to the first article on the subject calls the group a "kind of hybrid of the ideas of Lev Tolstoy and Vladimir Ulianov [Lenin]."[57] It is difficult to see precisely what their beliefs and practices have to do with either Tolstoy or Lenin: the group supposedly advocates "absolute freedom, conscience and uncompromising-ness," and practices free love, theft, prostitution, and murder.[58] Their children are raised on an eclectic diet of literature whose enumeration says much about the cultural agenda of the reporter, Nikolai Popov: "the children study the classics from Aristotle to Berdiaev, from Ovid to Pushkin, from Pythagoras to Lobachevsky." By arranging the names as a series of contrasts between ancient Greek and Russian culture figures, Popov treats the Russian patrimony and the Greeks as two equally valuable (and equally dead) traditions. Moreover, Popov recapitulates a classic Russian millenarian pattern by implying that, in all fields of endeavor, it is Russia that completes the march to progress begun by the Greeks. To the best of my knowledge, no other newspaper picked up the Tolstoyite story; and given the reputation of *Megalopolis Express* and the sensational nature of the articles, it is more than likely that the Tolstoyites are the product of the reporter's imagination. Yet even if the Tolstoyites are a fabrication, the use of a classic Russian author as inspiration for the sect suggests that a concern with Russia's cultural heritage is an essential part of the deep structure underlying new religious movements in Russia today: it is the Russian *spetsifika* (specific character) that makes the forgery at least somewhat convincing.[59]

Totalisectarians

The existence of so many different new religious movements created a problem for ambitious groups such as the Great White Brotherhood. Inevitably, the leaders of the Brotherhood found themselves hurling invective not only at the "usual suspects" such as Patriarch Aleksii II, Yeltsin, and Leonid Kravchuk (then president of Ukraine), but also at rival prophets who were equally sure that *they* were the authors of a new and final testament. For all its talk of unity, the Great White Brotherhood encountered the same problem faced by utopian visionaries throughout history: the Brotherhood's pretensions to global truth easily revealed themselves to be parochial. Indeed, the very term most commonly used to describe new religious movements in Russia (*sekta*) connotes factionalism and obscurantism dating back to the Schism of the seventeenth century, thereby implicitly relativizing any new religious movement's claim to global truth. The competing claims of so many would-be messiahs diminishes their "divine" status; the Promised Land begins to resemble a feudal estate divided among so many quarrelsome godlings.

In between diatribes on the evils of contemporary Orthodoxy, Tsvigun and Krivonogov used the pages of *IUSMALOS* to fulminate against Ioann Bereslavsky's Mother of God Center. Although it has garnered far less media attention than the Great White Brotherhood, the Mother of God Center appeared on the scene several years before Maria Devi. Early in his prophetic career, Bereslavsky was quoted as saying that Moscow's streets would be filled with thousands of plague-infested corpses if the city failed to accept his teachings; but by the time Maria Devi won her *succès du scandale,* Bereslavsky had tuned his rhetoric down several notches.[60] Maria Devi's lurid description of the hellish fate reserved for nonbelievers is a classic millenarian vision, while the reformed teachings of Bereslavsky might well be called "apocalypticism with a human face": the world is to be transformed rather than destroyed, all thanks to the mercy of the Mother of God.[61] Even discounting the differences in their respective scenarios for the culmination of history, the nature of Bereslavsky's center ensured that he and the White Brotherhood would be mortal enemies. Where Tsvigun claimed to be both Christ and the Mother of God incarnated in one form, Bereslavsky built his center around the worship of Christ's mother and declared himself her messenger.[62] In a poem dated March 20, 1993, Tsvigun declares Bereslavsky a "false prophet" and "traitor" who has sold himself to Satan.[63] On June 14, 1993, followers of Maria Devi disrupted a Mother of God service in St. Petersburg and distributed pamphlets referring to Bereslavsky as "kike filth" (*nechist' zhidovskaia*). Bereslavsky responded by calling "Maria Bludevi" (Maria Devi Slut) a "village cow and androgynous freak" whose genitals were invaded by an evil spirit while her soul was making one of its periodic trips into space.[64] Such fierce turf battles between the two cults could scarcely have had a salutary effect on the image of either organization.

Nevertheless, it is the totalizing ambitions of some new religious movements, rather than their intramural sparring, that provoke popular concern. Perhaps the clearest indication that new religious movements serve as a barometer for anxiety over the totalitarian legacy is the manner in which "cults" have been tarred with the brush of totalitarianism. The same authors who call for greater state control over religious affairs, and for an increased role of the Orthodox Church in public life, routinely refer to new religious movements as "totalitarian sects."[65] This term, which is used to describe religious movements that aspire to total control of the believer's life, has cold war roots that are even deeper than one might suspect. The accusation leveled at "totalitarian sects" by their critics is that they engage in "coding" (*kodirovanie*) or "modeling" (*modelirovanie*), the Russian equivalent of brainwashing. According to a Ukrainian Ministry of Internal Affairs (MVD) dossier on White Brotherhood leader Yuri Krivonogov, the Brotherhood's guru "is a master of bio-energetics and hypnosis, which he uses to neutralize a person's will and make him obedient and incapable of resistance." Krivonogov's "coding" turns his victims into "zombies" (*zombi*) "during their 'christening' or 'initiation' into the 'Great White Brotherhood.' "[66] Where did Krivonogov and other would-be messiahs develop these skills? In the laboratories of the KGB, of course.

Here we are dealing with the justifiable paranoia of a culture in which psychiatry was used as a weapon against dissidents rather than a tool to treat the sick, and in which the information vacuum left by the state-controlled press was filled largely by a formidable rumor mill whose productive capacity outstripped that of any actual Soviet factory. Ironically, the KGB served (and continues to serve) the same function fulfilled by "Communists" in the fantasies of right-wing extremists in the West: they can always be invoked to explain the inexplicable. As Boris Falikov puts it, "There are more than enough specialists in demonology in our country, which is, in itself, symptomatic." Falikov reports hearing his acquaintances argue that the entire White Brotherhood was a KGB mind-control experiment gone wrong, a theory that had earlier been used to explain the equally baffling phenomenon of Vladimir Zhirinovsky's popularity.[67] A number of sources claimed that Krivonogov had worked as an engineer or computer scientist in a laboratory specializing in "psychotropic weaponry."[68] One journalist insists that the young Krivonogov learned to "zombify" people while working at an artificial intelligence laboratory: "According to reliable data . . . the laboratory was dedicated not only to the creation of electronic intelligence, but also to the transformation of human intelligence into artificial intelligence."[69] The fact that such a claim would make no sense to anyone with even the vaguest understanding of the nature of artificial intelligence is of little import; with this rhetorical sleight-of-hand, the post-Soviet cult is revealed to be a totalitarian genie let out of a KGB-manufactured bottle.

The irony of such charges of brainwashing is twofold. The accusations leveled at "totalitarian sects" betray an implicit faith in the claims of cult leaders to possess supernatural powers. In the frequent accusations of "zombification" and "coding," as well as in the tendency to treat science, religion, and mysticism as merely a verbal repertoire from which one may mix and match elements, we see evidence that the leaders of new religious movements and their opponents in the mass media turn to the same sources to frame their arguments. Maria Devi Khristos, the Living God of the Great White Brotherhood, claimed that the servants of the Antichrist were "subjecting thousands of naive people to his influence with the help of their television and radio programs," and that Russian Orthodox priests had been "adding a special psychotropic element" to the Eucharist, "making the parishioners into weak-willed slaves of the Satanists."[70] Throughout Russian history, religious dissenters have painted the authorities as servants of Satan on earth; Peter the Great, whose attempts to transform the country along Western models alienated a large segment of the population, and Patriarch Nikon, whose reforms in church ritual led to the Schism, are perhaps the most prominent figures to be identified with the Antichrist.[71] Yet the attempt to identify "coding" with a plot to destroy traditional Russian values has itself been infected by foreign discourse: Russian critics are echoing the "brainwashing" debate in the United States, which itself grew out of the experience of Western POWs in communist reeducation camps.[72] In America, the debate over brainwashing constituted the translation of the Red Scare into the realm of religion; now it has been appropriated by the defenders of Orthodoxy in the name of Russian cultural purity.

Relatively Russian

The irony surrounding the anxiety provoked by new religious movements in Russia is almost palpable: while the opponents of "cults" routinely charge that the phenomenon is the result of pernicious foreign influences, their own discourse has been colonized by the rhetoric of the Western "anticult" movement, which, for its part, displays cold war roots. In these unstable first years of the post-Soviet era, appeals to a simpler, more authentically "Russian" past are by no means uncommon, as demonstrated not only by Stanislav Govorukhin's popular documentary *The Russia We Have Lost* (1992), but also by the frequency with which Russian historical and folk heroes appear in television commercials and by the massive circulation of pictures and calendars bearing the images of the last Romanovs. The propagandists both for and against new religious movements in Russia are fighting over more than the souls of potential believers: the prize at stake is the Russian cultural patrimony itself. Each side claims to be the heir to the Russia of a long-lost golden age, when the quarrelsome, unruly peoples that now populate the Russian Federation, Ukraine, and Belarus were supposedly of one faith, one blood, and one mind. Yet their competing claims for authenticity are inevitably a pastiche of myths, symbols, and rhetoric whose sources cannot be considered exclusively or fundamentally "Russian." Rather than simply debunking their opponents, those who purport to be the bearers of indisputable truth, whether they be Orthodox, nationalist, White Brothers, or worshippers of the Mother of God, manage only to further relativize both their own claims and those of their enemies. Even totalitarianism has been cut down to size: if the term *totalitarian sect* is a rhetorical hand-me-down from the cold war era, it is one that subjects the totalitarian model to significant alterations, since, despite all pretensions to the contrary, postcommunist cults function on a drastically smaller scale than that of the Soviet government.

While the ideological struggles between new religious movements and the establishment (i.e., the press, the government, and the Orthodox Church) lead only to further relativism, they can also be seen as evidence of an oblique tendency toward a rather unexpected form of unity. All parties to the debate speak the same language: a language that combines nostalgia for a long-lost, mythical past and strong faith in the supernatural with the fear of an impending apocalypse, whether it be the end of the world forecast by the likes of Maria Devi or the huge social upheaval expected by her opponents as a result of her predictions. Both cultists and anticultists offer versions of the same eschatological narrative to an anxious public. Inundated with propaganda both for and against new religious movements, contemporary Russia has proved itself to be their ideal audience, providing what authors of fantasy have traditionally demanded: the willing suspension of disbelief.

Notes

1 "Russia's Strongman Lebed Supports Yeltsin's Reforms," Reuters, June 27, 1996.
2 Michael R. Golden, "Russian Vote Sets Off Battle, This Time in Yeltsin's Camp," *New York Times,* July 6, 1996, p. 1.

3 The Russian words for "Mormon" (*mormon*) and "Mason" (*mason*) are both stressed on the final syllable, and thus sound much more similar than do their English counterparts.

4 "Russia's Lebed, on Eve of Vote, Wants More Powers," Reuters, July 2, 1996.

5 Reliable statistics on the number of foreign missionaries on Russian soil are hard to come by, in part because the anecdotal evidence of their presence is so overwhelming as to obviate the need for a survey. Recent statistics released by the Department of Ethics and Law in *Moskovskie novosti* claim that the "missionary boom" has peaked: 1995 saw the number of registered missions decrease from 318 to 209 (*Moskovskie novosti,* March 17–24, 1996, p. 34, trans. in *Current Digest of the Post-Soviet Press* 48, no. 13 [1996]: 20). The number of unregistered missions is, of course, unknown.

6 Because "cult" carries a heavy load of ideological baggage, I will place the word in quotes. Many contemporary religious scholars prefer the term "new religious movement" to avoid the negative connotations associated with the word "cult." For an extended discussion of the problem with terminology, see James T. Richardson, "Definitions of Cult: From Sociological-Technical to Popular Negative," *Review of Religious Research* 34, no. 4 (1993): 348–56. I am grateful to Professor Richardson for sharing his unpublished manuscript, coauthored with Jane Dillon, "The 'Cult' Concept and Ideological Hegemony: A Politics of Representation Analysis."

7 Sergei Filatov claims that more than 70 percent of urban Russians believe in astrology, although he does not cite any source for this statistic (Filatov, "Sovremennaia Rossiia i sekty," *Inostrannaia literatura,* no. 8 [1996]). Kashpirovsky is a faith healer who repeatedly appeared on Soviet television during the perestroika era, using his "powers" to cure the diseases of both his studio audience and viewers at home (David Remnick, *Lenin's Tomb: The Last Days of the Soviet Empire* [New York: Vintage Books, 1994], pp. 255–63). Evgeniia "Dzhuna" Davitashvili attracted Brezhnev's attention in 1980; her psychic powers prompted him to give her a government job as what she obliquely calls "sort of a Kremlin doctor" for Brezhnev and others. Like Kashpirovsky, Dzhuna claims that she can cure a wide range of ailments, from allergies to AIDS, using either her hands or the "Dzhuna stimulator," a machine with a picture of her hands on it ("Russians Turn to Mystic Healer," Associated Press, April 23, 1995.

8 Mikhail N. Epstein, *After the Future: The Paradoxes of Postmodernism and Contemporary Russian Culture,* trans. from Russian by Anesa Miller-Pogacar (Amherst: University of Massachusetts Press, 1995), p. 161.

9 Ibid., p. 159.

10 Ibid., p. 160.

11 Mikhail Epstein, "Response: 'Post-' and Beyond," *Slavic and East European Journal* 39, no. 3 (1995): 363.

12 The results of these two surveys were presented in a round table published by *Voprosy filosofii* in 1992, and subsequently reprinted in English translation as "Religion and Politics in Postcommunist Russia," *Russian Studies in Philosophy* 33, no. 1 (1994): 50–95. The surveys were conducted in Moscow, Pskov, "and a number of other cities and villages in July–September 1990 and in August–October 1991"

(p. 52). The survey was sponsored by the Russian Academy of Sciences and interpreted by D. E. Furman and S. B. Filatov; the size and composition of the sample were not specified. As L. N. Mitrokhin argued in the round-table discussion, the results must be taken with a grain of salt (p. 92) because of both the unreliability of survey techniques in the Russian Federation and the traditional reluctance of Russians to speak openly to pollsters. Nevertheless, even with a wide margin for error, the data can be considered indicative of general trends in the early 1990s.

13 The very existence of "Christians in general," or generic "believers," can easily be underrepresented by surveys, especially if the results are taken out of context. The 1996 *Moskovskie novosti* survey claims that the Orthodox "account for 75 percent of the religious believers in Russia" (*Moskovskie novosti,* March 17–24, 1996, p. 34). The wording is, however, misleading because the article reports a study of religious centers, congregations, and other organizations rather than of believers. By definition, "Christians in general," or "believers," would be absent from the results because they do not form a congregation.

14 Furman, "Religion and Politics," p. 57.

15 David Lyon suggests that the New Age and postmodernism share a number of common features, including "the critique of secularization, itself seen less as a description of religious doctrine than as part of a metanarrative of secular modernity" (David Lyon, "A Bit of a Circus: Notes on Postmodernity and New Age," *Religion* 23 [1993]: 119).

16 L. Ron Hubbard is the founder of Scientology. Scientology came to Russia in 1991, and by 1992 the organization sponsored management courses for "New Russians" throughout the cities. *Dianetics,* Scientology's primary text, was published in a Russian translation in 1993 (Filatov, "Sovremennaia Rossiia i sekty").

17 Filatov, "Sovremennaia Rossiia i sekty"; Peter Rutland, "Sects Infiltrating Schools," *OMRI Daily Digest,* December 27, 1995.

18 The arms purchases, both successful and attempted, are discussed in a number of publications, including Murray Sayle, "Nerve Gas and the Four Noble Truths," *New Yorker,* April 1, 1996, p. 66; and David E. Kaplan and Andrew Marshall, *The Cult at the End of the World* (New York: Crown, 1996), pp. 69–76, 190–205.

19 Oxana Antic, "The Spread of Modern Cults in the USSR," in *Religious Policy in the Soviet Union,* ed. Sabrina Petra Ramet (Cambridge: Cambridge University Press, 1993), pp. 260–61.

20 Sabrina Petra Ramet cites an article in *Moscow Magazine* claiming that the number of Krishna followers in the USSR grew from 3,000 to 100,000 between 1988 and 1990 ("Religious Policy in the Era of Gorbachev," in Ramet, ed., *Religious Policy in the Soviet Union,* p. 31). Whether or not the numbers are accurate, the Krishna movement has certainly become much more visible in the past decade. The 1996 *Moskovskie novosti* survey cites the Hare Krishnas as the largest new religious movement in the Russian Federation, with an estimated 10,000 followers (*Moskovskie novosti,* March 17–24, 1996, p. 34). For a history of the Krishnas in the USSR, see Antic, "Spread of Modern Cults," pp. 260–68.

21 "Russia's Lebed."

22 Furman, "Religion and Politics," p. 58.

23 Ibid., p. 59.

24 On the role of the occult in contemporary Russian chauvinist circles, see Walter Laqueur, *Black Hundred: The Rise of the Extreme Right in Russia* (New York: HarperCollins, 1993), pp. 149–53.

25 *Chernyi sled "Belogo bratstva": Danilovskii listok* (Izdatel'stvo Sviato-Danilova monastyria), p. 3.

26 Detailed English-language summaries of the rise and fall of the Great White Brotherhood can be found in Eliot Borenstein, "Articles of Faith: The Media Response to Maria Devi Khristos," *Religion* 25 (1995): 249–66; and Borenstein, "Maria Devi Khristos: A Post-Soviet Cult without Personality," *Mind and Human Interaction* 5, no. 3 (1994): 110–22.

27 Although the focus of this essay is the Russian Federation, the Great White Brotherhood was equally active in Ukraine and Belarus. The significance of Maria Devi's "pan–East Slavic" perspective is discussed below.

28 "Vyrezh' i zaklei Mariiu Devi!," *Komsomol'skaia pravda*, Ekstrennyi vypusk, November 12, 1993, p. 22.

29 [Marina Tsvigun], *Ia Esm' Liubov'! Sbornik Bozhestvennoi poezii* (*IUSMALOS*, no. 8 [1993]), p. 128. This official biography, along with Tsvigun's credentials, was disputed in the Russian and Ukrainian press. For more on Tsvigun's "earthly" life, see Borenstein, "Articles of Faith," pp. 251–52.

30 Aleksandr Marsuk, "A mama zhdet svoiu boginiu . . . ," *Komsomol'skaia pravda*, November 10, 1993, p. 2. The implications of the roots of Tsvigun's delusions of godhood in a botched abortion were not lost on observers of the movement. Aleksandr P'iankov (*Vechernii klub*, November 12, 1993) ironically refers to Tsvigun as "that victim of Soviet gynecology," while Valerii Vyzhtovich ("Epidemiia 'Belogo bratstva': Istoriia bolezni," *Izvestiia*, November 26, 1993, p. 6) reports that Tsvigun's ex-husband explained on Ukrainian television, "It all started after her seventh abortion." Andrei Igruev ("Mariia Devi Khristos: Zhizn' i tvorchestvo. Zhizn' kak tvorchestvo," *Nezavisimaia gazeta*, July 12, 1993, p. 5) asserts that Tsvigun's greatest problem is "an unquenched thirst for motherhood," which explains not only her rather bizarre poems to her baby son Jesus, but also the motive behind her participation in the cult: she is a childless woman who steals other people's children.

31 *IUSMALOS*, no. 8 (1993), pp. 1–2. Although the idea of "God the Mother" could be considered simply an obvious addition to the Christian "divine family," it seems, like much of the Brotherhood's doctrine, to have its roots in the Theosophy of H. P. Blavatsky. Blavatsky describes the three "Logoi" (Father, Mother, and Son) who were the "antetype" of the Christian trinity in *Collected Writings*, vol. 10 (Wheaton, Ill.: Theosophical Publishing House, 1978), p. 332. Even the name of Maria Devi's religious movement seems to be lifted from Theosophy: Blavatsky claimed that her writings came to her through a mystic link to a "Great White Brotherhood" of mysterious *mahatmas* (Maria Carlson, *No Religion Higher Than Truth* [Princeton:

Princeton University Press, 1993], p. 31). Although the name "Great White Brotherhood" has definite racist overtones, such connotations were not explored in Maria Devi's literature.

32 *Uchenie Marii Devi Khristos* (Nauka o Svete i ego transformatsii. Osnovnye formuly, 1993), p. 13.

33 *IUSMALOS,* no. 8 (1993), p. 2.

34 *Uchenie,* pp. 21–22.

35 *IUSMALOS,* no. 8 (1993), p. 2.

36 *IUSMALOS,* no. 11 (1993), p. 7. The view that both Krivonogov and Tsvigun were to be killed is supported by Filatov ("Sovremennaia Rossiia i sekty").

37 V. Ignatov, "Maria Devi gotovitsia k raspiatiiu, a kievskaia militsiia—k massovym besporiadkam," *Segodnia,* November 4, 1993, p. 1.

38 Ibid., p. 1; Leonid Kapeliushnikov and Natalia Zinets, " 'Beloe bratstvo' v predverii kontsa sveta," *Izvestiia,* November 2, 1993, p. 6.

39 Kapeliushnikov and Zinets, "Law Enforcement Organs Appeal to Public Order," *Uryadovyy kuryer,* October 30, 1993 (rpt. in FBIS, *Daily Report—Central Eurasia* [November 3, 1993], pp. 61–62); Kapeliushnikov and Zinets, " 'Beloe bratstvo,' " p. 6; Halyna Kryvenko, "Sect Mass Suicide Threat Moved Ahead to 14 Nov.," *Molod Ukrayiny,* November 5, 1993 (rpt. in FBIS *Daily Report—Central Eurasia* [November 9, 1993], p. 58); "Appeal on Activity of Sect," *Uryadovyy kuryer,* November 4, 1993 (rpt. in FBIS, *Daily Report—Central Eurasia* [November 5, 1993], p. 58); " 'White Brotherhood' Members on Hunger Strike," *Molod Ukrayiny,* November 2, 1993 (rpt. in FBIS *Daily Report—Central Eurasia* [November 5, 1993], p. 57).

40 Oleg Karmaza, "Reportazh s kontsa sveta," *Komsomol'skaia pravda,* November 16, 1993, p. 3; Kapeliushnikov and Zinets, " 'Beloe bratstvo,' " p. 1.

41 Mariia Starozhitskaia, "Zaderzhany 700 chlenov 'Belogo bratstva.' Konets sveta otmeniaetsia . . . ," *Izvestiia,* November 26, 1993.

42 Andrei Borodin and Sergei Kisilev, "End of the World Postponed—Leaders of White Brotherhood Arrested in Kiev," *Segodnia,* November 13, 1993, p. 1, trans. in *Current Digest of the Post-Soviet Press* 45–46 (1993): 27.

43 "Ukraine Court Sentences Doomsday Cult Leaders," Reuters, February 9, 1996.

44 Filatov, "Sovremennaia Rossiia i sekty"; Boris Falikov, "Beloe bratsvo," *Znamia,* no. 8 (1996), p. 192.

45 Borenstein, "Articles of Faith," pp. 249–66.

46 Borodin and Kisilyov, "End of the World," p. 27; Starozhitskaia, "Zaderzhany 700 chlenov," p. 1. For a more detailed discussion of the role of this misperception in the Maria Devi hysteria, see Borenstein, "Articles of Faith," pp. 254–55.

47 Nowhere in any of the Brotherhood's materials that I have examined is there a mention of mass suicide; instead, only Maria Devi (and perhaps Krivonogov) were to die on the cross. For a discussion of the roots of this misconception, see Borenstein, "Articles of Faith," pp. 253–54.

48 Even the name "Maria Devi Khristos" suggests a cross-cultural hybrid: "Khristos"

is, of course, both the Russian word for "Christ" and a distinctly Greek lexical import, while "Devi" comes from the Sanskrit word for "goddess."

49 ITAR-Tass, "Kstati," *Komsomol'skaia pravda*, November 16, 1993, p. 3. Tsvigun's litany of countries she visited can be found in the pamphlet *Stupaite za mnoi, deti moi!*

50 *Stupaite za mnoi,* emphasis in the original.

51 Serge Zenkovsky, ed., *Medieval Russia's Epics, Chronicles, and Tales* (New York: Meridian Books, 1974), p. 447; Anonymous, "Ispoved' byvshego sviashchenika (ili o merzosti zapusteniia v sviatykh mestakh)," *IUSMALOS*, no. 8 (1993), p. 6. The author notes that the numbers on the license plates of top church officials add up to 666: "Do you think this is by accident?"

52 *Stupaite za mnoi.*

53 "Peite moiu vodu zhivuiu," *IUSMALOS*, no. 10 (1993), p. 3.

54 S. Kisilev, "Belaia goriachka'. Pochemu chekisty ne mogut naiti shtab 'Belogo bratstva,' " *Novaia gazeta*, November 10, 1993. One sign of the near universal recognition of Maria Devi's image is a parodic series of "xerox art" produced by Ekaterinburg artist Sasha Shaburov. In photo after photo, Shrburov put his own face on a number of classic cultural icons, from Vera Mukhina's monumental statue "The Worker and Collective Farmer" to the bust of Nefertiti. Included in the series is a portrait of the artist as Maria Devi, over the inscription "Sasha Shaburov Khristos."

55 Filatov, "Sovremennaia Rossiia i sekty."

56 All my information on the Bazhov Academy comes from Filatov, "Sovremennaia Rossiia i sekty."

57 Nikolai Popov, "Sect in the Moscow Catacombs," *Megalopolis Express*, no. 13, March 25, 1992, p. 7, trans. in *Current Digest of the Post-Soviet Press* 44, no. 12 (1992): 32–33.

58 Popov, "Sect in the Moscow Catacombs."

59 Inventing nonexistent "cults" in order to advance a cultural agenda is hardly the sole purview of tabloid journalists; in his monograph *New Sectarianism,* Mikhail Epstein describes more than a dozen different sects that have been formed in Russia since the 1970s: "Khazarians," "Blood Worshippers," and even "Pushkinites." The result is both a commentary on recent cultural trends and an extended Borgesian joke (fiction in the form of scholarship). See Mikhail Epshtein, *Novoe sektantstvo* (Holyoke: New England Publishing Co., 1993).

60 Svetlana Kolosovskaia, "Chumnaia volna," *Smena* 3 (1994), pp. 20–36.

61 Filatov, "Sovremennaia Rossiia i sekty."

62 Bereslavsky's center did, however, predate the Great White Brotherhood; Falikov claims that it was Bereslavsky's prophecy of the Mother of God's imminent reappearance in March 1990 that led Tsvigun to believe she was the Mother of the World (Falikov, "Beloe bratstvo," p. 186).

63 Mother of the World Maria Devi Khristos, "Moskovskomu Izheproproku o. Ioannu (Bereslavskomu) (direktoru Bogorodichnogo tsentra)," *IUSMALOS*, no. 4 (1993), p. 3.

64 Aleksandr Shchipkov, " 'Bran'' Bogorodichnogo tsentra s 'Belym bratstvom': Ko-mediia, perekhodiashchaia v dramu," *Nezavisimaia gazeta,* June 16, 1993, p. 2.

65 The term *totalitarian sects* appears throughout the Russian-language literature on new religious movements; for an example in English, see "Boom of Religious Cults in Russia Provokes Fear," Reuters, May 11, 1995.

66 Georgii Alekseev, "Khishchniki v belykh odezhdakh, ili kuda ischezaiut nashi deti?" *Shchit i mech,* July 8, 1993, p. 8; Viktor Smirnov, "Brat'ia, apostoly . . . i propavshie deti," *Rossiiskie vesti,* November 10, 1993; Aleksandr Shipkin, "Lzhe-proroki v Kieve," *Rossiiskie vesti,* November 13, 1993. None of the Brothers who were detained after the Kiev incidents confirmed such rumors, even after they had been "cured" by Ukrainian psychiatrists and released into the custody of their parents (Vyzhutovich "Epidemiia," p. 6). Nonetheless, the living conditions for the brotherhood's rank and file did not exactly encourage freedom of thought. Ludmila Grigorieva a researcher in Russian sectarianism from Krasnoyarsk, infiltrated the White Brotherhood and spent two months with them. Her findings confirmed some of the stories found frequently in the popular press: Maria Devi's followers fasted throughout most of the day and ate a small portion of food only at night; most of their day was spent in prayer; "Brothers" were rarely allowed to sleep longer than four or five hours at a time. While these methods are, arguably, coercive, neither drugs nor the supernatural appear to have played a role (Filatov, "Sovremennaia Rossiia i sekty").

67 Falikov, "Beloe bratstvo," p. 191.

68 Alekseev, "Khishchniki," p. 8; Nikolai Burbyga and Aleksei Grigor'ev, " 'Otets nebesny' i 'Mater' Mira' pokhishchaiut detei, sovershaiut finansovye afery v psev-doreligioznoi sekte 'Beloe bratstvo,' " *Izvestiia,* July 28, 1993, p. 3.

69 Valerii Lapikura, " 'Beloe bratstvo': zombi ili fanatiki?" *Rossiiskaia gazeta,* No-vember 9, 1993, p. 5. Boris Falikov also makes much of the "artificial intelligence" connection, calling the "program" of IUSMALOS a "cosmic computer game, in which God battles the devil" (Falikov, "Beloe bratstvo," p. 189).

70 *IUSMALOS,* no. 8, 1993, p. 1.

71 James Billington, *The Icon and the Axe: An Interpretive History of Russian Culture* (New York: Vintage Books, 1970), pp. 142–44, 158, 180.

72 The "brainwashing" controversy was inaugurated by Edward Hunter, who intro-duced the term in his study of Chinese "thought reform techniques" (*Brainwashing: The Story of the Men Who Defied It* [New York: W. W. Norton, 1956]). The term was appropriated by the anticult movement to describe alleged coercive indoctrination techniques. The debate continues to the present day, although a number of convinc-ing studies have found flaws in the brainwashing model. For more on this debate, see David G. Bromley and James Richardson, eds., *The Brainwashing/Deprogramming Controversy: Sociological, Psychological, Legal, and Historical Perspectives* (New York: Edwin Mellen Press, 1983).

CONTRIBUTORS

Adele Marie Barker is Associate Professor of Russian and Comparative Cultural and Literary Studies at the University of Arizona. She is the author of *The Mother Syndrome in the Russian Folk Imagination* (Slavica, 1986); coauthor with Susan Aiken, Maya Koreneva, and Ekaterina Stetsenko of *Dialogues/Dialogi: Literary and Cultural Exchanges between (ex) Soviet and American Women* (Duke University Press, 1994), and coeditor with Jehanne Gheith of *The History of Women's Writing in Russia* (forthcoming from Cambridge University Press).

Eliot Borenstein is Assistant Professor of Russian and Slavic Studies at New York University. He is the author of *Men without Women: Masculinity and Revolution in Early Soviet Fiction* (forthcoming from Duke University Press) and the editor and cotranslator of Mark Lipovetsky's *Russian Postmodernism: Dialogue with Chaos* (M. E. Sharpe). He is currently at work on a book-length study of contemporary Russian popular culture.

Svetlana Boym is Professor of Slavic and Comparative Literature at Harvard University. She is the author of *Common Places: Mythologies of Everyday Life in Russia* (Harvard University Press, 1994) and *Death in Quotation Marks: Cultural Myths of the Modern Poet* (Harvard University Press, 1991). She is currently working on a book on nostalgia.

John Bushnell is Professor of History at Northwestern University. He is the author of *Mutiny amid Repression: Russian Soldiers in the Revolution of 1905–1906* (Indiana University Press, 1985) and *Moscow Graffiti: Language and Subculture* (Unwin Hyman, 1990).

Nancy Condee is the director of the Graduate Program for Cultural Studies at the University of Pittsburgh. Her publications include *Soviet Hieroglyphics: Visual Culture in Late Twentieth-Century Russia* (Indiana University Press/British Film Institute, 1995) and *Endquote: Sots-Art Literature and Soviet Empire Style* (coedited with Marina Balina and Evgeny Dobrenko, forthcoming from Northwestern University Press).

Robert Edelman is Professor of Russian History at the University of California at San Diego. He is the author of *Serious Fun: A History of Spectator Sport in the USSR* (Oxford University Press, 1993). He is presently working on a study of the relationship between the Moscow working class and the Spartak soccer team.

Laurie Essig received her Ph.D. in sociology from Columbia University. She is the author of *Queer in Russia: A Story of Sex, Self, and the Other* (Duke University Press, 1999). She also writes a syndicated column on queer parenting called "Baby Boom."

Julia P. Friedman is a graduate student in art history at Brown University.

Paul W. Goldschmidt is Adjunct Professor of Political Science at the University of Wisconsin-Platteville. He is the author of *Democracy and Pornography: Legislating Obscenity in Post-Communist Russia* (Westview Press, 1999).

Judith Deutsch Kornblatt is Professor of Slavic Languages and Literatures at the University of Wisconsin at Madison, where she is also a member of the Jewish Studies and Religious Studies Programs. She is the author of *The Cossack Hero in Russian Literature: A Study in Cultural Mythology* (University of Wisconsin Press, 1992), and the coeditor with Richard F. Gustafson of *Russian Religious Thought* (University of Wisconsin Press, 1996). She is currently at work on a book entitled *Meeting of the Chosen Peoples: Modern Russian Orthodox Thought and the Jews*.

Anna Krylova is a Ph.D. candidate at Johns Hopkins University. Her dissertation is entitled "Gendering Sovetskii Chelovek: The Great Fatherland War and Soviet Identity 1943–1946." Her essay "In Their Own Words: Soviet Women Writers and the Search for Self" appears in *A History of Women's Writing in Russia,* edited by Adele Barker and Jehanne Gheith (forthcoming from Cambridge University Press).

Susan Larsen is Assistant Professor of Russian Literature at the University of California, San Diego. Her most recent publications have focused on contemporary Russian cinema, but her current book project is a study of girls' culture in late imperial Russia.

Catharine Theimer Nepomnyashchy is Associate Professor of Russian Literature at Barnard College. She is the author of *Abram Tertz and the Poetics of Crime* (Yale University Press, 1995) and the cotranslator of Abram Tertz, *Strolls with Pushkin* (Yale University Press, 1993). She is current at work on two books: *The Politics of Tradition: The Rerooting of Russian Literature after Stalin* and *Under the Sky of My Africa: Aleksandr Pushkin and Blackness*.

Theresa Sabonis-Chafee received her Ph.D. in Political Science from Emory University. She lives in Almaty, Kazakhstan, where she is Energy and Environment Policy Resident Advisor to the Harvard Institute for International Development.

Tim Scholl is Associate Professor of Russian at Oberlin College. He is the author of *From Petipa to Balanchine: Classical Revival and the Modernization of Ballet* (Routledge, 1994) and is at work on a second volume entitled *Balanchine's Romanticism* (forthcoming from Yale University Press).

Adam Weiner is Assistant Professor of Russian at Wellesley College and the author of *By Authors Possessed: The Demonic Novel in Russia* (Northwestern University Press, 1998).

Alexei Yurchak is Assistant Professor of Anthropology at the University of California at Berkeley. His essay "The Cynical Reason of Late Socialism: Power, Pretense and the Anekdot" appeared in *Popular Culture*, 1997. He is currently completing a book entitled *The Cynical Reason of Late Socialism: Language, Culture, and Ideology of the Last Soviet Generation.*

Elizabeth Kristofovich Zelensky is a professorial lecturer at Georgetown University. She has published several essays on the function of liminality within the cultural system of the Russian state. She is currently collaborating on a textbook entitled *Childhood: Social Construct, Literary Genre and Celluloid Image.*

INDEX

Library of Congress Cataloging-in-Publication Data

Consuming Russia: popular culture, sex, and society since Gorbachev / edited by Adele
Marie Barker.

p.   cm.

Includes index.

ISBN 0-8223-2281-1 (cloth : alk. paper). — ISBN 0-8223-2313-3 (pbk. : alk. paper)

1. Russia (Federation) — Civilization.   2. Popular culture — Russia (Federation)

3. Sex — Russia (Federation) I. Barker, Adele Marie

DK510.762.C66 1999

947.086 — DC21   98-50856